'This book contains the wisdom of some of the world's best specialists in the field of business archives. They have arduously assembled a wealth of information which makes it easy to set up a new business archive and to nurture it to becoming a useful asset for its sponsors. This book should be compulsory reading not only for archivists but also for business leaders who are interested in managing the continuity of their businesses.'

Alexander L. Bieri, Chair, Section on Business Archives,
International Council on Archives

'Business archivists are unsung heroes. They are the guardians of the secrets of how capitalist enterprises in the past have driven innovation and created wealth. This impressive volume brings together both professional archivists and business historians to provide a robust and compelling intellectual foundation for the successful management of business archives in the digital age.'

Geoffrey Jones, Harvard Business School, Harvard University, USA

'This ambitious book fills an important gap in the archival literature, starting with context-setting essays and moving through both academic analyses and pragmatic advice on the fundamentals of managing business archives. The editor and authors are to be congratulated for providing the most in-depth examination of business archives issues in decades – perhaps ever. Students, experienced practitioners, and business executives considering an investment in business archives should consider this book a "must read."'

Elizabeth Adkins, Former President of the Society of American Archivists

'The book brings together practical and stimulating contributions from leading business archivists and business historians. In its breadth of scope and coverage, it will undoubtedly become the standard reference work on the nature and context of business archives, their management and their use.'

Michael Anson, Chair, Business Archives Council, UK

'This volume helps fill a 20-year gap in the professional archival literature related to business archives. Of equal importance, however, it provides lessons learned and best practices for archives of all types. All too often, business archivists find themselves talking to one another. With this volume, the conversation should expand to archivists of all types on both sides of the Atlantic.'

Gregory S. Hunter, Long Island University, USA;
Editor-in-Chief, The American Archivist

'As reputations have become the most important corporate asset, business archives have become the tangible legacy of public trust. This volume brings together historians and archivists to show how to get value from corporate records. A practical guide on these invaluable resources, this handbook helps business executives better manage the future by leveraging their past.'

Christopher McKenna, Said Business School, University of Oxford, UK

T0360950

The International Business Archives Handbook

The *International Business Archives Handbook* provides up-to-date information and guidance on key issues relating to the understanding and management of the historical records of businesses.

Key features include:

- Chapter contributions from a range of experts in their respective fields.
- Coverage of business archive and business history initiatives around the world.
- Practical advice combined with thought-provoking discussion.
- Discussion of both well-established issues and those that have previously received little attention.
- Useful quick-reference tables, case study examples from a range of countries, and further reading suggestions.

The handbook is an invaluable guide for students, archive professionals and business historians alike. It is also an important reference tool for business professionals involved in information management more generally.

Alison Turton has been Head of Archives at The Royal Bank of Scotland Group, UK, for over 28 years. Her previous edited handbook, *Managing Business Archives* (1991) has served as a key text in the field for over 25 years.

The International Business Archives Handbook

Understanding and Managing the
Historical Records of Business

Edited by
Alison Turton

Routledge
Taylor & Francis Group

LONDON AND NEW YORK

First published 2017
by Routledge

2 Park Square, Milton Park, Abingdon, Oxfordshire OX14 4RN
52 Vanderbilt Avenue, New York, NY 10017

Routledge is an imprint of the Taylor & Francis Group, an informa business

First issued in paperback 2019

Copyright © 2017 selection and editorial matter, Alison Turton; individual chapters, the contributors

The right of Alison Turton to be identified as the author of the editorial material, and of the authors for their individual chapters, has been asserted in accordance with sections 77 and 78 of the Copyright, Designs and Patents Act 1988.

All rights reserved. No part of this book may be reprinted or reproduced or utilised in any form or by any electronic, mechanical, or other means, now known or hereafter invented, including photocopying and recording, or in any information storage or retrieval system, without permission in writing from the publishers.

Notice:
Product or corporate names may be trademarks or registered trademarks, and are used only for identification and explanation without intent to infringe.

British Library Cataloguing in Publication Data
A catalogue record for this book is available from the British Library

Library of Congress Cataloging in Publication Data
A catalog reference for this book has been requested

ISBN: 978-0-7546-4663-1 (hbk)
ISBN: 978-0-367-88244-0 (pbk)

Typeset in Bembo and Gill Sans
by Florence Production Ltd, Stoodleigh, Devon, UK

To dedicated archivists the world over
who are ensuring that our business heritage
is preserved and used

Contents

Tables

Boxes

Figures

Contributors

Roy Edwards is a lecturer in Accounting at Southampton Business School where he teaches financial accounting and business history. He studied economic history at the LSE as a mature student before switching to accounting teaching. He has published on the history of the London Midland & Scottish Railway as well as the history of General Electric. He is a trustee of the Business Archives Council and the co-founder of the Archives and Artefacts Study Network.

Leslie Hannah is Honorary Distinguished Professor at the Cardiff Business School and divides his time between the United Kingdom and Japan. He spent most of his academic career at the London School of Economics, eventually as Pro-Director. He also held posts at Oxford, Essex, Cambridge, Harvard and Tokyo and served as dean of two European business schools. He has published on the corporate economy, management strategy, entrepreneurship, pensions, the electricity industry, tobacco and banking. Latterly he has specialised in internationally comparative business history, publishing articles on logistics and plant size (*Journal of Economic History*, 2008), the divorce of ownership from control (*Business History*, 2007, *Economic History Review*, 2012), investment banking (*Business History Review*, 2011), the international spread of the corporate form (*Economic History Review*, 2015) and stock exchanges (forthcoming).

William Kilbride is Executive Director of the Digital Preservation Coalition (DPC), a not-for-profit membership organisation providing advocacy, workforce development, capacity and partnership in digital preservation. He started his career in archaeology in the 1990s when the discipline's enthusiasm for new technology outstripped its capacity to manage the resulting data. He joined the DPC from Glasgow Museums where he was Research Manager and previously Assistant Director of the Archaeology Data Service in the University of York. Before that he was a lecturer in archaeology at the University of Glasgow where he retains an honorary position.

Sara Kinsey is Head of Archives at the Nationwide Building Society. She has been a professional archivist for over 20 years, working in business archives for the majority of her career. She joined HSBC Archives in 1993, becoming the Global History Manager in 2007 and most recently running the bank's 150th anniversary programme. In 2016 she moved to the Nationwide to set up its first archive service. Between 2000 and 2012 she taught on the business archives module for prospective archivists at Liverpool University's Centre for Archive Studies. She joined the executive council of the Business

Archives Council in 2003 and held the post of vice-chair between 2007 and 2010. During her time with the Business Archives Council she was instrumental in guiding the work to produce the United Kingdom's first national strategy on business archives. She was the chair of the Wadsworth Prize for Business History in 2013.

Paul C. Lasewicz is the archivist at McKinsey and Company, one of the world's leading management consulting firms. Before joining McKinsey in 2014, he was the corporate archivist at IBM and Aetna Life and Casualty, two Fortune 100 corporations with extensive global operations. While managing the archives programmes at those two companies, he served on the IBM Centennial Core Team (for which he received a 2012 Best of IBM award), two IBM Academy of Technology studies on digital preservation, the Aetna Y2K committee and the original Aetna intranet steering committee. Over his 25 years in the profession, he has held leadership positions in local, regional and national professional associations. A frequent presenter on topics in corporate archivy at domestic and international conferences, he has written for regional, national and international archives publications. He is also a multiple winner of the coveted Society of American Archivists' Golf Open's Keiner Cup.

Katey Logan developed the United Kingdom's national strategy for business archives, published 2009, and authored various publications including the website *Managing business archives* that supported strategy implementation. For a period of ten years, she was an executive member of the Business Archives Council, most recently with a remit for international liaison. As a career archivist from 1987 to 2007 she established the Castrol Archive (now part of BP), and an integrated archive and records management function for Boots The Chemists (now Walgreens Boots Alliance). She has worked as a consultant, lectured on business archives at Liverpool University and published articles on a range of professional issues. Katey recently returned to the United Kingdom after a four-year period living in Asia, and is currently a doctoral researcher at Warwick Business School.

James Mortlock is the Digital Archives Manager at HSBC. James qualified as an archivist in 2010 and previously worked for Lloyds Banking Group prior to joining HSBC. At HSBC he initially worked administering the bank's United Kingdom collection before moving on to lead the implementation and subsequent development of the bank's digital archives system. James organised the Business Archives Council's Business Archives Training Day for several years and was the Archives and Records Association's Section for Business Record training officer between 2011 and 2015.

Michael Moss is professor of archival science at the University of Northumbria. He was previously research professor in archival studies in the Humanities Advanced Technology and Information Institute (HATII) at the University of Glasgow, where he directed the Information Management and Preservation MSc programme. Prior to being appointed to HATII, he was archivist of the University from 1974 to 2003. He was educated at the University of Oxford and trained in the Bodleian Library. He is a non-executive director of the National Records of Scotland and until 2014 a member of the Lord Chancellor's Advisory Council on National Archives and Records. He was Miegunyah Distinguished Fellow in the e-Scholarship Research Centre at the University of Melbourne in 2014. He researches and writes in the fields of history and the information sciences. His recent publications include: 'Archival research in organisations in a digital age' (in D. Buchanan and A. Bryman, eds, *Handbook of organizational research methods*, 2009); 'Brussels sprouts and empire: putting down roots' (in D. O'Brien, ed., *Gardening – philosophy for everyone*, 2010); 'The high price of heaven – the 6th Earl of Glasgow and the College of the Holy Spirit on the Isle of Cumbrae' (*Journal of the Architectural History Society of Scotland*, 2012); 'Where have all the files gone, lost in action points every one?' (*Journal of Contemporary History*, 2012); 'From cannon to steam propulsion: the origins of Clyde marine engineering' (*Mariner's Mirror*, 2013); and 'La campagne en faveur des économies de guerre en Grande Bretagne: naissance d'une politique modern de l'epargne' (in F. Descamps and L. Quennouelle-Corre, *La mobilisation financiére pendant la Grande Guerre*, 2015).

John Orbell was Archivist of Baring Brothers from 1978, retiring from ING Bank London Branch in 2004. Prior to that he worked for the Business Archives Council where, *inter alia* he completed a survey of the historical records of British banking, which was later published with Professor L. S. Pressnell and in a second edition with Alison Turton. His other publications include, with Richard Storey, *Business history explorer: bibliography of UK business and industrial history* (2011), which is available online, and *A guide to tracing the history of a business* (2nd ed., 2009). In retirement he continues to write about business history and business archives.

Lesley Richmond is the Deputy Director of the Library and University Archivist at the University of Glasgow, which is home to one of the largest collections of business records in Europe. Currently, chair of the Business Archives Council of Scotland and the Section of Business Archives of the International Council on Archives, she has been involved with business archives throughout her professional life in Scotland, the United Kingdom and internationally. Lesley has written extensively in the field of business archives in the area of the appraisal, ethics and research and cultural values of business records and has produced several directories and guides to business archives. Experienced in maximising heritage assets to enable reputational gain and global reach through temporal connections, she aims to develop community identity and pride in past business endeavours, and create events and resources that inspire today's designers of tomorrow's products.

Tina Staples is Global Head of Archives at HSBC. Tina qualified as an archivist in 1999 and initially spent a year at the Victoria & Albert Museum as the Archivist for the Arts Council of Great Britain. In 2000 she joined the HSBC Archives team in London. She advised on the development of the bank's regional archives for Asia-Pacific in 2004. Having then taken over responsibility for the department in 2007, she also established a new United States function. She now manages a team across London, Hong Kong, Paris and New York – with the collections meeting high demand from internal and external stakeholders around the globe. Major projects in recent years have included the initiation of a new records management policy unit; relocation of the London archives to a purpose-built centre; regeneration of the bank's United Kingdom art collection; and the introduction of HSBC's digital archives system.

Jeannette Strickland has been an independent archive and records consultant since leaving her post as Head of Art, Archives and Records Management with Unilever plc in 2014. A qualified archivist and records manager, Jeannette has also worked in local government and for a major charity. She took Unilever Archives and Records Management successfully through submissions for Designation of Unilever's collections and The National Archives' accreditation process; implemented a digital preservation programme; and was responsible for writing the company's record retention policy and global retention schedule. She has written several papers, spoken at a number of conferences and organised the International Council on Archives' Section for Business Archives conference in 2014. Active throughout her career in both the Archives and Records Association (ARA) and the Business Archives Council, her current professional activities include membership of ARA's Qualifications Accreditation Panel and acting as a mentor on the ARA Registration Scheme. She is also studying for a PhD.

Kevin Tennent is lecturer in Management at The York Management School, University of York. He researches management history topics relating to international management and sport, is a trustee of the Business Archives Council, chairs the British Academy of Management's Management and Business History Track, and is on the editorial board of the *Journal of Management History*.

Alison Turton, a registered archivist who gained a Masters in Archive Studies at University College London, has been Head of Archives at Royal Bank of Scotland since 1988. There she has led many major archival projects, including the construction of two purpose-built archive stores, the development of several websites, a wide range of promotional initiatives and successful submission for Archive Service Accreditation under The National Archives' scheme. She also manages the bank's art collection. Prior to 1988 Alison worked in archive and records management roles at Glasgow University, House of Fraser, the Business Archives Council and Babcock FKI. Her publications include *Managing business archives* (1991); the *Business archives* module for University of Liverpool's distance learning Diploma in Professional Studies: Archives and Records Management (2001); and jointly with other authors *Bitter sweet: the history of Fletcher & Stewart 1838–1988* (1988); *A legend of retailing . . . House of Fraser* (1989); *The brewing industry: a guide to historical records* (1990); *The banking industry: a guide to historical records* (2001) and *The pharmaceutical industry: a guide to historical records* (2003). She has also contributed articles to a number of journals and biographical dictionaries. Alison chaired the implementation group of the National Strategy for Business Archives in Scotland 2010–16 and sits on the executive committees of Business Archives Council Scotland and the Section on Business Archives of the International Council on Archives.

Richard Wiltshire is Senior Archivist for Business Archives at London Metropolitan Archives (LMA), the City and pan-London local authority archive, managed by the City of London Corporation. Richard qualified as an archivist in 2001 and joined LMA, which holds an extensive collection of business archives, in 2002 where he was previously responsible for acquisitions. He is a trustee of the Business Archives Council.

Preface

I have spent my whole career as a corporate archivist. It was a field that I stumbled upon quite by chance 40 years ago, but one that has provided me with huge satisfaction and a host of exciting and enriching experiences. It has also brought me into contact with some extraordinary people, among them many dedicated archivists who have also spent much of their working lives ensuring that business archives of all kinds are preserved and used, and that their importance and value is fully recognised.

The first archival handbook I edited, *Managing business archives*, was published in 1991. It brought together in a single volume the experience of many of the United Kingdom's pioneering business archivists and set out the practical information that those working in a corporate archive, or with the historical records of business in a collecting repository, needed to have at their fingertips. At the time, it was the first book specifically published to support practitioners with the management of business archives. Yet, even as that first handbook was published, much was changing.

In 1997 *The records of American business* appeared, published by the Society of American Archivists. Perusing its pages, crammed with views and ideas from experienced archivists across the Atlantic, the British-centric approach of *Managing business archives* already seemed too parochial, too restrictive. A path-finding international conference held in Glasgow that same year, sponsored by the Business Archives Council, brought together 300 business archivists and business historians from around the world for the first time. It made it amply clear that there was an international network of like-minded archive professionals ready to share their knowledge and expertise and to reflect on the need for new approaches and standards. Business archivists globally held much in common and had much to learn from each other.

This book was born when I stood up in 1997 to speak at that conference, but has been two decades in the making. Several archivists who were at the same event, and who have been on similar professional journeys, have kindly lent their expertise to this new book as contributors or peer reviewers. We have all learned a great deal over the intervening years as technological and business change has utterly transformed the environments in which we work. Yet the international dialogue has continued, and indeed deepened, through the work of the Section on Business Archives of the International Council on Archives and the knowledge and experience shared through its annual conferences and occasional publications. So too within the United Kingdom, with the dual five-year national strategies on business archives in England and Wales and in Scotland recently completed, the profile of the historical records of business and the joint working between business archivists is at an all time high.

Looking back at the beginning of my career the pace of work at that time now seems rather slow and the range of knowledge and skills required fairly limited. Today managers of business archives must be masters of so much – not only traditional archive skills, but also digital preservation, social media use, historical research, web authoring, media liaison, change management and so much more. The purpose of this book, and the 13 contributions it contains, is not to provide a complete guide to the subject of managing business archives, but to set out key principles and practices and to signpost useful further reading and online sources of information. It also aims to place the United Kingdom's experience in an international context and in so doing to demonstrate not only the worldwide strength and depth of the business archives sector, but also the striking commonalities.

This publication would not have been possible without the contributions and expert advice of a very large number of people. First and foremost, I am immensely grateful to the 14 chapter authors who have worked tirelessly to distil and share their knowledge and who have borne with good humour my unreasonable demands and the numerous frustrations and delays as work on the book has run its course. I am humbled by their patience, dedication and expertise. I also owe a huge debt to over a 100 practising archivists and historians from Britain and across the world who have willingly peer reviewed the chapters and provided the authors with case studies, exemplars and good-practice policies and procedures. Without their help this book would not be so complete nor would it have been possible to append that important international dimension to the United Kingdom experience. Their support is testimony to the professional generosity and kindness that I have always found inherent in the sector. Additionally I would like to thank my current employer, The Royal Bank of Scotland, which has always encouraged my involvement in the wider archive profession and provided so many opportunities to continue to develop my own skills and knowledge. A final debt is owed to my parents – much loved and much missed – who nurtured my passion for history and delighted in my archive career.

All the royalties that this book earns will be passed to a charitable body, the Business Archives Council, and used to support the future preservation and promotion of business archives. I hope that in some small way it will also help every archivist who comes across it to look after our shared business heritage with a little more ease and confidence than before.

Alison Turton, April 2017

Part I

Business archives in context

Chapter 1

An introduction to business archives

Katey Logan

The role of business in global development

Business touches everything in the modern world. Business archives, though less well understood, constitute the written record of business, and are the key to unlocking our knowledge of it. This opening chapter shows how an increasing interest in and care of business archives is shaping our academic and general understanding of business development, at a time of phenomenal change in global commercial activity.

Western economies

In advanced economies, business and industry is the economic nucleus, commanding a position in society first held by royalty and then by government. Initially industry was regarded by some with suspicion – as, although a wealth creator, it was associated in the nineteenth and twentieth centuries with exploitation of workers, degradation of the environment, and ruthlessness in the pursuit of profit and the destruction of competition. While industry stripped society of free time and green spaces, astute governments through taxation of the new industrial and middle classes, established health and social services, cultural sponsorship and patronage, and education for all, and even employed large sectors of the population in nationalised industries – born out of the political need to control key strategic assets.

Public and private industry

By the twenty-first century there has been a further shift as the nationalised sector has been re-privatised by some governments keen to relinquish large, unionised industrial workforces and their burdensome on-costs.[1] As a result a much larger proportion of the working population exists within the private sector and the old battle lines of public/private sector are softening. As the 2008 global financial crisis has demonstrated in spectacular form, the success and failure of large corporations impact economic and social wellbeing across all sections of society. As a new political equilibrium is arrived at, the state is publicly recognising the role of the private sector as paymaster to the economy, and to counter nascent anti-globalisation movements, the private sector is stepping up to the challenge of engaging in the social and welfare agenda. In progressive societies, a new discourse is emerging and the era of big business is becoming the era of responsible and ethical business.

Emerging economies

In emerging economies, where rapid industrialisation has come relatively recently,[2] fed by globalisation, low-cost efficient shipping of containers and bulk commodities as well as access to cheap labour and technology, the lessons of the West's industrial revolutions cannot be ignored. The example of China's dramatic industrialisation and positioning as an economic powerhouse is tempered by the suffocation of its urban populations by toxic air pollution and the unremitting news stories in *China Daily*[3] of mining tragedies, food scandals, land degradation and climate change. The ubiquitous 'Made in China' product may be cheap, but comes at a high cost to the country and its hard-working population. Its government faces challenges so great, not least its handling of the capitalist/communist dichotomy, that the rest of the world can only spectate and hope for success and the 'best possible'[4] outcome.

Globalisation of trade

A truly global economy is becoming a reality as business, profoundly impacted by ever-more sophisticated technology and improved infrastructure, connects diverse corners of the globe. 'Third world' economies demonstrate industrialisation at unprecedented speed. Change is palpable, and as global citizens connected by the internet struggle to understand the changing world order, business and capitalism are perceived as a global panacea and global curse. Unable to imagine the technological future the information technology (IT) gurus are designing, today's global population is striving to learn how to progress without descending into chaotic environmental disaster, war, political meltdown and human exploitation.

Twenty-first century connectivity

Of course global trade is not a new activity. But the inter-connectedness of countries geographically separated is now a given, and as business models and cultures converge so too does the education of the political and business elite. The bureaucrats running China's civil service are as likely to have an MBA from Harvard as from Beijing, while Asian MBA schools are attracting increasing numbers of European and North American graduates.[5] Similarly the legal and regulatory framework in which business operates is becoming, paradoxically, both simplified and more complex as businesses trade across markets and economic zones, sharing common supply chains and manufacturing. The volume of regulation increases, but it is becoming more standardised globally. For example, regulations created by the European Union are adapted and implemented by the emerging economies as a cheap, 'ready-made' solution to making products and services compatible and competitive with European and North American markets.[6]

Internet and communications revolution

As participants in contemporary business we forget, or sometimes cannot see, the unprecedented changes happening around us. Office workers in the 1990s witnessed the installation of the first desktop computers in a rather more orderly manner than

---

Box 1.1 Restoring the first internet page

Sometimes it is difficult to know what will have historical value in the future. Years after the invention of the World Wide Web in 1989, the team at the European Organisation for Nuclear Research (CERN) have kept the computer of Tim Berners-Lee, inventor of the internet, and in 2013 restored the world's first website to its original address – thereby preserving some of the digital assets that are associated with the birth of the web. The earliest existing internet page is available online at http://home.web.cern.ch/topics/birth-web [Accessed 3 September 2016].

---

eighteenth-century weavers accepted the mechanisation of hand-looms.[7] Yet the impact of this step change in office technology was to make companies, office environments and working relationships almost unrecognisable. Business computers with the capacity to transform world trade are now igniting the civil liberties debate as electronic surveillance, cyber-security and corporate hacking scandals[8] counter the democratic trending towards transparency and freedom of information.

Business leadership

In an exciting and unexpected development the new role models of business – multi-million dollar teenage internet entrepreneurs – are providing significant inspiration to the next generation of would-be business leaders. The combination of immediate financial success, the 'dressed down' accessibility of young entrepreneurs, and the ingenuity and desirability of tech products and ideas has made a career in business unexpectedly 'cool'. The best-selling autobiography, and subsequent Oscar-winning film about Apple entrepreneur Steve Jobs, and *The social network*, the film of Mark Zuckerberg's creation of Facebook, demonstrate an alignment of the business world with youth and popular culture.

Understanding business through academic research

Facts and context

Across continents as business takes a more central position in everyday life, there is an academic, socio-cultural and economic need to learn more about it, and a key way to do that effectively is to study performance over time through the investigation and analysis of primary and secondary source material, that is business records. Published and unpublished business data is 'past' data, literally historical data. Records of business activity are necessary to understand and communicate business change and development and business's impact on societal change. However much business commentators and investors talk about the here and now of 'bottom line' performance; there has to be a line, a computation, an explanatory context. Facts and context are the essential components of business archives.

Transparency and accountability

The efficient management of business records and archives enables business to become transparent and accountable, a prerequisite to gain trust in an era of public scrutiny of business ethics and product safety. Newly-empowered and vocal consumers discuss through social media the actions or inactions of major corporations that in turn monitor and increasingly utilise social media sites such as Twitter, Facebook and Weibo.[9] While consumer choice used to be a key driver of better business, consumer voice can now seriously impact a commercial activity for better or worse; in sectors ranging from luxury goods and pharmaceutical companies focusing on counterfeit product, to clothing retailers drawn into the scandal of third world factory conditions,[10] businesses seek to know and make public aspects of their supply chain from ethical sourcing to product manufacture, packaging and even advertising.[11]

Business and economic history

Current business leaders and business historians alike need to understand business success and failure whether their goal is to educate, theorise and publish papers, or to 'copycat' format or strategy in creating new businesses. Journalist Chris Cobb writing in *Ottawa Citizen* encapsulates the value of archival research: 'Researchers and writers . . . do the work for the rest of us' (Cobb, 2013). Cobb also cites the work of Canadian television broadcasters in creating accessible histories for mass audiences. Likewise European broadcasters are finding a global market for populist business and economic history. For example, historian Niall Ferguson's published economic histories of China, Europe and the United States make successful television programmes that are syndicated worldwide.[12] Today business journalists make careers of studying individual corporations, business trends and sectors, but behind contemporary analysis and research lies a body of disciplined historical research. As Terry Cook, Canadian archivist and academic, wrote 'You may have 100 people who read an academic historian's book, but those academic books of scholarship fuel the bestselling authors who write books that tens of thousands or hundreds of thousands . . . read' (Cobb, 2013).

Box 1.2 Transparency in history

In 1944, almost half of Daimler–Benz's 63,610 employees were civilian forced labourers, prisoners of war or concentration camp detainees 'loaned out' by the Nazi regime in exchange for money. After the war, Daimler–Benz admitted its links with the Nazis, and also became involved in the German Industry Foundation's initiative 'Remembrance, Responsibility and Future', the work of which included the provision of humanitarian aid for former forced labourers.

Source: Daimler–Benz in the Nazi Era (1933–1945) at www.daimler.com [Accessed 3 September 2016].

> **Box 1.3 Chandler's legacy**
>
> American historian Alfred Chandler (1977) disputed Adam Smith's interpretation of the free economy dictating economic development and replaced it with the notion that corporate management of companies directly stimulated a company's growth or decline, citing the United States giants Du Pont, General Motors, Sears Roebuck and Standard Oil as templates for universal economic success. His writing excited a generation of industrialists and historians alike.

Historical research

Historians have been investigating business and economic history since the 1920s and 1930s when universities started to acknowledge and support these new disciplines.[13] As the world's first industrial nation (Mathias, 1969) the history of the United Kingdom's industrial revolution and its business leaders captured the imagination of academics. Business histories written in the early nineteenth century tended to focus on business biography or discrete business initiatives, but the academic discipline now attracts historians interested in the comparative nature of businesses – how sectors are developing and how principles and practice differ and coalesce in international markets. The pressure on academics to provide explanation and de-mystify successful business practice is increasing as projected population growth demands that the energy, agriculture and water industries in particular continue to innovate and develop in order to sustain global populations. Academic journals such as *Business History*, *Business History Review*, *Enterprise and Society*, *Management and Organisational History* and *Accounting History Review* provide a body of knowledge and research on many key business challenges.

Development of the business archives sector

In tandem with the development of economic and business history, pioneering archivists have sought to collect business papers and archives in public institutions, recognising that business enterprise is a formidable part of economic and cultural life that should be preserved as part of the national record. Canada's first archivist, Douglas Brymner, acquired business archives from the outset for what became the Public Archives of Canada, and as early as 1926 his successor procured relevant records from the finance house Baring Brothers & Company, joint London agent to the government of Canada (and the predecessor Province of Canada) in the nineteenth century (Salmon, 2003). In the private sector archivists began to 'infiltrate' corporations in significant numbers in the 1980s as the expansion of regulation as well as the volume of records created in the digital age had companies looking for record-keeping expertise beyond the traditional company secretarial role. In 2001 the archive and records management community developed an international standard for the management of business records (International Organization for Standardization, 2001) with the intent of significantly impacting the way businesses managed their records. Robert McLean, International Organization for Standardization (ISO) committee member, quoted in the ISO news release, explained that the 'standard enables organisations to develop policies, strategies and programmes which will ensure that information assets have the essential characteristics of accuracy, integrity and reliability'.

For companies interested in outsourcing their archives and records management functions, suppliers exist that offer records and data storage, retrieval and destruction, the more progressive offer records retention advice. It is harder to outsource historical archives management, but American specialists The History Factory, History Associates and The Winthrop Group, currently provide such services to a range of large, medium and small businesses interested in the benefits of keeping archives but unwilling to resource an in-house archive.

Development of archival theory

With archival practice comes archival theory. The two most celebrated proponents of archival theory are Hilary Jenkinson (1922) and Theodore Schellenberg (1956). Jenkinson writing in the 1920s established the concepts of original order and provenance, and explained the stages of records' life-cycle – that is, that records change status over time from current record (used regularly), to semi-current record (used occasionally), to permanent archive (used rarely). American academic Theodore Schellenberg, writing in the 1950s, described the primary and secondary value of archives. He believed that archives were of primary value to the originating agency, and of secondary value to other external agencies. Looking specifically at business archives, this translates as business archives having primary importance to the company that produces them, but having secondary value to other stakeholders such as academics, journalists and company employees, their families and communities. For example, the 50-year-old packaging and design archives of a biscuit manufacturer could be important to the company today for legal, pubic relations and marketing purposes, but the records may also be vital to planning officials interested in the reclamation or reuse of the industrial site, or genealogists, business biographers, brand or design historians, or even tourists and local history groups.

Schellenberg also introduced the idea of classifying records in line with functions, activities and transactions, another early archival concept with resonance in the business sphere. In more recent years archival theory has developed to take into account digital records and the ongoing accessibility of information. The records continuum[14] theory explains records and archives as existing in a dynamic environment, moving back and forwards between Jenkinson's 'life' stages as the information within is reused, manipulated and re-valued by diverse users.

Training opportunities for business archivists

Both private and public sector business archives have expanded in the last few decades as archival theory and practice have developed. The depth and scope of work, and the skills set of the archivist vary between sectors, but all have to be advocates for the sector and market the advantages of investing in business archives to their stakeholders. Traditionally company archivists were long-serving staff members seconded to the role of archivist because of their personal knowledge of the company history. This is still the most common route into the role in Japanese companies where long-service is an integral part of business life. Elsewhere, where business archives professionals are more common, university courses have adapted to the demand for more specialist training.

Box 1.4 Japanese *shashi*

Japan has a fascinating and unique style of business writing called the *shashi*. Since the Meiji era (1868–1912) over 13,000 *shashi* have been produced. Initially the *shashi* took the form of a chronological listing of historical events, but by the 1960s this was changing into the more scientifically researched, 'authentic' business history of which around 200 are produced annually.

Source: Matsuzaki, 2013.

Although there is limited postgraduate education specifically targeted at business, in recent years some archive studies courses in the United Kingdom have developed business archives modules for archive trainees.[15] There are also training events and conferences, including those hosted by the International Council on Archives[16] targeted at business archivists and records managers. In the United States of America, United Kingdom, Finland and France there are training opportunities in business archives organised by universities and government authorities, some on an annual and biannual basis, others more sporadic.[17]

Business archives defined

To research and analyse business records we need to know what they constitute and how and by whom they are created. In simple terms the archives of a business are like those of any other organisation: they record its activities and transactions. They can be created by anyone within the business or in business-to-business transactions or by third parties working as suppliers or agents or consumers of the business's products and services. The processes from business start-up to liquidation are captured by statutory record-keeping, while daily business operation relies on records as evidence of customer and supplier activity, financial transaction, communications, agreements and contracts, and business strategy and management.

The business entity itself can be broad in scope. Trading organisations are obvious candidates, but institutions providing secondary and tertiary education, medical research and provision, and charitable and non-governmental organisation (NGO) activities, can fall within a wider definition of business practice.

Definition of archives

The international community defines records as 'information created, received and maintained as evidence and information by an organisation or person in pursuance of legal obligations or the transaction of business' (International Organization for Standardization, 2001). Some professionals regard archives specifically as 'historical records', those records that are retained permanently, but, in simple terms, all business records at source are potential archives so it is common to use the terms interchangeably. Records and archives are produced by the organisation as it exists and conducts its business. As unpublished products of the business process they are called primary sources. They have unique provenance – they relate and belong to the organisation and are understood (only) in the context of that organisation.

Archives complexity and format

Business sectors include, for example, food and beverages, pharmaceuticals, oil and gas, communications, media, financial services and transportation. While we can imagine a range of activity – the production of our daily bread and milk, clothes, medicines, transport, consumer products and financial services – when we investigate the records of business they are fairly generic, and it is the commonality of records that allow career archivists and records managers to move easily from one company and sector to another, unfazed by variation in operational records and archives. Archives can take the form of paper documentation, digital records and images, disparate photographic and video media and more recently dynamic websites and databases. Change in record formats is endemic as companies seek from new technologies both greater business efficiency and competitor advantage.

Location of business archives

The majority of business records reside with the business institution itself and are managed by company personnel. Under the guidance of the company secretariat, statutory records will be retained for as long as legally necessary and dependent on the size of the enterprise, other records created for regulatory reasons will similarly be kept and made available to regulatory inspectors as appropriate. Professional staff with responsibility for functions such as human resources, finance and legal should have a good knowledge of the value of their records and how long they need to be kept in line with professional standards and best practice. After periods of retention are up they are routinely destroyed, ignored or managed.

A growing proportion of businesses, usually large multinationals with significant brand-related heritage, have set up corporate archive functions by hiring professional archivists to actively manage and exploit their archive collections. The archives are usually located at the company headquarters (or, if off-site, within the country of company registration) but for transnational enterprises with subsidiary companies worldwide, records relating to 'overseas' business may be kept in the appropriate region where they can be exploited locally. This is becoming more common as it is deemed ethical to honour the geographic provenance of the archives, and with digitisation capability copies can be made available internationally. While relocation of records does take place with company merger and acquisition, where professional staff are in place this can be done smoothly with appropriate safeguards in place.

The biggest proportion of managed business archives can, however, be found in public sector records repositories, museums, libraries and university archives. Business records migrate to the public sector by various means:

1   records are transferred to public ownership by parent companies perhaps as a public relations initiative at a moment of company relocation, takeover, or downsizing, or as companies take advantage of government incentives to deposit their archives;

2   records earmarked for destruction by company managers or liquidators are saved by employees or by proactive public sector archivists who organise their deposit in local museums, records offices, university archives or community archives;

3   businesses are nationalised and their records transferred to government departments and ultimately to national archive services;

4   government records relating to companies are transferred over time to national archives;

5   professional associations supporting business make their archives publicly available as private organisations providing a public archive service;

6   company records are managed by charitable trusts or community archives.

Archives and records types

A business can be a multinational or state-owned enterprise employing hundreds of thousands of people or a sole trader selling sweetmeats on a street corner. The mass and complexity of the business's records increase in proportion to the scale of the business operation, and the management of those archives as a business asset can similarly vary enormously. There will always be individual record types that are unique and of exceptional significance to particular companies, but the majority of records fall into defined classes, since they are products of the legislative and regulatory framework that spawns them. Later chapters[18] will discuss both core and industry-specific records in more detail – their form and function – but as a generic starter they can be grouped under the following headings.

Corporate records

Records are created by law to establish and maintain a business, from initial filing of key information[19] through to the submission of annual financial returns showing the company's economic health. Legislation generally dictates that even failed companies have to provide records of liquidation and bankruptcy. Other corporate records include directors' minute books – recording the decisions of the board of directors – as well as shareholders' registers (for public companies) showing ownership of the company in terms of private and institutional shareholding. So long as the company remains in business some of these record classes have to be kept, so for older companies, records that look and feel like archives are still technically active administrative papers.

Finance records

Company accountants create financial records that illustrate every aspect of the company's income and expenditure. These records can be complex, and like statistical data, are manipulated by trained professionals to create multi-faceted profit and loss statements. Fortune 500 companies can have income and expenditure amounting from hundreds of millions to billions of dollars/euros per annum, and financial records at all levels of the accounting hierarchy will account for purchase and payment of all goods, services and resources, as well as the macro-finance of company merger, acquisition and debt (servicing company flotation or privatisation).

Management records

Records are created by executive and management committees to organise and record their activities and thinking, as well as interaction and inter-relations with a company's functions or divisions. Records relating to the management of a business offer an intriguing insight into day-to-day market opportunities, the growth and organisational development of the business as well as analysis of business success and failure. Well-established records series such as management committee minute books and some of the more contemporary records such as company-wide risk registers and business continuity plans offer interesting snapshots of business opportunities and vulnerabilities.

Communications records

Communications records seek to reach and influence diverse stakeholder groups from investors and regulators to pensioners and competitors. Outward-facing communiqués relate to public relations and brand management, and include advertisements, press releases and internet communication. These are carefully controlled messages, communicated continuously through diverse media channels that position corporate and commercial brands in the marketplace. Internally-facing communications records include company confidential communiqués that set out and explain company strategy, marketing campaigns, employee issues, human resources policy and the like.

Legal records

Legal records are evidence of the contractual activities of companies. Legal teams cover a range of work including land purchase and lease (factories, offices, transport, distribution centres, retail outlets), the creation of partnerships, engagement of employees and suppliers, establishment of infrastructure such as IT and telecommunications, and managing litigation arising from customer complaints, personal injury and contractual failure. In addition, the company's intellectual property is formalised and protected through the establishment of patents and trademarks and assertions of design and literary copyright.

Regulatory records

External regulation enforces a plethora of record keeping about a company's activities and internal processes – from manufacturing, to workplace safety, to product development. In the research, development and manufacture of pharmaceuticals and foods, where the end products are physically consumed, the supply chain is rigorously controlled by adherence to and inspection of standard operating procedures documenting process minutiae. Regulation is heavier in some sectors than others, and overseen by different regulatory bodies; all ensuring a safe and ethical landscape in which to trade, protecting consumers across many sectors. In areas such as health and safety at work, and duty of care to employees, regulations are in place across all industries.

Product records

All companies have a product to sell, whether it is a physical item or a service. The records relating to products are multi-faceted ranging from those measuring manufacturing output or equipment calibration, to product samples such as mortgages and insurance policies, toy cars, rivets, confectionery and clothes. Records relating to products are kept as part of the company's intellectual property, as well as to show quality, range and technical innovation. There should also be complementary files on product innovation, development, production, marketing and advertising.

Business archives as a company asset

Most classes of records can be discarded as soon as the statutory or regulatory need to keep them has elapsed. Yet many millions of business records are kept beyond these defined retention periods. Is there a rationale for this, and what are the outcomes for the business and for society at large? Why do businesses retain their records when their immediate use is over?

Exploiting business archives – primary value

Some companies recognise that archives can be used as a commercial asset. They employ professional archivists to manage their archives, funding company archive repositories and records centres. These businesses tend to be of an age at which the history of the company or brand begins to provide some competitive advantage over others in the marketplace. Alternatively the company may approach archive management passively as a result of modern records and data management where the information specialists decide to keep 'antiquated' or 'historical' materials as they sense they may have some historical or even public relations value.

Advantages of in-house corporate archives

An in-house archive is a rich source of information. In tandem with selective records management programmes, the archive will have a depth and quality of information and completeness. Corporate archivists can appeal to ex-employees to fill gaps in the corporate records, or make deals with public archives for the repatriation of material. Archivists will be able to extract a mass of diverse information from the records and be able through research to understand, explain and communicate the company's past. The best professionals will proactively push information to stakeholders whose needs they will ascertain. Where possible they will make the archives accessible to external researchers in a controlled and supervised environment – thus releasing the archives' secondary value to external communities. For academics working with corporate archivists it is an easier and more efficient way to exploit the archives than being given access to an uncatalogued archive, or having to use secondary source material, oral reminiscence, or 'unofficial' company records stashed in the chairman's home, as the basis of research.[20]

The company archivist can deliver the twin benefits of commercial and public relations impact. Depending on the sector and circumstances of the business, these benefits will come from various channels,[21] including brand knowledge and marketing; innovation;

evidence, compliance and management information; corporate identity; corporate responsibility; and employee recruitment, engagement and retention. Each of these channels is explored below.

1 Brand knowledge and marketing

For long-established brands, historical records can chart their birth and development, and provide insight into brand values and differentiation. Smart companies use targeted video, training materials, intranet communications as well as seminar or conference environments to inculcate their sales forces with brand achievements and history. These training opportunities allow time and space for the history of the brand to be absorbed by front-line sales teams; so enthusiasm and brand knowledge is instilled in employees tasked with ever increasing sales targets. From the consumer's point of view a brand with longevity is often associated with quality and consumer trust so long as public relations messages are backed up with authoritative and genuine archival data. Michael Brock, Managing Director, Mercedes-Benz Museum GmbH noted in 2013 that: 'The Mercedes-Benz Museum is the best and only place in the world where, from the beginnings down to the present, one can experience the history of the automobile and the legend embodied by the Mercedes-Benz brand in a completely new and fascinating way'.

Today the internet is an essential tool for companies to illustrate brand history. The richness and diversity and volume of audio–visual collections (at one time the unusable Achilles' heel of most archives) are a perfect fit for internet capability and dissemination of brand values. Many companies take this further by promoting their brands through heritage exhibitions created in-house or in partnership with external cultural organisations.

Box 1.5 Case study: Jack Daniel's Tennessee Whiskey, United States of America

Jack Daniel's Tennessee Whiskey internet site is packed with nineteenth century stories and images of the brand, including young Jack's first purchase of a whiskey still in 1863 (aged 13), the introduction in 1895 of the distinctive square bottle, images of brand labels and awards, and personalised stories about the Daniel family, including the audio life story of business's founder Jack Daniel. Many drinks companies take the same approach and archival images, documents, even handwritten dockets are reproduced on contemporary product packaging – lending historical weight to a product made from fresh twenty-first century raw materials in sterile state-of-the-art production facilities regulated by stringent FDA protocols.

Source: Website available at http://store.jackdaniels.co.uk/world-of-jack/heritage?p=1 [Accessed 3 September 2016].

---

2 Innovation

Innovation is by its very nature about the new, the novel, the untried – but the best innovators need inspiration. Company archives can be a great inspiration to contemporary designers or scientists or business leaders as they offer ideas from past generations that can be adapted to fit today's marketplace. If the company makes products and has an archive of product samples going back over decades, some of the designs, the packaging, the structures, the components that may be regarded as dated can take on new resonance when placed in today's commercial environment. Plenty of examples exist from clothing and perfumes through to wallpapers and household goods where the company archive has inspired new consumer products. The same is true for less tangible consumer products and services in telecommunications, transport, banking and financial services where contemporary creativity can be stimulated by referencing archival data from previous markets.

Box 1.6 Case study: Marks & Spencer, archive by Alexa, United Kingdom

In April 2016, UK designer Alexa Chung collaborated with UK fashion retailer Marks & Spencer (M&S) to launch a new M&S fashion collection called *Archive by Alexa*. She used the company's Leeds-based archive as creative inspiration and all the pieces in the collection were inspired by the archive and unashamedly promoted as such in the media and in the company's stores. Her aim was 'bringing back to life the golden oldies she felt were missing from the modern high street', ranging from vests and knitwear to a classic trench coat.

Source: Sykes, 2016.

Box 1.7 Case study: Ladybird Books, centenary archive-based book series, United Kingdom

To mark the centenary of Ladybird Books in 2015, publisher Penguin Random House agreed to produce a series of satirical Ladybird books for 'grown-ups' framing contemporary relationships and topics in a way that affectionately recalled the children's books of the 1960s to 1970s. The books, with titles such as *Dating*, *The hangover* and *The husband*, adopted the same format as the original children's books and were illustrated with existing drawings from the Ladybird archive. The books were hugely popular, selling more than 600,000 copies in the two months running up to Christmas.

Source: Brown, 2015.

3 Evidence, compliance and management information

Records management and information governance offer structured frameworks for records creation, usage and disposal that ensure records are kept and destroyed appropriately, meeting legal and regulatory obligations. To participate in records management programmes, company managers must have awareness of record keeping issues and have knowledge of information their teams generate and keep. This discipline in itself creates a more efficient and effective working environment when data can be shared as needed and not subject to long searches or re-creation via IT back-up. In addition the intellectual property of a company – its trademarks and patents – is essential to protect the business in local and overseas markets, trademark disputes and copyright infringements. Often, positive evidence of trading activity such as historic sales and marketing information is needed to protect against trademark infringement, illegal patent usage and counterfeit product in undeveloped markets.

Despite evidence that companies destroy documentation as protection against legal discovery, either through rigorous records management programmes or as in some high-profile cases as the company faces court proceedings, in general the archives can be an invaluable and unique asset when companies are subject to adverse litigation. When facing litigation, speedy location of records and information from a well-managed archive is a huge bonus and saving in time and money. Records can demonstrate that business practice and activities were conducted in good faith and with due diligence. As banking historian Reis Roowaan wrote in 2009:

> Destruction of possibly damaging documents is almost certainly a losing defensive strategy ... it makes sense to maintain a complete archive in order to properly reconstruct and document events so that the lawyers are not taken by surprise by the sudden and unexpected appearance of an unknown, yet crucial document.
>
> (Roowaan, 2009, pp. 23–24)

Box 1.8 Case study: BP plc, United Kingdom

Castrol GTX is one of the best-known engine oil brands in the world, but with commercial success comes the threat of counterfeit. Where trademarks are infringed, the BP team is regularly called upon to prove that Castrol GTX has been continuously advertised and sold in particular territories. They do this by exploiting Castrol's comprehensive archive of historic packaging, pricing and advertising material. Although the intellectual property in the archive is historic, material perceived as out-of-date can be used as evidence of commercial development over time, and is invaluable for protecting current brands, and ultimately BP's business.

Source: Business Archives Council's *Managing business archives* website, 2012, at www.managingbusinessarchives.co.uk/materials/2785_managing_business_archives_lr.pdf/ [Accessed 3 September 2016].

---

4 Corporate identity

For many companies, identity and reputation are critical to their position in the marketplace and are proactively managed by executive teams. Heritage management can be used to support their endeavours. Through effective public relations strategies companies position themselves as trustworthy and capable of riding economic storms or other social or political events such as war and regime change. Indeed by embracing and making public their version of history, companies thwart attempts of potential detractors to write alternative histories. For example some of those European companies implicated in Nazi activity during the mid-twentieth century are now funding research into this period of history in an attempt to demonstrate transparency and honesty about the past. As Pontus Staunstrup explains: 'If management does not embrace and define the past, someone else inside or outside the company will, and controlling the message will become impossible' (Roowaan, 2009, p. 37).

5 Corporate responsibility

Over the last couple of decades, demonstrating ethical trading and corporate responsibility in business activity has become an agenda item for company boards. As businesses have lowered their costs by outsourcing company production and services to different and cheaper international markets, in particular Asia, there has been a consumer backlash against media stories emerging about the exploitation of native workers and resources. In response companies have taken a holistic approach when formulating their sustainability strategies aimed at clarifying their impact on and their commitment to society and the environment not only by using archival data as evidence of their actions, but also using the archives themselves as a public relations tool to support the corporate responsibility (CR) agenda.

Box 1.9 Case study: Kraft Foods Inc. (now Mondelēz International Inc.), United States of America

During company takeover and merger the use of authentic archival 'stories' to disseminate company culture and values can be a persuasive tool in the propaganda war that can spill into company and media sensibility. The hostile takeover of British confectioner Cadbury in 2010 by United States conglomerate Kraft Foods Inc. was portrayed in the United Kingdom media as predatorial and an outrage on British business and 'values'. Throughout months of negotiation and hostile media attention, the Kraft archive team worked to provide information and data about the roots and values of the Kraft organisation, particularly to the former Cadbury employees to help the change management process run its course more smoothly and less stressfully.

Source: Tousey, 2012, Seaman and Smith, 2012.

Box 1.10 Case study: Scotiabank, Canada

In 2013 the Archives Association of Ontario awarded Scotiabank's Archives, Corporate Records and Fine Art Department with the Corporate Award for excellence in archives. Scotiabank was the first Canadian bank to allow external researchers to research its holdings and the company's Director of Corporate Archives and Fine Art stated: 'We are committed to archival professionalism and have long believed that arts, culture and heritage deeply enrich our communities and should be accessible to everyone'.

Source: Scotiabank press release, 30 May 2013. *Canada's only corporate archives fully available to the public recognised by the Archives Association of Ontario.*

For example British retailer Marks & Spencer (M&S) used the announcement of their joint educational venture with the University of Leeds – the establishment of a new purpose-built company archive and research centre – as a key strand of their CR strategy. Head of the M&S company archive, Alison Houston, declared: 'We feel it is our duty to protect and conserve our retail heritage and make it available for both our internal and external users' (The National Archives, 2009. p. 13).

The companies that can use archival information to back their ethical credentials dispel the cynicism that clouds those whose CR schemes are regarded by investigative journalists and social activists as a diversionary front behind which can loom large-scale corporate tax evasion or labour force or environmental exploitation.

6 Employee recruitment, engagement and retention

Company archives and history tell the story of business development and achievement, and can be used in understanding the fabric of company culture. Often an important part of the employer proposition, companies understand that their history – available on all good corporate websites – will be investigated by potential employees before job applications or interviews. Once recruited, new employees respond well to stories about the past to get an understanding of the organisation they have joined. For many, the emotional engagement starts when the collective past is shared and they learn where the company has come from and how it has achieved its market position. For many large companies, the employee induction programme, whether conducted through formal presentations or computer-based learning, uses company history as scene-setter, teaching the new recruit about the company and its values with messages that dovetail with contemporary mission statements and strategic goals.

Beyond induction programmes, ongoing collection and curation of business narratives can be used as part of employee education and training, a form of transferable business intelligence.

Box 1.11 Knowledge transfer through reminiscence capture

A growing number of businesses capture employee reminiscences on film or audio so that experiences can be captured and knowledge transferred to the next generation. United Kingdom telecommunications business BT pioneered a programme whereby graduates and apprentices engaged in interviews with the company's senior managers, while some newly established high-tech companies reportedly interview their staff during key strategic events, creating 'real-life' history.

Source: Clegg, 2010.

International comparison of corporate archives

The Fortune 500 Global List ranks companies by revenue worldwide. Table 1.1 lists the top 10 countries represented on the list. There are three in Asia (China, Japan and South Korea), two in North America (United States of America and Canada) and the rest in Europe (France, Germany, United Kingdom, Switzerland, Netherlands). Of the 29 companies headquartered in the United Kingdom, approximately two-thirds have professionally-managed archives whose staff are active in promoting the archives' services or online research resources. This is probably the highest percentage of the European countries and is due to the well-established corporate archives sector in Britain. For North American companies, research needs to be conducted to discover whether a similar trend exists. However, a summary investigation of online sources indicates that North American companies, of which there is the highest number in the Fortune 500 list, have a good representation of managed business archives. The picture in the three Asian countries is different. In China, industrialisation started after Mao's 1949 revolution but the massive economic change that makes China home to almost one-fifth of today's Fortune 500

Table 1.1 Fortune 500 Companies with corporate archives, breakdown by country, 2015

Country	Number of Fortune 500 companies, 2015
Canada	11
China	98
France	31
Germany	28
Japan	54
Netherlands	13
South Korea	17
Switzerland	12
UK	29
USA	127

Source: List of Fortune 500 Companies. [online] Available at: http://fortune.com/rankings/ [Accessed 3 September 2016].

companies is a recent phenomenon and the Western model of long-established firms is not applicable. Alternatively in Japan, there is a centuries-old tradition of large-scale business enterprise and published business histories. Using local knowledge of Japanese business archives, Yuko Matsuzaki suggests that one-third of the Japanese Fortune 500 companies may have programme archives.[22] There is no known research on South Korea at this time.

As these are the most successful companies worldwide they are role models for many more. There is a good chance that through the trickle-down effect smaller companies will follow suit and certainly in the United Kingdom there are around 100 companies with corporate membership of professional archive associations.[23] Conversely, as the balance of global wealth changes, the proportion of highly successful companies from developing countries should increase markedly. It will be interesting to see what value these new corporations will put on archive management and record-keeping.

Business archives as cultural and community asset

Despite these examples of businesses exploiting their archives in-house, the traditional use of business archives is by historians interested in research potential. This is Schellenberg's 'secondary' value of archives – where the records have value not only to the originating organisation, but also to external parties. Economic and business history have developed as academic disciplines in response to societies' interest in the explosion of wealth and scientific growth arising from the industrial revolutions worldwide. Business archives, which are managed by the public archive services, are used by researchers in pursuit of new academic knowledge.

The strength of business collections managed within the public sector is their sheer breadth, including good coverage of the small- and medium-sized enterprises that may have been important local institutions but were not large enough to ever employ professional archive staff. Second, the collections are available on general access and not the restricted access of some of the corporate archives, allowing objective academic research. So how do business collections end up as public sector archives? Six routes are identified:

I Public sector archives – donated corporate archives

In some European countries such as Denmark and Norway, legislation is in place to encourage large companies to donate their historical archives to public institutions to make them available for research.[24] In the legislation these records come under a 'private archives' jurisdiction covering the records of science and technology or specifically businessmen and women of distinction. Some multinational corporations have taken advantage of this opportunity, but may also donate records to support research and development in the industry by transferring archives to universities with the appropriate academic expertise. For example, the University of Aberdeen is key partner in the 'Capturing the Energy' project that documents North Sea oil exploration and development. The university works with partners such as French energy company Total, to ensure that deposited business records are available for research.

Box 1.12 Case study: Ekofisk Cultural Heritage Project, Norway

The Ekofisk Industrial Heritage project illustrates the development of the North Sea Ekofisk area for the period 1962–98 and provides access to key documentary sources about Norway's oil industry. It is the first time that 'cultural relics and environments' from the petroleum sector have been documented on a large scale. Ekofisk was Norway's first producing oil and gas field and the website aims to inform audiences about the oil fields and platforms, as well as the way of life of those who lived and worked there. The installations at Ekofisk are of national importance as 'cultural monuments' and the documentation project has emerged from the Cultural Heritage Act protecting Norway's industrial heritage. The documentation has inherent complexity as it covers multi-media and is sourced from a number of commercial partners managing North Sea exploration, including the field's operator ConocoPhillips, all working in partnership with the Directorate of Cultural Heritage.

Source: Website at www.kulturminne-ekofisk.no [Accessed 3 September 2016].

---

2 Rescued industrial records in state archives

The greatest concentration of business archives entering the public sector are derived from 'rescued' industrial records. In the United Kingdom, the economic recession of the 1970s resulted in a swathe of traditional industries failing and their records were often recovered from rubbish skips and derelict factories by local archive activists. Collections of steel, coal, rail and shipbuilding records have since been established in the city and county records offices where these industries once flourished, or indeed in local university collections or specialist museums.[25] The two largest business archive collections in the United Kingdom are London Metropolitan Archives and the Scottish Business Archive at the University of Glasgow. Both institutions have significant collections and dedicated business archivists managing them. In addition to managing records of failed industries, these archives have adapted a proactive relationship with the current business community offering records management, records storage, conservation and research services so that new archival deposits can be planned and managed; though the reactive support still carries on in times of austerity and recession.[26]

3 Records of nationalised industries in state archives

These are industries where company ownership has transferred from private into public sector as a result of political action. There has not been an international trend in this regard as some countries such as the United States of America have adopted a *laissez-faire* attitude to the private sector while others, for example France, United Kingdom

---

Box 1.13 Case study: Scottish Business Archive, Scotland

The Scottish Business Archive is based at the University of Glasgow and is recognised as the guardian of Scotland's business and industrial history with remit, 'to acquire, preserve and develop the use of these records by a local and global academic community and the wider public'. The existing collections date from the eighteenth century and were inaugurated in 1959 by the university's first professor of economic history, Sydney Checkland. The archive holds over 500 collections covering the records of individual entrepreneurs, family businesses and large conglomerates. Shipbuilding, heavy engineering, brewing and banking are well represented.

Source: Website at www.gla.ac.uk/services/archives/about/ [Accessed 3 September 2016].

---

and Russia, have had a more interventionist strategy. Often a country's commercial and industrial assets remain under state control as a strategic ownership to secure wealth and power for the state; depending on political strategy this is done autocratically, where the wealth and power remains within the political elite, or more democratically, where the wealth is then re-distributed to society at large. Regardless of political status, in times of war, social unrest or economic depression governments may step in to control the means of production or propaganda dissemination.

Box 1.14 State Archives, People's Republic of China

Prior to Mao's revolution in 1949, the economy was predominantly agricultural, with only local smaller-scale industry. Industrialisation happened as China borrowed technology from political allies, in particular East Germany and Russia. These allies helped China to build factory complexes and lent technology specifically in the engineering sector. In the early years after the revolution technical drawings were kept by the Chinese State Archives. Only in the 1980s did they begin to save other business records such as finance and management records. In contemporary China, where industry operates within state/private sector partnerships, sometimes in joint venture with Western companies, the State Archives service offers advice and training in records and archive practice, while some provincial authorities, recognising a skills-shortage, are sending delegations of archive practitioners to Europe to update knowledge.

Source: Private communication with Lan Wang, State Archives, Beijing.

---

4 Records of government departments in state archives

As early as Napoleonic France,[27] governments have supervised and regulated company activity and the records of government departments shed light on not only individual companies, but also the political policies that have shaped business regulation. In the United Kingdom government departments, the records of which appear in due course in national archives, include those relating to company registration, bankruptcies, designs, patents and trademarks. Political leaders make international alliances, set trade boundaries, create tax incentives and havens to stimulate economic activity and encourage business growth in their countries. The records of the European Union trade zone will provide future historians with primary source material on the single currency, the movement of labour, the development of agricultural policy, as well as the standardisation of manufacturing regulation.

5 Records of business associations and institutions, and support services

It is common for trade and professional associations to maintain records of membership and activities that influence political discussions and decisions, and their records provide an additional resource to researchers and a different perspective from traditional company archives. The records of these organisations are often well maintained and available for public research. Examples in the United Kingdom include the Institute of Electrical Engineers, the Royal Institute of British Architecture, Trades Union Congress[28] and the History of Advertising Trust. In addition the City of London livery companies and guilds supported medieval crafts' communities, like goldsmiths and drapers, and maintain records to this day.

6 Community archives and collections held as charitable trusts or not-for-profit

Community archives are collections of records saved from destruction by employees or ex-employees, enthusiasts and collectors whose private collections together form the basis of a community-wide archive. They are often created spontaneously when a community dependent on a single industry is impacted by the failure or relocation of that industry. The archive provides a community memory with documents and audio–visual records illustrating industrial practice, clubs, sports and societies, relating to the industry. For some companies that want to separate heritage management from their trading activities, independent charitable trusts have been set up. Examples of this in the United Kingdom include the archives of Sainsbury's, Rothschilds, Royal Mail, Cable & Wireless, *The Guardian* newspaper, Clarks Shoes and Barings Bank.[29] There are many types of charitable trusts managed independently of the parent company by a board of trustees. Although they can receive financial assistance from the parent company they are able to seek third party funding and generate income by trading in heritage memorabilia, or through licensing intellectual property. In general, by adopting charitable status the archive becomes less dependent on the parent company's balance sheet and is afforded a certain degree of stability during uncertain economic conditions. The downside of the creation of independent trusts is of course the removal of the archive from the parent company itself, in particular impacting its ability to future-proof collections, by acquiring contemporary records of the business to maintain the archive's chronological growth.

International comparison – managing business archives

Business records began to be regarded as interesting primary sources and collections appeared in the public domain throughout the twentieth century at both national and regional level. North America, Europe and Australasia have strong traditions of records and archive management.

Legislation relating to business archives

In most countries legislation relating to business records affects current record-keeping, that is to say that company law dictates what records should be kept by businesses and for how long.[30] Although there is a desire amongst archivists to extend this legislation to cover historical business archives, there has been little movement in this area as it is regarded by many governments as too intrusive to enforce, understanding that most companies are private enterprises and that public legislation to govern archives management would in some cases equal expropriation of privately-owned items. The most common legislation protects records over 50 years old being legally exported from a country of origin. In addition northern European countries have progressive legislation: in Norway the national archivist is empowered to define company archives of national value and force companies to preserve them, while in Denmark the state carries most of the ongoing cost of preserving archives regarded as having special scientific importance. France has a ministerial committee for the protection of industrial records, Australia has tax incentives for the transfer of cultural property to recognised public sector archive institutions, and in the United States grants exist to support preservation and access to corporate archives through State Historical Records Advisory Boards and the National Historic Publications and Records Commission.

National strategies for business archives

To date only Denmark, England (and Wales) and Scotland have developed national strategies to manage business archives. In 2003 the Danish State Archives formally adopted an archival policy for private archives including the archives of business. It states that the primary task of the State Archives in relation to private archives is to pre-serve those from persons or institutions that have a nationwide activity and national importance or are important in the history of Danish society. Denmark offers financial incentives to businesses preserving their archives, carrying 80 per cent of ongoing costs and making one-off payments to companies to catalogue their collection prior to transferring to public archives. In the United Kingdom, The National Archives published a National Strategy for Business Archives (England and Wales) in 2009. The strategy encouraged the development of corporate archives, through publicising the commercial benefits of managing business archives effectively, as well as encouraging cross-sectoral partnerships in business archive management. The strategy was supported by a group of professional associations that formed an implementation group with a five-year remit and created an online guide to managing business archives.[31] The National Archives promoted the strategy[32] and created a post of business archives advice manager to support strategy implementation. In 2011 a Scottish version of the strategy was launched, with its own implementation group and website.[33] In 2016, when the Scottish strategy came to an end, a Scottish Business History Network was set up to continue the outreach and advocacy work it had begun. In neither case were any financial incentives or legislative provision built into the strategy, nor was there a public relations budget for strategy implementation and awareness raising.

Dedicated centres for business archives

The United Kingdom has some designated centres for business archives such as the aforementioned Scottish Business Archive, and Aberdeen University's collections of oil and gas exploration archives. Other regional centres have collections of business records often related to the industrial heritage of the area for example centres of steel-making, shipbuilding, textiles or ceramics. In other countries designated centres for business archives have become the *de facto* home for millions of business records. Examples include the Noel Butlin Archives Centre in Australia, the People's Archive in Finland, the Center des Archives du Monde du Travail in France, regional business centres in the principalities of Germany, Harvard Business School (Historical Collections) and the Hagley Museum and Library in the United States. Special mention should be given to the Danish National Business Archives (established 1948), which became a government institution in 1963 with the purpose of collecting and managing records that illustrate the history and development of Danish trade and industry.[34]

Professional associations for business archivists

On the whole there are few professional institutions dedicated to business archives and business archivists, although some of the general archive/records associations have sections or special interest groups in this area. This trend has been growing in recent years with business groups appearing in the national network from the 1980s and 1990s, with the exception of the United Kingdom's Business Archives Council, which was established in 1934. Other sector-specific organisations include the Finnish Business Archives Association, the Italian Museum and Business Archives Association and the United States Corporate Archives Forum.[35]

Academic exploitation of business archives

Academic research can explain how business and labour have contributed to Western 'capitalist' society and values, and just as corporate archivists are helping businesses to understand their past and exploit it to meet today's corporate goals, so academics are helping to create a business and economic history that informs of society's progress and international competitiveness. Outside of economic history itself there are new areas of research where business archives can contribute to the academic debate, including the following subjects.

Anthropology

It is suggested that trade was the early instigator of the development of human writing as pre-industrial societies took account of the sale of produce and goods (or 'cargo' as indigenous peoples today have described late-twentieth century goods from industrialised economies). So primitive business archives – records of institutionalised trade – are as old as human 'civilisations' and help our understanding of nascent society interactions and behaviours, critical to the study of social evolution, and the socio-cultural and general history of pre-literate and subsequent societies (Diamond, 1997). Today's business records show another step-change in human development as the frenetic nature of social media impacts human communications, interactions and relations.

Architecture

Architectural history is linked closely with industry as business clients' needs have pushed architectural and construction development forwards. From the industrial villages of New Lanark, Bournville, Port Sunlight and Saltsmill in the United Kingdom and Munkebo in Denmark (all housing projects that leave evidence of contemporary design corresponding to the economic developments in the societies) to the high tech campus environments favoured by today's IT companies, the 'means of production' and their surroundings is as visible in our environment as the showcase downtown administrative centres where companies use sky-scraping architecture in an effort to compete for top class employees and blue chip clients. Contemporary architecture and construction records provide evidence and comment on today's commerce – edge-of-town retail parks, call centres and business parks – and the post-industrial regeneration of decaying inner-city sites, now housing an emerging sector of media, communications and financial services professionals.

Art and science

Beyond economic, financial and business history, business archives are increasingly being used in the study of other academic disciplines. For example, retail archives provide data about social and cultural trends, consumer markets and product design, and publishing archives deliver information about literary figures and trends in literature and language development. The records of manufacturing and technology companies reveal scientific progress, just as the records of energy and utility companies will yield information about changing environmental science. In fact the potential of business archives as sources is limited only by imagination, as business and commerce is intrinsic to every aspect of daily life in consumer societies.

Business management and business history

For developed economies that have generated their wealth from capitalist enterprise and industry, an understanding of how companies operate and achieve success is essential to building academic theory of business administration and management. The cumulative knowledge gained from primary research on business records is transferred to teaching programmes at higher education establishments, and can ultimately provide learnings for the next generation of business leaders studying for undergraduate and postgraduate degrees in business administration. In the words of Harvard Business School's Business history initiative: 'We seek to enable scholars, educators, and practitioners to learn from the past by providing rich and nuanced evidence on the key issues faced by the world today'.[36] Business management theory also filters through to the public sector at theoretical and practical level either through the diffusion of ideas, or through collaborative service provision initiatives.

Geography

In addition to the economic value of studying business records, societies' industrial legacies have also had a significant impact on the socio-cultural and environmental landscape. From the geography of city and towns to the development of infrastructure necessary to enable trade, for example, canals, railways and roads, the landscapes of countries bear the scars of industrial growth and decline. Examples in the United Kingdom include the closely-knit mining, shipbuilding and steel towns of Scotland, Wales and northern England, the cotton and textile cities of the English Midlands, the ports of Liverpool, Southampton and Bristol, and the agricultural communities of East Anglia and the South East that produced food for the industrial populations in Britain's major cities. The contemporary oil and gas industry and the newer renewable energy industries, such as solar and wind, are making new markers in the landscape.

International relations

The United Nations Educational, Scientific and Cultural Organisation (UNESCO) Memory of the World project, initiated in 1997, recognises archives that have significant cultural value worldwide. In addition to treaties and maps that document colonial jurisdictions, records of major trade routes, roads and canals, the register also has records of individual companies and commercial activity. The following enterprises are on the register, which is updated biennially: Danish Overseas Trading companies (1997), Officina Plantiniana (2001), Dutch East India Company (2003), Lumiere Films (2005), Hudson Bay Company (2007), Farquherson's Journal of Daily Life on a San Salvador Plantation (2009) and Trade Company of Middelburg and Dutch West India Company (2011).

Box 1.15 UNESCO Memory of the World: Dutch East India Company (VOC)

The Dutch East India Company . . . founded in 1602 and liquidated in 1795, was the largest and most impressive of the early modern European trading companies operating in Asia. About 25 million pages of VOC records have survived in repositories in Jakarta, Colombo, Chennai, Cape Town and The Hague. The VOC archives make up the most complete and extensive source on early modern world history anywhere with data relevant to the history of hundreds of Asia's and Africa's former local political and trade regions.

Source: Documentary heritage submitted by the Netherlands and recommended for inclusion in the UNESCO Memory of the World Register in 2003. See Memory of the World website available at www.unesco.org/new/en/communication-and-information/memory-of-the-world/homepage/ [Accessed 3 September 2016].

In parallel to the international Memory of the World register, many countries operate a national register for significant national archives. These national and international initiatives help raise public awareness of archive collections and business archives are well represented at both levels.

Politics

Business archives record social and political progress; in particular the involvement of government in business affairs. Over time political pressure has spawned the wholesale takeover of business enterprise such as railways or oil exploration to ensure national interests are best protected, and paradoxically, the sale or flotation of nationalised interests to fund government initiatives such as public services, wars or taxation relief. In particular company tax is a significant asset in funding public services and government fights an ongoing battle of wits and experience against company tax managers eager to secure greater returns for their organisation. This struggle between government and business protagonists plays out in the twenty-first century as governments worldwide try to strip back privacy in the corporate domain to enable investigation of the economic and communication footprints of terrorists, mercenaries and other proclaimed enemies of the state.

Social sciences and the arts

The wealth and poverty of regions has varied over time as industry has flourished and declined, and this leaves its mark not only on the populations but also on their public buildings, language and cultural organisations. As company records from the nineteenth century demonstrate, paternalism was expressed through the funding of company sports and social clubs, exemplified by the colliery band or the in-house football team. In the late twentieth century companies made a more public statement of their charity by developing sophisticated corporate sponsorship of the arts programmes, supporting major cultural and sporting events. In the twenty-first century the scope of outward-facing charitable giving has shifted to investment in corporate responsibility programmes typified by well-publicised support of charities and educational initiatives. Social scientists are interested not only in the explicit relationship between companies and communities but also the theory and practice of business communications, employee behaviours and the cultural impact of business organisation.

Conclusion

Business archives are coming of age – as business tools, academic sources and cultural assets. Their accessibility and usability is continually enhanced by the digital landscape they inhabit, with company and public service archivists under increasing pressure to promote their use and expose their secrets. It can only be a good thing that our commercial heritage is better understood as it is the key driver for economic development. Through competition in business we advance science, technology, medicine, electronics and communications. As those countries saddled with the label 'third world' know to their cost, without economic development there is no social welfare, education and social stability.

An introduction to business archives offers a glimpse of possibilities and futures for the profession, as well as examples of how the exploitation of business archives can give us knowledge, insight and even commercial advantage. Those managing either public or private sector business archives will need to respond quickly and positively to ever-changing technology and customer expectations, and those working to preserve and research business archives will need new skill-sets and an abundance of intellectual creativity. But above all, archive custodians and researchers alike must borrow the strategies of successful commerce – they must market and promote their work, publish their research, and ensure that the academic and cultural value of business archives is explained and understood by the widest international community.

Acknowledgements

The author would like to thank Morgan Henning, Yuko Matsuzaki, Vrunda Pathare and Becky Tousey for reviewing the chapter and contributing helpful information.

Notes

1 Only 10 countries worldwide have over 20 per cent of their labour force in public service employment. They are (from highest to lowest per cent): Norway, Denmark, Russia, France, Finland, Slovenia, Estonia, Poland, Netherlands and Greece. Four of these nation states were historically part of the communist USSR where state ownership and control of industry and agriculture was prevalent for most of the twentieth century. Source: *The Economist*, 2012. *Pocket world in figure: 2013 edition*. London: Profile Books.
2 Economies that are amongst the wealthiest in the world, but which have only achieved ascendency in the last 10–20 years, referred to as BRICS, are Brazil, Russia, India, China and South Africa.
3 China's English language daily newspaper, produced in Beijing with a circulation of over 200,000. Source: *China Daily*, Wikipedia [Accessed 3 September 2016].
4 Reference to Voltaire's ever–optimistic protagonist in the satirical novella *Candide*, published in 1759.
5 MBA is the postgraduate degree of Master of Business Administration.
6 For example the Euro4 Directive on passenger car vehicle emissions is now compulsory in China's large cities, Singapore has introduced food-labelling legislation based on European and Australasian regulatory practice and ASEAN countries follow European directives for testing on chemical componentry in both consumer and commercial products.
7 In the English Midlands in the eighteenth century angry followers of Ned Ludd reputedly smashed up machinery in new mechanised textile mills as a protest against their job-stealing efficiency.
8 BBC News reports that 'There is no precedent for how to deal with hacking attack on the scale of that which hit Sony Pictures'. Source: Rawlinson, K., 2015. *Sony boss: 'no playbook' for dealing with hack attack*. [online] Available at: www.bbc.co.uk/news/technology-30744834 [Accessed 3 September 2016].
9 In January 2015 there were reported to be over 2 billion active social media accounts worldwide.
10 In 2013 over 1,000 people died (over 2,000 injured) when a sub-standard building collapsed in the town of Savar near the capital city Dhaka. Some Western businesses responded by campaigning to support improved conditions for factory workers in Bangladesh.
11 Ford Motor Company's unauthorised advertisement depicting women held prisoner in a car boot was condemned by women's rights groups after its erroneous publication by Ford's Indian advertising agency. Source: Article in *International Business Times*, 24 March 2013. [online] Available at: www.ibtimes.co.in/ford-india-sorry-for-offensive-figo-ad-showing-gagged-women-449655 [Accessed 3 September 2016].

12 Television documentaries, each with a related book, include *Empire: how Britain made the modern world* (2003), *Colossus: the rise and fall of the American empire* (2004) and *The ascent of money: a financial history of the world* (2008). Source: Niall Ferguson, Wikipedia [Accessed 3 September 2016].

13 See Chapter 13 for a full historiography.

14 The records continuum concept was developed by the Records Continuum Research Group at Monash University, Melbourne, Australia.

15 There are seven postgraduate archive administration and records management courses in the United Kingdom. All cover business records to some extent and two have dedicated (though optional) modules on business archives. Several corporate archives in the United Kingdom also offer year-long trainee positions for graduates prior to qualification. Professional archival and records management bodies regularly hold training days and conferences on business archives.

16 See website available at: www.ica.org/en [Accessed 3 September 2016].

17 The Society of American Archivists holds a short course on business archives annually. The Finnish Business Archives Association provides training exclusively for business archival management in a course held every two years, as well as short courses and seminars on topical themes for business archivists. Since 1984 the Centre de formation (training centre) of the Association des Archivistes Français has organised courses about business archives and since 1951 the Direction des Archives de France has run three-month international training course that include a business archives element.

18 See Chapters 4 and 5.

19 At Companies House in the United Kingdom. In the United States company registration takes place at state level by the offices of the Secretary of State, while the Internal Revenue Service is the federal institution.

20 This was common methodology before the advent of the corporate archivist.

21 The six channels described here are identified on the Business Archives Council's Managing Business Archives website, 2012. [pdf] Available at: www.managingbusinessarchives.co.uk/materials/2785_managing_business_archives_lr.pdf [Accessed 3 September 2016].

22 Private communication from Yuko Matsuzaki, Information Resources Centre (Shibusawa Eii'ichi Memorial Foundation), Tokyo.

23 Private Communication from the Business Archives Council.

24 In Denmark Erhvervsarkivet (The Business Archives) is a separate entity in the National Archives organisation.

25 In England and Wales there is a network of over 100 county and city records offices and around a dozen universities with collecting policies that include business records. This remains unusual from an international perspective.

26 This work is enabled by funding partnerships between private and public sector. The Scottish Business Archive is funded by the University of Glasgow in partnership with the business community. Partnerships are individually tailored and may be long-term contractual arrangements, individual projects for specific tasks, or one-off gifts to demonstrate general support of the aims of the university in preserving Scotland's rich business history. Similarly London Metropolitan Archives negotiates with most major business depositors for funding for their archives and this is written into collecting/acquisitions policy. Funding is secured for cataloguing and packaging costs (rather than storage and retrieval) including digitisation projects and collection-based outreach and events.

27 The Napoleonic Code enacted in 1804, mandated businesses to make annual returns to the *Tribeaux de Commerce*.

28 The Trades Union Congress (TUC) archives are deposited with the University of Warwick's Modern Records Centre.

29 For further information see Chapter 6.

30 A useful survey is available in ICA Section on Business and Labour Archives, 2004. *Business Archives in International Comparison*. [online] Available at: www.ica.org/2719/activities-and-projects/business-archives-in-international-comparison.html [Accessed 3 September 2016].

31 Available at: www.managingbusinessarchives.co.uk [Accessed 3 September 2016].

32 Available at: www.nationalarchives.gov.uk/documents/information-management/corporate-memory.pdf [Accessed 3 September 2016].
33 Available at: www.scottisharchives.org.uk/projects/business_archives/national_strategy [Accessed 3 September 2016].
34 Information on the Danish Business Archives is available online at www.sa.dk [Accessed 3 September 2016].
35 A list of professional associations, including those with business archives sections, is available through the International Council on Archives at www.ica.org [Accessed 3 September 2016].
36 Available on Harvard Business School's website. [online] Available at: www.hbs.edu/businesshistory/Pages/default.aspx [Accessed 3 September 2016].

References

Brown, M., 2015. Ladybird's foray into grown-up world tops Christmas book sales, *The Guardian*, 23 December, p. 9.

Chandler, A. D., 1977. *The visible hand: the managerial revolution in American business*. Cambridge, MA: Harvard University Press.

Clegg, A., 2010. The memory-makers. *Financial Times*, 11 January.

Cobb, C., 2013. Record breaking. *Ottawa Citizen*, 3 May.

Diamond, J., 1997. Guns, germs, and steel. The fates of human societies. New York: W.W. Norton & Co Ltd.

International Organization for Standardization, 2001. *ISO 15489–1:2001. Information and documentation – records management*. Switzerland: International Organization for Standardization.

Jenkinson, H., 1922. *A manual of archive administration*. Oxford: Clarendon Press.

Mathias, P., 1969. *The first industrial nation: an economic history of Britain 1700–1914*. London: Methuen.

Matsuzaki, Y., 2013. *Overview of business archives in Japan*. Japan: Shibusawa Eiichi Memorial Foundation.

Roowaan, R., 2009. *A business case for business history*. Amsterdam: Boom.

Salmon, M. S., 2003. The future of business archives in the post-modern world. *The future of economic history: a Canadian conference*. Guelph, Ontario, October 2003. [pdf] Available at: www.uoguelph.ca/~cneh/pdfs/salmon.pdf [Accessed 3 September 2016].

Schellenberg, T., 1956. *Modern archives: principles and techniques*. Chicago, IL: University of Chicago Press.

Seaman, J. T. and Smith, G. D., 2012. Your company's history as a leadership tool, *Harvard Business Review*, December. pp. 45–52.

Sykes, P., 2016. The Alexa factor, *The Sunday Times, Style*, 20 March, p. 42.

The National Archives, 2009. *Corporate memory: a guide to managing business archives*. London: HMSO.

Tousey, B. H., 2012. Proud histories: the use of heritage stories in post-acquisition integration. In: Resource Center for the History of Entrepreneurship, ed., 2012. *Leveraging corporate assets: new global directions for business archives*. Japan: Shibusawa Eiichi Memorial Foundation. pp. 81–86. [pdf] Available at: www.shibusawa.or.jp/english/center/network/pdf/Leveraging_all_hr.pdf [Accessed 3 September 2016].

Chapter 2

The development of international business

Roy Edwards and Kevin Tennent

The purpose of this chapter is first to provide some context to the development of international business with reference to how organisations changed, the processes of decision making and identification of issues surrounding international business. In other words the emphasis will be on the processes that lead to the generation of archives. Of necessity, there will be limits to such an introductory approach: the chapter is necessarily British 'centric' because of the expertise of the authors, but this is less of an issue as the role of Britain in the internationalisation of business has been significant and she continues to be in the forefront of international trade and commerce. Second, we will outline the development of transport and communications that has facilitated the development of an international economy by reducing the cost of transacting, while increasing its geographical scope, making it easier for instance to arrange finance internationally. Such background will hopefully prompt curiosity about the organisational and informational context that generates the archive. Inevitably there are limits: increasingly, what a nation is constantly changes, both temporally (in terms of time) and spatially (in terms of geography). Further, as well as commercial organisations there is the potential to explore other kinds of international organisations, which have had a global influence, including sporting bodies such as the International Olympic Committee and FIFA, or religious bodies such as the Catholic Church or the Anglican Communion. We limit our coverage in this chapter to those organisations directly engaged in international business – the delivery of goods, services and commodities across national boundaries as these are the best understood. However, it should be recognised that there is research being conducted on a wider range of international organisations and that our understanding of industries such as sport, should improve (Tennent and Gillett, 2015). Finally, this chapter focuses on the business side of international management and business history as a foundation and introduction, although there are also areas of political, social and cultural history that will be informed by the study of international business. We justify this by our belief that a basic knowledge of how such organisations and transactions were managed is a necessary prerequisite to understanding how the archival record should be used.

We also need to reflect on the boundary of our analysis: Is 'global' the same as international? The *Oxford English Dictionary* offers the following 'relating to or encompassing the whole of anything or any group of things, categories, etc.; comprehensive, universal, total, overall. Of, relating to, or involving the whole world, worldwide; (also in later use) of or relating to the world considered in a planetary context'. Globalisation seems to have subsumed the use of international within the literature on business history. For example the *Oxford handbook of business history* (Jones and Zeitlin, 2007) has a chapter on globalisation rather than international business. Few organisations fully encompass the whole world in their operations; many are really regional in focus. The emphasis on international management implies an organisational approach to understanding business, that is to say: 'The study of the functions, structure, relationships, and behaviour of organisations, and their relationships with the external environment' (Bullock *et al.*, 1988, p. 614). The number of organisations that can be said to encompass the whole world as their sphere of operations has generally increased over time, as the speed of transactions has generally increased, making increasingly complex international capital flows and business models possible. As companies operate in more countries the 'dual taxation' of international business, where companies have to pay tax in more than one country has become a bigger issue with practices such as thin capitalisation and transfer pricing emerging to attempt to avoid it (Mollan and Tennent, 2015, pp. 1055–1057).

The study of international management is an emerging, divergent field from international business, with an emphasis on the ongoing management of organisations and decision making. While international business history has drawn from the Chandlerian view of the firm, the study of management processes suggests that we need to define what is meant by strategy and how it relates to the study of international business organisations. Chandler (1962) defines strategy as 'the determination of the long-run goals and objectives of an enterprise and the adoption of courses of action and the allocation of resource necessary for carrying out these goals'. With international business strategy this will involve the development of capabilities to collect information about potential overseas opportunities and the ability to co-ordinate activity over distance. Of course the nature of the transactions – manufacturing, services or primary products reflects the organisational structures and the nature of the archive. International businesses require a greater span of control and have specific informational requirements but at heart they are the same as 'domestic' business.

The chapter proceeds as follows. First, we introduce the nature of international economic activity before providing a chronology that defines how the organisation of corporations changed over time. Our main focus is inevitably on the corporate form and the importance of trade and transport in creating the modern globalised economy. In so doing we pay scant attention to other important actors – the role of markets structures, the involvement of the state, the political and administrative processes of government and international political organisations, the development of institutional regimes and the wider international business environment as characterised by social, technological and legal factors (Deresky, 2014, pp. 22–56).

The nature of international economic activity

At its most basic, international business is the management and organisation of business activity across national borders, or, in the past, often between polities and jurisdictions within the same Empire, such as the British, French, Spanish, Portuguese, Dutch, German, Belgian, Danish or Japanese. This cross-border activity includes the movement and co-ordination of people, capital, commodities, goods, services and technology. It also encompasses the transfer of knowledge and information through people and organisations, as well as via communications networks. International business history, then, consists of the study of international business activity in the past. It is concerned with the continuities and discontinuities of how international business has been undertaken over time. There are a variety of literatures relating to 'varieties of capitalism', and 'national innovation systems' that inform our understanding of what international business is. While these histories are not strictly 'transnational' in character (that is 'across' borders), they are international in the sense that they compare different experiences of business *between* nations. This involves making a judgement about what the limits of international business might be. We realise that there are international institutions, like the International Monetary Fund and World Bank, which are crucial to understanding the context within which business developed. These organisations became increasingly influential in setting the scope for international business; especially after 1945. National record offices may have much that will relate to the inter-governmental negotiations that shaped these entities as well as the ongoing governance and management of them. We deliberately draw the line at such organisations. This chapter explores the organisations more directly associated with changing technology and economic growth. Inevitably this is selective but it does give a sense of what the critical issues are and the nature of the debate on international business.

To appreciate the structure of international business we have to appreciate both the organisational structures and how they are framed within society. The business corporation is a 'social' technology that helps to structure and frame transactions – and as such is a product of the nation state. Certainly legislatures can be influenced by invaders and empires – such as the Code Napoleon in Europe. The sheer number of countries does not make it practical to review each and every set of rules. However, as this publication explores the management of business archives in Britain from an international perspective the importance of British company law to many former colonies and overseas territories should be recognised. Hence we will briefly explore the historic structure of British company law and associated financial reporting.

The development of British business forms

It is important to remember that for many years the sole trader and partnership were the dominant means of organising economic activity. Up until the nineteenth century enterprise might be a partnership under contract law or incorporated using trust law established by a deed of settlement and governed by trustees rather than shareholders. In addition entrepreneurs could attempt to obtain an Act of Parliament. The latter mechanism was popular for all manner of infrastructure projects including railways and public utilities.

In England it was still possible to be imprisoned for debt, and reputation was a strong signal as to economic performance and with no welfare safety, unlimited liability was a deterrent to investors. With increasing demands for capital and surplus funds seeking investment opportunities, it was perhaps only a matter of time before a mechanism for limiting liability was under consideration. After the Restoration in 1660 there had been a wave of company promotions guaranteed by parliament, but this ended with a bang in 1720 when shareholders in the South Sea Company had parliament pass a bill prohibiting further incorporations in order to push their share price higher (Freeman *et al.*, 2012). The resulting act, the Bubble Act, has been claimed to have prevented the earlier development of limited liability. This act was finally repealed in 1825 but it was not until further legislation, beginning in 1844 with the Joint Stock Companies Act, that formal financial reporting was required. This required disclosure in the form of an annual balance sheet together with an annual general meeting. Limited liability was introduced

Table 2.1 Select list of legislation, which impacted United Kingdom business governance and record keeping

Year	Legislation	Impact
1720	Bubble Act	Prohibited joint-stock companies unless authorised by royal charter or Act of Parliament.
1825	Repeal of the Bubble Act	Board of Trade authorised to grant privileges of corporate status under letters patent, but the legal status of such corporations remained unclear.
1826	Banking Copartnership Act/ Country Bankers Act	Allowed for joint-stock status banks outside London (extended to London in 1833).
1834	Trading Companies Act	Required the public registration of members.
1837	Chartered Companies Act	Board of Trade conferred corporate status by letters patent and members' liability limited to the amount stated in the letters patent.
1844	Act for the Registration, Incorporation and Regulation of Joint Stock Companies	Made acquisition of joint-stock status legal, cheap and easy. All existing partnerships with 25+ members and transferrable shares had to become companies. Companies to be registered with, and return certain records to the newly created Registrar of Joint Stock Companies (the first in the world). Each company had to keep specific records including books of account, registers of directors and members and board minute books. A 'full and fair' audited balance sheet had to be presented to each meeting of shareholders.
1847	Act to Amend an Act for the Registration, Incorporation and Regulation of Joint Stock Companies	Amended the Act for the Registration, Incorporation and Regulation of Joint Stock Companies 1844.
1855	An Act for Limiting the Liability of Members of Certain Joint Stock Companies	Introduced limited liability.
1856	Joint Stock Companies Act	Superseded and consolidated previous acts. Established separate registers in Scotland and Ireland. Memorandum and articles of association (which defined the company's name and objectives) had to be lodged with the Registrar. Audited balance sheet no longer mandatory.
1862	Joint Stock Companies (Consolidation) Act	Consolidated existing legislation. Extended limited liability to insurance companies. Made record keeping recommendations but no longer required balance sheets to be lodged with the Registrar or board or shareholder meeting minutes to be kept. Companies did have to maintain a register of mortgages.
1867	Companies Act	Amended the Joint Stock Companies Act 1862.
1869	Limited Partnership Act	Allowed partnerships to accept long-term loans at variable interest rates, permitting sleeping partnerships.
1890	Companies (Winding Up) Act	Extended the role of Official Receiver to companies in compulsory liquidation.

Table 2.1 Continued

1890 Partnership Act	Number of partners in a business limited to 20 (10 for banks). Partnerships no longer automatically dissolved upon the death of a partner.
1900 Companies (Amendment) Act	Made external annual audit mandatory for all registered companies. Required prospectuses with standard information and registers of mortgages to be submitted to the Registrar.
1907 Companies Act	All public companies had to lodge annual balance sheet with Registrar. Recognised and provided limited liability and non disclosure to certain private companies.
1907 Limited Partnership Act	Attempted to create partnerships with limited liability, allowing sleeping partners to have limited liability.
1908 Companies (Consolidation) Act	Consolidated existing legislation.
1928 Companies Act	Required profit and loss and balance sheet accounts to be circulated to members prior to annual general meetings, prescribed balance sheet format and demanded directors provide lists of other directorships. Set out the kind of minute books and accounts a company should maintain.
1929 Act to Consolidate the Companies Acts 1908 to 1928	Consolidated existing legislation.
1948 Companies Act	Made consolidated accounts and independent audit mandatory. Profit and loss accounts to be lodged with the Registrar. Prospectuses, registers of directors, shareholders and mortgages, memorandum and articles of association and special resolutions to be kept and disclosed. Content of directors' reports prescribed.
1967 Companies Act	Abolished exempt private companies so all limited companies now had to provide the Registrar with certain records.
1980 Companies Act	Introduced public limited company (PLC) title for publicly quoted companies and aligned United Kingdom legislation with Europe following 1973 entry into European Economic Community.
1985 Companies Act	Consolidated existing legislation repealing acts of 1948, 1967, 1976, 1980 and 1981, and introduced more modern wording.
2006 Companies Act	Superseded the Companies Act 1985. Codified and changed almost every aspect of United Kingdom company law. Currently the primary source of United Kingdom company law.

by the eponymous Act of 1855. A further Act of 1856 consolidated previous legislation but also repealed financial reporting requirements. It is important to recognise the link between legislation reflecting corporate organisation and the associated financial reporting to investors and creditors. Acts in 1928 and 1947 gradually introduced the reporting requirements of audited profit and loss and balance sheets, in both single business entities and consolidated groups. By the 1960s financial reporting was increasingly used by investors in finance models, but the quality of accounting left something to be desired because of a general lack of accountability. In 1970 this was addressed by the creation by the Institute of Chartered Accountants England and Wales of an Accounting Standards Board. This became a focus for the accounting profession to develop accounting 'standards' to allow greater comparability between accounts. This culminated in a global move toward international standardisation known as IFRS (International Financial Reporting Standards). For archivists it is important to appreciate the legal and accounting foundation of organisations and their records. Printed public accounts are not the same as internal financial and management accounts. Modern financial reporting enables a comprehensive story to be told about a business – albeit one that requires a great deal of expertise and some caution in interpretation (Armstrong, 1991; Berland and Boyns, 2002; Edwards, 1988). Table 2.1 provides a select list of the key legislation that has impacted the governance and record keeping of British companies, but for further detail see the works of R. Harris (2000) and B. C. Hunt (1936).

The origins of international business

Trade unifies studies of the pre-historic and the modern. In this sense we will have to delineate our analysis of the past to include the emergence of trade and international business from the seventeenth century. This makes sense if we view our story as one of changing ways of organising economic activity over time; a gradual shift in how nation states came to acquire resources and facilitate the selling of output. Rosenberg and Birdzell (1986) begin their analysis of Western economic development in the Middle Ages, and there is good reason to view this as a critical juncture in international business. Practices and techniques supportive of commerce spread throughout Europe, including double entry bookkeeping, and varieties of contract law – the Lex Mercantoria. These, combined with the exploration and discovery of the 'new world', created an environment that required new ways of organising production, distribution and selling. The dominant form of trade activity was often based upon individual voyages with partnerships dissolved when the ship returned. The risks associated with these ventures led to early insurance contracts such as the 'bottomry and respondentia' bond. Marine insurance markets developed in London and Amsterdam, and eventually specialist brokers offered an increasingly wide range of products that supported not just marine transactions but also industrial insurance.

With the development of new ship design, allied to an enthusiasm among many states for overseas expansion and conquest, further opportunities for wealth acquisition emerged. Indeed the pursuit of empire itself was a significant administrative operation, requiring administrative capabilities that could be applied in business (Darwin, 2009). Indeed in some cases the boundary between governmental and commercial was not always clear. The granting of corporate status to companies intended to develop trade in overseas markets is a case in point.

From the seventeenth century corporations emerged to take advantage of these opportunities, often associated with a specific region, becoming some of the largest organisations then in existence. The Dutch East India Company (established 1602) and the English East India Company (established 1600) set up operations in Asia and the Hudson's Bay Company (established 1670) in Canada (Dari-Mattiacci et al., 2013, p. 1; Michie, 1999, p. 15). Some, such as the ill-fated Company of Scotland Trading to

---

Box 2.1 Case study: Company of Scotland Trading to Africa and the Indies 1695–1707

The Company of Scotland Trading to Africa and the Indies was created in 1695 to set up a Scottish trading settlement in Central America. Snubbed by the English King and Parliament, the enterprise became a national patriotic cause in Scotland and attracted a large and diverse group of Scottish investors.

The subscription list opened in Edinburgh in February 1696, inviting investments from a minimum of £100 up to a maximum of £3,000. Such was the popularity of the scheme that on the first day alone 69 subscriptions were taken, worth £50,400. A second book was later opened in Glasgow and soon the full target of £400,000 sterling had been reached. Subscribers were initially required to pay one quarter of the total they had signed up to invest, with the remaining sum being paid in smaller instalments as and when requested by the directors. Investors included nobility, landed gentry, doctors, lawyers, ministers, farmers and merchants as well as a number of city and town councils.

The company was managed by an elected court of up to 50 directors – the first 25 elected by the subscribers, with up to a further 25 elected by the first 25 electees. Subscribers with a holding of £1,000 or more could stand for election. The first 25 directors were elected in May 1696.

Two expeditions of settlers set sail and a colony was established. However, the expected trading opportunities did not materialise, the settlement was decimated by disease and attacked by the Spanish who considered the territory their own. The company was finally wound up in 1707 and in its failure Scotland lost a quarter of its liquid assets. The Company of Scotland archives are held by the Royal Bank of Scotland's Archives and the National Library of Scotland and their historical significance has been recognised by UNESCO.

For further information see Prebble, 1968.

Africa and the Indies (established 1695), better known as the Darien project, failed spectacularly (Prebble, 1968). Perhaps the most infamous was the South Sea Company (established 1711) established to trade in the South Seas and America, and, almost as an afterthought, to encourage the development of fishing. It was the South Sea Company that collapsed because of fraud leading to the Bubble Act of 1720 that constrained joint stock incorporation in Britain until well into the nineteenth century (Dale, 2004; Paul, 2011).

These companies were quasi-governmental in character but had a secondary market in shares. In an age of uncertainty and communications inhibited by distance, they enabled investors to pool risk, while delegated powers to boards of directors provided what passed for accountability. Such structures had permanence then rarely afforded to a partnership usually based on a specific voyage or specified projects such as a mine. The death of a partner or the need to realise funds when faced with a call on cash, meant that the lifetime of any partnership was limited with no guarantee when such events might occur. This affected planning horizons and hence the nature of the projects/products provided by the entity. These chartered corporations had elements of limited liability, and were often supported by the granting of monopolies by their respective governments. They were allowed separate legal personality and the ability to transfer ownership – significant innovations that provided a more hospitable environment to invest. So corporate organisation was not just government monopoly and it was during the seventeenth and eighteenth centuries that a richer variety of corporate forms emerged to suit the particular operating and commercial conditions. According to Harris' analysis:

> Because of their peculiar path of historical development and their distinct economic circumstances, shipping and mining had a unique framework for business organisation: the part ownership in ships and the cost book partnership system in mining.
>
> (Harris, 2000, p. 31)

The law that affected international business developed piecemeal from custom and practice before being codified within statute law by sympathetic judges. By the nineteenth century, the chartered companies were generally unable to protect their monopolies and the political will to maintain monopoly had receded.

The emergence of international business

The formal legal structuring of transactions within some organisational format was clearly important for enabling business activity to be planned. However these were often the result of pre-existing activity that was later formalised, thereby codifying relationships for future performance. For example, syndicates of independent merchants and intermediaries were involved in creating global networks to facilitate trade, such as Jardine, Matheson & Co. and Butterfield & Swire in the China trade (Jones, 2000, pp. 162–163). Jones illustrates how Butterfield & Swire, known as John Swire & Son by 1914, operated a number of branches in China and Japan in addition to four 'affiliated' companies, all registered in London (Jones, 2000, pp. 165–166) – a shipping company – the China Navigation Co., a sugar refining company – the Taikoo Sugar Refining Co, the Tientsin Lighter Co., which provided 'lighter' services for loading and unloading ships, and the Taikoo Dockyard and Engineering Co. Swire did not fully own these companies, but generally took the largest stake, allowing the group to gain outside capital for its ventures without loss of control. Single project companies were incorporated by such merchants in association with solicitors and accountants, and encouraged the growth of London, and to a lesser extent Liverpool, Glasgow, Edinburgh and Dundee as 'headquarters cities' (Jackson, 1968; Wilkins, 1988, pp. 265–270; Wilkins, 1989; Wilkins and Schröter, 1998; Tennent, 2009; Miller, 1998, pp. 228–229).

Institutional changes made corporate organisation both cheaper and easier to get. Limited liability was introduced in Britain through the Companies Acts of 1854 and 1862 (Maltby, 1998); France saw limited liability in 1867 (Murphy, 2004, p. 19), and Germany in 1870 (Herrigel, 2007, pp. 474–475). However, it was often the case that investor protection was weak even in the United Kingdom for domestic business. Shareholders had few rights compared to today, the role of directors was not clearly prescribed except that they had to exist, shareholders were only allowed one vote per share, and the need for audited balance sheets as had existed in the unpopular 1844 Companies Act was removed in 1854. In the Victorian era, the United Kingdom's standards of corporate governance were basically equivalent to one of today's 'offshore havens'. The position of Britain as a centre of empire and trade attracted overseas companies to register in the United Kingdom too. Reporting requirements were a little more onerous as additional information was required for entry into the *Stock Exchange yearbook*. In general companies were cheap to set up, and the only reporting necessary was the head office address and an update on issued capital every year. The level of information required to be disclosed slowly increased in the early twentieth century – by 1901 the auditing of balance sheets was required, by 1907 'public' companies had to publish a balance sheet and by 1930 a profit and loss account, although it was not until the post-war period that full reports of subsidiary companies would be required (Napier, 2010). This gradual move toward transparency in financial reporting was replicated across the Western world as the twentieth century progressed, but for most of this period – and for most companies – formal public disclosure was at a minimum. This meant that the true nature of inter-national activities could be concealed within a corporate structure while their promoters faced limited risk.

The expansion of economic activity from the classical 'Industrial Revolution' to 1914 saw a mix of direct investment and portfolio investment, whereby domestic investors supported overseas activity. The twentieth century would see business expand-ing from the 'core' to the periphery, but lacking the stability of the nineteenth century. Prior to 1914 many manufacturing companies simply exported as tariffs were low, currencies were pegged to gold and intermediary firms, such as S. Hoffnung & Co. in Australia, could sell British manufactured goods into underdeveloped colonial markets (Mollan, 2010). Where internationalisation developed as a strategy was in markets where products were heavy, technologically sensitive or perishable, such as Vickers' overseas investments in the armaments industry, the Sheffield steel maker's overseas invest-ments, or even the Mackintosh confectionery company's establishment of factories in Germany and the United States (Jones, 1986, pp. 6–7). After the First World War and especially in the 1930s, tariffs rose significantly, with markets both within Europe and overseas attempting to become more self-sufficient by developing home industry to increase export substitution. This tendency created more opportunity for 'export substitution' internationalisation as manufacturing behind tariff barriers was the only way to ensure access to markets (Jones 1986, p. 9). The disruption created by two world wars began a gradual shift of economic power that had the effect of increasing international barriers – especially the introduction of tariffs and the fixing of currency through the agreements reached at Bretton Woods.

The gradual and messy end to European empire also changed how business was organised. Some British firms, such as ICI, had expanded by targeting the British Dominions, replicating their British operations in Australia, New Zealand and South Africa (Owen, 1999). In a world increasingly shaped by nationalism, foreign business was at risk of nationalisation often without compensation. This created an unstable business environment, as entrepreneurs and managers sought to manage increasingly nationalist economic and business policies. But the gradual liberalisation of tariffs from the 1970s onwards led to trade barriers falling and an export substitution strategy gradually became less advantageous for manufacturers. Falling tariffs, transport costs, deregulation, privatisation and better technology meant by the 1980s and 1990s that replicating manufacturing in many markets was no longer necessary. Manufacturing could instead be spread around the world according to the relative cost of production.

The development of international business before 1914, particularly that based in the United Kingdom and to a lesser extent other European countries, did not just follow the structure of domestic business. A more nuanced view held that the specific problems associated with long distance, the need to be informed of local conditions in what were increasingly global markets, led to the formation of companies that were involved in investment using a bilateral business model. Emerging from her research into British foreign direct investment (FDI) into the United States, Mira Wilkins found a tranche of companies that did not fit the typical headquarters-subsidiary fashion associated with later FDI – thus emerged the notion of the Free Standing Company (FSC) (Wilkins, 1986; Wilkins, 1988; Wilkins, 1989; Wilkins and Schröter, 1998). FSCs had a headquarters in, for example, Britain, and a registered office, but did not have any operations in the domestic economy (known as the 'home country' in international business nomenclature). The Free Standing Company 'business model' may be illustrated with a hypothetical example: suppose a prospector discovered gold deposits in Ghana. He could register a company at his existing place of business, for instance in London and 'sell' the company secretarial services. He could then use his networks and the financial press to seek capital from investors. In addition, expertise in mineral extraction and geology might be bought in from consultants in mining engineering who would also be based in London. Then it was a matter of investing sufficient seed capital to establish the business in Ghana. The output of the mine could then be sold through the metal exchanges and other networks in London, and if the project turned out to be less productive than thought, the mine could be closed and mothballed or shut completely, winding up the corporate entity.

Free Standing Companies were not unique to the British experience and have been found headquartered in France, Belgium, the Netherlands, Germany, Switzerland and the United States of America, investing all over the world (Wilkins and Schröter, 1998). They were established in a variety of industries across the primary, secondary and tertiary sectors. There were 8,400 mining companies registered in London during the period 1870–1914 (Harvey and Press, 1990). Another important area of activity was investment in plantation operations, particularly in tropical crops, such as tea in India, rubber in India and Brazil, as well as coffee, indigo, silk, and jute among others (Schmitz, 1997; Chapman, 1998). In livestock farming free-standing companies also facilitated the meat supply chain as well as the associated processing of dairy products. This was crucial in developing the economies of countries such as Australia and New Zealand, the United States of America, Uruguay and Argentina (Jones, 1997; Tennent, 2009; Tennent, 2013). The financing of these enterprises were supported by finance and infrastructure projects, and free-standing banks, such as the London and River Plate Bank, and the Bank of British West Africa, provided additional support to these projects (Jones, 1998, p. 346).

Physical infrastructure was provided by funds channelled across borders by these institutions – railways, port facilities, electricity, gas, water, tramways, inland shipping – especially in Latin America, but also to some extent in Asian and African colonies (Jones, 1997; Miller, 1998; López, 2003; Boughey, 2009). Management capabilities were developed both in the home, and in the host country (the country where the operations lay), although the extent to which strategy was developed in the home or host country has been controversial, with empirical studies finding a range of outcomes (Tennent,

2009). In any event, this geographical separation of ownership and control necessitated frequent communication between headquarters and the outlying enterprise. It is difficult to generalise across the experiences of the many types of company. Some of the larger businesses such as Rio Tinto internalised with multiple 'projects', effectively following a portfolio approach to investment. This approach required management hierarchy and associated career structures that enabled the business to acquire – and keep – the relevant skills (Harvey, 1981). Other, cosmetically smaller mining companies – such as Anglo-American, Goldfields of SA, London Tin Co., Selection Trust and affiliates – used the free-standing structure as a vehicle to spread risk around a 'central' firm, which was essentially a hollowed out entity arranging financial services and mining expertise for the affiliated free-standing companies (Johnson, 1987, p. 28). In the extreme some were simply a 'brass plate' corporation, with little evidence of formal corporate structure. They had a headquarters and were only operational overseas and all knowledge and strategic resources came from outside the firm. See Box 2.2 for a case study of the Edinburgh-based New Zealand and Australian Land Company Ltd, one of the largest Scottish free-standing companies.

The FSC could also emerge from the host economy. Dalgety & Co. were an Australian company founded in Melbourne in the mid nineteenth century as general merchants who developed specialist expertise in the management of wool exports to London (Daunton, 1989). They co-ordinated between home operations and London, but found difficulties in overcoming distance from the market and moved to London in 1854, relying on family members as agents to manage business in Australia. The ephemeral nature of some FSCs was undoubtedly because they were established on a project-by-project basis and had 'completed' their task and exited. Others evolved into multinational corporations (MNCs), as we shall see below.

Mira Wilkins argued that over time, the Multinational Enterprise (MNE) superseded the Free Standing Company. But was the latter really an inferior mode of international management? Wilkins, a diehard Chandlerian, argued that management processes were likely absent with no centralised managerial resources and this was possibly a weakness in the long run (Wilkins, 1988; Wilkins and Schröter, 1998). It appeared that many of these companies lacked their own strategic capability, being a purely financial vehicle for a specific project. There was often no pooling of risk between multiple projects or international holdings within one corporate unit, nor transfer of resources or capabilities such as people, practices or plant between them. However, it may well be that strategic management was conceptualised differently by the British and one of the issues for historians is to tease out from the remaining archives what form this might have taken. Nor was the FSC the final word in corporate endeavour as it was always possible to transition into a 'mainstream' corporation when the time was right. More importantly for the decline of the FSC over the twentieth century was the changing institutional environment, as described above.

Other factors helped to shape these entities. Taxation, and in particular the problem of double taxation, shaped the organisational structure of the FSC, beginning from after the First World War (Mollan and Tennent, 2015). The FSC was vulnerable to corporation tax both in its home and host countries. In some cases this prompted mergers between FSCs and the central co-ordinating firms, with local domiciling of subsidiaries, and strategies of transfer pricing or thin capitalisation between entities to manage tax liabilities.

***

**Box 2.2 Case study: New Zealand and Australian
Land Company Ltd, 1866–1968**

The New Zealand and Australian Land Company (NZALC) was a free-standing company set up by the Glaswegian financier James Morton, together with his business associates, in 1866 to bring limited liability to 38 disparate land holdings on the South Island of New Zealand and in Queensland, Victoria and New South Wales. Initially capitalised at £2 million the company developed a managerial hierarchy in Australasia to manage its properties, which farmed sheep and cattle on a mass scale. The company contributed to the development of industrialised farming in both countries, pioneering the export of frozen sheep carcasses from New Zealand to London in 1882, before copying Canadian and Danish dairy production techniques to move into cheese and butter production.

Strategic management remained concentrated at the company's headquarters in Glasgow, and later Edinburgh, and under the iron-fisted control of the company's General Manager, William Soltau Davidson, who served from 1878 until 1916. Davidson exhorted the company's farm managers to 'place yourselves in the position of proprietors, and make every effort to work the places as economically and as profitably as if they were your own'. Over time the company consolidated its holdings, pursuing greater economies of scale, gradually selling out of New Zealand and reinvesting in larger properties in Australia. NZALC bought its first property in Western Australia in 1906, and continued to invest in Australia until its purchase by the Anglo-Australian group Dalgety in 1968.

The NZALC archives, including the company's minutes, letters and property maps remain accessible in the National Archives of Scotland in Edinburgh, providing evidence of the company's headquarters organisation. Microfilmed copies are also available at the National Library of Australia in Canberra.

For further information see Tennent, 2009, pp. 101–198; Tennent, 2013.

***

The nature of the FSC changed as technology and economic circumstance dictated and transition could take a myriad of forms. For example, by the 1970s, many mining companies listed in London had evolved into 'mining finance' companies that lent to mining exploration and extraction companies who were locally registered. Even with the decline of the mining FSC, there were still 369 overseas mining companies listed on the London Stock Exchange in 1950 (London Stock Exchange, 1950). So the industry was the same, but the business model had changed.

The multinational enterprise

The multinational enterprise (MNE) is perhaps the best known and arguably the most important form of international business, with a rich and varied history. Some MNEs grew out of FSCs while others grew out of domestic operations – particularly in manufacturing or services, some through licensing or replicating a business model in new markets. These are essentially assumed to be classic Chandlerian (1962; 1977; 1990) corporations spreading after establishing domestic competitive advantage, so that comparative advantage – technology, knowledge and so on, in the home country is spread through the corporate form. The MNE developed in many cases out of companies seeking to substitute for exports by locating in the host market. Post 1918 many United States and European MNEs expanded into developed countries by simply replicating their manufacturing activities and even their research and development work. For example the American company NCR expanded into Britain and located significant research facilities in Dundee, retaining research and development facilities there even after the main factory had closed (BBC News, 2009). Others, like Ford and Mars, created subsidiaries around the world to which they delegated considerable managerial independence. This allowed them to recruit local employees with appropriate skills sets to complement the capabilities being imported and to develop branding relevant to domestic markets. Domestic competition was often weak as these were often so-called 'second industrial revolution industries' where first mover advantages were spread more evenly around the developed world. Some businesses followed a multinational strategy in order to gain competitive advantage by integrating backward into primary industries in Africa or Asia. For example Unilever – formed of a merger between British soapmaker Lever Brothers and Dutch margarine producer Antoon Jurgen (by then Margarine Unie) – was created in 1929 (Wilson, 1968). Both needed to secure supplies of palm oil, an ingredient in both detergents and margarine, and established business throughout Africa thereby securing their supply chain.

The creation of such trading networks was common in industries such as food, drinks and tobacco wherever there was a need for commodities as inputs. These might take the form of direct ownership of plantations as in the case of tea and coffee. Other organisational solutions were found through the development of trading networks – often found in palm oil, cocoa, bananas (Jones, 2000). Services were also internationalised as they developed more sophisticated, replicable business models. F. W. Woolworth pioneered discount retailing in the United States of America, before entering Britain in 1909, and Germany in 1927 (Seaton, 2009).

From the 1950s onwards franchised-based business models were often used in industries such as fast food (McDonalds), hotels (Hilton) and car rental (Avis) (Hackett, 1976). This was followed in the 1970s by more direct and widespread investment. This trend was continued into the 1980s when deregulation and privatisation policies, alongside of free movement for capital, established a rationale (however contested) for private, often foreign ownership of infrastructure business. More widespread investment in utilities – such as in railways (Deutsche Bahn), waste management (Veolia), and gas and electricity (EDF) – became possible after domestic markets were liberalised. Political ideology also influenced the behaviour of overseas enterprise. Perhaps one of the most marked examples of this has been the 'Africanisation' process seen in the 1960s and 1970s, in newly independent West African colonies, and after the end of apartheid in South Africa as subsidiaries of MNEs came under pressure to employ more African managers and even localise their sources of capital (Decker, 2005; 2007; 2008; 2010). For a useful case study in terms of service internationalisation, that of Stagecoach's entry into the Malawian bus industry, see Box 2.3.

Box 2.3 Case study: Stagecoach Malawi 1989–1996

Stagecoach Malawi is an illustrative case of misplaced internationalisation. Stagecoach plc is a United Kingdom bus and rail operator, which grew from one bus in 1980 to a turnover of £36.8m and pre-tax profits of £3.5m by 1989. The company's founders, brother and sister Brian Souter and Ann Gloag, looked for overseas expansion opportunities and found one in the former British colony of Malawi, where the bus system was run as a monopoly concession by a British company, British Electric Traction, who wanted to pull out. The expansion seemed logical for Stagecoach as English was the country's official language, and left-hand driving meant that buses could easily be transferred to the country. Stagecoach were able to bring in spare double decker buses from another of their overseas subsidiaries in Hong Kong, and the Commonwealth Development Corporation funded further fleet improvement. All was successful until 1993, the subsidiary generating profits of about £1.6m a year. But in November of that year two accountants set fire to the company's head office in Blantyre to conceal their own embezzlement. Cracks began to show, as it proved increasingly difficult to hire well-qualified professionals to run the back office, as they preferred to work for the government. Worse was to come, as President Hastings Banda, who had been favourable to Stagecoach, was overthrown in 1994. The new government refused to enforce Stagecoach's monopoly, and the company soon found its operations become unprofitable as they were overtaken by competition from unlicensed minibuses. The acquisition was not completely unsuccessful as its initial cost to Stagecoach was repaid within two years, but in exiting the company was forced to hand its subsidiary back to the Malawian government for free.

The company had been unprepared for the cultural and psychic distance between the United Kingdom and Malawi. While its brightly coloured buses, considered banal in the United Kingdom, were popular with Malawian passengers, the company had struggled to import its management style into such an alien environment. It failed to motivate local employees and fell out with government, ultimately becoming victim to a deregulation, a cause the company had ironically championed in its home country.

For further information see Wolmar, 1998, pp. 106–111.

During the 1990s yet more political changes changed the operating environment of the MNE, as the Soviet Union broke up and the Chinese embraced their own modified form of capitalism. Coupled with earlier liberalisation, and the free movement of capital, manufacturing and services could be produced anywhere in the world. The globalised supply chain created a world of connection that changed yet again the nature of international business.

The new MNE? Businesses that are born global

International New Ventures (INV) are rapidly globalising firms, post 1990, that bring together capabilities from more than one country from their initial formation (Oviatt and McDougall, 1994). For example in software, a programming team that might be based in several countries drawing upon specific strengths of a location, while avoiding any of the pitfalls, and being able to develop specific capabilities that match the business model of the enterprise.

In the digital age many firms really are 'born global' as the transaction costs associated with international business have declined, with the use of email and video conferencing building on the transport innovations wrought by cheap air fares. Examples include Uber, founded 2009, now in 53 countries and worth US$40bn, and Airbnb, founded in 2008 with properties in 192 countries. Crucially both of these companies are able to offer service products in a wide spread of countries without direct investment into them.

Back to the future?

International New Ventures (INVs) are a type of firm organised through the internalisation of some transactions and reliance on alternative governance structures to access resources, such as capital or productive assets from multiple countries. So these organisations are 'created international' at birth, like Wilkins' free-standing companies – but are they the same thing? There are clear similarities in that neither entity established successful domestic operations before going overseas and both tend to be primary or service sector firms. Geographical location still matters, although this might involve tax advantages rather than a primary resource or access to markets behind a trade barrier. Both also had to overcome the problems of working at distance and managing the relationships necessary to conduct business effectively overseas. Certainly, where the FSC existed as more than a cipher both have centralised strategic decision making at a head office. However there are still significant differences: the INV may operate in the home country as well as draw resources from it and is perhaps more likely to internalise knowledge and managerial resources and may be more likely to be a distinct corporate entity of its own.

Finally, it's worth noting that FSC-like structures are still attracted to 'offshore jurisdictions' that are often still notionally under the control of the United Kingdom or other former colonial powers, such as Isle of Man, Channel Islands, Cayman Isles, British Virgin Islands and Bermuda. These locations still offer low (or no) corporation tax, low shareholder protection, low disclosure requirements, anonymity, and the like, although in recent years these powers have come under attack by governments concerned by the domestic political ramifications of tax avoidance schemes and the use of such havens by terrorists (Wojcik, 2012). To summarise the FSC, MNE and INV, have, at different points in history, been attractive structures for international business.

The MNE is probably the most well known form of international business activity as it involves the setting up of a subsidiary in every country, but the FSC and INV have more flexibility and are especially well adapted to deliver on project-like endeavours. For the FSCs, history has largely forgotten their role until relatively recently and there is still much to be learnt of their contribution to international business. Wilkins argued that they declined because they did not have the 'managerial infrastructure' of the MNE,

Table 2.2 International business forms in history – a taxonomy

Type	Features	Approximate period	Examples
Mercantile partnership/ Trading company	Partnership or limited company structure based around a network of offices around the world, often organised by family. Facilitates and organises trade. Promotes free-standing companies (FSCs), domestic companies and later MNEs to spread risk and create side-bets.	c.1700– present	Jardine Matheson James Finlay & Company Harrisons & Crossfield
Chartered company	Chartered and guaranteed by home government to protect and monopolise trading interests in a certain part of the world. Some primitive arrangements for secondary sale of shares. Builds networks of forts and military infrastructure to protect trade.	c.1600–1900	Dutch East India Company East India Company (United Kingdom) Hudson's Bay Company Niger Company
Free Standing Company (FSC)	Registered and notional head office in home country, operations entirely in host country. Usually extractive (mining or farming), or utility sector. Often trade oriented with home country.	c.1860– 1960s	Roan Antelope Copper Mines New Zealand and Australian Land Company Matador Land and Cattle Co. Midland Railway of Western Australia Anglo–Argentine Tramways Co.
Multinational Enterprise (MNE)	Diversified set of operations across a number of countries, potentially globally. Typically 'stage' internationalisation, starting with exports, then moving manufacturing abroad to substitute for export. May invest to circumvent tariff barriers. Increasing retreat from this model towards networked structure with outsourced production, activities located for optimal factor conditions, and FDI supporting distribution only.	c.1860– present	Anglo–American Corporation Electrical & Musical Industries Unilever Shell Transport & Trading Hong Kong and Shanghai Banking Corporation
International New Venture (INV)	Network model – head office often notionally at place of registration. Activities spread around world wherever factor conditions suit. Draws capabilities from around the world. Can use technology to operate in host economies without direct investment.	c.1990– present	Uber AirBnB

but this is likely to be an oversimplification as many FSC structures gradually evolved into MNEs while those wishing to remain small and nimble may have moved to less visible headquarters locations. The financial reporting requirements of such businesses when privately held are not as great and hence their activity is rarely in the news and may get overlooked by the media.

Transport and the international economy

The emergence of international business was facilitated by changes in transport and communication. The recent analysis presented by Miller (2012) is a useful corrective to the view that 1914 saw a demarcation between an international economy that was open, followed by years of autarchy and protectionism. While there is an element of truth in this view, Miller notes that there is more to international business than market integration. His work draws upon a vast range of archives, and explores the business, social and economic connections forged by banks, shippers and other institutions of commerce, that supported international trade. This historical perspective is augmented by interview evidence that places the analysis within its operational and commercial context. He emphasises the importance of individual experience, both of workers and entrepreneurs in shaping perceptions of international trade and associated business entities. As Miller points out from 1945 the world of trade became less Eurocentric, and saw the demise of the traditional technology associated with port cities that had long been associated with trade such as London, Liverpool and Amsterdam. Of course the legacy of trade and commerce helped to create the City of London even though by the late twentieth century there was little left of the old docks and the new container terminal had been built further down the river at Tilbury. The financial institutions that had supported trade remained and transformed into global providers of financial services. Kynaston (1994; 1995; 2000; 2002) provides an excellent narrative of this process and how the domestic linked to the international in the City. Miller notes the interaction between finance and trade. Capital market deregulation in the late twentieth century led to a variety of new financial instruments and funds – for example the euro-dollar market that emerged in London during the 1960s, prompting investment in trade. The process of containerisation led to demand for investment in new port and ship infrastructure.

It is usual to place the development of trade alongside the steamship, railway and telegraph in the nineteenth century. However, it is in the twentieth century that the notion of integrated logistics conceived as a supply chain – food from field to fork, manufactured products from forge to factory and final delivery to the customer – emerged. This is most often represented by the process of containerisation and the invention of standardised, stackable metal containers that could be transferred from rail to ship to road (Levinson, 2006). This revolutionised the haulage of freight and the utilisation of assets. The use of pallets and fork lift trucks, alongside a host of mechanical handling innovations decreased the cost of transportation. Miller notes that the 1967 Rotterdam container cost one fiftieth of conventional cargo (Miller, 2012, p. 337). The loading of pallets into containers further eased the process of haulage. The speed of change was astonishing. The first trans-Atlantic container was hauled in 1966 and by 1970 70 per cent of general cargo was in containers. The implication for port cities was clear, although it often took time for the now outdated infrastructure to be demolished or turned over to new uses.

The development of containerisation increasingly relied on the use of computers and mathematical models to ensure safe stacking of ships and complemented the wider use of such models in logistics. However, it is often left unappreciated that this was only possible with more general innovation in standards of packaging to ensure that the product arrived safely. The shift from sacks and wooden barrels to the cardboard box and metal containers meant that the quality of haulage improved throughout the twentieth century. The history of packaging from a functional, rather than as an artistic or advertising endeavour has yet to be written.

The corporations involved in the container trades were often not the traditional shipping companies, although some were able to make the transition through buying early movers. For example, the first Sea-land Services Inc., founded by Malcom Mclean in 1960, would be bought by a railway (US railway CSX) before finally being purchased in 1999 by Maersk. The Mediterranean Shipping Company was founded in Italy (1970) and by 2005 it had its headquarters in Switzerland and was second only to Maersk (Miller, 2012, p. 354). Other entities, such as American Presidents Line (APL), were able to transform themselves into what were effectively logistics companies. APL introduced dedicated container trains, established wagon leasing services, designed schedules for terminal operations and liaising with haulage of containers bought into port by APL ships (Miller, 2012, p. 344).

The global nature of trade and the ability of corporate entities to function more effectively relied on a variety of innovations associated with information technology and the rise of cheap air travel that enabled rapid exchange of staff for the purpose of supervision and training. It became easier to understand international cultures by visiting host economies and sharing visions of strategy and operations.

Conclusion

This chapter has presented a broad sweep of international business history. Early forms of international business developed supported often by European expansion into the Americas, Asia, Africa or Australasia. Some of the earliest business structures, such as the chartered companies, evolved to support directly the governance of empire. This in some ways reflects the fact that empire itself was, at least before the late nineteenth century, a commercial activity with expected returns for the home country. As time moved on the emergence of limited liability structures allowed for more entrepreneurialism to develop independently of the state and indeed of imperial structures. British capitalists were able to set up business groups, and float free-standing companies affiliated to them that could target areas of the world such as India, Australasia and sub-Saharan Africa that the British dominated – but they were also able to target other European dominated settler countries such as Argentina and Uruguay. Over time these structures, which allowed for risk parcelling, permitted business groups to rapidly expand their interests, while attracting surplus funds from European economies.

Multinational companies based on spreading competitive advantage in manufacturing also started to emerge in the second half of the nineteenth century. These companies typically made products that were costly to trade internationally, as they were heavy or perishable, such as motor vehicles or margarine. These companies were often able to develop along similar trading pathways to the free-standing company groups, but they also had the advantage of having developed their business model in the home economy, typically the United States of America or a European country. After the First World War, governments, including most strikingly the United Kingdom, started to raise tariff barriers and pursue protectionist and autarchic industrial policies more. Corporation tax also increased in a number of countries making double taxation more of a threat to international business. These changes ironically did not encourage domestic entrepreneurs, although they did make the bilateral form of the free-standing company less attractive, but often encouraged 'multinational enterprise' type structures to flourish as manufacturing firms sought advantage by manufacturing behind tariff barriers. This form of international manufacturing continued to flourish after the Second World War, while free-standing companies often merged together or changed their structure towards finance to avoid direct double taxation. By the 1970s, this tendency created the gnomic impression that the multinational enterprise was the natural form of international business – but the liberalisation and financialisation processes seen since the 1970s have started to reverse the dominance of the traditional MNE.

Manufacturing multinationals have increasingly been able to move their production around the world to locations with the most favourable 'comparable advantage'. This has meant targeting places with the best factor conditions, whether price of land or labour. Originally this was done within the firm, but increasingly offshoring takes places outside of the firm, and so we have seen something of a retreat from multinational manufacturing operations. We have also seen something of an evolution back towards free-standing company type structures, particularly where the opportunity of registering in a low disclosure, tax and regulation jurisdiction is available. Further technology allows for teams of workers located around the world to work together in logistics or service based multinationals, allowing large numbers of countries to benefit from services without foreign direct investment. Generally today we see more international business activity than ever before, but direct FDI is not as important as it once was. Where MNEs are important it is often in franchise based service industries or in terms of organisations from emerging markets seeking technological resources or markets abroad. Meanwhile, the legacy of the pre-First World War era of FDI continues to be felt in terms of the lingering legacy of colonialism across the developing world, and in business structures there that often continue to reflect the dynamics of north–south relations in some way.

Acknowledgements

The authors would like to thank Terry Gourvish, Michael Moss and especially the editor – for her forbearance and help to the authors.

References

Armstrong, J., 1991. The development of British business and company law since 1750. In: A. Turton, ed., 1991. *Managing business archives*. Oxford: Butterworth-Heinemann, ch. 2.

BBC News, 2009. Hundreds of jobs to be cut at NCR. [online] Available at: http://news.bbc.co.uk/1/hi/scotland/tayside_and_central/7939476.stm [Accessed 14 August 2016].

Berland, N. and Boyns, T., 2002. The development of budgetary control in France and Britain from the 1920s to the 1960s: a comparison. *European Accounting Review*, 11(2), pp. 329–356.

Boughey, D., 2009. British overseas railways as free-standing companies, 1900–1915. *Business History*, 51(3), pp. 484–500.

Bullock, A., Stallybrass, O. and Trombly, S., eds, 1988. *The Fontana dictionary of modern thought.* London: Fontana.

Chandler, A. D., 1962. *Strategy and structure: chapters in the history of the industrial enterprise.* Cambridge, MA: The MIT Press.

Chandler, A. D., 1977. *Visible hand: the managerial revolution in American business.* Cambridge, MA: Harvard University Press.

Chandler, A. D., 1990. *Scale and scope: the dynamics of industrial capitalism.* Cambridge, MA: Harvard University Press.

Chapman, S., 1998. British free-standing companies and investment groups in India and the Far East. In: M. Wilkins and H. Schröter, eds, 1998. *The free-standing company in the world economy, 1830–1996.* Oxford: Oxford University Press, pp. 202–217.

Dale, R., 2004. *The first crash: lessons from the South Sea Bubble.* Princeton, NJ: Princeton University Press.

Dari-Mattiacci, G., Gelderblum, O., Jonker, J. and Perotti, E. C., 2013. *The emergence of the corporate form.* [online] Available at: http://papers.ssrn.com/sol3/papers.cfm?abstract_id=2223905 [Accessed 14 August 2016].

Darwin, J., 2009. *The Empire project: the rise and fall of the British world-system, 1830–1970.* Cambridge: Cambridge University Press.

Daunton, M. J., 1989. Firm and family in the City of London in the nineteenth century: the case of F. G. Dalgety. *Historical Research*, 62(148), pp. 154–177.

Decker, S., 2005. Decolonising Barclays Bank DCO? Corporate Africanisation in Nigeria, 1945–69. *The Journal of Imperial and Commonwealth History*, 33(3), pp. 419–440.

Decker, S., 2007. Corporate legitimacy and advertising: British companies and the rhetoric of development in West Africa, 1950–1970. *Business History Review*, 81(1), pp. 59–86.

Decker, S., 2008. Building up goodwill: British business, development and economic nationalism in Ghana and Nigeria, 1945–1977. *Enterprise & Society*, 9(4), pp. 602–613.

Decker, S., 2010. Postcolonial transitions in Africa: decolonisation in West Africa and present day South Africa. *Journal of Management Studies*, 47(5), pp. 791–813.

Deresky, H., 2014. *International management: managing across borders and cultures.* 8th ed. Harlow: Pearson Education.

Edwards, J. R., 1988. *A history of financial accounting.* Abingdon: Routledge.

Freeman, M., Pearson, R. and Taylor, J., 2012. *Shareholder democracies? Corporate governance in Britain and Ireland before 1850.* Chicago, IL: University of Chicago Press.

Hackett, D. W., 1976. The international expansion of U.S. franchise systems: status and strategies. *Journal of International Business Studies*, 7(1), pp. 65–75.

Harris, R., 2000. *Industrializing English law: entrepreneurship and business organization, 1720–1844.* Cambridge: Cambridge University Press.

Harvey, C., 1981. *The Rio Tinto Company: an economic history of a leading international mining concern: 1873–1954.* Penzance: Alison Hodge.

Harvey, C. and Press, J., 1990. The City and international mining, 1870–1914. *Business History*, 32(3), pp. 98–119.

Herrigel, G., 2007. Corporate governance. In: G. Jones and J. Zeitlin, eds, 2007. *The Oxford handbook of business history.* Oxford: Oxford University Press, pp. 470–497.

Hunt, B. C., 1936. *The development of the business corporation in England, 1800–1867.* Cambridge, MA: Harvard University Press.

Jackson, W. T., 1968. *The enterprising Scot: investors in the American West after 1873.* Edinburgh: Edinburgh University Press.

Johnson, P., 1987. *Gold fields: a centenary portrait.* London: Weidenfield and Nicholson.

Jones, C., 1997. Institutional forms of British foreign direct investment in South America. *Business History*, 39(2), pp. 21–41.

Jones, G., 1986. Origins, management and performance. In: G. Jones, ed., 1986. *British multinationals: origins, management and performance*. Aldershot: Gower.

Jones, G., 1998. British overseas banks as free-standing companies, 1830–1996. In: M. Wilkins and H. Schröter, eds, 1998. *The free-standing company in the world economy, 1830–1996*. Oxford: Oxford University Press.

Jones, G., 2000. *Merchants to multinationals: British trading companies in the nineteenth and twentieth centuries*. Oxford: Oxford University Press.

Jones, G. and Zeitlin, J., eds, 2007. *The Oxford handbook of business history*. Oxford: Oxford University Press.

Kynaston, D., 1994. *The City of London: Vol.I. A world of its own, 1815–1890*. London: Chatto & Windus.

Kynaston, D., 1995. *The City of London: Vol.II. Golden years 1890–1914*. London: Chatto & Windus.

Kynaston, D., 2000. *The City of London: Vol.III. Illusions of gold, 1914–45*. London: Chatto & Windus.

Kynaston, D., 2002. *The City of London: Vol.IV. Club no more 1945–2000*. London: Chatto & Windus.

Levinson, M., 2006. *The box: how the shipping container made the world smaller and the world economy bigger*. Princeton, NJ: Princeton University Press.

London Stock Exchange, 1950. *The Stock Exchange official year-book*. London: Stock Exchange.

López, A. M., 2003. Belgian investment in tramways and light railways: An international approach, 1892–1935. *The Journal of Transport History*, 24(1), pp. 59–77.

Maltby, J., 1998. UK joint stock companies legislation 1844–1900: accounting publicity and 'mercantile caution'. *Accounting History*, 3(1), pp. 9–32.

Michie, R. C., 1999. *The London Stock Exchange: a history*. Oxford: Oxford University Press.

Miller, R., 1998. British free-standing companies on the west coast of South America. In: Miller, M., 2012. *Europe and the maritime world: a twentieth century history*. Cambridge: Cambridge University Press.

Mollan, S., 2010. S. Hoffnung and Co. 1851–1980: the case of a market intermediary in Australia. *Consumption, Markets & Culture*, 13(1), pp. 7–29.

Mollan, S. and Tennent, K. D., 2015. International taxation and corporate strategy: evidence from British overseas business, circa 1900–1965. *Business History*, 57(7), pp. 1054–1081.

Murphy, A. E., 2004. Corporate ownership in France: the importance of history. [online] Available at: www.nber.org/papers/w10716 [Accessed 14 August 2016].

Napier, C., 2010. United Kingdom. In: G. Previts, P. Walton and P. Wolnizer, eds, 2010. *A global history of accounting, financial reporting and public policy*. Bingley: Emerald.

Oviatt, B. M. and McDougall, P. P., 1994. Toward a theory of international new ventures. *Journal of International Business Studies*, 25(1), pp. 45–64.

Owen, G., 1999. *From Empire to Europe: the decline and revival of british industry since the Second World War*. London: Harper Collins.

Paul, H., 2011. Limiting the witch hunt: recovering from the South Sea Bubble. In: Past, Present and Policy: 4th International Conference. The sub–prime crisis and how it changed the past. Geneva.

Prebble, J., 1968. *The Darien disaster*. London: Secker & Warburg.

Rosenberg, N. and Birdzell, L. E., 1986. *How the West grew rich: the economic transformation of the industrial world*. London: Tarus.

Schmitz, C., 1997. The nature and dimensions of Scottish foreign investment, 1860–1914. *Business History*, 39(2), pp. 42–68.

Seaton, P., 2009. *A sixpenny romance: celebrating a century of value at Woolworths*. London: 3d and 6d Pictures.

Tennent, K. D., 2009. Owned, monitored, but not always controlled: understanding the success and failure of Scottish free-standing companies, 1862–1910. Ph.D. London School of Economics.

Tennent, K. D., 2013. Management and the free-standing company: the New Zealand and Australia Land Company c.1866–1900. *The Journal of Imperial and Commonwealth History*, 41(1), pp. 81–97.

Tennent, K. D. and Gillett, A., 2015. Football's first trip home: behind the scenes before, during and after the 1966 FIFA World Cup. In: British Academy of Management Conference, Portsmouth 2015.

Wilkins, M., 1986. Defining a firm: history and theory. In P. Hertner and G. Jones, eds, 1986. *Multinationals: theory and history*. Aldershot: Ashgate.

Wilkins, M., 1988. The free-standing company, 1870–1914: an important type of British foreign direct investment. *The Economic History Review*, 41(2), pp. 259–282.

Wilkins, M., 1989. *The history of foreign investment in the United States to 1914*. Cambridge, MA: Harvard University Press.

Wilkins, M. and Schröter, H., 1998. *The free-standing company in the world economy, 1830–1996*. Oxford: Oxford University Press.

Wilson, C., 1968. *The history of Unilever: a study in economic growth and social change*. New York: Praeger.

Wojcik, D., 2012. Where governance fails: advanced business services and the offshore world. *Progress in Human Geography*, 37(3), pp. 330–347.

Wolmar, C., 1998. *Stagecoach: a classic rags-to-riches tale from the frontiers of capitalism*. London: Orion.

Chapter 3

Changes in office technology

John Orbell

Introduction

An understanding of the evolution of office technology in its broadest sense, and of the ways in which it has been harnessed through history, is especially useful for business archivists. This is because it gives insight into how, when and why the many different record types making up a business archive were created, something especially important as the archives of businesses are generally more varied and complex than those of other organisations with the probable exception of large government departments and agencies. It also sheds light on the business itself through its adoption of new technology as a path to greater competitive advantage. Equally it explains changes in office organisation resulting from the innovation of new technology; knowledge of organisational change is always of importance to the archivist. At a more practical level, it helps with day-to-day issues relating to particular documents such as dating, appraisal and conservation.

This chapter, therefore, surveys in necessarily broad brush strokes the different technologies involved; it covers the period from the eighteenth century to the personal computer (PC) revolution of the 1980s and 1990s. It embraces a wide definition of office technology that ranges from present day equipment to the very basic technology upon which eighteenth- and early nineteenth-century businesses depended. The former is, of course, well known to us. The latter comprises paper, quill pens and account books together with the external services of a rudimentary postal system. These tools of the eighteenth-century office – in so far as an office then existed – were rooted in a simple yet hard won technology.

Two issues occur and reoccur in this chapter. One is on the supply side. The pace of change in office technology accelerated greatly from the mid-nineteenth century with the introduction of the telegraph, typewriter, telephone, duplicator, tabulating machine and microphotography and again from the mid-twentieth century with photocopying, telex and facsimile machines, the mainframe computer, the personal computer and its associated software, email and the web. This acceleration came on the back of advancements in materials and mechanical and electro-mechanical engineering; latterly its basis was electronics. The result was mass production, cost reduction, widespread innovation and increased office productivity.

The other issue is to be found in the office. Another important element in driving productivity was the ever-increasing empowerment of the individual office worker. A characteristic of late-nineteenth-century technology was the need for specialists to operate new technologies – typists, telegraph operators, telephonists, duplicator operators, printers and so on. A feature of late-twentieth-century advances was their empowerment of the individual worker through his or her direct access to new technology via cheap telephone calls, facsimile and photocopying machines, PCs and email.

However, whatever the period and the technology associated with it, the information needs of business have always been constant and can be broken down into four well-defined areas: recording information, copying information, communicating information and organising and analysing information. This chapter deals in turn with each of these functions.

Recording information

Paper and parchment

Parchment, otherwise known as vellum, was the earliest form of writing material and was made from sheep, calf or goat's skin. It was invariably produced in sheets that were durable but stiff and difficult to fold, especially relative to paper. The smoothness of its surface varied according to the age and breed of the animal from which it came and the resource put into its preparation. Its durability made it particularly suitable for contractual documents such as property deeds, articles of partnership and apprenticeship agreements, but it did not find significant wider use due to its rising cost relative to paper and its unsuitability as a medium on which to print, although printing on to it was possible. By the later Middle Ages paper had begun to replace parchment significantly although the latter's durability meant that its widespread use for contracts persisted until the late nineteenth century and occasionally thereafter. Indeed, official copies of British Acts of Parliament continue to be printed on vellum, the House of Commons in 2016 opposing a proposal to move to archival paper.

Paper was first produced in China in very early times and introduced into Europe via Spain and Italy; its production reached Britain in the fifteenth century although it had been in use there very much earlier. Before the nineteenth century, it was made by hand. Cellulose fibre, its basic component, was obtained from rags, the quality and colour of which determined its grade. Before the availability of bleaches in about 1800, white paper for writing and printing was derived from ship sails or garments that could sometimes be whitened further by placing them in sunlight; coloured or badly soiled rags made less expensive brown paper used in marginal tasks such as packaging.

The early process for producing paper involved sorting and dampening rags, leaving them to rot (a process which could be quickened by the addition of lime but at the cost of imparting a creamy colour to the paper), pulping them in water and then spreading the pulp across a wire-covered mould on which a 'film' of cellulose formed after the water had drained away. This film was then dried and sized to give it strength; it thus became a sheet of paper. Such 'handmade' or 'laid' paper is readily identified by the grid marks the wire imparts to the paper and which are visible when the paper is held up to the light.

This 'laid' paper varied slightly in thickness even within a single sheet creating unevenness that caused problems both for the printer and the writer whose pen tended to dig into the paper's surface. 'Wove' paper, although expensive, addressed these problems. First used in Britain in the 1750s, it was made on finely woven wire resulting in a relatively smoother finish the quality of which steadily improved over the years.

The introduction of watermarks into paper is a long-standing practice that evolved in Italy in about the thirteenth century. Such marks were unique to a papermaker or manufacturing stationer, taking on some aspects of a trademark; some paper carried the marks of both maker and stationer. They were formed by introducing fine wire into the mould, fashioned in the form of the maker's and/or seller's mark. Early designs were simple, comprising just a letter or symbol; they grew in complexity from the eighteenth century, notably in the production of security paper including banknote paper. Standard forms of watermarks evolved to denote paper size. In late-eighteenth-century England, for example, those in common use were a *fleur-de-lys*, a fool's cap and a post horn sometimes inserted within a shield with the maker's name below. Also at this time, especially in Europe, tin foil shapes might be inserted into the watermark wire to create light areas in addition to lines. 'Watermarked ruling' was introduced in the late eighteenth century, to assist writing in straight lines, while experiments to create coloured watermarks were first successful around 1819, but such marks were seldom used.

Watermarks give the archivist all sorts of clues to the approximate date of an otherwise undated document as well as to the place of manufacture of the paper on which the document is written. This dating process is helped by the introduction into the watermark of, say, a year of manufacture, which might be required by legislation, as in Britain in 1794 for books intended for export without payment of duty. Once adopted, this tradition of dating paper might continue for long after the abolition of the relevant legislation. Obvious caution needs to be exercised, however, when dating documents from watermarks as a document might have been created long after the paper was manufactured.

In the nineteenth century new production techniques meant that paper made by machine largely replaced handmade paper; by 1850 90 per cent of paper in Britain was machine-made. Significant reduction in paper costs resulting from this led to more extensive document creation although other factors were also at work including greater literacy and numeracy, the more complex requirements of larger businesses, and a more demanding legal and regulatory environment. Most notable were the commercial introduction of the Fourdrinier machine in 1807 and the substitution of rags for esparto grass from around 1840 and by wood pulp from the mid-nineteenth century.

New manufacturing processes and raw materials brought with them a decline in paper quality as the nineteenth century progressed. Writers as early as the 1820s reckoned the causes were the introduction of alum in the size, of gypsum to ensure whiteness and of bleach in excessive amounts in the preparation of rags. All reacted adversely with cellulose fibres. As significant was the use of wood pulp, which contained components such as lignin, a cause of yellowing and brittleness, which has created real challenges for conservators.

Identifying hand-made from machine-made papers is not difficult. The former, when held up to the light, show the lines of the wire mesh as well as light and dark patches, the latter reflecting an uneven spread of cellulose on the wire mould however skilled the papermaker. Another indicator is the absence of grain in handmade paper resulting from the dispersal of fibres in the mould. By contrast, the fibres of machine-made paper are aligned in a single direction enabling paper to bend more readily in one direction.

Writing instruments

The quill pen, fashioned from the stem of a bird feather, was the standard writing instrument before the early nineteenth century. Although inexpensive, its tip needed frequent yet careful sharpening to give legible writing and to prevent it digging into the paper. Steel nibs, mass produced from the 1820s, were widely used by the 1840s as prices fell and as improvements in nib design gave greater flexibility and enabled easier writing. A flourishing pen-making industry developed in Britain at Birmingham and came to serve the world. But as with quills, steel nibs suffered the tiresome disadvantage of needing replenishment with ink every few words. From at least the eighteenth-century efforts were made to manufacture a pen with its own ink reservoir, but were commercially successful only when L. E. Waterman of New York perfected his fountain pen in the 1880s leading to mass production. From 1900 until the 1960s fountain pens were widely used.

The ball point pen was the next significant innovation; it was marketed from as early as the 1880s but only came into its own in 1938 when Laszlo and George Biro realised its potential for applying quick-drying, non-blotting ink similar to that used by printers. After the Second World War, the modern ball point, which early on also came in a range of coloured inks other than black and blue, notably red and green, went on regular sale. By the late 1950s sales outstripped those of fountain pens and were boosted by better reliability and the arrival of the throw away Bic 'biro'.

Despite its ancient origins, the pencil has always been of secondary importance to pens in record keeping. One obvious reason for this is that pencil writing can be erased resulting in the fraudulent alteration of text although the ability to erase text can sometimes be useful, say, when annotating drafts. The modern pencil dates from the sixteenth century when a form of carbon called graphite was discovered in Cumbria, Britain. Initially sticks of graphite were used perhaps wrapped with string or encased in wood and mass production commenced in Germany in the mid-seventeenth century. In France in 1795 a technique was developed to give pencils different grades of hardness and softness while the indelible pencil was introduced in the United States in about the 1870s. Propelling pencils were available at least as early as the 1820s but were used by few.

Typewriters

Document creation in business was revolutionised by the typewriter; it heralded the arrival in the office of the mechanical age. Speed, in terms of both document creation and copymaking, was the typewriter's most attractive feature for businesses while presentation, legibility and accuracy of copies were of secondary importance. Typewriters came to be used for creating not just letters and memoranda but also index cards, invoices, minutes and accounts, the last two uses also being facilitated by the introduction of loose-leaf books by 1900. They also impacted on the office environment and workflow with typists, often centralised in specialised typing pools, replacing copy-clerks.

After many attempts at perfecting a viable typewriter, the first marketable machine was developed by Sholes & Gidden and manufactured and sold by Remingtons in the United States in the early 1870s. Known in 1876 as the Remington Number One, it turned out to be neither technically reliable nor commercially successful, although some 4,000 machines were sold. The Number Two, introduced in 1878, addressed its shortcomings. This could type in both upper and lower case and was equipped with a range of punctuation keys but continued to suffer the disadvantage of writing 'non-visibly', so that the typist was unable to see the text being typed. The first 'modern' machine, capable of typing 'visibly', was introduced in the 1880s.

Other developments included keyboard standardisation, notably the introduction of the 'Universal Keyboard' from the 1870s and its general application in the early twentieth century. The first typewriter with an integral tabulator was marketed by 1900; these were to become important in the creation of accounts and tables of statistics, which might need to be spread across large sheets of paper. Two-colour typewriter ribbons were in use by 1909, perhaps earlier. Electric typewriters, notable for the even impression of their type, appeared shortly before the Second World War; the first to encounter significant commercial success was marketed by International Business Machines (IBM) from 1935. From the early 1940s IBM machines incorporated proportional spacing between characters enabling the creation of text resembling a printed page. The first 'golf ball' typewriter, the IBM Selectric, which was characterised by an interchangeable typing head allowing a given typewriter to produce text in a variety of fonts, made its appearance in the early 1960s. A magnetic tape was soon incorporated into the Selectric introducing memory and enabling the editing of stored text; it was the precursor to word processing. From the 1970s in a small way but especially in the 1980s and 1990s, the word processor, later the PC, supplanted the typewriter in virtually all its functions in the western world; when retained it was used for specialist needs such as envelope addressing. In developing countries it found regular use for much longer.

From the early 1880s the use of typewriters expanded very rapidly in the United States although less quickly in Europe where Remington sales agencies were established, for example, in Germany in 1883, France a year later, the Netherlands in 1890 and Greece in 1896. Mass production reduced prices, which stimulated demand; by the 1890s typewriters started to become commonplace in offices in the United States. At the same time, machines became less cumbersome and more user-friendly resulting in greater output by the typist and productivity for the business. Machines of the early 1870s were capable of 30 to 40 words a minute while by 1887 Remington claimed speeds of up to 100 words. Electric typewriters required less exertion by typists and consequently were capable of still greater output.

The concept of the typewriter and its keyboard was harnessed for other functions such as the cutting of stencils for duplication. Early attempts at stencil-making were frustrated for want of suitable material but in 1886 Gestetner discovered a Japanese tissue, Yoshino, out of which, from the 1890s, the typewriter could cut high quality stencils for mass copying.

Associated with the arrival of the typewriter, but in fact significantly predating it, was shorthand writing based on phonetic principles. The first 'modern' systems date back to the sixteenth century and were well established in Britain, France and Germany by the eighteenth century. By 1840 they had been more or less perfected, most notably by Isaac Pitman whose system found use throughout the English-speaking world. Post 1945 shorthand was supplemented significantly by 'Dictaphones', the trademark of an eponymous United States business, as a means of recording copy for transcription, although 'dictation machines' had been in business use for very much longer. Usage increased especially from the 1970s as Dictaphones became more compact, user-friendly and portable.

Inks

Writing inks date back to ancient times. They are quite distinct from printing inks, which have a more complex composition, and which have dominated the ink making industry since the advent of printing. Only writing inks are dealt with here.

Prior to the introduction of aniline inks from the mid–1850s, two basic types of writing ink existed. Carbon ink was made from carbon substances such as soot. The other, more frequently encountered, was iron gall ink, made from iron salts such as ferrous sulphate. The precise composition of these inks varied between ink makers and it was not uncommon for individual users to make their own ink. A relatively few ink makers emerged from this large body of producers, Henry Stephens, 1796–1864, being the most noted in Britain from the mid-nineteenth century. Stephens Ink, promoted by innovative marketing and advertising, quickly became a national brand leader. By the late 1830s the firm was making ink in a range of colours such as black and blue and also red for 'contrast writing'. Steel pen makers also made ink partly because 'quill ink' caused steel nibs to corrode.

Ink is of greatest interest to archivists for conservation reasons. In certain circumstances it can fade and in others its corrosive composition can burn holes in paper and cause it to become brittle. That said, carbon ink is more stable than the more widely used iron gall ink. The discovery of aniline dyes in the mid-nineteenth century greatly affected the composition of ink; the resulting synthetic inks eliminated some corrosive properties. The post-1945 world has witnessed a broadening in the types of pens for handwriting using particular inks which over time fade, most notably the ball point and felt tip, presenting additional challenges for conservators.

The introduction of the typewriter led to a dramatic decline in the number of formal handwritten documents generated by businesses and thus in the use of ink for writing. In place of liquid ink, the typewriter used typewriter ribbons, which were impregnated with synthetic ink, which dried quickly on contact with paper. The production of a copy or multi-copies was via carbon paper, a robust paper coated on one side with a dry synthetic ink and placed ink-side down on to copying paper. This process could result in some smudging especially when multiple copies were made.

Entirely new principles for printing emerged alongside the development of the computer and the photocopier, especially from the late 1970s and 1980s, replacing impact copying associated with the typewriter. These are inkjet and laser printers, the first propelling liquid ink onto paper, the second applying an electrostatically formed image to paper via a powdered ink called toner.

Addressing machines

Addressing machines, or addressographs, were developed in the United States from the mid-nineteenth century with commercial application dating from the 1870s and 1880s. Big businesses with wide customer bases and long mailing lists were the first users, but cheaper hand-operated models were soon developed for businesses with more modest requirements. Apart from addressing envelopes and postcards, they could also be used to create the heading text for ledger cards, to address invoices and to record information on record cards.

There were two early forms, one based on stencils, the other on embossed metal plates or rubber type. The latter gave the clearest print but the former offered greatest flexibility as they could more easily be made in-house. Metal plates had generally to be made externally, although by 1910 big users could acquire specialist machinery to make them in-house. Over time, of course, addressographs developed greater capacity and flexibility; by 1900, for example, treadle-operated machines were available and by the 1930s automatic selection of address plates and selection of only certain fields for printing was possible.

By the 1890s the market leader in the United States was the Addressograph Co.; by 1907 it claimed to have 30,000 machines in use. It expanded internationally, for example setting up a British subsidiary in around 1900. Related machinery appeared at an early date such as machines for sealing envelopes (c.1899), folding letters (c.1907) and opening envelopes (c.1912).

Audio and moving images

Business processes were facilitated by use of audio and moving image recording and reproducing devices. Audio and moving image recording was technically possible from the late nineteenth century and by the 1920s both technologies were sufficiently reliable and cost effective to be harnessed for use by the biggest businesses. They were especially useful when sound and image could be combined in 'talkies', notably for advertising, marketing, training and education purposes. Much later on these functions were facilitated by the introduction of video recording and display technology. Although technically available from the 1950s, this was very widely exploited from the early 1970s when user-friendly video cassettes offered greater flexibility and cost effectiveness (although, of course, the creative costs of video film making remained relatively high). Video-based films became much more commonplace in the office, especially for marketing 'presentations', while the medium found new users in specialist areas of record creation such as surveillance and multi-location conferencing. In the late 1990s video technology was succeeded by the DVD format.

Sound recording was also significant both in communicating information, especially via advertising, and also in terms of document creation via recording interviews of meetings and recording text via Dictaphones. Reel-to-reel technology was succeeded by sound cassettes from the mid-1970s and the latter by compact discs especially from the early 1990s. Both image and sound recording greatly benefitted from the introduction of magnetic tape from the 1950s.

Copying information

Early practices

It was not until the late nineteenth century that effective mechanical devices, most notably the typewriter and duplicator, were introduced for making multiple copies of documents. Before then, for the most part, the copy clerk or 'writer' ruled supreme, although the use of the copy press grew substantially as the nineteenth century progressed. Other early devices such as the polygraph (or multipen) were, relatively speaking, seldom used.

Pressing dampened sheets against an original in a copying press was the earliest means of effective copying, dating to the mid-seventeenth century. A letter, written in ink on robust paper, was copied when dry by placing it between damp tissues in a screw or roller copying press. This left an impression in reverse, which was readable from the underside of the paper.

Despite a tendency for copies to be smudged and feint, use of this process steadily gathered pace in the nineteenth century. This was especially so from the mid-nineteenth century following the introduction of aniline ink, based on newly discovered synthetic chemicals, and improved tissue paper, which led to clearer copies. Often copies were made direct into books of tissue paper, rather than loose paper, which thereby became copy out-letter books. The natural order of such copies was, of course, by date and thus, for easy access, pages required indexing. When loose copies were required, say for attachment to related in-letters, a roller press was equally practicable. A notable development was James Watt's portable press patented in 1780 although its impact was relatively limited; apparently 150 copies were made in the first year of its production.

The press was put to use throughout the world and even in some Western countries continued to be used by a few businesses until well into the twentieth century. It was, however, increasingly marginalised in the late nineteenth century by the arrival of carbon paper and the typewriter. 'Carbonated' paper, coated in carbon black, had been available from at least the 1820s but quills and steel nibs did not work well with it. Until the introduction of ballpoint-type pens, writing instruments failed to apply the even pressure needed for the making of clear copy of handwritten documents; therefore carbon paper-copying tended to be relegated to marginal tasks such as for copying receipts and orders. Its effectiveness improved with the arrival of aniline dyes and the development of so-called 'clean' carbon paper in the United States at the end of the century. However, the typewriter had greater impact on its use given the firm pressure it applied. Up to 10 copies, although in practice significantly fewer, could be made simultaneously, perhaps distinguished by paper colour in order to identify the function of each copy, such as whether intended for a day, correspondent or project/case file.

Carbon paper was supplemented in the 1950s by clean carbonless paper developed by the National Cash Register Corporation (and therefore sometimes referred to as NCR paper). The reverse of such paper was coated with micro-encapsulated dye, the capsules breaking on the application of pressure from handwriting or type to form an image on sheets below.

Printing

Whereas typewriters were suitable for making a few copies, other methods were needed for making multiple copies for wide circulation, especially by businesses that had large numbers of customers and shareholders or at least had geographically dispersed ones, when quality of presentation was at a premium.

Printing, of course, was one means by which businesses generated multiple copies and plenty of examples date to the seventeenth century. Merchants at an especially early date used printed *pro-forma* documents, such as bills of lading, required for commodity transactions and shipments. In the early nineteenth century later generations of merchants trading internationally mailed printed circular letters giving details of local commodity prices and market conditions to their correspondents in other trading centres. From the early eighteenth century many businesses made use of printed trade cards while by the late century banks sent various printed *pro-forma* letters to customers, say to accompany remittances or to give notice of stock or dividend transactions. The arrival of numerous big, multisite, incorporated businesses from the early and, especially, mid-nineteenth century brought new requirements; not only did they need multiple copies of documents in dealing with their customers and shareholders, they also needed them for the effective operation of their internal administration. Railway companies form a particularly important example of such businesses but there were many others such as chartered companies trading internationally, joint-stock banks, insurance businesses and so on.

Printing was, of course, an old-established craft, but from the early nineteenth century technical improvements and cost reduction facilitated its greater use as did in Britain the removal mid-century of tax, established from 1712, on certain printed documents such as newspapers and advertisements. The introduction of small-scale jobbing presses from the mid-nineteenth century was especially important in meeting the needs of smaller businesses while a steady stream of improvements in lithographic printing made the production of images much cheaper. Increasingly big businesses established their own printing units but for the vast majority the use of in-house printing of documents was rarely justified, even in recent times, on grounds of cost although cost considerations could sometimes be overridden should confidentiality or speed of production be necessary.

Duplication

A more effective solution, especially for internal use when presentation might not be important, lay in duplication using stencils initially cut by handheld pens. This process, for the most part, was based on the principle of using a pen to make patterns of fine holes in impermeable paper through which ink was subsequently forced to create an image of handwriting on sheets of paper below. The earliest commercially viable stencil copying product, the papyrograph, was patented in 1874; by the 1880s it was claimed that many thousands of apparatus had been sold in the United States and elsewhere. Improvements followed in quick succession with the introduction in the mid-1870s of a duplicating product based on the 'Edison Electric Pen', a stencil-cutting pen propelled by electric power, and, in England, of David Gestetner's 1881 Cyclostyle wheeled pen, which worked on waxed paper and which was of much greater importance.

By the late 1880s hundreds of thousands of duplicating apparatus were in use worldwide. Innovation had been aided by more easily manipulated pens, clearer copies, cleaner and less laborious processes, faster equipment and stencils capable of generating greater numbers of copies. By the 1890s it was reckoned that a single copy could be generated within 10 seconds and 2,000 copies could be made from a single stencil. A hugely important advance was made in the mid-1880s when for the first time stencils could be cut successfully by typewriter, which improved speed of production and, not least, presentation.

Additional improvements to duplicating machines followed quickly such as automatic inking, replacement of fluid by paste-like ink and the introduction of rotary machines in which the stencil was fitted around a cylinder. In the 1920s a spirit duplicator was introduced that dispensed with ink and produced cheaper but generally poor quality copy suitable for internal use by organisations, such as for intra-business communications. Copy was often printed in distinctive purples, greens and blues and is particularly susceptible to fading.

From the early twentieth century copy quality had improved so much that the output of specialised duplicating machines could mimic typed letters. Shortly after 1900 the modern duplicator was in place; models developed in the nineteenth century were still in use after 1945 while newer models aped nineteenth-century technology. By the twentieth century market leaders included A. B. Dick of the United States and Gestetner and Roneo of Britain.

Photocopying

From the 1960s duplicating machines and other copying methods discussed above were rapidly replaced by the photocopier. This technology commonly involved creating an electrostatic image and fusing it by heat to paper by means of a powdered ink called toner. However, an earlier technology, developed by 3M in the United States in the early 1950s and marketed as Thermo Fax, involved placing a heat-sensitive sheet of paper over the document to be copied and exposing the two to infrared light. The copy produced was subject to fading while the process was difficult to manipulate resulting in its eventual relegation to marginal and specialised tasks.

The electrostatic photocopier had its roots in the United States in the late 1930s and was developed in the late 1940s by a business known from 1961 as Xerox Corporation. Its first machine, although somewhat slow and dirty, was marketed in 1949 and met with modest success. It was the fully-automatic Xerox 914, marketed at the end of the 1950s and capable of seven copies a minute, that really made an impact; this was the first modern photocopier and some 10,000 machines had been sold worldwide by the close of 1962.

Improvements followed quickly. The first desktop machine appeared in 1963. By 1968 an output of 60 copies a minute was possible. By 1970 the automatic two-side copier had been introduced closely followed by the colour copier although high costs prohibited the widespread application of the latter until about the late 1980s.

The photocopier's impact on record keeping has been substantial. It did away with other methods of duplication and copying. It introduced much greater flexibility in the production of copies and of work processes, in particularly empowering office workers to make copies in whatever numbers as and when required. It raised important copyright and evidential issues and, with colour photocopying especially, gave rise to forgery. It increased security issues as copies could now be made illicitly. As copies were increasingly cheap and quick to make, it encouraged excessive copying and fuelled an explosion in record accumulation with consequent damage to effective record organisation; it was now possible for each interested party to have a copy of a document that once could only have been circulated between them. Photocopying also created important conservation issues as early copies had a strong tendency to fade.

Table 3.1 Some important dates for document copying

Period	Document copying method
From early times	Copying clerk making hand copies
From seventeenth century	Copying press
From seventeenth century	Printing, especially of forms
1780	James Watt's portable copying press
1850s	Microphotography, widely adapted from the 1990s
1870s	Typewriters with carbon paper
1870s	Stencil duplicating
1950s	Typewriters with carbonless paper
1950s	Thermo fax photocopying
1950s	Electrostatic photocopying

Photography

Photography enables facsimile copies of documents to be made and, before the age of the photocopier, had several uses in record keeping. First, it provided day-to-day working copies of annotated and signed documents. Second, it enabled copying of documents such as tables of statistics, accounts, plans, drawings and diagrams, which it would otherwise be impractical to copy on grounds of high costs. Third, it provided surrogate or back up copies for use in the event of originals being lost or damaged. Fourth, through miniaturisation via microfilm or microfiche, it could facilitate effective storage especially in secure and, therefore, high cost, environments. Very often, of course, these factors were interlinked.

On account of high processing costs and, in the case of microfilm, high access costs relative to paper records, photography was only used in exceptional circumstances. For the most part it was undertaken by out-of-office specialist agencies such as Photostat Ltd (which gave rise to the generic term), established in London in 1923. Early on invariably they made white on black copies.

The production of microphotographs was possible by the early 1850s and the first microfilm patent was registered in France in 1859; much initial development was focused there before shifting across the Atlantic in the 1880s. Such early developments did not foresee microfilm as a format for record keeping; its use in 1871 to copy the records of a French insurance company was exceptional. The next known application in business was Century Publishing Company's microfilming in New York in 1887 of 25,000 sheets of galley proofs for back up purposes.

By 1900 the broad technical advances needed for microfilming were in place. George Eastman had already made vast strides in perfecting, *inter alia*, nitrocellulose film. Film standards (35mm and 16mm) were being established on a *de facto* basis. A microfilming camera had been patented in 1890 followed by an 'automated' camera for cheque microfilming in 1899. It seems, however, that the first commercially viable device for mass microfilming originated in New York in the early 1920s and was acquired by Eastman Kodak in 1928. A subsidiary, Recordak Corp., was established in New York, with a subsidiary in London in 1935, to provide outsourced microfilming services for banks and insurance companies in particular; it grew into a major business, boosted in the late 1930s by the need for copies in the event of war. Microfilm reading machines were available from at least 1919 when the first was patented in the United States. At some stage post 1945, reels of microfilm were supplemented, and subsequently to a great extent replaced, by microfiche 'sheets', which substantially improved ease of interrogation by users but at the risk of fiche being misfiled and lost.

From about the 1970s to the 1990s the use of microfilm received a major boost through the download of computer held data reports to microfiche via 'Computer Output Microfilm' (COM). This was a response to limited computer capacity and the high costs of storing computer generated reports in paper form should this be needed. This was succeeded by Computer Output to Laser Disk (COLD).

Communicating information

Postal systems

The first means of business communication was via post or courier/messenger services. Their availability – provided they were reliable, easily accessible and relatively inexpensive – is a fundamental requirement of a modern society as underlined by their early provision and close regulation by the state. The early modern public systems were rooted in Western Europe and North America in the seventeenth century. Britain's General Post Office was first created in 1657, although public services existed earlier, and enjoyed a monopoly – in theory if not in practice – in home and overseas mail. Its post offices and post roads, in due course, came to traverse the whole country. North America's postal system dates to the 1690s; it was reconstituted in 1775 as the United States Post Office and subsequently as the United States Post Office Department.

Early on, postal charges were generally paid by the recipient, although prepayment was possible, and for the most part were calculated according to distance carried and number of sheets enclosed. This was inherently inefficient and often government subsidies made good revenue shortfalls. Exceptions existed. For example, superimposed on the British postal system in 1680 was a prepaid penny post for delivery within London, which survived into the nineteenth century; its success meant the establishment of similar posts in other cities.

By the mid-nineteenth century reform of postal systems was underway in developed countries based on the concept of universal postage whereby charges were calculated according to weight and not by other criteria. Vital to its effectiveness was prepayment by the sender evidenced by postage stamps or other postmarks, generally referred to as franking. The system first appeared in 1840 in Britain for inland mails and in the early 1880s for parcels and was rapidly copied elsewhere – Brazil and Switzerland, for example, in 1843, the United States in 1847 and France, Belgium and Bavaria in 1849. These reforms massively boosted mail volumes. Franking was used especially for bulk mail sent by business and government. Automatic franking machines were introduced around 1900; the British Post Office adopted them shortly afterwards.

International mailing was, and still is, facilitated by international reciprocity agreements under the aegis of the Universal Postal Union. Before its establishment in 1874, international mails were based on a combination of state and private enterprise; in theory a letter crossing an international boundary needed to carry postage for both countries. The Union established important conventions – flat postage rates from one country to another, acceptance by one country of the postage stamps of another, and retention of revenue by the post office of the country of origin. The mailing of parcels internationally was agreed in 1885; it represented a massive step forward in international communication.

Historically, sending mail internationally took an exceptionally long time, especially if it was sent overseas by sailing ship; in the early nineteenth-century delivery of British mail to Australia could take many weeks. Steamships quickened the process while telegrams were to become, when practicable on cost and other grounds, the preferred option. In international posting, aircraft had by far the greatest impact. Initially airmail services were commonly operated within country boundaries; the first scheduled service, albeit short lived, was between two relatively close English towns, Windsor and Hendon, in 1911. After 1918, with improvements in aircraft design, scheduled airmail services developed apace. This was especially so in the United States where, from 1918 a service operated between Washington DC and New York City. By 1920 it is reckoned that services in the United States had carried some 50 million items.

Text, markings, stamps and stickers appearing on letter covers and envelopes provide a series of clues to date, provenance, recipient and, less often, sender; for archivists and historians they are invaluable should the contents include no date, address or names. Early on addresses could be brief and imprecise but latterly well-defined, especially after the introduction of post/zip codes, for example in Germany in 1941, Britain in 1959 and United States in 1963. Location codes for cities were established much earlier than zip codes, for example they existed for London from the 1850s although at that stage seldom written onto envelopes by senders. Stamps indicate country of origin and, using collectors' catalogues, can sometimes be precisely dated. Stamp cancellation marks sometimes show date, time and place of postage. Predating stamps are postmarks, introduced as early as the mid-seventeenth century by the British Post Office to indicate, *inter alia*, month and day of postage as a step to improving reliability. Franking marks, used instead of stamps to denote prepayment especially for bulk mail, indicate place and date of postage. The introduction of metered mail around 1910 enabled in-house franking and paved the way for customised franking marks. Airmail gave rise to a whole set of special envelopes, stickers and lightweight stationery; the first dedicated airmail stamp was issued in Italy in 1917.

Historically postal systems have been state monopolies although sometimes the latter permitted a degree of competition, notably in parcel services. Also, of course, individual businesses could distribute their own mail between sites, and externally to customers and associates. As the twentieth century progressed state monopolies were challenged by private enterprise, the case of United Parcel Services (UPS) in the United States providing an early example. Privatisation of state systems or the introduction of competition from private enterprise has been a feature of recent decades. The privatisation of the Dutch state postal and telecommunication systems in 1989 was an early and extreme example; the postal system was demerged from telecoms in 1998 when it combined with TNT, an internationally spread logistics business. The British Post Office was privatised between 2013 and 2015 although many of its services had been opened to competition several years earlier.

Envelopes

Until the introduction of the envelope as a separate item of stationery, letters were either wrapped within a separate sheet of paper or, if the reverse of the letter was not written upon, folded on itself and the address written on the unused side. They were then secured by either sealing wax (often marked with the sender's signet) or a wafer (a moistened disc made of flour mixed with gum and colouring).

Before the nineteenth century, envelopes were rarely used on account of high costs of manufacture and postage, although they existed at least from the seventeenth century when used in France. By the mid-nineteenth century envelope usage expanded rapidly as postage was now generally calculated by weight rather than by number of sheets, as mass production methods were applied to envelope making and as paper costs fell. The firm of Thomas de la Rue's envelope-folding machine led the way in 1845 and improvements followed thick and fast in the 1850s and 1860s. Notably, the first successful envelope self-gumming and folding machine, for example, was invented in the United States in the 1860s. By 1876 John Dickinson & Sons of Britain was turning out some three million envelopes a week.

Envelopes soon came in varying sizes for different purposes. By the late 1850s two basic types were marketed – 'pocket' envelopes, which opened on the short side and 'bankers' envelopes, which opened on the long side. 'Burnished' envelopes, resistant to wet and characterised by a glazed finish, were another innovation at this time. By the 1880s Dickinson alone was manufacturing over 1,000 different envelope types. Around 1900 the first window envelopes were patented in the United States and were being manufactured in Europe by 1905. The arrival of regular airmail services after 1918 resulted in the introduction of lightweight stationery including envelopes, writing paper and 'aerograms' as a response to high postal charges; they remained popular into the 1970s.

Business letters

Early on record creation, including letter writing, by businessmen and women must have been relatively uncommon, most notably in small businesses, which formed the great majority. Widespread illiteracy, an undemanding legal environment and relatively high paper and postage costs must have contributed to this by reducing the need for written documents. Also tight-knit local business networks linking a business with its customers, suppliers and competitors may have been another factor in reducing letter writing over what it would otherwise have been.

Letters were then written on plain paper with the sender recording the date and his or her address at the top of the first page; the latter might comprise just the name of a village, town or, in the case of well-known businesses, city. At the end of the nineteenth century a much more formulaic approach was adopted resulting from the emergence of house style based on best practice letter layouts as encouraged by agencies such as Pitmans. Generally speaking such practices have endured to recent times (although have not been redefined for electronic documents).

Writing paper carrying relatively simple printed decoration appeared in Europe from the mid-eighteenth century and was later adopted in America. But it was not until the mid-nineteenth century, with the advancement of printing technology, notably lithography, and its associated lower costs, that illustrated writing paper began to appear in quantity; it soon became commonplace especially with manufacturing and marketing businesses who chose their products and plant as illustrative material. By the 1940s its use was in decline being replaced with simpler styles later dominated by logos.

Such writing paper in business had its antecedence in the trade card, a printed and invariably illustrated single sheet giving details of the name, address, products and activities of a business; it was used by business people as an *aide-memoir* for existing customers and as an advertisement for potential ones. The earliest date to the beginning of the seventeenth century, but their heyday was the eighteenth and early nineteenth centuries when they tended to become increasingly decorative. From the early nineteenth century the plates from which they were printed found use in the production of a suite of other business stationery, notably writing or typing paper, price lists and invoices.

Telegraph

The introduction of telegraphy, in particular submarine telegraphy, represented an enormous step forward in business communication, especially in international trading, banking and insurance. Messages that once took weeks to reach their destination could now be received within hours, something that brought massive increases in business efficiency. That said, the telegraph had major and obvious limitations over the letter post. Telegrams were expensive so were only used for essential business; when used text was abbreviated and cryptic; notwithstanding the use of codes confidentiality and anonymity were compromised; authenticity was less clear; only certain formats of text could be transmitted and, of course, not images; and so on.

The first practical electrical telegraph equipment was patented in 1837, coincidentally in Britain and America, and put to commercial use shortly afterwards; by the mid-1840s inland telegraphy was on a firm footing. The earliest systems were associated with railway companies, which constructed telegraph lines along their tracks initially for their own use. By the 1850s most major towns in Western Europe and North America were linked by telegraph, by 1861 the east and west coasts of America were linked and by 1872 Australia was crossed from north to south. Usage of inland telegraphy grew steadily, peaking in developed countries in the early years of the twentieth century. In Britain, for example, inland messages rose from 6.5 million in 1865 to 90 million in 1910 before falling away to 35 million in 1935 and 7.7 million in 1970, a collapse that resulted in the winding up of telegraphy from the early 1980s. By the beginning of the twenty-first century services in most countries had been reduced to a shadow of their former selves. The cause of this decline was the progressive rise of telephone services and subsequently other forms of immediate communication, which were cheaper and more convenient.

In 1851 the first submarine cable linked France and Britain, by 1866 Europe was linked to North America and by 1870 a link between Europe and India was completed (although earlier communication had been possible by a combination of submarine and land lines). Extension followed at breakneck speed and by 1871 a cable reached Australia. By 1902 the Pacific Ocean had been crossed, linking North America directly with Australia and Asia. Wireless technology was soon a competitor. Guglielmo Marconi, in 1897, sent his first wireless message over water and, in 1901, across the Atlantic, heralding the arrival of effective wireless communication whether by telegraphy or telephony in the early years of the twentieth century. However wireless communication complemented and did not replace submarine telegraphy; when Britain's international telegraphy companies were consolidated into a single unit in 1928 it embraced both and from 1934 was known as Cable & Wireless Ltd.

Telegraphy is perhaps at the very root of the paperwork explosion through an increase both in the number of messages sent and received and in the volume of paper created per message. Procedures, of course, varied from business to business but could be as follows: an initial handwritten and/or typed-message was created along with a coded copy if required and sent to the telegraph office for dispatch; an incoming message, either printed or handwritten, was received; if in code, a decoded copy might be made; letters might then be mailed confirming outgoing and incoming messages; typed copies of messages might be made for inclusion in working files. All of this resulted in far more record creation than hitherto and the position was later significantly compounded by the introduction of telex communication. Code books – both those of the recipient and of the sender –

Table 3.2 Dates of establishment of early submarine telegraph cables

Year	Telegraph cable connection
1851	United Kingdom–France
1853	United Kingdom–Ireland
1866	Buenos Aires–Montevideo
1866	United Kingdom–Canada (the first successful transatlantic line)
1866	Florida–Cuba
1868	Malta–Alexandria
1870	United Kingdom–Gibraltar
1870	Gibraltar–Malta
1870	Egypt–Mumbai
1870	India–Singapore
1871	Singapore–Java
1871	Java–Australia (thereby linking Europe and Australia)
1875	Rio de Janeiro–Montevideo
1876	Sydney–New Zealand
1901	Mauritius–Australia
1902	Australia–Canada (via Pacific)
1903	United States of America–Philippines (via Pacific)

In some cases earlier telegraph links were possible using a combination of submarine and landlines.

Source: Baglehole, 1969.

would also be kept to facilitate message coding and decoding. However, inland-letters always had the upper hand over inland-telegrams for anything other than the most routine messages and confirmations. In 1865, for example, when inland-telegraphy was fully operational in the Britain, for every telegram sent 150 letters were posted.

Telex messages sent via teleprinters were a development of telegraphy although subsequently operated via the telephone network. Teleprinters were developed in the late nineteenth century and for many years operated in a very limited way on a point-to-point basis. They resembled a typewriter and sent messages that were printed automatically as text at the receiving end. Public telex services became available from the 1930s but telex was only used in a relatively limited way until the 1950s. Then rapid technical advances resulted in a dedicated telex network, each line identified by a unique telex address and each accessed from within the business's offices by its own specialist telex operator. Easily accessible by direct dialling, confidential, fast and relatively inexpensive, telex brought text communication under the business's direct control; from the 1950s until facsimiles, email and cheap international telephone calls heralded its decline from the late 1970s, it was a hugely important means of business communication internationally. This was especially so for routine traffic, such as intra-company messages, confirmation of settlement instructions, account queries, and so on, when written copy was vital for checking and evidential purposes. Telex numbers came to appear alongside telephone numbers on business notepaper.

Telephone

For most of its existence, the telephone did not give rise to particular record formats – other than file notes recording telephone conversations and, early on, letters to other parties confirming points raised in telephone conversations. That said, it certainly affected the creation of other formats, in particular leading to an absolute reduction in telegrams and of letters from a level that would otherwise have been attained. In recent years, the audio recording of telephone conversations and/or the registration of calls made and received, undertaken for regulatory, evidential and training purposes, has created other record formats.

In the mid–1870s the telephone developed out of the principles of telegraphy and was quickly put into business use, notably in the United States. Centralised switchboards in telephone exchanges very quickly followed. For the first time a user was offered immediate and direct communication with a third party, whether within or without the business; as with the stream of electro-mechanical and electronic devices that followed, it directly empowered the business user. In Europe innovation was far slower than in the United States where there were 135,000 subscribers by the early 1880s. In Britain, for example, where the Post Office had recently bought up inland telegraphy companies, its introduction was carefully regulated. Subscribers totalled only 13,000 by 1884, although a sizable number of private networks also existed for intra-business use. By the mid-1880s inter-urban trunk lines were permitted on condition that no written message delivery service was provided so as to compete with telegraphy. Only in 1890 was London linked by trunk line to the Midlands and North and only in 1912, when most of the telephone network was taken into Post Office ownership and management, did telephone usage accelerate. By 1920 Britain had almost one million telephones but, that said, most British homes still did not have one by the 1960s.

The first submarine telephone cable was laid in 1891, linking Paris and London and providing the first tiny step to a global telephone network. However, the establishment of longer distance services came far later and, when they arrived, were radio based. Transatlantic telephone services, linking New York with London, were initiated in 1927 and quickly expanded to encompass Europe and North America. Shortly afterwards a sustained conversation between Britain and Australia was possible. But needless to say, such services were for many years prohibitively expensive and telegraphy remained the clear leader. A good time later, in 1956, the first transatlantic telephone cable opened for business and this, together with a quick succession of related improvements resulted in steadily falling costs, higher quality reception, greater security and easier access, not least via direct dialling within Europe from the early 1960s and across the Atlantic from 1970. Other changes, including the introduction of satellites, the use of fibre optical cables and restructuring of the telecommunications industry, meant that by the 1990s international telephone communication was cheap and routine. This restructuring of the industry was characterised by privatisation. Telephone services in some parts of the world, most notably the United States, have always been in private ownership but early on those in most Western countries were nationalised. Privatisation of nationalised systems was a feature of the late twentieth century, in 1981 in the case of Britain.

The most recent advance in telephony has been via cell – or mobile – phones that have supplemented landline phones and have transformed communications with businesspeople when travelling. They have their business roots in car radio telephone services introduced in the United States from the late 1940s, which enabled commercial vehicles such as taxis to operate more effectively and for senior executives to communicate with their peers when travelling. The first mobile call from a handset – albeit a very large one – was made on an experimental basis by Motorola, a United States corporation, in the early 1970s while the first automated cellular network was offered in Japan in 1979 and in the United States shortly afterwards. By 1990 there were reckoned to be 12 million cell phone subscribers worldwide, a figure that expanded to over six billion in the following decade on the back of a steep and sustained fall in service and handset costs.

From the mid-1980s the development of successive generations of cell phone technology led to the introduction of additional functionality such as text messaging (from the early 1990s), photography, wireless email, internet connectivity and web browsing. From the mid-1990s this combination of cell phone with computing capability created a multi-functional device, referred to generically as a smartphone. Inevitably their usefulness was diminished by the smallness of the smartphone screen.

Facsimile machines

The introduction of the facsimile machine from the mid-1960s made a very substantial contribution to the communication of documentation. Its significance was at the same level as that of the photocopier for copying documentation. It was more versatile than telex. At one level it communicated images rather than text and these images included signed, annotated and handwritten documents, tabulated information such as statistics and accounts and plans and drawings. At another level it was a device that empowered office workers who themselves could communicate documentation, in due course from their desktops, without having to do so through a third party.

The antecedence of facsimile communication is surprisingly long, dating to mid-nineteenth-century experiments. In early commercial use transmission was over telegraph wires; later it was via wireless and telephone lines. The American Bank Note Co. in the 1890s is the first recorded sender of facsimiles via telegraphy for commercial use and by 1910 newspapers were commonly exchanging facsimile images of photographs. On account of high costs and to a lesser extent slow operation, use for a long time was restricted to sending images that were urgently required and which could not be sent quickly by other means. Telegraphy was wholly unsuitable as, of course, it could not send images.

A huge stride forward was made in the mid-1960s through the introduction of the modern fax machine by Xerox Corporation. This was compact, easily connected to the telephone network, relatively user friendly and relatively inexpensive although transmission times could be slow and quality of copy not good. Improvements soon followed and by the early 1970s some 30,000 machines were at work in the United States. New digital technology resulting in cost reduction, easier operation and enhanced image quality led to widespread innovation from the late 1970s. By 1988 the United Kingdom alone had almost 400,000 machines (but just 112,000 telex machines), which reflected their dispersal from central stations to departmental and, in some cases, to individual desk-top level. Fax numbers, alongside telex and telephone numbers, became commonplace on business notepaper. Another advance was the introduction of laser printing from the mid-1980s, which produced clearer images and facilitated the use of plain paper in place of chemically-treated 'thermal paper'. Text printed on to the latter had a marked tendency to fade. But technology marched on; by the 1990s the use of facsimile machines was in substantial decline in the face of internet communication but they continued in use for specialist tasks in the early twenty-first century.

Internet, electronic mail and world wide web

Information transfer by facsimile and telex was overtaken in the 1990s by the internet, which ultimately enabled the sending of electronic mail and attachments and the more passive publishing and exchange of information via sites on the web. It continued the process of empowering the individual office worker by enabling the near-immediate communication of messages and a wide range of documentation to a single or to multiple destinations. Messages could be of whatever length or formality, and could also replace or supplement telephone communication. The near-immediate communication between two parties who might not be available simultaneously was enabled. All of this resulted in substantial changes in office organisation and increases in office productivity but also in the creation of vast quantities of information and the information management challenges associated with it.

As with the development of so much advanced information technology in the post-war period, the initial stimulus was the interconnected needs of scientific and military research, especially the need for institutions and individuals working at a distance from one another to share information. In all of this the United States was well ahead of other countries.

The roots of the internet lay in linking individual terminals with a common mainframe. The first linking of two remote university computers via a telephone line was achieved in the mid-1960s. From the late 1960s several networking systems were developed, notably the ARPANET in the United States in 1969, which linked computers in four United States universities; it very soon incorporated many others. In the United Kingdom in the 1970s several networks were established to serve scientific and other academic institutions and which were consolidated into the JANET network in the early 1980s. In the 1970s and 1980s inter-networking emerged on the back of internet protocols to facilitate the joining up of individual networks and from this the global internet emerged. In 1989 the first commercial internet service providers were established to offer network access and other facilities and this heralded the opening up of the internet to worldwide business and personal use especially from the early 1990s.

Email developed alongside the internet from its earliest days; in the early 1960s it was first possible for multi-users of a given mainframe computer network to exchange messages. An email facility was developed for the ARPANET in 1971, establishing the principles on which email operates today and not least the concept of the individual mail box and the term 'user@host'. By the end of the 1980s the basic functionality associated with email was largely in place. The first commercial use of email – on an experimental basis – is recorded in the United States in 1988 and in 1993 commercial internet service providers began to offer email services over the internet. Many large- and medium-sized businesses, however, operated their email systems over internal networks.

The web (otherwise known as the World Wide Web) is the other vital information product associated with the internet. The underlying technology, especially hypertext, was developed in the 1980s and use of the web was massively facilitated from the early 1990s with the introduction of effective web browsers such as Netscape Navigator and Internet Explorer. The latter had achieved dominance by 2000 when bundled as part of Microsoft's Windows operating system. Exploitation of the web was further enhanced through the introduction of advanced search engines such as Google in 1998 and Safari in 2003.

By the mid-1990s big corporations had come to view a presence on the web as an indispensable component of their corporate communication with both the world at large and with specific groups such as their customers and shareholders. For them in particular the web offered low cost and easily updated publishing, while for the user it offered immediate access. It was only a step from this, albeit a revolutionary and expensive one in which the economic benefits would have been uncertain, to engagement with associates, suppliers and, most particularly, customers in a more dynamic and focused way. For businesses providing services this meant giving customers online access to account information and enabling them to provide online instructions for account movements. For retailers and other sellers of goods, it enabled customers to select from online catalogues, to deliver instructions, pay for purchases, and to track the relating transaction process. This has led to dramatic changes in the way companies transact their business, to the records they create in place of hard copy records and to the way in which they retain long-term records of these activities.

The same principles also applied from the early 1990s to internal communications within a business through the setting up of intranet sites to distribute information only to staff, or groups of staff, at as many geographical locations as it possessed. This means of information distribution quickly replaced hard copy records such as staff newsletters, circulars, procedural manuals, management accounts and sales analysis. Intranets also had a transactional dimension facilitating internal work processes across sites. All of this, coupled with such social media tools as Facebook, Twitter and Skype, which became available after 2000, have enabled businesses operating from multiple sites, especially internationally spread ones, to engage customers and staff in a more cohesive and effective way.

Organising and analysing information

Books and binders

The earliest means of organising information was through the making up of accounts, which were invariably held in bound volumes to preserve the integrity of their content, for example by preventing loss of sheets and reducing opportunities for fraud. However, high paper costs, an undemanding tax and regulatory environment and widespread illiteracy and innumeracy probably mitigated against most small businesses creating few, if any, accounts until well into the nineteenth century. High paper costs manifested themselves in several ways in early record keeping; in ledgers individual accounts were carried forward to non-adjacent pages or half pages in order to ensure that as few pages as possible went unused. From mid-century account-keeping spread quickly as business size increased, as paper costs fell, as ownership and management of businesses became more separate, and as business legislation, especially connected with company law and registration, required the keeping of certain types of record.

Bound books for record keeping were made in the same way as printed books but were usually manufactured by stationers who invariably were also jobbing printers. Some big firms, such as Robinsons of Bristol and Barclay & Fry of London, produced standard ranges for national sale but, until well into the twentieth century, many if not most were manufactured locally. Some were made to the customer's specification meaning that over time a run of identical books accumulated for a particular function; reordering was facilitated by quoting the manufacturer's reference number written on a label inside, often on the inside-front cover.

Loose-leaf books for holding accounts, minutes, and the like, were originally made in the United States and were introduced into Europe around 1900; in Britain Kalamazoo and Twinlock were early brand leaders. Their use was widespread from the 1920s having overcome initial reservations about the loss of integrity through the removal and/or replacement of pages; here locking and other devices sometimes came to be employed as a safeguard. Loose leaf offered many advantages over bound volumes: pages could be kept in alphabetical order of account name, obviating the need for book or card indexes; content could be typed; dormant pages could be transferred from the current book to a dormant book; sub-division of content into two or more books was possible meaning that no ledger became too unwieldy to handle; and so on. Derivatives of the loose-leaf ledger included card ledgers where pages were held together on rods and not in binders.

Filing systems

Individual letters and other messages together with unbound documents such as invoices, contracts, memoranda, printed papers and the like are invariably organised in files, which together formed a substantial part of a business's information resources. File organisation might be by document type, by name of correspondent or by transaction and, within that structure, by date or serial number. At the heart of a filing system is the dual need to preserve the integrity of documentation and to ensure that it is properly and consistently organised so that it can be located and tell a narrative in a comprehensive way.

Early 'filing' systems used no conventional file stationery and were basic; the 'stationery' might simply be a series of metal spikes on to which letters were attached in some simple order. Such primitive systems would only be effective when record volumes were relatively small, as was the case with the vast majority of businesses before the nineteenth century; early large businesses such as the Bank of England, the East India Company, Lloyds of London and the like were then very few and far between. But as a footnote to this, albeit one outside the scope of this chapter, the organisational needs of large government departments and agencies should not be forgotten, especially those supplying materials, say, to the Admiralty and Army.

Spikes apart, a typical early system might be based on pigeon holes ordered in an alphabetical sequence, perhaps contained within a lockable cabinet. Letters were docketed with the name of correspondent, possibly the subject and more often the date of reply, and allotted to a pigeon hole according to the name or geographical location of the correspondent. When non-current, they might be bundled in date order and stored, possibly in a deed box. Copies of outgoing correspondence might be kept separate, perhaps in a copy letter book.

By the last decade or so of the nineteenth century a range of filing stationery had appeared. 'Expanding alphabet cases' or concertina files, which held papers in pockets, were the first and simplest devices; early ones, made from leather, can be found in the mid-nineteenth century. Greater integrity was offered by devices that secured papers on spikes; possibly the earliest, marketed under the Shannon brand, was described in 1906 as a 'substantial board to which is attached a perforator, a double spring arch over which the letters are placed and a cover on which a spring presses to protect the letters from dust' (Dicksee and Blain, 1906, p. 43). The standard and enduring 'manila' file was introduced shortly before 1900. Here letters were 'placed in a strong paper or linen cover (which can be had in various colours to distinguish departments, subjects, geographical division) on the back of which are placed metal strips, which pass through corresponding holes pierced in the document, the ends of the strips being bent down over the top letter and held in place with a clip' (Dicksee and Blain, 1906, p. 43).

The establishment of far more big businesses from the mid-nineteenth century, especially railway, bank and insurance companies, created a need not just for relatively sophisticated file stationery, but also for complex filing systems subject to greater intellectual control. This was especially so for 'strategic' information, say about a particular project, transaction or policy, as opposed to 'routine' information such as invoices and remittance advices or papers relating to, say, an insurance policy or bank account. A very basic requirement for the keeping of 'strategic' files was the filing of in and out correspondence and related papers in a single and logical sequence, something facilitated by carbon copies generated easily and cheaply by typewriters. Other features involved the creation at the front of files of an index to correspondents and subjects and also, perhaps, of a central card index to the filing system as a whole. More sophisticated was the introduction of an intellectually-derived file structure for the whole file population, which acknowledged the information organisation and access requirements of users and the need for accuracy, consistency and continuity in organisation. This was the stuff of effective file registries established by big businesses (and certainly not least government departments).

The nature of these registries varied with the nature of their contents and the needs of users. Simple registries, handling relatively few papers per correspondent or transaction, might employ a numerical system. Here in-letters, marked with a reference number and date of receipt, might be recorded in-letter registers supported by a cumulative index of correspondents. Out-letters sent in reply might carry this reference together with the page number of the letter book where the copy of the out-letter was to be found. Any subsequent incoming letter would be filed with the first in-letter. Therefore a typical letter reference, say A2/16/1234, is interpreted as follows: A for department name, 2 for out-letter book number, 16 for folio number of the letter book and 1234 for letter(s) reference. A later derivative of this system might comprise in- and out-letters held in a dedicated file within a numerical sequence and supported by a cumulative index.

At the other end of the spectrum, filing systems for complex transactions, embracing a wide variety of document types, could be highly sophisticated and demand substantial intellectual input. That of Baring Brothers, London merchant bankers, serves as an excellent example. Around 1900 a registry system was introduced to handle papers created and received by senior managers in connection with, *inter alia*, bond issues and project finance. In- and out-letters and telegrams along with their enclosures, minutes of meetings and conversations, contracts and other supporting papers were filed in date order. Each file – and several volumes could relate to a given transaction – was supported by a sophisticated correspondent and subject index. See Box 3.1 for a case study of this filing system.

The design of such systems brought into being specialist businesses dedicated to advising businesses on best practice. The Roneo Company provides a good example with the 1908 establishment of a filing systems division, which devised systems and supplied associated stationery.

Box 3.1 Case study: the registry filing system of Barings Bank, London, United Kingdom

The registry filing system introduced at Baring Brothers, the leading London merchant bank, in the first years of the twentieth century provides a good example of a sophisticated registry filing system. It served the six or so partners of the firm and was known as Partners' Filing. Its introduction was urgently needed as in the last decades of the nineteenth century the pre-existing system at Barings had all but collapsed under the weight of increased volumes and changing technologies.

The new system organised all documentation created and received by the Baring partners. As they handled all the major bond issue and other financial transactions, relationships with key correspondent firms in Europe and North and South America and internal administration policy, it was by far the firm's most important source of 'strategic' information.

For the most part documents were organised by transaction or by name of correspondent or by name of administration matter; there were other files but these are the most important. The underlying philosophy was that the files should contain all documentation required to give a very clear understanding of the matter to which the file related. Thus if a given document covered, say, two transactions, a typed copy would be made and it would be filed on both transaction files.

Documents were filed in date order unless there was an intellectual need to adopt a different order. All relevant in- and out-letters, telegrams, notes of telephone conversations, meeting minutes, conversation memoranda, press cuttings, contracts, and so on, would be filed. Each document on the file was numbered sequentially and each document was marked with the page number of the previous and subsequent document that directly related to it. At the front of each file was a typed index, presumably made when the file was closed, organised by name of correspondent and subject matter. A card index, serving the whole accumulation of files, was maintained; it contained much cross referencing.

Consistency, continuity and accuracy were the hallmarks of the system. A hallmark of a different kind was the intellectual control that was imposed on the system by the secretaries and filers involved who, by necessity, were of high intelligence and had a profound knowledge of the underlying business. No information is available about the agency that introduced the system at Barings.

A massive increase in information and its creation and delivery in a variety of formats put traditional registry filing systems under increasing pressure after 1945; this gathered pace with the introduction of telex and photocopies from the 1950s. Many hitherto effective systems succumbed under the sheer volume of documents for filing and were hampered in cost-benefit analysis by the inherent difficulty of demonstrating intangible benefits over easily calculated costs. Centralised intellectual control of the registry gave way to devolved systems that often lacked the vital requirements of consistency, continuity and accuracy. In the late 1990s, with a large proportion of records by then received and created in electronic format and with paper records capable of electronic conversion via scanning, electronic records management became, in theory, an effective successor to the traditional registry.

A major problem with the handling of electronic documents – whether text, spreadsheets, data tables, presentations or email – is that historically the tools made available to the creator and/or recipient by software developers have only permitted documents to be organised in a fairly rudimentary way. This, amongst other reason, has led to the development of electronic document management systems whose chief functionality allows the 'collection' of documents created or received by the population served by the system; the 'tagging' of these documents by date, correspondent name, project name, and so on; and the searching for 'strings' of labelled documents according to criteria defined by the user. Security protocols permit document integrity, version control, access rights linked to user status, and the like. Such systems, in theory, provide massive benefits, for example, in allowing users speedy access to up-to-date, shared information; in serving a user population spread across sites and countries; and in revealing ways in which general work processes can be adjusted to operate more effectively. In practice, the key to the success of such systems – most notably those where document types and linkages are complex and the number of users numerous – is competent centralised intellectual control to ensure consistency, continuity and accuracy in the organisation of documents. Historically the importance of this has often been underestimated, with an over-reliance placed on the users and creators of documents as organisers of documents, meaning that systems fell far short of their full potential.

Calculating and bookkeeping machines

Calculating devices, most notably the abacus have their roots in ancient times and from the seventeenth century were joined by such aids as logarithm tables and slide rules. Mechanical devices also date from this time but while representing important steps in knowledge development had no commercial significance. Things changed around the mid-nineteenth century. On the production side knowledge accumulation and material developments were no doubt vital but on the demand side businesses (but also government departments) increasingly needed labour saving and accurate devices to handle their calculations. A very small number of very large businesses had existed for a long time but in the nineteenth century big businesses increased very rapidly in number in Britain, the rest of Europe and especially in the United States. They included railways, banks, insurance and shipping companies, international trading concerns, armaments producers and, increasingly, businesses operating across a wide spectrum of manufacturing. Their administration and products grew large and complex and all needed machinery for use in functions such as account-keeping, cost analysis, statistics production say for marketing and management control and, more specifically, for actuarial predictions, design and construction, research and the like.

While some commercial application of calculating machines began in the early-nineteenth century, it was only from the mid-1880s that they attained any significant impact. As with so much office technology, the United States dominated production and innovation, the first notable machines being produced there in the mid-1880s by Felt & Tarrant whose keyboard-based models became known as Comptometers. Soon afterwards William Burroughs, of what came to be Burroughs Corporation, took calculating machines a step further by incorporating functionality that printed and totalled the numbers inputted. It was a market winner and Burroughs's company came to dominate the early market, buying up emerging competitors if need be, and had sold almost 300 machines by 1895 and 50,000 some 20 years later; by 1926 the company claimed to have supplied one million machines since its foundation. Burroughs' products were usually known as Adder-Lister or Adding-Listing machines.

From the outset model development was rapid with specific machines being developed for particular tasks. They could be big or small, expensive or cheap. Some very large machines were developed for accounting applications such as bookkeeping and billing. By 1905, for example, some machines could print two rows of figures simultaneously or could print ancillary information such as page, invoice and policy number. In the 1920s bookkeeping machines that enabled a ledger narrative to be typed alongside rows of listed and totalled figures were introduced.

Traditional electro-mechanical calculating machines were displaced from the early 1960s by electronic desktop calculators. Pocket calculators, designed for a mass market, appeared in the early 1970s. Both greatly empowered individual office workers. The arrival of mainframe and personal computers was to diminish the use of both.

Tabulating machines and computers

Calculating machines filled one relatively straightforward requirement of business for the mechanical handling of certain data but there were other requirements, which still had to be met, albeit ones hardly articulated by late-nineteenth-century businessmen. These involved the recording, processing and analysis of data about a wide range of business components: sales, output, costs, performance, personnel and the like. This requirement was already manifested in the nineteenth-century archives of some big businesses in which tables or even books of statistics, graphs and other forms of data analysis and presentation are to be found. But statistics were laborious and costly to compile, hugely costly to analyse and subject to the inaccuracies inherent in repetitive tasks. Adding machines certainly assisted in these processes, especially with small datasets, but they fell far short of what was required. The tabulating machine and its successor, the computer, changed all of this, revolutionising the means and speed of analysing business information.

Heroic attempts to develop mechanically-driven computing machines were made in the nineteenth and earlier centuries, those of Charles Babbage being especially well known, but none had any commercial significance until the advent of the tabulating machine. The origins of the latter date to 1890 when Herman Hollerith devised an electro-mechanical machine, which 'counted' and thereby analysed data recorded in a pattern of holes (or lack of them) punched into a batch of punch cards. Put another way, the batches of punch cards formed machine-readable data for processing by the tabulating machine.

It is interesting that the Hollerith machine was not prompted by business requirements but was first developed to facilitate the fast counting and analysis of data collected by the decennial United States Census of 1890, a process so time consuming if conducted manually that the data would be obsolete before its analysis was complete. The location of holes on the card denoted different criteria per person and these holes were read by the machine to give, via a set of dials, individual totals for each criterion.

Hollerith in 1896 set up his own business to make and sell his machine; in 1911 it was subsumed into an amalgamation of businesses under the name of Computing-Tabulating-Recording Co., from 1924 known as International Business Machines, or IBM. This name belied the take up of this United States technology internationally and associated businesses were soon established in Europe such as the British Tabulating Co. Ltd and the Accounting & Tabulating Machine Co. of Great Britain Ltd. Soon machines were developed that could print results in tables or as accounts, from at least the 1920s on fan-fold paper. Data handling capacity also improved. By 1912, for example, a punch card holding some 45 pieces of information could be handled, a capacity that roughly doubled by the late 1920s when IBM introduced an 80-piece card, which was to become the industry standard.

At this stage, generally speaking, business usage was restricted to the very largest corporations and this remained so until the late 1930s. In Britain big business users included the likes of Great Western Railway Co.; the government printing organisation, HMSO; the Prudential life insurance business; the engineering and armaments giant, Vickers; and leading food processors such as Cadbury Brothers. The United States, as in other areas of information technology, was far and away the most enthusiastic innovator. Much earlier than in Europe tabulating machines were adopted by many medium-sized businesses, while in the 1930s service bureaux opened to cater for those businesses which could not afford such heavy investment.

Applications could be wide ranging even within the same business. Here the leading Scottish insurer, Standard Life, makes a good case study. Its first tabulating machine was installed as late as 1927 but nevertheless the business 'quickly emerged as a pioneer in the mechanisation of life assurance records'. Initially its machine facilitated valuation and the issue of bonus certificates but this soon extended to 'calculation of annuity payments and associated tax, the compilation of new business statistics . . . the tracking of lapses and revivals, payment of invoices, and stock control' (Moss, 2000, p. 205). This example also underlines the slowness of British business in taking up this new technology, something generally attributed to high costs. Only in the late 1930s did innovation gather pace; it was sustained until the mid-1960s after which the electro-mechanical tabulating machine was deposed by the electronic computer. Professor Martin Campbell-Kelly has produced several case studies of the introduction of data processing by leading United Kingdom businesses and institutions including Prudential Assurance, Post Office Savings Bank, Railway Clearing House and the British Census (Campbell-Kelly, 1992; 1993; 1996; 1998).

There were of course many parallels between the tabulator and the computer, but the latter had powerful advantages, which over time came more and more into their own. The computer stored and processed information electronically and as such was far faster and more powerful than the tabulator. Not least, in due course, it obviated the cumbersome handling of punch cards and their careful storage in thousands. But the abandonment of punch cards was not fast and they were still in evidence in the 1970s. They continued as the input-output medium for early computers, before being replaced by magnetic tape, and eased the transition of businesses from tabulating machines as their existing work processes and parts of their existing tabulating machinery could be used in conjunction with their new computer. But by the 1960s the era of the tabulating machine was fast approaching its end in the face of competition from the commercially-viable computer.

The electronic computer made its debut in the United States and Britain for government work in the Second World War; as with other aspects of electronic information technology, its early days were dominated by the combined needs of government and their military and scientific agencies. A defining feature of a computer is its programmability; it acts on a set of instructions written by programmers and parcelled up into a programme. An important early breakthrough in the mid- and late 1940s was the development of the 'stored program computer', which laid down fundamental design principles for future computer development.

Early on programmes were introduced to the computer manually via punch cards or paper tapes whereas the stored program computer was to hold them internally in memory. Latterly they were introduced via source code written on a keyboard in a programming language. A vital feature of programming from the 1960s onwards was the development of relatively friendly programme languages of words and figures, such as BASIC. This stood for Beginner's All Purpose Symbolic Instruction Code, a choice of words that announced the accessibility of programming to a far wider constituency.

Memory is another vital feature of the computer. Memory size dictates the computer's capacity to hold both programme instructions and data and early on manifested itself in an array of bulky components such as electrostatic storage tubes. By the 1960s these were largely replaced in new computers by magnetic core memories and from the 1970s by integrated circuit, semiconductor memory. At each stage this led to relative miniaturisation, improved reliability, cost reduction and, certainly not least, increased computing capacity. It also led to the mass production of computers, with IBM in the vanguard, and widespread innovation of them by business.

Early computers used punched cards for both input and output with printed output being obtained by passing cards through a tabulator. Around 1960 it became possible to obtain printed output of data and of its analysis ('hard copy') direct from the computer for perusal, checking and annotation by office workers; it was invariably obtained on A3 'fan-fold' continuous stationery (as monitor access then was unavailable to the vast majority of office workers). Fan-fold stationery became a permeating feature of the office landscape but, such was its bulk, retaining printed output long term for information and legal reasons was impracticable. This gave rise to the capture of reports on microfilm/microfiche and their access on a working basis by office workers via readers. Known as COM (Computer Output Microfilm), it was possible from the 1970s and was widely used. Otherwise computer data came to be downloaded onto magnetic tape on a regular periodic basis for short-term backup and for long-term retention. Due to its strategic importance it was held in secure, environmentally suitable conditions; this was also necessary as in the long term it could become unstable.

An early, if unlikely, pioneer in the development of electronic computing was the caterer and food processor, J. Lyons & Co. Ltd, a top-tier British catering business; a study of its unique response to data management in the 1940s and early 1950s highlights computing issues then confronted by big business. In the 1930s Lyons' business experienced phenomenal expansion based, as it was, on a vast number of transactions each with an infinitesimally small profit margin. Its determination to manage this effectively led to the use by the 1930s of some 250 business machines of one sort or another; it emerged as a leader in corporate information processing. After 1945 its natural progression in the absence of commercially produced computers – albeit a progression demanding substantial management courage – was to develop an 'in-house' computing facility in conjunction with Cambridge University. The result was LEO – or Lyons' Electronic Office – introduced in 1953, the first computer 'designed and built to undertake general commercial work as distinct from mere mathematical or scientific calculations'. Its first task was to manage part of Lyons' payroll. Its operators discovered it could handle a transaction in 1.5 seconds, which would have taken an office worker eight minutes to perform. LEO went on to undertake a wide range of other tasks and, although it had a relatively short life, it graphically demonstrated the capability of computing and the pressing need of business for it. Such needs were to be met through the mass production of computers from the early 1960s onwards.

By the mid-1950s IBM, with an extensive internationally-spread manufacturing, research and sales infrastructure, was the leading player in the information technology industry; it led the way in the development of commercial computers globally. In the early 1950s it marketed its 701 machine and quickly achieved domination of the relatively small but growing big business market. Its 360 machine, introduced in the mid-1960s with an emphasis on range, compatibility and ease of upgrade, confirmed its market dominance and finally upturned the tabulating machine. Computers were now brought within the buying power of medium-sized businesses and demand soared. By 1967 Western Europe had some 10,000 machines at work, a number that was doubling every two years.

This widespread installation heralded unprecedented change in information processing although the tasks undertaken in the 1970s remained narrow compared with future achievements. In the office, as opposed to on the factory floor, these tasks fell into five broad areas, namely invoice writing, payroll preparation, bookkeeping and other routine clerical tasks; data analysis to provide management information about key areas such as performance, costs, sales, pricing and stocks; new product design; comparison of real with hypothetical data to measure differences and aid decision making; and customer-facing processes such as airline ticket reservation facilities for travel agents and statement generation for bank customers.

Hugely significant advances in the technology used in the manufacture of computers in the 1970s, resulted in the introduction of what came to be commonly termed personal, and later also laptop, computers (PCs). It was the beginning of the end for the large mainframe with its desktop terminal linkages and, at the other end of the spectrum, for the typewriter. Commodore and Apple were early leaders in PC production in the late 1970s, followed by IBM at the beginning of the 1980s, a commitment by the latter that legitimated the PC as a vital business machine. These early machines were, however, relatively expensive and initially found use in big companies for specialist tasks, especially accounting and administration, but before long a million had been sold worldwide. By the end of the 1980s other manufacturers, notably new entrants to the information technology sector, were marketing small and cheap home computers such as, in Britain, the Amstrad PC and the BBC Microcomputer. These were relatively user friendly and widely used and had huge impact on small businesses and on the acquisition of computer literacy by employees.

Whilst the arrival of new manufacturers created greater competition, entrepreneurship and innovation, other vital reasons also contributed to a dramatic fall in computer prices and their greater use. One was the onward march of miniaturisation referred to above, especially that enabled by integrated circuit technology and the development of silicon chips with ever-greater capacity. As important was the development of off-the-shelf software developed by a burgeoning software products industry, obviating programming by the user. The biggest contribution came from the development of operating systems by Microsoft.

The Microsoft business was established in 1975 and subsequently provided an operating system for IBM's new IBM PC. This was named PC DOS. Alongside this Microsoft marketed the product to other PC manufacturers as MS DOS. From this emerged the hugely successful Microsoft Windows operating system and its associated office software marketed as Microsoft Office. Their first product, Microsoft Windows (Windows 1), was marketed in 1985 and new and enhanced products appeared in quick succession, most notably the very successful Microsoft Office product in 1989 with its package of word processor, spreadsheet and database applications. By the mid-1990s Microsoft provided operating systems to 90 per cent of the world's PCs.

Computers, and the PC in particular, led to the creation of a range of record formats connected with the storage, transfer and sharing of information. Historically data from mainframes was downloaded via punch cards and magnetic tapes, later cassettes, for storage and back up. Disk drives replaced these. PCs came with their own storage, transfer and back up devices: floppy disks from the 1980s, CDs from the mid-1990s and flash drives from the late 1990s, including the memory stick at the turn of the century.

By the mid-1990s the availability of the PC as an individual workstation had continued the process of empowering the office worker, although in this instance more than ever before. It enabled text document creation by software such as Word, accounting document creation and analysis via Excel, data recording and analysis via Access, presentation documentation via Power Point. In all these cases searching for specific pieces of information was a vital part of functionality. Another was the ability to share information via networked machines; documents could be stored in shared directories and accessed by multiple workers via password protocols. Hard copy could be achieved via printers, electronic copy via CDs. By the 1990s PCs held email functionality, which permitted communication with others including document communication as attachments. Web browsing was also, of course, possible for the acquisition of knowledge and passive communication via websites. It can be seen, therefore, that by the 1990s all the components of office technology – document creation, copying, communication and analysis – had been deposited in the office worker's workstation completing a transition in empowerment that had for long been in progress.

Massive changes in office organisation and culture resulted from the 1980s. New technology led to the reduction and in some cases disappearance of a wide range of office functions such as the typing pool, secretaries, the print room, the post room, and telex operation. Their place was taken by a huge army of information technologists – technicians, programmers, designers, security personnel and the like; they along with the hardware and software they administered meant a newly arrived cost base of similarly huge proportions. Effective remote working from a centralised office became possible. Many traditional record formats disappeared from the office scene – account books, books of statistics, indexes, record cards, registers of various sorts, internal memos, artwork – while others were in sharp decline such as letters and photographs. Existing technologies became redundant or at least near-redundant such as the typewriter, telex machine, facsimile machine and printing press. Office workers had to learn new skills, at the least the ability to use a keyboard efficiently, to manipulate software and to organise electronic documents effectively.

All of this, however, did not come without its problems. Chief amongst these was a general decline in the management of documentation associated with increases in volumes and types and in fragmentation in creation and storage. By the 1990s centralised intellectual control with its emphasis on comprehensive collection of documents, their organisation in a structured and consistent way, their controlled accessibility and security and, not least, their scheduled destruction had became increasingly difficult to implement.

Acknowledgements

The author would like to thank Martin Campbell-Kelly, Paul Lasewicz and Julia Sheppard for kindly commenting on the chapter as a whole. Linda Ramsay made some useful suggestions on early papermaking.

References

Baglehole, K. C., 1969. *A century of service. A brief history of Cable & Wireless Ltd, 1868–1968*. London: Cable & Wireless Ltd.

Campbell-Kelly, M., 1992. Large scale data processing in the Prudential, 1850–1930. *Accounting, Business and Financial History*, 2, pp. 117–139.

Campbell-Kelly, M., 1993. Railway Clearing House and Victorian data processing. In: L. Bud-Frierman, ed., 1994. *Information and acumen. The understanding and use of knowledge in modern business*. London: Routledge.

Campbell-Kelly, M., 1996. Information technology and organizational change in the British census, 1801–1911. *Information Systems Research*, 7, pp. 22–36.

Campbell-Kelly, M., 1998. Data processing and technological change. The Post Office Savings Bank, 1861–1930. *Technology & Culture*, 39, pp. 1–32.

Dicksee, L. R. and Blain, H. E., 1906. *Office organisation and management*. London: Pitman.

Moss, M., 2000. *The building of Europe's largest mutual life company. Standard Life, 1825–2000*. Edinburgh: Mainstream.

Further reading

General

Dale, R. and Weaver, R., 1993. *Machines in the office*. Oxford: Oxford University Press.

Delgado, A., 1979. *The enormous file. A social history of the office*. London: John Murray.

Dicksee, L. R. and Blain, H. E., 1906. *Office organisation and management*. 1st ed. London: Pitman.

Recording information

Adler, M. H., 1973. *The writing machine*. London: Allen & Unwin.

Anon., 1977. As fast as speech. *An outline history of shorthand from 2400BC*. London: Pitman.

Beeching, W. A., 1990. *Century of the typewriter*. 2nd ed. Bournemouth: British Typewriter Museum Publishing.

Current, R. N., 1988. *The typewriter and the men who made it*. 2nd ed. Arcadia: Post-Era Books.

Grattan, D. W., ed., 1993. *Saving the twentieth century. The conservation of modern materials*. Ottawa: Canadian Conservation Institute.

Heawood, E., 1924. Use of watermarks in dating old maps and documents. *Geographical Journal*, 63(5), pp. 120–127.

Heawood, E., 1950. *Watermarks, mainly of the seventeenth and eighteenth centuries.* Hilversum: Paper Publications Society.

Hills, R. L., 1988. *Papermaking in Britain, 1488–1988. A short history.* London: Athlone Press.

Hunter, D., 1978. *Papermaking. The history and technique of an ancient craft.* 2nd ed. London: Constable.

Kissel, E. and Vigneau, E., 2009. *Architectural photoreproductions. A manual for identification and care.* New Castle, DE: Oak Knoll Press.

Mares, G. C., 1909. *History of the typewriter; being an illustrated account of the origin, rise and development of the writing machine.* London: Guilbert Pitman.

Mell, G., 2010. *Writing antiques.* Botley: Shire Publications.

Nickell, J., 1990. *Pen, ink and evidence. A study of writing and materials for the penman, collector and document detective.* Lexington, KY: University of Kentucky Press.

Richards, G. T., 1964. *The history and development of typewriters.* 2nd ed. London: HMSO.

Whalley, J. I., 1975. *Writing implements and accessories. From the Roman stylus to the typewriter.* Newton Abbott: David & Charles.

Early office museum, 2000–2015, [online]. Available at: www.officemuseum.com [Accessed 19 September 2016].

Copying information

De Sola, R., 1944. *Microfilming.* New York: Essential Books.

Desborough, W., 1930. *Duplicating and copying processes.* London: Pitman.

Dorlay, J. S., 1978. *The Roneo story.* Croydon: Roneo.

Gauntlett, M. D., 1978. *A history of Kodak Ltd to 1977.* Harrow: Kodak.

Hills, R. L., 1996. James Watt and his copying machine. In: P. Bower, ed.,1996. *Proceedings of the British Association of Paper Historians fourth annual conference.* London: British Association of Paper Historians, pp. 81–88.

Luther, F., 1959. *Microfilm. A history, 1839–1900.* Annapolis, MD: National Microfilm Association.

Proudfoot, W. B., 1972. *The origin of stencil duplicating.* London: Hutchinson.

Early office museum, 2000–2015, [online]. Available at: www.officemuseum.com [Accessed 19 September 2016].

Communicating information

Abbate, J., 1999. *Inventing the internet.* Cambridge, MA: MIT Press.

Alcock, R. C. and Holland, F. C., 1943–56. *The postmarks of Great Britain and Ireland.* Cheltenham: R.C. Alcock.

Allaz, C., 2004. *The history of air cargo and air mail from the eighteenth century.* London: Foyle Publishing.

Barty-King, H., 1979. *Girdle round the earth. The story of Cable & Wireless.* London: Heinemann.

Browne, C., 1993. *Getting the message. The story of the British Post Office.* Stroud: Alan Sutton.

Cahn, W., 1961. *The story of Pitney Bowes.* New York: Harper & Bros.

Campbell-Smith, D., 2011. *Masters of the post. The authorised history of the Royal Mail.* London: Allen Lane.

Daunton, M. J., 1985. *Royal Mail. The Post Office since 1840.* London: Athlone Press.

Evans, J., 1955. *The endless web. John Dickinson & Co Ltd, 1804–1954.* London: Jonathan Cape [for envelope manufacture].

Flinn, B. and Yang, D., eds., 2009. *Communicating under the seas. The evolving cable network and its implications.* Cambridge, MA: MIT Press.

Gillies, J. and Cailliau, R., 2000. *How the web was born. The story of the world wide web.* Oxford: Oxford University Press.

Hargest, G. E., 1975. *History of letter post communication between the United States and Europe, 1845–1875*. Lawrence, MA: Quarterman.

Holmes, D. B., 1981. *Air mail. An illustrated history, 1793–1981*. New York: C. N. Potter.

Johannessen, N., ed., 1991. *'Ring up Britain'. The early years of the telephone in the United Kingdom*. London: British Telecom.

Kieve, J. L., 1973. *The electric telegraph. A social and economic history*. Newton Abbot: David & Charles.

Laakso, S. R., 2007. *Across the oceans. Development of overseas business information transmission, 1815–1875*. Helsinki: Finnish Literature Society.

Michaelis, A. R., 1965. *From semaphore to satellite*. Geneva: International Telecommunication Union.

Milne, G. J., 2007. British business and the telephone. *Business History*, 49(2), pp. 163–185.

Naughton, J., 1999. *A brief history of the future. The origins of the internet*. London: Weidenfeld & Nicolson.

Roberts, S. T., 1975. *History of Pitney Bowes Limited*. Harlow: Pitney Bowes [for franking].

Robinson, H., 1953. *Britain's Post Office. A history of the development from the beginnings to the present day*. London: Oxford University Press.

Robinson, H., 1964. *Carrying British mails overseas*. London: Allen & Unwin.

Scott, P., 2011. Still a niche communication medium. The diffusion and uses of the telephone system in interwar Britain. *Business History*, 53(6), pp. 801–820.

Solymar, L., 1999. *Getting the message. A history of communications*. Oxford: Oxford University Press.

Staff, F., 1956. *The transatlantic mail*. New York: Adlard Coles.

Staff, F., 1993. *The penny post, 1680–1918*. 2nd ed. London: Lutterworth Press.

Standage, T., 1998. *The Victorian internet. The remarkable story of the telegraph and the nineteenth century's online pioneers*. New York: Berkley Books.

Winston, B., 1998. *Media technology and society. A history from the telegraph to the internet*. London: Routledge.

Young, P., 1991. *Person to person. The international impact of the telephone*. Cambridge: Granta.

Early office museum, 2000–2015, [online]. Available at: www.officemuseum.com [Accessed 19 September 2016].

Organising and analysing information

Broadberry, S. N. and Sayantan, G., 2002. From the counting house to the modern office. Explaining Anglo-American productivity differences in services, 1870–1990. *Journal of Economic History*, 62(4), pp. 967–998.

Campbell-Kelly, M., 1992. Large scale data processing in the Prudential, 1850–1930. *Accounting, Business and Financial History*, 2, pp. 117–139.

Campbell-Kelly, M., 1993. Railway Clearing House and Victorian data processing. In: L. Bud-Frierman, ed., 1994. *Information and acumen. The understanding and use of knowledge in modern business*. London: Routledge.

Campbell-Kelly, M., 1998. Data processing and technological change. The Post Office Savings Bank, 1861–1930. *Technology & Culture*, 39, pp. 1–32.

Campbell-Kelly, M., 2003. *From airline reservations to Sonic the hedgehog. A history of the software industry*. Cambridge, MA: MIT Press.

Campbell-Kelly, M., 2014. *The computer. A history of the information machine*. 3rd ed. Boulder, CO: Westview.

Coopey, R., 1999. Management and the introduction of computing in British industry, 1945–70. *Contemporary British History*, 13(3), pp. 59–71.

Cortada, J. W., 1993. *Before the computer. IBM, NCR, Burroughs and Remington Rand and the industry they created, 1865–1956*. Princeton, NJ: Princeton University Press.

Evans, C., 1981. *The making of the micro. A history of the computer*. London: Victor Gollancz.

Ferry, G., 2003. *A computer called LEO. Lyons teashops and the world's first office computer.* London: Fourth Estate.

Kemp, K., 2014. Early commercial computing, *Bristol Industrial Archaeological Society Journal,* 47, pp. 21–34.

Morgan, B. S., 1953. *Total to date. The evolution of the adding machine. The story of Burroughs.* London: Burroughs Adding Machine Ltd.

Powers-Samas Accounting Machines Ltd, 1950s. *Powers-Samas Accounting Machines.* London: the firm [marketing document explaining tabulating machines and punch cards in non-technical jargon].

Simmons, J. R. M., 1962. *LEO and the managers.* London: Macdonald.

Tweedale, G., 1990. *Calculating machines and computers.* Princes Risborough: Shire Publications.

Tweedale, G., 1993. A machine on every desk. The development of the mass market in computers. In: R. S. Tedlow and G. Jones, ed., 1993. *The rise and fall of mass marketing.* London: Routledge.

Early office museum, 2000–2015, [online]. Available at: www.officemuseum.com [Accessed 19 September 2016].

Part 2

The nature of business records

Chapter 4

Understanding core business records

Michael Moss

Introduction

The foundation of any enterprise is a transaction or exchange between individuals or corporate bodies, which is based on trust that each party will honour its obligations. In tight-knit communities trusted relationships depended and still depend on social connections, but as businesses were extended and became more complex tokens were introduced to help guarantee trust, which could be upheld by courts of law. Tight-knit communities do not necessarily have to be local: they can be international. The Masonic order and similar associations, such as the professional bodies set up in the United Kingdom in the nineteenth century, had and still have global connections. Particularly in the wake of the financial crisis there has been a great deal of interest in the nature of these trusted relationships by politicians, regulators, anthropologists, economists, historians, moral philosophers, sociologists and even archivists (see for example Fukuyama, 1995; Hosking, 2010; Moss, 2010; O'Neill, 2002; Selden, 2011). This has sparked an interest in the core records and their evidential value (Borland, 2009; Ellerbrock, 2005; Iacovino, 2006). Never before has there been such interest in the 'trusted' management of records in the corporate world, although the role and functions of records managers and archivists are rarely mentioned.

How transactions are recorded

Even today in oral cultures a transaction does not necessarily need to leave any physical record, for example when it is simply an exchange of goods or services by way of barter. The evidence is the good or service that is exchanged. The Yao people in Malawi, Mozambique and Tanzania to this day still conduct all their business by word of mouth with not a trace of a written record (Mitchell, 1956). Sometimes transactions are sealed by the exchange or giving of objects, such as conch shells in the Pacific, or in China and Europe by cutting notches in tally sticks, which were then split with each party holding a matching half, or knotting strings as amongst the Inca peoples of South America and the Chinese (Krishnamurthy, 1997; Kan, 1991; Jenkinson, 1925; Urton, 2003). Interestingly many of these practices, particularly tally sticks, subsisted long after the invention of paper (Kan, 1991; Clanchy, 2009; Classen, 2015, pp. 1209–1212). It is difficult for those familiar with written cultures, and the evidential base that written texts support, to understand how large enterprises can be managed using what appear to be such primitive forms of textuality. As such they need to be approached with an open mind, as it is easy to assume that the absence of the secure audit trail, familiar in written cultures, smacks of corruption. The use of writing to record transactions dates back thousands of years in Asia, the Middle East and much of Europe. The evidence is scanty and depends on the chance survival of clay and wax tablets, and bark, which was widely used as a writing surface in many parts of the world, and of course paper. Bark and paper easily decompose and only survive in exceptionally dry conditions or when petrified (Franklin, 2002). Such finds as have been made suggest that the use of writing to record business transactions began at much the same time as it did for administrative purposes, possibly as early as the Neolithic period (9500 BCE).

Today the majority of records of enterprise throughout the world is in writing and conforms to international standards and agreed ways of conducting business, even though cultural differences persist, which reflect different record keeping and information seeking traditions. At a local level, however, in many parts of the world enterprises interact with older traditions, such as the oral cultures of East Africa or barter, which is still a commonplace in parts of the eastern Mediterranean and throughout Asia. Such practices need not concern us here, except to be aware they exist and that in some parts of the world the written record will only provide partial evidence for the history of enterprise. The business archivist can take comfort from knowing that across the historical sciences and in many other disciplines the notion that the written record is the only 'secure' evidence is no longer tenable. Ethnographers want to know the circumstances in which the written record was constructed, what were the power relationships within the office hierarchy, were there external pressures that might shape the ontology of the record (Heath and Luff, 2007a and b). Anthropologists, philosophers and sociologists have similar concerns about power relations and the culture surrounding record-keeping practices that might so distort the record by disguising as much as it reveals as to make it almost valueless for retrospective investigation (Strathern, 2000; Ess, 2010; Giddens, 1987; Hurley, 1995; Mackenzie, 2009; 2011; O'Neill, 2010; US Securities and Exchange Commission, 2003). These and other disciplinary perspectives take the archival principle of context on to a higher plane and raise questions about the relationship in a corporate setting of archives and records management and how far archivists can be expected to capture such contextual information unless they are willing to redefine what is meant by 'core business records' (Kiran and Verbeek, 2010).

The docquet

In written cultures the document that underpins the keeping of business records is the record of the transaction, usually recorded on a single sheet of paper and, at least in Europe, from the thirteenth century, if not earlier, referred to as the docquet. Like many record keeping practices its use originates in state bureaucracies and was adopted by the legal profession and business communities. There is evidence to suggest that in written cultures the docquet is ubiquitous, because it was and is so obviously the way to record individual transactions. In some sense the bark manuscripts of the Roman Empire can be described as docquets. It represents an exchange, an invoice for a good or service supplied and a receipt for payment, which makes for an unambiguous audit trail. There has been very little research into this humble but foundational document in record keeping systems and almost no cross-cultural comparisons. What seems universally to be the case is that they were endorsed with their date and a brief description of their context so that they could be easily retrieved by busy clerks. Dorit Raines has concluded that in Venice endorsed docquets were widely used from the sixteenth century by notaries and in the courts to provide rapid access to a vast number of documents without having to go to the trouble of reading the contents of every one (Raines, 2012). Edward Laurence, in the third edition of his book *The duty and office of a land steward: represented under several plain and distinct articles*, published in London in 1731, gave advice on how docquets were to be made and stored:

> *N.B.* Every Steward that is curious should take particular Care to have *all* his Bills and Vouchers drawn out upon a sheet or half sheet of paper, according to the bigness of the Bill, and to *fold* them all up *exactly* of equal Bigness, and to *indorse* them on the backside, and also to number them . . . The being exact in this, will make easy the examining all sorts of Accompts.
>
> (Laurence, 1743, p. 197)

Docqueting was not only used for accounting records, but also for correspondence, minutes and other papers. In the British civil administration from the middle of the nineteenth century more important documents were placed in jackets, which carried the endorsement on the outside cover, and stored flat instead of being folded as had been the case before. The jacket was attached to the docquet by means of what became known as a Treasury tag (a piece of string with a metal fastener at either end).

In docquet cultures there were various ways of organising them. The preferred method in Europe and North America was the 'pigeon hole' where current docquets were placed in order for easy access (Yates, 1989, pp. 28–31). This could be by subject or by function or from the eighteenth-century Enlightenment by letter of the alphabet. As Jeffrey Garrett argues, it was in response to an epistemological crisis as much as the vast increase in holdings that led Martin Schrettinger, an Austrian monk and librarian, to put in place 'a search-and-find-machinery, beholden only to its own laws that in turn are dictated by the demands placed upon it by modern science' (1999). Such practices persisted well into the twentieth century. Special furniture was manufactured for the purpose from the seventeenth century. In *Our mutual friend*, by Charles Dickens, Eugene Wrayburn described just such a piece of furniture to his friend Mortimer Lightwood:

> Secretaire, you see, an abstruse set of solid mahogany pigeon-holes, one for every letter of the alphabet. To what use do I devote them? I receive a bill – say from Jones. I docket it neatly at the secretaire, JONES, and I put it into pigeonhole J. It's the next thing to a receipt and is quite as satisfactory to ME.

Writing in 1870 R. W. Lapper, who worked at the headquarters of the London and North Western Railway, Euston Station in London, commented in his book *Registration of correspondence. A new system applicable to large offices, etc.*:

> In some offices, and by private individuals, the method of filing away letters is by means of endorsing on the back of the letter the name of the writer and date of the letter, and placing them in alphabetical pigeon–holes.
>
> (1870b, p. 11)

The practice of docqueting and pigeon-holing by the mid-nineteenth century was synonymous with bureaucracy and red-tape. To say that something was pigeon-holed was to imply that it lay forgotten in the records. Yet authors of books about business practice resolutely defended the practice as making for efficient and effective administration. R. W. Lapper calculated by combining his improved index books with pigeon holes – 'an average of one minute will suffice for discovering any one record in 35,000' (1870a, p. 5). Not all docquets were pigeon-holed, many were simply placed on billhooks, or strung together with wire or cord, awaiting either disposal or registration.

Nowadays instead of duplicates of such receipts being sorted and stored in pigeon-holes, they are stored in databases, the digital equivalent. Embedded codes permit allocation by subject, function and name, as will be seen in the discussion of the migration of record-keeping systems to the digital environment.

Putting away

When docquets ceased to be current, normally after six months or a year, they were and still are 'put away'. In much of Northern Europe this took the form of what were known as 'long bundles' in which docquets either relating to a particular subject or function, or in alphabetical (by correspondent) or numerical order, were tied up in bundles and stored for future reference. R. W. Lapper recommended placing the contents of the pigeon holes in wooden boxes (1870a, p. 2). In some cases docquets ordered either alphabetically or numerically were withdrawn and put together with those relating to similar subjects to form additional long bundles. Such practice when combined with the jacketing of docquets led in the British civil administration progressively from the 1840s to the creation of the 'file' containing all the papers on a given subject. In Southern Europe and in Japan docquets were bound up together in books, which made it very difficult to remove papers from a sequence, but made re-ordering and appraisal impossible. In whatever form docquets were put away, they tended to suffer from benign neglect, particularly when there was ample room to store them, and as a result archivists are often confronted with large accumulations of neatly wrapped or bound series of docquets that cry out for retention.

Registration and abstraction

Management of any organisation depends on the registration and abstraction of information from docquets. This is the basis of all accounting systems (Edwards and Walker, 2009). Until the development of double entry book-keeping in the Renaissance period, the common practice was to list all outgoings (disbursements or discharges) and all income (charges) and strike a balance by subtracting the total of one from that of the other. It was a convenient way for those delegated to take care of accounts to report their stewardship as each entry at audit could be compared with the docquets and verified. This was known in Europe as 'single entry' and was best suited to cash transactions, such as the payment of rents or tradesmen (Reininghaus and Hoock, 1997). It was widely used particularly by government, public bodies, corporate bodies, such as universities and schools, landed estates and the legal profession long after double entry (see below) was introduced. It survived particularly in organisations or for functions where funds could not be carried forward from one year to another and any surplus was disbursed or losses recouped or written off either at the audit or when a legal process was complete. The administration of the estates of the deceased and bankrupts were and are nearly always in the form of single entry. Single entry can at times be hard to follow as discharges usually outweigh charges and entries are often muddled up with minutes and notices of meetings (see below). It can be many pages before a balance is struck by setting all the discharges against the charges. In creating lists of charges and discharges the date, the endorsements on the docquets and the reference number were usually included in the table to provide an evidential trail (Boyns, Boyns and Edwards, 2000, pp. 8–18).

Single entry, however, does not provide very helpful management information. Patrick Kelly in his book on the *Elements of book-keeping, both by single and double entry, comprising a system of merchants' accounts, etc.* published in 1801, commented:

> . . . Book-keeping, by Single Entry, is essentially defective as it affords no method of ascertaining the State of a Merchant's affairs, without taking stock; a task which is both laborious and liable to error, and at which best affords no adequate means of preventing embezzlement or detecting fraud; but these objects are attained by Double Entry, perhaps as effectively as human ingenuity can devise.
>
> (1801, p. 5)

It is not possible in single entry, for example, to find out at a glance the state of the financial relationships of an organisation with a client – what is the turnover on the account, how much does the client owe, is the account in arrears and so on? It is also difficult to carry forward transactions from one year to another after a balance has been struck. For this reason it is common to find double entry mixed up with single entry accounts, for example in bringing together the annual accounts of a large estate or in the final accounts of a bankrupt's estate. As European trade developed in the fifteenth century merchant ventures could extend over several years and involve partners in different countries and later different continents. A more sophisticated system of registration and abstraction was needed.

In the Islamic world and in Europe an improved system of accounting tailored to the needs of management, particularly of enterprise, began to emerge from the twelfth and thirteenth centuries. It was known as double entry because the charge (credits or assets) and discharge (debits or liabilities) are displayed on facing pages unlike in single entry. If a good or service is sold, for example, it should be balanced by a payment for the good or service received. There is a debate about whether Islamic practice, which was heavily influenced by the need to show business practice conformed to Shari'ah law, influenced European practice (Napier, 2007). As Carnegie and Napier have observed: 'what appear to be similar accounting approaches at a high level of generality may turn out to be quite different at a closer level of analysis' (2002, p. 711). Double entry has been regarded as a cornerstone in the development of Western capitalism by authors such as Max Weber, because it allowed merchants and tradesman to exercise greater control over their business, for example by calculating profit and loss on various ventures or branches of an enterprise and the capital employed (Weber, Baehr and Wells, 2002). By the fifteenth century Venetian merchants were generally using double entry, which was codified by Fra Luca Bartolomeo de Pacioli, a Franciscan (1446/7–1517) in his book *Summa de arithmetica, geometria, proportioni et proportionalita*, published in 1494. As a result double entry was often referred to as the Italian or Venetian method of accounting. It was slow to spread to other parts of Europe and it was not until the eighteenth century that it became universal amongst the merchants and manufacturers.

The core record series of the double entry system were originally the waste books and journals (the books of prime entry) and the ledgers. The information on the docquets was originally entered or registered in the waste books in much the same way as in the single entry system. The waste book was a daily register of transactions that was to serve as a memorial before they were posted in double entry form to the journal:

> In this book must be daily written whatever occurs in the way of trade; buying, selling, receiving, delivering, bargaining, shipping &c. without omission of anything either bought, sold or borrowed &c. . . . In this book anyone may write, and on occasion any thing may be blotted out, if not well entered, or any error made.
>
> (Murray, 1821, p. 144)

The use of waste books seems to have declined in the early nineteenth century and transactions entered directly into books of prime entry. The principal book of prime entry was the journal, where, unlike the waste book, entries had to be made in a fair hand, 'without any alteration of ciphers or figures' (Murray, 1821, p. 144), and laid out in such a way as to distinguish credit and debits. For this reason the journal was often referred to as the 'organiser', as it was here that accounts were put in order before 'posting' to the ledger. Where an enterprise had a very large volume of transactions, such as an auctioneer or shopkeeper, day books and cash books were often introduced to supplement the journal as books of prime entry. They usually take the form of sales and purchase day books. Summarised transactions were usually posted directly to the ledger. In other instances the journal itself was broken up, for example into the private journal, sales journal, purchase journal and so on. The private journals were often locked and held separately from other accounts, as they contained the key management accounts and details of partners' transactions. Cashbooks, as the name implies, just contained details of cash transactions that were totalled and posted to the ledger. They, too, could be divided up. Petty cash books were used for office expenditure, such as postage and the purchase of stationery.

THE LEDGER

> Is the chief book of accounts to which all the rest are subservient. Into this all the several articles, which belong to the same person or account, and are dispersed into different parts of the *Waste–book*, and sometimes in other *Auxiliary Books*, are gathered, and reduced each to its particular and distinct head, or proper folio, or place. So that the merchant at one view may see how stands the account of each person he deals with, and each sort of good he deals in, or any part or branch of his trade, the state of which he desires to know.
>
> (Dowling and Jackson, 1801, p. 4)

Manuals, such as those by Dowling, stressed the importance of accuracy and the clarity and neatness of writing in the ledger. It might be expected that the detail entered in the journal would be fuller than that for entries posted to the ledger, but this is not always the case. When an entry was posted to the ledger, it might appear more than once, for example the purchase or sale of timber would be entered under the name of the seller or the purchaser (a personal entry) but also under 'timber' (a nominal entry). Any profit or loss on the sale would be posted internally in the ledger to the profit and loss account. A characteristic of all double entry accounts is elaborate cross-referencing to make it easy to follow transactions and to avoid the danger of double counting. Cross-references usually appear in a separate column and are often in different colours to distinguish a reference back or forwards from the ledger to the journal or to the docquets, and in the ledger to denote internal transactions within the ledger. Internal transactions could also be posted to the journal. Accounts were normally, but not always, balanced annually and the credit and debit balances posted to the profit and loss account or, if accounts were outstanding, they were posted to the balance sheet, which were sometimes referred to as current assets or liabilities. Originally the balance sheet and profit and loss account appeared in the ledger; but gradually, particularly in large and complex organisations and those registered as limited liability companies, the balance sheet and profit and loss accounts were separated and prepared on folio sheets. They are often to be found bundled up with other papers, such as trial balances, used in making up the annual accounts and in the conduct of the audit. After the introduction of limited liability, these internal records were used to prepare the published annual report and accounts.

Just like journals, ledgers could also be subdivided into private, purchase, sales, nominal, impersonal and personal ledgers and so on. When this happened the key management information was held in the private ledger, often held under lock and key away from prying eyes. This was the core financial record, containing the balance sheet and profit and loss account, details of borrowings and advances, the partners' private accounts and so on. The titles of other ledgers replicate the journal series. Where a firm had a very large number of suppliers or customers, the sales and purchase ledgers became very bulky and may even have been broken up alphabetically. The most bulky are those from banks where each customer had a separate entry in the account ledgers. It is not uncommon to find a ledger for every letter of the alphabet. Such accounts with sufficient detail can be very revealing and may provide information that cannot be found elsewhere about linkages and patterns of income and expenditure. The bank accounts of the landscape gardener Lancelot 'Capability' Brown (1716–83) with London-based Drummonds Bank have allowed researchers to identify gardens designed by him that were hitherto unknown (Wild, 2013). Likewise in Australia, Leanne John and Simon Ville have explored business and networks in colonial Sydney between 1817 and 1824 by analysing the ledgers of the Bank of New South Wales (John and Ville, 2012). However, account ledgers present data protection problems that will inevitably involve long periods of closure. Some financial institutions insist that permission of descendants is secured before access is granted.

The best way for archivists to learn how to find their way around all accounting records is to use them to trace transactions, especially in a set of accounts kept in double entry. In using any accounting series it is essential to examine them carefully as practice often changes over time. There are many accountancy handbooks that explain the system, even if today accountants brought up in digital systems no longer necessarily understand these records. It must be emphasised that double entry is not prescriptive. It provides a framework for keeping accounts, but implementation varied from business to business to suit individual needs and circumstances. In some jurisdictions and for some types of organisations, for example, charities in the United Kingdom, there are mandated standards for financial records; but these can often mislead as much as inform.

Bill books

Until the twentieth century, one of the principal means of funding enterprises, especially overseas trade, was by means of bills of exchange, normally defined as: 'an unconditional order in writing addressed by one person to another, signed by the person or company giving it, requiring the person or company to whom it is addressed to pay on demand or at fixed or determinable future time a sum certain in money to, or to the order of, a specified person or company, or to bearer' (see for example Gerrard & National plc, 1981, p. 55).

Bills were usually payable in three to six months, but could be renewed if a trade, for example the import or export of goods or commodities, had not been completed (Nishimura, 1971, p. 30). They were used largely to finance overseas trade in what was termed the 'consignment system' whereby commission merchants bought and sold goods to be delivered in several months time at a price they judged would yield a handsome return – see the section on marketing and sales below (Nishimura, 1971, p. 31). Interest rates were typically set at one per cent above bank rate. Longer dated bills were used for expensive capital products, such as ships and machinery. The political economist Walter Bagehot observed in his essay of 1873 on *Lombard Street* – the financial heart of the City of London: 'English trade is carried on upon borrowed capital to an extent of which few foreigners have an idea . . . ' (Barrington, 1915, p. 15).

Bills payable and receivable books were integral to double entry book-keeping systems as they represented current liabilities and assets, which could have serious repercussions for cash flow. Patrick Kelly in his book *The elements of book-keeping, both by single and double entry, a system of merchants' accounts founded on real business and adapted to modern practice*, published in 1801, explained:

> The Bill-book is an Index or Register of Bills of Exchange whether *Receivable* or *Payable*. Bills Receivable are those which the Merchant receives in payment of some Debt or Contract, and Bills payable are such as are drawn upon him, and which he must pay when due.
>
> (1801, p. 58)

Both bills receivable and payable could be sold at less than their face value, a practice known as discounting, either locally or more commonly on the London discount market (Gerrard & National plc, 1981, p. 8). Bagehot remarked in the same essay: 'In every district small traders have arisen, who "discount their bills" largely, and with the capital so borrowed harass and press upon, if they do not eradicate the old capitalists'. He went on to explain how by resorting to bill finance a merchant could make a much better return than by relying solely on their own capital (Barrington, 1915, p. 15). There were risks. If no one would accept a merchant's bills then this was a portent that failure was only a little time off. In such circumstances a company would stop payment on its bills payable, as it no longer had access to cash to support its operations. This happened, for example, in 1890 when Barings, the London bankers, were unable to meet their liabilities. The consignment system had its critics, who believed it served simply to drive up prices. Although with the development of alternative forms of finance, notably overdrafts, use of bills declined towards the end of the nineteenth century, they continue to play an important role in providing short-term liquidity (Gerrard & National plc, 1981, p. 55). Bill books provide useful evidence of a business's linkages and connections.

Registers of mortgages and mortgagees and of sealing

Concerns and individuals with portfolios of land and property and other fixed assets have for hundreds of years secured loans against their value. Such loans are usually referred to as mortgages and the practice of using collateral to secure loans as hypothecation. In some jurisdictions where the registration of land transactions is a statutory function, such as Scotland, mortgages are a matter of public record. In other jurisdictions, particularly common law countries, they are simply a contract between two parties. The borrower retains control of the assets unless there is a default in repayments, when the lender has the right to resort to legal remedies to take possession. Just like bills of exchange, mortgages can be bought and sold on the discount market. The mortgage documents will most likely be found amongst the papers held by a company's lawyers.

From the time the first companies were formed by charter, they used seals to certify documents, just like members of the landed aristocracy, religious houses and civic corporations. They usually maintained registers of every time the seal was applied so as to prevent fraud (Callahan, 2004). All companies with limited liability are required to keep registers of sealing.

Cost and order books

All manufacturing companies generated cost records, sometimes, particularly in the case of large products such as ships and locomotives, these were abstracted from the general ledger and purchase day books into a separate ledger series. More commonly cost books were held in a separate series of records that detailed all the inputs including materials, wages and overheads. Such cost books were usually cross-referenced to order books, specifications and drawings and wage records. They formed a vital record, as they were used to calculate prices when tendering for the supply of spare parts and, as importantly, new orders in the future. The process of tendering was sometimes recorded in tender books and confirmed orders in order books. The costs and prices of all completed orders should appear in summary form in the ledger against the customer's name, with the costs appearing on the debit or expenditure side and the payments from the customer on the credit side. The difference between the two will represent the actual profit or loss that will be posted to the profit and loss account. The price of the contract may not be included in the ledger; but it may be possible to compute it from the total payments. In some instances, particularly for bulk products and common services for example fertilisers and shipping freight rates, prices were governed by trade agreements that were often international in their scope. In the shipping industry these were known as conferences (Deakin and Seward, 1973). The archivist should always be on the lookout for papers relating to such implicit cartelisation or restrictive practices. They are now illegal, but were a commonplace in the nineteenth and well into the twentieth century.

The introduction of scientific management techniques in the late nineteenth century 'focussed . . . attention on predetermining "standard" rates at which material and labor should be consumed in manufacturing tasks' (Taylor, 1911; Johnson and Kaplan, 1987, pp. 49–50). The introduction of scientific management techniques led to the standardisation of products and components and to the standardisation of costing and greater attention to cost control of both direct inputs and overheads. Organisation and Methods

(O&M) departments were set up by larger concerns and a new discipline of cost accounting emerged (Garcke and Fells, 1887; Norton, 1889). Cost accounting stressed the importance of maintaining up-to-date inventories of plant and stock and integrating production or factory accounts with the general ledger. The use of such techniques encouraged the introduction of technology into costing departments from the late 1880s, especially the Hollerith tabulating machine (Edwards and Walker, 2009, p. 124). Such developments began in the United States, the home of scientific management; but soon spread to Japan, India, Europe and its colonies. Standardised costing coupled with the use of regulations, circulars and forms are seen by some as an effort to normalise corporate behaviour (Fleischman, 2000, p. 599). Cost and order books can be very voluminous and, with a few exceptions, very little used by researchers.

Salary, time and wages books

In most companies until the late twentieth century, the number of salaried staff was small and details of remuneration, especially of senior staff, was often recorded in the minutes. Until restrictive practices were outlawed in many sectors and industries wage rates were set by trade associations in negotiation with trade unions. Consequently, it is unusual to find papers relating to such negotiations in companies, although there will be papers dealing with local demarcation disputes that do not involve national policy. In large organisations wage records were voluminous and do not often survive. Where they do, particularly before the twentieth century, they can be revealing, containing, for example, details of enforced saving through subscriptions to burial societies or the purchase of hand tools. Since many people engaged in manufacturing industries were employed on piece rates, time books were used to calculate wages and to allocate costs to contracts. Like wages books, they rarely survive. With the emergence of cost accounting such records were used to calculate productivity. The only employment records that do survive consistently are registers of apprentices that were kept for reference purposes. In the late nineteenth century many larger companies established pension schemes, usually in collaboration with a life assurance company. Such schemes are usually, but not always, administered by separate trustees and can survive long after the sponsoring company has ceased to exist.

Premises, plant, moveables and stock

The ownership of premises and plant depended until the twentieth century on the treatment of depreciation and land by the fiscal authorities that varies from country to country. In the United Kingdom, for example, until 1894 landed property was exempt from death duties and consequently mercantile and industrial property tended to be owned personally by individuals and leased to the enterprise. There were also issues about the way in which depreciation on plant and stock was treated by the Inland Revenue for tax purposes on individuals and corporations (Sabine, 1966, p. 115). In these circumstances premises and plant will not appear in the balance sheet. However, when they do, inventory books of plant and machinery sometimes survive. In some cases assets, notably ships and then later property, were transferred to separate independent companies to protect them from losses on trading activities and to free up working capital. In a few cases inventories of plant, machinery and loose tools are included in the internal annual accounts; but normally they are held in separate volumes with a variety of titles such as asset registers or registers of plant and machinery. Occasionally inventories of premises and plant are accompanied by independent valuations undertaken by surveyors for balance sheet purposes. Quite often little survives and the only records are general photographs of buildings and offices and plans of the premises and essential services, which are required for care and maintenance purposes or in case of emergency. Environmental legislation and international regulation today require companies to keep accurate records of land use, for which they can be held accountable in court. Inventories of stock are infrequently found, with the exception of those made up for valuation purposes, for example at the time of the death of a partner or in the case of bankruptcy. In most cases the only information about stock in hand is to be found in the ledger with a summary figure in the balance sheet. The exception is 'bills of lading' detailing the shipment of goods that were required for custom and excise purposes.

Access and appraisal of financial and related records in the analogue

In its most complete form, the ledger will contain all the information most users might want to know about an enterprise, the balance sheet, profit and loss account, partners' accounts, accounts with suppliers and customers, details of all the business activities and ventures the enterprise was engaged in. One of the most ambitious projects to make available on line details from such ledgers is The Borromei Bank Research Project at Queen Mary College, London, which is publishing details from two ledgers of Filippo Borromei & Co., one from its Bruges house for the year 1438, and one for its London house for the years 1436–39.[1] The partners' accounts in such ledgers often contain details of other ventures they were engaged in (see for example Morgan and Moss, 1989). Since the balances in the partners' accounts before the introduction of limited liability in the mid-nineteenth century represented the capital of the enterprise, the partners used their accounts rather like private bank accounts to buy and sell goods and services and make investments on their own accounts. When limited liability was introduced such transactions disappeared from the financial records, because the directors' (usually the former partners) personal trading activities could not be protected in this way or at least not under the umbrella of the new company. Since ledgers and other books of account are sequential and form a series, there is no point in only retaining single volumes as representative. Whole runs should either be taken or destroyed. The most important ledgers to select for preservation are those with the partners' private accounts and the balance sheets and profit and loss accounts. That being said financial records require time and effort to learn to use effectively, something many historians are unwilling to do. As a result long runs of ledgers and journals lie unused in repositories. If lack of use persists, then they may need to be de-accessioned. It is a matter of judgement as to whether related records should be accessioned, particularly in collecting repositories, and will depend on the character and significance of the company concerned. Few archivists would accession late nineteenth- and twentieth-century receipts and invoices; but many have taken such records for earlier periods for no very good reason except their age.

Mechanisation of financial records and the transition to the digital

Mechanisation of financial records has a long history, dating back to the mid-twentieth century (Andersson, 2010). At first the introduction of machines changed the physical format of the records, particularly the introduction of loose-leaf journals, day books and ledgers. These are often a nightmare for the archivist, as most entries are in numerical code and pages when filled were arbitrarily removed and bundled up into the twentieth century equivalent of long bundles, in which the pages often have become confused. With the introduction of digital technology financial records were an early and obvious candidate for conversion. In the process of migrating such records to the digital environment the long tradition of book-keeping was abandoned for the simple reason there was no longer any reason for it to exist. Instead of the labour of entering details in the journal and other books of prime entry and posting them to the ledger, individual receipts and invoices could be coded up when they were being entered in the database to ensure they found their correct place unambiguously in any aggregation. As a result in most financial software programmes individual transactions subsist and are aggregated and disaggregated as the need arises. Apart from the data protection and privacy issues that surround such records, few, if any, archivists could contemplate accessioning such resources and the only response can be to take the outputs, such as the balance sheet and the profit and loss accounts and even these may be seriously circumscribed. Such strategies combined with other factors, such as the encroaching culture of audit, will inevitably reduce the usefulness of such records to the researcher (Moss, 2010).

Marketing and sales

Aligned with financial records are those relating to marketing and sales of goods and services. Until the twentieth century sales of many manufactured goods as well as commodities were made through commission merchants, so-called because they charged a flat rate percentage on costs, normally somewhere between 2.5 and 5 per cent. As James Kempson, a Philadelphia cotton manufacturer, explained in the *Mechanics' Magazine* of New York in 1834: 'The manufacturer sends his goods to a commission merchant at the shipping ports, who receives five per cent, for selling and guaranteeing' (p. 35). Even expensive goods, such as ships, railway locomotives, civil engineering structures and whole factories were sold on commission. In these cases progress payments were made as work proceeded and from the 1880s photographs were used extensively to provide evidence of how much of the contract had been completed. Commission merchants often operated from very small premises, but could execute huge quantities of business without ever taking delivery of any goods. Their normal practice was to accept goods on consignment and to sell what they could at a profit, sometimes direct to customers and sometimes through brokers. In overseas markets this could prove difficult and often led to complaints and legal proceedings. However, before the development of the international telegraph in the mid-nineteenth century and even afterwards in many parts of the world, it was the only practical way of doing business. Futures trading only became practical with the telegraph and was pioneered by the London commission agents, Lewis & Peat, which led rapidly to the development of the international commodity market (Lewis & Peat, 1975). Commission merchants made most of their sales through personal contacts and had little interest in promoting the goods and services of one supplier over another, although they would instruct manufacturers about the type and quality of goods that were likely to sell. The only advertisements were to be found on letter-heads, receipts and invoices and bags and wrapping paper, mostly using wood blocks. Widely used from the late eighteenth century, they can be very attractive.

It was not until the second half of the nineteenth century with the advent of mass-production of goods, especially food and drink, that branding, registered trade marks and supporting advertising began (Tedlow and Jones, 1993, pp. 11–13; Jones and Morgan, 1994, pp. 25–29). The financial services sector, which was both consolidating and expanding nationally and internationally, adopted similar strategies. The growth in marketing and branding stimulated the expansion of the trade press, which often carried extensive descriptions of individual firms and their products that included photographs of plant and premises. Sometimes these were published separately as books or booklets for promotion and publicity. Although trademarks have a long history extending back to prehistoric times, legislation establishing registers of trademarks was only introduced in the second half of the nineteenth century. In 1857 France established the first trademark register in the world and other countries slowly followed suit, the United States in 1870, Germany in 1874, the United Kingdom in 1875 and Japan in 1884.[2] Trademarks only enjoy legal protection, if they are actively on the register. Advertising and promotion was and is a function of available technologies and itself depended on techniques of mass production, such as developments during the nineteenth century of printing, which allowed newspapers and periodicals to include illustrations, and of colour printing and the manufacture of ceramics, cans and glass-bottles that made it possible to package products in distinctive containers with attractive labels. Branded containers have become very collectable. Photography, either in-house or contracted out, was used extensively from the 1880s to support promotion and sales. In the twentieth century many companies began to use film and after the Second World War television to advertise their products.

Companies with a strong brand identity either sold products direct or appointed tied agents who bore the costs of marketing the product in their area. This practice still persists in some industries. Although advertisements and marketing literature was produced in considerable quantities, few companies take the trouble systematically to preserve copies. This is largely because most advertising copy was prepared by specialist advertising agents, such as J. Walter Thompson. Where companies have preserved copies, they are usually pasted into guard books. Nevertheless impressive collections of advertisement and promotional literature survive, particularly in the retail sector.

Brand protection is vital to many companies, especially those with a global reach, such as Coca-Cola, McDonald's and Johnnie Walker Whisky. It is not simply enough to ensure that trademark registration is up-to-date in various jurisdictions, advertising standards agencies and other regulatory bodies need evidence that claims made in advertisements and promotional literature can be justified, for example the date of the foundation of an enterprise or introduction of a product or entry to a particular market. In collaboration with corporate lawyers, the archivist and the archive become in a very real sense the guardians of corporate history and identity, which often finds expression in in-house museums or displays. Brand protection is not a role that a collecting archive can safely perform without very strong legal safeguards. If related records find their way into a collecting archive it is often by accident following a corporate collapse.

Correspondence and the emergence of the file

In the words of Lord Panmure, the United Kingdom's Secretary of State for War, in 1855: 'The great desiderata for the easy and efficient discharge of the duty of a public office is a simple and efficient system of registration of the papers of the department'.[3] Not only did registration make for business efficiency, it also provided an unambiguous audit trail if a document had to be produced as evidence in a court of law. Writing in 1804 Edward Turner, Secretary of the United States Treasury, advocated: 'I think that the filing of documents with the register, for the purpose of recording, constitutes the legal date of the record . . . ' (Anon., 1838, p. 661). In a judgement in the Scottish Court of Session in 1831 the court found that 'a document merely found within the walls of Register House [now the National Registers of Scotland]' that had not been formally registered could not be given 'the character of a record' without the authority of the court (Shaw et al., 1831, p. 864). Many individuals and businesses routinely registered documents, such as partnership agreements, contracts and so on, with courts to ensure that they could later be produced as evidence. The process of registering correspondence within a system had the same effect. Charles Edwards Lester in his *Life and voyages of Americus Vespucius*, published in 1853, refers to the practice of registering all the records relating to the Americas irrespective of their nature in the library of King Alphonso V (1432–81) (1853, p. 398). The system of registering papers in European governments had its origins at this time and was often located in libraries. It was replicated in many other organisations, for example in landed estates, universities, monastic houses and in the emerging banking and commercial houses. It is not surprising that such practices should emerge in government bureaucracies as they were the largest 'business' organisations at the time or that landowners, bankers and businessmen, such as the Corsinis and the Fuggers, should have learned sophisticated techniques of record keeping from them (Beale et al., 2011).

Both in- and out-letters were treated in much the same way as invoices with endorsements, folding, sorting in pigeon holes and putting away. In large organisations, such as bureaucracies, all the docquets were registered in index books or ledgers. By the late eighteenth century the registries in the great European departments of state had become sophisticated. Each docquet was given a unique identifier and stored sequentially. To facilitate easy retrieval sometimes years after they had been put away, the endorsements were used by the clerks to register the docquets by subject in separate volumes. The subject headings in some ways corresponded to a modern file plan. Access was strictly controlled. If docquets were recalled for reference, they had to be signed in and out, and returned in the order they were delivered. Non-current docquets were regularly weeded to remove what were considered to be trivial papers. Such practices were only adopted by the largest commercial concerns, such as the railway companies or great merchant houses. As R. W. Lapper of the London and North Western Railway Company explained:

> The only way in which miscellaneous office papers can be kept in order and immediately referred to, is by means of an Index Book in which the papers are indexed away under their subject to a consecutive number.
>
> (Lapper, 1870a, p. 2)

In 1780 James Watt invented the wet copy process that did away with the labour of copying all outgoing correspondence or noting a reply had been sent on the endorsement to the docquet. Wet copying involved pressing a damp thin tissue paper on the outgoing letter, the moisture dissolved the dye in the ink and a mirror image of the original was imprinted on the tissue paper by means of a press. This could then be viewed on the reverse side of the tissue, known as a 'flimsy' the right way round (Andersson, 2010, pp. 59–61; Dube, 1998). When wet copying was introduced, flimsies were bundled up with the docquets. Wet copying quickly became popular in both Europe and North America. In some cases incoming correspondence and the flimsy were pasted into guard books, a practice adopted by North American railroad companies (Yates, 1989, p. 32). Copying letters was a thankless and dirty task performed by lowly clerks, such as Bob Cratchit immortalised by the novelist Charles Dickens in his novel *A Christmas Carol*, published in 1843, who is described 'copying letters' in a 'dismal little cell'. Nevertheless according to JoAnne Yates businesses on both sides of the Atlantic were slow to adopt wet copying, largely because there was no pressing need to do so because the volume of business was small (1989, p. 27).

With the introduction of wet copy letter books in the 1850s coupled with the growth of business and accompanying expansion in correspondence, wet copying became ubiquitous. In copy letter books, each letter was cross-referenced internally, with references both forward and backwards, and indexed for easy retrieval. Incoming correspondence on the other hand continued to be tied up in bundles when it was put away. As a result outgoing correspondence bound in letter books is more likely to survive than incoming letters, probably because no one has the heart to throw them away. Letter book series, just like those of journals and ledgers, are often divided up by function. The most important for management purposes were the 'private' letter books, which would contain the confidential correspondence of partners and directors. In many cases letter books continued to be used after the introduction of filing (see below) as a means of providing a register of all outgoing correspondence. In many organisations they continued in use until the time that computers began to be introduced for word processing.

As has been explained above the correspondence file emerged from the system of registering docquets in the British civil administration in about 1840. By the end of the century filing had become standard practice in British civil administration and by extension in all its imperial and colonial possessions. Filing continued to be administered by registries, which retained many existing practices, such as the registration of incoming correspondence and papers and the signing in and out files. Files were organised in a file plan, which in the case of the Foreign and Colonial Offices was based on the Dewey Decimal System and mandated for colonial governments in year books (Lihoma and Tough, 2012). The huge increase in government business during the First World War strained the registries and in 1919 the Treasury Organisation and Methods Division was established specifically to oversee registry provision in the home civil service (Craig, 2002). The file quickly became an essential management tool across commerce and industry, particularly after the First World War. During the war many businessmen had come into contact with the way of doing business in government. Business administration manuals began to be published, which recommended the use of files and filing cabinets, such as those published by Sir Isaac Pitman in the United Kingdom from the 1890s and translated into many languages (Pitman, 1897), or that by John William Schulze, *The American office its organization, management and records* published in 1914. The use of files was made easier by the widespread introduction of the typewriter and accompanying carbon copies at about the turn of the century in most offices.

Circulars, memoranda and forms

In her book *Control through communication: the rise of system in American management*, published in 1989, JoAnne Yates identifies the evolution of management circulars, memoranda and forms as tools for 'imposing system on people and processes' in large organisations in North America (p. 65). These are in a sense another form of docquet. As Luciana Duranti has shown Italian notaries from the fifteenth century used forms when registering instruments in their protocol books to ensure legal admissibility rather then for management purposes (1998). Following notarial practice they were widely adopted commercially to provide irrefutable evidence for such purposes as bills of exchange, apprenticeship agreements and applications for life assurance. The use of circulars and forms as a management tool is associated with Benthamite utilitarianism of the late eighteenth and early nineteenth century with its preoccupation with order and control through the collection of statistics, particularly in civil and military administration but also by business. As Yates points out circulars and forms were widely adopted from the mid-nineteenth century by railway companies to ensure 'safety and efficiency' (p. 68) and later more generally by much North American business to support the 'scientific management' pioneered by Fredrick Taylor (1911). From a scientific management perspective circulars and forms were a means not simply of collecting data but also of enforcing corporate rules and regulations. Although some European companies adopted forms for such purposes, they seem to be much less common than in the United States. European companies seem to have preferred to manage subsidiaries or plants remote from their headquarters at arms length, rather than imposing tight rule-based controls. It is, however, easy for the archivist to overlook tokens of scientific management, such as rulebooks and circulars, as they can often appear insignificant. Frustratingly for the historian the introduction of new management techniques often went unrecorded in minutes or memoranda and the only evidence tends to be such tokens.

Access and appraisal of correspondence and papers in the analogue

It is unusual in business to encounter the centralised registry systems, familiar in large bureaucracies, unless there was a business need as for example in Fuggers bank (Kluger, 2014). Most often filing was carried out at a departmental or office or branch level. The critical files are usually those held at the head office by the secretariat. They are difficult to appraise, as, unlike British government files, they are frequently not held together by Treasury tags and easily become disorganised when removed from current storage. In most companies the core files are held in the headquarters or divisional head offices and it is only practical to select these for permanent retention. In most companies with a long history few bundles of docquets survive, with the notable exception of landed estates where they can extend back for centuries. However, letter books survive in abundance, often over long periods of time. They can be bulky and contain only fragments, often important fragments, of useful information. The archivist has to decide if they justify the shelf space.

Where series have been divided up, the private letter books should receive priority in any acquisition strategy. Interestingly new networking software makes it possible to visualise the links within such structured collections of correspondence (History Lab, 2015).

Migration to the digital

There is a large and burgeoning literature on management information systems, which is often dominated by technology and ignores past practice and rarely is concerned with questions of preservation and long-term access. In engaging with this literature archivists and other information professionals need to be much more precise about the concepts and terminology they employ, as the ethnographers Susan Leigh Star and Karen Ruhleder warn:

> Most of us, in speaking loosely of infrastructure, mean those tools which are fairly transparent for most people we know about, wide in both temporal and spatial scope, embedded in familiar structures . . . That loose talk is perfectly adequate for most everyday usage but is dangerous when applied to the design of powerful tools on a wide scale . . .
>
> (Yates and Van Maanen, 2001, p. 309)

As they perceptively point out paradoxically technology is 'both an engine and barrier for change, both customizable and rigid, both inside and outside organisational practice. It is product and process' (p. 306). The sociologist Anthony Giddens termed this paradox structuration, on which the Australian archivist Frank Upward built his continuum model for managing records and archives in the early 1990s (McKemmish *et al.*, 2005). Such new approaches to archival thinking mirrors management thought more widely, particularly in organisational and the more critical literature about management information systems that draw heavily on theoretical paradigms, such as the work of the German philosophers Martin Heidegger and Eric Kittler or the French philosopher Michel Foucault. Much of this theoretical work is concerned with the complex issue of the social construction of knowledge. These developments need not be of concern here, except to be aware that it is the context in which archivists need to work in approaching digital content (Levy, 2001).

When networked personal computers (PCs) were introduced into the workplace from the 1980s, the long established practices of registration and filing collapsed as managers began to process their own correspondence rather than relying on their secretaries. The processes that had been developed over hundreds of years in the analogue were abandoned. In the British civil administration the consequences are very evident in the evidence submitted to the Hutton Inquiry, the investigation into the circumstances surrounding the death of weapons inspector Dr David Kelly (Moss, 2005). Documents, even key documents, were stored locally and not filed in any meaningful sense (Moss, 2012). As early as 1977 Barbara Pym in her novel *Quartet in Autumn* predicted the likely consequences when describing the retirement of the two central female characters from a commercial registry:

> The (acting) deputy assistant director, who had been commanded to make the presentation speech wasn't quite sure what it was that Miss Crowe and Miss Ivory

did or had done during their working lives. The activity of their department seemed to be shrouded in mystery – something to do with records or filing, it was thought, nobody knew for certain, but it was evidently 'women's work', the kind of thing that could easily be replaced by a computer.

(Pym, 2004, p. 86)

The response from the computing science community was the introduction of Electronic Document and Record Management Systems, which, like accounting systems, hold documents as single instantiations that can be aggregated into files and disaggregated at will. Such systems depend heavily on the creators of documents adding the necessary metadata or coding to ensure that they can be retrieved within the appropriate contexts. This they will only do if it can be shown to add value to their work (Currall *et al.*, 2001). As Sir Alex Allan showed in 2014 and 2015 in two reports for the United Kingdom government such systems have largely failed to deliver (Allan, 2014; 2015).

Existing systems which require individual users to identify documents that should constitute official records, and then to save them into an EDRMS or corporate file plan, have not worked well. The processes have been burdensome and compliance poor. As a result, almost all departments have a mass of digital data stored on shared drives that is poorly organised and indexed.

(Allan, 2015)

Capturing content where it exists from such systems or from elsewhere presents the archivist with huge challenges, which are discussed by Ross Harvey in *Preserving digital materials*, where he argues that traditional appraisal techniques are no longer practical (2005, p. 61). It is very difficult to review digital records for sensitive content and most would have to remain closed for long periods, in the United Kingdom up to 120 years, because of data protection concerns, not only within the jurisdiction in which they were created but internationally. This is arguably the biggest obstacle to preserving digital content, which is all indexed by ubiquitous search engines and therefore easily discoverable. In any event it is unlikely that audit and risk management committees would sanction the release of such content, because of concerns about any contingent liabilities that might reside within it. To manage such contingent risks in their record keeping systems many organisations aggressively destroy records when they reach their statutory or regulatory limitation period, if not earlier (Power, 2004; 2007). Despite all the scare stories about changing file formats, preserving digital objects is relatively straightforward and increasingly less expensive (Gollins, 2009). Where unstructured records are retained, the bulk can be reduced by the removal of duplicates and redundancy, as experiments with the Enron collection of emails has shown (Klimt and Yang, 2004). There are also ways of making sense of large accumulations of digitally born records, being pioneered mostly in the United States for example by the History Lab at Columbia University (History Lab, 2015) and the Visualizing History Project at Harvard University (Harvard University, 2015). Such tools are in their infancy, but they have the potential to radically change historiography (Bernstein, 2015; Gauldi, 2014). They must, however, be treated with caution (Pechenick *et al.*, 2015).

Limited liability, corporate governance and the minute book

The keeping of minutes of meetings has a long history, particularly in public administration or in organisations that acted in a fiduciary capacity, such as town councils, charities and other trustee bodies, schools and universities and so on. In the corporate sector they are usually to be found in organisations that operated for the mutual advantage of the shareholders, such as ports, canals, railways, exchanges of various sorts, guilds, trade associations, commercial and savings banks, life assurance companies, friendly societies, and so on. In these corporate businesses minutes could be very detailed and extensive. In United Kingdom life assurance companies, for example, not only was every life assured minuted so were all investment decisions. Although the chartered companies, such as the Russian Company established in the United Kingdom in 1557 and the Company of Royal Adventurers Trading to Africa established in 1660, both with boards of management, kept minutes, few other straightforward commercial partnerships, even those with very large business operations, did and relied entirely on financial ledgers for management information and evidence of decision making. When the partners in the London merchant bank of Barings chose to have their portrait painted by Thomas Lawrence in 1806/7, they were depicted, not with a minute book, but with an open ledger surrounded by docquets (Holmes, 2011, pp. 41–42).

At the beginning of the nineteenth century in the United States, France and the United Kingdom there were moves to limit liability of the partners and shareholders in companies, because of the dire consequences of bankruptcy. Legislation was passed in the United Kingdom in 1856, followed shortly by France and by the end of the decade most states in America had enacted similar legislation. Germany lagged behind and only introduced legislation, authorising *Gesellschaft mit beschrnkter Haftung* (GmbH) in 1892 (Ellerbrock, 2005; Fohlin, 2005). Limited liability required companies to draw up articles of association, to register and for shareholders (often the former partners) to subscribe capital and to remove their private trading activities from the business. In many jurisdictions, for example in Scotland, there had been ways in which partnerships could register their contacts of co-partnery (Payne, 1960) or, for example, in parts of Europe covered by the Code Napoleon were legally obliged to be registered with the *tribunaux de commerce* (Jobert and Moss, 1990, pp. 3–10).

Limited liability companies were and are required to keep minutes, a list of shareholders and publish annual accounts. Minute books vary greatly in quality and detail. Most, however, are perfunctory and only record information needed for statutory or legal purposes, such as details of documents sealed under the company's seal. Larger companies, particularly those that floated their shares on the stock market or attracted outside capital, usually keep more detailed minutes of their board meetings and decisions taken. By the end of the nineteenth century it became standard practice in such boards for papers in support of agenda items to be prepared. Such papers are usually referred to in minutes, but rarely either engrossed in them or even kept with them. When they survive, they are very revealing and are key core records, allowing the researcher to chart the development of the enterprise. They usually contain minutes and memoranda on corporate planning, investment opportunities and takeover targets, detailed financial and production reports, information about the fixing of prices and wage rates through trade associations and so on. When restrictive practices were outlawed in the 1970s in much of Europe and North America and the competition authorities had the right to inspect company minutes, they became less informative. Sensitive documents, such as the corporate plan and agreements with suppliers and key customers are usually stored separately from other papers under lock and key.

Annual returns, reports, balance sheets and shareholders meetings

All limited liability companies are required to make annual returns to registrars of companies in the jurisdiction in which they are registered. This normally consists of lists of directors and their interests, lists of shareholders and in some, but not all cases, an audited balance sheet and a statement of the use of the funds in the form of a profit and loss account. All public companies are required to publish their accounts together with an annual report to shareholders, and to hold an annual meeting in public. Minutes of annual meetings are sometimes recorded in separate books. Such documents can often disguise as much as they reveal, even if they have been audited. There will inevitably be differences between the internal balance sheet and profit and loss account and the published versions. Archivists should never assume that because they have secured the published balance sheet, even for relatively small concerns, it is safe to discard internal accounts and related papers. It is possible that in the future, because of the risks embedded in internal documents and the migration of record keeping systems to the digital environment, that the only record left for researchers will be such published accounts and related papers mandated by international regulation and local jurisdiction (Moss, 2010, p. 462). This will have serious implications for research in the future that will need to rely largely on press comment. Even before these changes began to make an impact, Michael Nash of the Hagley Museum in the United States observed a 'declining reliance on archival resources' that had characterised the case studies of the Harvard Business School (Nash, 1997, p. 35). He attributed this to the wealth of secondary literature that was by then available.

Registers of shareholders and bonds

All charter companies, which issued stock, such as the United Kingdom East India Company, or partnerships with extended membership, such as the ill-fated City of Glasgow Bank, maintained registers of members so that dividends could be paid or demands made to cover losses. It is axiomatic that limited liability companies should maintain registers of shareholders and bonds, which are returned annually to the registrar of companies in the jurisdiction in which the company is registered. Such registers can be bulky and as a result do not often survive. However, they are a useful source for the historian, showing those who were behind a company's flotation that may not be obvious from the articles of association. (Green, 1991, p. 5). This can provide useful clues to the linkages between entrepreneurs and companies. Edwin Green has used them to identify customers of banks and other joint-stock companies (Acheson et al., 2012; Ellerbrock, 2006/7; Holmes and Green, 1986, pp. 37–38).

Corporate histories

Many companies have commissioned corporate histories, designed either for promotional purposes or more commonly largely for internal consumption and, if published at all, with only a limited circulation. In Japan this practice is widespread and known as *shashi*, 'a publication in which a company provides an account of its own history based on its own archives and assumes responsibility for it' (Murahashi, 2002, pp. 2–3). At least 13,000 were produced during the Meiji period from 1868–1912 (Matsuzaki, 2007, p. 6). *Shashi* were also produced by Chinese firms, but only some 2,000 survive including journal articles.[4] Like many company histories in other parts of the world, *shashi* are compiled on an *ad hoc* basis and distributed in a variety of formats from formal publications to internet resources. The Business Archives Association of Japan puts on regular seminars and training events to encourage the compilation of *shashi* (Matsuzaki, 2007, p. 7).

It is important for the archivist to remember that most enterprises are both small and short-lived. Although big enterprises with long histories represent a larger share of the economy, they are not necessarily representative of a sector either locally, nationally or internationally. Collecting business records has to be a matter of judgement, particularly when space is at a premium and usage low. It is equally difficult to provide hard and fast guidance about which records can be considered as 'core', as practice varies widely from firm to firm. Logic may suggest that ledgers are more useful than journals and other books of prime entry; but this will not universally be the case. Such appraisal decisions are made more complex by requests to take collections at times of crisis, such as takeover, sale or failure, when there is almost no time to make a considered judgement. Surveying is, probably, the most effective way of identifying core records that might be considered for acquisition by a collecting archive, but even then not all the core records may be disclosed particularly in a large concern operating over multiple sites. It may be that in future bulky collections should be accessioned on a temporary basis to be subsequently destroyed if no users emerge. Inevitably an in-house archive will accession more records than a collecting archive, as it has different priorities and responsibilities, such as brand protection and safeguarding corporate memory. Few collecting archives would wish to take the whole contents of an in-house archive unless there were powerful financial incentives (Ellen *et al.*, 2004).

Acknowledgements

The author would like to thank the following for their assistance in writing this chapter Professor Takeshi Abe of the Kokushikon University, Matts Andersson, archivist of Swedbank, Edwin Green, Professor Pui-tak Lee of Hong Kong University, Jennifer Meehan, Yale University, Sachiko Morimoto, the University of Tokyo Archives, Professor Christopher Napier for permission to quote his paper on Islamic accounting, José Manuel Neira Agra, of Confederación Española de Cajas de Ahorros, Dorit Raines, Universita Ca' Foscari, Venice, Professor Peter Stallybrass, University of Pennsylvania, for permission to quote his work on docquets, Dr David Thoms, Dr Thorsten Wehber, Deutscher Sparkassen und Giroverband, Germany, and Yuko Matsuzaki of the Information Resources Center, Shibusawa Eii'ichi Memorial Foundation.

Notes

1   See www.queenmaryhistoricalresearch.org/roundhouse/default.aspx [Accessed 3 September 2016].
2   See *The history of trademark law*. [pdf] Available at: www.iip.or.jp/translation/ono/ch2.pdf [Accessed 3 September 2016].
3   The National Archives, London, WO 32/9310.
4   Private communication from Professor Pui Tak Lee, University of Hong Kong.

References

Acheson, G. G., Turner, J. D. and Ye, Q., 2012. The character and denomination of shares in the Victorian equity market. *Economic History Review*, 65, pp. 862–886.

Allan, A., 2014, *Records review*. Cabinet Office and The National Archives. [online] Available at: www.gov.uk/government/publications/records-review-by-sir-alex-allan [Accessed 3 September 2016].

Allan, A., 2015. *Government digital records and archives review*. Cabinet Office and The National Archives. [online] Available at: www.gov.uk/government/publications/government-digital-records-and-archives-review-by-sir-alex-allan [Accessed 3 September 2016].

Andersson, M., 2010. *Tekniken i bankarbetet*. Stockholm: SparbanksAkademin.

Anon., 1838. *General Public Acts of Congress*. Washington, WA: Gales and Seaton.

Barrington, R., ed., 1915. *The works and life of Walter Bagehot. Vol.6*. London: Longmans, Green and Co.

Beale, P., Almond, A. and Archer, M. S., eds, 2011. *The Corsini letters*. Stroud: Amberley.

Bernstein, J., 2015. Can an algorithm do the job of a historian?, *BuzzFeedNews*. [online] Available at: www.buzzfeed.com/josephbernstein/can-a-computer-algorithm-do-the-job-of-a-historian [Accessed 3 September 2016].

Borland, J., 2009. *Trust and the records professional*. Masters dissertation, University of British Columbia. [pdf] Available at: www.armaedfoundation.org/pdfs/JBorland_ScholarshipEssay.pdf [Accessed 3 September 2016].

Boyns, R. E., Boyns, T. and Edwards, J. R., 2000. *Historical accounting records: a guide for archivists and researchers*. London: Society of Archivists.

Callahan, D., 2004. *The cheating culture: why more Americans are doing wrong to get ahead*. New York: Harcourt.

Carnegie, G. D. and Napier, C. J., 2002. Exploring comparative international accounting history. *Accounting, Auditing and Accountability Journal*, 15(5), pp. 689–718.

Clanchy, M. T., 2009. *From memory to the written record 1066–1307*. 2nd ed. Chichester: Wiley Blackwell.

Classen, A., ed., 2015. *Handbook of medieval culture*, vol. 2. Basel: De Gruyter.

Craig, B., 2002. Rethinking formal knowledge and its practices in the organization. The British Treasury's registry between 1900 and 1950. *Archives Science*, 4(1), pp. 111–136.

Currall, J., Johnson, C. E., Johnston, P., Moss, M. S. and Richmond, L. M., 2001. '*No going back?*' *The final report of the Effective Records Management Project*. Glasgow: University of Glasgow. [pdf] Available at: www.gla.ac.uk/InfoStrat/ERM/Docs/ERM–Final.pdf [Accessed 3 September 2016].

Deakin, B. M. and Seward, T., 1973. *Shipping conferences: a study of their origins, development and economic practices*. Cambridge: Cambridge University Press.

Dowling, D. and Jackson, W., 1801. *Book-keeping in the true Italian form*. Dublin: John Gough.

Dube, L., 1998. The copying pencil: composition, history, and conservation implications. *The Book and Paper Group Annual*, 17. [online] Available at: http://cool.conservation-us.org/coolaic/sg/bpg/annual/v17/bp17-05.html [Accessed 3 September 2016].

Duranti, L., 1998. *Diplomatics: new uses for an old science*. Chicago, IL: Scarecrow Press.

Edwards, J. R. and Walker, S. P., 2009. *The Routledge companion to accounting history*. London: Routledge.

Ellen, J., Hart, T., Piggott, M. and Merrett, D., 2004. Making archival choices for business history. *Australian Economic History Review*, 44(2), pp. 185–196.

Ellerbrock, K. P., 2005. Wirtschaftsarchive in Deutschland: zu den anfängen und zur gegenwärtigen rolle der regionalen wirtschaftsarchive vor den herausforderungen von strukturwandel und globalisierung, *Archiv und Wirtschaft*, 1, pp. 16–25.

Ellerbrock, K. P., 2006/7. Archivmarketing: zielgruppen und netzwerke zwischen wissenschaftlicher kommunikation und eventkultur. In: H. Schmitt. *Archive und Öffentlichkeit, Tagungsdokumentation, Deutschen Archivtag*. Essen: Fulda, 76, pp. 175–182.

Ess, C., 2010. Trust and new communication technologies. *Knowledge, Technology and Policy*, 23, pp. 287–305.

Fleischman, R., 2000. Completing the triangle: Taylorism and the paradigms. *Accounting, Auditing and Accountability Journal*, 15(5), pp. 597–624.

Fohlin, C., 2005. The history of corporate ownership and control in Germany. In: R. K. Morck, *A history of corporate governance around the world: family business groups to professional managers*. Chicago, IL: University of Chicago Press, pp. 223–282.

Franklin, S., 2002. *Writing, society and culture in early Russia, c.950–1300*. Cambridge: Cambridge University Press.

Fukuyama, F., 1995. *Trust the social virtues and the creation of prosperity*. London: Hamish Hamilton.

Garcke, E. and Fells, J. M., 1887. *Factory accounts, their principles and practice; a handbook for accountants and manufacturers, with appendices, etc*. London: Crosby, Lockwood & Co.

Garrett, J., 1999. Redefining order in the German library, 1775–1825. *Eighteenth-Century Studies*, 33(1), pp. 103–123.

Gauldi, J. and Armitage, D., 2014. *History manifesto*. Cambridge: Cambridge University Press.

Gerrard & National plc., 1981. *The London discount market: a guide to its role in the economy and its contribution to industry and commerce*. London: Gerrard & National plc.

Giddens, A., 1987. *Social theory and modern sociology*. Cambridge: Polity Press.

Gollins, T., 2009. *Parsimonious preservation: preventing pointless processes! (The small simple steps that take digital preservation a long way forward)*. London: The National Archives.

Green, E., 1991. Business archives in the United Kingdom: history, conspectus, prospectus. In: A. Turton, ed., 1991. *Managing business archives*. Oxford: Butterworth-Heinemann.

Harvard University (Center for History and Economics), 2015. *Visualizing historical network*. [online] Available at: www.fas.harvard.edu/~histecon/visualizing/ [Accessed 3 September 2016].

Harvey, R., 2005. *Preserving digital materials*. Munich: K. G. Saur.

Heath, C. and Luff, P., 2007a. Ordering competition: the interactional accomplishment of the sale of fine art and antiques at auction. *British Journal of Sociology*, 58(1), pp. 63–85.

Heath, C. and Luff, P. 2007b. Gesture and institutional interaction: figuring bids in auctions of fine art and antiques. *Gesture*, 7(2), pp. 215–241.

History Lab, 2015. *How do we find something, when we do not know what we are looking for?* [online] Available at: www.history-lab.org/ [Accessed 3 September 2016].

Holmes, A. R. and Green, E., 1986. *Midland: 150 years of banking business*. London: Batsford.

Holmes, R., 2011. *Thomas Lawrence portraits*. London: National Portrait Gallery.

Hosking, G., 2010. *Trust: money, markets and society (Manifesto for the 21st century)*. Chicago, IL: University of Chicago Press.

Hurley, C., 1995. Ambient functions – abandoned children to zoos. *Archivaria*, 40 (Fall), pp. 21–39.

Iacovino, L., 2006. *Recordkeeping, ethics and law: regulatory models, participant relationships and rights and responsibilities in the online world*. Dordrecht: Springer.

Jenkinson, H., 1925. Medieval tallies, public and private. *Archaeologica*, 74, pp. 289–351.

Jobert, P. and Moss, M., 1990. *The birth and death of companies*. New York: Parthenon Publishing.

John, L. and Ville, S., 2012. Banking records, business and networks in Colonial Sydney, 1817–24. *Australian Economic History Review*, 52(2), pp. 167–190.

Johnson, H. T. and Kaplan, R. S., 1987. *Relevance lost: the rise and fall of management accounting*. Boston, MA: Harvard Business School Press.

Jones, G. and Morgan, N. J., 1994. *Adding value: brands and marketing in food and drink*. London: Routledge.

Kan, L., 1991. The use of the tally in China. In: D. T. Roy and T. Tsuen-Lsui, eds, 1991. *Ancient China: studies in early civilization*. Hong Kong: Chinese University Press.

Kelly, P., 1801. *Elements of book-keeping, both by single and double entry, comprising a system of merchants' accounts, etc.* London: J. Johnson.

Kempson, J., 1834. The state of manufacturing in America. *Mechanics' Magazine and Register of Inventions and Improvements*. New York: D. K. Munro and J. K. Challis.

Kiran, A. H. and Verbeek, P. P., 2010. Trusting our selves to technology. *Knowledge Technology & Policy*, 23 (Dec.), pp. 409–427.

Klimt, B. and Yang, Y., 2004. *Introducing the Enron corpus*. Pittsburgh, PA: Carnegie Mellon University. [pdf] Available at: http://nl.ijs.si/janes/wp-content/uploads/2014/09/klimtyang04a.pdf [Accessed 3 September 2016].

Kluger, M., 2014. *The Fugger dynasty in Augsburg merchants, mining entrepreneurs, bankers and benefactors*. Augsburg: Context Verlag.

Krishnamurthy, R., 1997. *Sangam age Tamil coins*. Madras: Garnet Publications.

Lapper, R. W., 1870a. *A new method of filing away miscellaneous office papers for immediate reference etc.* London: Waterston.

Lapper, R. W., 1870b. *Registration of correspondence. A new system applicable to large offices, etc.* London: Waterston.

Laurence, E., 1743. *The duty and office of a land steward: represented under several plain and distinct articles*. 3rd ed. London: J. & J. Knapton.

Lester, C. E., assisted by Foster, A., 1853. *Life and voyages of Americus Vespucius*. New Haven: Horace Mansfield.

Levy, D. M., 2001. *Scrolling forward: making sense of documents in the digital age*. New York: Arcade Publishing.

Lewis & Peat, 1975. *Two centuries of Lewis & Peat (now the Guinness Peat Group) 1775–1975*. London: Guinness Peat Group.

Lihoma, P. and Tough, A., 2012. The development of record keeping systems in the British Empire and Commonwealth, 1870s–1960s, *Archives & Manuscripts*, 40(3), pp. 191–216.

McKemmish, S., Piggott, M., Reed, B. and Upward, F., 2005. *Archives: recordkeeping in society*. Wagga Wagga, Australia: Centre for Information Studies, Charles Stuart University.

Mackenzie, D., 2009. Beneath all the toxic acronyms lies a basic cultural issue. *Financial Times*, 26 Nov., p. 36.

Mackenzie, D., 2011. The credit crisis as a problem in the sociology of knowledge. *American Journal of Sociology*, 116(6), pp. 1778–1841.

Matsuzaki, Y., 2007. Business archives in Japan: an overview and access issues, Japan–US Archives Seminar, May 2007. [pdf] Available at: www.archivists.org/publications/proceedings/accesstoarchives/06_Yuko_MATSUZAKI.pdf [Accessed 3 September 2016].

Mitchell, J. C., 1956. *The Yao village: a study in the social structure of a Malawian tribe*. Manchester: Manchester University Press.

Morgan, N. J. and Moss, M.S., 1989. Wealthy and titled persons – the accumulation of riches in Victorian Britain – The case of Peter Denny. In: C. Harvey, ed., *Business History Concepts and Measurement*. London: Cass.

Moss, M., 2005. The Hutton inquiry, the president of Nigeria and what the Butler hoped to see? *English Historical Review*, CXX, 487, pp. 577–592.

Moss, M., 2010. Archival research in organizations in a digital age. In: D. Buchanan and A. Bryman, eds, *The Sage handbook of organizational research methods*. London: Sage, pp. 395–408.

Moss, M., 2012. Where have all the files gone? Lost in action points every one? *Journal of Contemporary History*, 47(4), pp. 860–875.

Murahashi, M., 2002. *Shashi no kenkyu* (A study of company histories). Tokyo: Diamond, Inc.

Murray, L., 1821. *The young man's best companion, and book of general knowledge; containing English grammar, book-keeping, drawing . . . general observations on gardening . . . a brief sketch of naval and military affairs, an account of the various religious sects . . . observations on behaviour and manners, with rules for conversation. Also a choice selection of the most useful and important receipts in the different branches of art and science.* London: Thomas Kelly.

Napier, C., 2007. *Other cultures, other accountings? Islamic accounting from past to present.* Paper presented at the 5th Accounting History International Conference, Banff, Canada.

Nash, M., 1997. Business history and archival practice. In: J. O'Toole, ed., 1997. *The records of American business.* Chicago, IL: Society of American Archivists.

Nishimura, S., 1971. *The decline of inland bills of exchange in the London money market, 1855–1913.* Cambridge: Cambridge University Press.

Norton, G. P., 1889, *Textile manufacturers' book-keeping for the counting house, mill and warehouse, etc.* Huddersfield: A. Jubb.

O'Neill, O., 2002. *A question of trust.* BBC Reith Lectures. [online] Available at: www.bbc.co.uk/radio4/reith2002/ [Accessed 3 September 2016].

O'Neill, O., 2010. *Keynote address: finance in question/finance in crisis conference.* ESRC Centre for Research on Socio-Cultural Change, University of Manchester.

Pacioli, L. B., 1494. *Summa de arithmetica, geometria, proportioni et proportionalita.* Venice.

Payne, P. L., 1960. *The early Scottish limited companies, 1856–1895.* Edinburgh: Scottish Academic Press.

Pechenick, E. A., Danforth, C. M. and Dodds, P. S., 2015. Characterizing the Google Books corpus: strong limits to inferences of socio-cultural and linguistic evolution. *PLOS One*, 10(10). [online] Available at: http://journals.plos.org/plosone/article?id=10.1371/journal.pone.0137041 [Accessed 3 September 2016].

Pitman, Sir I., 1897. *Pitman's manual of business training.* London: Sir Isaac Pitman & Sons.

Power, M., 2004. *The risk management of everything – rethinking the politics of uncertainty.* London: Demos.

Power, M., 2007. *Organized uncertainty – designing a world of risk management.* Oxford: Oxford University Press.

Pym, B., 2004. *Quartet in autumn.* Basingstoke and Oxford: Macmillan.

Raines, D., 2012. Public or private records? The family archives of the Venetian patriciate in the fifteenth–eighteenth centuries. In: M. de Lurdes Rosa, ed., 2012. *Arquivos de família, seculos XIII–XX: que presente, que futuro?* Lisboa: IEM (Instituto de Estudos Medievais)/CHAM (Centro de História de Além–Mar/Caminhos Romanos), pp. 535–548.

Reininghaus, W. and Hoock, J., 1997. *Kaufleute in Europa. Handelshäuser und ihre Überlieferung in vor– und frühindustrieller Zeit. Beiträge der tagung Westfälischen Wirtschaftsarchiv 9.–11. Mai 1996.* Dortmund, Verlag: Gesellschaft für westf. Wirtschaftsgeschichte.

Sabine, B. E. V., 1966. *A history of income tax.* London: George Allen & Unwin.

Schulze, J. W., 1914. *The American office its organization, management and records.* New York: The Ronald Press Co.

Selden, A., 2011. *Trust. How we lost it and how to get it back.* London: Biteback Publishing.

Shaw, P. A., Dunlop, A., Bell, J. M. and Napier, M., 1831. *Cases decided in the Court of Session, from 1830 to 1831.* Edinburgh: William Blackwood.

Strathern, M., 2000. Abstraction and decontextualisation: an anthropological comment or: e for ethnography. [online]. Available at: http://virtualsociety.sbs.ox.ac.uk/GRpapers/strathern.htm [Accessed 3 September 2016].

Taylor, F. W., 1911. *The principles of scientific management.* New York and London: Harper & Brothers.

Tedlow, R. S. and Jones, G., 1993. *The rise and fall of mass marketing*. London: Routledge.

Urton, G. 2003. *Signs of the Inka Khipu: binary coding in the Andean knotted-string records*. Austin, TX: University of Texas Press.

US Securities and Exchange Commission, 2003. *Final judgement against Henry McKelvey Blodgett.* [online] Available at: www.sec.gov/litigation/litreleases/judg18115b.htm [Accessed 3 September 2016].

Weber, M., Baehr, P. R. and Wells, G. C., 2002. *The Protestant ethic and the 'spirit' of capitalism and other writings*. London: Penguin.

Wild, A. M., 2013. Capability Brown, the aristocracy, and the cultivation of the eighteenth-century British landscaping industry. *Enterprise and Society*, 14(2), pp. 237–270.

Yates, J., 1989. *Control through communication: the rise of system in American management*. Baltimore, MD: Johns Hopkins University Press.

Yates, J. and Van Maanen, J., eds, 2001. *Information technology and organizational transformation: history, rhetoric, and practice*. Thousand Oaks, CA and London: Sage Publications.

Chapter 5

Understanding industry-specific business records

Lesley Richmond

Records are created by organisations in the course of their day-to-day activities as a means to remember or provide evidence for administrative, legislative and operational purposes. Commercial organisations of all shapes and sizes throughout the world create records in order to be able to go about their business. Transactions are recorded in order that the information, the action, the concept, the right, the instruction, the agreement, the process or the product is put into a lasting form, which can be recalled if and when required. Records allow an organisation to be accountable and thus trustworthy to shareholders, investors, regulators and other stakeholders.[1]

All businesses have commercial goals, which are pursued through functions. Records are created as the result of the transactions undertaken in the course of the activities performed to fulfil those functions. Functions are intangible and abstract, whereas activities are concrete actions, performed by actual 'departments' of the business.

The functions of a business of any size, structure or location are broadly the same. External legislation and regulations, both generic (such as company, employment, health and safety and marketing regulations) and specific (such as banking, pharmaceutical and insurance regulations), will affect the types of records created as the law or regulation affects the activities required to comply with it. Some of this legislation is global, such as accounting for companies quoted on stock exchanges, but most of it is defined by both business sector and national legislation. The growth of a global economy has resulted in more universal legislation and regulations.[2]

Surprisingly, no generic model of the functions and activities performed by a business has been developed to date, although examples have been set out for other organisations and specific business sectors (Bruemmer, 1997, pp. 137–60).[3] In order to understand business records, core or specific, for a local or global commercial organisation it is necessary to be aware of the goals, functions and activities of a business. A generic model of the functions of a business is given in Table 5.1. An example of a function and activity model for a specific industry – the retail industry – can be found later in this chapter in Box 5.2.

The creation and retention of records of activities carried out in order to fulfil the functions of a business is dependent on the structure and size of a business and the industrial sector within which it operates. A sole trader functions within an environment in which few statutory requirements exist for either the establishment or operation of the business. A large company producing and marketing thousands of products will require activities in place to ensure the flow of materials, products, information and finances. The majority of these activities will create records. So whilst the basic functions of a

Table 5.1 Function and activity model for a commercial organisation

Function	Description
Governance	Self-regulation and setting of the boundaries in which the business operates, including the legal framework; ensuring compliance with all relevant legislation; developing the corporate governance structure and rules; and conducting the business of the corporate body and the executive committees in accordance with those rules.
Strategic planning and performance management	Developing and establishing the direction of the business; setting targets to develop financial gain and investment; and managing performance in attaining targets.
Production management	Developing and managing the creation of the products of the business.
Merchandising	Buying and selling products.
Marketing	Identifying customers and advertising products and services.
Financial management	Managing the financial resources of the business.
Investor management	Creating the financial growth of the business with responsibilities for shareholding activities.
Audit	Conducting audits of the affairs and operations of the business to ensure compliance with corporate, industry, legal or regulatory requirements.
Legal affairs law management	Managing the legal affairs of the business; ensuring compliance with and regulation; and defending and prosecuting the interests of the business in the courts.
Quality management	Managing the overall quality of the services, products administration and compliance of the business.
Risk management	Managing all risks to and within the business.
Organisational development	Developing the business structure and culture of the business.
Health and safety management	Identifying and managing the risks associated with health and safety within the business and ensuring compliance with legislation.
Environment management/ Sustainability	Managing the impact of the business and its operations on the environment and ensuring compliance with environmental legislation.
Estate and facilities management	Managing the real property of the business.
Human resources management	Managing the workforce of the business.
Information resources management	Managing the information resources generated or acquired by the business in the course of its work.
Communications management	Managing the external and internal communication and relationships with the public, media and staff of the business.
Purchasing and procurement	Acquiring ownership or use of goods or services other than property.
Equipment and consumables management	Managing equipment and consumables purchased and used by the business – often now outsourced.
Supply chain management	Managing the flow of materials, products, information and finances as they move in the operation of the business.

Acknowledgement: Glasgow University Archive Services.

business are the same, particular functions and related activities may predominate depending on the goal of the business. A commercial organisation, which distributes services or goods directly to the public will, for example, create records focused on merchandising and marketing, whilst a business exploiting raw natural resources will have a special emphasis on environmental management.

Commercial organisations operating within the same business sector do tend to have similar goals related to the production of goods or services. The diversity of business sectors is large. The United Kingdom's Office for National Statistics arranges 'economic activities' into 21 sections, 88 divisions, 272 groups, 615 classes and 191 subclasses.[4] Although it is impossible to prescribe the specific types of records created within business sectors, there are more than enough similarities to provide a guide to the types of records created. Production records, in particular, vary greatly between service providing businesses and those that manufacture products and amongst different types of manufacturing concerns. The production records of pharmaceutical, retailing, brewing, mining, heavy engineering and financial services businesses, for example, are very different.

The size of a business and its organisation also affect the nature and types of records that are created. In a small business in one location where the managers are familiar with all employees, staff records may not be as detailed as those in a much larger organisation based in several locations. In general, in small firms departments or other units are fewer than in large firms, and the boundaries between units can often be blurred. Functions in small businesses are often combined in one unit where in a larger firm the function may be managed separately or even split over many different units. An extreme example is the sole trader, operating out of a market stall with no employees, who manages and is responsible for all the functions of the business – from governance to supply chain management – but usually concentrates on merchandising, marketing and financial management. The structure of a small engineering firm may be organised along general management and technical and production functions rather than, as is often the case in a large firm, by a number of specialised departments responsible for particular functions or activities. The smaller firm for instance may have combined its drawing, costing and estimating functions in a single unit. These different workflows and procedures will create different record series within businesses in the same industrial sector. Understanding the internal organisation of a business and its procedures and processes is essential to understanding its record creation, as is the regulatory environment within which it works and its purpose and goals.

There are at least five organisational types of business: simple, functionally departmentalised, holding company, multi-divisional and global. The sole trader or single proprietor may originally carry out all functions but over time, if growth occurs, will gather functionally specialist employees. Firms may be set up with functional departments and 'depending on the nature of the business may be further departmentalised by geographic, process, market channel or client lines' (Baer, 1997, p. 88). Geographic departmentalisation tends to duplicate activities such as accounting and human resources management at regional or national levels, ensuring support skills are available to hand. Process departmentalisation groups activities based on their role in a production process, for example in the textile industry, where activities directly or indirectly related to spinning, weaving, dyeing and printing will be grouped together to form a department. Market channel follows the markets in which the firm is involved, such as wholesale or retail, and client departmentalisation follows customer groups, such as domestic or international customers.

As companies expand further by vertical integration or horizontal growth by acquisition, they adopt a form of structure to deal with the issues of co-ordinating so many different companies. In the holding company form, a small head office loosely controls a number of subsidiary companies as decentralised profit centres. The subsidiaries are separate companies, often with directors of the main board holding multiple appointments within them. This form of control usually ensures that more of the activities of the subsidiary are recorded in the documents of the parent than when the two are entirely separate.

A tighter form of control than that of the holding company is the multi-divisional form, which is designed to improve efficiency. Here the organisation of the holding company is decentralised and each market or product line is managed by a semi-autonomous division, which acts like a separate, functionally departmentalised firm. Support services and the co-ordination of the whole company are provided centrally. Multi-divisional firms often evolve into global ones, producing multiple products and spreading their functions out across many countries. The global form is usually a matrix of product, functional and geographic units, creating their own records, subject to different national laws, which may never be brought together under a single control.

This chapter will describe the types of records created by businesses linked by product and organisation within a small selection of industrial sectors as a way of exploring the wide variety of records that businesses create. The sectors explored are shipping, ship-building, textiles, insurance, chartered accountancy, banking, pharmaceuticals, chemicals, consumer goods, brewing, architects, utilities, extraction, mechanical engineering and retailing.[5]

Shipping

Shipping played an important part in the economic development of many nations. It is one of the most low-cost modes of transport and continues to play a vital and significant role in today's global economy, facilitating 90 per cent of world trade. It makes possible the bulk movement of raw materials and the import and export of affordable food and manufactured goods.

Commercial shipping can be traced back to Phoenician merchants who carried goods across the Mediterranean and until the nineteenth century the industry was dominated by merchants. The first trans-Atlantic freight service was established in 1818 and the industry boomed after the opening of the Suez Canal in 1869 facilitated faster trade between Europe and Asia. The introduction of engines, first steam and later diesel, as well as the propeller in steel ships, revolutionised shipping and meant ship owners could offer more reliable services. Meanwhile, new means of communication via cable improved information flow and reduced risk. In the 1970s and 1980s the container shipping sector grew exponentially. Ship owners make their vessels available to importers and exporters through a highly efficient international network of shipping brokers. The main trades in shipping are bulk (crude oil/product/gas tankers or bulk carriers transporting grain, coal, iron ore and the like), container liner shipping (fixed schedules on routes) and special vessels (such as car carriers, supply vessels and refrigerated ships). Depending on the trade the ships are operated commercially in very different ways. Brokers can be contracted to buy and sell ships, obtain cargoes and service ships when in port.

The distinctive records of the shipping industry relate to financial, human resource, production and equipment management and marketing. As the weather and sea conditions impacted on the profits of each voyage, ship owners required detailed accounts to be maintained on all sailings, both for on board costs and in port costs, such as stevedoring, pilots, landing, tugs and repairs. Financial records were voluminous. Specific voyage data books recorded consumption of coal and oil and average speed and log books recorded the movements and incidents on board. It was also vital for records to be retained relating to the purchase of ships, including specifications, agreements, contracts, plans, drawings, photographs and even models of vessels commissioned from shipbuilding companies. Ships are very expensive assets and their potential owners required evidence of construction progress and adherence to the agreement in terms of both physical specification and timetable of production. Depending on the type of ship and the contract details, similar records, especially certificates for insurance and operational purposes, can be required when ships are traded second hand.

The cargo carried by the ships, whether human, mail or freight, was also very valuable and registers of passengers, mails and cargo were created and agreements for services and supplies retained in case of dispute. Statistics on cargos and passengers were gathered and reports on services commissioned. Log books were kept for the whole voyage, as well as for specific vital areas of the ship such as the engine room, refrigerators and the decks. Agreements with agents, local managers and the officers and crew were vital records. The captain of a ship and his senior crew were in sole charge of a highly valuable asset and had to be trustworthy and capable. Certificates, registers and record books abound for senior officers as well as lists of crew members. Instructions issued to officers and crew members were also retained in case of a dispute or legal process.

The voyages and associated services were advertised through timetables, brochures, posters and handbills, and latterly through videos, television commercials, websites and other promotional material. Freight tariffs and passenger rates and fares were printed on posters and in handbooks. The firms operating the luxury liner market also created items such as menus, entertainment programmes and other at sea material issued to passengers.

Shipbuilding

From earliest times boat and shipbuilding has been a complex industry, involving the assembly of materials from a variety of specialist suppliers – from timber to anchors. The introduction of steam propulsion and iron and later steel shipbuilding in the early nineteenth century added further complexity to the industry. Shipbuilders used conventional business record keeping practices to manage the construction of very expensive products but also developed some to suit their own needs.

Shipbuilders won business by submitting competitive tenders to their potential customers. Documentation included design drawings meeting the specifications drawn up by customers and an estimate of the costs of construction. The estimates were recorded in estimating or tender books. On acceptance of a tender, a contract was drawn up between the customer and the shipbuilder, specifying in general terms the size and type of vessel to be constructed, the delivery date, the price and the method of payment. Initially, contracts consisted of a few pages of text but, as ship design became more complex and strict international regulations were established to control methods of construction and operation, contracts became very bulky documents. Once the contract was signed the ship was allocated a number, usually referred to as the new building number. Most shipyards maintain registers of hull and engine numbers, detailing the date the contract was signed, the date of launching, the name of the ship's sponsor at the launch and the date of completion. A detailed technical specification of the hull and the engine was usually associated with the contract.

Before work could begin on either the hull or the engines, detailed designs had to be prepared in accordance with the agreed specification. For even a relatively small craft there would have been several hundreds of drawings, from a general arrangement to very detailed drawings of individual components, not all of which require to be selected for preservation. These drawings were located by means of plan registers and normally stored by new building number or contract number. The final principal paper drawings prepared in the nineteenth century are often works of art, carefully tinted in various colours to indicate the material used in the construction.

The construction of a ship generated a vast quantity of correspondence and papers relating to the delivery of materials and equipment from sub-contractors and technical issues. These were originally bound up in letter books and later held in files by new building number or contract number.

It was essential that costs related to each new building number – labour, materials, equipment and overheads – were accurately recorded and controlled during construction. The recording of costs generated many series of records, including wages books and materials books, which were usually brought together under the new building number or contract number in cost books. As the contract progressed these were often entered in progressive cost books and when complete recorded in finished cost books. Finished and estimated costs were often compared, creating a separate record series.

One of the main reasons that cost had to be recorded in detail as construction progressed was that payment was related to estimated expenditure at certain stages specified in the contract, usually retrospectively. Customers required evidence, in the form of reports, that work had progressed according to the specification and contract terms before payment was made. Earlier customers would send a representative to inspect the construction at certain stages, often coinciding with the time payment was to be made. In recent times customers often set up an inspectors' office at the shipyard to facilitate ongoing supervision of the construction. To complement the reports made to customers' inspectors many firms created a comprehensive photographic record series to demonstrate progress. Sometimes changes to the details of the design occurred and such extra modifications were usually recorded in separate registers known as 'extras books', detailing the modification and the cost, which were agreed with the customer after delivery of the ship.

The launch of a vessel was the most important event during the construction process, usually marked by formal celebrations. A sponsor named the ship in front of guests representing the owners, sub-contractors, financiers, insurers, brokers and agents. Firms maintained scrapbooks of invitations and orders of proceedings, together with photographs and press comment. For shipyards using building berths, as opposed to building docks where the ship was not launched into the sea, technical launch books were also maintained recording such things as the weights of the drag chains used, the height of the tide and the setting of the launching gear.

Box 5.1 Appraising shipbuilding technical drawings

The following are the core technical records that should be kept for each vessel or series of vessels:

- General arrangement: pictorial to scale, last plan to be produced, not used for construction of the ship.
- Rigging: winching equipment, superstructure.
- Accommodation: specifications for fitting out crew and passenger quarters.
- Lines: used for hull design it describes the shape of the ship in three perspectives – profile, body and plan.
- Shell expansion: shows individual plate on keel.
- Midship section: shows a cross section at the middle of the ship and often illustrates the construction technique and materials.
- Profile and decks: construction drawing showing plating.
- Sternframe and rudder: plans of same.
- Offsets: table-based on lines plan.
- Pumping: internal and external pipelines.
- Cargo pumping: primarily oil tankers, internal and external pipelines.
- Docking: dry-docking information such as dimensions.
- Capacity: holds and oil tank dimensions/capacity.
- Hydrostatics: graphs of vessel stability.

In addition, the following plans should be kept:

- All relevant plans for any vessel deemed to be of particular historical interest. Is it a classic example of what the company produced? Is it a detail of a significant part of the vessel (if the ship was a bucket dredger, for example, the plan showing the bucket dredging machinery should be kept)? Is it a famous vessel or was it involved in a historically important event?
- Major plans of all naval vessels.
- Plans showing details of wartime modifications to merchant ships.
- Arrangement plans for first and subsequent designs for a series of ships.

There is normally no need to keep the following records:

- Dyeline prints and blueprints where the originals survive (but look out for signed copies or handwritten notes of importance).
- Plans of small parts, details, plate plans or sub–contractors' plans.

Although sailing ships were normally launched complete, fully rigged and fitted and so ready for sea trials, machine-propelled vessels were normally launched before the fitting out of the interior. Once fitting out was completed the vessel's performance had to be tested against the specifications before delivery. From the early nineteenth century this was done in elaborate trials, involving the testing and inspection of every item of equipment on board. Trials were carried out at the out-fitting quay at the shipyard as well as at sea, where the vessel was run at progressively faster speeds over measured distances, the results being recorded, usually, in separate trial books.

In order to know if the actual cargo capacity corresponded with the specification laid down at the contract signing, the customer required to know the exact weight of the vessel delivered, so the weight of material incorporated into the vessel had to be recorded throughout construction in weights books, or tonnage and dimension books. Such information was normally brought together in finished weight books in which the final weight of the vessel was calculated.

The first round of trials were known as 'builder's trials', which eventually led to the final round of trials, the 'acceptance trials', with the owners' representatives present. When these had been successfully completed and any faults rectified, the builder and the owner would sign a completion certificate and the vessel was formally handed over. Owners normally retained a percentage of the final price to be paid at a specified period after delivery to ensure that any faults revealed in service would be rectified by the yard. Sea trials were sometimes extensively photographed and filmed. On delivery an extensive photographic record of the exterior and interior was often made for use in the publicity of both the yard and the owner. A final 'as fitted' or 'as built' set of drawings of the vessel were also given to the owner as part of the contract along with sets of comprehensive manuals and instruction books explaining the workings of the vessel and engines for use by the crew.

Some shipyards built ships, some repaired ships and some offered both services. A customer decided when a ship required docking for maintenance or repairs and this generally did not take place at the shipyard where the ship was built. If offering such services, the shipyard created records that documented every activity from when the ship arrived until it departed, both as technical documentation for the owner and to document the costs of the docking operation. Repair and maintenance jobs were normally given separate contract numbers from the ship/engine number series. These were recorded in repair registers, detailing the date of arrival of the vessel, the work carried out and the date of departure. Sometimes repairs included major modifications to the layout of accommodation or the replacement of engines and so would create nearly as many records as the contract for a new vessel.

Shipyards and marine engine works represented the largest concentrations of capital and employment in many national economies. As in the case of other manufacturing companies, the plant could be very extensive, covering several acres with a number of buildings and masses of equipment and tools, all of which required maintainence and ratings. Details of plant and equipment were recorded in plant and property registers, including a description, the name of the manufacturer or builder, the date of acquisition, the cost, depreciation and the date of disposal and price realised.

Every shipyard employed men from a number of trades who had to work together in the construction and fitting out of the hull. Who did what was specified in a demarcation agreement, often printed in a rulebook carried by each tradesman. Nevertheless, demarcation disputes were a regular occurrence, requiring arbitration by the management or in serious cases by external experts.

Textiles

The manufacture of textile is one of the oldest of human technologies. Fibre is used to create a (usually spun) yarn, which is processed (knitted or woven) into cloth. The fibre or cloth is dyed and can later be printed for decoration. The textile industry was, and is, a worldwide business drawing on raw materials produced all over the globe. It was the lead sector in many countries during their industrial revolutions. Textile manufacturers, in the form of cotton masters, pioneered the industrial revolution in the United Kingdom from the 1760s. During the nineteenth century the industry saw vast concentration in capital and resources caused by advances in technology and the organisation of raw material supply, marketing, production and distribution. New forms of technology, power generation, finance and labour and industrial organisation were combined in a textile mill on a scale that foreshadowed today's industrialised and urbanised society.

Specialism has always existed in the industry by fibre and/or product and by function – design, manufacture, distribution and retail. The largest companies often carried out all the functions in one or various locations. In the United Kingdom there was also a trend in the late nineteenth and early twentieth centuries for amalgamations of different branches of the industry – bleachers, dyers, printers and sewers.

Textile manufacturers employed huge national and later international workforces. In the eighteenth and early nineteenth centuries, factories were built near a source of water, for power as well as for washing. Sometimes, in isolated areas, the firm took on the role of a local government authority, recording population statistics, as well as providing housing, welfare facilities, education and entertainment. Textile factories were regulated like other places of production and maintained statutory registers, such as those to record accidents and young employees.

Technical innovation was initially protected by secrecy and later by the rule of law through patents and licences, while fashionable developments in designs were protected by trademarks. Machinery and equipment were important components in the production of material and the costs involved, having a major bearing on the number of people required to be employed and the time it took to produce the finished product. Plans and drawings of plant and machinery were important to ensure speedy repairs and maintenance registers provided proof of upkeep. Inventories of plant and equipment were vital for insurance purposes and depreciation.

Production records are distinctive. Records recording quantity of fibre or cloth produced by various processes on a periodic basis, such as spinning, drawing, weaving, hand-loom, carding and dyeing books, were created often with wage and other costs recorded. Purchases and stock books were required to control costs and ensure efficient and timely availability of raw materials required in the processes. Textile pattern books are the most distinctive design and production records created by the industry. They were created for inventory control, to facilitate sales and for the purpose of design intelligence. They consisted of painted, printed or drawn fabric designs or samples of fabric with additional notes recording the pattern, weave and quality and orders completed. Pattern books were a record of the process from design to production, a record of orders completed and a record of what was available for a customer to purchase. The equivalent in the dyeing branch of the industry were more akin to recipe books, noting the ingredients used to produce the sample colour of fibre or cloth pasted in the volume. Sample books were developed to provide customers with a catalogue of the full range of products produced by a company.

Insurance

Insurance is a form of risk management used for centuries to protect against the risk of an uncertain loss. The insured enters into a contract with the insurer for insurance cover, paying the premium calculated by the insurer who in return guarantees to compensate the insured in the case of personal or financial loss. The insured receives a contract, the insurance policy, which details the conditions and circumstances under which they will be compensated.

The insurance industry historically consists of four distinct categories – marine, fire, life and accident – with firms being classified into two groups, life and non-life. Life insurance companies sold life insurance, annuities and later pensions products, while non-life insurance companies sold other types of insurance, such as property or casualty insurance. Life and non-life insurers were, in most countries, subject to different regulatory regimes and different tax and accounting rules. The main reason for the distinction was and is the period of the length of risk. Non-life insurance cover usually covered a short period, often a year, while life, annuity and pension business covered a much longer period – potentially the lifetime of a person.

Marine insurance gives financial protection from total loss or partial damage of sea-going vessels and cargoes and requires an assessment of the nature, size and value of the risk. The underwriter calculates the premium according to quality of ship or cargo and destination and route of the voyage at risk. The earliest examples of modern marine insurance date from thirteenth-century Genoa and the marine insurance policy was the earliest example of a printed business form in the United Kingdom (Cockerell and Green, 1994, pp. 4–5). The first two corporate marine businesses in Europe were established in 1720 by royal charter, Royal Exchange Assurance and London Assurance.

Fire insurance offices were established in the United Kingdom in London in the late seventeenth century and in other major cities in the early eighteenth century. The major London-based companies operated through a network of agents throughout Britain, which went global in the late nineteenth century. Often insurance firms were established for a particular geographical area or class of risk.

Life insurance in the form of term assurance (payment on death during a fixed period) was available from at least the sixteenth century in the United Kingdom, although life assurance (certain payment on the death of the policy holder) was not available until the eighteenth century. It was the use of actuarial research into mortality statistics developed by Equitable Life Assurance Society (established 1762) which allowed the business to expand with a range of contracts. Endowment policies, providing payment of a sum of money at the end of a fixed period or the death of the policy holder, were introduced in the 1830s. Accident insurance covers all other forms of commercial insurance, such as personal accident, sickness, vehicle, damage to property and legal liability, and was introduced in the nineteenth century.

The distinctive records of the industry are created from the transactions and mechanisms required to provide insurance cover. These include proposal and claims files; risk/voyage books (marine); policy registers that record details of the items or lives to be insured and the term of insurance; registers of lapsed copies; actuarial reports (life); surveyors' reports; inspection reports (boiler); claims registers (claimant name, item, location, settlement detail); death registers; salvage books (marine); endorsement/renewal registers and loss registers.

Insurance companies invested the premiums received to cover the costs of insurance payouts and so investment registers have a particular significance. Efficient accounting systems were required to deal with the multitude of customers who made small premiums payments. Agents kept customer records to secure repeat business and commission account books to record premiums received and commissions paid. Other records of agents include agreements, accounts, instructions from head office, policy registers and endorsements books. The structure of insurance companies over time has also been diverse and impacted the records created, with partnership, mutual benefit or joint-stock corporate forms prevailing depending on the nature of the business.

Chartered accountancy

Accountancy as a service industry, offering professional expertise in a number of areas, such as taxation and auditing, liquidation and management consultancies, began in the United Kingdom in the early nineteenth century. Some firms specialised in one area, while others, often larger organisations, offered many different services.

The records generated by a firm of chartered accountants usually consist of two groups; records, mainly partnership, dealing with the internal affairs of the business and the records created by the work undertaken for clients. The distinctive nature of the records generated by the industry is the result of the particular work of accountants and the fees charged.

Chartered accountants have mainly been constituted as sole traders or partnerships and so the main governance documents have been the partnership agreement, which can be local, national or international in nature, and minutes of the partners' meetings. Partners' professional diaries, in the form of notebooks, pre-printed volumes or computer generated, provide a daily record of work undertaken for clients. The detail has always varied in nature but acts as an informal record or an *aide-memoire* for billing purposes.

Time records are the means by which accountants account for the time they charge to their clients. Time sheets maintained on a periodic basis summarise the time spent per client. Summaries were transferred via time daybooks or journals to time ledgers building up the total amount spent on a client's work. The detail varies from general to specific detail and can contain the number and grade of staff working on particular work and in total.

The amount of time spent on a client's work is converted into a fee (cost) by applying the charge-out rate for the grade of staff involved and the client is billed (invoiced) accordingly. Copies of the bills may be recorded in the bills delivered books and details of the fees recorded in accounts/fees rendered books. Fees were also recorded in the fees or bills journal, which would be posted to fee or clients' ledgers. Firms also recovered exceptional expenditure – travel and accommodation expenses – incurred on clients' business and these were recorded in client disbursements books, and then recharged to the client as part of the fee. Clients' papers on which accountants' worked are also accumulated by accountancy firms.

Banking

The modern banking industry began in medieval and early Renaissance Italy, in the northern cities of Florence, Venice and Genoa, where merchants could exchange and validate foreign currencies and hold surplus funds. Banking offices continued to be located near centres of trade. In the late seventeenth and early eighteenth centuries private banks were established in the United Kingdom, initially in London and later in the provinces.

These banks obtained their capital from partnerships with unlimited liability, restricted in law to six people, and offered a number of banking services to customers, including the receipt of cash and other valuable items on deposit, the purchase and discounting of bills of exchange, the provision of advances and, in many cases, the issue of bank notes. By the end of the eighteenth century, the clearing bank system was established, by which cheques could be exchanged and accounts between the banks settled on a daily basis.

Joint-stock banks, owned by a large number of shareholders rather than a handful of wealthy individuals, already commonplace in Scotland, were established in England and Wales after the passage of the Banking Copartnership Act in 1826. The joint-stock form spread risk and increased capitalisation, allowing the new banks to grow much larger. By the end of the nineteenth century, national clearing banks with head offices in London and national branch networks had been formed. During the twentieth century, the banking industry in the United Kingdom underwent major concentration, as a result of mergers, diversified its business and saw massive changes in technology.

The distinctive records of the banking industry fall into two main groups: those created by the bank's internal affairs and those created by its interaction with customers. The governance records of banks created as partnerships include partners' agreements, which record the constitution of the bank and the manner in which the partners could act. Partnership ledgers often recorded general accounts of the bank, including balance sheets and profit and loss accounts, as well as the contribution and distribution accounts of the partners. Partnership meetings were also held and sometimes, but not always, minuted.

Joint-stock banks were more heavily regulated and required to create and maintain more records than private banks. The constitution of these banks was the deed of settlement, later the memorandum and articles of association. Share registers originally recorded the names of shareholders with their addresses and occupations, their size of holding and date of acquisition and sale of shares. Dividend books recorded profit allocation to shareholders. Annual and general meetings of shareholders were recorded in minute books and generally were concerned with changes in share or loan capital, the election or retirement of directors, and profit and loss. Sometimes details of local, regional and national events or sectoral trends were also recorded. These meetings were initially the only way that shareholders were advised by directors about the performance of a bank, but printed annual reports were later issued. Originally these reports were only a profit and loss account, but increasingly included lists of branches, the names of branch managers and a chairman's report. By the latter half of the twentieth century reports were highly illustrative glossy booklets, but in recent years have increasingly been offered online in electronic format.

Most of the internal accounting records of the banking industry consist of the usual range of account books. Income accounts will include, for example, interest received from funds placed at call with discount houses; commission received from discounting; charges received from customers for the provision of services; commissions received from accepting, underwriting or issuing; and profits from securities transactions. Bank branches often maintained their own account books and head office ledgers recorded transactions between branches and head office.

Staff records are very similar to those created by other industries, but some types of records are particular to banks such as staff fidelity bonds and declarations of secrecy. In the United Kingdom from the eighteenth century banks required employees in positions of trust to provide personal sureties, fidelity bonds, to make good any loss arising from the conduct of the person guaranteed. During the second half of the nineteenth century, specialised insurance companies were formed to cover the risk and produced printed forms for all staff to complete. New bank staff were required to sign an undertaking not to reveal the confidential affairs of the bank or its customers to a third party. Such records gradually assumed a standard printed form.

Administration records do vary by type of bank. Merchant and overseas banks whose agents, branches and customers were potentially worldwide required a robust communication system. Letters were the original communication and recording medium, originally filed in bundles and then kept in indexed letter books. By the 1920s subject files became the norm. Today such communication with customers and clients is created and retained electronically. Large banks with vast branch networks required a means to quickly communicate standard information concerning changes in services and procedures to managers. This was done from the early twentieth century through the issue of printed or duplicated circulars. Instruction books or procedural manuals were issued to branches from the late nineteenth century. Originally printed books, these assumed loose-leaf form from the 1960s.

Customer records are distinctive in the banking industry. In the United Kingdom customer account ledgers from the seventeenth century to the introduction of account mechanisation, between the 1930s and 1960s, were recorded in single- or double-entry ledgers showing daily payments in or out of each customer's account. By the mid-nineteenth century most banks were making the distinction between current and deposit accounts by maintaining separate deposit ledgers and since then have created new ledger series for other types of account, such as savings and dormant accounts.

Customer securities or investments were recorded in a security register and customer property was recorded in a safe deposit register. From the mid-eighteenth century, in the United Kingdom, customers were issued with a passbook for each of their accounts as a personal record of transactions and these continued to be used until account processing was mechanised. They were then superseded by printed customer statements. Signature books were compiled from the eighteenth century to provide samples of customer signatures for the validation of authorities. Customer character or opinion books were kept to document the character and resources of customers in order to assess lending risks. Banks also created a range of financial instruments for customers to support financial transactions, including bills of exchange, post bills, cheques and banknotes and their issue and destruction were recorded in registers.

Merchant banks created a particular series of customer records within their three main areas of specialisation: merchanting and agency work, finance of international trade and the issuance of securities. Records relating to merchanting comprise accounts of trading in commodities, memorandum books describing trade procedures and the characteristics of different commodities and commodity markets, intelligence circulars, correspondence concerning transactions, papers relating to legal disputes and papers relating to ship management, insurance, warehousing and so on. Trade finance records include accounts relating to the operation of customers' credits, credit agreements, customer character reports, trade finance business and financial market papers. Security issuance records cover the negotiation and process of the issue, including correspondence and papers, prospectuses, certificates and registers of subscribers.

Pharmaceuticals

The roots of a large portion of the pharmaceutical industry lie in the European apothecaries of the fourteenth to sixteenth centuries who mixed and compounded drugs prescribed by physicians. By the seventeenth and eighteenth centuries these apothecaries had become druggists and chemists. In the nineteenth century a new profession of pharmacy emerged, developing advances in drug manufacture and creating some of the current multinational firms, such as F. Hoffmann–La Roche and GlaxoSmithKline. However, some companies, such as the large German manufacturers Hoechst or Bayer or in Switzerland Ciba, Geigy or Sandoz, developed out of the dyestuffs industry. They extracted dyes from natural resources and then, adopting chemical synthesis in around 1855, eventually ventured also into pharmaceuticals. Other companies, such as Burroughs Wellcome and Roche, have never been apothecaries but were founded as industrial pharmaceutical enterprises. In the latter half of the twentieth century pharmaceuticals became the world's fastest growing high-technology industry and one of the most profitable of all businesses.

As an industry it covers both retailing and manufacturing and is highly regulated in such areas as research and product approval by national and international bodies, including the International Conference on Harmonisation of Technical Requirements for Registration of Pharmaceuticals for Human Use, European Medicines Agency and US Food and Drug Administration. Within the research-based pharmaceutical industry, the biggest bulk of records accumulates during the clinical trials, which may last up to ten years. The storage of these highly personal records is strictly regulated. The distinctive records of the industry have always been, and remain, in merchandising, marketing and production management.

From the earliest days of the industry there was a strong requirement to ensure that processes and procedures were recorded. Apothecaries, chemists and druggists who made up drugs recorded their ingredients carefully in laboratory logs and prescription books. By the nineteenth and early twentieth centuries, orders and recipes involving drugs classed as 'dangerous' had to be appropriately noted. In the United Kingdom the Dangerous Drugs Act of 1920 affected all aspects of pharmacy – manufacturing, wholesale and retail – requiring the employment of trained and qualified personnel to carry out many of its demanding requirements. The Pharmacy and Poisons Act of 1933 further tightened the regulations concerning the selling and dispensing of listed poisons and controlled drugs, which could only be carried out by registered members of the professional body. Such regulations created records in the form of registers of dangerous drugs and poisons. The dispensing and licensing controls for drugs are, currently, even more extensive. Drug profiles are produced and retained in case of toxic side-effects. Drug development from concept to market takes years, involving numerous experiments, human trials and eventual licensing, creating massive data files.

The nineteenth-century chemists and druggists who developed into manufacturers of chemicals and drugs began with a rudimentary chemical laboratory on their premises. Each day's work in the laboratory was carefully recorded and eventually each entry would note the source, the date, the ingredients, the quantity, the time, the cost and the person making each batch of medicine or chemicals. Overlapping with laboratory records are formularies and prescription books. In these, the chemist and druggist recorded each prescription as it was made up as an important source of reference for future prescriptions and, if an unusual reaction occurred, as a record of past transactions. The pharmaceutical industry has always required systematic book-keeping as in both buying raw materials and selling to customers large numbers of people are involved globally and locally. Raw materials for drugs, in particular, have always been a worldwide market and customers, since the late nineteenth century, have become increasingly international.

Individual firms and chemists and druggists traded on the reputation of their products and so displayed testimonials and appointments to royalty and others in their shops and on their advertising material. The developers and sellers of proprietary medicines, many of whom were 'quacks', and prominent chemists and druggists, sold medicines over the counter at their own shops and created advertising material, which demonstrated the success of their pills, powders, creams and other treatment. Some proprietary drugs were patented and many were trademarked as brands. By 1875, in the United Kingdom, trademarks had been given statutory protection, with a national register of trademarks and the protection of the law to counter infringement. The pharmaceutical industry was a pioneer in advertising techniques. British firms led by Thomas Beecham, Thomas Holloway, James C. Eno and Jesse Boot became experts at running advertising promotions, devising striking brochures and trade advertisements. Illustrated trade catalogues, of all sizes, were produced in large numbers.

By the late nineteenth century, the modern pharmaceutical industry began to emerge. Chemists and druggists transformed the scale of their operations and the retail sector also changed dramatically. By the 1900s the pharmaceutical industry had become multinational with British and American companies opening overseas subsidiaries around the globe. By the early twentieth century German and American companies began to make major scientific advances in research and development, followed by British companies after 1945. Records created to record research developed from details of experiments and other data recorded in chemist's and pharmacist's diaries as money was spent on advancing new drugs and the status and importance of research and development within companies grew. Separate research divisions were established with their own budgets, research plans and strategies.

The pharmaceutical industry has been among the first to embrace a truly global organisational culture. From the 1990s, the country-based organisations of the past made way for global departments spanning a large number of countries. This development also came as a reaction to the governing bodies (such as the European Medicines Agency and the US Food and Drug Administration) around the world, which increasingly extended their influence across their nations' borders to factories overseas, as long as these were supplying the agency's respective home market. In order to fulfil these agencies' demands for better accountability in production and quality control, electronic records management systems to administer, on a global scale, the huge mass of procedural documents made their appearance in the mid-1990s. Pharmaceutical companies continue to be at the forefront of introducing and managing sophisticated global records management programmes.

Chemicals

The chemical industry converts raw materials, oil, natural gas, air, water, metals and minerals into industrial chemicals, plastic and polymers making up the largest percentage of products. The largest corporate producers worldwide have plants in several countries.

The chemical industry is and has been concentrated in three areas of the world, Western Europe, North America and Japan.

The distinctive records of the industry are similar to those of the pharmaceutical industry with emphasis on laboratory notebooks and research and development records. Documentation and records of processes undertaken were also created, the equivalent of recipe books. Plans of work and plant were also vital to the production process as were operating handbooks and maintenance records. The plant could be very extensive, covering several acres with a number of buildings all of which required to be maintained and leased or purchased. Details of plant and equipment were recorded in plant and property registers, including a description, the name of the manufacturer or builder, the date of acquisition, the cost, depreciation and the date of disposal and price realised.

Correspondence and documentation concerning patents, processes, supply of raw materials and licensing agreements are distinctive for the industry. Leading companies producing particular chemicals were often involved with international consortia of other producers established to share technical knowledge, patents and personnel. Such consortia created minutes of meetings, report and correspondence files.

Consumer goods

Most long-established consumer goods companies have their origins in small single-product factories, often established in the nineteenth century, which went on to swallow up their rivals and acquire related businesses. They often went on to sell their products overseas and then establish manufacturing bases there, until they became global enterprises like Unilever, Procter & Gamble and Nestlé. Unilever, for example, was formed from the merger of Lever Brothers in the United Kingdom and the Margarine Union, a combine of family firms in The Netherlands and Eastern Europe. William Lever was the first manufacturer to produce and sell individually wrapped bars of household soap. In the 1880s, when he started manufacturing, soap production in the United Kingdom was locally based, with every major town having its own soap company. He used increasing industrialisation and transport improvements to ship his products across the United Kingdom, and later the globe, buying up his rivals along the way. Using the same raw materials he expanded into margarine manufacture and came into competition with the Van den Bergh and Jurgens families (who went on to form the Margarine Union).

All three companies were tapping into an increasingly prosperous working class, which saw soap and margarine as necessities of life, not luxuries. They, Procter & Gamble and other manufacturers took advantage of increasingly cheaper printing costs to advertise their products to the housewife, promoting many of them as a means of easing her workload. Examples of the sheer quantity and quality of the advertising from the nineteenth and early twentieth centuries and the myriad ways in which Lever and his peers sought to promote their products, from on-pack coupons, to gift offers for wrappers collected and sent in, to the use of fine art[6] and publicity stunts[7] can all be found in a company's archives.

Today, the key activity for any consumer goods company is still marketing. Promotional campaigns create a wide range of records, not all in the form of traditional document-based archival materials. There will probably also be many three dimensional artefacts, such as packaging and point-of-sale items and also film and sound archives related to television and radio advertising. Paper records may include scripts for commercials, price lists, brochures and press releases.

Many companies have their own research and development laboratories and the records created are similar in scope to those described in relation to the pharmaceutical industry, such as laboratory notebooks, technical specifications and clinical trials, but also include recipes and formulae, shelf life evaluations and consumer panel test reports. There are also records relating to quality control, ISO 14001[8] certification and environmental concerns, such as emissions and waste disposal. The manufacturing process is recorded in production plans, production logs and stock control and analysis, whilst the sourcing and transport of raw materials and the delivery of finished goods to retailers within the supply chain are largely reflected in financial records such as purchase orders, invoices and shipping documents, and also legal contracts.

Brewing

The brewing industry is based on a number of processes that transform basic raw materials – malt, hops, water and yeast – into beer to be delivered to a wholesale or retail customer in either bulk or small individual containers. The change from a domestic to a commercial industry, which began in the United Kingdom in the late eighteenth century, ensured that records were created for the first time and technology, legislation and the size and structure of the industry has affected record creation subsequently. By the second half of the twentieth century, the industry became one of large-plant technology, mass-production, mass marketing and control of retailing with global companies such as Anheuser-Busch InBev, SABMiller, Heineken, Carlsberg and China Resources Enterprise, concentrating production and brands worldwide.

Investment capital was required to start or expand a brewery and the brewery industry by the nineteenth century was dominated by large partnerships, which required governance records in order to manage partners' shareholdings at year end or upon the withdrawal of a partner. Breweries required premises and equipment for initial production, ancillary operations, storage for raw material and final product and ancillary workshops (container production or storage). This created particular real estate records within the industry – title deeds, rent and rate books, insurance records and other property books. From the late nineteenth century British brewers 'tied' their retail trade to their beer and property records may document investment in retail outlets to both stop competitors selling rival beers within their area and create outlets within a transportable area of production. Breweries lending to publicans also created such records as loan ledgers and bond books.

Beer also had to be transported, initially by horses and later by steam and diesel, owned or outsourced. Records were created relating to the maintenance and use of transport; such as purchase, depreciation and repair ledgers. However, the most distinctive records were those of production. Documentation was elaborate as the industry's raw material, along with the product, was excised. Brewers had to declare to excise gaugers (tax officials) the quantities intended for each gyle (brewing) of beer brewed and the timing of the different processes. The record created was called a gauge book and was entered up weekly for the excise official who also kept his own records. Brewers also kept exact records of production in case of dispute over surveys and to be able to claim allowances for batches that went bad and such like. They were also required to keep records to ensure that they could make timely orders for raw materials such as hops or malt (often cultivated out of their region and later out of their country) and to keep control of materials bought on commission or account to stop cheating – if excised goods were lost or damaged the tax could be reclaimed. Efficient records of production, quantities and prices in buying, and stocks were essential to run a successful business.

Systematic accounting was essential as the business was made up of a multitude of small sums to and from numerous suppliers and customers. Beer was often supplied on six months' credit, so again careful accounting was required. Beer is a relatively cheap, bulky product and so the amount of profit on individual transactions was small. To ensure that the business prospered and stakeholders received a return, efficient book-keeping was essential to minimise fraud, waste, bad debts and inefficient operations.

Brewers also needed to keep good documentation about raw materials (as do all business that use recipes) to ensure that the various ingredients were mixed correctly in order to obtain a consistent standard of strength, colour and flavour. Profitable brewing businesses were always matching price against quality and consistency in product with suppliers to ensure their profit margins and market share. It was vital for brewing firms to continually scrutinise the entries in malt, hop and other stock books, the detailed production record of the ingredients of each brew and the costs of the raw materials against the output of beers of different strengths and flavour. So, as Peter Mathias (1990, p. 30) states, the only records particular to the brewing industry are the brewing books recording the details of each brew – brew books, waste books, fermenting books, racking books, licensed house property and tenancy records and return books. All other records found in the brewing industry – purchasing, plant, marketing records and so on – are shared with other kinds of business.

During the latter half of the twentieth century the design and packaging of beer and bottles, and point of sales advertising became an important part of a firm's sales and marketing strategy. New product designs, labelling and packaging, including docu-mentation concerning their introduction were accumulated as a record of product marketing.

Architects

Architectural practices are usually sole traders or partnerships. In the United Kingdom, the first non-family firms began to appear in the mid-nineteenth century. Architects win commissions for buildings through competitive tendering, entering a competition or by selection, the means usually being dependent on the client, whether public or private. Once commissioned, or earlier, if competition or tendering was the means of selection, the initial practical records to be created will be sketches and preliminary design drawings, often presented in a portfolio or other elaborate presentation in video or digital format. On acceptance of the design, more drawings are undertaken. Historically, with the development of technology, drawings have grown larger and more detailed.

The most distinctive records of the architectural practice are the drawings. To construct a building detailed working drawings were required giving a complete survey of the proposed building in scale drawings comprising plans, elevations and sections. Copies of the drawings were made for sub-contractors to be able to tender for the building work and to comply with local building and planning regulations. Contract

Table 5.2 Architectural drawing types

Plan	Information shown on the drawing
Block plan	Shows buildings and layouts in simplified, undetailed form.
Detail drawing	Shows a small part of the construction at a larger scale, to show how the component parts fit together.
Elevations	Shows a vertical view of a building or object seen from one side, a flat representation of one façade.
Floor plan	The view from above of a building, to illustrate the arrangement of spaces/rooms in a building.
Site plan	Shows the whole context of a building or group of buildings. Gives an overview of the entire scope of the work.
Section/ cross-sectional	Shows a view of the building or object cut along an axis to reveal the interior.

drawings, a complete set of working drawings, were signed by the client, architect and main contractors. Technology has progressively transformed the creation and copying of drawings. Initially created on starched linen and tracing paper, the arrival of chemical processes and then photography introduced blueprints and dyelines, while most recently computer technology has revolutionised their production and form. From the early nineteenth century in the United Kingdom, the 'artist's impression' of the finished building in its surrounding environment also became a key drawing. Models, fulfilling a similar function, were also created. Each project was given a job number and recorded in job books, which were used to identify drawings.

In order to control building projects architects require good means of communication to stay in touch with progress. Initially this was achieved by means of letters, subsequently supplemented by reports and photographic evidence. As the building process was formalised more records series were created such as detailed specifications for quantity surveyors, fee books recording income from clients, certificates recording satisfactory completion of various phases of construction and diaries and time records recording the time spent on work for particular clients so that fees could be calculated.

Utilities

In the United Kingdom, utility companies – providers of gas, water and electricity – were privately owned joint-stock companies until the mid-twentieth century when they became state owned. They were denationalised from the 1980s. Utility companies are large undertakings with substantial plant, infrastructure and large numbers of employees. Vital records for utility companies are their plant records and operational reports. Companies created and maintained 'as built' drawings of plant layouts and distribution systems, design drawings and construction specifications for original plant and modifications and many series of photographs of plant, component and operational conditions. Constant monitoring of the performance and state of equipment and infrastructure as well as production was carried out, resulting in consulting engineers' and managers' periodic and annual reports.

Extraction – mining minerals, oil and gas

The industrial revolution in the United Kingdom transformed mining as new machinery – steam-driven pumps, engines and drills – expanded existing mines and established new ones. The growing use of technology required increasing finance, leading to joint-stock companies being formed. Many mining concerns are now huge international or multinational concerns with vast financial resources as large sums of money are often invested for many years before any return is made. The mining industry also requires a strong public relations function as businesses liaise with the general public and other bodies, maintain the corporate image against criticism, and convince local and national environmental groups of their case. Records created include reports, press releases, films and other presentations of projects and technical leaflets.

At each stage of a mining project, local government regulations have to be taken into account. Concessions usually require a licence to proceed at every stage of exploration – for prospecting and reconnaissance, exploration, exploitation, refinery and treatment plants, pipelines and transportation. Such concessions result in legal contracts, agreements and licences with supporting correspondence and papers. The extraction of minerals by licence involves the payment of taxes and royalties to the owner of the minerals. Royalty records detailing production and the price per unit of the mineral with the royalty due are maintained.

Technical records are also distinctive and cover all aspects of exploration from preliminary survey to full-scale production and distribution. In the preliminary study stage existing information and records are re-examined and reports and images from remote sensing images created. Reconnaissance and follow-up surveys can create geological maps, plans, reports and field notebooks; samples, data from samples, maps, laboratory notebooks and geochemical reports; geophysical survey sheets, maps and plans, notebooks, computer modelling and imaging results. The exploratory drilling stage tests the results of the preliminary surveys to determine the extent of the mineralisation. Core samples are logged and the samples and other materials are analysed.

A feasibility study is then undertaken to evaluate the legal, economic, social and environmental and technical factors required to operate the project. If the study is favourable, production may begin either as a pilot for a set period or full-scale. Once it has been agreed that a project is feasible the infrastructure has to be put in place – communication routes, accommodation, plant and equipment – and contracts put out for tender. Operations will begin, the mineral extracted, processed and transported. Quality control samples are taken at all stages of processing, waste products are monitored and regeneration and reclamation carried out as appropriate. Records created or accumulated at this stage include government regulations, concessions, royalty records, labour agreements, tenders, contracts, licences, maps and plans, photographs and models, specifications and drawings, operating manuals for plant and machinery, service contracts, quality control records, production registers, sales records, shipment records, staff records and environmental monitoring records.

Mechanical engineering

The earliest mechanical engineering firms were formed in the United Kingdom during the industrial revolution when iron replaced wood as the material with which to construct machines. Other advances made at this time were improvements in the steam engine, the mechanisation of the textile industry and the development of hydraulic engineering. Initially, the industry consisted of small workshops which could not guarantee accuracy of manufacture and standardisation and the interchange of parts was impossible. From the early nineteenth century engineers began to develop machine tools, such as lathes, steam hammers and planing and drilling machines, which allowed faster and more accurate production. Huge works began to be built where the foundry and production shops could be accommodated together, but until the second half of the century these were rarely specialised but made a wide range of machinery for many different industries.

Cheap open-hearth steel became available from the 1850s and other inventions followed, such as the safety boiler, steam turbine and the internal combustion engine at the end of the century. Many engineering firms began to specialise in machinery or parts for a particular purpose or product and sub-division of labour led to many new series of records being created as managers strove to inform and control production. By 1900 specialised engineers had emerged with expertise in contracting, erecting, and later production, and the First World War accelerated mass-production. Specialisation continued throughout the twentieth century as technology advanced introducing new materials and new fields such as nuclear engineering.

The records of engineering firms are distinctive in the way in which their production records are created and referenced. Engineering firms usually win business or jobs by transforming enquiries from potential customers into confirmed orders, by supplying a quote via a tendering process. Different systems to manage the potential order from tender to finished product will have existed over time and were often described in a contract or order procedure book, which explained the process. Initially an enquiry to the sales department would be allocated a reference number and be recorded in an enquiry or order book. Each confirmed order would be given a unique contract/order/job number and all contract work and any modifications or extras would be carried out under this number. Later replacement parts could be recorded in a separate series and/or a supplementary number. Contract/job books were ordered by contract number and the sales day book or sales book or sales index cards would provide details of the customer, via the contract number. Different firms had different practices for allocating contract numbers: single series or blocks, separate series for different products or markets or alphabetical sections for different parts of the plant ordered. Distinct prefixes may have been used for contract materials, drawing, erection, transport and so on; whilst sub-contractors used their own contract number series and where products were mass produced, rather than custom made, batch numbers were often employed.

Once an enquiry was made the design office or projects department prepared original sketches and, for new tenders, approved detailed calculations and drawings and collected data on tests. The unit determined the materials required and how far the customer specifications could be met. The records that it created included project books, drawings and sketches, design studies and technical papers, including calculations and test reports. The costing department was involved with the contract at both the estimating and the production stages, providing information on basic costs from which the estimating department could calculate prices and also control the costs of production. The records created include works, time materials and overhead cost books, cost and weight books, stock books and cost control accounts.

The estimating department, often part of the costing department, calculated the price of a job and often retained information on scales of wages and rates of production and weight registers from previous jobs. Records created include estimate cost sheets and books, offer letter, tender approval forms, specification forms detailing requirements, delivery date and method and standard conditions. The contracting or sales department administered the contracts once the tender had been accepted by co-ordinating the activities of the various processing departments. Records created include contract/job/order books and indexes, spares order books, estimate books and contract records.

The drawing office created the various types of designs and drawings required for product production; general arrangements, major sub-assemblies and details. For firms with a standard product, such as a specific machine tool, one set of drawings might be used for hundreds of thousands of products. Firms producing a product built to the specifications of a particular customer, such as locomotives, ships or boilers, prepared a set of drawings for each bespoke product. Drawing registers resulted, recording drawing numbers and providing a brief description of the contents. Table 5.3 describes the most common types of mechanical engineering drawings. Much of the information required to describe technical drawings is often present on the drawing itself in the form of a title block. A title block refers to the practice, which emerged in the twentieth century, of recording information in one corner of the drawing. The block generally provides the title and type of plan, date, order/job/contract numbers and scale used. The names of the business, architects/engineer/designer and draughtsmen who worked on the drawing may also be recorded.

The purchasing/buying department was responsible for the purchasing of materials and parts and the control of stock. The records created by this department include bought/purchase ledgers, buyers' abstract books, detailing materials to be ordered and dates required, ordered and delivered, material specification/works material books, stock books, stock inventories and valuations and inventory books.

The control and organisation of production varied greatly between firms. Records created included job inspection books, quality assurance manuals, machine books, weekly production statements, forward load assessments, production diaries, pattern registers, metal mixture books, assembly work books, actual and estimate cost comparison books, duplicate job books, drawings and photographs.

The dispatch department was responsible for the packing and shipping of completed plant and spares. It created records including dispatch books; goods sent out daybooks;

Table 5.3 Common mechanical engineering drawing types

Plan	Information shown on the drawing
Assembly drawing	Shows how a product is put together and illustrates fit and function.
Detail drawing	Shows a small part of the construction at a larger scale, to show how the component parts fit together.
Elevation	Shows a vertical view of an object seen from one side, a flat representation of one aspect of it.
General arrangement	Shows an overall view of the product and may also show how the component parts fit together.
Section/ cross-sectional	Shows a view of the object cut along an axis to reveal the interior.

and shipping documents. The erecting department was responsible for the assembly and commissioning of plant on site and created erecting instructions and manuals, erecting engineers' notebooks and reports, test reports, inspection and test certificates, technical circulars to erectors and photographs. The servicing and maintenance department was responsible for setting, testing and maintaining plant supplied by the firm by training customer staff and undertaking repairs, refurbishment and general maintenance. It created such records as repairs books, technical circulars to service engineers, service engineers' notebooks and reports and photographs.

If the firm had important patent rights to administer and protect, this activity might be administered by a patents department. Firms with extensive work premises created records relating to the buildings, plant and machine tools, such as property registers, architectural drawings, inventories and valuations and insurance policies.

Retailing

The modern retailing industry with fixed shops began, in the United Kingdom, in the eighteenth century and soon ranged in scale from small, specialised local shops to large department or chain stores. Many retailers expanded by vertical integration into wholesaling, distribution and financial services and by merger. Distinctive records created by the industry include marketing records – newspaper advertisements, handbills, price lists, catalogues and videos and films of television commercials and other advertising and records relating to campaigns launching new products. Records were also created of packaging products and design in order to develop and protect brands.

Customer records include accounts, receipts and passbooks, circulars, correspondence and credit agreements. Buying records include suppliers' correspondence and notebooks but rarely survive in quantity. Box 5.2 provides a function and activity model for the arrangement of the industry's records.

Selecting records for preservation

In-house corporate archivists will have the kind of clear understanding of the goals, functions and activities of the business, to which a collecting archivist can only aspire. Corporate archivists are consequently well placed to choose what functions and activities need to be documented in order to fulfil the mission and aims of their archives and the businesses they serve. For companies who trade on their brand (such as food and drink companies) the mission of the archive may be to protect and promote the brand and so the key records to be selected will come from the marketing function. By understanding the activities of a business the corporate archivist can choose to document the activities of most value and importance to the company. These can cover many functions and many activities within each function.

For archivists in collecting archives the opportunities for selection are limited, by both a lack of understanding of the functions and activities of the business concerned and the access to surviving records. Selection is often made from a much-reduced pool of records, which have survived the winnowing hand of time – what records happen to remain in a geographical area, a former factory, a sales office or a head office building. The potential of the once complete fonds needs to be envisaged as selection is made. The core records of a business may always be important for evidential purposes, but the informational value

Box 5.2 Function and activity model for the United Kingdom retail industry

1. Governance

Description of function:

The function of self-regulation and setting of the boundaries within which the company operates. It includes developing the company's legal framework and ensuring compliance with all relevant legislation, developing the corporate governance structure and rules, and conducting the business of the corporate body and the executive committees in accordance with those rules.

List of activities:

1.1 Legal compliance management
1.2 Legal framework development
1.3 Governance structure development
1.4 Corporate body management
1.5 Executive committee management
1.6 Senior officers' appointments management

2. Strategic planning and performance management

Description of function:

The function of developing and establishing the direction of the company, setting targets to develop financial gain and investment and managing the performance of the company in attaining targets at an overall company level (not individual outlet level).

List of activities:

2.1 Corporate policy development
2.2 Corporate procedures development
2.3 Corporate strategy development
2.4 Corporate strategic planning
2.5 Corporate strategic performance management

3. Corporate retail management

Description of function:

The function of joined-up management of the company and its retail outlets.

List of activities:

3.1 Retail strategy development
3.2 Retail management planning
3.3 Retail management performance management
3.4 Retail management policy development
3.5 Retail management procedures development
3.6 Retail outlet proposal development
3.7 Retail outlet planning
3.8 Retail outlet promotion

4. Merchandising

Description of function:

The function of buying and selling.

List of activities:

4.1 Merchandise planning
4.2 Buying management
4.3 Stock management
4.4 Pricing management
4.5 Sales management
4.6 Customer services management

5. Marketing

Description of function:

The function of identifying customers and advertising, promoting and displaying goods.

List of activities:

5.1 Market research management
5.2 Advertising management
5.3 Sales promotion management
5.4 Display management

6. Financial management

Description of function:

The function of managing the company's financial resources.

List of activities:

6.1 Finance strategy development
6.2 Finance management planning
6.3 Finance management performance management
6.4 Finance management policy development
6.5 Finance management procedures development
6.6 Financial audit
6.7 Financial accounting
6.8 Management accounting
6.9 Statutory accounting
6.10 Internal accounting
6.11 Budget management
6.12 Payroll administration
6.13 Pension contributions administration
6.14 Tax management
6.15 Cash management
6.16 Asset management

7. Investment management

Description of function:

The function of creating the financial growth of the company with responsibilities for shareholding activities.

List of activities:

7.1 Investment planning and strategy development
7.2 Investment performance management
7.3 Investment monitoring
7.4 Ethical investment monitoring
7.5 Shareholding administration

8. Audit

Description of function:

The function of conducting audits of the company's affairs and operations to ensure compliance with corporate, industry, legal or regulatory requirements. These consist of both internal and external audits and can focus on a particular function or activity.

List of activities:

8.1 Procedures audit

8.2 Records audit
8.3 Business process audit
8.4 Performance audit

9. Legal affairs management

Description of function:

The function of managing the company's legal affairs including ensuring regulation and compliance requirements are met.

List of activities:

9.1 Contracts and agreements management
9.2 Legal claims management
9.3 Litigation management
9.4 Legal and interpretation advice provision

10. Quality management

Description of function:

The function of managing the overall quality of the company. This includes quality of services, products and company administration and compliance.

List of activities:

10.1 Quality level setting and prompt setting
10.2 Business process inspection
10.3 Quality level check
10.4 Staff and customer feedback

11. Risk management

Description of function:

The function of managing risks to the company and within the company. These can be financial, legal, compliance and regulatory, operational, environmental and confidentiality risks.

List of activities:

11.1 Insurance management
11.2 Risk identification and assessment
11.3 Business continuity planning
11.4 Disaster planning

12. Organisational development

Description of function:

The function of developing the company structure and culture.

List of activities:

12.1 Organisational restructuring management
12.2 Change management
12.3 Organisational review
12.4 Benchmarking
12.5 Membership of industry and professional organisations

13. Health and safety management

Description of function:

The function of identifying and managing the risks associated with health and safety within an organisation, ensuring compliance with legislation.

List of activities:

13.1 Health and safety consultation
13.2 Health and safety information, inspection and training provision
13.3 Health and safety hazard identification and risk assessment
13.4 Hazardous substance exposure control
13.5 Health and safety inspection
13.6 Health and safety recording, reporting and investigation
13.7 Employee health surveillance
13.8 Emergency planning

14. Environment management

Description of function:

The function of managing the impact of the company and its business on the environment and ensuring compliance with environmental legislation.

List of activities:

14.1 Environmental hazard identification and risk assessment
14.2 Environmental management scheme accredited management
14.3 Environmental awareness promotion
14.4 Environmental incident reporting, recording and investigation
14.5 Energy management
14.6 Waste management

15. Estate management

Description of function:

The function of managing the company's real property such as land, buildings and fixed structures.

List of activities:

15.1 Property acquisition
15.2 Property development
15.3 Property maintenance (including grounds maintenance)
15.4 Property disposal
15.5 Property and facility compliance management
15.6 Property and facility security management
15.7 Property leasing out
15.8 Facility development
15.9 Facility maintenance
15.10 Facility relocation management

16. Human resources management

Description of function:

The function of managing the company's workforce as a whole, and individual employees, whether permanent or fixed.

List of activities:

16.1 Workforce planning
16.2 Workforce recruitment
16.3 Workforce induction
16.4 Workforce training and development
16.5 Workforce performance management
16.6 Workforce remuneration and reward management
16.7 Workforce welfare management
16.8 Workforce relations management
16.9 Employee contract management
16.10 Industrial relations management
16.11 Pension schemes administration

17. Information resources management

Description of function:

The function of managing the information resources generated or acquired by the company in the course of its work to support its work.

List of activities:

17.1 Data Protection Act compliance management
17.2 Freedom of Information Act compliance management
17.3 Copyright compliance management
17.4 Records management
17.5 Archives management
17.6 Library materials management
17.7 Publications management
17.8 Information and communications technology (ICT) systems development
17.9 ICT systems operations management
17.10 ICT systems security management
17.11 ICT systems user support

18. Communications management

Description of function:

The function of managing the company's external communication and relationships with the public and media.

List of activities:

18.1 Public communication management
18.2 Public relations event management
18.3 Corporate identity and brand management
18.4 Media communication management
18.5 Industry communication management
18.6 Community relations communication and event management

19. Purchasing and procurement

Description of function:

The function of acquiring ownership or use of goods, works or services apart from property acquisition.

List of activities:

19.1 Supplier approval
19.2 Supply contract tendering
19.3 Supply contract management
19.4 Purchasing administration

20. Equipment and consumables management

Description of function:

The function of managing the equipment and consumables purchased and used by the company.

List of activities:

20.1 Equipment and consumables selection
20.2 Equipment and consumables storage
20.3 Equipment and consumables commissioning and installation
20.4 Equipment and consumables inspection and testing
20.5 Equipment and consumables maintenance
20.6 Equipment and consumables disposal

21. Supply chain management (including wholesale, transportation and storage)

Description of function:

The function of managing the flow of materials (products), information and finances as they move in a process from supplier to manufacturer to wholesaler to retailer to consumer.

List of activities:

21.1 Customer service management
21.2 Procurement
21.3 Product development and commercialisation
21.4 Manufacturing flow management and support
21.5 Physical distribution
21.6 Outsourcing and partnerships
21.7 Performance measurement (for the above activities)

Acknowledgement: Glasgow University Archive Services.

of the non-core records of a business of a specific industry may be of value to an archive attempting to document variety or speciality within a region. In fact, the records of a business within a particular industry may be of no value without the records specific to that industry. Other variables such as the size or importance of a company to the region in which it operated will also be of importance if an appraisal strategy, involving a documentation strategy and/or collection and functional analysis, such as the Minnesota method, is being used by a collecting archive (Greene and Daniels-Howell, 1997).

Understanding the objectives, organisation and functions of a business, and the activities covered by its extant records, are a vital first stage in selecting business records of value for permanent preservation as archives. For most archivists, industry-specific records, which can include a preponderance of quite technical records, can be very daunting, as gaining an understanding of the informational content of such records often involves gaining some understanding of the technical processes involved in the production of long-disused material by long-abandoned techniques. Acquiring an insight into the nature of such records can often only be achieved by reading contemporary manuals and technical histories or by consulting technical experts.

Acknowledgements

The author is very grateful to all the contributors and reviewers who improved this chapter with their knowledge and expertise. The following read and commented on the chapter as a whole, Alex Bieri (Roche), Dr Karl-Peter Ellerbrock (Westfälisches Wirtschaftsarchiv), Terry Gourvish (London School of Economics), Morgan Henning (A. P. Moller–Maersk), Yuko Matsuzaki (Shibusawa Eii'ichi Memorial Foundation), Michael Moss (Northumbria University) and Bruce Smith (archive consultant, Australia). Additionally Jeannette Strickland (consultant, United Kingdom), Shona Sinclair (Hawick Museum) and Helen Taylor (Heriot-Watt University) provided expert advice on particular record types. Special thanks go to Kiara King (University of Glasgow and The Ballast Trust) for compiling the technical record tables and providing comment that has improved the chapter overall.

Notes

1   For the reasons why records are created see International Organization for Standardization (ISO), 2001. *BS ISO 15489–1:2001. Information and documentation. Records management. General.* Geneva: ISO.
2   For example 'Basel III' (or the Third Basel Accord) is a comprehensive set of reform measures, developed by the Basel Committee on Banking Supervision, to strengthen the regulation, supervision and risk management of the banking sector. [online] Available at: www.bis.org/bcbs/basel3.htm [Accessed 3 September 2016].
3   The development of generic models of organisations' functions and activities provides a useful tool to support archivists undertaking archival appraisal of records and applying retention schedules and also enhances user understanding of archival finding aids. For a model for institutions of higher education see www.jiscinfonet.ac.uk/partnerships/records-retention-he [Accessed 3 September 2016] and *Developing archival context standards for functions in the higher education sector: final report.* [pdf] Glasgow University Archive Services. Available at: www.gashe.ac.uk/news/final_report.pdf [Accessed 3 September 2016].
4   Office for National Statistics, UK standard industrial classification of economic activities 2007. [online] Available at: www.ons.gov.uk/ons/guide-method/classifications/current-standard-classifications/standard-industrial-classification/index.html [Accessed 3 September 2016].
5   In the United Kingdom surveys of the surviving records of many of these business sectors have been undertaken by the Business Archives Council and published in a series entitled *Studies in British business archives*, details of which are listed in the further reading bibliography at the end of the chapter.
6   The use of fine art in advertising was pioneered by Thomas Barratt when he purchased a painting from the artist John Everett Millais to which he added a bar of soap in the foreground, renaming it 'Bubbles', and used it for advertising Pears' soap.

7   For example, Barratt had the name 'Pears' stamped on French centimes, which passed into usage in the United Kingdom, resulting in a law being passed making it illegal to deface foreign currency.
8   *ISO 14001:2015* is the international standard for environmental management systems.

References

Baer, C. T., 1997. Strategy, structure, detail, functions: four parameters for the appraisal of business records. In: J. M. O'Toole, ed., 1997. *The records of American business*. Chicago, IL: Society of American Archivists. Ch.5.

Bruemmer, B. E., 1997. Avoiding accidents of evidence: functional analysis in the appraisal of business records. In: J. M. O'Toole, ed., 1997. *The records of American business*, Chicago, IL: Society of American Archivists. Ch. 6.

Cockerell, H. A. L. and Green, E., 1994. *The British insurance business, 1547–1970*. 2nd ed. Sheffield: Sheffield Academic Press.

Greene, M. A. and Daniels-Howell, T. J., 1997. Documentation with an attitude: a pragmatist's guide to the selection and acquisition of modern business records. In: J. M. O'Toole, ed., 1997. *The records of American business*. Chicago, IL: Society of American Archivists. Ch.7.

Mathias, P., 1990. Brewing archives: their nature and use. In: L. Richmond and A. Turton, *The brewing industry: a guide to historical records*. Manchester: Manchester University Press.

Further reading

Appleby, R. C., 1994. *Modern business administration*, 6th ed. Harlow: Pearson Education.

Armstrong, J. and Jones, S., 1987. *Business documents. Their origins, sources and uses in historical research*. London: Mansell.

Boyns, R., Boyns, T. and Edwards, J., 2000. *Historical accounting records: a guide for archivists and researches*. Northampton: Society of Archivists.

Business Archives Council and Society of Archivists, 1989. Papers of Business Archives Council and Society of Archivists joint working party on business records 1987–1989. Unpublished.

Cockerell, H. A. L. and Green, E., 1994. *The British insurance business, 1547–1970*. 2nd ed. Sheffield: Sheffield Academic Press.

Edwards, C., 2001. *Railway records: a guide to sources*. London: Public Records Office.

Giffen, L., 2009. *How the Scots financed the modern world*. Edinburgh: Luath Press.

Greene, M. A. and Daniels-Howell, T. J., 1997. Documentation with an attitude: a pragmatist's guide to the selection and acquisition of modern business records. In J. M. O'Toole, ed., 1997. *The records of American business*. Chicago, IL: Society of American Archivists. Ch. 7.

Hapgood, W., 1994. *Chartered accountants: a guide to historical records*. Manchester: Manchester University Press.

Hatheway, A. W., 2012. *Remediation of former manufactured gas plants and other coal-tar sites*. London: CRC Press.

Hudson, P., 1975. *The West Riding wool textile industry: a catalogue of business records from the sixteenth to the twentieth century*. Pasold Occasional Papers, III. Edington: Pasold Research Fund.

Hunter, P., 2004. *Veterinary medicine: a guide to historical sources*. Aldershot: Ashgate Press.

International Council on Archives Architectural Records Section, 2000. *A guide to the archival care of architectural records 19–20th centuries*. Paris: International Council on Archives.

Mathias, P. and Pearsall, A. W. H., 1971. *Shipping: a survey of historical records*. Newton Abbot: David & Charles.

Moss, M. S. and Hume, J. R., 1977. *Workshop of the British Empire. Engineering and shipbuilding in the west of Scotland*. London: Heinemann.

Orbell, M. J. and Turton, A., 2001. *Banking: a guide to historical records*. Manchester: Manchester University Press.

Orbell, M. J., 2009. *A guide to tracing the history of a business*. 2nd ed. Chichester: Phillimore & Co.

O'Toole, J. M., 1997. *The records of American business*. Chicago, IL: The Society of American Archivists.

Richmond, L. and Stockford, B., 1986. *Company archives: the survey of the records of 1000 of the first registered companies in England and Wales*. Aldershot: Gower.

Richmond, L. and Turton, A., 1990. *The brewing industry: a guide to historical records*. Manchester: Manchester University Press.

Richmond, L., Stevenson, J. and Turton, A., 2003. *The pharmaceutical industry: a guide to historical records*. Aldershot: Ashgate Press.

Ritchie, A., 1992. *The shipbuilding industry: a guide to historical records*. Manchester: Manchester University Press.

The Royal Commission on Historical Manuscripts, 1990. *Records of British business and industry: 1760–1914: textiles and leather*. London: HMSO.

The Royal Commission on Historical Manuscripts, 1994. *Records of British business and industry: 1760–1914: metal processing and engineering*. London: HMSO.

Part 3

Managing business archives

Chapter 6

Organisation and objectives

Jeannette Strickland

If asked to characterise a business archive, many people would describe either an archivist working entirely on their own, or a state of the art service with a large budget at its disposal; both sitting firmly within the company itself administratively speaking, even if physically located remotely from the head office. However, neither is an accurate representation of business archives in general. What this chapter will explore is the wide diversity of business archive services and how they are run and organised. It will demonstrate that there is no single best practice model.

Where are business archives usually located?

In-house

The most obvious location for a business archive is within the parent company itself. There are many examples of this from a wide of range of different sectors around the world, including BT (telecommunications), Fortnum & Mason (retail) and Unilever (consumer goods) in the United Kingdom; Guinness (brewing) in Ireland; Coca-Cola (soft drinks), McKinsey (management consultancy) and Procter & Gamble (consumer goods) in the United States; Godrej (a business conglomerate) in India; F. Hoffmann–La Roche (pharmaceuticals) in Switzerland; A. P. Moller–Maersk (shipping) and Grundfos (pump manufacturers) in Denmark; Evonik (chemicals) in Germany; Intesa Sanpaolo (banking) in Italy; and SNCF (railways) in France. Some in-house business archives operate across several countries to reflect the global nature of their parent business. HSBC, for example, has archive units in the United Kingdom, France, Hong Kong and the United States of America, whilst Mondelēz International, primarily based in the United States of America, has branches in the United Kingdom, Germany and Australia.

In the United Kingdom, The National Archives (2009) estimates that 20 per cent of FTSE companies, as well as many smaller concerns, employ an archivist to manage their archives in-house. In some instances the tradition of record keeping is a long one. BP has found references to an archive in 1921, albeit not necessarily an archive in the sense we understand it today, but certainly an ambition that information should be captured for posterity. The Royal Bank of Scotland has an example of a retention schedule dating from 1874 and Unilever from 1935, demonstrating that organising records and information has long been of importance to companies. The Bank of England led the way in the United Kingdom business sector with the appointment of an archivist in the 1930s, but the appointment of in-house archivists did not really gather pace until four decades later. In the United States there was also a considerable rise in the number of archives being established by major corporations in the 1970s and 1980s as they started to recognise the value of archives to defend intellectual property and help with their marketing campaigns (Adkins, 1997). For many businesses the key benefit in maintaining an in-house archive is the safeguarding of its data, a corporate asset, which is easily retrievable when information is needed, whilst its own archivists have in-depth knowledge of both the company and its collections, so can provide a tailor-made service and not only respond quickly, but also anticipate demand. The archivists are also aware of the sensitivities and confidentiality of commercially valuable records.

What all these in-house business archives have in common is that they are naturally accruing archives, in other words their primary function is to collect and care for the records of their parent company. In many cases this will also include predecessor and subsidiary companies and, possibly, the papers of the family which established the business. Some may also accept donations of material from the general public, pensioners and current staff, whilst others actively collect related material such as the personal papers of board members. All these archives, however, at heart, contain simply the records of the parent business and it is this that sets the in-house service apart from business archives held in most other institutions.

Charitable trusts

In many ways a business archive sitting within a charitable trust is very similar to an in-house service, as the collection will, primarily, be that of the founding company and the company will also be one of the major clients of the trust, and perhaps the only one. The main differences lie in the governance and funding of the service, both of which will be discussed later in this chapter. So why would a company set up a charitable trust in which to place its archives? The main driver could be to ring-fence and protect the archive. There is a growing trend in the United Kingdom for museums to move from local authority control to an independent trust in an attempt to avoid funding cuts, building closures or the mothballing of collections.[1] Archive services in local government and the private sector may increasingly be forced down the same route. Some of the intangible benefits include less bureaucracy and greater scope for entrepreneurialism, as well as more flexibility and the freedom to make decisions and be more responsive to new opportunities. Tangible benefits, certainly in the United Kingdom, include the ability to bid for external grants and benefit from reduced business rates for premises.

It is vital to retain a good working relationship with the former parent organisation as it will, usually, be the major funder of the trust. This will be particularly important if the funding is transferred by annual subsidy rather than an investment endowment. So it is also essential to appoint trustees who not only understand the archive, but are also capable of managing investments and the expectations of the funders. Reasons for retaining amicable links include keeping open communication channels so that the trust is aware of any developments in the parent organisation that may affect the trust, and also to ensure the continued flow of material into the archive from the records management service. If there is no such service then the trust's archivists will need to work even harder to ensure that the archive continues to grow naturally.

There are downsides to running a business archive service within a trust. The most common is overestimating the amount of funding that the trust will be able to raise, whether from investments or grant applications, leaving the trust open to the risk of an annual shortfall in income. In some local authority services a belief among ratepayers that museums and archives should remain in public ownership could also be a deterrent to moving to trust status. For services in both the public and private sectors the potential loss of access to the parent organisation's facilities, such as legal and human resources services, could pose additional problems, whilst the amount of time and resources that have to be expended on running the trust could cost more than the service charges paid to the former parent organisation. Also, whilst staff transferring to the trust may retain by law the same terms and conditions of employment, any newly appointed staff could be on completely different contracts, which may lead to dissension. In drawing up any agreement the trust must take care not to leave itself open to threat of sale to meet company losses, as in the case of the Wedgwood Archive. When Waterford Wedgwood went into administration in 2009 the company had a pension deficit of £134 million. As the museum (of which the archive was a part) was still solvent and five employees were in the pension plan, pension law meant that the full debt was transferred to the museum, which then also went into administration. The High Court ruled that the museum and archive collections should be sold and only through the efforts of The Arts Council, Heritage Lottery Fund and public donations was the necessary £15.75 million raised to purchase the collection for the nation.

Examples of business archives held within trusts in the United Kingdom include the Royal Mail archives, held by The Postal Museum, the archives of C. & J. Clark Ltd, shoemakers, held by the Alfred Gillett Trust, The Baring Archive and The Rothschild Archive, but the governance models and funding arrangements vary substantially. For example, in return for the gift of the Rothschild archive, the trustees signed a licence with the bank to permit it, on condition of its support in terms of premises, staff and budget, to exploit the collection. The Rothschild family play an important role in the care of the archive, with several of them serving as trustees, because it is their family heritage as much as it is that of the bank, which gives them a vested interest in ensuring its longevity. The Postal Heritage Trust, now branded as The Postal Museum, was set up by Royal Mail in 2004 to safeguard its postal heritage in response to large-scale changes in the management and delivery of postal services. It is a much larger trust than The Rothschild Archive with a communications manager and an access and learning manager, as well as archive and museum professionals, as part of its compliment of staff. Similar trusts have been set up overseas including the Alfried Krupp von Bohlen und Halbach Foundation (Krupp) in Germany, the Iron Library Foundation (Georg Fischer) in Switzerland and the Fondazione Pirelli in Italy.

A development from the trust model is the creation of 'fund raising foundations', which are garnering interest in the heritage sector. The governance model stays the same, with the archive or museum reporting to its parent organisation but, by creating a charitable body to fund raise, it provides access to the same grants and tax breaks as trusts and offers a new way to bring in revenue from sources that might not otherwise be accessible. Examples include Tyne & Wear Archives & Museums Development Trust set up in 2010, Norfolk Museums' Development Foundation in 2013 and Explore York in 2014.

Specialist repositories

Business archives may also be found in specialist repositories, which are either dedicated to business archives or which take in business records as part of a broader mission. In the United Kingdom many such specialist repositories are linked to universities, but there

Table 6.1 The different structures for charitable archive trusts

Aspect	Options	Comment
Governance	Archives owned by the trust, for example Rothschild Archives loaned by the parent company, for example the Baring Archive loaned by ING to The Baring Archive Ltd, a charitable company Ownership of collections split between the trust and parent company, for example the records of the Royal Mail and Post Office Ltd are public records so ownership of the deposited collections remains with the creating companies, but the former National Postal Museum collections were donated to The Postal Heritage Trust (now known as The Postal Museum)	The archives may be more secure, but the agreement needs to have watertight funding arrangements The trust will need an agreement to ensure the long-term stability and viability of the archive A deposit agreement will also be needed that should include agreed levels of service in return for support
Funding	From the parent company, for example Rothschild and Baring for premises and operating budget Endowments, family bequests, income from company shares – for example the Alfred Gillett Trust is funded by a combination of all three	A delicate juggling act may be needed to satisfy both the company and the trustees Such an arrangement will need staff or trustees with the financial acumen to manage diverse funding streams
Staffing	Employed by the parent company, for example Rothschild Employed by the trust, for example The Postal Museum and Alfred Gillett Trust	Trusts set up like this need to be aware of the financial liabilities under pensions law as reflected in the Wedgwood case (see page 153) The trust needs to have the capacity for some activities that the parent company would have offered, such as human resources support

are also a few standalone collecting archives, such as the independent History of Advertising Trust, which collects records relating to brand communication and marketing.

In the United States of America in particular, these often take the form of historical societies, which, because of the way they have been established, sit in the private sector. The Minnesota Historical Society (MNHS), founded in 1849, is one example. It is a private, non-profit educational and cultural institution dedicated to preserving the history of the state of Minnesota. MNHS is responsible for 26 museums and historic sites and the Minnesota State Archives and the State Historic Preservation Office are run as departments within it. Its library actively collects corporate records, the records of trade associations and the papers of prominent businessmen to reflect the diversity of economic enterprise across the state from fur trading in the seventeenth century through agribusiness, timber trades and shipbuilding to milling and mining and much more, and holds collections from well-known companies such as 3M, Honeywell and Northwest Airlines. Such repositories may be the solution for small businesses, which do not wish to set up and maintain their own archive or which cannot justify the expense of employing an archivist and creating bespoke storage for a few linear metres of records.

Similarly The History Factory and History Associates, also in the United States of America, which started by providing heritage consultancy, have developed over the years to provide a wide range of services to their clients, including the provision of storage for archive collections. Such consulting firms can also help with the creation of publications, online exhibitions and the celebration of anniversaries.

Regional and national business archives

Another solution for businesses that do not wish to set up and maintain their own archive could be to deposit their records with a regional or national business archive. As with specialist repositories, this need not simply be for archival storage; the organisation may offer additional services, such as help with publications, exhibitions, and so on. There is a strong tradition in northern Europe of regional and national business archives, such as Centrum för Näringslivshistoria (The Centre for Business History), a national archive for business archives in Sweden founded in 1974 as a not-for-profit organisation owned by its members. The centre cares for the archives of nearly 7,000 companies and its mission is to preserve corporate history and help their member companies to use it more effectively. Suomen Elinkeinoelämän Keskuarkisto or ELKA (The Central Archives for Finnish Business Records) has been the centralised national repository for collecting Finnish business records since 1981. ELKA was established as a partnership of academic and business organisations with the aim of preserving not just business records, but also those of industrial organisations and the personal papers of leading businessmen. In recent years ELKA has been working to build a digital repository in which all the video, film and photographs can be preserved. The Erhvervsarkivet (The Danish National Business Archives) is a public institution, which is part of the State Archives of Denmark. Established in 1948, it has a collection of about 33 shelf miles of business records from all sectors of Danish business, as well as trade and industry associations and the private papers of prominent individuals in business in those organisations. It regularly undertakes collecting programmes in particular business sectors, such as the tourism industry, to identify records at potential risk of loss.

In Germany there is a network of regional business archives and, in a spirit of co-operation, they often feature an alliance of archives and businesses with the local chamber of commerce involved in the foundation and ongoing running of the repository. These archives have a long tradition with the first such service being established in Cologne in 1906 for Rhein-Westfalia, whilst the Stiftung Westfälisches Wirtschaftsarchiv, a regional archive for businesses in Westphalia and Lippe, was founded in 1914. The most recent, the Bayerisches Wirtschaftsarchiv (Bavarian Industry Archive), was founded in Munich in 1994 specifically for any business archive that cannot be 'appropriately maintained on site or is in danger of extinction'. The Archives de France comprises three services with national jurisdiction: Archives Nationales (National Archives), Archives Nationales d'Outre–mer (Overseas National Archives) and Archives Nationales du Monde du Travail (Working World National Archives). The Archives Nationales du Monde du Travail was established in 1993 in a former cotton mill in Roubaix in an industrial region of northern France, but came under the jurisdiction of the French Ministry of Culture in 2006 alongside the other national services. It collects the archives of businesses, trade unions and associations, and describes its mission as being to 'collect, process, preserve and make available to the public the archives called "the world of work"'.

Universities

Business archive collections can also be found in universities across the world, although the arrangements may differ greatly. The University of Glasgow in the United Kingdom, The Noel Butlin Archives Centre, part of the Australian National University (ANU) and the Swiss Economic Archive in the University of Basel all actively collect business archives as part of their remit: in Glasgow's case, records of Scottish business from the nineteenth to the twenty-first centuries, in particular from the West of Scotland, including shipbuilding, the drinks industry, banking and tourism,[2] whilst ANU collects business and labour records from Australian companies, trade unions, industry bodies and professional organisations from all states and territories[3] and the Swiss Economic Archive mainly collects the archives of defunct companies. Although not constituted as one, because it does collect other types of archives, Glasgow is the closest thing in the United Kingdom to a regional business archive.

Since its foundation in 1911, the Baker Library at Harvard Business School in the United States has collected archives focusing on the evolution of business and industry covering a broad range of business activity from agriculture and manufacturing to publishing and transportation.[4] So too has Duke University in North Carolina. In 1987 J. Walter Thompson (JWT) advertising agency in the United States donated its archive of advertising in all media to Duke University's John W. Hartman Center for Sales, Advertising and Marketing History. According to the *New York Times* the company deposited more than three million items because 'it was running out of storage space'.[5] Processing of the collection to create online finding aids was partly funded by JWT. BP came to a different arrangement by leasing space for the archive at a peppercorn rent from the University of Warwick, after investing jointly with the university in a new extension to the university library known as the Modern Records Centre. The BP archive moved to Warwick from London in 1993 in a bid to make the collection publicly accessible as part of a wider corporate strategy of openness. The archive occupies its own managed space within the Modern Records Centre, creating a positive working relationship with the BP researchers and also allowing the BP archive to tap into an existing pool of researchers at an established centre for business history.

Also in the United Kingdom retailer Marks & Spencer entered into a special partnership arrangement with the University of Leeds to relocate its archive to the university campus, which has provided benefits to both bodies. The aim of the 125th anniversary of the company in 2009 was to celebrate its long history, reinforce the brand and reconnect with customers, but it was also the catalyst that led the company and its archivists to investigate options for providing better archive accommodation and service going forward. The archive was benchmarked and academically assessed for its educational value and the proposed partnership with the University of Leeds was unanimously supported by the Marks & Spencer board, leading to the move of the archive back to the company's original home in Leeds. The fields of textiles, colour technology and food science are core to Marks & Spencer's product manufacture and the relocation of the archive complemented existing research synergies in textiles and food technology between the company and the university. It was believed that the move would increase use of the archive and enhance teaching and research at the university, whilst also supporting the business's principles around education, value and trust.[6]

The Marks & Spencer Archive is also unusual in the United Kingdom in being constituted as a Community Interest Company (CIC).[7] A CIC is a company limited by guarantee and is taxable, but it is not run for profit as it is intended to provide services and facilities to the public as well as the company, particularly in the area of educational engagement.

Museums

Museums are another possible home for business archives with synergies around preserving heritage and providing access to information but, like universities, the models vary. The museum may be at a national or a local level. For example, the National Railway Museum and the Victoria & Albert Museum in the United Kingdom both have a national collecting remit, the former for railway archives and the latter for archives relating to the fields of design and fashion, whilst museums in the Sheffield Museums Trust hold the archives of very local steel and cutlery-making firms. Archives may be held as a stand-alone collection, such as the Sainsbury Archive, which was transferred to an independent charitable trust in 2003 and is currently on long-term loan to the Museum of London to facilitate researcher access. The archive is described as 'a living record of Sainsbury's and new material continues to be transferred to the archive when it has passed out of current business use' (Museum of London, n.d.). Whereas The Museum of English Rural Life within the University of Reading is a more traditional collecting repository, acquiring the archives of agricultural manufacturing firms, agricultural organisations and co-operatives and company accounts of farms from across England and the Museum of Science and Industry in Manchester collects archives that relate to and complement its collections of artefacts that are used together to tell the story of Manchester as the world's first industrial city.

Business archives within a museum environment may benefit from access to cultural and economic initiatives and consequent funding streams, to promotional and marketing facilities to help broaden their user base and to in-house conservation studios. Optimising services can result in cost savings and, by placing its archive in a museum, the public's perception of a company may be improved. A report about library, museum and school partnerships in the United States, observed that 'collaboration may enable . . . museums and libraries to strengthen their public standing, improve services and programs, and better meet the needs of larger and more diverse cross-sections of learners' (Institute of Museum and Library Services, 2004), which could equally apply to partnerships between museums and archives. On the downside there may be a lack of understanding of archives and their needs amongst museum personnel, which will have to be overcome with training and communication. Working practices and principles may differ and the aims of the museum may conflict in some ways with those of an archive, so compromises may have to be made, such as using museum cataloguing software which is not compliant with such standards as ISAD(G) or archival metadata requirements.

Public archives

In the public sector, most, if not all, city and county record offices in the United Kingdom hold business archives, whilst the National Records of Scotland and the Public Record Office of Northern Ireland also hold large collections of business archives. London Metropolitan Archives (LMA), for example, is part of the City of London Corporation, which provides local government services for the City of London. The City is home to all manner of financial institutions, including merchant banks, insurance companies, stockbroking firms and trading companies, many of which are long-established and operate globally. LMA actively collects business records from these businesses by donation or deposit and holds more business archives than any other local government record office in England and Wales. The businesses usually deposit, rather than donate, their records in case they wish to retrieve them in the future, and occasionally provide funding for the archive to be catalogued. Often depositing companies are too small to maintain their own archives or simply have no interest in their own heritage.

However, the bulk of business archives held in local authority record offices are from defunct companies, which may have been donated voluntarily or acquired when the business was liquidated. There are also many stories of archivists who have entered derelict and crumbling buildings in order to rescue industrial records. The financial crisis of recent years has seen increasing numbers of long-established businesses fold. In response to this

Table 6.2 Advantages and disadvantages of depositing business records in a public archive

Advantages	Disadvantages
Depositing may be more cost effective than employing an archivist and creating bespoke storage if a business has only a small archive.	The company and archive will need to work in close co-operation to overcome differences in perspective or inadvertent misunderstandings.
Depositing may offer protection to a historical collection where a business lacks interest in its own heritage.	The archive may only accept donations of records, not deposits.
Depositing may help a business meet its corporate social responsibility obligations by being more open and providing greater access to its archives than might be possible in-house.	The archive may not have the storage capacity to accept large collections. If so, is the business willing to permit the appraisal and weeding of its collection?
Tax breaks may be available for donating archives to public institutions, for example in the United States, so businesses may be more inclined to provide funding for the cataloguing and preservation of their collections as part of the donation.	Some archives are selective about what they will accept, which may not include artefacts or ephemera, key elements of many business collections.
The business may be able to obtain records management advice from the archive.	The archivists may lack the knowledge to catalogue the records of a specialist business.
A proactive arrangement, with interested individuals on both sides, could bring greater involvement in the local community and some positive public relations.	Cataloguing the collection may be a low priority unless it is accompanied by funding. Public archives have a policy of open access to records but, for valid reasons of commercial confidentiality or protection of intellectual property, the company may be reluctant to deposit some records leaving gaps in the collection, unless closure periods can be negotiated.
Researchers have access to related collections all in one place in a public repository and may become a source of useful historical information that the company can use but of which it might otherwise have been unaware.	Records, once deposited in a public repository, may be subject to freedom of information legislation. An ongoing relationship will need to be maintained in order for the record office to secure continuous deposits of future records, as failure to do so will leave the collection frozen in time.

Table 6.3 Definition of terms relating to archive deposit

Deposit	The depositor retains legal ownership whilst placing archives in the care of another organisation. The period may be open-ended or the deposit agreement may specify a minimum period of deposit including a penalty for requesting early withdrawal.
Long-term loan	A form of deposit where the expectation is that the depositor will leave the archives on loan for an extended period of time, which may or may not be specified.
Indefinite loan	A form of deposit where the expectation is that the depositor will leave the archives indefinitely, as if they had been donated, whilst ownership remains with the depositor.
Donation	Gift involving the transfer of legal ownership as well as the custody of the archives.

one of the principal recommendations of the recent national strategies for business archives in England, Wales and Scotland[8] was the formation of a shared crisis management team to act when businesses go into administration, receivership or liquidation or when records are potentially at risk due to takeovers. It has grown from a team of three to eight archivists, academics and other specialists and has had some notable successes in securing the deposit of 'at risk' records.

Sadly, business collections are often at the bottom of a public record office's list of cataloguing priorities, especially if the archivists lack the skills and knowledge to deal with business records. They can, however, be prioritised if funding becomes available, as with the British Steel Archive project on Teesside and the Powering the World project in Wales, described later in this chapter. Once catalogued, the key benefit for researchers is that business collections are usually held alongside the records of the local authority, as well as those relating to local religious institutions, schools, hospitals, associations and families, allowing them to study the business archives in a wider context.

In conclusion, there is no clear cut-model for how or where a business archive might be held. Where it can be supported in the longer term the in-house model is usually the most desirable, but may not be feasible for smaller or vulnerable businesses. If the decision is taken to deposit or donate a company's archive, careful consideration must be given to the terms of the transfer and issues regarding confidentiality and access. The National Archives provides guidance on loan (deposit) agreements for privately-owned archives.[9]

Governance

Whether in the public or the private sector organisations operate within a framework of rules and practices, overlaid with regulatory compliance and risk management, through which the governing body will ensure accountability, fairness and transparency in its relationships and dealings with its stakeholders, be they customers, suppliers, employees, electors, ratepayers or the community in general. Governance also provides a framework for setting and achieving the organisation's objectives and goals by means of action plans and performance measurement, from the highest corporate level down to an individual's personal target setting and performance development. For some organisations this may include a Corporate Social Responsibility (CSR) agenda. CSR is defined by the European Union as 'the responsibility of enterprises for their impacts on society'.[10] This involves the organisation taking responsibility for its own actions by adopting ethical standards and practices and incorporating them directly into its business strategy in a way that will have a positive impact on the environment, encourage sustainability and support social welfare.

Mission statements

A mission statement defines what an organisation is and why it exists, a purpose and focus that often changes little over time. It can also be called a corporate purpose. All major businesses and other large organisations now have mission statements, but this is not always necessarily the case with their archive. However, a mission statement is a good way of encapsulating the purpose of the archive in a sound bite format. Some may adapt or take their inspiration from the mission statement of their parent organisation, or may even be required to do so, in which case you may see words such as culture, values and reputation amongst other more archivally-related phrases. Creating a specifically archival mission statement is appealing, particularly if the parent one is liable to change, but it is important not to contradict the parent organisation's mission in any way.

Archival mission statements, as shown by the examples in Box 6.1, may be brief and to the point, as with Roche, or more detailed, as with A. P. Moller–Maersk, but most include key words about the main focus of the archive, such as 'protect' and 'preserve'. Some business archives will refer to their role in the legal and compliance aspects of record keeping, whilst corporate archives that are more public-facing, such as the BT archive which holds some public records and therefore has a duty to make them available, or trusts which have a requirement to provide access under their charitable status, such as The Postal Museum, focus on openness and accessibility. Even where a business archive does not have a mission statement the opening sentences on its website will usually include similar words about preservation, uniqueness and corporate memory.

Some services may also have a vision as well as a mission statement. A vision statement differs from a mission statement because the latter is based in the here and now, whereas the former is more aspirational and a description of what the organisation would like to achieve in the future. It can also be an emotional stimulus to help drive the delivery of the vision. The Postal Museum's vision is 'to connect people through the evolving story of communications past and present'. Such statements can ensure that everyone in the team has an 'elevator pitch' in case they ever have the opportunity to speak to a senior executive, and this should encompass the vision for the service; not just what the archive does but also what it aspires to do.

Policies, plans and procedures

Most organisations will have policies concerning the management of finance and people, including recruitment and performance management and health and safety, which the archive service will be expected to follow, largely to ensure legal compliance. Whether or not the archive is obliged by its parent to create one, an archival policy is a vital tool that defines the position and role of the archive and its scope of work. It can act as a mandate for present activities and future planning. A policy may be one document or

---

Box 6.1 Examples of corporate archive mission statements

British Telecom (United Kingdom):

To ensure the best possible care and preservation of our past and future heritage on behalf of the nation, and to make it as accessible and relevant as possible to everyone everywhere.

The Postal Museum (United Kingdom):

British postal services helped to shape the modern world. We work to ensure that this human story of communication, industry and innovation is available and enjoyable for all.

Aviva (United Kingdom):

Our mission is to protect, develop and exploit the unique resource of which we are custodians.

The Roche Historical Collection (Switzerland):

The Roche Historical Collection is the core provider for the long–term legal protection of company information.

Barclays Group Archives (United Kingdom):

Barclays Group Archives exists to maintain the Group's corporate memory by preserving and providing access to records, in any format, with permanent business value or historic importance.

A. P. Moller–Maersk (Denmark):

History documentation will: – Ensure compliance with the regulatory environment and accountability with stakeholder expectations for records retention. – Establish and maintain efficient and auditable procedures and guidelines for archive management. – Research and document historical facts. – Support our culture, values and reputation. – Communicate timely and correct information to a relevant audience by means of any available channel.

---

a series of linked documents covering areas such as collections management and repository control, which should link back to the service's mission statement or overall objectives. The archive should also have forward-looking plans in order to deliver its mission and/or objectives and procedures that document processes and activities. They may be formalised in a procedural or best practice manual and should form part of the induction training of all new staff. Such a consistent approach provides the archive service with a structure, sets standards and helps the archive both run its present service effectively and efficiently and to plan for the future. Examples of the type of documents an archive should have as good practice are set out in Table 6.4.

The recent introduction of an Archive Service Accreditation Scheme by The National Archives (TNA) in the United Kingdom[11] is a major step forward in promoting good practice. It is open to repositories in all sectors that meet the criteria for eligibility and the scheme's scalability means that repositories large and small can apply. TNA's view is that the scheme 'offers a badge of external recognition and endorsement of [the archive] service' and that it will bring benefits across seven keys areas: professionalism, performance, profile, people, partnerships, planning and patronage. It is also central to TNA's desire to promote more effective and sustainable archives. Several United Kingdom corporate archives have gained accredited status and having appropriate policies, plans and procedures in place are key to a successful application.

Table 6.4 Examples of some key archive policy documents

Archive policy	Policy documents	Supporting documentation
Governance	Archive policy (if you do not have separate policies as listed below)	Mission statement Annual plan/Forward plans Risk register Job descriptions/roles and responsibilities Key performance indicators (KPIs) Budget
Collections management and development	Acquisition policy/ statement of collecting policy Collections information policy Appraisal policy Cataloguing policy	Deposit agreement/terms of deposit Depositor receipt Accession register Collections information plan to address cataloguing priorities and backlogs Digital strategy De-accessioning guidelines Collections development plan Listing templates Authority files
Repository management	Disaster and recovery planning Collections care and conservation policy	Disaster plan (regularly tested) Environmental readings Expansion strategy Security guidelines/incident reporting Handling guidelines
Stakeholders	Service delivery policy Access policy Outreach policy Volunteer policy	Service level agreements Analysis of stakeholder requirements Closure periods statement Searchroom rules Reproduction guidelines Enquiry handling guidelines Outreach aims, objectives and strategy Exhibition guidelines Publications strategy Online strategy Volunteer agreement

Service goals

Corporate culture, the pervasive values, beliefs and attitudes that guide a company's activities and interactions with its stakeholders, changes over time and will influence the approach taken by the archive. Archive services may be expected to conform to their organisation's governance principles and to echo these in their own objectives. Even if not required by the parent organisation, an annual business plan gives the archive structure in its daily work and provides focus. Although longer-term plans may not be feasible in a fast changing business environment it can be useful to document a long-term vision for the service. Both types of plan can be a means of obtaining additional funding for specific projects, such as anniversaries, and for creating SMART[12] targets for team members linked to their personal performance appraisals. London Metropolitan Archives describe the linking of their mission through to individual work targets as a 'golden thread'. At large corporates the process is more formal as targets filter down from the overall global objectives, through to functions, and from there to teams and individuals. A little creativity may be needed for an archive to reflect the annual objectives of a manufacturing company where production and the customer are the key focus. The archive may also find it useful to have a set of key performance indicators (KPIs) to measure operational activities and maintain statistical data, such as numbers of enquiries received and research visits hosted, as quantitative evidence to demonstrate an exponential growth in service and to justify allocated or additional resources.

Structure

Whilst some business archives operate with just one archivist, the sustainability of such a service must always be a risk. At the other end of the scale there are well-staffed services with not only archivists, but also administrative and specialist support staff. Where the archive is placed in the organisation and how it is managed will also determine its long-term sustainability.

Position in the organisation

As managing archives is a specialist function many working in the field believe that the archive (and records management) should exist as an independent standalone unit, ideally reporting to the chief executive or board but, realistically, an archive service would never be perceived as being of enough importance to sit at this level. In the private sector archive services may report into the legal, secretariat, marketing, public relations (or communications as it's now more commonly known) functions, to name but a few. They may remain in one department for many years, whilst others find themselves moved on a regular basis and have to adapt accordingly. Experienced practitioners generally believe that the level of senior management support and being able to align with the company's objectives may be more important than the department in which the archive service sits.

In the United Kingdom public sector archives traditionally sat in county secretary and solicitor's offices, but very few still have that reporting line and most have been moved over to the libraries, community services or social services departments. Archives usually operated as a combined service with records management but, with the growth of data protection, and freedom of information regulation and ever increasing importance of

Table 6.5 Advantages and disadvantages of where an archive function is positioned within a business

Department	Advantages	Disadvantages
Board/Executive committee	At the heart of decision making Quicker decision making Easier access to resource Understanding of accountability and reputation linked with poor record keeping	Visible at times of economic difficulties Subject to executive whim or vanity projects Executive changes may require the archive to repeatedly justify its existence
Legal/Company Secretary/ Compliance	Governance is their responsibility, so the legal and compliance elements of archive work are taken seriously Close to the board and their records Within one of the major record-producing departments Less challenge on the time such processes as cataloguing take Involvement in mergers, acquisitions and disposals	Can tend to advise rather than lead implementation so may not provide the leverage an archive service needs May have an over-cautious attitude to projects and allowing access to the archive May lack creativity and vision to support advocacy May not be seen as a priority in the department
Marketing	Interest in the brands Usually have large budgets for promotional activity	Narrow focus on their work and a lack of interest in non-brand material Want to tell good stories, sometimes regardless of the facts May impose unrealistic deadlines Fail to see why the archive should not be digitised and the originals destroyed
Public relations/ Communications	At the heart of information dissemination The best place for promotion of the archive Links with journalists Usually have large budgets for promotional activity Access to digital delivery channels like websites and social media	Narrow focus Keen on reputation and so may be cautious about allowing access to the archive or promoting its use
Human Resources (HR)	May be speedier recruiting Resourcing of training Support with performance management issues Support with including heritage in induction and other training	Lack of interest in what the archive does and can do Have to work harder to raise awareness in other departments
Finance	Major record producing department Has an interest in compliance	Lack of interest in what the archive does and can do Have to work harder to raise awareness in other departments Emphasis on cost saving

Facilities management/ Office services	Links with every department and business unit	The drive of many facilities management departments is cost cutting May see archives as just 'boxes on shelves' May be an outsourced service
Technology services	The right place for digital preservation Knowledge of IT trends and developments Easier to obtain new IT hardware and software	Focus on electronic record keeping, not paper Short-term rather than long-term views A lack of understanding of the concept of 'permanence' Challenge to digitise archives through lack of understanding
Property	Help in finding new or additional accommodation	Lack of interest in what the archive does and can do Have to work harder to raise awareness in other departments
Procurement/ Supply Chain	Possible economies of scale in purchasing	Have to work harder to raise awareness in other departments Looking for large-scale cost savings
Cultural heritage/ Libraries	Interest in the company history Access to complementary printed materials	May treat archives the same way as printed sources May have to use library software

electronic data, the records management service now tends to find itself left behind in the legal team or moved to the IT department. To some extent, this reflects the ever-changing structure of local government in the face of size reduction, outsourcing of services and merger with other public sector functions.

Overall the legal or company secretary's department would appear to have the edge over other functions in an organisation, but an interdependency with IT is vital if the archive is to stay one step ahead in preserving and managing digital archives. However, where an archive is located does not seem to matter as much as the level of senior management support and commitment, as this affects how the service is championed and protected. Open channels of communication and being positioned as close as possible to the top level management, rather than a long way down a hierarchical chain of command, are vital to the sustainability of the service.

Funding

Every archive should have a budget, but what a business archive may receive differs greatly from organisation to organisation. In some cases, the budget may cover everything from premises and staff costs through to all manner of consumables, whilst in others premises and salary costs are covered by another budget. Annually allocated budgets generally cover revenue costs, whilst capital expenditure on new buildings or large pieces of equipment usually have to be bid for separately with a robust business case. So the archive must be prepared to justify its spend and may have to fight for additional resources. As Davies puts it 'the allocation of a budget . . . ensures support for and justification of the work-plan and defines the services of the department. In effect a budget legitimizes the position of the archive in the hierarchy of the company' (Davies, 1991, p. 450).

Funding for a business archive can come from a variety of sources:

- *From the parent body.* Most in-house archive services are exclusively funded this way, for example HSBC, The Roche Historical Collection and Unilever are all funded directly by their parent company. Within business and government budgets are usually prepared annually in advance and are monitored to ensure that there is no overspend as part of a financial cycle. It is the responsibility of the archivist carefully to plan for the archive's financial requirements in the coming year. For some archives this will be an annually calculated sum based on all the costs the archive will incur, whilst others may be obliged to recharge other parts of the business for their services or pay another department for their accommodation and facilities support.
- *Through the formation of a trust.* The Postal Museum and The Rothschild Archive, for example, are funded in this way. Arrangements can be simple or complex depending on how much is devolved to the trust and how much is managed jointly between the trust and the former parent organisation. The trust could be set up by means of an endowment, which the trustees then have to invest and manage, or there could be an agreement to receive an annual subsidy from the parent organisation. In the latter case there will be a need for a robust service level agreement in order to manage the expectations of the parent body in return for funding and the trust will have to work hard to continue to prove its worth. Trustees with good financial acumen need to be appointed so that they can anticipate any shortfalls in funding and act accordingly. Where trusts have been set up by family-run companies the financial situation may be more secure as none of the family members would, presumably, wish to be seen as the one who puts the family heritage at risk by withdrawing or reducing funding.
- *As a joint service*, where the key financial driver is reduced overheads, largely through the use of shared premises or resources. Examples include the use of shared premises by BP and University of Warwick and Marks & Spencer and University of Leeds. A slightly different model is provided by the Scottish Brewing Archive (SBA), which was set up in 1982 as a co-operative venture between several companies in the brewing industry in Scotland to safeguard their archives. Each company makes a financial contribution to the upkeep of their collection, which includes the salary of an archivist. The collections are deposited at Glasgow University's Scottish Business Archive where the archivist is also based.
- *Through joint funding.* The British Steel Archive Project was a partnership that pooled the resources of Teesside Archives and the University of Teesside in Middlesbrough in the north east of England, once a heavily industrialised area. Funds were raised from Corus Group (now Tata Steel), university grants, the Heritage Lottery Fund and corporate and individual donations. The university provided organisational support and management skills and employed the archive project staff, whilst the record office provided office accommodation for them, use of archive software and server space. Dr Joan Heggie, who led the project, described the partnership as 'a new model for the preservation of business archives' (2009, p. 31).
- *Through partnerships.* Since 2008 Archives and Records Council Wales (ARCW), together with CyMAL (Museums, Libraries and Archives Wales) and the Richard Burton Archives at Swansea University have collaborated on a number of business archive projects. 'Powering the World: Looking at Welsh Industry through Archives'

used an innovative model whereby two archivists were based in two repositories and the archives of ten of the most valuable uncatalogued business collections in Wales were transferred to them to be catalogued before being returned to their home repository (Capner, 2011, pp. 26–27). Follow-on funding in 2011 for 'Profiting from Powering the World' was used to show potential researchers, by means of a travelling exhibition, leaflets and a website, that business archives can be invaluable in providing wider context to more commonly used collections, as well as to encourage further deposits of business records and promote their use in teaching. Other examples of partnership funding include the John Johnson Collection, an archive of eighteenth- to early twentieth-century printed ephemera, including a wealth of advertising held by the Bodleian Library, which was conserved, catalogued and digitised in a partnership with ProQuest, an information-content and technology company, and funded through the Joint Information Systems Committee's (JISC) digitisation programme. Likewise, BT entered into a partnership with the University of Coventry and The National Archives to catalogue, digitise and publish online almost half a million images.[13] Through partnerships these projects have widened access to previously inaccessible or under-used collections.

- *From government.* National museums in the United Kingdom, for example, receive their core funding from grants allocated by the Department for Culture, Media and Sport, such as the Science Museum Group, of which the Museum of Science & Industry (in Manchester) and the National Railway Museum (and their respective archives) are part.
- *By charging depositors and donors.* Examples here include the regional and national business archives in Europe, which levy charges on the companies using their services. These can be fees for storage, cataloguing, writing histories or providing a historical enquiry service or marketing support. To a lesser extent, most business archives will charge their users for certain services, such as photocopying, or undertaking research on the user's behalf, but the income raised in this way will be limited. The cost of processing such payments has to be taken into account to consider whether it is, in fact, worthwhile making any charges.
- *By setting up an enterprise arm* to generate income through retail, publishing and licensing, including branded merchandise, shop sales (physically and on-line) and picture library sales. This only works in a larger-scale organisation, due to the sizeable set up and running costs. Examples include The Postal Museum, the Victoria & Albert Museum and the National Railway Museum in the United Kingdom, which all draw on their archive collections to generate income in this way.
- *Donations, bequests and grant applications.* Relying on these methods of funding alone would lead to a precarious life for any archive as the income stream would vary from year to year making it impossible to plan ahead and putting the service in jeopardy if insufficient funds were forthcoming. Some larger organisations, particularly museums, may have their own development team tasked specifically with fundraising via sponsorship and applications to charitable trusts. Donations and bequests only tend to be made to archives which make their collections publicly available and grant applications are something for which, in the United Kingdom at least, corporate archives are usually ineligible. There are ways around this: some business archives have been successful by entering into a joint bid with a public service, either a local authority archive or museum or a university, whilst archives that have been transferred to

charitable trusts are usually eligible to apply in their own right for grant aid. The Postal Museum, for example, received Heritage Lottery Funding to produce learning packs for schools to accompany its exhibition 'Last Post: Remembering the First World War'.

A combination of any of the above funding streams is possible and also more likely to occur in the public sector, where the core work of the archive is funded by the parent body, but grants are sought for specific projects and users may be charged for services. If the archive is reliant on funding beyond that received from its parent organisation, what always needs to be borne in mind is the hidden cost of staff time when planning and taking part in fund-raising activities.

Geographical location

Location of the archive function in a company's head office is ideal. Such a location allows relationships to be built with senior stakeholders, as services can easily be provided and visits to the archive hosted. The archivists remain visible and tend to receive earlier notice of changes and initiatives that may impact the service or provide an opportunity for the deployment of heritage assets. However, head office space is generally costly making onsite storage of archives inappropriate and, for reasons of economy, some in-house archive services find themselves located at a distance from their head office. Unilever Archives, for example, is in Port Sunlight and Barclays Archives is located just outside Manchester, both over 200 miles from their London head offices. This can bring its own challenges, including inadequate support for issues around personnel, IT and premises. Remoteness from the headquarters can also instil a feeling of 'out of sight, out of mind'. In such instances the archivists may need to be more proactive in raising their profile and demonstrating their value to the business. Budgetary restrictions may mean that visits to head office are restricted, so careful planning and use of video- and telephone-conferencing facilities will be important. A good online presence and regular feeds of news stories can also help to maintain the service's profile. Networking will also play a vital role in building up a solid cadre of contacts who will help to spread positive messages about the service.

Related information and heritage functions

In many cases the archive service does not sit alone, but has responsibility for other internal information or heritage functions inside the company or must liaise on a regular basis with the providers of these services. These could include records management, information or library services, art collections or museums. Where the archive includes other functions the archivist may have direct responsibility for specialists such as records managers, librarians, education officers and museum or art curators. Responsibility for a museum open to the public adds a different dimension.

Records management

Records management may form part of the archive service or vice versa, or the archivist may find him or herself managing an outsourced storage contract for records management. Combined archive and records management services are not common in business, but were the norm in many local authority records offices in the United Kingdom until the recent increase in born-digital records and paperless ways of working led to many records management services being moved into IT functions. A joint archive and records management service has the great advantage of ensuring that there is harmonious dialogue between the archivists and records managers and a seamless flow of records of historical value into the archive. There are also economies of scale to be made in the form of shared resources and expertise. Where the archive and records management services are not part of the same team, and particularly when they are not even in the same department, then communication and good working relationships are vital. Records management is currently moving towards becoming a separate discipline and many records managers, without a traditional grounding in archives, have little interest in the historical record. Archival input to filing structures can help in identifying archival material at the point of creation, so that the correct disposition is applied in the retention schedules. Archivists may otherwise lose intellectual control of the appraisal process and archives may be selected for preservation without archival input.

Table 6.6 Advantages and disadvantages of a combined archive and records management service

Advantages	Disadvantages
Holistic service reduces risk management in record keeping	More difficult to keep the team cohesive where there are different processes
Intellectual control of all records created by the organisation	Explaining the differences to users who see archives as any non-current records
Seamless flow of records into the archive	Corporate focus on risk confers greater importance and resource to records management
Shared resources including staff and storage	
Greater knowledge and understanding of how the business works	

Museums

Whilst most business archives include artefacts, demanding some knowledge of the management of museum-style holdings, a number of archivists are directly responsible for museum buildings, whether purposely or by default. Lloyds Banking Group archives has managed the bank's Museum on the Mound since it opened in Edinburgh in 2006 in the bank's former headquarters, leaving the archivist in charge with a museum curator, front of house and security staff to manage as well as an archive team. Similarly, the archivist to the Alfred Gillett Trust (Clarks shoes) has found that the administration of the company museum has fallen by default to the archives. Diageo's historical collections in Ireland are open to the public via the Guinness Storehouse in Dublin, which claims to be Ireland's top visitor attraction. The archive is physically located in the building and a wide range of advertising and packaging from the collections is used in the exhibition spaces. Marks & Spencer have a similar set up where the museum showcases the best of the collections and the archive is situated in the same building. The archivist of the Roche Historical Collection manages three museums in Switzerland, two relating to the history of the business and an eleventh-century castle.

There are benefits to running a museum, not least the ready-made exhibition spaces and the opportunity to showcase treasures from the archives, as well as shared resources, such as a search room. Indeed, archives can add context to the objects on display. Archives based in a larger museum may also have access to a library and in-house conservators. The major downsides for an archivist in charge are the recruitment and management of specialist staff in a different discipline and responsibility for public access space and the inherent logistical and security issues.

These problems do not exist with online or virtual museums. A number of archives host online exhibits on their websites, but BT went a step further when it took the decision to close its telecommunications museum in London in 1997 and dispersed the collection to a number of partner museums specialising in science and technology, which the company felt were better placed to care for its heritage. A virtual museum, 'Connected Earth',[14] which was launched in 2002, features artefacts from the BT collections in the partner museums across the United Kingdom, as well as archives, photographs and film footage, interactive games and an education centre.

Table 6.7 Advantages and disadvantages of a combined archive and museum

Advantages	Disadvantages
Objects are more visually appealing than archives in exhibitions and online, so attract stakeholders and users	Responsibility for managing a specialist public space
Shared resources, such as a searchroom and library	Potentially managing a service beyond normal weekday hours
Possible synergies in cataloguing and conservation	Recruiting and managing staff with different specialist conservation requirements
Greater likelihood of in-house conservation services	Possible multiple databases to manage collections or compromise over cataloguing standards
More outreach opportunities	
Greater involvement with the local community, if desired, for example through an educational service	

Art collections

Many business archivists find themselves taking responsibility for artwork, usually in the form of portraits of the founding partners or more recent chairmen and directors, which can be seen as a part of the historical collections. Including historical artwork in the archive policy can benefit the archive as visual items may have more appeal to senior management and link the company more obviously to its roots. This remit may even be widened to encompass heritage-linked silverware and furniture. The Rothschild Archive, for example, displays pieces of furniture and artwork connected with the family in their search room.

There are other United Kingdom business archivists, however, who manage broad fine art collections as part of their role. These include Aviva, Lloyds Banking Group, Royal Bank of Scotland, HSBC, Unilever and the Baring Archive. The artwork is usually displayed in head office and other company buildings and has to be documented, valued and managed. Moving artwork requires specialist suppliers and can take up a good deal of time, particularly in a business undergoing considerable change in its property portfolio. However, requests from art galleries to borrow historical works can be used to help raise

Table 6.8 Advantages and disadvantages of managing an art collection with an archive

Advantages	Disadvantages
Allows heritage artworks to be documented and protected alongside the archive	Managing security and move issues
Artworks are more visually appealing than archives in exhibitions and online so engage stakeholders and users	Recruiting and managing staff with different qualifications and skill sets
Profile raising through greater public access or loan to external galleries	Cost of using consultants if a curator is not employed
Works can be displayed globally so, through good labelling, can help with archive profile raising	Possibly multiple databases to manage collections or compromises over standards
There may be synergies in cataloguing and conservation	Managing loans, both internal and external

the archive's profile via internal news channels. It is rare for a qualified art curator to be part of the team so, unless the archivist has a fine art background, he or she will need a network of specialist external suppliers and art consultants and perhaps a panel of experts to advise on acquisitions and the promotion of the collection.

Libraries and information services

As more and more publications are appearing either solely online or both in print and electronically, many businesses have taken the step of closing their in-house libraries and simply purchase online subscriptions to the journals that are needed. Some archives may always have incorporated a small library into their service as a means of providing complementary background to the collections but, if they are required to take on the organisation's principal library as well, there will be issues over the recruitment and management of specialist staff and different procedures required for acquisitions, subscriptions and loans.

Table 6.9 Advantages and disadvantages of a combined archive and library service

Advantages	Disadvantages
Printed and published works which complement the archives	Recruiting and managing staff with different qualifications and skills sets
Access to printed resources will assist research for staff and users	Possibly multiple databases to manage collections or compromises over standards
Shared resources, such as a search room	Managing user expectations, for example users may expect to borrow archive material like books
Larger budget for purchasing printed materials and online subscriptions	
There may be synergies in cataloguing	

As can be seen from Tables 6.6–6.9 there may be advantages in managing another allied specialism alongside a corporate archive. Control of records management in particular may ensure intellectual control over the flow of material into the archive and greater resources.

There are also promotional opportunities to be gained from a museum or art collection, but managing such collections can be a drain on time and resources and can cause problems in recruiting and managing individuals from a different professional background. Alternately, the archivist may have to manage other specialist activities without dedicated professional support and find that they have to become a jack of all trades.

Conclusion

There are a wide diversity of business archive collections and services sitting within many different organisations. Where business archives are held and where an archive service sits within its parent organisation can influence dramatically how that archive is perceived and used and, ultimately, its long-term viability. What is clear is that no one size fits all, but the most successful business archive services are those with sound policies and procedures, good internal communication and senior management buy-in.

Acknowledgements

This chapter is based on responses, received from business archivists around the world, to the author's questionnaire about how their services are run. Without their help this chapter could not have been written. Thanks are also due to Alex Bieri for kindly commenting on the chapter as a whole.

Notes

1 The English Arts Council's accreditation scheme statistics show a fall of 9% in museums registered as 'local authority' between 2011 and 2014. The most likely explanation is thought to be that many have changed their legal status. Source: www.artscouncil.org.uk/what-we-do/supporting-museums/accreditation-scheme/accreditation-statistics/ [Accessed 15 August 2016].
2 www.gla.ac.uk/media/media_61203_en.pdf [Accessed 15 August 2016].
3 http://archives.anu.edu.au/collections [Accessed 15 August 2016].
4 www.library.hbs.edu/hc/ [Accessed 15 August 2016].
5 www.nytimes.com/1987/12/01/business/advertising-j-walter-thompson-donates-its-archives.html and http://library.duke.edu/rubenstein/hartman/ [Accessed 15 August 2016].
6 http://corporate.marksandspencer.com/blog/stories/working-in-partnership-to-spark-innovation-within-business [Accessed 15 August 2016].
7 For more information about CICs see www.gov.uk/government/organisations/office-of-the-regulator-of-community-interest-companies [Accessed 15 August 2016].
8 For England and Wales see www.businessarchivescouncil.org.uk/materials/national_strategy_for_business_archives.pdf and for Scotland see www.scottisharchives.org.uk/business/business_case_studies/1national-strategy-for-business-archives-in-scotland.pdf [Accessed 15 August 2016].
9 See www.nationalarchives.gov.uk/documents/archives/loanagreement.pdf [Accessed 15 August 2016].
10 http://ec.europa.eu/growth/industry/corporate-social-responsibility/index_en.htm [Accessed 15 August 2016].
11 www.nationalarchives.gov.uk/archives-sector/archive-service-accreditation.htm [Accessed 15 August 2016].
12 SMART objectives are easier to understand and to know when they have been achieved. SMART is a mnemonic acronym standing for specific, measurable, achievable, realistic and time-limited.
13 See www.digitalarchives.bt.com/web/arena [Accessed 15 August 2016].
14 See www.connected-earth.com/ [Accessed 15 August 2016].

References

Adkins, E. W., 1997. The development of business archives in the United States: an overview and a personal perspective. *American Archivist*, 60(1), pp. 8–33.

Capner, S., 2011. Powering the world: looking at Welsh industry through archives, *CyMAL Magazine*, 11, pp. 26–27.

Davies, V., 1991. The business archivist as manager. In: Turton, A., ed., *Managing business archives*. Oxford: Butterworth-Heinemann. Ch. 17.

Heggie, J. K. F., 2009. The British Steel Archive Project: forging new kinds of partnerships to preserve significant business archives. *Business Archives: Principles and Practice*, 98, p. 31.

Institute of Museum and Library Services, 2004. *Charting the landscape, mapping new paths: museums, libraries and K–12 learning*. Washington: Institute of Museum and Library Services.

Museum of London, n.d. *Other collections and archives: the Sainsbury archive*. [online] Available at: www.museumoflondon.org.uk/collections/other-collection-databases-and-libraries/sainsbury-archive [Accessed 23 April 2016].

The National Archives, 2009. *National strategy for business archives (England and Wales)*. [pdf] Available at: www.businessarchivescouncil.org.uk/materials/national_strategy_for_business_archives.pdf [Accessed 15 August 2016].

Further reading

Bettington, J., *et al.*, 2008. *Keeping archives*. Canberra: Australian Society of Archivists.

International Council on Archives (ICA), Section on Business and Labour Archives, 2004. *Business archives in international comparison*. Vienna: ICA.

Turton, A., ed., 1991. *Managing business archives*. Oxford: Butterworth-Heinemann.

Williams, C., 2006. *Managing archives: foundations, principles and practice*. Oxford: Chandos.

Articles on business archives referenced in this chapter

Berry, C. and Crumplin, T. E., 2012. Pastures new: unlocking the heritage collections at the Alfred Gillett Trust. *Business Archives: Sources and History*, 105, pp. 18–34.

Giffen, L. and Shields, K., 2010. Going back to our roots: the partnership between the Marks & Spencer company archive and the University of Leeds. *Business Archives: Principles and Practice*, 100, pp. 27–40.

Heggie, J. K. F., 2009. The British Steel Archive Project: forging new kinds of partnerships to preserve significant business archives. *Business Archives: Principles and Practice*, 98, pp. 16–32.

Hollier, A. and Johnson, V., 1994. Moving and opening the BP Archive. *Business Archive: Principles and Practice*, 67, pp. 1–12.

Rea, V., 2007. 'We've got to get together before we fall apart': collaboration and partnership as the way forward for business archives. *Business Archives: Principles and Practice*, 93, pp. 30–45.

Ritchie, A., 2014. The work of the business archives crisis management team. *Business Archives: Principles and Practice*, 108, pp. 63–72.

Strickland, J., 2000. A suitable home for an archive? *Business Archives: Principles and Practice*, 79, pp. 57–74.

Swinnerton, H., 2007. The initiative to build in Hong Kong a regional archive for HSBC in the Asia Pacific. *Business Archives: Principles and Practice*, 93, pp. 46–55.

To identify where business archive collections in the United Kingdom are located see The National Archives' online Discovery database. Available at: http://discovery.nationalarchives.gov.uk/find-an-archive [Accessed 15 August 2016].

Chapter 7

Acquisition, appraisal, arrangement and description

Richard Wiltshire

Introduction

Business records are rarely generated for the purpose of building a historical archive. A series of decisions and actions must be taken if records are to be preserved as archives for the long term. Once potential historical records have been identified, they must undergo accessioning, appraisal and cataloguing to enable their future use. The importance of these key activities is often overlooked and they may not be given due consideration when other priorities arise. Companies naturally focus on the achievement of business objectives that impact the bottom line and archivists managing their archives in-house must both prioritise internal requests and align collections to support wider corporate strategies. In the public archives environment, bulky, complex business archives often compete for attention with more heavily used or smaller collections which are easier to process.

This chapter is concerned with the key activities of deciding which records should be kept, and which should be consigned for disposal, and of influencing others to ensure that comprehensive, high quality archive collections survive to bear witness to past business activities. The art of describing business archives to professional archival standards, within the context of a corporate or collecting archive, is also covered. All actions undertaken in acquiring and cataloguing archives should adhere to the archive profession's recognised international code of ethics (International Council on Archives, 1996).

Rescuing business records

Business archives under threat

Given the multitude of businesses that have existed, the archives of a relatively small proportion of firms have survived. Those collections that do remain tend to relate to successful firms. In some countries businesses are legally required to retain certain records and make them accessible, for example to shareholders or legal or tax agencies. Business archives are, however, by their nature essentially private property and can generally be managed and disposed of as their owners wish. It has been acknowledged that 'we cannot make sure that business records are kept. If a company wants to destroy its archives, it can do so . . . What we can do is to try to persuade the owners of business records that they have an obligation to keep their records and make them available for historical research' (International Council on Archives, 2004a, p. 3).

Most businesses do not maintain formal in-house archives and those which do are subject to periods of flux and change, which may in turn favour or threaten their archive collections. Drastic changes, caused by the discontinuation of the parent business or part of its operations, particularly put such corporate archives at risk and may include:

- sale, merger or takeover by another company or by the state;
- diminished economic well-being, which prompts the relocation of operations or disposal of property thereby forcing decisions to be made on the retention of accumulated records;
- discontinuation or loss of a brand name or change in a company name, commonly after a merger, disposal or switch in product or service focus;
- insolvency, where an insolvency agent acts on the behalf of creditors or other stake-holders to recapitalise the business; wind down or sell the firm and any assets it owns wholesale; or split off viable elements that are saleable. In some national jurisdictions, such as the United Kingdom, insolvency includes companies entering administration, liquidation or receivership.

Other factors that can threaten business archives include:

- negligence or whim of those in power, or snap decisions made by individuals or departments unaware of policies in place on archives retention;
- lack of awareness of a corporate archive and its potential value to the business or wider society due to its failure to build an adequate profile;
- lack of a robust records management system and unsuitable storage or security measures for record keeping;
- wider political, social, economic or climatic upheaval, such as that caused by war, financial crisis or environmental disaster.

Planning a rescue

Rescue, in this context, refers to policy decisions and practical actions, which can be taken to help save business archives at immediate risk. This chapter does not cover disaster planning and linked conservation practices, which are described in Chapters 8 and 11. The decision to rescue a set of records, whether by a collecting archive externally or corporate archivists internally, must be arrived at with full awareness of the related business case and the budget and resources available.

Attempts by a collecting archive to save records can on the one hand be expensive, time-consuming and ultimately fruitless, but on the other could be vital in securing rare archives or key historical records which evidence the development of the business in question. The would-be rescuer should contact a person with the knowledge to identify the records and sufficient level of authority to support the rescue effort. The ownership of salvaged records could be in question and needs to be established from the outset. The rescuer must expect disappointments along the way, but should persist in the face of negativity and lack of momentum on the part of the record owners. Time may well be of the essence and other work may need to be put aside to focus on the rescue, although it should not be allowed to compromise the essential activity of an archive service.

The following questions should be asked in planning a rescue:

- can the archive team cover all key activities? Do they have the necessary equipment?
- is the scope and scale of planning appropriate to the situation in hand?
- which records should be prioritised for rescue?
- can a response be made without compromising the archive material?
- in cases where records have to be salvaged due to physical damage, what are the stabilisation, handling, packing and restoration options?
- should contact be made with a specialised conservation or storage supplier where items cannot be physically accommodated immediately within the repository?

The rescuer may also be able to look to regional or international networks to provide support or intelligence. In the United Kingdom, for example, a business archives crisis management team was set up in 2009. The team, comprising archivists and historians, watches for potential threats to business archives and works with relevant repositories to ensure their survival in appropriate hands.[1] Globally the International Committee of the Blue Shield supports the protection of world cultural heritage, including archives, threatened by natural and human-made disasters.[2]

Within a business, robust and well-observed record management processes are by far the best way of ensuring key archival series survive intact and are transferred to the archive. However, the sale of subsidiary businesses, the disposal or refurbishment of properties and the clearance of legacy records in commercial storage may frequently give rise to the need for rescue efforts to save potential archives at sudden risk. Occasionally a company's entire archive is put in jeopardy by financial failure, merger or acquisition. In-house corporate archives may wish to ensure a channel of communication is kept open with a relevant external collecting repository. The flow of advice and expertise can benefit both parties and allows sharing of information on issues which might affect the future integrity of the collection. It will then be no surprise for the collecting repository should the archives suddenly need to be deposited externally. Sometimes businesses at risk establish a short-lived trust, by deed of declaration, by which trustees agree to dispose of any heritage assets to a collecting archive.

Dealing with insolvent companies

The archives of companies entering insolvency are at immediate risk. Contact should be made with both the company, if still in operation, and the named insolvency agent. The rescuer should telephone the advertised number, describe the archive's interest and ask to whom they should speak. The contact is likely to ask for details in writing (see Box 7.1). It is important to mention in any written communication that the note of interest will be followed up, in order to imply that the request cannot be easily ignored.

Identifying archival material

The insolvency agent and/or the contact at the business in question may well not be at liberty to make arrangements or discuss matters further until more detailed plans have been made for the future of the business. Regular communication should, however, be maintained to keep up to date with progress and related deadlines. At this stage it may

Box 7.1 Archivist's letter to the insolvency agent for a business

Dear _____

My name is _____ and my role is _____.

[Note the background to the enquiry, including any previous contact, the importance of the company/likely records and the evidence, if any, of the existence of records.] My main concern is that the historical records of X [*company*] are identified and protected for future generations. If there is any question of destroying or otherwise disposing of the records, Y [*archive repository*] would offer to house the collection or work with relevant parties to make sure that it is preserved.

I am seeking contact details for the appropriate person or department within X [*company*] with whom I can discuss protecting this important historical business archive.

I have also spoken to Z [*mention any wider body or person of historical authority who has also been contacted*] and they will contact you separately with regard to protecting the archives of X [*company*].

I will follow this letter up with a telephone call next week.

Yours sincerely, _____

---

not even be clear whether any archives have survived. An attempt should be made to consult existing listings and view records *in situ* before they are removed or the buildings housing them are sold. Records that are not required by an insolvency agent are routinely left behind in business premises, which may then be sold on. The complexity of who controls, can access and own records increases once they are in the hands of third parties.

Insolvency agents will not want to incur any costs. The collecting archive must therefore have an agreed budget in place to fund the opening up and viewing of records in abandoned buildings or retrieval of boxes held in off-site storage. The rescuer should contact company staff, where these can still be found, to ask them to share any listings, explain where key record series are located and provide any other relevant information. This is especially important in the case of born-digital material held on servers or hard drives protected by passwords. Using such insider knowledge may considerably reduce the time that has to be spent on the identification and selection of records.

The insolvency agent will take all current records required for their purposes, some of which may have archival value and these may need to be earmarked for later transfer. Once their work has been completed and the business has been dissolved, records are routinely destroyed after a set period. Identification and negotiations must be completed before that retention period expires.

Repositories should ensure ownership of rescued records is transferred and a gift agreement is signed by the insolvency agent who relieves the donor of legal liability for the records once they are gifted. Box 7.2 explores lessons learned from the rescue of the archives of William Verry Ltd of London, while Box 7.3 demonstrates the value of

Box 7.2 Case study: the records of William Verry Ltd, London, United Kingdom

The background:

In 2009 William Verry Ltd, a 177-year-old London-based building contractor, went into administration following an economic downturn and cash flow problems. London Metropolitan Archives (LMA), the regional local authority repository for Greater London, was alerted by a depositor and contacted the administrators (insolvency agent) by telephone and email.

The lessons:

Be persistent. One of the company's properties was sold quickly, along with records left *in situ*; luckily the new owner retained volumes felt to be of historical value.

Expect difficulty in gaining access. Records were held at three sites (head office, off-site storage and Hertfordshire); at head office, health and safety issues were raised together with requirement that a visit could only be made when the administrator's estate agents were hosting prospective buyers. LMA had two hours to survey and identify a taxi-worth of records as the keys were literally being handed over to the new owner.

Insolvency agents cannot incur costs. LMA had to meet transportation and off-site storage company costs.

Records may be incomplete. Off-site storage listings revealed a vast series of building job files, but most records had been routinely destroyed after six years, including board reports summarising key project progress.

The outcome:

Archives donated via a signed gift agreement included minutes, reports, ledgers and cash books, pension scheme records and work in progress photographs. Job records for Walthamstow Mosque were selected as a sample, as the extent of the collection meant that the resource required to appraise the whole series was too great.

Acknowledgement: London Metropolitan Archives.

Box 7.3 Case study: Stoddard-Templeton heritage collection, Glasgow, United Kingdom

The background:

The Stoddard–Templeton heritage collection encompasses the design library, design archive corporate records and heritage carpet collection of James Templeton & Co. Ltd and Stoddard International plc, two of Scotland's most prominent carpet designers and manufacturers. Scotland's carpet industry had been in decline from the 1970s and in 2005 Stoddard International plc appointed Ernst & Young to manage the receivership of the company.

The partnership:

Recognising the historical significance of the collection, the joint receivers at Ernst & Young enlisted the help of Christie's auction house to catalogue and value the archive. This work was continued by KPMG, when Bair Nimmo was later appointed liquidator of the company. The collection comprised 3,800 design drawings and patterns; 2,000 design sketches; a design library of 1,500, titles including books and journals; 226 carpet pieces; and numerous albums of photographs. Interest in the collection was expressed by a number of parties from around the world. Fortunately, Ernst & Young and KPMG worked for several years with a Glasgow consortium of heritage institutions to keep the collection in Scotland as representative of the history of Scottish carpet manufacturing.

The outcome:

In 2008, following a scoping project and successful funding bids, the unique archive of designs, corporate records, patterns and carpets was bought by the University of Glasgow in conjunction with Glasgow School of Art and Glasgow Life, with the assistance of a £172,000 grant from the National Heritage Memorial Fund.

Acknowledgement: Glasgow University Archive Services.

working in partnership with a liquidator and other heritage services in the case of the Stoddard–Templeton Collection, Glasgow.

Sale of business archives

Most business archives are unlikely to have significant asset value. However, some collections can command market interest and high sale prices. Selling such collections in their entirety or in part may be an attractive proposition for the owners of failing businesses or their insolvency agents. A piecemeal sale is the worst possible outcome as the collection is then broken up making subsequent re-construction of the archive almost impossible. The letters of the seventeenth-century City of London merchants Clayton & Morris were, for example, acquired by purchase in a number of separate lots from a dealer over a period of more than a decade in the 1990s and 2000s by the predecessor to London Metropolitan Archives.

Purchase funds may be available from national or specialist-funding bodies to acquire records at risk, although matched funding is often required. Letters of support from potential users and related historians can be helpful. Founded in 1873, Poole Pottery Ltd of Dorset was well known for using the designs of significant twentieth-century artists. In 2003 the company entered administration and a year later – after controversy and public protest – the firm's entire archive, comprising both business records and working design patterns, was acquired wholesale by Dorset History Centre. The purchase price of £22,493 was supported by a grant from the Friends of The National Libraries.[3] Complementary pottery artefacts passed to Poole Museum. Another major example of a successful rescue campaign in the United Kingdom was the prevention of the threatened sale of the important UNESCO-recognised Wedgwood archive (see Box 7.4 for further information).

Surveying business archives

Surveys can vary widely in scope from the perusal of a simple paper or digital list of records or dropping in on a department and appraising a couple of files, to working through an entire storage area of hundreds of boxes. The degree of formality and detail appropriate to a survey will depend upon the scope and circumstance. The following guidelines outline best practice for a large formal records survey.

Planning a survey visit

Visits should only be undertaken for important or large collections of potential archives, or where face-to-face contact may enhance future collecting and build useful relationships with departmental contacts within a business or between a business and a collecting archive. Small straightforward record accumulations made up of defined series with existing lists, or labelled digital records in folders using software that can be easily shared, should not require a visit. Often these records can just be sent to the archive on the basis that any unwanted items are either confidentially destroyed or securely returned. Guidance can also be offered to depositors regarding which record types might have archival value so they can then report items of potential historical interest. Where a business has regional, national or international branches or subsidiaries and budgets cannot support a visit, a

Box 7.4 Case study: archives of Josiah Wedgwood & Sons, Barlaston, United Kingdom

The background:

Josiah Wedgwood & Sons, founded in 1759, is one of the United Kingdom's oldest and most iconic pottery firms. In 2011 the Wedgwood Archive, managed and held in trust by the Wedgwood Museum Trust at Barlaston, Staffordshire, was added to UNESCO's United Kingdom Memory of the World Register as 'one of the most complete ceramic manufacturing archives in existence'.

The threat:

In 2009 a major threat arose when the firm's successor company, Waterford Wedgwood plc went into administration with a major pension shortfall. The Wedgwood Museum Trust faced a large demand from the Wedgwood Pension Plan following the administration of Wedgwood Group companies. This was as a result of a series of entirely unforeseen and unusual circumstances and an unintended consequence of pension law introduced in 2008. The Trust was served with a notice of a £134 million pension debt. At the end of 2011, a High Court Ruling agreed that the Wedgwood collection of artefacts, art and archives, valued at £11–18 million, could be sold to help meet the pension deficit. The Trustees' priority was to ensure the preservation and continued display of the Trust's unique heritage collection at its award-winning museum at Barlaston, Stoke-on-Trent, and the retention of its small specialist curatorial team and support staff.

The outcome:

The model of placing collections in a trust to safeguard an archive was shaken. Efforts were made to secure funds to protect the collection from being lost with support from cultural and archive sector associations, Wedgwood family members and local people. The archive and museum sectors highlighted the lack of protection for important business archive collections and lamented a dangerous precedent for viewing items purely in terms of their financial value. The Art Fund raised £15.75 million in total, including £2.74 million through a public appeal, and in 2014 the collection was saved for the nation. The Art Fund gifted the collection to the V&A, which loaned it back to Waterford Wedgwood Royal Doulton to ensure it remained at the Wedgwood Museum in Barlaston.

Acknowledgement: The Wedgwood Museum Trust.

'virtual' survey may well be the solution. Samples of digital records or screenshots of folder contents may also be emailed to allow remote appraisal.

If a visit is needed the surveyor should find out the following information to plan their visit:

- Who will host the visit. What their position, contact details and relationship with the records is. This helps with assessment of the contact's responsibility for and level of experience and knowledge of the records and suggests whether he or she will have sufficient authority to deposit the archives.
- Where the survey is to take place. This assists journey planning, understanding of the equipment required and other practical considerations.
- The physical condition of the records and storage area. If the records are kept in poor conditions, the surveyor should bring appropriate equipment.
- The extent of records to be surveyed. This will help to plan how long will be needed and how many staff should attend.
- Whether any listings of the records exist. Inventories may, for example, have been compiled by the creating department, which can be used to check off or identify records. Additionally in the United Kingdom many private business records have been surveyed in the past and historic listings may be available via Discovery, hosted by The National Archives,[4] or The National Register of Archives for Scotland, hosted by The National Records of Scotland.[5]
- The background to the structure and responsibilities of the individuals, businesses or departments that created the records. Such details help the surveyor to gain an understanding of the relevance of the records to the archive's collection policy and what is likely to be reflected in the records.

Surveys should be arranged when the contact or individual who knows the records well will be able to attend. It may be appropriate for the surveyor to suggest a short discussion at the beginning of the survey, and then offer to work alone with the records. In this brief meeting, the origin and general content of the records can be clarified together with any rules for the visit, such as which items can or cannot be surveyed, whether everything must be left in place and whether boxes can be labelled. It is advisable for the surveyor to find out if records can be rearranged or items removed, or if everything should be left where it is until further discussions have taken place after the survey. The surveyor should take whatever equipment will be useful during the survey (see Box 7.5).

Conducting the onsite survey

Good communication skills are important to leading successful surveys. The surveyor should judge the situation, listen, ask pertinent questions and be sensitive to any emotional ties to the records. In some cases, the host may not initially like items handled, in others, they will assume that the surveyor can be left to delve into boxes at will. The surveyor should be vigilant on site and not afraid to ask about anything that looks as if it might be archival. They should, however, stick to the aims of the survey and keep an eye on the time allotted. They should be diplomatic, honest and show interest but not to an extent which might compromise future decision making. The surveyor should not agree to accept or take any records unless this is agreed or authorised by both the record owner

---

Box 7.5 Equipment checklist for a site survey of physical records

- Mobile phone.
- Laptop, for creating a survey report.
- Bound paper to take notes/draft the survey report. Bound paper is preferable to loose sheets to avoid pages getting lost or out of order.
- Overalls, particularly if records are reported to be stored somewhere dirty.
- Torch, in case there are unlit areas.
- Mask and gloves, these are essential even if the contact does not give warning of the records' physical condition – they may not recognise the signs of damp and mould which can cause health risks including skin and respiratory problems.
- Scrap paper that can be left as markers on shelving or boxes to identify records of potential interest. This is particularly important in cases where it has been agreed not to disturb the existing arrangement, and may avoid the need for a return visit if it is later decided that the records are to be transferred.
- General stationery supplies, including pencils, scissors to cut tightly-tied bundles, and adhesive tape for attaching notes to shelving or boxes.
- Digital camera, for taking photographs to record the original order and arrangement, extent and format sizes. Seek permission before taking photographs.
- Business card and leaflets to promote the archive and its services.
- Sample archive transfer forms/agreements, to be shared with the contact should this be appropriate.
- Personal safety alarms can be reassuring, especially when working alone.

---

and the repository. It should be explained clearly why and how the repository takes in records and how and when they are processed and made accessible after deposit. A surveyor left to work alone should make sure they have the means to contact someone locally who can help with any queries, or whom they can notify when they are ready to leave.

The visit should aim to cover all aspects of the record accumulation and related factors, which can be summarised in a survey report (see Box 7.6). Where the survey is informal or the records few, it may be appropriate to create a simpler document or summarise findings in a brief email.

The survey report should be compiled soon after the visit whilst the records and circumstances are still fresh in the memory. The report may be sent to the contact and/or used to make a decision over which records should be transferred. The value of the records, depositor expectations, deadlines, charges or funding and practical arrangements should all be considered in making the decision and it may be useful to set these out on a decision-making form (see Box 7.7).

The records earmarked as archives should, where the repository is able to accommodate them, be taken in as soon as possible whilst the list is still current and the contact is in post, as even documented and clearly labelled records could be at risk if left on site. In the context of a collecting archive it may take months or years before a deposit of records can be negotiated and made. Contact details, survey and decision-making documentation

---

Box 7.6 Suggested content for an archive survey report

1. Title page:

Include the date of the survey; surveyor's name; the contact's name, role and address; the department/business the records relate to; the address, the physical whereabouts and extent of the records surveyed; and any accession number(s) arising from the survey.

2. Background:

Can include:
*   details of any circumstances requiring immediate action;
*   the motivations of the contact and/or owner in allowing or proposing a survey (such as an anniversary, lack of space, reorganisation, building closure) and their expectations or requirements (for example, requiring records to be catalogued soon after transfer);
*   information on the background to the records and their storage;
*   information on the history of the business and/or department which created them that will also be useful for compiling an administrative history. Record the name changes of the firm/department(s), registered offices/premises, main business activities and remit, key impacts on local and wider society, the existence of subsidiary companies, branches and/or relevant key individuals or families;
*   the names and contact details of any individuals who could shed more light on the records, in case these prove useful to the future cataloguer.

3. Scope notes:

It should be made clear what the notes cover. For example, a general summary (which is best for more extensive material and where a list is already available), everything seen, or only items deemed archival and suitable for transfer. Record the following:

*   Scope, dates and extent with summarised details of key series. A list can be made at the appropriate level of detail (such as file-by-file; shelf-by-shelf; cabinet-by-cabinet). Include dates of creation, and where appropriate, record the physical location of the item (for example, '2nd cabinet from left, 3rd shelf down, left hand side'). It can be useful to record physical appearance, to aid identification later (for example, 'orange file cover' or '7-centimetre pile of papers tied with string'). If everything is noted (not just items of interest), include details on appraisal, for example 'Not for archives', 'Archival' or 'Keep a sample'. A sketched plan of the storage area can provide a useful reminder back at the office.
*   How well records are organised and the type of packaging.

- How much appraisal may be required for any bulky series and whether this can be done *in situ* or post transfer.
- Details of digital records, their format types and metadata on their creation and modification, how these are saved and arranged (for example, screenshots of directories could be included), which servers and/or hardware they are saved on and how these complement or duplicate hard-copy sources.
- Existence of listings, checking for any reference sequences on boxes or volumes which suggest an original order or the likely existence of earlier listings.
- Physical condition and related practicalities affecting access/ability to receive records in their current state. For example, items in poor state of preservation caused by water, mould or insect damage or issues presented by the format of items.
- Details on access to storage pertinent to practicalities of any future transportation – such as the position of lifts or existence of a loading bay.

4. Past and current access:

Expected access demands and details of related records held elsewhere.

5. Recommended outcome(s):

A recommendation should be made, together with the type of agreement likely upon transfer of records. Include confirmation of ownership and level of responsibility of the contact.

Details of what actually happened. For example, 'Recommended transfer of items marked ★ in the list above; items transferred *[date]* as accession *[reference number]*'.

should be filed for future reference and eventually moved to the accession file upon transfer of the records. Should the repository not be in a position to accept digital format records immediately, guidance should be provided on their backup and retention so that they can be retrieved and transferred at a later date. For further details see the information on accessioning later in this chapter.

Surveying digital records

Surveying digital records requires a different approach to physical records as they are:

- often stored in proprietary file formats, databases or email accounts;
- generally extensive and can be technical in nature;
- often perceived as current business assets;
- rarely more than 20 years old and often confidential;
- at risk of being made inaccessible by technological obsolescence;
- sometimes available as hard copy records too.

Box 7.7 Potential acquisition decision–making forms

Name of creating business/department, person or family:

1. The background:

- Contact name and details;
- Urgency;
- Background/previous work progress;
- Brief administrative history (company/department name changes, registered head office/regional or departmental address(es), remit/geographical scope).

2. The records:

- Brief scope of records (series, dates);
- Extent (linear metres or boxes with sizes);
- Whether well organised/existing listings;
- Notes on digital, audio–visual and other special record formats;
- Conservation issues.

3. Access, value and likely significance:

- Existing or likely future demand/restrictions;
- Company's local/national/regional or department's corporate importance;
- Documents a key business, department or product, constitutes a complete series, is of display or other value;
- Whether additional to or fills a gap in existing holdings;
- Related material and presence of other formats/surrogates.

4. Decision/funding:

- Decision/reasons;
- Budget/charging;
- Date/names of decision maker(s).

Acknowledgement: London Metropolitan Archives.

Most businesses would be unable to allow an external surveyor access to their shared network drives for reasons of security. Furthermore, the bulk and technical detail of what exists may be difficult to assess without significant input from the record owners. Owner advice can support quicker identification of the most important records generated by particular business activities and those that should be retained as archives. The survey should aim to document information regarding the infrastructure in which the digital records are held, the various digital record formats which require preservation and the scale of the records to be dealt with. The section in Chapter 10 entitled 'From theory to practice: key actions and common challenges' provides more detailed guidance on the practical steps that should be taken when surveying digital records. Depositors may see allowing access to digital records as fraught with risks, as they often contain recent information prompting corporate fearfulness of reputational damage from leaks of digital material. As a result archivists need to demonstrate that the level of risk is no different to that attached to paper records.

Collection policy and deposit agreements

Collection policy

An archive repository should define its remit and the range of material, which is accepted through a collection policy. This policy underpins all collecting activities and should therefore be endorsed by senior management, published, adhered to and regularly updated. It should be linked to the repository's overall mission statement and be kept simple, clear and concise to ensure that it is easily understandable and fit for purpose. Corporate archives' policies should position their collecting activities in a way that serves the company's commercial objectives, and supports executive, colleague, customer and shareholder needs. Collecting for a broader audience, such as academic researchers, should also be considered to ensure that the wider importance of the business's story is also documented.

The policy statement should outline the following:

1   Repository details: give the name, address and governing body, or authorised department within the business.
2   Legal status and authority to collect: specify any legislation or constitutional foundation bestowing the power to collect archives and set out any official external recognition of the repository.
3   Scope and limitations: define what archives are by describing the variety of record formats and underlining that they are records, which are preserved for their continuing value for a range of long-term uses, often other than those for which they were originally intended. The policy should also outline the scope of collecting activities, such as the subject area within which records are sought, any geographical or chronological restrictions and the types of formats that can be handled. Include reference to digital, audio-visual and other records requiring specialised equipment and any related non-archival material such as reference publications and artefacts.
4   Alignment of collecting activities with those of related repositories: explain how collaboration actively seeks to avoid conflict and duplication with the collecting policies of other repositories (The National Archives, 2004, p. 7). 'Cherry-picking' should be avoided to prevent collections being unnecessarily fragmented. Collecting repositories should underline that they only accept business records where a company is not in a position to retain them or where deposit will particularly benefit future access and preservation.
5   Process of collection: state how records are acquired including the types of agreement used. In-house corporate archives will more naturally focus on internal sources for the deposit of material. It should be stated that the repository seeks to be satisfied as to the authority or title of depositors. The policy should also indicate how records

are accessioned, appraised and de-accessioned and outline how the repository actively engages in survey and rescue work.

Ideally the policy statement would seamlessly integrate the acquisition of digital records alongside traditional physical records collection. But if the repository is in the early stages of digital archives management it may be necessary to add some specific content in that regard. As one author has acknowledged 'electronic records will not survive to become archives unless early decisions are made about how to maintain their authenticity, reliability and accessibility throughout their current and archival lives' (Williams, 2006, p. 36). In practice this may involve advice to depositors on document-naming conventions and folder structures, liaising with information technology colleagues on software changes and setting up simple tracking lists to support the future migration of digital records to the archive.

Box 7.8 sets out a template for a corporate archive collection policy. The policy should ideally be aligned to the collection policies of other local or national archive repositories to mitigate duplication of effort and maximise the use of available resources. The policy should also form part of an integrated collections management framework[6] linked to forward planning and objective setting (ranging from strategic three or five year plans to annual business/departmental/individual performance goals) and procedures or guidelines setting out how proactive and passive accessioning activities will be carried out by staff.

Deposit agreements

Company records deposited with a collecting repository

Clarifying the ownership of records is as important as safeguarding their evidential value or preservation. If the legal status of a collection is prejudiced, there can be serious repercussions for its future management, including related authorisations and copyright-related queries. Also there is the danger that staff time and conservation resources spent on records in legal limbo may be wasted if ownership is challenged by a third party and the records are later removed. Potential legal ramifications can also have a major impact on the integrity and reputation of the repository.

Agreements are important in defining ownership and avoiding future disputes. Confirming the ownership of some archives can be practically impossible, for example in the case of client records held by businesses such as solicitors' firms or banks. In such cases the repository may have to accept them despite the possibility that a third party might claim ownership in the future. Agreements also set out the responsibilities of the depositor and repository and outline any terms and conditions linked to the transfer of records. They should be signed by both parties and exchanged at the time of transfer. Collecting repositories should also encourage firms to minute the deposit decision at board level and provide a senior signatory.

Internal records deposited within a company

An in-house corporate repository should acquire archives from all key functions in order to fully document the business's history. This may require archivists to proactively identify potential archives by developing relationships with business partners in each function to

Box 7.8 Information to include in a corporate archive collection policy

1. **Acquisitions policy** – set out the overall collecting objective.
   For example: The acquisitions objective of X is to identify, collect and preserve the documentary heritage of X and its constituents past and present in whatever media, with the aims of:
   - exploiting it to the benefit of X, by providing business information and supporting brand identity and reputation;
   - making it available to researchers in a manner compatible with X's interests;
   - preserving archives of local or national significance in the public interest.

2. **Authority to acquire archives** – set out the basis of the authority of archive X to collect and retain records, whether that stems from a board minute, procedural circular or records management policy.

3. **Records considered for collection** – set out the scope of that authority to collect, including record provenance, format and dates. Reference links to the wider records management process.
   For example: 'Records considered for collection are those generated or received by X in any format, relating to its business worldwide including past and present constituents and associates, regional/local offices, divisions and departments. The archive also collects selected material relating to past proprietors, directors, staff and customers. Material is collected up to the current date. Historical records classes/types are flagged on records retention schedules'.

4. **Terms of acquisition** – set out how records are acquired.
   For example: 'Most material is acquired by in-house transfer. Gifts and bequests of relevant material, for example from staff, pensioners and customers, are accepted. Records are rarely purchased. No records are accepted on loan. Ownership and relevant copyright in deposited records passes to the archive.'

5. **Appraisal and de-accessioning** – set out the circumstances under which records may be de-accessioned.
   For example: 'Once appraised and catalogued archive material is only de-accessioned and removed from the finding aids in exceptional circumstances. For example disposal of part of X's business or property or re-appraisal of record types considered worthy of preservation due to prolonged absence of use. Where the depositing or creating body still exists (for example the creating department or its successor) – depending what was agreed at the time of accession – archives will contact them and offer to return the records before destroying them.'

6. **Disposal** – set out how records are destroyed.
   For example: 'All material deemed unworthy of permanent preservation is destroyed as confidential waste.'
   State the name of the policy owner and intervals at which the policy will be reviewed and updated.

Acknowledgement: Royal Bank of Scotland Archives.

support record inventorying and scheduling and to deal with the implications of office moves and closures. Transfers to the archive should be evidenced by transmittal forms (see Box 7.9), which require depositors to briefly describe the deposited records and advise if there are any ongoing access or destruction restrictions. Clear guidance should be provided to depositors and the terms of transfer set out in an internal records policy endorsed by management. Depositing departments should be discouraged from the expectation that they will be able to withdraw items temporarily in the future. Instead, records should only be transferred when there is no longer a regular demand for reference or retrieval or because reference copies have been retained locally.

Terms of deposit agreements

Gift, loan and internal transmittal are the commonest types of legal transfer used for business archives. Table 7.1 outlines each option and the related benefits and limitations of each in the context of an in-house corporate archive and a collecting repository. In-house corporate archives generally accept only internal transfers or gifts from third parties like customers and pensioners. Boxes 7.10 and 7.11 summarise the key information to include in gift and deposit agreements.

Agreements should be clear and easily understandable. Standard forms, or letters of proposal, which are countersigned can be cheaper alternatives to bespoke deposit agreements, but may prove too inflexible. All agreement pro-formas should be reviewed by the company's legal department or by a solicitor on behalf of a collecting repository.[7] Depositors may, of course, request alterations, but only minor amendments should generally be accepted. Major variations between agreements may make the management of the collections difficult and encourage inconsistency in the treatment of depositors. A balance must be struck between the importance of the records in question and the

---

Box 7.9 Information to include in an internal corporate archive transmittal form

1. **Contact details of sender:**
   Company, department and section name
   Sender name, job title, address, email and telephone number(s).
2. **Transfer details:**
   Agreed date of transfer
   Departmental consignment reference number
   Description of records transferred including: box reference; file or file series description; dates (from/to); quantity/type (for example '1 file'); whether adds to a series previously deposited; and whether there are any access or destruction restrictions.
3. **Instructions and guidance:**
   Information to help the sender complete the form and guidance on how records should be transferred, including the archive's address and contact details.
4. **Repository administration:**
   Date of receipt and acknowledgement and accession number.

demands of the depositor. The repository may need to walk away from negotiations if excessive access restrictions, rights or requirements are being requested that cannot be met.

Accessioning

Accession register

The term 'acquisition' relates to the transfer process by which new archival records are received by a repository. The accession register is a fundamental collection management tool, which logs essential information on the nature and circumstances of each acquisition, including provenance and ownership. The register is essential for providing a repository with overall intellectual control over incoming records.

The minimum data elements required in such a register are the date of receipt, a brief description of the records including the extent, the creator(s) (including company and/or departmental name changes and names of notable subsidiaries where relevant), the legal terms of the transfer, the name, position and address of the person transferring the material, and the accession reference number to enable the records and any related documentation to be traced in the future. Complex transfers that reflect multiple businesses may require more than one accession record. Box 7.12 sets out the information to be included in an accession register with a fictional example of an accession entry. The accession register is now commonly part of a relational database containing other key record-related data, such as the descriptive catalogue. Accession registers should be kept secure and depositor details protected. Many repositories keep hard copy accession registers as an additional back up because of their crucial importance. Accession registers should be earmarked for permanent retention.

Collecting repositories may wish to make the accession register, with the exception of depositors' contact details, which should be restricted, available to users via either the repository itself or a national register. This alerts users to new business record holdings and enables demand to prioritise future cataloguing. Publicising key new accessions can also help advocate the work of a repository, but should be done only where it is in a position to allow immediate access.

Accessioning process

There are a number of tasks that must be performed as soon as possible once a deposit has been transferred:

1   An initial receipt should be sent to the depositor providing an accession number where this has been allocated. The full extent and detail may not be known until the records have been surveyed and checked, a process that for larger collections may take some weeks. A receipt (see Box 7.13) and letter of acknowledgement outlining future access and any other relevant matters should eventually be issued to the depositor.
2   The accession register should be completed. Where the register is electronic, descriptions should ideally be linked to the related catalogue, location, conservation and depositor databases.

Table 7.1 Legal transfer options – the benefits to and limitations for corporate and collecting archives

Transfer type and related agreement	Benefits to and limitations for corporate archives	Benefits to and limitations for collecting archives
Gift: also known as a donation. Transfers ownership and any rights in the items. Use a gift agreement or deed of gift.	**Benefits:** Corporate archives mainly collect records pertinent to their business. Gifts are the main way in which corporate archives acquire externally-held records, such as those offered by former employees or customers. Donations secure legal ownership and allow control over the records on a par with the main owned collection, including copyright and disposal rights. Gift agreements simplify long-term collections management as they do not require an ongoing relationship with the depositor. **Limitations:** A potential depositor may not agree to gift the records and associated rights.	**Benefits:** Gift agreements should be mainly used for records of defunct companies, and those collected by former employees or other individuals. Donations secure legal ownership and allow control over the records on a par with the main owned collection, including copyright and disposal rights. Gift agreements simplify long-term collections management as they do not require an ongoing relationship with the depositor. A one-time or ongoing financial donation may be secured from the business at the time of transfer. Gifted archives may also be eligible for wider funding streams. **Limitations:** A potential depositor may not agree to gift the records and associated rights. It may not be appropriate to accept gifts from a live business where records are required regularly by the company, for example semi-current records especially those under 5–10 years old, and assets not to be seen by competitors such as recipes and designs. No organisation can better use the archive content in support of a company's brand than the firm itself. Complex rights and responsibilities (for example, author rights and licensing in the case of a publishing company) could be transferred to the repository which it may not be in a position to handle. For insolvent businesses the repository may have to take responsibility for future liabilities which an insolvency agent will not accept. In the United Kingdom, freedom of information legislation no longer allows public sector repositories or donors to impose access restrictions to donated records other than restrictions which adhere to data protection legislation.
Bequest: where a donor wishes to gift records but does not wish to relinquish control until after their death. Outlined in a will.	**Benefits:** Eventual benefits as above. **Limitations:** The archive must agree to terms and conditions before the decease of the donor.	**Benefits:** Eventual benefits as above. Limitations: As above.
Deposit on loan: where ownership is retained by the depositor along with associated	**Benefits:** May provide access to records crucial to the history of a business. This option may be appropriate where ownership cannot be ascertained (for example for records of business clients who cannot be traced)	**Benefits:** Often appropriate for an archive collection supporting an active business brand as the repository does not have to take responsibility for any complex ownership, access or copyright issues. The agreement can outline a commercial partnership arrangement between a business and a collecting repository where a charge can be levied for storage

rights including copyright, and allows for depositors to withdraw items. Use a loan or deposit agreement.

Limitations:
This option restricts the repository's control and should rarely be used by a corporate archive.
There is also a risk to the depositor where the loaned archive function is discontinued that the loaned material is assumed to belong to the company and may be inadvertently disposed of or published without reference to the depositor.

This option may be appropriate where ownership cannot be ascertained (for example for records of business clients who cannot be traced).
Loan agreements can encourage transfer of under-represented businesses.
Retaining ownership can be particularly important to owners of business archives from small, family businesses.

Limitations:
The withdrawal of all or part of the deposit temporarily or permanently can be damaging if no safeguards are written into the agreement to recompense the repository for work done on the collection and for users who can no longer access the records.
The repository has to manage and document temporary withdrawals. Such withdrawals can, however, encourage ongoing dialogue with the owner over collections development. Permanent withdrawal can be beneficial if the collection, and any users, would benefit from a change of keeper.
Requires regular maintenance of contacts with the depositor and can lead to ownership queries over time. Repositories may have difficulty in the long-term in locating the owner to seek permissions, amend terms or seek a conversion to a gift, particularly in the case of takeovers and mergers and where a business is no longer in existence.
'Permanent' loans can lead to future confusion over ownership and should be avoided. An agreed term of years should be included or a gift negotiated.
Not applicable.

Transfer: where records are owned within the business and transferred internally. Use a transmittal form.

This is the most common transfer type for in-house corporate archives. The terms should be defined in company records management policy and process and should allow sufficient access and flexibility to support ongoing business activity without constraining the repository's management.

Benefits:
This secures ownership and related control over item(s) (as in the gift option above).

Purchase: where money is paid for item(s) upon which ownership passes to repository. This does not require an agreement, although evidence of payment should be retained.

Benefits:
This secures ownership and related control over item(s) (as in the gift option above).

Limitations:
Costs can be high. The act of purchasing encourages a market for business archives. A purchase should only be made where records are rare, plug key collection gaps, have significant business value and fully meet the collections policy.
Provenance and background information may be difficult to ascertain and can be disputed by third parties.

Benefits:
This secures ownership and related control over item(s) (as in the gift option above).

**Box 7.10 Information to include in gift agreements/
deeds of gift**

1. **Parties and ownership:** date of agreement; contact details of the parties: the owner/donor and the repository and its parent body; and definition of the meaning of the terminology used.
2. **Records:**
   Material to be deposited: detail creators, content scope and dates (normally presented in a schedule listing), extent, repository accession number(s) and date(s) of transfer.
3. **Declaration of the donor:**
   As to their legal title and lawful right to gift records; that they are not aware of third party claim to the records; and that that as from the date of transfer (normally the date of receipt by the repository) the donor agrees to assign all legal ownership and rights in the records to the repository outright and forever.
4. **Declaration of the repository:**
   That records are accepted as an unconditional gift outlining relevant legislation or constitutional rules under which the repository accepts gifts.
5. **The donor's acceptance of the following terms:**
   - Limit of liability: that the repository will not accept any liability for any loss, damage or claim which is the result of the acceptance, display, use or destruction of the records. The clause can also outline that the donor will financially cover the repository against loss or costs incurred by any future contest over ownership by a third party. [Note: Some donors may not want to accept any legal or financial repercussions. The removal of this clause should be weighed up against the importance of the records or any likely future claim. Insolvency agents and individuals will be unlikely to accept any ongoing liability. This should be acknowledged in the agreement with details of the background and role of the signatory included under section 1].
   - Access: outline reasonable availability, and any rights of the repository to withhold access including in accordance with legislation.
   - Copyright (where applicable): that the donor assigns all copyright and other intellectual property rights where they are held in the records. That the donor will advise the repository of any rights held by third parties. That the repository is entitled to use, copy and reproduce items for its own use or sale, and for others, in accordance with legislation.
   - Preservation: outline reasonable effort to retain, conserve and preserve items, but indicate that the repository cannot agree to retain or preserve items indefinitely.
   - Return of records: outline the rights of the repository where records will not be retained to either return or destroy them. Set out also whether the repository will contact the donor, the period of time between contact being made and destruction if no reply is received, and the responsibility of the donor in providing current contact details if they should wish to be contacted in such circumstances.

- Finding aids: indicate that catalogues are produced at the discretion of the repository, that copyright in catalogues is retained by the repository and that the repository may rearrange and mark the records. The repository may offer to send a copy of the catalogue to the donor.
- Receipt: that a receipt will be provided for the items.
- Law: that the terms and any dispute arising out of them shall be subject to local legislation and courts.

6. **Signatures:** donor, witness and repository's parent body. In addition to signatures, names should be printed with job positions included where appropriate.

Box 7.11 Information to include in deposit agreements

1. **Parties and ownership:**
   - Date of agreement and any dates of periodic revisions.
   - Contact details of both parties, the owner (and depositor if not owner) and the repository and its parent body.
   - Outline any meanings of terminology used.
   - Declaration of depositor as to their legal title and lawful right to deposit records, and that they are not aware of third party claim to the records.
   - Outline responsibility for notification of changes of address for both parties, details of next of kin or heirs. Include terms to resolve situations where contacts are lost and where ownership is in question, in favour of conversion of the deposit into a gift to the repository.
2. **The records and their selection:** material to be deposited. Detail creators, content scope and dates (mention any attached schedule listing), extent, condition, arrangements for destruction or return of unwanted material, repository accession number(s) and date(s) of transfer.
3. **Loan period:** outline the minimum period (normally up to 50 years or indefinite) and procedure for additional future records.
4. **Finding aids:** detail how cataloguing will be done, responsibilities for funding, depositor's responsibilities for providing contextual information to the records such as provenance, history and prior research usage, and how catalogues and other finding aids will be disseminated. Outline any rights to descriptions produced. Mention records will be packaged appropriately for their protection and numbered with reference codes.
5. **Access:** add conditions of access for both before and after cataloguing has been completed. Include restrictions subject to current legislation/policy or stated restrictions on use required by the depositor, and any charges for access.
6. **Conservation and preservation:** outline how work will be prioritised. Usually minor repairs undertaken by the repository, but major work often at the discretion and cost of the depositor. Include details on surrogates (copies to be made for security or preservation reasons), formats and responsibility for

costs. Any recognition that certain formats, such as film and digital records, are particularly subject to deterioration over time or dependence on available software or hardware.

7. **Storage and maintenance:** compliance with standards, type of storage and liabilities for loss, damage, theft to records (usually states every reasonable precaution would be taken by the repository without accepting liability for loss or damage).

8. **Insurance:** state provision, usually repair not replacement, and at whose cost.

9. **Copies and publication:** state permissions for copying are usually given, provided the process does not damage items, and records may be published or exhibited in line with local copyright legislation. Include responsibilities of depositor to highlight copyright ownership or any related licences to third parties. The repository may request rights to reproduction fees and to use the records for promotion without permission.

10. **Withdrawal:**
    - temporary withdrawal by the depositor or third parties (for administrative use, exhibition, research elsewhere) – period of notice required and any related permissions or proof of ownership requirements;
    - permanent withdrawal – period of notice required, arising charges and responsibility for costs incurred to date, liability of the depositor to offer first refusal to the repository to purchase the records, in case of sale, or the opportunity to make copies prior to withdrawal.

11. **Law:** set out the terms and any dispute arising out of them shall be subject to local legislation and courts.

12. **Signatures:** confirmation that both parties have a) the authority to sign the agreement and b) that they have read and accept the terms. In addition to signatures, names and positions should be printed on behalf of both parties.

Box 7.12 Typical information to include in an accession register

1. **Repository name:** include the name of the parent body and the address.

2. **Reference numbers:** include accession number, prospective or final catalogue reference code(s).

3. **Records:** include date received, type of records classification, whether or not additional to an existing collection held by the repository, title (usually the name of creator – business or person, the same as the collection fonds); content summary only with specific dates where necessary together with details on relevant departments and name changes; extent in terms of bulk and linear metres; overall covering dates; details on related material held elsewhere; notes on affect of condition on handling and access.

4. **Terms of transfer:** such as departmental transfer, loan, gift, purchase (include price paid). Detail any income received with the deposit; indicate whether

power to destroy has been granted; specify who holds the main copyright (repository, depositor, third-party) and detail rules on reproduction.

5. **Access:** state whether records are generally available or subject to specific permissions and/or restrictions under legislation.

6. **Listing:** give details of interim lists, updates on cataloguing status (whether part or fully catalogued) with cataloguing archivist's name and position, and date completed.

7. **Depositor/transfer contacts:** include depositor's name, position, organisation or business department, address, telephone and email. Include contact details for any intermediate party.

8. **Repository administration:** include name and job title of staff accessioning the records (record locations should be recorded separately).

9. **De-accessioning and appraisal:** include details of decisions and records affected, any authorisations received, staff name and position, whether de-accessioned for return to depositor, destruction or transfer to a third-party, for which details should be added.

For example:

THE PLANETARY ARCHIVE OF MARS, MARTIAN GOVERNMENT

Crater Nine, 345 Star Boulevard, Mars

Reference codes: Accession number: 2167/057; Proposed final catalogue reference code: 0671

Records:

Date received: 23 June 2167

Records classification: BUSINESSES

Title: **CRATER SETTLEMENT COMPANY OF MARS LTD**

Description: Board minutes (2101–2150), reports, staff lists (2110–2143), plans and other estate records, publications. Includes chairman's copies of minutes and other records of Mars Crater Enthusiasts' Association (2088–2140).

Dates: 2088–2160

Extent: 457 digital Mars bytes

Additional to existing collection.

Related material: Crater Exploratory Mission (reference code 0055)

Condition: some bytes corrupted.

Terms of transfer: gift, power to destroy, copyright vested in repository.

Access: generally available, except Association membership details.

Listing: interim list available.

Depositor contact information: Mr T. B. Bloggs, Secretary, Crater Settlement Company of Mars Ltd, Red Crater, Mars.

Repository administration: accessioned by Mrs Tyra Syra, Archivist.

De-accessioning and appraisal: estate relating to occupation of minor craters destroyed 21 May 2168 by Mrs Tyra Syra, Archivist, as authorised by Head Archivist (see appraisal report 6771).

3   The newly acquired records may need to be quarantined before they enter the repository's main storage area, or server in the case of digital records. An assessment should then be made to ensure they will not detrimentally impact the physical or digital records in the repository's existing holdings. For example, in the case of physical records this could include inspection for mould or insect activity and in the case of digital records hazards could include viruses. Issues affecting access to the records, ongoing preservation or the health and safety of users and staff should be recorded for reference. A survey (see Box 7.6) should have identified any major problems prior to deposit.

4   Transfers, particularly those made by the parent business, should be accompanied by sufficient information to allow full understanding of the records. The accessioning archivist should create a summary list to check that all agreed records have been received. This should identify bulky series for appraisal and decide whether any items should be returned to the depositor or destroyed. Storage media, such as boxes, should be reviewed to reduce the shelf extent. The deposit should be organised and numbered. Each storage unit can be numbered (for example accession and part-number 2016/014/001 of 100) or original numbers used where they exist and match a list, or a concordance made with the list. Numbering allows each unit of the deposit to be individually entered onto the repository's location index and for staff to identify and retrieve specific units of the accession using a temporary listing. In this way a repository can provide access to items prior to cataloguing and avoid time wasted looking through boxes with unknown contents.

5   Accession files, either physical or electronic, should be created for storing relevant documentation, including correspondence, agreements, receipts, listings and notes for future reference. Files can be arranged by accession number, collection title (name of business, department or individual), or depositor name, and should be kept permanently.

De-accessioning refers to the reversal of accessioning, whereby a deposit, either wholly or in part, is disposed of. Disposal involves the return of the deposit to the depositor, transfer to a third-party, or destruction. The process can be motivated by the repository's own appraisal decisions, at the behest of a depositor wanting to end a loan agreement or in-house department transfer arrangement. It can also occur where assets

---

Box 7.13 Information to include in an accession receipt

Include accession reference number(s), title of collection, any future catalogue reference number(s), scope description, extent in bulk or shelf metres.

Outline who the records are from giving the full name, position, department, organisation and address. Give the date the accession was received by the repository and by what legal means, such as transfer, gift, loan, bequest or purchase.

Allow space for the signature of the authorised archivist, their job title and date.

Explain that the receipt is issued by the repository, and provide address and governing body to which correspondence should be addressed.

such as subsidiary or brand are sold to another business, requiring associated records to be permanently transferred. Details must be recorded on the accession register and the appropriate authorisation sought and documented. A positive example of de-accessioning was the recent opening of a heritage room at Ede and Ravenscroft Ltd, tailors, robe makers and wig makers of London founded in 1689. This led the company to request return of archives on deposit at London Metropolitan Archives, to be used in an exhibition at their new heritage room and to join the extensive records and textiles still retained by the business. Subsequently an Archivist and Collections Manager was recruited with responsibility for these records.[8]

Documentation strategies

'Documentation' is a term that American archivists coined[9] to refer to proactive measures to ensure that core human activity is documented, which may not otherwise be properly recorded for posterity. This strategy helps assert a degree of consideration and control given the abundance of records and the limited resources of archive repositories. In the context of business archives, it ensures through collecting policies that the whole story of industry in a particular area, region or country, or of a single business if a corporate archive, is adequately documented in the archive collections that are retained. Documentation advocates that the archives of businesses of all kinds should be retained, from all sectors and of all types and sizes; failed and successful, local, national and international, family-run businesses, partnerships and public limited companies. Table 7.2 compares recent documentation theory to traditional early twentieth-century archival theory on collecting, alongside opinions on appraisal.

A documentation strategy takes a functional top-down approach and prioritises activity by focusing on areas of economic value to the business. For example, an in-house corporate archive may focus selection of records on the parent firm's head office and major branches and agencies, letting records from other parts of the business be disposed of unless they are proactively offered to the archive. A collecting repository with responsibility for a geographical area might concentrate on the industrial sectors, which have been most significant in the region's development.

Positive action can be taken by stepping back to review collections strategically rather than always responding to offers of 'more of the same'. The existing collection policy and holdings should be assessed and an analysis made of their strengths and weaknesses. Corporate archives should check whether all departments and business functions are documented. Collecting archives can consult trade directories, national guides to archival holdings and academic studies of particular business sectors and contact local or similar repositories or related bodies with potentially conflicting collecting policies. Results should be fed into an active collections policy (see Box 7.8) with a linked business plan focused on bridging known gaps.

A long-term plan with key targets can be set to prioritise and approach certain areas of a business or sector, which are ill-documented in existing collections. Cold calling can be time consuming and is rarely successful. Repositories should instead consult stakeholders in this process, such as internal management and departmental contacts, external researchers and interest groups. Records relating to past contacts and archive surveys can be revisited and may support future negotiations.[10]

Table 7.2 Collecting and appraisal theory

Aspects of collecting and appraisal theory	Traditional theory	Documentation theory	Comment
Decision-making: once made is it forever?	Once the decision is made it cannot be reversed as it documents what society felt should be kept at that time.	Reviewing the continuing value of material requires ongoing re-assessment of appraised records, particularly where space is at a premium.	There is always value in re-assessing collections against wider holdings, particularly as more records are accumulated. This helps repositories to avoid duplication and free up space.
Methodology: which is best?	Ideally avoid appraisal altogether and leave the creators to decide what will survive, thereby avoiding an appraiser imposing their subjective value judgements and bias. For example, an individual may only keep material which meets research requirements at that time or their own personal interests. This opinion was a key feature of the theory of pioneering archivist Hilary Jenkinson (1965), but is an extreme approach not widely adhered to in recent times. If appraisal is carried out at all it should adopt micro-appraisal methodology only; examining each record 'file-by-file' from the 'bottom-up'.	Appraisal should always be a top priority. An appraiser should adopt a 'top-down' approach where records are appraised according to the importance of the functions and activities of an individual, department or business. Only a minority of records need to be assessed to reach a decision over their retention. 'Macro' large-scale appraisal may be used at collection-level to assess the relative economic value of the creating department to the business or of the business to society, and to keep only those archives which reflect a major contribution.	Appraisal has to happen or a repository would soon fill up and access to records would be compromised due to bulky, low-grade, uncatalogued collections. Researchers' views should not dictate decision-making. They can have narrow interests which do not consider all parts of a collection or the future needs of society. However, an in-house archive is likely to retain certain types of material which may benefit the wider business which a collecting repository would not keep, or would sample. Drastic decisions can be made if the appraiser has not carried out a pre-assessment or pilot: key files of high informational value may be missed, particularly if material is not well organised. A 'high-handed' approach may consequently be damaging to a repository's collection and reputation.
Collections development: how best should collections be developed?	A repository should accept all items it is offered in a passive way. Deposits should not be proactively encouraged. If a repository stands back and sees what records society thinks are worth keeping, the archive becomes a truer reflection of society and its values.	The 'Minnesota Method' (Greene and Daniels-Howell, 1997) reviews and samples records of businesses to reflect all aspects of society. As part of documentation this method proactively collects records in order to fill the gaps in consultation with other bodies. The role of an archive is to be part of society and, in turn, should mould it through use. Repositories should advocate their role and capture records as evidence for their continuing value. For example an archive should proactively work together with records creators and managers to determine retention schedules.	Strategies should help ensure material is not one-sided. Diverse businesses and communities should be made aware of archives and their value. Such campaigns will help ensure that they will be documented in the long-term, so that a repository reflects all facets of society, rather than simply one aspect. Co-operation with others and partnerships help a repository to document a business or section of society. Without proactive intervention and systems in place, records, especially digital items, may not be offered to the repository.

Successful collecting is closely linked with advocacy and outreach,[11] the reputation that a repository develops and the quality of the service that it provides to its stakeholders. Building relationships with key influencers and educating the wider business or community about the value of archives is particularly important in attracting collections. For example, the archives of Eric and Jessica Huntley, founders of Bogle-L'Ouverture Publications Ltd, international Black African Caribbean booksellers and publishers, deposited in 2005 at London Metropolitan Archives, have acted as a 'hub' collection leading to the subsequent deposit of related community collections.[12] Working closely with trade associations can help open doors to particular business sectors. In the United Kingdom, a fairly comprehensive documentation of the pensions industry has been achieved by The Pensions Archive Trust. The Trust is formed of individuals from the sector with strong contacts in the industry, working in partnership with London Metropolitan Archives where most of the collections are deposited.[13] The case study of the Odense Steel Shipyard in Denmark (see Box 7.14) shows how stakeholder support can be rallied following closure of a key business in a region. Similarly, within a company the deposit of records perceived as significant and confidential, such as recent board meeting documentation, and the provision of an efficient helpful retrieval and advice service, may encourage record owners to trust the archive and deposit records more freely.

Documenting a business is often best achieved internally in liaison with the in-house records management team where one exists. Archivists should work closely with the company's records managers to develop strategies and processes that ensure historical records are identified on retention schedules and that records owners are clear how and when to send historical records to the archive (see Box 7.15). Retention schedules list different types of records and state how long they should be kept for legal, regulatory or operational reasons. Retention periods are generally based on a period of years from a retention event particular to the records in question, such as the date of creation, sale of a property or end of a customer relationship. Some records, however, may be better taken into the archive at the point of creation if they are known to be historical, such as regularly produced in-house publications or press releases or key series of committee minutes. Often such ongoing immediate accessions, negotiated direct with the record creators, will provide better assurance of comprehensive collecting.

Where a company does not have a records manager or formal retention schedule, or where key staff and departments are known not to use a records management system, the company archivist will have to be far more proactive, determining where records of historical importance may be created and working directly with those departments to identify and secure the transfer of key archives. Many of the records created at executive or senior level will be archival as these key records concern the overall strategy, policy and operations of the company. At business unit level a smaller proportion of documentation is likely to be historical because of the more administrative and transactional character of the records created.

The globalisation of businesses has major consequences for the documentation of their archives. How should a repository approach the almost impossible task of documenting worldwide operations? There are two approaches: the first is the centralised solution, where the repository proactively collects records representing the company's global activities, transferring them to the headquarters of the parent company. This demands large budgets and significant repository space to handle such a broad remit. The second is the decentralised approach, where the repository creates 'satellite' archive programmes

Box 7.14 Case study: the Odense Steel Shipyard 1918–2012, Denmark

The background:

The Odense Steel Shipyard was established in 1918 and eventually became a leading industrial company in Denmark. International competition led to declining profitability and in 2009 the owner, A. P. Moller–Maersk, decided to cease shipbuilding. The last ship left the shipyard in 2012. Upon the announcement of the cessation of shipbuilding the A. P. Moller–Maersk corporate archives initiated a project to secure the heritage of the Odense Steel Shipyard.

The lessons:

1. A rapid decision was made to secure the archives and related heritage in 2009 allowing time to establish and execute the project.
2. Positive and proactive communication with the business management about the vision and the plan laid the foundation for a constructive engagement in the project from all levels in the shipyard's organisation.
3. The project used the local press and the former employees to establish good-will and visibility among its external stakeholders, both proved effective communication channels to reach the 2,000+ workforce, their families and friends.
4. Economically and socially the closing of the shipyard had a negative impact on the locality, but a project aimed at securing the history of the company was perceived positively by all stakeholders. This underlying perception, based on the communication effort, made it easier to implement the project.

The outcome:

A project commenced in early 2010 to a) map the physical environment at the shipyard, b) identify relevant themes to describe the company history and c) secure the retention of any relevant records. Following on from this project the owning company decided to fund the production of a company history. A group of subject matter expert historians were contracted, research started in late 2012 and a two-volume book was published in 2016. The Odense Steel Shipyard archives have been retained in the A. P. Moller–Maersk archive.

Acknowledgement: Henning Morgen, A. P. Moller–Maersk Archives, by private communication.

Box 7.15 Case study: archives and records management at Unilever plc, United Kingdom

The background:

Archives and records management are fully integrated in Unilever in a holistic service, so the majority of records flow naturally from current use to the archive. However, the archivists are faced with a backlog of appraisal because details of all boxes, once they reach the end of their retention, have to be made up into appraisal packs and checked before a decision whether to transfer to archives or to destroy is made.

Archivists sought ways to streamline the process by classifying records on arrival into records management. Using the archive classification scheme and a selection of old transfer sheets and appraisal decision sheets as a guide, a list of records always transferred to archives and a list of records that were always to be destroyed was drawn up. The records management transfer sheet then had an additional tick box added at the bottom with the letters A, C and D. Records management support staff were given training to identify the classes of records on arrival and mark up the transfer sheets accordingly with A for anything to transfer directly to archives at the end of the retention period, D for anything to be destroyed without further inspection, and C for any material that might need appraisal at the end of its retention period. Only 29 per cent of records subsequently fell into the C category and required appraisal, as opposed to checking every box as previously.

Advantages:

- Creates a clear list of material suitable for preservation as archives.
- Creates a clear list of material to be routinely destroyed when retention periods expire.
- Far less time is spent on preparing appraisal packs and appraising records.
- Appraisal takes place more quickly.
- There are more clearly documented audit trails.

Requirements:

This system only works if the records management team is strict about accepting only boxes that contain the same class of records, and not mixed contents.

Source: Contributed by Jeannette Strickland, Archives Consultant, formerly Head of Art, Archives and Records Management, Unilever plc, by private communication.

in key regions or markets of the company, which maintain records locally, or deposits records externally in local collecting archives. The latter option is more commonly adopted for practical purposes and in the light of legal and language constraints. Local legislation can forbid the export of archives, as in Algeria and China, or require licenses to be procured, as in the Republic of Ireland. While for linguistic reasons it may not be useful to bring back to a repository based in Western Europe archives written in Arabic or oriental characters, which can not be read or understood. The life of a company can be unstable and subsidiaries based in different regions sold off and it would be a waste of resources for a centralised archive repository to import and process archives only to have to return them later. Both Mondelēz International (consumer goods) and HSBC (banking) are multinational companies, which operate satellite archive keeping programmes.

Appraisal – definitions, theory and practice

Appraisal is the crucial process, which helps the archivist select the records to be preserved as archives for the long term. Only a tiny percentage of all records generated are normally retained as archives. Records that are kept are deemed to have continuing value in evidencing past actions, supporting business operation and accountability and providing information for research. Each record has a lifecycle, from gestation and creation through active and semi-active use. Records that are no longer required are appraised and those selected for permanent preservation as archives are refined into an efficient, stream lined unit for ongoing business and/or research use. Appraisal is also a strategic management tool, ensuring budgets are spent storing high quality collections and that space is available for their continued growth.

There is no single right way to appraise business records. Terry Cook has called for an archival theory of appraisal, a theory of value developed by archivists and not by creators, users or society at large. Cook argued that only once an archival theory of appraisal has been defined, can an appraisal strategy, methodology and practice, be implemented (Cook, 2001). Archivists determining historical value will inevitably inject their own values into all decision making. However, if the archivist documents their appraisal decisions fully, their assumptions and actions will be accountable and explicable to users and others in the future.

Decision making can be contentious and subject to ethical debate. Reasons can always be found to keep material that someone might want to see and decisions will inevitably be subjective, based on the appraiser's knowledge, interests, experience and their repository's resources. When the archives of Standard Chartered Bank held in London were offered at short notice to Guildhall Library in 1989, with an ultimatum that they would be destroyed if not accepted, the archivist had to take tough decisions, including placing cut-off dates on the record series transferred (Freeth, 1991). For corporate archives, appraisal decisions will certainly be impacted by business requirements and strategy as archivists need to consider legal and operational requirements as well as the historical value of records to both the business and to external researchers. The appraiser cannot control the past, but their decisions will impact the way the past is documented and perceived. Table 7.2 compares the variety of professional opinion on appraisal.

Planning

It is important, given the sheer bulk of records created during the past two centuries, to start from the position of disposal and consider why the material should be kept at all. The appraiser will, with experience, develop their confidence and ability to think strategically and to justify the retention of records as archives. They should aim to make an informed selection based on the following planning considerations:

- Methodology should be linked to the repository's collections policy which provides a framework for decision making.
- A sound understanding of the organisational context of the business that created the records should be gained. The appraiser should check the accession file, and may seek advice from colleagues, company staff, historians or user groups.
- The evidential and informational value of the records should be weighed against the resources and costs required to maintain them. Storage budgets, for example, will be a key consideration in the case of large collections of physical and digital records. A lack of digital archives expertise may prove to be a stumbling block when appraising obscure file formats and complex IT infrastructure. Finding the right balance may be achieved by selecting records that document key information in a concise way. For live businesses, records of ongoing importance for administrative, financial, legal, operational or promotional purposes should be prioritised and retained more fully. According to archival theorist Theodore Schellenberg (1956), the primary value of records is for the originating business, the secondary value is for researchers.
- Records retention and disposal schedules should be in place to identify series of potential long-term value requiring appraisal and those for systematic destruction.
- Criteria should be adopted in line with local and international legislation on retention of information together with reference to good commercial practice and law.[14] Material should not be destroyed without checking if it still has a current purpose, for example, unregistered property deeds or plans may be needed to establish legal title and company law may require certain recent records to be available for shareholder consultation.
- The repository should make the intention to dispose of any items clear at the time records are acquired and this should be referenced in agreements along with any necessary consents. It is advisable to arrange confidential destruction of unwanted items to avoid accidental re-circulation of items or inappropriate access and this may anyway be required by a company's records management policy.

Business series for appraisal

Business records benefit from a systematic approach towards their appraisal. Table 7.3 suggests a way to approach appraisal by setting out the retention values applicable to each business function and considering the opportunities for appraisal.

The appraiser should consider if 'patchy' records of minor, defunct subsidiaries or branches are worth keeping. An in-house corporate archive may decide that they are not core records and may consider depositing them with a local collecting repository if they are felt to have local or wider informational value. Non-core records should be

Table 7.3 Opportunities for appraisal

Functions or categories	Record types	Value for evidence of business decisions or wider informational value	Opportunities for appraisal
Corporate and administrative	Constitutional records such as memoranda and articles of association, certificates of incorporation, executive minutes, policies, plans, reports, procedures, files of individuals in key positions or departments.	These series are vital in safeguarding evidence of a business's foundation, governance and operations and support consistent decision making. They have legal value. These records provide a useful distilled overview for researchers.	There is less opportunity to appraise these records. These series distil information held in bulkier operational series. Departmental files usually require appraisal.
Shareholding	Registers of shareholders, application and allotment books, debenture registers, transfer registers, probate registers, dividend books.		These series should be appraised. They do not add greatly to knowledge of a business and rarely give detailed information on individual shareholders. They are also bulky and may need to be heavily weeded. It is suggested the earliest volumes of large series are kept as evidence of the establishment of the business.
Legal and premises	Contracts and agreements, statutory reports, patents and licences to operate, instruments including delegation of authority, property records including deeds, plans and inventories.	These records are proof of an event or agreement. They document the obligations, commitments, rights and delegations of authority. These records are core evidential records subject to longer retention periods as semi-current records. There is no security or foundation for past decision making if these are not retained.	Advice should be sought where records reflect a business which is still active, or where buildings are still in use. Records reflecting minor arrangements and building works such as repairs, and installation of utility services (for example, heating and air-conditioning) should be appraised rigorously.
Financial	Annual statements of account, returns, audit and statutory reports, budget policy and planning, reports on exceptional	These series should be kept as proof of honest and fair conduct of affairs, and to support the financial standing of the	Annual reports and statements of account distil information contained in lower financial series but they may simply offer the picture a company

Category		
results, ledgers and other series recording financial transactions.	business. Financial records are important in gaining an understanding of a business's transactions and successes and failures.	wishes to project. More detailed series such as ledgers and journals should also be retained. The lowest financial series should be appraised rigorously. These can include petty cash books, bank pass books, invoices and routine taxation records.
Production and operational (relating to the purpose of the business)	Plant, factory and sales records (these vary considerably from one business sector to another). For further information see Chapters 4 and 5.	These should be kept as a record of a company's processes and products, transactions, successes (especially key assets such as recipes, inventions and designs) and failures.	Production and operational series may be sampled (see Box 7.17).
Staff	Staff and employment records.	These are core evidential records subject to longer retention periods as semi-current records.	Staff files should normally be sampled or rejected due to their bulk and restrictions required to protect personal information. Some salary books give limited information such as name and payment only and therefore should not always be retained.
Marketing	These records can include advertising posters, press material, photographic series and audio-visual footage.	These records tend to have high informational and display value but are not core evidential records.	Retain final sets, original artwork and designs, and appraise proofs and press items which will be found elsewhere in publications.
Reference material	Records not created by the company.	These records may have related informational value but are not core evidential records.	Heavily appraise 'collected' items not created by the business. These can include reference material which might be more appropriately retained in a library.

compared with key head office record series to ensure distilled information about the activities of subsidiaries, branches and minor functions are held elsewhere. Lower level records detailing routine activities or transactions may lend themselves to sampling or macro-appraisal where only records of units of key importance to the business are retained.

Methodologies

Different approaches can be instigated in appraising records:

- File-by-file, also known as micro-appraisal, is a methodology that involves the analysis of each record. A set of values and criteria are applied to assess the evidential and informational value of each record. This methodology is useful for ensuring that all records are seen and assessed and nothing is missed, and should be used for series produced by a key individual or function, or for multiple small, unsorted series.
- Functional analysis, also known as macro-appraisal, involves consideration of the functions of a business and their wider context. Criteria are applied to the records based on the relative importance of the function that created them. This method is useful for bulky, large series, which are well organised, listed and their content generally known. Not all records need to be looked at, and this approach can therefore be an efficient, less costly way of appraising records. However, this method may overlook the potential research value of some information held at file level.
- Sampling methodology can be applied where the validity of keeping a whole series of records is doubtful, but where full destruction is felt to be too drastic. Sampling is best used for large series of routine case files, which may have some high informational value but demonstrate little value for ongoing operational business use. Sampling can be either selective, which involves subjective choices; systematic, where a selection is made according to a pattern, for example topographic or numeric such as every tenth numbered file; chronological, such as retention of all files for every fifth year only; or random. Larger samples tend to provide a better retention result, and work well where a robust records management system is in place. Sampling can also show how a business documented or performed particular activities without retaining complete record series.

Box 7.16 gives an example of an appraisal plan using sampling and file-by-file methodologies to reduce a large record series.

The appraiser should ask the following questions of the records being assessed in order to make decisions:[15]

- Do they conform to the collection policy?
- Are there existing appraisal guidelines?
- Are they core records of the business; do they cover the origins, structure and policy of the creating business?
- Do they document the rights of the business?
- Do they document the financial responsibilities of the business?
- Do they offer useful, 'low level' informational material for research or would they help answer queries often received by the repository?
- Do they offer potential for promotional purposes or display?

Box 7.16 Case study: an appraisal plan for a large production series from the archives of Chubb Fire Security Ltd, United Kingdom

The collection:

- Title and brief history: Chubb Fire Security Ltd, Pyrene Division (formerly Pyrene Company Ltd, acquired by Chubb & Son Ltd, 1967), of Hanworth Air Park and Victoria Road, Feltham, London.
- Accession number: 1999/062.
- Extent: 21.5 shelf metres (170 boxes containing around 1,290 files).
- Legal status: records owned by City of London, London Metropolitan Archives.
- Scope of records: centralised series of factory files (1960s–80s) containing product specifications and correspondence, material lists, drawings, inspection reports, export papers. Files record the production of fire-fighting vehicles and equipment produced for global export to customers for airfields, oil refineries and other uses.
- Created by: W. Hall, Vehicle Production Controller (VPC), D. Biggs, Factory Manager and Mr Wooden, Chief Draughtsman of Vehicle Drawing Office.
- Arrangement: arranged and labelled by sales reference number giving customer name, product type, country destination, and vehicle chassis type.

Listings give reference numbers and summarise product range and customer base.

Justification and methodology:

This series complements other company records but is bulky with over 50 per cent of files covering routine products with little information on the customers or countries they were exported to. The method is to sample files to document the range produced using the listing to select reference numbers, then conduct a file-by-file check for any 'outstanding' files giving detailed information on customers and countries.

Step	Procedure	Estimated time
Step one: sampling	Keep sample of vehicles manufactured (most important) by reviewing list and extracting a ratio of files covering 56 different vehicles identified from the lists. Sample to also reflect a range of countries and vehicle chassis types.	0.5 days
Step two: file-by-file review	Select any remaining outstanding files showing major issues/impact of customers/countries on production. For example: File 7737 High Altitude Airfield Crashtender for High Commission of India includes correspondence on impact of Indian Standards.	3 days (based on pilot on 4 shelf metres)

Step three: disposal and finishing off	Re-box and relocate files for retention, and organise confidential disposal of unwanted material. No permissions required. Record decisions in accession file. Dispose of unwanted files including minor products: for example two-wheel rubber suspension units, foam trailers, conversions, dry powder/jet monitor, carbon dioxide cylinders (all of which are covered in major orders).	1–1.5 days

Summary and targets:

Estimated time: 1 week for 1 person. Space likely to be saved: 18.8 shelf metres (or if only a file-by-file review adopted: 10.5 metres – based on pilot).

Acknowledgement: London Metropolitan Archives. Prepared by the author with assistance from K. Rawson.

If the answer is yes, to one or more of the above, consider retaining the records.

- Are they mainly incoherent, incomplete series, which will be less useful for systematic research?
- Are they duplicated or maintained elsewhere in another form or in a higher level series such as reports or minutes?
- Is the quantity too great to retain for the quality of information that the records provide?
- Does their format and condition pose retention problems?

If the answer is yes to one or more of the above, consider disposing of the records. Duplicates should only be retained if they can be used as secondary copies for display use. Other considerations may include:

- Do they require access restrictions to maintain the privacy of the business, its staff and customers? External repositories may not be in a position to justify maintaining deposited business records which are restricted for years or decades to come.
- Do they relate to other records already held or kept elsewhere? This may support their retention, or their disposal by destruction or transfer to another repository.
- Do the records have existing finding aids such as classification schemes, filing references, plans, registers or indexes that can assist the appraisal process?
- Are the records part of larger production or case series that might lend themselves to file-by-file or sampling appraisal?
- Are the records well-organised with a discernible arrangement, which supports their retention as they are easy to maintain and catalogue later?

The appraiser should record their decision making in appraisal documentation, which should be kept by the repository in the accession file and noted in the catalogue once the collection has been listed. See Box 7.17 for an example of an appraisal report with authorisations for record disposal.

Box 7.17 Example (fictitious) of appraisal decision–making documentation

1. Context:

Company: GOING BANANAS (IMPORT AND EXPORT) INC, Sunny Island, Tropicana Sea, Southern Ocean.

Description and formats: Head Office Management Department subject files (250 hardcopy files, 7 linear metres) and 9,000 digital documents on main registry B Drive.

Accession reference(s): 2013/018.

Dates of creation: c.1970s–2006.

Administrative history of series: Centralised record keeping began in 1970 under the Administrative Manager. In 1984 changed name to become Office Management Department. In 2013 the department was abolished with the sale of Banana House, Sunny Island head office. Activities were de-centralised to banana-producing offices.

Custodial history of series: Records remained under control of the Office Management Department until 2013.

2. Findings:

Need for review/extent of evidential and informational value: The series adds value to the board and committees series covering policy, reporting, circulars, asset management and information on a wide variety of subjects which are not covered in detail elsewhere. However, many items relate to property refurbishments and orders for banana-picking equipment which do not contain unique historical information.

Link and relationship with collecting policy: Contains core records (see Collections Policy version 2).

Related records: As above.

Restrictions on access and use: Files contain staffing matters which are to be restricted.

Condition of records: Good, files were kept in office conditions.

Future accruals: None. Later files were handed to banana-producing offices for business reasons and will be added to their own registries.

3. Record of appraisal:

Details of record series appraised	Criteria used	Extents disposed and kept, and time taken
Subject files 1970s–1990s, 250 files (7 linear metres)	Disposal of files on minor works and routine administrative banana equipment orders (Retention Policy version 9).	100 files (3 linear metres) disposed of. 150 files (4 linear metres) retained. 6 hours
9,000 digital documents on main registry B drive	Disposal of draft report registry (1999–2003), equipment order folders A–Z (2000–2006) and duplicate versions (Retention Policy version 9 and Digital Record Ingest Procedure Note). Further appraisal required once ingested.	3,000 documents (56 GB) disposed of. 6,000 documents (90 GB) retained. 2 days

4. Disposal information and authorisation:

Disposal type (destruction, return to depositor or third party): Destruction.

Depositor consent and repository authorisations/dates/signatures: Authorised by [name], Office Manager, 11 June 2016. See email on file. Authorised by [name], Lead Archivist, 25 June 2016. [Signed].

5. Catalogue update

Appraisal field in catalogue description updated: Catalogue series reference code: 21/01 (subject files only).

Date/cataloguer name: [Name], Cataloguing Archivist, 25 June 2018.

Finding aids

Archives cannot be easily understood, accessed or effectively managed without finding aids. These can encompass temporary box lists, full catalogues, indexes and guides. Finding aids represent and interpret the context and content of archives. They enable repository staff and users to make choices and searches in a variety of different ways, and protect records by limiting access to those with appropriate rights. Finding aids should aim to incorporate the expertise and knowledge gained by a cataloguer or indexer, and convey that understanding to the user in an easily intelligible way.

Archival arrangement and description are the main processes in cataloguing. They reflect a truly intellectual art. Unlike the published book, which neatly presents its own independent description, an archival item cannot be understood and actually loses its value without reference to the wider context in which it was created. Archives can often be loose and unsorted and individual items do not always tell the cataloguer all that they need to know in order to describe them. Large, complex business archives can present even greater challenges because they can contain items reflecting multiple companies subject to constantly changing organisational structure and nomenclature.

The task of cataloguing can, however, be made easier if carried out in compliance with national or international cataloguing and indexing standards. These conventions outline how records should be described and are recognised by professional archive bodies. They provide consistency for users and facilitate the sharing of information. The following section focuses on the main steps in the creation of catalogues and indexes. Proprietary archival cataloguing software packages are widely available, but tend to be national in distribution and common use. Such software is often compliant with international cataloguing standards and provides an easy way to ensure all data elements are appropriately captured and that large amounts of descriptive information can be easily searched and manipulated. Tabular spreadsheets may, however, be sufficient for small repositories without proprietary archival software. Spreadsheets enable data to be entered into pre-defined fields that can be prepared and migrated into an archival software system later. Software databases should ideally be relational so that the finding aid database's fields are shared with those in related accessions, loans, conservation and locations databases. They should also allow easy migration of datasets, and dissemination of data as, for example, is provided by Encoded Archival Description (EAD).[16] Ideally any digital preservation repository system will be linked to, or integrated with, the catalogue to seamlessly connect related information and activity. Digital archives software should allow users the opportunity to view descriptions within their wider hierarchical context and not compromise the implementation of professional descriptive standards.

The intended final form of, and access to, a catalogue will determine which of the following steps are required, and their relative importance. For example, if the catalogue is only intended to exist as a database, and to be accessed solely by a business's archive staff, then the requirements and cataloguing processes will be very different from those of a collecting repository that will provide a catalogue and related indexes for public use.

Step one – temporary lists

The quantity of accessions received by a repository may not always be matched by the same rate of cataloguing. It is always preferable to list archive accessions as soon as they are received so that the cataloguer can reach out to the depositing business department for contextual and technical information as records are described and create well-informed authority records (see Step Six). However, there are practical solutions for repositories that must establish the content of their collections, but that lack the resources to embark immediately on full-scale cataloguing. Temporary transfer schedules completed by depositors or box lists are invaluable in allowing content to be quickly ascertained. Table 7.4 gives an example of a summary box list and the data elements that can be recorded. Temporary numbers can be given to each box or volume that can be replaced by final references and more detailed descriptions when they are fully catalogued in the long term.

Temporary lists should never be seen as an alternative to catalogues, however tempting this might be where other priorities compete for archivists' time. The disadvantages of temporary lists, as shown in Table 7.4, are that they lack detail, tend to be unstructured,

Table 7.4 Extract from a sample temporary list

Include accession reference, collection name, and date and by whom list completed.

Temporary number	Sub-creator (if known)	Brief description	Dates	Extent	Notes on appraisal, access or condition
001 of 203	Company Secretary	Private letter books on policy and staff	1934–1989	8 volumes	Access restrictions apply
001 of 203	Company Secretary	Subject files and correspondence	1970s	22 files and 1 bundle	Require appraisal
002 of 203	Marketing Department	Advertising proofs and adverts	1960s	1 box	Pages stuck together
003 of 203	Accountant	Cash books	1967–1989	1 box	
004 of 203	Mixed/ unknown	Digital records on CD and audio-cassettes	2000s	1 box	Content requires upload to server and further identification
005–010 of 203	Marketing Department	Price lists and leaflets	1930s–1980s	6 boxes	

in that there may be no order between one part of the collection and another, and may have a degree of inaccuracy where material has been assessed quickly and hidden content missed. Consequently, much contextual information about an archive as a whole is missing and the list cannot permit easy use or a high level of control by the repository over a collection. For example, in making uncatalogued collections available there is an increased likelihood that unnumbered records may unknowingly be misplaced. In addition there is an increased danger that records in poor condition or subject to access restrictions are accidentally made available to users. Such risks can make archive repositories wary of making uncatalogued items publicly available.

Step two – prioritising and resourcing cataloguing

All accessions should be assigned a cataloguing priority based on their relative importance and likely user demand, balanced against the collection's complexity and size in the light of cataloguing resource and likely future accruals. For example, in-house corporate archives may prioritise head office executive level records for their key evidential value or photographs for their promotional value over those of less significant functions in order to meet core business needs.

The accession file, existing lists and the records themselves should be checked and further information sought from contextual histories or reports and from the depositor. Details of likely accruals, access restrictions, conservation needs and the degree of appraisal, sorting, description and packaging required should also be considered. These will impact on the level of experience the cataloguer requires and whether specialist support is needed from the record owners or other experts. Larger cataloguing projects can benefit from the process being split into stages aligned to the staff expertise required, after an archivist has sorted and appraised the records and ascertained the catalogue structure. Simple series with similar content could, where appropriate, be delegated to a para-professional or volunteer who would also label and package items as directed by the archivist. For example, Wolverhampton City Archives' project *Taking account of our past* cataloguing the archive collection of Smith, Son & Wilkie, chartered accountants, benefitted from this phased approach, which saw about 1,800 hours of volunteer input over 18 months in repackaging, basic conservation, research and indexing of records already listed by the project archivist. The selection and cataloguing of technical series can also benefit from input from record creators and industry specialists who understand them best. The Ballast Trust, for example, is a charitable foundation established in 1988 to support the preservation and cataloguing of the archives of the shipbuilding and heavy industries of the west of Scotland. The Trust is staffed by volunteers with an industrial background supervised by an archivist. Together, they catalogue technical records on behalf of archive repositories, drawing on the expertise of their voluntary workers.[17]

Cataloguing should be project managed with realistic targets set and monitored to ensure completion. It is suggested a 10 per cent time contingency is included in large-scale projects to allow for any unforeseen challenges, such as staffing changes. In-house corporate archives should negotiate and allocate internal resources, but at the same time be prepared to defend the activity and demonstrate the benefits which archive cataloguing brings to the business. An imminent anniversary can, for example, be utilised to demonstrate the importance and value of examining and describing records fully. In the case of a collecting repository funding should be sought for cataloguing deposited archives from the live business before looking to wider national, lottery or charitable funding streams. Negotiations for funding may be better at the point of acquisition when there is support for retention and consequent next steps relating to the records at decision-making levels. Some repositories may request companies to pay an annual management fee for storage, however many depositors prefer to avoid being locked into an annual arrangement and would rather agree one-off payments that are matched to defined activities. A budget proposal to the owner can be the simplest and swiftest way of obtaining funding (see Box 7.18). Business-funded projects may involve a less onerous degree of reporting compared to other funding scenarios as well as encouraging ongoing dialogue between the depositing company and the repository.

Step three – arrangement

Hierarchy of levels and ISAD(G)

The arrangement of an archive collection is an intellectual process, which requires careful analysis of provenance, content and interrelations between records. The order of and relationship between items should ideally be based on the structure or functions of the originating business or individual. Arrangement of a collection should not always be designed for the convenience of staff or users, even though they will expect it. The end product should enable users to understand and evaluate documents in the context of the creating unit, function or individual, as well as on their own merits. Index terms (see Step six below) can help users get around the difficulties such arrangement may lead to, such as records relating to the same customer or same premises being held in different file series.

Box 7.18 Proposal for a budget for business-funded cataloguing

1. Title [name of the collection]

   Include the date; the name, position and department/business of the individual the report is for; and the name and contact details of repository staff who prepared the proposal.

2. Summary: Outline how the proposal fits with the business's objectives, for example a major anniversary or a particular research demand such as a new corporate history publication. Summarise the proposal's recommendations for future development of the archives, with the request for funding for employment of staff to catalogue the records and related archive packaging, conservation and/or digitisation. Include where appropriate details of opportunities for staff learning and development and the involvement of volunteers. Provide a brief explanation of the repository, including where it is based, and its purpose and provide links to further information.

3. The archives:

   a) Background: Include details on previous work progress including surveys, information on agreements and names of past liaison contacts.

   b) Scope and access: Outline the value of the records for the business/for wider research. Give a brief description, extent and covering dates including known further records to be deposited. Explain the current lack of finding aids to the collection and related limitations, and evidence of demand for access with examples.

4. Funding/budget: Outline the proposed project dates and reiterate how this fits with any time-bound targets and policy. Provide a breakdown of the proposed budget in a table with brief explanations and provisos; for example 'this figure is subject to a survey which may reveal more records'. Figures should include any additional costs such as tax.

Aspect of work	Details and explanation	Cost
Employment of cataloguing staff		
Supervision/management (for example 10 per cent of staff cost above)		
Archival packaging		
Related aspects such as conservation, digitisation and outreach (including exhibition and events)		
Total		

5. Conclusion: Summarise recommendations and the next steps. Include a request to the contact to raise the proposal with decision maker(s) and an invitation to discuss the recommendations further.

Arrangement must be demonstrated through hierarchical levels of description (see Table 7.5) as defined by *General international standard archival description* (International Council on Archives, 2000). This standard, familiarly known as ISAD(G), is the most widely recognised standard for arranging and describing archives and was first adopted by the International Council on Archives in 1994. The fonds or collection level normally refers to the main creator and is the top level. The series is the highest level that describes actual records, and file level is the commonly-used description linked to retrievable volumes, digital files or bundles in a collection.

There is no requirement for physical arrangement, unless that will aid retrieval, and in the case of large collections it is unlikely that rearrangements would be practical or necessary as long as accurate information on the location of records is maintained. Indeed, random physical storage may be preferred as an aid to security.

Arrangement in practice

The key to arranging archival material is to review content and establish a structured set of groupings according to the main creators. In the context of cataloguing, the term 'creator' can mean the last active business user of a record, not necessarily its original author or compiler. In an ideal scenario the cataloguer should, therefore, first gain an understanding of the business or department and its function, activities, transactions as well as its structure and key players. However, there will usually not be the time to undertake this research in advance and such information may only become apparent during the process of cataloguing. The accession file should be checked for notes, together with relevant publications and articles. Other archival items, such as internal staff handbooks, organisational charts and telephone directories, can be very useful to track provenance and functional fit. The depositor of the records or specialist researchers may also be of assistance if insufficient information is available elsewhere. The cataloguer should compile lists of names and roles for reference and put together administrative or biographical histories, including name changes of particular departments or functions, as work progresses. This information will also form part of the catalogue description.[18]

Where feasible, a survey of the collection, using any existing lists, should also be conducted to ascertain the record types and corresponding creating department(s), staff positions, and activities and transactions, which generated them. This will help the cataloguer to arrange and describe the records in line with their creators, business function and original order. The survey also helps ensure that all records are accounted for from the start and avoids unnecessary re-arrangement of records later to slot items in. A temporary list (see Table 7.4) may help the cataloguer avoid problems presented by limited sorting space by supporting the ability to select specific items from storage for cataloguing.

If resource is limited it may be more practical to list records randomly within their fonds, after identifying key series, assigning each record the next running reference number. Each record could be assigned a functional label (based on a scheme similar to that in Table 7.6) to enable sorting of records within a fonds (in a database this label could exist as a dedicated field within each record). Alternatively items could be assigned a temporary number during cataloguing, which could be replaced with a permanent number once the collection had been arranged intellectually on the completion of the

Table 7.5 Explanation of hierarchical levels of archive description

Level	Concerns creators or records	Explanation	Examples
Fonds	Creators	This level relates to the collection as a whole and reflects records usually derived from a common source consisting of one or more accessions. The records have a common history of creation and function, although the history of custody may vary according to where records have accrued over time.	Great Entertainments plc
Sub-fonds Sub-sub fonds	Creators	These levels relate to sub-divisions of a main creator, usually reflecting linked companies, business functions, departments or named individuals.	Operations Events Manager
Series (and further divisions as sub-series and so on)	Records	The highest level representing records in the collection. These are normally groups of records resulting from the same accumulation, filing process or activity often with alphabetical, chronological or numerical attributes.	Music band files
File	Records	This level concerns an organised unit of documents, grouped together because they relate to the same subject, activity or transaction. File level is the most commonly used in the hierarchy for handling, production and citation of records.	'Rainbow Parrots Rock: 2–5 May 1997' (original event file)
Item	Records	This is the smallest intellectually indivisible unit of a record.	Single page in the file of an outgoing copy letter from the Events Manager concerning band's failure to turn up and ticket refunds (3 May 1997)

cataloguing. Such an approach allows for the inevitable ongoing additions to the deposit from a live business.

The key to discovering the creator, the creating function and its provenance is to question each record by asking:

- 'By or for whom were you created?' to work out the creator;
- 'For what purpose?' to identify the function; and
- 'Why were you found where you were?' to highlight the provenance of the record.

For example, in correspondence files incoming letters should be checked to establish to whom they have been written and ascertain if there is a common name and/or position, which may point to the name of the creator(s) who accumulated the file. The cataloguer should beware of copy or blind-copies of letters that were sent between third parties, and draft letters that were never sent at all. Cataloguers should also avoid making complex structures for passively collected items that do not represent active corporate entities. For example, unsigned minutes of company X, which were received for reference purposes by staff of organisation Y, do not constitute part of the true records of company X. The minutes should therefore either be arranged under department or staff role of organisation Y, which received them, or disposed of if they are patchy or known to duplicate the archives of company X.

The cataloguer's findings should be used to sketch out an outline scheme using ISAD(G) hierarchical levels. The cataloguer should be able to justify why material has been arranged in a particular way and understand the impact of the decisions he or she has taken on the evidential quality of the records and the way in which they will be accessed. Table 7.6 provides guidance on good and bad practice in archival arrangement.

Business classification by both function and creator

A compromise can be made between creator, provenance and function in the arrangement of company archives, but it should be made clear where such an order has been used to artificially structure a collection. Box 7.19 provides a detailed arrangement scheme template, which matches each of the functions against a business's creating departments, individual positions and other entities and orders the records accordingly. Despite the inherent uniqueness of each company and the information content of the archives generated, similar record-types will be encountered from one business archive to another because such records are generated in accordance with prevailing legislative and administrative procedures. This model improves consistency in arrangement and avoids re-thinking structures, helping both staff and users. Care should be taken not to use broad functional categories such as subjects, placing items in one category simply because that is what the archives are about without regard to their origin or context.

Subsidiaries and predecessors

Records of a company's predecessors and subsidiaries should be arranged within the main firm's archival structure but remain distinct from their parent as they have their own legal entity. A business's subsidiaries may be sold off at a future date and their records may well have to be separated out and transferred to a new owner. Records of amalgamated companies should remain separate prior to the takeover and then under the same section as the pre-merger company, which technically made the takeover. Where the merger has taken place on an equal basis and neither of the pre-existing companies has continued, the newly formed company should be given a new section.[19] Box 7.19 offers guidance on reference codes for subsidiary and acquired companies and Box 7.20 provides an example of hierarchical arrangement for a complex business.

There is no single right way to arrange business archives. The broad classification described above is not useful for small collections with no further accruals expected. A much simpler structure, such as fonds, series and file level, or fonds and file level, would be more suitable. Such a simple structure is also likely to be relevant for in-house corporate archives serving a live business, where there needs to be sufficient flexibility to accommodate likely additions and ongoing changes to organisational structures and functions.

Table 7.6 Best practice tips for archival arrangement

Aspect of arrangement	Good practice	Poor practice
Creators (fonds, sub-fonds)	Always arrange records by their creator. For example, by the company, then (where known with certainty) by the sub-creators such as departments, offices and branches which created, received or accumulated and used the records as part of the business. This arrangement is sometimes reflected in the provenance of items, but often cannot easily be determined. It helps protect the chain of custody and provenance of archival material; it respects who originally handled the records, establishing their authenticity and integrity. In practice, arrangement by sub-creators works best in cases where businesses had rigid departments which did not change greatly over time, although this is in reality a rare scenario. Companies often change name during their lifetime reflecting partnerships changes, name change registration, and so on, but they remain the same entity and their records should accordingly be kept together.	Never mix records from different creators or sources unless there is a good reason to do so. An exception might be where business records have been separated in the past, such as those taken home by a former employee and later offered back by their family. Never split a collection unless this conforms to the repository's collections policy. For example, head office records may be kept separate from branches or subsidiaries held locally or in external repositories. Never 'invent' creating departments where there is no evidence that they existed.
Functions and activities (fonds, sub-fonds)	Always arrange records by main creator(s), then by business function where creating departments are generally unknown. Arrangement by function suits company archives as it can reflect departments which were radically reorganised over time, but where the function and record series remained the same. It also helps standardise arrangements and assists organisation of personal collections where individuals had various interests.	Remember that functional arrangement is artificially imposed. Problems of attribution can occur. For example, whether wage books are to be catalogued under the staff function or, as a financial record, under finance. Beware treating functions as subjects and splitting known original groupings of records. For example, the secretariat's files on business property should not be removed from other subject files, to go under premises. A more practical arrangement might be to avoid any artificially-imposed structure and instead add a functional classification or marker to each record which is independent of the arrangement but which allows for sorting of records into a recognisable order.

Ordering by importance	Where it is intended to produce some form of ordered catalogue, always arrange the list according to the relative importance of creators and functions to the continuation of the business. Arrange items from high level corporate documents such as memoranda and articles of association and board minutes generated by the executive and secretariat, down to lower level business unit working files (see Box 7.20). There will be no need for such ordering where the catalogue will exist solely in the form of a database.	Never plan an overall arrangement by the oldest, most used, or monetarily most 'valuable' records.
Original order (series to item level)	Always use the original order of records where it is present, makes sense and adds to understanding of the provenance and custodial history of a series. Make this clear in final catalogues by highlighting original files and noting former references. The reason for reconstructing the order when archives were managed as live records is that it helps reveal a business's culture and organisation independent of the content of the records themselves. The original order of records will often have changed during the course of their life and there may be evidence of this on file covers. Sometimes the records may be so haphazard that it will be impossible to tell how they were originally kept. Common sense must prevail in such instances and an artificial re-order that makes sense to the user, such as by subject, chronology or other arrangement should be made explicit and documented.	Never 'break-up' or re-order meaningful original files. For example, remove an annotated newsletter found in an original file containing related correspondence, and add the issue to a newsletter series. Add related unit description to the series to alert users to the presence of the item. It is appropriate to remove certain formats from original files such as photographs which require different storage conditions for their preservation. The archive catalogue description of the photographs should appear adjacent to the description of the rest of the file. The removal should be made clear and stated in each description, for example 'originally found in [reference code]' and 'See [reference code] for photographs originally found in this file'.
Formats (series to item level)	At lower levels below creators and functions always arrange records in coherent series which have a common 'look' or informational content. These will often have a chronological or alphabetical sequence resulting from a filing process.	Never arrange archives by record format without reference to the creator. For example, the signed minutes of a holding company and its constituent subsidiaries should not be kept under one series, unless they are composite and bound together. Similarly, files contained on discs should not necessarily be grouped together under one 'digital records' section, however easier this may make it to manage that record format.

Box 7.19 Classification arrangement for business archives

Each section below refers to a sub-fonds, and departments as sub-sub-fonds. The record types refer to series level. Each section is numbered and is suggested as a scheme for sub-fonds reference codes.

A: Corporate bodies (use for records from businesses)

01: Corporate

This section normally reflects key records of the corporate body rather than departmental copies and come under the Secretary's responsibility

Foundation records: charters, acts, deeds of settlement, memoranda and articles of association (mode of conducting business and internal organisation), partnership and liquidation agreements

Signed minutes of meetings of managing body (board of directors or partners) and records relating to these meetings including agendas, presented papers, resolutions of meetings

Signed minutes of annual general meeting and other meetings of shareholders and related records including annual reports and proceedings

Committee minutes and related records

Registers of directors and so on

Seal registers

Powers of attorney

02: Shares (records marked with a star should be sampled or rejected)

Share records will normally reflect the Secretary's or Registrar's responsibility

Prospectuses

Registers of shareholders★

Application and allotment books★

Debenture registers★

Transfer registers★

Probate registers★

Dividend books★

Annual returns to Registrar of Companies

Amalgamation/liquidation records, for example notices to shareholders

03: Administration (internal records of the head office)

Normally arranged under department or individual name, for example, Chairman, Secretary's Department or General Manager's Department

General letter books and correspondence

Memoranda books

Subject files, reports, project papers, business plans and organisational charts

General legal papers, for example counsel's opinions

Speeches

04: Accounting and financial (internal records of the head office)
Include records of financial and taxation departments
Balance sheets and profit and loss accounts (not for shareholders)
Trial balances
Private ledgers
General ledgers
Nominal ledgers
Sales and purchase ledgers (and other specialised ledgers)
Journals/cash books/income or expenditure accounts
Bills receivable/payable – registers and other items
Bad and doubtful debt books/creditors books
Investment books (except where investment is the business of the company)

05: Legal (internal records of the head office, other than property or premises)
Include here records of legal department or legal representative
Cases
Opinions and solicitors' papers

06: Operation/Production
This section is reserved for records of the factory, or operational departments
– see also Agency/Branch below
Production series (vary according to business, for example reflecting customers/
manufacturing, events or estate businesses)
Estimate and order books
Daybooks, production cost ledgers and estimates
Distribution books
Letter books and correspondence
Technical specifications, drawings and plans
Patents and related licences
Equipment and product stock and inventories
Research and development records such as laboratory notebooks and major
projects
Photographs

07: Marketing and advertising
This section can be used for publicity departments
Event, sales promotion and publicity records including marketing research and
policy reports, sale catalogues, leaflets, advertisements, photographs, audio-
visual material, websites.

08: Staff and employment
Use for records of human resources departments
Staff registers
Wages and salaries books
Selected recruitment forms and papers and staff files

Staff rules and manuals
Pension scheme records
Industrial relations records
Recreation clubs' and societies' records
Newsletters
Photographs

09: Premises and property (except where property is the business of company. Use for records of Premises and Estates Departments)
Premises including building agreements, drawings, plant registers, inventories
Property records including rentals, valuations and surveys
Title deeds

10: History
Unpublished histories, photographs, audio-visual material (not used for marketing and advertising) including oral history recordings.

11: Agency/branch (distinct from head office)
Records created and kept by these entities. This section should not be used for material recorded or submitted to head office or other business entities about agencies or branches.

12: Family
Records of families are often closely linked with their business, and can be impossible to separate from 'true' business records.

13: Subsidiaries/Acquired companies (use next number for each or adopt a letter code using the name(s) of the business(es) in reference codes to denote each one)
Archives of each company can be given its own section and records can take a similar arrangement as shown above.

B: Individuals (use for personal collections which are to be kept together as one unit. These archives may well present a mixture of business and non-business elements)
Arrange under the name of the individual records of each business interest or organisation with which the individual was involved:
- A–Z by name of organisation or by the chronology the individual's involvement.
- grouped by functional theme where multiple interests such as directorships are represented. For example sub–fonds may include 'Agriculture', 'Glass', 'Shipping' and 'Steel'.
- in simple series for small collections or a single business enterprise run by the individual(s).

Acknowledgement: London Metropolitan Archives. Adapted from a business classification scheme originally developed by the predecessor to London Metropolitan Archives.

Box 7.20 Hierarchical arrangement showing the context of four file-level descriptions (marked in bold)

CLC/B/207 STANDARD CHARTERED BANK (fonds)

CLC/B/207/CH CHARTERED BANK OF INDIA, AUSTRALIA AND CHINA (sub-fonds)

CH01 CORPORATE (sub–sub-fonds)

CH01/01 Foundation (sub–sub–sub-fonds)

CH01/02 Board (sub–sub–sub-fonds)

CH01/03 Annual general meetings (sub–sub–sub-fonds)

CH02 SHARES (sub–sub-fonds)

CH03 ADMINISTRATION (sub–sub-fonds)

CH03/01 Secretary's department (sub–sub–sub-fonds)

CH03/01/01 Letter books (series)

CLC/B/207/CH03/01/01/001 'A' Letters to Hong Kong (file)

CH03/01/02 Circulars (series)

CH03/01/03 Half-yearly letters (series)

CH03/01/04 Special advices to branches (series)

CH03/02 General manager's department (sub–sub–sub-fonds)

CH03/03 Inspection department (sub–sub–sub-fonds)

CH04 ACCOUNTING AND FINANCIAL (sub–sub-fonds)

CH05 OPERATIONS (sub–sub-fonds)

CH06 LEGAL (sub–sub-fonds)

CH07 BRANCHES AND AGENCIES (sub–sub-fonds)

CH07/01 Hong Kong Branch (sub–sub–sub-fonds)

CLC/B/207/CH07/01/001 Head office circulars (file)

CH07/02 Rangoon Evacuation Branch (sub–sub–sub-fonds)

CH08 STAFF AND EMPLOYMENT (sub–sub-fonds)

CH09 PREMISES AND PROPERTY (sub–sub-fonds)

CH09/08 Photographs (series)

CH09/08/01 Albums (sub-series)

CLC/B/207/CH09/08/01/001 Premises album (unbound pages) (file)

001/003 Alor Setar, Kedah State, Malaysia photograph (item)

CH10 HISTORY (sub–sub-fonds)

CLC/B/207/ST STANDARD BANK OF SOUTH AFRICA LIMITED (fonds)

ST01 CORPORATE (sub–sub-fonds)

ST01/01 Foundation (sub–sub–sub-fonds)

ST01/02 Board (sub–sub–sub-fonds)

ST01/02/01 Minutes (series) *[series held by depositor]*

CLC/B/207/ST01/02/01/001 Minute book (file)

Acknowledgements: London Metropolitan Archives and Standard Chartered Bank. Standard Chartered Bank's archives are held by London Metropolitan Archives.

Step four – description and ISAD(G)

Description relates to the activity referred to as 'listing' or 'cataloguing'. According to *General international standard archival description* (International Council on Archives, 2000), the term refers to 'the creation of an accurate representation of a unit of description . . . by (processing) any information that serves to identify archival material and explain the context and records system within it'. The catalogue is made up of descriptive units, each referring to 'a document or set of documents . . . treated as an entity and as such forming the basis of a single description'.

Rules

The fundamental rule of ISAD(G) dictates that description should be made from the general to the specific through the hierarchical levels described above. A hierarchical structure represents the creative context of the individual items. The beauty of this system is that the hierarchy provides a position for, and links, each unit of description. However, as noted above, there might be good reasons to have only a limited number of levels in the hierarchy. In the case of published catalogues, the use of ISAD(G) levels streamlines the amount of information required by reducing the need for repetition, but in a database catalogue sufficient information (for instance the name of the record creator) will need to be entered at each level to make each database record meaningful when presented in a search result. Details must be relevant to the level of description. In general, information at upper levels should summarise and provide ranges to their constituent parts.

The cataloguer should aim to help identify items of interest to users by giving contextual and interpretative guidance highlighting special attributes of records, access restrictions and related sources. Each description should be concise and designed to 'sell' the research value of the component of a collection it represents by appropriately conveying its content. The catalogue should, however, remain impartial and the cataloguer should avoid conveying his or her own personal interests in its construction. Sentences written in first person and subjective adjectives such as 'interesting' or 'important' should be avoided, and any gaps clearly highlighted to avoid user disappointment.

Cataloguers should not assume future users will have any prior knowledge. Catalogues should explain unusual terminology and be consistent and free from jargon and abbreviations. Adherence to ISAD(G) will help the cataloguer create high-quality lists and allow the potential for integration and exchange of descriptions between repositories. Local listing conventions should be adopted to promote consistency and quality in the catalogues produced by each archive.

Elements of description

ISAD(G) outlines 26 elements of description that come under seven information areas. Only the five descriptive elements that all come under ISAD(G) Identity Statement Information Area are compulsory: namely, unique reference code, title, dates of creation, extent and level of description. Table 7.7 outlines commonly-used elements with comments and tips for their application. Archivists must decide which of these elements are appropriate to their requirements. It is possible that an in-house corporate archive might need to adapt or add elements to meet their particular requirements, and in creating

Table 7.7 ISAD(G) descriptions: rules and tips for commonly-used fields

ISAD(G) information area and description type	Comment and tips
3.1: Identity Statement Information Area: mandatory information which must be supplied in a catalogue at all levels	
Reference code(s): mandatory field where reference codes must be unique.	ISAD(G) anticipates that references reflect changes in level, linking lower units back to the fonds. Codes can consist of a mixture of alpha and numerical characters, normally with a forward slash to reflect changes in level. Use leading zeros to ensure descriptions appear in order in databases. The prime function of a reference code is to allow the location and retrieval of a requested file or item. Multiple hierarchical levels can result in long, unwieldy reference codes which can be difficult for staff and users to follow. The cataloguer should avoid choosing an overly complex arrangement which complicates access. Use abbreviated letter codes for subsidiaries in larger business collections.
	Referencing should be consistent and expandable. One way is to number each function in the classification (Box 7.20) and use numbers accordingly. Additional material to an existing catalogued collection should use the same scheme imposed by the existing catalogue. It is appropriate to leave gaps for known functions or missing files or volumes. For example if a series of general ledgers numbered with original volumes numbers 2–22 are catalogued, catalogue as /002–022 and leave /001 for volume 1 which may be deposited later.
	Include separately (in a database, in a separate field) any former references assigned to records, either used before deposit to denote original order (for example a file with a registry number), or as part of a former listing to help identify material which has previously been used for research.
Title: mandatory field with a short, free text description.	At fonds to sub-fonds level the title is usually the latest or current name of the business or person, or the name current at the time the records were created. Names should conform to indexing rules. At series to item level the title should give the record series name, or title given to the file or item. In a printed catalogue it may be appropriate at the lowest levels to leave this field blank where there is no variation in the title and the description is covered by the level above, but in a database the essential information about a record should be capable of being understood without reference to records at higher levels.
	Avoid making up titles. Always use existing titles given to material where they make sense. Use quote marks to denote that the title has been taken from the original, for example a file titled 'Australia and New Zealand' or a publication titled 'Do you tire of your hair? New Fashion Tips 1988/89'. Use semi-colons in sentences to reduce the length of descriptions. Avoid using phrases such as 'records of . . . ' or 'photograph relating to' where details are already apparent in extent or scope and content.

Table 7.7 continued

ISAD(G) information area and description type	Comment and tips
Date(s): mandatory field giving the covering dates of when material was created.	Save time by recording only the year range, unless adding month or date helps to establish chronology in detailed series or identifies key items. This field should not be used to record the period of time covered by the information held within the unit of description. Beware photocopied items or back-filled volumes which were created later than the period they cover. Give the date the copy was made and provide further details in scope and content. Database software may determine the precise date formats which can be accommodated. Examples: 1823–1982 1 January 1823–2 August 1982 18—–19— for undated material where only estimated centuries can be given 187– – 189– or 1870s–1890s for estimated decades 1873? or c.1873 for an estimated year. The use of 'undated' is unhelpful and should be avoided unless estimation is impossible. 'Rogue' dates of items outside the date range of the main unit of description should be highlighted, such as '1870–1922, 2003' and explained in scope and content, unless database software prevents this.
Level of description: mandatory field.	See Table 7.5. Levels should be recorded in databases and reflected in catalogues by the font size and style.
Extent and medium: mandatory field providing a measure of the volume of material.	At fonds to sub-fonds level describe the total number of producible units or formats at file level, and/or the linear shelf metres or digital space taken up by the relevant section of the collection. At series to item level record the number of pieces and the format, for example '1 volume', '1 file', '3 documents', '3 digital PDF files'. The number of items within a file or bundle should specified, where feasible for document security reasons. For example '1 bundle of 17 items'. Numbering of every item should only be done for key items but generally avoided where packaging keeps items secure as this demands considerable time. An original file which does not fit new archival packaging should be made into parts and numbered. The catalogue should still state '1 file in 5 parts' to record that the repackaged file was originally a single file, and be made accessible to the user as one unit.
3.2: Context Information Area: gives contextual background, origin and custody details	Where a catalogue is to be produced in printed form only, complete fonds to sub-fonds levels. For database catalogues name of creator(s), for example, will need to be included at all levels to make each record meaningful.
Name of creator(s)	Use indexing rules to give all name changes of a company or individual.
Administrative/ Biographical history	A brief outline of the history should be filled in at fonds level and in larger collections at lower levels. Details should not take the place of existing history publications.

For records of businesses give details of the establishment, purpose and coverage of the business, department, agency or branch including production, commodities and geographical range. Include details of all name changes and any key mergers, subsidiaries and associated companies. Also include information on any major developments, events and key individuals reflected in the archives. Addresses of head office and operational premises with dates of occupation should also be supplied.

For personal and family collections, a brief biography of the major figure(s) is appropriate.

Never copy text directly from a published source, as this can be an infringement of copyright law. Always paraphrase text and add a credit.

Custodial history	Provide information about previous transfers of ownership or custody of the records with dates. Only include details if such transfers are significant for the authenticity, integrity and interpretation of the archive. It should not be used to record the deposit unless as part of a more complicated chain of custody.
Immediate source of acquisition	Give relevant accession numbers and dates of transfer. Supply details at fonds level and also lower levels in the case of additional accession(s). Only include information about depositors where this does not infringe their privacy.

3.3: Content and Structure Information Area: gives details on the subjects covered and arrangement

Scope and content	This field should be used at all levels as it is important in providing significant details which are not supplied by the title field. Give a brief summary of content with examples and an indication of the main formats. Unusual items in the content should be drawn to the attention of the user. Include individual covering dates where possible and note missing information or gaps, for example where a series of departmental staff lists lack individual names. Avoid using words such as 'miscellaneous' or 'general' unless they refer to original descriptions. Record details such as whether a record is signed or unsigned, indexed or unindexed, latter half blank, part missing and so on. Use quote marks to denote where a description is derived from the document itself.
Appraisal, destruction and scheduling information	Include details where past action (for example by an archivist) might affect the user's interpretation of the material. State whether an appraisal report exists (see Box 7.17).
Accruals	This field should be used at fonds to series level by those repositories receiving regular transfers of business records. Indicate where records are expected in the future, and how regularly accruals are received.
System of arrangement	Give information on the arrangement of the material. This can be presented as a table of contents at highest levels, and at lower levels whether chronological, alphabetical and so on.

3.4: Conditions of Access and Use Information Area: details on conditions affecting access

Table 7.7 continued

ISAD(G) information area and description type	Comment and tips
Conditions governing access	Give details on conditions which restrict access at all levels. For records containing private personal information on staff or customers subject to any local privacy legislation, use a brief description such as 'not available for general access until [year]'. To calculate restrictions based on 100 year closure use the following guidelines: where individuals are exclusively adult, assume an age of 16 years and close for 84 years from the end date of the item. Where individuals are deceased, the item will normally be 'Open' or 'Available for general access'. Some series or collections may be available for consultation by users only with permission of a business or department, usually where commercial sensitivities exist. Use 'Access by permission only'. For records available in an alternative format, for example digital scans or microfilm, normally restrict access to the surrogate for preservation reasons. Use 'Not available for general access' and provide information about the surrogate. Where items are in poor condition and unfit for consultation use 'Not available for general access' or 'Unfit for production'.
Physical characteristics and technical requirements	If the condition of the document limits its use, use 'Unfit for production' or 'At risk'. Status can be confirmed by a professional conservator. For unfit items change the access restrictions to 'Not available for general access' or 'Unfit for production'.
Copyright	Give information about conditions governing the use or reproduction of the material after access has been provided. For records which transferred to an in-house corporate repository by a department or are deposited as a gift, most copyright will be 'owned' but details should be checked first. Record details where copyright remains the property of the depositor or a third-party.
Language/scripts of material	The use of the main language where the repository is based is always assumed, only specify details if it is not the main language. However, if there is more than one language used, record them all.
Finding aids	Details of other finding aids including guides and indexes.
3.5: Allied Materials Information Area: related material	Details can be provided on the existence and location of originals and copies, and related units. Record details of whether relevant material (including non-archival sources) is held elsewhere signposting users to other sources. This is important for collections of one fonds split across sites or countries. The publication note field should be used to record histories and articles using the collection.
3.6: Notes Information Area	Include specialised information which cannot be accommodated elsewhere.
3.7: Description Control Information Area: how and who compiled the description	Includes details of the cataloguer and when the catalogue was compiled, conventions or standards used and any acknowledgements.

Acknowledgement: London Metropolitan Archives. Adapted from the cataloguing description conventions used by London Metropolitan Archives.

database records there may be a need to incorporate index elements alongside ISAD(G) elements, and also to include location information within (or linked to) each database record.

International standards, for both cataloguing and the construction of authority records and index terms, are subject to periodic revision, so catalogues constructed in accordance with them may cease to be compliant. It may then be impractical to re-structure existing catalogues and indexes to meet the revised standards. However, the currently available standards do provide a very useful framework for archival description. Boxes 7.21–7.23 give examples of sub-fonds, sub-sub-fonds and series and file level descriptions using ISAD(G).

Depth of description

The degree of description should reflect a balance between the repository's time and resources, user demand (including that of the business for an in-house archive) and the need to safeguard items both physically and intellectually. Where an archive is stored off-site there may be a requirement for more detailed cataloguing in order to reduce the cost and physical wear and tear involved in retrieving items unnecessarily. The cataloguer should aim to supply sufficient descriptive information for the likely relevance of a document to be clear to users, but not 'calendar'[20] the records or let the descriptions take the place of the documents that they concern. It is therefore usually appropriate only to catalogue to file level (that is by volume, file or bundle), rather than to item level (every single page in a file or sheet in a bundle). The latter can be time consuming and result in overly detailed databases or catalogues that are difficult to use.

Certain series may warrant in-depth description. Some in-house corporate archives may decide to catalogue selected categories of material to item level to save retrieval time and ensure the fastest enquiry response rates to the parent business. Other records, which are collectable or have high market value, may be catalogued to item level for security reasons, such as letters written by famous individuals, banknotes or envelopes carrying rare postage stamps. Where there is likely to be a heavy demand for visual material, more detailed descriptions of individual photographs and past advertising or packaging might be required. Scrapbooks containing diverse material may also be worth item listing as they may contain items of particular or unexpected interest. Indeed, photographs and scrapbooks (in which items are fixed in place) may suit item-by-item listing by volunteers in a way which resourcing may render impossible for archivists themselves to achieve. Box 7.24 provides an example of item-level cataloguing achieved by volunteers.

Describing business archives in practice – physical records

ISAD(G) does not prescribe how a cataloguer should describe certain record types. Other guidelines have therefore been developed to help formulate descriptions.[21] The following, alongside Table 7.7, provides tips on describing commonly-encountered business archives, although the level of detail required will vary greatly depending on the intended use of the catalogue and archive:

- **Files and volumes**: Check carefully front and back and add any unusual or unexpected use and dates to the description. Partially-used volumes should be noted.

Box 7.21   Example of a sub-fonds description relating to Standard Chartered Bank based on ISAD(G)

Level: sub–fonds part of Standard Chartered Bank (fonds)
Title: Chartered Bank
Creator: Chartered Bank of India, Australia and China | Chartered Bank
Reference code: CLC/B/207/CH
Dates: 1851–1986
Extent: 167 linear metres

Administrative history:

Chartered Bank of India, Australia and China, known from 1956 as Chartered Bank, was established by Royal Charter in 1853. It was an overseas exchange bank, based in and controlled from the City of London. It was established to take advantage of the end of the East India Company's monopoly in 1853.

The bank operated in India and throughout the Far East – in China, Hong Kong, Vietnam, Cambodia, Siam [Thailand], Burma [Myanmar], Singapore, Malacca, Penang and the Malay States, the Philippines, Japan, Java, Sumatra, Ceylon [Sri Lanka], North Borneo, Brunei, Sarawak, Pakistan and East Pakistan [Bangladesh]. There were also branches in New York [United States of America] and Hamburg [Germany]. Despite its name, the bank never operated in Australia.

The bank's activities in the Far East were severely disrupted by the Second World War and nationalist post-war governments in the region. The takeover in 1957 of rival Eastern Bank presented new opportunities. Eastern Bank was active in Chartered Bank's traditional areas of operation, but also had branches in the Middle East – in Iraq, Bahrain, Yemen, Lebanon, Qatar, Sharjah, Abu Dhabi, Dubai and Oman. In the same year, Chartered Bank purchased the Ionian Bank's interests in Cyprus.

The bank's City of London head office addresses: 1852 first two meetings of directors at 8 Austin Friars; November 1852 offices acquired at 21 Moorgate; December 1853–55 rented offices at South Sea House, Threadneedle Street; 1855 rented offices at 34 Gresham House, Old Broad Street; June 1857–66 rented offices in the City Bank building at Threadneedle Street; 1867 former Hatton Court building on Threadneedle Street. In 1909 the bank moved into newly built premises on the former site of Crosby Hall where it was still located at the time of the merger with Standard Bank in 1969 to form Standard Chartered Bank.

For further information on the history of the bank see Sir Compton Mackenzie, *Realms of silver: one hundred years of banking in the East* (London, 1954) and Geoffrey Jones, *British multinational banking 1830–1990* (Oxford, 1993).

Scope and content:

Records cover the operation and management of the business covering branches, agencies and head office. There is information relating to premises and staff, inspection of branches and customer accounts, some records of legal actions as well as general administrative records created and maintained by the secretaries and general managers.

Highlights include records relating to the bank during times of war, from accounts of local rebellions and riots through to the Second World War which saw two thirds of the bank's branches occupied by the Japanese and over 100 of the bank's European officers interned. There is a series of letters within the records of the Secretary and a number of personal reminiscences recounting the courageous actions of trustworthy staff members trying to salvage bank records from being seized by the Japanese and experiences in internment camps and conditions in occupied countries (CLC/B/207/CH03/01/07) and a register of employees interned in prisoner of war camps or killed during enemy action (CLC/B/207/CH08/01/004).

There is a series of posterity files (CLC/B/207/CH03/01/09–13) consisting of over 1,300 documents which were retained by the Secretary as a research resource and for historical interest covering a remarkable range of subjects such as legal wrangles and reports on trading conditions in particular countries reflecting how the bank was responsive to early economic development and new trade when seeking to expand its network of branches.

The *Realms of silver* centenary publication research files are a valuable source on the history of the bank (CLC/B/207/CH03/01/14–17) covering a range of topics such as key commodities in particular areas, they show staff enduring disease, plague, famine and drought, rebellion and revolution, earthquakes, floods and fire and highlight how the activities of the bank have touched upon events of world history as well as of local development, often reflecting creative solutions that the bank employed to overcome such problems.

There is an extensive collection of premises records (CLC/B/207/CH09) including plans of the branches and often subsequent upgrades and developments of branches and agencies in response to growing business needs. There are also photographs which show not only bank premises but also create a pictorial history reflecting the international operations of Chartered Bank as well as showing local flora, fauna and methods of trade, for example, in Cebu the use of buffalo to move hemp and in Burma the use of elephants in the emerging logging trade. They also reflect local tragedies such as the effects of the Yokohama Earthquake in Japan in 1923 (CLC/B/207/CH09/08; CLC/B/207/CH08/04; CLC/B/207/CH03/01/16).

There is an extensive series of records relating to accounting and financial matters (CLC/B/207/CH04), including general ledgers; a comprehensive series of half-yearly balance sheets from branches and records of the Taxation and Statistics Department (which appears to have fallen under the auspices of the Chief Accountant).

There are also records relating to staff (CLC/B/207/CH08), which give details on the bank's application and registration process, and progress and activities of named staff when they took up their posts. These records include registers of staff (1874–1920), some staff applications and employment agreements (1900–30) and an extensive series of half-yearly schedules of staff in overseas branches (1863–1960).

Immediate source of acquisition:

The bank's archives were deposited in the Manuscripts Section of Guildhall Library in 1989 and after. Guildhall Library's Manuscripts Section merged with London Metropolitan Archives, City of London in 2009. Accession numbers: 1989/040, 1994/076, B11/068, B12/009, B12/025, B12/068, B13/020.

Access restrictions:

48 hours' notice required for access. Access to records less than 45 years old should be sought from the depositor. These records are available for public inspection, although records containing personal information are subject to access restrictions under the Data Protection Act, 1998.

Related material:

Some key records of the bank have been retained by Standard Chartered Bank. These comprise all of the board and committee minutes, and all the records of shareholders. In addition, not all the records listed in L. S. Pressnell and J. Orbell, *Guide to the historical records of British banking* (1985), or by the Business Archives Council in 1979–80, have been deposited in the Manuscripts Section. The whereabouts of these other records are unknown.

HSBC Group Archives holds archives of the Hong Kong & Shanghai Banking Corporation which document Chartered Bank.

Arrangement:

[See Box 7.19 above]

Appraisal:

The records were appraised prior to cataloguing. See S. G. H. Freeth, Destroying archives: a case study of the records of Standard Chartered Bank, *Journal of the Society of Archivists*, 12(2), Autumn 1991, pp. 85–94.

Language:

Mainly English, other language details given at file-level.

Acknowledgements: London Metropolitan Archives and Standard Chartered Bank.

Box 7.22 Example of a departmental administrative history relating to Standard Chartered Bank's predecessor Chartered Bank at sub-sub-fonds using ISAD(G)

GENERAL MANAGER'S DEPARTMENT

The General Manager's Department was situated at London Head Office and responsible for managing and directing the network of overseas branches which had little independent autonomy. The first General Manager, George Ure Adams, was appointed in 1857 and remained in post until 1870. He died aged 71 on 7 June 1874. As a result of the growth of the overseas branch network the General Manager's Department gradually expanded and by the 1960s consisted of a Chief General Manager, Joint General Manager and a number of Assistant General Managers.

General Managers whose records are represented in the collection include:

– John Howard Gwyther began his employment with the bank serving in the Singapore and Shanghai branches from 1860. Following a break he returned to London and was appointed Secretary in 1868. In 1871, aged only 35, he took the post of General Manager. Gwyther served out the rest of his career with the bank, acting as director 1887–1904, retiring from the post of manager to become Managing Director in 1892 and serving as Chairman 1896–1904.

– William Marshall Cockburn joined Chartered Bank in 1911 and spent most of his early career in the branches in Vietnam, Malay States, Japan and China, especially Shanghai where in 1934 he was appointed sub-manager and in 1935 manager of the branch. In 1936 he was appointed a sub-manager at Head Office rising to Chief Manager in 1940 and to Chief General Manager in 1950, retiring in 1955, although remaining as a director until his death in September 1957. He was responsible for managing the bank during the Second World War, when all branches east of Calcutta, India, were effectively taken over by enemy forces, and for its reconstruction afterwards.

– William George Pullen was appointed sub-manager in 1950, Assistant General Manager in 1951 and Joint General Manager from 1952. Pullen would become Chairman and led the bank during the merger with Standard Bank in 1969 remaining Chairman of the Chartered Bank and Group Deputy Chairman of Standard Chartered Bank until his retirement in 1974.

– Arthur Thomson Hobbs, appointed in October 1956 as the first manager of the Bank in Iraq. He became an assistant general manager in London with particular responsibility for the India zone.

Acknowledgements: London Metropolitan Archives and Standard Chartered Bank. Standard Chartered Bank's archives are held by London Metropolitan Archives.

Box 7.23 Sample of subject files description at series and file level using ISAD(G)

Upper levels: Chubb and Son Ltd locksmiths and safe manufacturers: (fonds) Administration (sub-fonds): William E. Randall, Managing Director and Chairman (sub-sub-fonds)

Title: Geographical subject files (series):

Reference code: CLC/B/002/03/02/04

Dates: 1969–83

Extent: 14 files

Scope and content: Original files containing correspondence, reports and related papers concerning overseas subsidiaries and acquisitions in Australia and New Zealand (1969–83); Europe (1975–82); Indonesia (1980–81); Malaysia (1979–83); North America (1976–83); and South Africa (1977–82).

Access restrictions: 48 hours' notice required for access. Some files subject to restriction as they contain personal information on named staff.

Arrangement: Arranged alphabetically by country or continent using original file names.

Reference code(s) Access	Title Scope and content Extent	Dates
CLC/B/002/03/02/04/001 Former reference: WER/11/1 Box 208 Not available for general access until 2066	'Australia and New Zealand' Concerning Chubb's Australian Company Ltd. Includes directors' appointments for Chubb Lock and Safe Company Proprietary Ltd (1972) 1 file	1969 May– 1981 Feb.
CLC/B/002/03/02/04/002 Former reference: WER/11/2 Box 208 48 hours' notice required for access	'Australia and New Zealand' Includes Chubb New Zealand Ltd and Chubb Australia Ltd copy board minutes and managing director's reports. Also visit itinerary with cocktail party menu (1983) 1 file	1981 Mar.– 1983 Feb.
CLC/B/002/03/02/04/003 Former reference: WER/11/3 Box 139 48 hours' notice required for access	'Australia and New Zealand' Mainly concerns Chubb Australia Ltd with copy documents relating to James Hardie Industries Ltd's offer to purchase ordinary stock units in Fire Fighting Enterprises Ltd and related correspondence concerning Chubb's partial bid for the latter 1 file	1983 Mar.– 1983 Jun.

CLC/B/002/03/02/04/004 Former reference: WER/8 Box 208 Not available for general access until 2067	'Europe' Correspondence with Fichet–Bauche, Paris, France concerning a legal case regarding unfair competition, with related code of conduct in fair commercial practice, subsequent tribunal and anti-Chubb campaign. Also reports on staff management issues in Marseilles. Correspondence with Lips and Gispen BV 1 file	1975 Jan.– 1982 Mar. Includes French
CLC/B/002/03/02/04/005 Former reference: WER/13 Box 139 48 hours' notice required for access	'Indonesia' Mainly concerning P. T. Chubb Lips. Also special opening of new factory in Jakarta (1980 Nov.) 1 file	1980 Jan.– 1981 Mar.
CLC/B/002/03/02/04/006 Former reference: WER/14/1 Box 139, RCL/1/10 Box 290 Not available for general access until 2066	'Malaysia' Correspondence with Chubb Malaysia Sdn Bhd including change in Chief Executive, also Josiah Parkes and Sons Ltd, Josiah Parkes (Singapore) Private Ltd, Chubb Singapore Private Ltd, and papers concerning discussions with Pernas Sime Darby Holdings Sdn Bhd, Kuala Lumpur with shareholders' agreement (1981 Apr.). Includes photographs of P. T. Chubb Lips factory opening in Jakarta, Indonesia (1980) 1 file	1979 Jul.– 1981 Dec.
CLC/B/002/03/02/04/007 Former reference: WER/14/2 Box 139 Not available for general access until 2068	'Malaysia' Includes operations reports, property acquisition of Berger Paints factory site, Petaling Jaya (1982 Jun.) 1 file	1982 Jan.– 1983 Mar.

Acknowledgement: London Metropolitan Archives. Chubb and Son Ltd's archives are owned and held by London Metropolitan Archives.

Box 7.24 Example of item–level cataloguing by volunteers

Upper levels: Chubb and Son Ltd (fonds), lock and safemakers

History (sub-fonds)

Chubb Collectanea (series)

Scrapbook 1860–62 [actual coverage: 180– –1975] CLC/B/002/10/01/008 1 volume (file)

Original volume re-bound in 4 parts (indexed in CLC/B/002/10/01/007)

140/3/C3. Volume '3' Part 2

Reference code(s) Access	Title Scope and content Extent	Dates
CLC/B/002/10/01/008/053D 48 hours' notice required for access Former reference: 103	'Monster Iron Safe'. *Midland Counties Express* Reprinted from newspaper. Report of a large bullion safe made for export to China by Thomas Perry and Son of Highfields, near Bilston, Staffordshire. A celebratory dinner held inside for 17 guests before it is shipped 1 advertisement	1861 Sep. 7
CLC/B/002/10/01/008/054 48 hours' notice required for access Former reference: 105	'List of Articles Invented, Manufactured, and Sold by Joseph Bramah and Son, Engineers' Page 1 lists their locks, page 2 water closets, pumps and fire extinguishing equipment, page 3 patent letter copying presses, travelling desks, beer machines and portable water closets. Printing date is 1805, front page is annotated 1806 1 leaflet of 3 pages	1805–1806
CLC/B/002/10/01/008/055 48 hours' notice required for access Former reference: 105	'List of Articles Invented, Manufactured, and Sold by Joseph Bramah and Son, Engineers' Lists locks, with specifications and prices [Only one side legible because sheet is pasted down]. 1 leaflet of 1 page	1820
CLC/B/002/10/01/008/056 48 hours' notice required for access Former reference: 107	'The Perfect Inviolable Lock, For Which Letters of Patent Have Been Granted To T. Ruxton, Esquire'. *The Repertory for Arts* Description of the lock, with 3 images showing the lock open, closed and with its key. With technical details concerning operation 1 leaflet of 3 pages	1816 Aug.

CLC/B/002/10/01/008/057 48 hours' notice required for access Former reference: 108	'Robert Kemp's Patent Union Lock', Manufactured by Farmer, Kemp, and Farmer, Wolverhampton, Staffordshire 1 leaflet of 3 pages	181–
CLC/B/002/10/01/008/058 48 hours' notice required for access Former reference: 109	'Strutt's Patent Lock. Instructions for Use' Printed by H. Teape, Tower Hill, City of London 1 leaflet	181––185–
CLC/B/002/10/01/008/059 48 hours' notice required for access Former reference: 110	William Kingston, Master Millwright, Portsmouth Yard, Hampshire to Chubb: testimonial that Chubb's Patent lock no.137 'has been thrown 378,240 times without the least possible derangement' 1 letter	1819 Dec. 13

Acknowledgement: London Metropolitan Archives. Chubb and Son Ltd's archives are owned and held by London Metropolitan Archives.

Loose papers found in bound volumes should be reviewed and noted in descriptions. In some cases loose papers may be removed, kept and described separately in a way that links them to their original location.

- **Minutes**: Changes in board or committee names should be recorded at file level or at series level if there is more than one record. Records should also be checked for mixed minutes where multiple categories of meetings are recorded within the same volumes such as directors' and general meeting minutes. Descriptions should also record if minutes are signed, draft or indexed and reference any papers presented and included.
- **Correspondence**: Indicate whether letters are incoming, outgoing, copies, drafts, marked (for example as 'private' or with receipt stamps) or general circulars. Subject files should be given sufficient scope and content details to highlight unusual content. See the Chubb and Son Ltd example set out in Box 7.23.
- **Financial, operational and staff series**: Scope and content descriptions should be adequate to indicate the nature of the information records contain and it may be helpful to list the main entry headings used within records especially where there is a known research need. See the example of the Rio Tinto staff books in Box 7.25 below.
- **Photographs**: Describe the format, whether black and white or colour, the photographer's name where known and the subject matter depicted, naming individuals and places where possible. Also reference any copyright constraints.
- **Films and oral histories**: Describe the film medium, type and length, makers' names, title, genre and scope. Also note copyright and access constraints.
- **Plans**: Describe the place or object, type of drawing (such as site, block, elevation, section, plans, impressions), format of drawing (such as dyeline, CAD (computer-aided design), CAM (computer-aided manufacturing), and so on), architect's or engineer's names, and scale.

Box 7.25 Example of detailed series description using ISAD(G) for records with a high user demand, with file level descriptions

Rio Tinto plc (mining company) (fonds)
Rio Tinto Company Ltd (sub-fonds): Staff and Employment (sub-sub-fonds): Staff books and registers (series):
Title: Staff book: (sub-series)
Reference code: LMA/4543/09/01/01
Dates: 1873–1957
Extent: 6 volumes

Scope and content:

Details include name, appointments, amendments to salary, allowances, bonuses, pensions, details on leaving and other comments. Later volumes give birth date and references to board or committee minutes. Entries are mainly arranged and indexed by surname within each volume. Note: dates given in this catalogue relate to appointment entries. Continuations from previous volumes for staff still in post are included in later volumes.

The books mainly cover United Kingdom-based staff and United Kingdom nationals at Rio Tinto Spanish mine and elsewhere. Entries also include some staff of The Pyrites Company Ltd. LMA/4543/09/01/01/003 states that it is a 'record of staff in London, at Cumavon, at Foreign Sampling Stations, in Spain on English agreement and the following foreigners, Technical Manager at Mines, Legal Representative at Huelva, Representatives in Madrid, Sales Agent in North America'. In January 1947 it was agreed that information concerning Spanish staff was 'not such as to enable us to keep a reliable record of salaries' and Spanish staff were therefore excluded after that date (see note in LMA/4543/09/01/01/004).

Other finding aids:

A comprehensive electronic index to the staff names, 1873–1956, contained in LMA/4543/09/01/01/001–005, is available. Enquirers are advised to contact staff to check the electronic index before making a visit to request whether a particular name is contained in the original volumes.

Access restrictions:

These records are available for public inspection, although records containing personal information are subject to access restrictions under the Data Protection Act 1998.

Reference code(s) Access	Title Scope and content Extent	Dates
LMA/4543/09/01/01/001 Former reference: SRR/31	Staff book number '1' 1 volume	1873–1885
LMA/4543/09/01/01/002 Former reference: SRR/32	Staff book number '2' 1 volume	1885–1899
LMA/4543/09/01/01/003 Former reference: SRR/33	Staff book number '3' 1 volume	1899–1929
LMA/4543/09/01/01/004 Former reference: SRR/34 Not available for general access until 2032	Staff book number '4' 1 volume	1929–1947
LMA/4543/09/01/01/005 Former reference: SRR/35 Not available for general access until 2041	Staff book number '5' 1 volume	1947–1956
LMA/4543/09/01/01/006 Former reference: CAR/80 Not available for general access until 2042	Staff book 1 volume	1956–1957

Acknowledgements: London Metropolitan Archives and Rio Tinto plc. Rio Tinto plc's archives are held by London Metropolitan Archives.

- **Maps**: Describe the place, title, type, surveyor, colour, scale (ratio, original scale), size and medium (for example, on linen).
- **Property deeds**: Record the name and address(es) of the property/properties, main parties and type of deed, and reference if any plans are included. Describe as bundles where detail is not immediately required to assist with legal evidence of title.
- **Printed and published material**: Record the names(s) of author(s) or editor(s), title, publisher's name, details on editions and number of pages. Note any annotations.

Describing business archives in practice – digital records

There is currently no agreed standard for cataloguing born-digital and digitised records and ISAD(G) offers the archivist no assistance with the challenges of describing digital records. This is not surprising given that the standard was last revised 16 years ago and archivists must accept that the description of digital objects is an evolving art. Bulk makes the arrangement, appraisal and description both difficult and time consuming, whilst the searchability of digital documents may reduce the need for detailed cataloguing. Where the content of documents can be keyword searched, detailed descriptions and complex hierarchies are no longer essential or even achievable. The availability of existing mechanised file metadata also changes how catalogue descriptions are created. It is crucial that metadata accompanies the digital record as it is an integral part of it. Metadata forms the whole record and can come from sources that would not be traditionally viewed as part of the record. For example, metadata may not be embedded into the file in an original management system, such as an electronic document and records management system (EDRMS) data dictionaries or other associated files that provide a key to interpreting the record (Brown, 2013, pp. 155–158).

Metadata is multifunctional, it has many forms and can serve many purposes, one of which is archival description. It is possible to separate metadata into two broad categories, that of technical and descriptive metadata. Descriptive metadata concerns the conceptual information object, whereas technical metadata describes purely the technical characteristics of the object, often in a consistent form (Brown, 2013, p. 156). Descriptive metadata can be embedded in the digital object and extracted to form part of the catalogue description, it can also come purely from the archivist's own description of the object. Technical metadata will always be harvested from the digital object and will not always provide a user-friendly output that will be easily intelligible for researchers (for example the bit rate of a sample of audio), however it is important for providing access to the object and its long-term preservation.

When cataloguing digital objects it is the harvesting and subsequent structuring of this metadata that will make digital records 'discoverable'. Following metadata standards can help make digital records accessible, improving the way their data is structured and viewable. There are a myriad of standards available and these are discussed in more detail in Chapter 10. Consistency, however, is crucial. Archives should look at adopting one or more standards that work best for the types of digital records typically being preserved within the organisation.

Arrangement of digital records can also conflict with traditional archival practices in the physical world. The improved options for searching digital records, via the metadata available alongside the record, can render the need for hierarchical arrangement unnecessary, or at least not essential for a set of digital records that might also have their own folder structure. Archivists do not have to abandon the hierarchical arrangement in favour of maintaining the digital records original folder structure, these can co-exist. When receiving large volumes of digital records it is often not possible or a worthwhile use of time to carry out item or even folder level appraisal. Providing there is a strong accompanying set of metadata arranged within a widely accepted standard, and there is a strong evidential value in maintaining it, the original folder structure can be retained within a digital repository underneath a series or file level description within the existing catalogue's tree structure.

Step five – catalogue completion

Good project plans for cataloguing factor in enough time for completion. Catalogues should be reviewed and edited for adherence to standards, errors, consistency and accuracy. Catalogue layouts will vary as the final version may be used both online and in printed format, but they should be clearly laid out and, in hard copy, include introductory and contents pages. For an example of a catalogue page laid out in columnar format see Boxes 7.23–7.25. Where the catalogue will only exist and be used as a database, including online, consideration should be given to the optimal screen size, positioning and fonts for the display of fields within records. A final completion checklist may include:

- Ensuring disposal of appraised records is carried out with necessary permissions obtained and information added to the catalogue in the appraisal field.
- Updating the accession register to reflect the completion of cataloguing.
- Locating catalogued material, ideally by format for efficient storage, taking account of the environmental conditions required for specific formats such as photographs, audio-visual material and digital records.[22]
- Summarising cataloguing statistics, such as time spent and quantities appraised, for future planning and compiling reports where appropriate.
- Promoting catalogued collections where appropriate via online collection guides, staff induction, events, social media, related archive repositories, libraries and museums, and user groups.
- Releasing the catalogue for use online and/or in hard copy.

Policy on who should have access to catalogues should be formally determined and disseminated. In-house corporate archives may decide not to release catalogues to the public, but use them instead to efficiently provide support advice to internal and external users. Collecting repositories with deposited archives may distribute catalogues to related repositories or other interested parties. Each repository should have its own code number, usually controlled nationally, which provides a prefix reference number to support the international exchange of catalogues. The highest-level prefix is the appropriate country code as identified in *ISO 3166* (International Organization for Standardization, 1999). Catalogues should be updated with the inclusion of additional catalogued material, and amended as a result of feedback from informed depositors and users concerning content and context. Catalogues can therefore evolve as the collection to which they relate is used and augmented.

Step six – indexes or access points

The inclusion of keyword searches helps identify items described in digital catalogues and enables users to undertake multiple searches (including Boolean searches where true and false values are evaluated) to refine, expand and narrow hit lists in order to identify relevant records. Users of printed catalogues, however, often need to use related finding aids to get the best out of larger catalogues. Guides and indexes help researchers navigate records scattered across catalogues of archives arranged according to creator, provenance and original order.

The general principles of indexing are the same whether the catalogue takes the form of a database or a printed list. Given the summary nature of archive descriptions, indexing may only be possible or meaningful in relation to descriptions at higher archival hierarchical levels, such as administrative histories and scopes at fonds and sub-fonds levels, which anyway reflect the content of most items in a collection. Box 7.26 gives business guide entries with indexes compiled from fonds and sub-fonds descriptions for users to navigate multiple collections held by collecting repositories.

Box 7.26 Business collections guide with trade and geographical subject indexes

Introduction and explanation:

Outline the purpose of the guide, for example, to enable researchers to identify particular collections through a summarised list arranged alphabetically by organisation name. Give an explanation of how the list entries are also indexed by trade and geographical remit in two separate indexes. Highlight titles and reference codes explaining how researchers can use these to refer to any online catalogue or other finding aids for detailed information on particular collections of interest. Outline which collections are covered and those which are not; for example, uncatalogued and/or minor/incomplete collections may not be included. Note any access restrictions and link to the repository's access policy.

Alphabetical list:

Standard layout of main entries as follows:
Company title, trade title, business address(es) (with dates of residence); name changes (with date ranges of name changes).
Brief details of amalgamations, takeovers and connections between companies together with any other essential information.
Date range of the records held (note: details are given if the collection is small).
Catalogue reference code(s).
Details of any access restrictions or related entries.
Where the name of the firm is that of a private individual, it will appear in the form of surname, forename.
Include separate entries for former names or key business sites and refer to the main entry, for example: Company title, see Company title.

Subject indexes to the alphabetical list:

Arranged by heading, then an alphabetical list of names.
For example:
Trade subject: list of company/personal names:
Geographical place, region or country: list of company/personal names:

Acknowledgement: London Metropolitan Archives. Descriptive elements are adapted from the business guide published by London Metropolitan Archives.

An alternative to detailed indexing is the creation of administrative research documents, databases or topic-based files to support response to frequent enquiries. In particular, these can enable an in-house corporate archive to answer internal enquiries very quickly. Index terms should comprise names, keywords or concepts drawn from archival descriptions, with pointers to relevant material. These terms form access points, which are in turn governed by authority control, where only one term in the vocabulary used represents any one particular concept. This control ensures the use of terms is broadly consistent. Where possible corporate, personal, place name and/or subject indexes should be constructed from catalogues soon after their completion. Where the catalogue exists as a database, the index terms might be incorporated within a catalogue record (either within a free-text description or within specific keyword fields) or the catalogue records might be linked to (multiple) separate authority records or thesauri. There are a number of standards, which help maintain consistency and enable data sharing, but application of these standards may not be feasible or desirable in all circumstances. For example, an in-house corporate archive may decide that it is only feasible to create name authority records for its own subsidiary and predecessor companies and branches, rather than for all institutions and people referred to in its records – in this case it may be sufficient to use keywords within records (rather than authority records) for names of staff and customers.

ISAAR

The international standard archival authority record for corporate bodies, persons and families (International Council on Archives, 2004b), also known as ISAAR (CPF), was like ISAD(G) developed by the International Council on Archives. The standard is concerned with the creation and use of indexes to describe corporate bodies, persons or families and does not cover subjects. ISAAR (CPF) allows identification of elements within three areas – the Authority Control Area, which gives the key terms; an Information Area giving details about the corporate bodies, persons and families summarising administrative or biographical history; and a Note Area on the creation and maintenance of the authority record. See Table 7.8 for a case study on the application of ISAAR (CPF).

Other standards

Other standards work alongside ISAAR. Construction of place names in the United Kingdom is assisted by *Rules for the construction of personal, place and corporate names* (National Council on Archives, England and Wales, 1997). For subjects, the Library of Congress and *UNESCO thesaurus* online[23] can be used for an alphabetical list of preferred and non-preferred words with cross references to link these words to related terms. UNESCO covers fields of education, science, social and human science, culture, communication and information. The standard uses equivalent terms, known as 'Used For' (UF); hierarchical terms, known as 'Main Term' (MT), Broad Term (BT) and Narrow Term (NT); and associative terms, known as 'Related Term' (RT) or 'see also'.

The main challenge in applying international standards is that they can be too general for specialist or local needs. Problems of subjectivity and selectivity in the formation of indexes also mean that these standards cannot ensure universal consistent application. They do at least set out some rules which improve consistency when a term is used.

Table 7.8 Example of the application of ISAAR (CPF), 1st edition, to the creation of authority records

ISAAR CPF (1st edition) element name	Authority record field name	Data
1.1 Identity code	Code	CRA
1.2 Type of record	Type	Bank history
1.3 Authority entry	Authorised form of name	Crawshay, Bailey & Co, bankers, Abergavenny, Wales; 1837–1868
1.5 Non-preferred terms	Alternative name	Abergavenny Old Bank
1.4 Parallel entries		*Not used*
2.1.1 Legal numbers		*Not used*
2.1.2 Names	Authority Name	Crawshay, Bailey & Co, bankers, Abergavenny, Wales
2.1.3 Dates and places of existence [date element only]	Dates of operation	1837–1868
2.1.4 Business location	Location [for bank authority records only]	Abergavenny, Wales
2.1.5 Legal status	Function	Bank
2.1.6 Mandate, functions, sphere of activity	Administrative history	This private bank was established in 1837 as Bailey, Morgan & Co by Sir Joseph Bailey and William Morgan. The Baileys were industrialists who owned the Cyfarthfa, Nantyglo and Beaufort ironworks and several collieries. It was also known as Monmouthshire Agricultural & Commercial Bank. By 1846 the bank was called Joseph Bailey, Crawshay Bailey, Thomas Gratrex and William Williams. Branches were established in Monmouth and Newport. The bank also took over National Provincial Bank of England's branch at Usk, but later closed it. In 1868 the bank was taken over by National Provincial Bank of England. At the time it was acquired it was known as Crawshay, Bailey & Co and the partners were Crawshay Bailey senior and junior, Thomas Gratrex and Philip Williams.
[2.1.7 Administrative structure]		*Not used*
2.1.8 Relationships		*Not used*
[2.1.9 Other significant information]		*Not used*
3.1 Archivist's note		
3.3 Date	Source [also used to record sources of information]	Created by [Archivist's name], [date]. Archive ref: 10676
3.2 Rules or conventions	Rules	ICA, *ISAAR (CPF)* 1st edition, 1997; NCA, *Rules for the construction of personal, place and corporate names*

Acknowledgement: Royal Bank of Scotland Archives.

Decisions in indexing

The indexer needs to decide which categories of information warrant the creation of index terms and at what level. These decisions may be very different between an in-house corporate archive and a collecting repository. The records (and catalogue, if created separately) should be examined, and key subjects and names identified to establish retrieval terms. These should be translated into a controlled system of vocabulary using chosen standards. It is not possible to cover indexing issues in detail in this chapter, although the bibliography signposts some further sources of information. However, indexers when they create or add to an existing index should:

- Tailor the finding aid to the holdings and needs of key users. For example, a business that regularly requires information on its branches would benefit from a detailed place name index. The indexer should keep up to date with current and potential future users and understand their needs in order to develop indexes.
- Carefully plan at initial stages the development of authority control over the use of index terms.
- Aim to make the indexes easy to understand and support self-sufficient user research by assuming no prior knowledge.
- Aim to be concise and not over index archive collections. The indexer should consider if the term clearly reflects a substantive potential research topic within a collection or file or is simply a subject referred to briefly in passing, which does not warrant a mention.
- Be consistent and avoid bias in the selection of terms presented.

In the case of printed or digital catalogues it is recommended that general indexes are constructed to reflect collection fonds to sub-fonds levels picking out corporate, personal, family and place names, and subjects reflecting trade activity. Separate indexes can adopt more specific terms to reflect important series. In the case of catalogues held in databases many of the higher-level index terms will be created in the process of entering data into fields relating to the ISAD(G) data elements.

Conclusion

Appropriate selection and cataloguing of business archives is fundamental in allowing companies to proactively derive value from their history, and for society to build collections, which document the impact of industrial and commercial activities around the globe. Business archives present unique challenges and risks. They need to be strategically managed in accordance with collections policy and wider standards, and in collaboration with others such as creators, depositors, records managers, users and related repositories.

In-house corporate archives should focus on activities that develop and align the records to the needs of the business. They should secure series through robust records management systems and self promotion to gain an appropriate and complete archive collection regardless of format and media. Deposited business archives held by collecting repositories should ideally be managed in partnership with the depositing business to promote use and attract corporate-funding and continuing development.

The process of surveying, acquiring, appraising and arranging business archives should take account of the origins, structures, functions, activities and transactions of the creating companies and individuals. The arrangement and description of business records can use a functional structure which respects creators and in which physical and digital records are integrated and not separated. Final catalogues and indexes should be concise and consistent to assist users and should embrace professional standards such as ISAD(G) and ISAAR (CPF). A repository should regularly review its collections development to ensure it fully documents a business or a business's local or national contribution to society.

Acknowledgements

The author is grateful to the following colleagues for their support or for commenting on all or parts of this chapter: Nicola Avery, Rachel Cole, Louise-Ann Hand, Louise Harrison, Geoff Pick, Katie Rawson, Joanne Ruff and Charlie Turpie, London Metropolitan Archives, City of London; Roger Nougaret, Bank Paribas, France; Lesley Richmond, University of Glasgow; Alison Turton and Philip Winterbottom, Royal Bank of Scotland; and Tina Staples and James Mortlock, HSBC. Thanks are also due to Stephen Freeth, formerly Keeper of Manuscripts, Guildhall Library, City of London, Henning Morgen, A. P. Moller–Maersk, Denmark, Becky Haglund Tousey, formerly of Mondelēz International, United States of America, Lucy Lead, Wedgwood Museum Trust, Jeannette Strickland, formerly of Unilever plc, and Claire Tunstall, Unilever plc, for kindly contributing to the case studies and exemplars.

Notes

1 See www.managingbusinessarchives.co.uk/getting_started/business_archives_at_risk/ [Accessed 19 August 2016].
2 The body arose in the aftermath of the Second World War in Europe when, in 1954, UNESCO adopted the Hague Convention with rules to protect cultural goods during armed conflicts. The Committee brings together the knowledge, experience and international networks of key organisations. Further information available at: http://icom.museum/ programmes/museums_emergency_programme/international_committee_of_the_blue_shield [Accessed 19 August 2016].
3 Friends of The National Libraries at: www.friendsofnationallibraries.org.uk [Accessed 19 August 2016].
4 See http://discovery.nationalarchives.gov.uk/ [Accessed 19 August 2016].
5 See www.nas.gov.uk/nras/ [Accessed 19 August 2016].
6 A recommended structure for an integrated collections management framework is laid out in *PAS 197: 2009. Code of practice for cultural collections management*. London: British Standards Institution. The application of *PAS 197* can be seen in the United Kingdom's Archive Service Accreditation Standard, 2013. [online] Available at: www.nationalarchives.gov.uk/archives-sector/archive-service-accreditation.htm [Accessed 19 August 2016].
7 For examples of agreements used in France see Nougaret, C. and Even, P., eds, 2008. *Les archives privées. Manuel pratique et juridique*. Paris: La Documentation Française.
8 For examples, including Danish businesses, see papers on de-accessioning in Richmond, L. M., ed., 1997. *Proceedings of the annual conference 1997*, pp. 141–168. London: Business Archives Council.
9 The term 'documentation strategy' was first defined at a session of the 1984 Society of American Archivists, according to Cox, R. J., 1990. *American archival analysis: the recent development of the archival profession in the United States*. Metuchen, NJ: Scarecrow.

10 Successful surveys, which turned cold calling into calling with a purpose, include industrial or regional surveys such as those undertaken by the Business Archives Council and Business Archives Council Scotland in the United Kingdom.

11 See Chapter 12.

12 Other collecting repositories, which have benefitted from such an effect include Minnesota Historical Society, United States of America and the Scottish Business Archive, University of Glasgow, Scotland.

13 See www.pensionsarchive.org.uk [Accessed 19 August 2016].

14 For example, Hamer, A. C., 2011. *The ICSA guide to document retention*. 3rd ed. London: Institute of Chartered Secretaries and Administrators.

15 These considerations are partly based on Ellis, J., ed. 1993. *Keeping archives*. Port Melbourne: Australian Society of Archivists.

16 *Encoded archival description application guidelines*. (online) Available at: www.loc.gov/ead/ [Accessed 19 August 2016].

17 See www.ballasttrust.org.uk [Accessed 19 August 2016].

18 See www.housefraserarchive.ac.uk/ [Accessed 19 August 2016] for an example of a catalogue to the archives of a department store retail company with attention to descriptive introductions to multiple creators reflecting 200 company names, including predecessor, acquired and subsidiary firms, and staff names.

19 See Chapter 5.

20 A full descriptive summary (according to the British meaning of the word) where significant elements in the text are recorded so that the majority of researchers do not need to consult the originals.

21 Some countries have adopted standards such as *Rules for archival description* (Canada), *Describing archives: a content standard* (United States of America) and *Manual for archival description* (United Kingdom) – see bibliography for details.

22 In the United Kingdom the standard for storage conditions is British Standards Institution (BSI), 2012. *PD 5454:2012. Guide for the storage and exhibition of archival materials*. London: BSI. For further information see Chapter 8.

23 *UNESCO thesaurus*. (online) Available at: http://databases.unesco.org/thesaurus/ [Accessed 19 August 2016].

References

Brown, A., 2013. *Practical digital preservation*. London: Facet Publishing.

Cook, T., 2001. Fashionable nonsense or professional rebirth: postmodernism and the practice of archives, *Archivaria*, 51, pp. 14–35.

Freeth, S., 1991. Destroying archives: a case study of the records of Standard Chartered Bank, *Journal of the Society of Archivists*, 12.2 (Oct), pp. 85–94.

Greene, M. A. and Daniels-Howell, T. J., 1997. Documentation with an attitude: a pragmatist's guide to the selection and acquisition of modern business records. In: J. M. O'Toole, ed., 1997. *The records of American business*. Chicago, IL: Society of American Archivists, ch. 7.

International Council on Archives (ICA), 1996. *ICA code of ethics*. [online] Available at: www.ica.org/en/ica-code-ethics [Accessed 19 August 2016].

International Council on Archives (ICA), 2000. *ISAD(G): General international standard archival description*, 2nd ed. Ottawa: International Council on Archives. [pdf] Available at: www.icacds.org.uk/eng/ISAD(G).pdf [Accessed 19 August 2016].

International Council on Archives (ICA), 2004a. *Business archives in international comparison. Report to ICA Congress 2004 Vienna, Austria*. [online] Available at: www.ica.org/en/business-archives-international-comparison [Accessed 19 August 2016].

International Council on Archives (ICA), 2004b. *ISAAR (CPF): International standard archival authority record for corporate bodies, persons and families*. 2nd ed. Ottawa: International Council on Archives. [pdf] Available at: www.icacds.org.uk/eng/ISAAR(CPF)2ed.pdf [Accessed 19 August 2016].

International Organization for Standardization (ISO), 1999. *ISO 3166. Codes for the representation of names of countries and their subdivisions.* 5th ed. Geneva: International Organization for Standardization.

Jenkinson, H., 1965. *A manual of archive administration.* 2nd ed. London: Lund Humphries.

National Council on Archives (NCA), 1997. *Rules for the construction of personal, place and corporate names.* [pdf] Available at: www.archives.org.uk/images/documents/namingrules.pdf [Accessed 19 August 2016].

Schellenberg, T. R., 1956. *Modern archives: principles and techniques.* Chicago, IL: University of Chicago Press.

The National Archives, 2004. *Archive collection policy statements. Checklist of suggested contents.* London: The National Archives. [pdf] Available at: www.nationalarchives.gov.uk/documents/archives/archive-collection-policy.pdf [Accessed 19 August 2016].

Williams, C., 2006. *Managing archives. Foundations, principles and practice.* Oxford: Chandos Publishing.

Further reading

Rescue and selection

Adkins, E. W., 2004. Local history versus corporate history: responsible archival management of international subsidiaries of multinational corporations, *Business Archives in International Comparison.* Vienna: ICA, pp. 62–68.

Dadson, E., 2012. *Emergency planning and responses for libraries, archives and museums.* London: Facet Publishing.

Fogerty, J. E., 1997. The present as prologue: documenting business in the international age, *Proceedings of the annual conference 1997.* London: Business Archives Council, pp. 31–42.

Greene, M. A. and Daniels-Howell, T. J., 1997. Documentation with an attitude: a pragmatist's guide to the selection and acquisition of modern business records. In: J. M. O'Toole, ed., 1997. *The records of American business.* Chicago, IL: Society of American Archivists, ch. 7.

Hamer, A. C., 2011. *The ICSA guide to document retention.* 3rd ed. London: Institute of Chartered Secretaries and Administrators (ICSA).

Ross, S., 2006. Approaching digital preservation holistically. In: A. Tough and M. S. Moss, eds, 2006. *Record keeping in a hybrid environment.* Oxford: Chandos, pp. 115–153.

The National Archives, 2004. *Archive collection policy statements. Checklist of suggested contents.* London: The National Archives. [pdf] Available at: www.nationalarchives.gov.uk/documents/archives/archive-collection-policy.pdf [Accessed 19 August 2016].

Wiltshire, R. A., ed., 2016. *Hunter gatherers: collecting today's business archives.* London: Business Archives Council. [online] Available at: www.businessarchivescouncil.org.uk [Accessed 19 August 2016].

Appraisal

Association des Archivistes Français, 1997. *Les archives dans l'entreprise. Guide des durées de conservation.* Paris: Association des Archivistes Français.

Associazione Bancaria Italiana, 2004. *Linee guida per la selezione dei documenti negli archivi delle banche.* Roma: Bancaria Editrice.

Baer, C. T., 1997. Strategy, structure, detail, function: four parameters for the appraisal of business records. In: J. M. O'Toole, ed., 1997. *The records of American business.* Chicago, IL: Society of American Archivists, ch. 5.

Bettington, J., *et al.*, eds., 2008. *Keeping archives,* 3rd ed. Canberra: Australian Society of Archivists.

Brown, C., 1999. Keeping or destroying archives, some current issues in retention, *Business Archives Principles and Practice*, 77 (May), pp. 31–44.

Centre Français d'Organisation et de Normalisation Bancaires, 2005. *La banque et les durées de conservation d'archives*. Paris: La Revue Banque.

Cook, T., 2001. Fashionable nonsense or professional rebirth: postmodernism and the practice of archives. *Archivaria*, 51 (Spring), pp. 14–35.

Cook, T., 2004. Macro–appraisal and functional analysis: documenting governance rather than government. *Journal of the Society of Archivists*, 25.1 (Apr.), pp. 5–18.

Craig, B., 2004. *Archival appraisal: theory and practice*. Munich: KG Saur.

Fogerty, J. E. and Greene, M. A., 1997. The records of American business; the project and an approach to appraisal. *Business Archives Principles and Practice*, 73 (May), pp. 1–19.

Freeth, S., 1991. Destroying archives: a case study of the records of Standard Chartered Bank, *Journal of the Society of Archivists*, 12.2 (Oct.), pp. 85–94.

Hosker, R. and Richmond, L., 2006. Seek and destroy – an archival appraisal theory and strategy. In: A. Tough and M. S. Moss, eds, 2006. *Record keeping in a hybrid environment*. Oxford: Chandos, ch. 7.

Nougaret, R. and Tortella, T., eds, 2004. *Appraising banking archive*. Frankfurt: European Association for Banking History.

Richmond, L., ed., 1997. *Proceedings of the annual conference, 1997*. London: Business Archives Council.

Schellenberg, T. R., 1956. *Modern archives: principles and techniques*. Chicago, IL: University of Chicago Press.

Cataloguing and indexing

Canadian Council on Archives, 2003. *Rules for archival description*. Ottawa: Canadian Council on Archives.

Community Archives and Heritage Group, 2009. *Cataloguing guidelines for community archives*. [online] Available at: www.communityarchives.org.uk/content/resources/resources [Accessed 19 August 2016].

Doherty, T., 2004. Who, what, when, why? ISAAR(CPF) – The forgotten standard?, *Business Archives Principles and Practice*, 87, pp. 31–49.

Freeth, S., 1991. Finding aids. In: A. Turton, ed., 1991. *Managing business archives*. Oxford: Butterworth-Heinemann, ch. 11.

International Council on Archives (ICA), 2000. *ISAD(G): General international standard archival description,* 2nd ed. Ottawa: International Council on Archives. [pdf] Available at: www.icacds.org.uk/eng/ISAD(G).pdf [Accessed 19 August 2016].

International Council on Archives (ICA), 2004. *ISAAR (CPF): International standard archival authority record for corporate bodies, persons and families*. 2nd ed. Ottawa: International Council on Archives. [pdf] Available at: www.icacds.org.uk/eng/ISAAR(CPF)2ed.pdf [Accessed 19 August 2016].

International Council on Archives (ICA), 2013. *Multilingual archival terminology*. [online] Available at: www.ica.org/en/online-resource-centre/multilingual-archival-terminology [Accessed 19 August 2016].

Library of Congress/Society of American Archivists, 1999. *Encoded archival description application guidelines*. Version 1. [online] Available at: www.loc.gov/ead/ [Accessed 19 August 2016].

National Council on Archives (NCA), 1997. *Rules for the construction of personal, place and corporate names*. [pdf] Available at: www.archives.org.uk/images/documents/namingrules.pdf [Accessed 19 August 2016].

Nougaret, C. and Galland, B., 1999. *Les instruments de recherche dans les archives*. Paris: La Documentation Française.

Pearce-Moses, R., 2013. *A glossary of archival and records terminology*. Chicago, IL: Society of American Archivists. [online] Available at: www2.archivists.org/glossary [Accessed 19 August 2016].

Proctor, M., and Cook, M., 2000. *Manual of archival description*. 3rd ed. Aldershot: Gower.

Society of American Archivists, 2004. *Describing archives: a content standard*. Chicago, IL: Society of American Archivists.

United Nations Educational, Scientific and Cultural Organization, 1977. *UNESCO thesaurus*. [online] Available at: http://databases.unesco.org/thesaurus/ [Accessed 19 August 2016].

General

Association des Archivistes Français, 2012. *Abrégé d'archivistique. Principes et pratiques du métier d'archiviste*. 3rd ed. Paris.

Boyns, R. E., Boyns, T. and Edwards, J. R., 2000. *Historical accounting records: a guide for archivists and researchers*. Northampton: Society of Archivists.

Brown, A., 2013. *Practical digital preservation*. London: Facet Publishing.

Business Archives Council and The National Archives. *Managing business archives: best practice online*. [online] Available at: www.managingbusinessarchives.co.uk/ [Accessed 19 August 2016].

Carucci, P. and Messina, M., 1998. *Manuale di archivistica per l'impresa*. Rome: Carocci Editore.

Digital Preservation Coalition (DPC), 2016. *Digital preservation handbook* (first compiled by N. Beagrie and M. Jones, subsequently maintained and updated by DPC). [online] Available at: www.dpconline.org/advice/preservationhandbook [Accessed 19 August 2016].

Gasson, M., 1997. Business archives: some principles and practices, *Journal of the Society of Archivists*, 18.2 (Oct), pp. 141–149.

Guérin–Brot, I., 1989. *Les archives d'entreprises. Conseil pratiques d'organisation*. Paris: Direction des Archives de France.

International Council on Archive (ICA), 1996. *ICA code of ethics*. [online] Available at: www.ica.org/en/ica-code-ethics [Accessed 19 August 2016].

Kransdorff, A., 1998. *Corporate amnesia: keeping know-how in the company*. Oxford: Butterworth–Heinemann.

McKemmish, S., Piggott, M., Reed, B. and Upward, F., eds., 2005. *Archives: recordkeeping in society*. Australia: Centre for Information Studies, Charles Stuart University.

Millar, L. A., 2010. *Archives principles and practices*. London: Facet Publishing.

Nougaret, C. and Even, P., eds, 2008. *Les archives privées*. Paris: La Documentation Française.

Perks, R., 2010. 'Corporations are people too!': business and corporate oral history in Britain, *Oral History*, 38.1 (Spring). pp. 36–54. Reprinted in R. Perks and A. Thomson, eds., 2016. *The oral history reader*. 3rd ed. London: Routledge.

Shepherd, E., and Yeo, G., 2003. *Managing records: a handbook of principles and practice*. London: Facet Publishing.

The National Archives (TNA), 2012. *Managing digital records without an electronic record management system*. London: Crown Copyright. [pdf] Available at: www.nationalarchives.gov.uk/documents/information-management/managing-electronic-records-without-an-erms-publication-edition.pdf [Accessed 19 August 2016].

The National Archives (TNA), 2015. *Archive service accreditation standard*. [online] Available at: www.nationalarchives.gov.uk/archives-sector/standards.htm [Accessed 19 August 2016].

Turton, A., ed., 1991. *Managing business archives*. Oxford: Butterworth-Heinemann.

Williams, C., 2006. *Managing archives. Foundations, principles and practice*. Oxford: Chandos Publishing.

Wiltshire, R. A., ed., 2016. *Hunter gatherers: collecting today's business archives*. London: Business Archives Council. [online] Available at: www.businessarchivescouncil.org.uk [Accessed 19 August 2016].

Chapter 8

Preservation

Alison Turton

Preservation of archives has been described as 'the means by which the survival of selected material is ensured for enduring access' (Forde and Rhys-Lewis, 2013, p. 1). Preservation should inform every activity undertaken in an archive. It encompasses a wide range of managerial, financial and technical considerations, such as security, storage, packaging, handling and conservation, all aimed at making sure that records taken into an archive survive indefinitely. Given the diversity of record types, formats and media that may be found in a business archive, ranging from parchment and paper, to photographic, film and digital materials, it is not surprising that preservation can be a huge challenge. However, it is something that can be done to a greater or lesser degree and a small business archive can therefore establish a policy and procedures in line with its own means and ambitions.

Preservation operates at all levels in an archive ranging from the archive's formal policy, strategy and standards to the behaviour of researchers in the reading room. Preservation is the responsibility of all – archivists and record users alike.

Archival storage

Storing archives in an appropriate way is the cornerstone of preservation and there are recognised standards that provide a framework of reference. The one which most United Kingdom archives seek to meet is that produced by the British Standards Institution (BSI), *PD 5454:2012* (British Standards Institution, 2012a). There is also a similar, overall less rigorous, international standard produced by the International Organization for Standardization (ISO), *ISO 11799:2015* (International Organization for Standardization, 2015). Additionally *PAS 198:2012* (British Standards Institution, 2012b) provides a framework for risk-based decision making. In the United Kingdom, The National Archives has introduced the Archive Service Accreditation framework to help archives to improve their efficiency and effectiveness through external validation and by identifying good practice.[1] All these standards cover the key storage provisions required to contribute to optimal archive preservation.

Many companies now outsource modern records storage to commercial suppliers, but due to the special expertise needed to handle and store archives safely, and the regular and multi-item access required to them, commercial storage is not advisable for archives. Corporate archives in the care of the creating or owning company are generally best stored in-house, if storage close to the preservation standard can be provided. Some businesses have, however, successfully developed partnerships with external commercial storage suppliers by occupying discrete space within their facilities or by using firms that specialise in archival storage and promotion.[2] Others have come to mutually beneficial deposit agreements with public or private archives.[3]

The building

The principal means of preserving any archive collection is the building in which it is stored. Archive buildings vary greatly in size, form and age, but regardless of the scale of the building, or the rooms in it that are occupied, it must protect the records.

One expert described this requirement as follows: 'Every aspect of an archive building must, in this order, serve (1) to protect the archives against all forces which might otherwise harm them: in particular fire and water, physical or chemical change resulting from polluted or under-regulated environment; dust, mould and vermin; theft and vandalism; and: (2) to promote also the work and well being of everyone (staff and public alike) going about there business there' (Kitching, 1993, p. 10). Another that 'A successful archive building is one that protects the materials within it from excessive heat or cold, fire, water, theft and pollution (and) provides appropriate, comfortable and secure access for those who wish to use the facility or work there' (Forde and Rhys-Lewis, 2013, p. 47).

The first thing to consider is the site and its location. If starting from scratch, and with a free choice of location, avoid sites which are liable to flooding or pollution or which are vulnerable to potential hazards, such as fire, explosions or pests from neighbouring properties. Often, however, corporate archivists will simply be presented with a space or choice of spaces already available in the company's property portfolio. Sometimes compromises will have to be made, mindful of the relative scale of risk. If the space on offer does not already fit archival requirements a business case should be compiled and championed, setting out whether and how it could be adapted to do so. The paper should state the likely reputational and budgetary risks of storing archives inappropriately.

When considering a building some key attributes should be sought. Certainly it should be secure. This means a secure perimeter with blocked windows and security doors fitted with locks and intruder alarms. If it is in a shared building, as will be the case for many business archives, the store must be capable of being isolated from the rest of the building to protect it not only from theft and vandalism but also from fire. It is particularly important that systems supplying gas, electricity or water should not run through the storage area unless required within it.

The roof, floors, walls and ceilings need to be robustly constructed to protect against unauthorised entry, fire, flood, damp, dust and pests and to allow environmental control. The flooring should not generate dust, it should be hard wearing, non slip, easy to clean and chemically stable in use and in the event of a fire. A light coloured finish allows dirt to be easily spotted and removed. The floor also needs to be strong as it will have to support the weight of the stored records for many years ahead. Upper floors or floors in older buildings in particular should be tested to ensure that they are suitable. All paint finishes to walls and doors should be fit for purpose. Where a repository has been newly constructed or refurbished the building should be allowed time to dry out and settle prior to use.

Light is also a significant hazard to archives. The storage area should ideally be window free to exclude daylight, but if there are windows these should be blocked up or screened with blinds and ultraviolet (UV) filtering. All records should ideally be boxed to protect them against light. If the records are not boxed or otherwise protected illumination should be no more than 200 lux at floor level, with a separate on/off switch, or movement sensor, so that the repository is lit only when in use. Fluorescent lamps should be fitted with diffusers and UV filters and incandescent lamps with heat absorbing filters. Particular attention should be paid to the location of the lighting, for example ensuring lighting runs along the aisles of static or mobile shelving to provide visibility, but is not located so close to archives on the upper shelves as to cause heat-related damage.

The building itself should offer space for not only the existing collection of archives, but also provide expansion room for 10 to 15 years ahead. Future space requirements can be quite tricky to estimate in a corporate setting where mergers, disposals and the rise of digital record keeping can make such predictions difficult, but some considerable allowance should certainly be made for future accessions.

Environmental control

Optimal preservation requires the control of temperature and humidity in the storage area, either by use of mechanical air conditioning systems or by thermal inertia resulting from the building's design or location.

The target storage environment for mixed archives should be a stable cool temperature and a stable relative humidity (RH) below the point (typically around 65 per cent RH) at which microbiological activity takes place. A stable temperature of 13–20 degrees Celsius and relative humidity of 35–60 per cent for frequently used material is preferred. These ranges are intended to accommodate gradual seasonal changes. Colder temperatures would be ideal for infrequently used archives and some non-paper media, but as these would require materials to be acclimatised before and after use, they are impractical for most business archives. A small number of items requiring specialist humidity levels could, however, be placed in enclosures in which the relative humidity is locally controlled using silica gel. See Table 8.1 for the ideal environmental conditions for the storage of different media.

Some temperature and humidity fluctuation can be accommodated within an acceptable range as it is now generally agreed that if documents are relatively densely packed and well packaged, they will be minimally affected by short-lived fluctuations, as there is not enough time for transfer of the change and equilibration inside enclosures. Records will eventually equilibrate to slow seasonal changes, but whether they are adversely affected depends on the range of the seasonal variation. Major fluctuations that occur slowly enough to be experienced inside boxes and other enclosures can cause physical damage to some types of records and accelerate chemical degradation. Dramatic temperature variations, which must be avoided, are generally caused by the storage of archives directly next to an exterior wall or floor, near a heater or air vents or in direct sunlight. Further information on managing environmental fluctuation can be found in *PD 5454:2012* (British Standards Institution, 2012a, pp. 10–12).

The storage environment needs to be regularly monitored and action taken swiftly if conditions deteriorate. Building management systems (BMSs) or continuous monitoring systems associated with air-conditioning equipment may be controlled remotely by a company's property team and the archivist should ensure that colleagues responsible for it understand the importance of environmental control, locate and calibrate the sensors

Table 8.1 Recommended environmental conditions for the storage of different media

Record type/format	Temperature in degrees Celsius	Humidity in per cent	Comment
Mixed archives Including paper, parchment, seals, photographs	13–20	35–60	Longevity decreases as temperature rises, so temperatures are best kept as low as possible
Paper Rarely-handled, boxed paper	5–25	25–60	
Photographs and microfilm Black and white polyester negatives/transparencies; black and white glass plates; black and white microfilm; black and white paper prints; colour and black and white ink-jet prints. Colour and black and white acetate negatives and transparencies; cellulose nitrate sheet film; colour photographic and ink jet prints.	Cool storage 5–18 Cold storage −15 +/-5	30–50 50 (maximum)	Protect from dust, dirt and pollutants. Ensure careful handling.
Moving film Polyester base Black and white acetate base Colour acetate base Cellulose nitrate base Video	15–18 10–15 0–5 5–8 10–15	40–45 35 35 35 35–40	Protect from dust. Store flat in inert metal/plastic containers, wound on plastic cores with emulsion side inwards. Containers should be perforated to allow air exchange. 35mm cinematographic film made prior to 1951 may be on a cellulose nitrate base and highly flammable.
Magnetic tape Polyester base – data and audio Acetate – data and audio	5–18 −15 +/-5	25 50	Keep clear of electronic equipment that might produce magnetic currents and erase records. Store in aluminium, acid-free board or inert plastic. Containers should be perforated to allow air exchange. Examine regularly to ensure timely refreshment or migration and maintain a robust back-up programme.
Optical disks Includes CDs and DVDs	5–18	30–50	Remove plastic surrounds, spokes and paper inserts and store in manufacturer's hard plastic cases.
Gramophone records Includes acetate, shellac and vinyl	5–18	30	Store upright in soft polyethylene inner covers inside a robust card outer cover with flap. Keep original cover separately.

Sources: Environmental recommendations based on British Standards Institution, 2012a, and British Film Institute, 2004 (moving film).

appropriately and retain the data in the long term in an accessible way. It is useful to have a local monitoring facility too, so that the archivist can review environmental conditions where the company's control centre is separate to the archive. Independently held monitors or sensors are useful for confirmatory or comparative purposes or for use in repositories that lack a continuous monitoring system.

The overall air infiltration rate should ideally not exceed two air changes a day, although this can be very difficult to measure in practice. The intention of this recommendation is to find a balance between maintaining a stable temperature and humidity and introducing sufficient air movement to remove any internally generated off-gassing of pollutants. Filtration should also be fitted to reduce the external pollutants and dust brought into the repository with the fresh air.

Fire and flood protection

Systems, equipment and procedures must be put in place to prevent, detect and suppress fire. The extent of what can be done will depend on the nature of the archive storage building and the budget available. Fire suppression systems have become ever more sophisticated and increasingly expensive and smaller archives may need to focus on prevention and alarm, rather than on mechanical extinction, and ensure that best practice disaster mitigation and recovery plans are in place.

The risk of fire can be considerably mitigated by a range of precautions, including:

- use of fire resistant building materials;
- plant that is both well maintained and located away from the repository;
- no smoking policies and close control of risky activities, like welding;
- removal of combustible materials, like reprographic or conservation chemicals and nitrate-based film.

Ideally the walls, floors and ceilings and doors of an archive store should have four-hour fire resistance and be built of non-combustible materials that do not emit harmful substances when burning. The storage area should also be fitted with monitored fire detection and ideally also an automatic gas- or water-based fire fighting system. The relative merits and risks of the affordable and feasible solutions will have to be weighed up.

Most companies will be accustomed to deploying fire detection systems, ranging from basic detectors to VESDA (Very Early Smoke Detection Apparatus) early warning air sampling systems, especially if businesses already manage data centres that require similar protection. Even so, deciding upon the best way to protect archives from the risk of fire should ideally involve seeking advice from specialists.[4]

The main options for fire suppression are either gas- or water-based systems. The most popular gas systems involve Argonite, a mixture of nitrogen and argon that reduces oxygen levels but that – for short periods – is acceptable for human inhalation. Argonite is an environmentally friendly version of Halon, which was once commonly used in archive systems. Inergen, a similar gas to Argonite, is also widely used. The main problem such suppression systems present, apart from cost, is the space required to store the canisters of gas and the fact that they are most effective in small airtight compartments.

Water-based systems are now much more sophisticated and work in ways that reduce the damage to archives if they are purposefully or accidentally set off. Three options are available – wet and dry pipe systems and mist systems. The latter dilutes the oxygen feeding the fire and are increasingly popular. All can be programmed to be set off only at the point of the fire rather than throughout the store. Usually all these systems are complimented by appropriate hand-held fire extinguishers dotted through the repository area.

Whatever fire detection and suppression systems are chosen staff need to be aware of how to operate them and how to ensure that they are appropriately maintained. In reality, fires are rare events in archives, but there have been a few high-profile destructive fires in United Kingdom archives in recent years and the issue must be taken seriously.[5]

Water, like fire, can cause considerable damage. Archive storage should not be created in basements or directly under large water systems (such as lavatories, kitchens and water pipes) and where there is a known risk of incoming water, detection systems should be set to alarm. Detection devices should also be placed in roof voids and around mechanical air conditioning units that involve condensers and pipework. If using a water-based fire suppression system that emits a considerable quantity of water, this should be coupled with provision for rapid drainage and storage of records off the ground in order to minimise the damage to archives. Fire fighting by the fire brigade will also generate large amounts of water.

It is vital to have a clear, tested disaster plan in place to mitigate the impact of fire and flood incidents. Disaster planning is discussed later in this chapter and in Chapter 11.

Shelving

Whether shelving is inherited or purchased it is important to understand what it should be made of and how it should be configured and used. Shelving should ideally be constructed of a strong, inert and non-combustible material that can both support the weight of the archives and not compromise their preservation. High quality carbon steel[6] shelving with a weight loading capacity of at least 100 kilograms per shelf would be ideal, although certain kinds of wood shelving units are also quite usable. A powder-coated or baked-enamel surface is very suitable, but whatever the surface finish it should be free from rust and paints or other materials that may be flammable or that could emit substances harmful to the documents over time or in the event of fire. If the collections include videos and other magnetic media the shelving on which they sit should ideally be non-magnetisable.

In order to ensure that archives can be easily retrieved the main gangways should be wider (at least 110 cm) than the aisles between individual runs of shelving. The width of aisles depends on the size of the items and boxes on the shelves, but should be at least shelving depth plus 45 cm, and 75 cm minimum, to allow easy removal of items and the use of trolleys and pulpit ladders.

The dimensions and configuration of the shelving of course depends upon the ceiling height of the store and the dimensions of the records or record boxes to be stored. Clearly the higher the shelving units the more records can be stored, but this needs to be balanced against the difficulty of accessing material out of ordinary reach and the risks associated with the use of kick stools or ladders. Where there is considerable vertical space the introduction of a mezzanine floor could be considered.

In order to maximise the storage capacity the height and depth of the shelves has to be carefully matched to the holdings, both to avoid wasted space and to ensure sufficient space to remove records with ease. The shelving should consequently be easily adjustable. The bottom shelf should be around 15 cm clear of floor level to allow cleaning and avoidance of water in the event of a flood and the top shelf short of any lighting or fire-fighting system piping. An upper lid should protect the items on the top shelf from dust and debris.

Remember that the usable space on each shelf will be less than the external dimensions provided by the manufacturer due to overhangs and protrusions from the shelving structure. The front edge of each shelf should be rounded and have no lip or overhang to catch documents being removed, either from that shelf or from the one below. Where shelves are adjacent to walls, there should be a spacer between the wall and the back of the shelving unit for cleaning and air circulation and the placing of shelving directly against an outside wall should be avoided. Records should not protrude beyond the edge of the shelf upon which they sit.

Ideally the shelving bays should be backless and the uprights between bays open to permit the free circulation of air. Cross-bracing of back-to-back bays should be kept to a minimum, so that where possible large items may be stored across the depth of the two bays. Occasional pull-out shelves at the shelving bay mid-height could be advantageous for laying out documents for consultation, but there are perfectly good alternative solutions such as the use of trolleys or nearby plan chests.

Mobile shelving maximises storage capacity, but is more costly to install and requires a level floor and one that can withstand a heavier load. It constrains access, as only one aisle can be used at once, and can allow the creation of microclimates encouraging the multiplication of moulds and pests. Mobile shelving also needs to be carefully installed and used to reduce any attendant risks to the archives they contain and is unsuitable for fragile formats such as glass plate negatives or gramophone records. Electric mobile units are popular, but a manual override facility is essential in case of power failure.

Processing and public areas

In addition to the archive storage area the building will need an area for receiving and processing new accessions of archives. In a small business archive this may mean no more than the archivists' office, but it is important that new material is examined for pests or mould, that might spread to the rest of the collections, cleaned, sorted and re-boxed before being permanently stored. A small area for storing and processing new material in quarantine is preferable to avoid cross contamination of collections. Specialist suppliers should be used appropriately to deal with any mould or pest problems evident in new accessions.

The archive also requires space for users to view records. In a small business archive this may simply mean offering existing hot desk space in the office to the occasional visitor. However, the desk needs to be large enough to accommodate the records without compromising their handling or support and should be uncluttered. At archives where researcher visits are more frequent it may mean a separate room. A discrete reading room, if space can be afforded, is ideal for both the archivists' privacy and to reduce distracting noise for the researcher. Dedicated space is also preferable from a preservation perspective as the space can be tailored to protect documents – with better facilities for viewing, handling and temporary storage – and can be kept permanently free of hazards like food and drink. There must, however, also be visibility for the archivist to supervise record users, perhaps by means of a glass wall.[7]

Health and safety

In order to manage an archive building safely there needs to be a good health and safety regime in place that is mindful of the special issues archive work routinely involves, such as lifting and transporting heavy boxes and processing deposits that may require such physical interventions as the de-framing of old drawings or opening of locked ledgers or tin chests.

An archive store should be well equipped with heavy duty, easy-to-steer trolleys and robust pulpit ladders and with first aid on hand. Lone working should ideally be avoided or measures put in place to mitigate the attendant risks.

Planning a new archive store

In corporate life change is a constant. Increasingly companies are focused on leaning their property portfolios and using their buildings more intensively. As a result corporate archivists are often required to move their collections to new buildings and to manage relocation projects. Many of the surrounding circumstances and constraints will be out of the control of the archivist, but recognising opportunities and being prepared to lobby to gain support for the kind of building needed is vital.

Once the construction of a new archive store or conversion of an existing building is underway archivists should ensure that they are involved in every stage of the process. A clear and complete brief for the new repository should be compiled, including mini briefs relating to important components such as shelving, flooring and fire suppression system, and an architect with experience in designing archive buildings should ideally be engaged. The briefs should be clear and include flowcharts or similar to show how the various activities and functions relate to each other.

Once the building project is underway the archivist should ensure that he or she sits on the supervising committee and intervenes to clarify and insist upon key requirements and to spot and deal with any arising issues at an early stage. Being appropriately informed involves not only study of the relevant standards and literature, but discussion with other archivists who have recently commissioned new buildings to fully understand the key priorities and pitfalls.[8] A large capital project is a once or twice in a career involvement and will therefore be a steep learning curve. When the time comes to move the archive the activity has to be carefully project managed to ensure that the records are both safely transported and that they can be appropriately stored, audited and retrieved in their new home (Bendix, 2013).

Sustainable buildings

Most companies are keen to reduce their carbon footprint and develop and use their property portfolios in a sustainable way. Consequently, any brand new archive buildings for mixed archive collections should, where practical, be designed to maintain appropriate environmental conditions without air conditioning. This approach may also minimise the resources used for the build, the impact of the repository building on the environment and the long-term running costs.

Measures could include commissioning building designs that maintain environmental conditions through insulation, ground source heat pumps, wind turbines and solar panels and that reduce energy consumption through the reduction of air changes or the use of energy saving bulbs. Some business archives have, in recent years, opted for more passive archive repositories, including the C & J Clark archive at Street in the United Kingdom (see the case study in Box 8.1).[9] The Irish Distillers archive at Midleton, Republic of Ireland, to which records were transferred in 2013, uses thermostatically-controlled heaters to regulate temperature and portable dehumidifiers to deal with humidity spikes (Quinn, 2015, p. 30), whilst Evonik Industries' archive in Hanau, Germany, completed in 2010, relies on a loam layer on the walls to help regulate relative humidity in parts of the repository.

Box 8.1 Case study: building a passive repository at C. & J. Clark Ltd, United Kingdom

In 2012 the C. & J. Clark archive (Alfred Gillett Trust) completed the construction of a passive repository to the rear of a heritage building on Clark's factory site in Street, to house a mixed archive collection of paper, photographs, film, shoes (leather, textile, patent, metal, plastics) and costumes (cotton, wool, synthetics). The company chose a passive construction model because it was not only more sustainable, but also reduced long-term care and maintenance costs. Specialist consultants were engaged.

Key building key features

- Heavy insulation.
- Thick concrete base (*in situ*), concrete block walls and concrete (*in situ* and pre-cast) ceilings.
- Air-tight and water-tight structure.
- Windowless.
- Breathable high-quality building materials.
- Reduced reliance on monitoring and evaluation systems.
- Control of relative humidity/temperature balance by dehumidification.
- Simple heating/de-humidification/air circulation/ventilation systems.
- Archival building envelope (repository) and buffer (circulation) spaces.
- Green roof – additional layer of insulation, controls water flows, a visual and environmental enhancement to the building.

Advantages

- Low energy, maintenance and running costs;
- Insulated to reduce heat loss from the building and to prevent over heating in hot weather;
- Air tight to minimise heat loss through air filtration;
- Optimising shape, size and orientation of building.

Disadvantages

- Passive archive approach generally depends on a repository being full (using paper as a thermal and moisture buffer) to support building environmental stability;
- Segregation of material types required as shoes are less dense than paper and hard to predict effects in advance;
- Materials in shoe manufacturing have differed through the years, and may off gas – this will be monitored and may result in the need for mechanical intervention;
- Building needs to 'dry out' from construction process before the optimum performance is achieved.

Performance

Appears satisfactory, but has not been rigorously monitored. The environment inside the store is not observed to be adversely affected by external climatic changes.

Source: Information provided by Charlotte Berry, Alfred Gillett Trust, by private communication.

Packaging

In order to protect records from environmental fluctuation, light, dust and the harmful substances inherent in their own composition, records should ideally be stored in archive-quality boxes, folders or other enclosures that provide an acid-free buffer. These are most commonly made of paper, card or polyester. If enclosures cannot be afforded for every item archivists should prioritise the most vulnerable records. Storage boxes are the first line of defence and provide protection from flood and fire, environmental change and handling. They can also facilitate transportation and high-density storage. Boxes made of strong acid-free board with brass staples and full depth lids will prove sturdy and are ideal for preservation. Boxes should fit records snugly, so that items do not move around inside, but they should never be over filled.[10]

Enclosures for individual items within the boxes can be acid-free envelopes, four-flap folders which fold over the item or transparent polyester sleeves that allow photographs and other items to be examined without removing them. Maps and plans are best stored flat in plan chests. If plan chests are unaffordable large format items can be kept less expensively in large, shallow acid-free boxes or interleaved between supporting archive quality board and shelved through back-to-back bays.

Bundles of paper or wrappings should be tied together using unbleached linen tape and identified using labels cut from acid-free card. Individual volumes and papers, or their enclosures, should be marked with their archive reference using a lead pencil so that the marking can be erased if necessary. Special marker pens can be purchased for permanently marking polyester sleeves.

Handling

Much of the damage archives routinely sustain results from poor handling. Such damage can be cumulative and not immediately apparent. Accordingly both staff and users need to understand how to handle archives appropriately.

In storage, archives should not be fitted so tightly into envelopes, boxes or shelves that they will be damaged during retrieval or replacement. Items kept on mobile shelving should be packed or supported in a way that ensures they will not slide or topple over when the shelves are moved.

When transporting archives, archivists should ensure that all items are supported carefully with two hands and that both hands are clean, dry and free of creams. Trolleys can be used to transport multiple or heavy items, but should not be overloaded. To ensure records are fully supported in transit and are not accidentally knocked against walls and doorways they should not be allowed to protrude over the trolley edge. Small more vulnerable items should not be stacked below heavier ones and trollies should be stabilised by loading heavier items on lower shelves.

In the search room users should be shown how to handle records and archivists should not be shy about intervening to offer advice. Gloves, tight-fitting nitrile or surgical gloves, should be provided for handling certain items, like photographs, but wearing gloves can in general make it difficult to handle documents adeptly due to a diminished sense of touch. Despite the common sight of television presenters examining archives sporting white cotton gloves the disadvantages generally outweigh the advantages. It is actually better to ensure archivists' and users' hands are clean and dry and that hand creams and licking fingers to turn pages is avoided. Weighted snakes or other smooth weights can be used to hold down volume pages and unrolled drawings or plans for examination. The ideal maximum angle to which bound volumes should be opened is 120 degrees, so book wedges should be provided to reduce the strain on volume spines and additional foam pads used to provide support when viewing the beginning or end of a volume. Users should also be instructed to support pages appropriately as they are turned, using the centre fore edge or top corner. Any appended seals should be supported on a foam pad.

Clear search room rules should be given to all researchers and displayed prominently in the search room. These should explain the key dos and don'ts for handling archival records, namely:

- do ensure hands are clean and well dried and avoid the use of hand creams;
- do ensure documents are fully supported, not hanging off desks or held when read;
- don't drink or eat;
- don't write in or mark records;

- do use pencil only, don't use erasers or ink;
- do handle records as little as possible and avoid touching writing or images, or using a paper marker to follow text;
- don't write or lean on records;
- don't put records on the floor;
- don't insert bookmarks, attach sticky notes or fold page corners.

There is, however, no substitute for having watchful staff on hand to assist readers in the search room.

Photocopying can cause particular preservation problems, due to both the physical handling involved and the associated exposure to heat, light and ozone. Photocopying can be particularly damaging to books on flat-bed copiers, which force book bindings to open to 180 degrees. Book pages falling toward the plate as the volume is lowered into position can also cause leaves to be creased, folded or torn. Every archive should have a photocopying policy, which explains clearly to both staff and users what can and can not be copied. The key principle should be that only copying that does not threaten preservation should be permitted. Ideally, photocopying should be avoided and self-service copying by users should certainly be prohibited.

Scanners are probably more frequently used in business archives nowadays and similar concerns apply. In order to ensure the same item is not repeatedly scanned it is wise to take a master high-resolution image, whenever scanning is done, which can be stored safely and then reduced in size as required. Photocopiers and scanners specifically designed for imaging archival records and books do exist, but companies' procurement controls usually mean that limited office equipment options are available to staff and specialist machines are generally not within their scope. Care should be taken using scanning equipment that requires a lid to be pressed down onto archival records as this can cause significant damage. The best way of copying archives is using digital photography that involves neither flash or lighting and minimises handling.

Surrogates

An important strategy in promoting preservation is the use of surrogates, that is to say copies of records that reduce the wear and tear on originals by channelling access through the copies. Surrogates are particularly useful if the original is fragile or frequently accessed and vulnerable due to its condition or media. They can also provide a back-up copy of vital or important records in the event of disaster, if stored separately, and a source for the creation of future copies.

The term copying could include hand copying, photographic copying, photo-copying, microfilming or digitising, but nowadays in an archival context commonly refers to microfilming, digital photography or scanning. Such surrogate records can also be effective in promoting access, particularly by using digital means to distribute records. However, it is costly as it will normally have to be outsourced to a specialist provider, and can also demand significant staff time to prepare the records, for example, removing clips and checking originals for potential issues such as missing or damaged pages, faded ink or dirt. Afterwards the copies also need to be checked for quality, order and completeness.

Archivists also need to consider the risks inherent in the copying process as records usually have to be transported to a supplier and stored and handled beyond the archivist's control. Certainly insurance needs to be in place and the archivist should be confident in the quality of the supplier's work and familiarity with handling archival materials. Recommendation from another archive that has used the firm would be ideal.

Advice should be taken from a conservator before embarking on a major microfilming or scanning programme as inappropriate copying can be damaging and there are issues to be considered, such as material in different size and formats, large volumes that require unbinding to copy folios and attachments such as seals. Guidance and standards on microfilming are available and should be considered (National Preservation Office, 2000). The preparation time for digital programmes should not be underestimated (Bulow and Ahmon, 2010).

Once surrogate copies are made policy has to be agreed on how to catalogue the copies for issue, how to package them and how to manage film retrieval and replacement and referencing. Copying and digital distribution can also increase demand and enquiries and the decision as to whether and how to create and use surrogate records depends on a particular archive's objectives and budget.

Surrogacy decisions should be informed by user statistics, preservation surveys and the promotional value of enhanced access. It can also save considerable staff time in production. Surrogates, like photocopies, microfilm and scans can also be used to provide copies without preservation implications.

Pests

In the United Kingdom pests are not as big a problem as in some other countries, but an archive store should ideally be constructed or adapted in a way that keeps them at bay by preventing their access. Vertebrates like mice, rats and birds will cause problems, by shredding or eating paper and by defecating and thereby giving rise to damage or mould. The main preservation issues are usually, however, caused by insects that can gain access through small cracks, breed and multiply. Insects feed on the cellulose in paper and starch or wood in bindings, boring holes or eating the paper surface. The most common United Kingdom pests are silverfish, clothes moths, book lice and certain beetles. Most of these breed at higher temperature and humidity levels than are archivally recommended, but maintaining the right environment will not prevent such pests from inhabiting storage spaces.

Additional steps that can be taken to mitigate the risk of pests include:

- blocking up access points, cracks and holes around the pipes, doors and windows;
- proper cleaning and ensuring any unused space is fully accessible for cleaning;
- regular checking of dark warm damp corners, fabric folds and other places that might host pests;
- quarantining new accessions until fully inspected;
- keeping the repository well organised and clear so there is no build up of rubbish;
- keeping insect food sources, such as pot plants, wool carpets, food and drink, out of storage areas.

As insects may not be easily visible, infestations can sometimes be spotted by droppings – although frass is not always easily identifiable – and from holes in archival materials or small piles of dust. Archivists should set up a monitoring system, which involves the laying of insect traps – either sticky traps that insects blunder into or pheromone lure traps – so that pests can be caught, identified and the scale of the problem understood. Blunder traps, normally cards covered with a sticky substance, are generally the most appropriate large-scale monitoring tools.

If a significant problem is identified the archivist may need support from a commercial supplier well-briefed in the requirements of archive buildings. All the affected material should be put into sealed plastic bags, the cause of the infestation identified and an approved means, preferably non toxic, to kill the insects sought, possibly by freezing or oxygen deprivation. However, it is far better to prevent an infestation by careful management. Integrated Pest Management (IPM) is a widely-used control strategy in many sectors, including archives, based primarily on preventive measures, ranging from simple good housekeeping to professional pest treatment.

Mould

The growth of mould can stain and weaken the full range of archival materials, including paper, parchment, bindings and magnetic tape. Mould spores are in the air all the time and simply need the right environmental conditions – moisture and an organic substrate – to germinate. There are a wide variety of types of mould and some archive materials are more susceptible than others. Mould will flourish in environments with a relative humidity above 65 per cent, so keeping relative humidity levels low is the best prevention measure. The damage caused by mould is irreversible and chemicals do not provide an effective treatment.

There are health and safety risks associated with mould. These are particularly associated with the respiratory system and mucus membranes. Depending on the type and state of the mould the risks may be quite low, but it is important to be aware that some species of moulds can carry higher risks. People who are pregnant or have respiratory problems or compromised immune systems are particularly vulnerable. An increased risk also applies to anyone who is repeatedly exposed as mould has a cumulative effect. Moulds that present a high health and safety risk are not commonly found in archival collections, but any risks must be mitigated by wearing appropriate personal protective equipment, such as P3 masks,[11] protective sleeves and disposable aprons. If staff are cleaning or handling items individually local exhaust ventilation equipment should be used.

Mould can exist in three states – active, dormant and non-viable (when the mould will no longer reactivate even in suitable conditions). Active mould, which presents the highest health and safety risk, should not be treated. In order to deal with an outbreak any active mould must be deactivated and driven into a dormant state in which it is no longer feeding or producing fruiting bodies (reproducing). This can be done by lowering the relative humidity as far as possible, although not lower than 35 per cent. Bear in mind that it can be difficult to tell when mould has been deactivated.

Mould outbreaks can give rise to major problems and are difficult to eradicate (Child, 2011; Forde and Rhys-Lewis, 2013, pp. 74–75). It is not advisable to tackle a sizeable outbreak in-house without proper facilities. Instead specialist contractors should be engaged. Generally the affected archives are speedily removed from the environment that facilitated growth, without opening the boxes, and taken to a well-ventilated space with a stable environment and relative humidity below 65 per cent. Meanwhile, the original storage area will be dried out, the environment stabilised, the shelves washed with an appropriate fungicide and the air-conditioning filters cleaned or replaced to avoid the re-circulation of mould contaminants. When the specialist contractor advises it is safe to do so, the treated records can be re-boxed and returned to the main archive repository, but should be checked regularly for at least a year for subsequent mould development. For a case study on how mould outbreaks were dealt with at The Rothschild Archive in the United Kingdom see Box 8.2.

In order to try to prevent mould outbreaks keep relative humidity below 65 per cent; never place damp documents or untreated records showing mould infestation into the repository; store all records away from cold or damp walls or unregulated air vents; and undertake regular box checking, particularly in known cold spots in the repository.

Box 8.2 Case study: successfully controlling a mould outbreak at The Rothschild Archive, United Kingdom

Background

For 15 years the Rothschild archives were stored in two tanked, air-conditioned stores in the basement of the bank's City of London office. Due to space considerations the stores, designed in compliance with the predecessor standard to *PD 5454:2012* (British Standards Institution, 2012a), were fitted with mobile shelving.

The outbreak

In 2006, over the course of a few months, the appearance of a few spots of mould on archive boxes progressed to a major infestation. As soon as spores were lifted from one set of boxes or volumes, another outbreak appeared elsewhere. The infestation affected both stores and spot cleaning soon became inadequate.

Initially the archivists tried to solve the problem in liaison with the company's own building specialists. When this proved unsuccessful, independent consultants that specialised in dealing with mould contaminants in archives were recruited. The consultants confirmed that the existing store conditions were appropriate and that the mould had not been imported with recent accessions to the archive.

Eventually the origin of the outbreak was tracked to an incident two years earlier when a rise in the relative humidity readings had prompted the company's property team to modify the air taken into the air-conditioning units, reducing the fresh air supply by 50 per cent. What had been intended as a temporary air supply change had never been reset.

Response

With specialist advice the following actions were taken to control the outbreak:

- introduction of fans and extractors as an immediate, temporary measure;
- adjustment of relative humidity levels and comprehensive monitoring of environmental conditions;
- use of lamps to detect incipient mould, often not visible to the naked eye;
- removal of all the hardboard that had been used to secure the closed shelving racks (it had become a focus for mould growth);
- institution of a preservation survey to assess the extent of the problem (which had coincidentally already been a planned action);
- introduction of more air vents in the raised floor to improve air flow;
- thorough cleaning of the entire store contents once the infestation was halted;
- implementation of a rigorous ongoing programme of cleaning and checking.

Learnings

- Dealing with a mould outbreak can be very costly in both staff time and budget and it is far better to focus on prevention.
- Even the most accurate readings of appropriate environmental conditions can be localised; microclimates within the shelves can be radically different to the ambient readings in the store.
- Adding data loggers to open shelves and to the boxes can provide more precise readings.
- Mould is always there, constant vigilance is required.
- Support from specialist consultants is often needed.
- Continue to check for mould in the longer-term.

In 2015 random box checking, instituted due to the previous mould outbreak, prompted discovery of a second outbreak in archive boxes containing material that had been in a damp basement and located on shelving opposite the door from the repository to the workspace. With data loggers specialist consultants quickly discovered that the problem was caused by a rush of warm air from the office meeting the cool metal shelves and condensing; a phenomenon known as 'thermal bridging'.

Source: Information provided by Melanie Aspey and Natalie Broad, Rothschild Archive, by private communication.

Preservation surveys

The simplest way to collect preservation-related information about archives – format, materials and condition – is to gather and record it as they are accessioned. Alternatively, a preservation survey can be undertaken on all or part of an existing collection. There are many surveying techniques that can be used. It is important to decide the purpose of the survey, for example, to discover if the storage environment is protecting the collection overall or that the conditions/requirements of a particular type of record are suitable. The records to be surveyed can then be prioritised and the information to be collected determined.

To allow decisions to be made about preservation issues, needs and priorities, the survey should record:

* date;
* location – including environment and shelving type;
* type of archival record – including format, size and date;
* condition – including appearance, tears, dirt, mould, insect damage and paper clips/staples;
* packaging – whether boxes/sleeves/envelopes and whether of archival quality;
* future access needs – whether likely to be frequently used;
* recommendation – repackage, clean, repair, remove sticky tape and/or relocate;
* priority.

Keep the survey simple and frame it in a way that will allow the gathering of consistent data that can be quantified and accessibly documented. Include guidelines for the surveying archivist on what to survey and how to fill in the survey forms. It is usual to sample during the survey, for example looking at only one in ten or one in 100 items. A survey might focus on particular types of records such as vital records, records known to have suffered from poor past storage or vulnerable records such as photographs, photocopies or digital objects. A descriptive glossary and agreed terminology will be helpful.

Archivists should also survey the overall building environment and security measures, as well as the condition of the archive, with preservation intent. Proactive preservation surveying may, however, not be feasible where resources are squeezed and other priorities jockey for attention.

In planning conservation priorities following a preservation survey, the following should be taken into account:

* the historical, promotional, operational and monetary value of the document;
* likely future research use of the document;
* the conservation needs;
* the most cost-effective and appropriate way to conserve or preserve the document.

Disaster planning

The purpose of disaster planning is both to reduce the likelihood of a disaster happening and to maximise the speed and efficiency of the response in the event that a disaster does affect the archive store. Planning should reduce the likelihood of important things being overlooked and therefore minimise damage to the archive and archive service, although no plan can prepare for every situation and difficult decisions will undoubtedly have to be taken as events unfold.

Ideally an archive should have both a disaster prevention plan and a disaster recovery plan, although these may be combined in a single document. A disaster prevention plan aims to both prevent a disaster and to mitigate the impact of any fire, flood or biodegradation incident that might occur. It does so by identifying and evaluating risks and establishing checks and actions to diminish and control them. Box 8.3 sets out the possible content of a prevention plan.

Box 8.3 Information to be included in a disaster prevention and mitigation plan

Main risks

Identify the main risks, for example:

Fire	Flood	Other
Wiring and electrical systems	Toilets/sinks/drains/taps overflow	Structural damage – for example ceiling collapse, bomb
Light fittings	Leaks from roof	Theft/vandalism
Portable appliances	Water main leak	Mould infestation
Discarded cigarettes	Internal water tank	Macro-organism infestation
Arson	Internal pipework leak	Micro-organism infestation
Terrorism/explosion	Storm flood	
Infestation – for example rats gnawing wires	Radiator/air-conditioning leak	

Main preventative measures

Be aware of the main risks and ensure the following key prohibitions are observed:

- no smoking in or near building;
- no food in the repository or search room;
- no unsupervised access to the repository;
- no storage of damp or fungal- or insect–infested accessions in the repository;
- no exposure of the repository to damaging substances;
- repository doors to be kept shut at all times;
- regular cleaning to remove dust or dirt.

Arrange the archive storage in a way that minimises damage in the event of a disaster:

- store items in boxes, wherever possible;
- encapsulate items in polyester sleeves or in archive folders within boxes, wherever possible;

- label formats requiring different recovery methods such as videos, CDs, microforms and photographs;
- identify key records with fluorescent stickers on boxes to allow rapid recovery in the event of disaster;
- avoid use of ends of runs and top and bottom shelves for key records
- keep all items off the floor;
- ensure there is a communication cascade out of hours/during holidays.

Undertake the following regular checks (note the interval and person responsible in a table):

- doors locked and keys secure;
- temperature and humidity monitored. Action taken on significant variants from norm;
- checks for water ingress;
- lights operating properly;
- unusual smells and sounds;
- electrical appliances unplugged and switched off out of hours;
- flashlights working;
- disaster battle box intact;
- insect bodies or dirt visible;
- pest traps monitored and changed;
- electrical appliances checked;
- smoke and temperature detectors working;
- audio alarms working.

Undertake the following regular actions (note the interval and person responsible in a table):

- update and redistribute the disaster recovery plan;
- accompany contractors/researchers/work-experience staff;
- clean the repositories;
- replace all items stored temporarily on trolleys/plan chests;
- monitor environmental conditions;
- spot check for bio-deterioration – books, photographs, microforms and plans;
- document all material removed from repository;
- check and update disaster battle box contents;
- label vital records.

Key contacts

List of contact details for key archive, property and security staff internally, and conservators and other damage recovery services, such as vacuum/freeze-drying, pest fumigation, crate hire and microfilm reprocessing, externally.

A disaster recovery plan, by contrast, sets out how an archive deals with and recovers from any disaster that does occur. In reacting to a disaster, the aim must be to complete the salvage of damaged holdings within 48 hours'. This is because the majority of incidents may be expected to result in water-related damage and mould growth will normally begin to develop on water-damaged records after this time period. Much advice is available regarding managing disasters (for example Forde and Rhys-Lewis, 2013, pp. 99–121; Dadson, 2012a) and many examples of archive disaster plans can be found online.

To ensure that disaster planning is given appropriate profile and attention the role of disaster recovery co-ordinator should be assigned to a particular archivist. The co-ordinator will:

- own, develop and update the plan;
- ensure that the necessary equipment, budget and relationships, with building maintenance and media staff and external conservators and freeze-drying specialists and so on, are in place;
- lead and manage activity during and after a disaster.

The disaster recovery, or emergency, plan should set out the call out procedure for staff and suppliers and list the key contacts and the location of all the equipment that might be needed. Indeed, much of the essential emergency equipment should be identified, assembled and kept in readiness in boxes in or close to the archive building. A disaster box might include items like protective clothing, polythene sheeting and bags, torches, buckets, absorbent paper, pens, labels and so on. More costly equipment, like pumps and dehumidifiers, should be pre-sourced in liaison with the company's property team.

In the event of a disaster the co-ordinator should assess the damage, notify suppliers, arrange staff call-outs, look after health and safety, brief staff fully and set up areas for storage of evacuated unaffected material, for receiving, sorting and storing different damage types, for cataloguing and packing freeze-dry materials and for laying out materials for air-drying (Dadson, 2012b). The co-ordinator should also manage communication with senior managers and the media. See Box 8.4 for guidance on the kind of information that should be included in the plan.

The disaster recovery plan should list the priority records that should be recovered first, if recovery is possible, and note how they can be identified. For a business these might include such key commercial or operational records as board minutes and papers, product recipes or designs or archives of particular historical or monetary value. The plan should also set out how the building should be recovered after the disaster and how to check for problems like mould. Freeze- and air-dried material should be rehabilitated away from the main collection in well-ventilated space with a relative humidity of less than 30–40 per cent and temperature of less than 18 degrees Celsius for six to 12 months. See Table 8.2 for guidance on the treatment of water-damaged material.

All staff should keep a copy of the disaster recovery plan at home in case called out unexpectedly and be trained how to handle and prepare records for freezing and air-drying. The call-out cascade and procedures should be tested regularly and all issued copies of the plan tracked and replaced when the information they contain, such as contact details, is updated. Small archives will need professional help at an early stage for any significant incidents and may want to set up reciprocal disaster recovery relationships with

Box 8.4 Disaster recover plan, possible content

Disaster recovery plan location and update

State who holds copies/how often it is tested, reviewed and updated.

Incident discovery

- Call out procedures for different types of emergency/alarm, may include flow diagrams.
- Guidelines for dealing with a minor incident.
- Guidelines for dealing with a major incident.

Stock salvage

- Define salvage priorities, including a list of priority archive materials and a plan of the repository area showing their location.
- Set out likely salvage team actions, including advice on how to prepare records for air-drying and freezing and how to deal with smoke and soot damage – air–drying (damp, partly wet), freezing (wet), vacuum freezing (valuable wet) and discard (badly-damaged replaceable or duplicate items).

Post–disaster recovery

- Guidance on how to recover the building for archive use.
- Guidance on the rehabilitation of freeze-dried or air-dried records.
- Guidance on how to monitor for mould going forward.

Possible appendices

- List of key internal and external contacts.
- List of emergency equipment box contents.
- Plans of the archive and recovery building showing sorting areas and key equipment.
- Risk assessment template forms for listing hazards – whom they might effect and what has been/should be done to mitigate them.
- Damage list template form – for listing records sent for freeze-drying, including archive reference number, damage description and where crated.
- Treatments for different kinds of water-damaged records.

Table 8.2 Treatments for salvage of different kinds of water-damaged records

Record format	Priority	Handling precautions	Packing method	Drying method
Paper documents	Freeze or air-dry as soon as possible (within 48 hours).	Do not separate single sheets.	Interleave document units and pack in crates.	Freeze-vacuum dry or air-dry if small number.
Books and booklets	Freeze as soon as possible (within 48 hours).	Do not open or close, do not separate covers.	Place in freezer bags if small scale or separate with freezer paper. Pack spine down in crates.	Freeze-vacuum dry or air-dry if small number.
Books with leather and vellum bindings	Freeze immediately or air-dry if not too wet.	Do not open or close, do not separate covers.	Retain shape with use of crepe bandaging, tied horizontally with the knot on the side of the book block. Pack spine down in crates.	Freeze-vacuum dry or air-dry if small number.
Photographs – prints, negatives, transparencies	Air-dry as soon as possible. Separate whilst still wet. Rinse if dirty in cool clean water (<18 degrees Celsius). Only freeze if unavoidable. Can keep wet for up to 48 hours. Salvage order: 1. colour prints 2. black and white prints 3. negatives/slides /transparencies. Remove cardboard slide mounts.	Do not touch image with bare hands.	Keep in cold water. Pack in containers lined with bin bags.	Air-dry spread flat with print/emulsion side up or hang on nylon line with plastic clips. If frozen thaw then air-dry or freeze-dry. Do not vacuum dry.
Plans and drawings	Freeze or air-dry as soon as possible (within 48 hours).	Do not separate single sheets.	Pack in map drawers, flat boxes or polythene covered plywood crates.	Freeze-vacuum dry or air-dry if small number.
Video and audio tape cassettes	Air-dry containers and external surfaces if damp and water/dirt not penetrated. Dry within 48 hours if possible. Do not freeze. Recopy later.	Do not touch magnetic media with bare hands.	Pack vertically in crates. Do not place heavy weights on cassette sides.	Contact specialist to salvage sealed cassettes.

Item				
Film and audio tape reels	Immediately rinse tape reels soaked by dirty water. Dry within 48 hours if possible, alternatively keep wet. Do not freeze. Recopy later.	Do not touch magnetic media with bare hands.	Keep wet in plastic bags. Pack vertically in crates. Do not place heavy weights on reel sides.	Air-dry or vacuum-dry. Don't apply heat.
Compact discs	Immediately dry discs. Dry paper enclosures as soon as possible. Rinse discs in cold clean water if necessary. Do not freeze discs. If a duplicate back-up discs. If a duplicate back-up is necessary make a new copy and discard original.	Do not scratch surface. Clean/dry from centre out with lint-free cloth.	Pack vertically in crates.	Air-dry. Allow to dry for 48 hours before re-boxing.
Memory (USB) sticks	Dry inside and outside of stick. If a duplicate back-up make a new copy and discard original.		Place in plastic bags and pack in crates.	Contact specialist conservator if necessary.
Microfilm rolls	Immediately rinse tapes soaked by dirty water in cold clean water. Dry within 48 hours.	Do not remove from boxes. Hold cartons together with rubber bands.	Keep wet in cold water in dark sealed containers lined with bin liners.	Arrange with microfilm processor to rewash and dry. Air-dry spread flat or hang on nylon line with plastic clips. Do not allow to dry in rolls.
Microfiche	Immediately rinse fiche soaked by dirty water in cold clean water. Dry within 48 hours. Freeze or keep wet.	Remove paper or plastic jackets.	Keep wet in cold water in dark sealed containers lined with bin liners.	Air-dry spread flat with emulsion side up or hang on nylon line with plastic clips.
Watercolours	Immediately freeze-dry.	Do not blot.	Interleave and pack in crates.	Air- or freeze-dry.
Non-watercolour paintings	Air-dry immediately.	Drain and carry horizontally.	Pack face up without touching paint.	Air-dry. Contact specialist conservator.
Artefacts, costumes, and so on			Place in plastic bags and pack in crates.	Contact specialist conservator.

other local public or private archives. The disaster recovery plan should also incorporate any digital archive store.

Thought needs to be given to how any fire, flood and environmental alarms relating to the archive store manifest themselves. They will be of no use if they only show in the building itself if it is unoccupied at weekends and in the evenings. Many large companies have central monitoring centres for all alarms and the archivist needs carefully to define what issues should cause action to be taken and what that should be for particular fire, flood and environmental issues.

The disaster recovery plan will normally sit alongside, and be additional to, the corporate archive unit's business continuity plan. The latter is generally focused on getting the activity of the department up and running as soon as possible after an incident that prevents access to a building or other key resources such as records and technology, but is often in a company-dictated format that does not allow scope for the specialist requirements of protecting archival records.

Conservation

At one time the terms conservation, restoration and preservation tended to be used interchangeably. Today conservation has a well-defined meaning, an intervention, to stabilise the condition of a document and to minimise the risk of further physical or chemical damage, which generally requires a skilled conservator. Conservation treatments may remain visually noticeable and the processes are largely reversible. By contrast restoration is the entire rebuilding of a document so it looks like the original, often using methods that cannot be reversed. Preservation tends to be passive and conservation a more active intervention.

Most business archives are unlikely to have an in-house conservator and will use external suppliers. Even though advised by a conservator its archivists still need to have a working knowledge of basic treatments and issues in order to understand what to commission and the implications. For example, what type of binding would be appropriate for conserved volumes and what would be the repercussions of extensive conservation treatment.

Choosing the right conservator is important, as is appropriately managing that conservator as a supplier. The following steps should be taken:

- identify a possible conservator and make contact;
- provide a clear written description of the work required and explain the future use of the item. Be prepared to discuss several conservation options to ensure the appropriate approach is taken;
- visit the conservator's workshop to ensure it is well-organised and that items undergoing treatment are being handled and stored safely;
- take up references and look at work previously undertaken;
- after examination of the item get an estimate for the work, agree a timetable and ensure appropriate security and insurance is in place;
- agree a written contract;
- agree arrangements for transportation of the items;
- ensure a report on the conservation work undertaken will be supplied;
- test the conservator with one document before work on a large number is commissioned.

Box 8.5 Preservation policy – content elements

Introduction

Describe the purpose of the archive and its attitude toward preservation. For example, that the company recognises its responsibility to ensure all archives in its care are appropriately cared for and conserved in a consistent and safe way. State any standards that the archive observes, for example, *PD 5454:2012 Recommendations for the storage and exhibition of archival documents, ISO 11799:2015 Information and documentation – document storage requirements for archive and library materials* and *ISO 14721:2012 Space data and information transfer systems – open archival information systems (OAIS) – reference model.*

Preventive conservation

- Describe the repository conditions for the long-term storage of the physical archive collections in a maintained environment, for example compliant with *PD 5454:2012* or *ISO 11799:2015*, security guard presence and 24/7 closed-circuit television security and visitor site access control.
- Describe the environmental conditions the repository should meet and allowable deviations and monitoring.
- Describe the archive packaging used.
- Advise how and why new acquisitions and incoming collections are held in quarantine pending full inspection before integration into the archive collections.
- Set out surrogate policy and how records are digitised or microfilmed.
- Describe how staff are provided with basic preservation training and knowledge, so that they can identify potential conservation issues and any related health and safety risks.
- Describe the preservation aspects of the display cases used in and beyond the archive building.
- Describe the repository cleaning regime.
- Describe how insect and vermin traps are placed in appropriate locations throughout the building and monitored/replaced periodically. Also reference how trapped insects are identified and assessed for their potential risk to the collections.

Handling, copying and moving

Describe how the archive considers preservation and conservation requirements when assessing whether and how records should be handled, copied or moved as detailed below:

- Correct handling procedures are followed by all staff and volunteers.
- Items that can be harmful to the long-term preservation of archives are removed at the time of cataloguing or when found.
- Material is not photocopied or scanned if doing so will damage it in any way. Large, fragile or faded documents are never photocopied.

- All new researchers are provided with a copy of the reader regulations before their arrival at the archive, which details correct handling procedures and restrictions around the provision of reprographic facilities due to preservation concerns.
- Researchers are supervised during their visit by an assigned archivist.
- Researchers are not permitted to use original items if a surrogate version is available in order to reduce unnecessary handling.
- Support equipment (weights, rests and the like) are provided in the search room and where appropriate, researchers are given guidance on how to use this equipment by an archivist.
- If items are being used internally or loaned externally for exhibition, the risk posed to the items from transport, environmental conditions, storage and display are assessed before an agreement is reached.
- Set out how archive deposits are transferred to the archives and how such deposits should be packaged.
- Note that the archive reserves the right to reject any access request if it is felt that the item is too vulnerable or damaged, or would be otherwise put at risk.

Electronic archives

- Describe the conditions for the storage, management, preservation and provision of access to the digital archive collections, for example in compliance with the Open Archival Information Systems (OAIS) international model and associated in-house guidance.
- Advise restrictions on access to the digital repository, for example it may be available to the archivists only.
- Note the preservation formats used by the archive and whether multiple copies are held, for example copies for preservation and viewing purposes.

Disaster prevention and recovery

- State whether disaster management plans and processes are in place and whether they are periodically reviewed, tested and updated.

Remedial conservation

- State that remedial conservation of objects and archives is undertaken when necessary to ensure the long-term survival of the item.
- Note whether the archive has trained specialist conservation staff and if not whether suppliers used are fully-qualified and accredited conservators. Note whether a risk assessment is carried out before archives go offsite for conservation.
- Describe whether archive staff are trained to carry out simple in-house conservation work.

Review and update

- State how often and when the preservation policy is reviewed.

In the United Kingdom conservators are accredited individually and there is an online register,[12] which allows local specialists to be identified. Some public records offices may also be prepared to offer advice.[13] Very basic conservation can, of course, be undertaken by untrained archivists, following appropriate induction, but due to the lack of specialist knowledge should be limited to simple tasks such as straightforward cleaning or tipping in torn pages (Bendix, 2011). A number of guidance booklets developed by the British Library Preservation Advisory Centre are provided online on the British Library's website[14] and are referenced in the bibliography at the end of this chapter.

Risks

Many archival activities involve risks to the preservation of archives including access, reprography, loans and display. The key here is in striking the right balance between using records now and preserving them for future generations. How decisions are taken depends on the nature and purpose of the archive and the use which is made of it. A company tends to meet the costs of retaining archives in order to promote its brands and build engagement with its staff and customers. So business archivists may occasionally have to show or display archives in-house in a way that would not be acceptable to a public archive. For further information on preservation risks see Chapter 11. In the United Kingdom an online risk awareness profiling tool (RAPT) developed by two museums in 2010 through a short questionnaire allows heritage organisations to assess risk awareness in the organisation and help to improve risk management.[15] Most companies also have wider business continuity management systems and plans.

Preservation policy

Every archive should ideally have a written preservation policy that sets out the archive's preservation policy, the decisions it has made and its objectives. It reminds staff and users of their obligations and evidences the importance placed upon preservation. It also allows an associated preservation strategy and preservation plans to be developed. General guidance is available on how to set out a policy (Foot, 2001) and many individual public archive service preservation and conservation policies are available online.[16]

Policy content will vary between archives and archivists should be both mindful of professional standards, but realistic regarding their own particular situation and context. It should focus on high-level principles so that it can be both long lasting and unhampered by the minutiae of requirements for different media and formats. The policy should include a general statement of purpose, objectives and responsibilities, followed by notes that will evidence:

- commitment to cost-effective solutions for preservation of archives;
- access that is mindful of the needs of archives as well as those of users;
- packaging in conservation material that will not have a long-term detrimental effect;
- provision of appropriate storage – secure, environmentally controlled, and so on;
- provision of resources for conservation by qualified conservators as needed;
- use of copying to support conservation when appropriate;
- supervision of reading room access;
- appropriate control of exhibition and loans.

The preservation policy may also link to separate, but related, retention, storage, access or copying policies or guidelines.

A small business archive with few resources might decide to focus on:

- good security of storage and reading room;
- regular premises inspection and cleaning;
- pest control;
- monitoring environmental changes;
- training staff and users in good handling;
- storing material on shelving and in boxes;
- backing up digital records.

A larger archive with more resources can aspire or commit to:

- new or converted storage compliant with national or international standards;
- improved shelving;
- conservation–grade packaging and boxes;
- digital preservation policy;
- improved environmental conditions through better lighting and enhanced temperature and humidity control;
- conservation budget;
- surrogacy programme.

Such a policy can be used to build evidence to make a business case for improved storage and facilities. A separate preservation policy may be required for digital records due to their special requirements.

Special format records

Ultimately archivists can control how they store and handle records, but have no control over the problems associated with the materials from which they are made. The best approach to preservation is a thorough knowledge of the collection and the particular needs of different record types so that the archivist can identify the records most at risk and store and otherwise manage them in a way that avoids deterioration.

Consequently, it is important to understand issues associated with different record types such as photographs, films, optical discs, digital records, pressed copy books, newspaper print, dot matrix- and laser-printed papers, parchment agreements, and so on. There is not space here to examine the preservation issues associated with all records formats, but a selection of those commonly found in business archives is considered below. See also Table 8.1 for information on the ideal environmental conditions for the storage of different media.

Photographs

Photographs, invented in the early nineteenth century, are both common and particularly vulnerable to physical, chemical, biological damage and deterioration. Handling and poor environmental conditions can have a significant impact causing images to fade, tarnish or discolour or emulsion and support to separate. Whilst there are many standards for the long-term storage of specific types of photograph, in reality these may be difficult to achieve in a corporate archive and different kinds of photographs will have to be stored in the same environment alongside other record formats like paper.[17]

A single archive can hold a wide range of photographic media. Print formats have a base layer usually of paper or glass and an emulsion of gelatine, albumen, collodion or modern synthetics. Negatives are usually on flexible film or glass and are generally the master photographic image. The most common photograph types can often be identified by their appearance and age (Clarke, 2009, pp. 4–5).

The longevity of photographs can be hugely increased by the use of appropriate packaging – such as acid-free or Photographic Activity Tested (PAT)[18] paper (glassine is not recommended), acid-free board or polyester enclosures – and by storing different kinds of photograph separately to avoid chemical damage (Clarke, 2009, pp. 14–15). A principal concern is avoiding the storage of either cellulose nitrate or cellulose acetate format photographs with any other collection materials. These film types should be separated out. Where possible, storing photographic prints with poor quality paper should also be avoided. Photograph albums can present problems as they are usually made of low-quality materials that may damage the images they contain. Albums should usually be kept intact, but interleaving of pages with suitable paper or polyester buffers should be considered.

Photographs should be handled as little as possible and with care. Hands should be clean or gloved and the images well supported and never stacked. Photographs should only be marked, on the reverse, with a soft HB lead pencil. Scanning photographs and providing access digitally can considerably decrease wear and tear. Original photographs should ideally not be displayed in exhibitions due to the impact of sustained exposure to light. Further guidance on storage is available from the Institute of Image Permanence.[19]

Moving images

Business archives often include sizeable film collections because of the use of the moving image, in film, video or digital format, for both external advertising and marketing and internal training and communication. Film recordings are fragile because of their chemical composition, the past impact of providing access and the obsolescence of playback equipment. Additionally for formats that are no longer manufactured, like videotape, the equipment is difficult to obtain and the number of technicians with the expertise to repair the hardware used for playback is fast disappearing.

Moving image film is a continuous film strip, a base layered with emulsions, wound around a core or on a metal or plastic reel. It is a composite material in the sense that a plastic (cellulose, acetate, polyester) is layered with organic compounds and oils (dyes, gelatines) and often also metals (silver halides in the gelatine layer, magnetic filings in the magnetic sound strips). Diurnal and annual environmental fluctuations that have a wide-range can cause extreme and differing expansion of the various layers and materials that make up the film causing it to fracture, warp, delaminate, shrink and distort. This makes the preservation of moving image film, like that of other composite items like magnetic tape, CDs and DVDs, much more difficult than paper. Ideally they should not be stored in a mixed archive repository.

Film dating prior to 1951 can present particular problems as its cellulose nitrate base decomposes easily and it may spontaneously combust. Such film, 35mm in format, needs to be identified quickly and handled by experts (Health and Safety Executive, 2013).[20] Corporate archives should contact a specialist repository for advice if they suspect they have nitrate film. Much film produced before the mid-1970s is acetate based, but from the mid-1970s polyester-based film is by far the most common type. Polyester film is inert and generally stable if stored in an appropriate environment.

The condition of an accessioned film will depend on how it has been stored during its lifetime. The chemical composition of film means that from the date it is manufactured it is in a state of decomposition. A pristine print stored from the outset in the correct environment may last hundreds of years. A film kept in a warm company basement for 50 years, on the other hand, will already have undergone an unknown degree of chemical decomposition and it is impossible to know how long it will be before it becomes too degraded to view. However, this process can be slowed down by low temperature storage, which also prevents the fading of colour dyes.

One of the main preservation problems for film is the onset of vinegar syndrome, the chemical decomposition of acetate film stock. If the acidity level becomes too great, a decomposing film could detrimentally affect films kept in neighbouring cans. Fungus growth can also cause significant problems. Film, like photographs, ideally requires storage at a temperature and relative humidity particular to each film type because it is composed of layers, each of which reacts differently. There is much published guidance available (Reilly, 1993; International Organization for Standardization, 1996; Lee, 2001; British Film Institute, 2004; Adelstein, 2009) and specialist film archives will often give advice. In practice, few archives can afford to maintain the low temperatures or different storage conditions ideally required for different types of film stock, so compromises must be made to achieve the best result within the budget available. Many specialist film archives tend to adhere to the standards set by the Technical Commission of the International Federation of Film Archives (FIAF), rather than *PD 5454:2012* (British Standards Institution, 2012a), namely storage at 'a moderate relative humidity and as low a temperature as the archive can afford', keeping 'both the relative humidity and the temperature as steady as possible' (International Federation of Film Archives Preservation Commission, 1989, p. 28). The proper conservation of videotape is particularly complicated because of the wide range of different video formats, such as U-matic (introduced 1970), Betamax (1975), Video Home System or VHS (1976), Betacam SP (1986) and Digital Betacam (1993). Obsolete playback equipment in good working condition is required for each format to ensure that videotape can be viewed and the best strategy is to digitise videotape collections as soon as possible. However, unlike film, which is itself considered the master and is generally digitised for access rather than preservation, videotape should be digitised to preservation standards and the currently recommended format – uncompressed .avi files – will occupy a large amount of digital storage space.

Whilst very high specification scans would be required to achieve a perfect clone of a film print, digitised copies can provide excellent viewing and access copies. Archives should consider creating such copies of each film in a number of different formats, including .avi or H.264/MPEG-4 (for high quality viewing or back-up video) and .wmv and DVD (for low-quality video viewing copies). The master preservation copies of moving images should only be viewed by experienced archive staff and access should instead be provided via surrogate copies. Any digitised moving image files that are intended to be kept for the longer term will need to be constantly migrated, an expensive and time-consuming process.

Consideration should be given to transferring moving images archives to a collecting repository with specialist storage and expertise. Businesses may not have the facilities to retain broadcast-quality copies, or even store and clone relatively low-quality copies, and an agreement can usually be reached that will meet both archives' requirements often allowing the company to retain copyright and the film archive to have non-commercial rights for education and access purposes.

Digital records

Corporate information exchange and storage has in recent years moved almost entirely from paper letters, memoranda, reports, leaflets and filing systems to electronic documents, email and social media messages, websites, intranets and databases. This means that it is vital for corporate archivists to tackle the issue of digital preservation head on. Whilst the preservation of digital records is far better understood than it was a decade ago, there is still no simple single model for implementation and a variety of techniques and strategies are still being explored (Forde and Rhys-Lewis, 2013, p. 25). In the United Kingdom advice on digital preservation can be sought from The National Archives[21] or organisations like the Digital Preservation Coalition (DPC). Archivists in other countries have similar support agencies, such as the National Digital Stewardship Alliance (NDSA) in the United States, the Netherlands Coalition for Digital Preservation (NCDD) and the Danish National Archives. Meanwhile many specialist archivists worldwide are working collaboratively to identify best practice for the preservation of particular digital formats, such as the film archive sector's work on born-digital moving images.

The proper preservation of digital media records creates particular preservation problems because:

- the software and hardware required to access digital records become unusable, obsolete or impossible to procure;
- data on digital media, like tapes and discs, can be lost without warning even if they do not appear to be damaged;
- the average life of digital records is generally much shorter than paper records;
- issues of context, authenticity and provenance are significant as digital records can be altered and copied. The relationship of digital records to other records is also easily lost;
- procedures must be continually changed as corporate technology and business processes change;
- the acquisition of a host of new skills and knowledge is required, and cooperation with other departments with divergent priorities, like IT functions;
- the cost of instituting digital preservation management solutions can be significant
- there is a lack of specialist preservation skills and resources.

Due to legislation and regulation corporate records management programmes, where they exist, should already be addressing issues around the proper retention of digital records. A number of corporate archives have worked with such teams to develop mutually workable solutions or have appointed dedicated digital archivists to focus specifically on the management of digital records. Corporate archives generally adopt a custodial solution by which digital archives are cared for in-house as business confidentialities and sensitivities usually demand some kind of owned solution.

Digital records cannot be understood without the mediation of appropriate software and/or hardware, and the challenge of digital preservation is to ensure continued access to records and their authenticity over time despite a variety of risks including, but not limited to, technological obsolescence. Essentially this requires finding a means to either 'develop new methods for accessing the object in its original form, or to convert the original object to a new form which can be accessed using current methods. These two basic strategies are known as emulation and migration' (Brown, 2006, p. 86). Emulation requires the recreation of the functionality of the software, operating system and related hardware used to access a digital object over time. This can quickly prove unsustainable. Most digital preservation strategies and systems are consequently currently based on migrating the digital records themselves to new and more accessible forms. This too can present challenges – such as loss of information and functionality – and a decision has to be made to decide whether to migrate digital records upon ingest (transfer into a repository), just before record formats become obsolete or only at the point when access is required (Brown, 2013, pp. 209–213).

If a corporate archive lacks access to an overarching digital preservation system and has more limited resources, the archivist may take a pragmatic approach and simply preserve digital records in their original format on a secure part of a company's shared networked drives; taking care to store two or three copies as preservation insurance and to keep the related metadata either with the records or linked to them. The aim of this strategy being simply to ensure digital records at least survive to be dealt with by a future generation of IT systems; what the United Kingdom's National Archives has styled 'a parsimonious approach to digital preservation' (Gollins, 2009). Some digital objects can be converted to a single preservation format to simplify future preservation, such as migration of PDF to PDF/A format – a subset of the Portable Document Format specification intended to offer long-term stability and accessibility (International Organization for Standardization, 2005). However, even these actions need to be considered in the light of what functionality might be lost when moving from the original to a preservation format (see Chapter 10, p. 331). Digital objects like Microsoft Excel or CAD/CAM (Computer-Aided Design and Manufacturing) records which are more dynamic, complex and specialised are likely to have to continue to be held in their original format to preserve functionality. Indeed, given the diversity and complexity of digital records there is much to recommend simply preserving everything in its original format. If an overarching specialist digital preservation system is warranted some companies may be able to provide or support an in-house system, others will need to use a commercial supplier. In 2015 the HSBC Archives, for example, established a system based on pairing two different proprietary software packages to create a solution for cataloguing, preservation and retrieval of digital archives.[22]

The Open Archival Information Systems Reference Model (OAIS) (see page 320), the main standard relating to digital archiving, which offers a high-level functional model for a digital repository, does not provide detailed guidance on preservation. However, in order to preserve digital records appropriately (Brown, 2006, pp. 100–105) a company's digital archive repository must:

- be secure. The servers are secured, the IT systems and storage are protected from intrusions and software attack or data change and that user access is controlled;
- allow integrity checking, to ensure the records and metadata (see page 319) are not corrupted, altered or deleted;
- store records on an appropriate physical medium that has longevity, robustness, and capacity and is affordable;
- store multiple copies, ideally three and including at least one in a different geographical location;
- support the management of content, subject to appropriate controls;
- allow the archivist and user to work only on a copy of the record not the original.

For further information on managing digital business archives and on how to establish a digital preservation programme see Chapter 10 and the published literature in the bibliography at the end of this chapter. A good starting point is Adrian Brown's practical how-to guide on digital preservation (Brown, 2013). The preservation of CDs, DVDs and websites, three digital record types often found in corporate archives, are also discussed in more detail below.

However, the most pressing current challenge in the curation of digital business archives may in fact be the failure to identify and capture a comprehensive set of digital format historical records in the first place, rather than the preservation issues that have been more commonly discussed in the professional literature. Successful digital archiving requires a business-wide awareness of the need to ensure potential historical records are appropriately named, backed up, migrated to new formats and transferred to the archive. A clearly articulated, achievable and proactively pursued collection policy and plan with due focus on digital record formats is the cornerstone to achieving this.

CDs and DVDs

The introduction of desktop computing into the office has resulted in digital records on a wide range of storage media appearing amongst the archives of business – magnetic tapes, hard drive disks, floppy disks, CDs (compact discs), DVDs (digital video discs), flash drives and memory cards. CDs and DVDs are amongst those most commonly found, as they have been extensively used by companies for promotional purposes, internal training and communication and as a portable means to transfer large digital files. Both CDs and DVDs are made of polycarbonate plastic and are read by a laser following a spiral datatrack from the centre outwards. Both are made in rewriteable and recordable formats.

Optical discs can be vulnerable to manufacturing defects and are easily scratched or soiled by poor handling in a way that will interrupt playback. The disks should be held by the edge or centre hole only and should never be flexed or subjected to weight. They should be kept in an appropriate environment, protected from light and polluted air and stored vertically in individual jewel cases. Any original card cases should be removed and stored separately. The discs should not be labelled – if necessary they can be marked with a suitable pen on the label side of the inner hub – and any existing labels should not be peeled off in case doing so causes delamination.

Preservation copies of optical discs should not be used for access, but they should be regularly checked for deterioration both visually and by playback. All playback machinery should be kept clean and in good working order. Obsolescence of hardware should be managed by monitoring changes in technology and by migration of data.

It is good practice always to retain the original file format (as opposed to the physical medium) and the inevitability of media and hardware obsolescence means it may be necessary to create an authenticated copy of an optical disk so that the record can still be accessed. There are different ways to achieve this, but in most situations it would be preferable to create an exact copy of the disk, called a 'disk image', rather than simply copying the data into a directory. A disk image maintains the complete sequence of bytes on the disk and thus includes hidden, deleted or corrupted content, which may not be otherwise visible. This safeguards the authenticity of the record and ensures access can be maintained beyond technical obsolescence. However, no physical storage medium should be considered archival – content will periodically need to be refreshed to new media over time.

Websites

The first website was published by Tim Berners-Lee in 1991 and four years later changes to the infrastructure supporting the internet encouraged its commercial use. Since then companies, at first tentatively and later with enthusiasm, have increasingly used the internet to describe and promote their services, to transact business and to engage customers, shareholders, the media and employees through an increasingly sophisticated and varied use of websites. This inevitably means that much crucial information that archivists would want to preserve is stored only on a company's website. To complicate matters such sites change constantly and the information they contain is rarely held in alternate formats in an accessible or similarly dynamic way.

The peculiar issues related to website preservation are that they:

- are interconnected, making it difficult to define the extent of a particular website or of particular content on it;
- are subject to continual and rapid change, impacting not only page content but also whole pages and whole websites;
- comprise varied information content and page types. Websites or individual pages may be static (a series of linked pre-existing web pages) or dynamic (virtual web pages generated when a browser request is received). Content may include text, images, PDFs, videos, social media, databases, transactions and links to other sites.

Selecting specific content for preservation (Brown, 2006, pp. 24–41) can be time consuming and the corporate archivist may simply decide to preserve the entire parent company and brand/subsidiary websites. Such a domain-based approach provides a simple, objective and comprehensive solution. Certainly a clear decision does need to be made about what is to be collected – whether whole websites or content identified by, for example, subject, creator or information type – and the collection frequency. A series of snapshots taken over time is a pragmatic approach, but may need to be flexed if a website undergoes significant change. Websites can be collected by direct acquisition from the host web server or remote harvesting by use of web crawlers. Collecting web content is, however, a complex process and the content collected must be quality assured to double check outcomes from the automated processing.

Box 8.6 Case study: web archiving at the Diageo Archives, Scotland, United Kingdom

Diageo is one of the world's leading premium drinks companies and uses numerous online platforms to market its brands and reach its consumers. A web archiving programme was established by the Diageo Archive in order to document the company's web presence as an archival record of its marketing activities, a key area of focus for the archive's collections.

The aim of the web archiving programme is to create a managed and accessible archive of Diageo's online marketing activity on websites and social media platforms in order to preserve web resources as artefacts of intrinsic value for historical or heritage purposes, as well as for improved eDiscovery and the ability to provide reliable evidence of online activity.

The main considerations taken into account were the ability of the web archiving programme to archive using the *ISO 28500* (International Organization for Standardization, 2009) standard WARC (Web ARChive) format, to crawl websites with age verification gateways (all of Diageo's websites require age verification to ensure users are over the legal drinking age), the ability to capture and playback complex, dynamic content such as embedded video, secure hosting of archived content, a high degree of defensibility and authenticity of content and a user-friendly interface for accessing content.

In establishing the programme, two approaches were scoped. The first approach considered was to create an in-house web archiving system using a combination of open-source tools. This solution would have required a significant amount of staff time and training, as well as investment in technical infrastructure including large amounts of digital storage, and was calculated to be more expensive than outsourcing to a commercial supplier. In addition, the complexities of crawling sites with age-gating could have become prohibitive with this approach.

The second approach was to outsource to a commercial provider which would be able to handle the required scale, including social media, as well as the complexity of the sign-in process for sites with age-gating. All of the crawls run and are stored on the supplier's infrastructure, so there are no hardware, storage or software costs to Diageo. It was agreed that this approach would meet the Diageo Archive's requirements better.

After a rigorous procurement process, a supplier was chosen and the programme was established. All of Diageo's websites (around 70 sites) are now captured on a monthly basis and social media accounts on a daily basis and the programme is providing a valuable record of Diageo's online marketing activities.

Source: Information provided by Heather Malcolm, Diageo, by private communication.

The long-term preservation of websites involves the same considerations as the preservation of other digital records, but presents particular problems because websites are very complicated digital objects requiring the preservation of not only the components, but also the relationships between them and the interaction with users. Commercial web archiving services are available that can offer simple and affordable ways to archive websites. For an example of one corporate archive's approach to establishing a web archiving programme see Box 8.6. For more detailed discussion of web archiving see Adrian Brown's *Archiving websites* (2006).

Conclusion

A key role of the corporate archivist is to provide the professional knowledge and expertise that will ensure that in a climate of continual changes in objectives, organisational structure, staff and buildings that a business's archival records are preserved. He or she needs to have a clear understanding of the way in which different kinds of archival records can best be stored and handled and when to seek specialist advice and intervention.

The corporate archivist generally centralises historical records into one or several regional repositories so that preservation principles and conservation treatments can be more easily applied. Clearly defined policy and processes are vital along with the archivist's preparedness to champion the preservation requirements of the archive. In this way the archives can be safely stored and made accessible for current use, whilst also ensuring their survival for future generations.

Acknowledgements

Thanks are due to Linda Ramsay of National Records of Scotland and Juergen Vervoorst, Hannah Clare, Costas Ntanos and Jacquie Moon of The National Archives for kindly commenting on the chapter as a whole; to Adrian Brown, James Mortlock, Tina Staples and William Kilbride for reviewing the content on digital records; to Ruth Washbrook for reviewing the content on moving images; and to Melanie Aspey, Natalie Broad and Charlotte Berry for providing information for the case studies.

Notes

1 The National Archive's Archive Service Accreditation scheme framework guidelines are available online at www.nationalarchives.gov.uk/archives-sector/standards.htm [Accessed 20 August 2016].
2 HSBC's archive was for some years based in part of a commercial storage facility in London and in the United States History Factory and History Associates Inc. provide specialist storage and services for corporate archives.
3 University of Glasgow's Scottish Business Archive and London Metropolitan Archive in the United Kingdom and the Centre for Business History in Stockholm all have ongoing relationships with companies that have deposited their archives.
4 See, for example, Kidd, S., 2010. *Fire safety management in traditional buildings*, Parts 1 & 2. Edinburgh: Historic Scotland.
5 Norfolk Record Office in 1994 and Glasgow School of Art in 2014.
6 In the United Kingdom manufactured in accordance with British Standard *BS1449–1* is recommended.
7 For further information on setting up and managing search rooms see Chapter 9.

8 In recent years several new archive buildings have been opened by corporate archives in the United Kingdom including Unilever (2004, converted factory, Port Sunlight), Royal Bank of Scotland (2005, converted warehouse, Edinburgh), Marks & Spencer (2011, purpose-built, Leeds), C. & J. Clark (2011, purpose-built, Street), HSBC (2011, converted warehouse, London) and Diageo (2014, purpose-built expansion of existing facility, Menstrie). Others have been opened by corporate archives overseas including Evonik Industries (2010, converted workshop, Germany), Citizens Financial (2013, purpose-built within a warehouse, Rhode Island, United States), Coca-Cola (2015, converted data centre, Atlanta, United States) and Ford (2015, former research laboratory Dearborn, United States).

9 Other passive archive buildings recently opened in the United Kingdom include the Britten-Pears Foundation, Aldeburgh, Suffolk, 2013, a new-build home for composer Benjamin Britten's archive, and the Hereford Archives and Records Centre, Herefordshire, 2015, the first new British archive building built to Passivhaus standard.

10 In the United Kingdom, The National Archives publishes specification of and guidance on choosing box board. See www.nationalarchives.gov.uk/about/collection-care-advice-guidance.htm [Accessed 20 August 2016].

11 A facemask with a particulate filter that filters at least 99.95 per cent of airborne particles (European standard *EN 143:2000*).

12 See The Institute of Conservation (ICON) conservation register at www.conservationregister.com/ [Accessed 20 August 2016].

13 The Institute of Conservation provides guidance on choosing and working with conservator-restorers at www.conservationregister.com/PIcon-WorkingWithAConservator.asp [Accessed 20 August 2016].

14 The British Library. *Collection care.* [online] Available at: www.bl.uk/blpac/disaster.html [Accessed 20 August 2016].

15 Available at: www.raptonline.org.uk [Accessed 20 August 2016].

16 London Metropolitan Archives at www.cityoflondon.gov.uk/things-to-do/london-metropolitan-archives/about/Documents/archive-preservation-and-conservation-policy.pdf [Accessed 20 August 2016] and Tyne & Wear Archives Service at www.tyneandwear archives.org.uk/publications/preservation.htm [Accessed 20 August 2016].

17 See Table 8.1.

18 An international standard test (*ISO 18916:2007*) for evaluating photo-storage and display products.

19 www.imagepermanenceinstitute.org/imaging/storage-guides [Accessed 20 August 2016].

20 For guidance on how to identify nitrate film stock see British Film Institute, 2004. *Moving image collections: guidance note.* Film Archive Forum, p. 6.

21 See www.nationalarchives.gov.uk/information-management/manage-information/preserving-digital–records/ [Accessed 20 August 2016].

22 For a brief description of the project see Information Governance Initiative (IGI), 2016, *The governance of long-term digital information*, p. 17. [pdf] Available at: http://preservica.com/wp-content/uploads/sites/3/2016/05/The-Governance-of-Long-Term-Digital-Information-IGI-Benchmark-2016.pdf [Accessed 20 August 2016].

References

Adelstein, P. Z., 2009. *IPI media storage quick reference guide.* Rochester NY: Image Permanence Institute.

Bendix, C., 2011. *Cleaning books and documents.* 3rd ed. London: Preservation Advisory Service, British Library.

Bendix, C., 2013. *Moving library and archive collections.* 2nd ed. London: Preservation Advisory Service, British Library.

British Film Institute, 2004. *Moving image collections: guidance note.* Film Archive Forum. [pdf] Available at: http://filmarchives.org.uk/site/wp-content/uploads/2013/03/guidancenotes.pdf [Accessed 9 September 2016].

British Standards Institution (BSI), 2012a. *PD 5454:2012. Guide for the storage and exhibition of archival materials*. London: British Standards Institution.

British Standards Institution (BSI), 2012b. *PAS 198:2012. Specification for managing environmental conditions for cultural collections*. London: British Standards Institution.

Brown, A., 2006. *Archiving websites. A practical guide for information management professionals*. London: Facet Publishing.

Brown, A., 2013. *Practical digital preservation: a how-to guide for organisations of any size*. London: Facet Publishing.

Bulow, A. and Ahmon, J., 2010. *Preparing collections for digitization*. London: Facet Publishing.

Child, R. E., 2011. *Mould outbreaks in library and archive collections*. 2nd ed. London: Preservation Advisory Service, British Library.

Clarke, S., 2009. *Preservation of photographic material*. 2nd ed. London: Preservation Advisory Service, British Library.

Dadson, E., 2012a. *Emergency planning and responses for libraries, archives and museums*. London: Facet Publishing.

Dadson, E., 2012b. *Salvaging library and archive collections*. London: Preservation Advisory Service, British Library.

Foot, M., 2001. *Building blocks for a preservation policy*. London: National Preservation Office.

Forde, H. and Rhys-Lewis, J., 2013. *Preserving archives*. 2nd ed. London: Facet Publishing.

Gollins, T., 2009. *Parsimonious preservation: preventing pointless processes! (The small steps that take digital preservation a long way forward)*. Online Information 2009 Proceeedings, pp. 75–78. [pdf] The National Archives. Available at: www.nationalarchives.gov.uk/documents/information-management/parsimonious-preservation.pdf [Accessed 20 August 2016].

Health and Safety Executive, 2013. *The dangers of cellulose nitrate film*. [pdf] Health and Safety Executive. Available at: www.hse.gov.uk/pubns/indg469.pdf [Accessed 20 August 2016].

International Federation of Film Archives (FIAF) Preservation Commission, 1989. *Preservation of moving image and sound*. 1st ed. FIAF.

International Organization for Standardization (ISO), 1996. *ISO 10356: Cinematography: storage and handling of nitrate-base motion picture films*. Geneva: International Organization for Standardization.

International Organization for Standardization (ISO), 2005. *ISO 19005–1:2005. Document management – electronic document file format for long-term preservation (PDF/A)*. Geneva: International Organization for Standardization.

International Organization for Standardization (ISO), 2009. *ISO 28500:2009 Information and documentation – WARC file format*. Geneva: International Organization for Standardization.

International Organization for Standardization (ISO), 2015. *ISO 11799:2015. Information and documentation – document storage requirements for archive and library materials*. Geneva: International Organization for Standardization.

Kitching, C., 1993. *Archive buildings in the United Kingdom 1977–1992*. London: HMSO.

Lee, D. M., 2001. *Film and sound archives in non-specialist repositories*. Taunton: Society of Archivists.

National Preservation Office, 2000. *Guide to preservation microfilming*. London: National Preservation Office [A development of the earlier British Library and National Preservation Office, 1992. *Mellon microfilming project: microfilming manual*. London: British Library].

Quinn, C., 2015. Establishing a corporate archive for Irish Distillers Limited. *Journal of the Irish Society for Archives*, 22.

Reilly, J. M., 1993. *IPI storage guide for acetate film*. Rochester, NY: Image Permanence Institute. Available at: www.imagepermanenceinstitute.org/webfm_send/299 [Accessed 20 August 2016].

Further reading

Standards

British Standards Institution (BSI), 2012. *PAS 198:2012. Specification for managing environmental conditions for cultural collections*. London: British Standards Institution. [Developed by BSI in collaboration with The National Archives and others].

British Standards Institution (BSI), 2012. *PD 5454:2012. Guide for the storage and exhibition of archival materials*. London: British Standards Institution.

International Organization for Standardization (ISO), 2015. *ISO 11799:2015. Information and documentation – document storage requirements for archive and library materials*. Geneva: International Organization for Standardization.

Preservation Advisory Service Publications

Guidance booklets published by the Preservation Advisory Service (previously the United Kingdom's National Preservation Office) are available at: www.bl.uk/aboutus/stratpolprog/collectioncare/publications/booklets/index.html [Accessed 20 August 2016].

Anon., 2013. *Using library and archive materials*. 2nd ed. London: Preservation Advisory Service, British Library.

Anon., 2013. *Self-service copying of library and archive materials*. 2nd ed. London: Preservation Advisory Service, British Library.

Bendix, C., 2013. *Moving library and archive collections*. 2nd ed. London: Preservation Advisory Service, British Library.

Bendix, C., 2011. *Cleaning books and documents*. 3rd ed. London: Preservation Advisory Service, British Library.

Child, R. E., 2011. *Mould outbreaks in library and archive collections*. 2nd ed. London: Preservation Advisory Service, British Library.

Clarke, S., 2009. *Preservation of photographic material*. 2nd ed. London: Preservation Advisory Service, British Library.

Dadson, E., 2012. *Salvaging library and archive collections*. London: Preservation Advisory Service, British Library.

Foot, M., 2013. *Building blocks for a preservation policy*. 2nd ed. London: Preservation Advisory Service, British Library.

Henderson, J., 2013. *Managing the library and archive environment*. 3rd ed. London: Preservation Advisory Service, British Library.

Pinneger, D., 2012. *Managing pests in paper-based collections*. London: Preservation Advisory Service, British Library.

Walker, A., 2013. *Basic preservation for archive collections*. 5th ed. London: Preservation Advisory Service, British Library.

Other publications

Brown, A., 2013. *Practical digital preservation: a how-to guide for organisations of any size*. London: Facet Publishing.

Day Thomson, S., 2016. *Preserving social media. DPC technology watch report 16–01*. [pdf] Digital Preservation Coalition. Available at: http://dx.doi.org/10.7207/twr16–01 [Accessed 20 August 2016].

Forde, H., 1991. Conservation. In: A. Turton, ed., 1991. *Managing business archives*. Oxford: Butterworth-Heinemann. Ch. 12.

Findlay, C., 2008. Digital recordkeeping. In: J. Bettington *et al.*, eds, 2008. *Keeping archives.* Canberra: Australian Society of Archivists. Ch. 4.

Forde, H, and Rhys-Lewis, J., 2013. *Preserving archives.* London: Facet Publishing.

Hadlow, E., 2008. Preservation. In: J. Bettington *et al.*, eds, 2008. *Keeping archives.* Canberra: Australian Society of Archivists. Ch. 4.

Hunter, G. S., 2004. *Developing and maintaining practical archives.* 2nd ed. New York: Neal-Schumann.

International Council on Archives (ICA), 2016. *Understanding digital records preservation initiatives.* Paris: ICA/IRMT.

Kitching, C., 2007. *Archive buildings in the United Kingdom 1993–2005.* Chichester: Phillimore.

Ling, T., 2008. Buildings and storage. In: J. Bettington, *et al.*, eds, 2008. *Keeping archives.* Canberra: Australian Society of Archivists. Ch. 3.

Pennock, M., 2013. *Web-archiving. DPC technology watch report 13–01.* [pdf] Digital Preservation Coalition. Available at: http://dx.doi.org/10.7207/twr13-01 [Accessed 20 August 2016].

Williams, C., 2006. *Managing archives: foundations, principles and practice.* Oxford: Chandos Publishing. pp. 167–200.

Chapter 9

Access

Alison Turton

The term access refers to the conditions under which documents and information from an archive are made available to users. Most companies that maintain formal archives in the United Kingdom accept and embrace the need to allow at least some public access to their collections for the purpose of historical research, as well as promoting and overseeing internal use. In recent years this has been encouraged by government promotion of increased access to records, as evidenced in the freedom of information legislation – which has tended to the presumption that records are open rather than closed – and social inclusion agenda supporting cultural access. Many countries in North America, Australasia and Europe also have freedom of information laws giving rights of access to certain public records, but few of them recognise the same imperative to allow public access to corporate archive collections as prevails in the United Kingdom. This is accounted for in part by the maturity of the United Kingdom's corporate archive network, along with the background and interests of its pioneering archivists.

As companies seek to improve service to customers, embed themselves in the communities where they trade and demonstrate corporate responsibility, allowing free access to their heritage resources has become increasingly appealing. Since the 1990s public questioning of the nature and extent of corporate involvement in the slave trade,[1] Holocaust[2] and Nazi forced labour,[3] and more recently in the financial crisis of 2007–2008,[4] has also tended to push many businesses toward a culture of heritage-related transparency, both to avoid claims that they were attempting to obscure culpability and to encourage trust.

Why manage access?

All companies do, of course, have some records that are sensitive or confidential, and the skill that an archivist brings to a business is the ability to formulate policy and procedure that will both protect the interests of the business, mitigating or avoiding risk, and recognise and fulfil the social obligation to make historical records available. Archivists should ideally promote impartial access to the archival material in their care, a responsibility recognised in their national and international codes of ethics. The code of ethics adopted by the International Council Archives in 1996 exemplifies this duty:

6. Archivists should promote the widest possible access to archival material and provide an impartial service to all users.

Archivists should produce both general and particular finding aids as appropriate, for all of the records in their custody. They should offer impartial advice to all, and employ available resources to provide a balanced range of services. Archivists should answer courteously and with a spirit of helpfulness all reasonable inquiries about their holdings, and encourage the use of them to the greatest extent possible, consistent with institutional policies, the preservation of holdings, legal considerations, individual rights, and donor agreements. They should explain pertinent restrictions to potential users, and apply them equitably. Archivists should discourage unreasonable restrictions on access and use but may suggest or accept as a condition for acquisition clearly stated restrictions of limited duration . . .

7. Archivists should respect both access and privacy, and act within the boundaries of relevant legislation.

Archivists should take care that corporate and personal privacy as well as national security are protected . . . They must respect the privacy of individuals who created or are the subjects of records, especially those who had no voice in the use or disposition of the materials (International Council on Archives, 1996, sections 6–7).

Several national archival bodies have compiled statements on access. For example, the Society of American Archivists' statement on archival access in the United States (1994) and the National Council on Archives' *Standard for access to archives* (2008) in the United Kingdom. Likewise, in 2012, the International Council on Archives (ICA) published *Principles of access to archives* to provide an international baseline against which archivists around the world could measure their policies and procedures:

Extract on access from *Principles of access to archives* adopted by the International Council on Archives (**International Council on Archives**, 2012), section 1:

The public has the right of access to archives of public bodies. Both public and private entities should open their archives to the greatest extent possible.

. . . Institutions, whether public or private, holding private archives do not have a legal obligation to open the private archives to external users unless specific legislation, legal requirement or regulation imposes this responsibility on them. However, many private archives hold institutional records and personal papers that have significant value for understanding social, economic, religious, community and personal history as well as for generating ideas and supporting development. Archivists working in private institutions and managing the institution's archives encourage their institution to provide public access to its archives, especially if the holdings will help protect rights or will benefit public interests (International Council on Archives, 2012, section 1).

However, a corporate archivist, as the ICA code of ethics recognises, also owes a duty to the mission and obligations of the parent business and must by definition be partial. Such archivists must necessarily begin from a position of allowing zero gratuitous access to a company's archive and move toward a degree of openness that each particular business can reasonably support. Usually the very presence of an archive function will encourage a company to offer better internal and external access, by providing a resource that can establish an access infrastructure, weigh up the related risks and advocate for greater access.

In the United Kingdom there is no legislation that makes giving access to business archives for the purpose of research compulsory, and freedom of information legislation affects only public bodies.[5] The Companies Act 2006 does require businesses to make some statutory books, for example recent minutes of directors and members and registers of directors and members, available for inspection upon request and to file annual returns at Companies House, but they are not required to keep anything permanently. Both public and private organisations must, however, comply with United Kingdom data protection (privacy) legislation.

In formulating a policy on access the main issues a business archivist must consider are what records should be made available, to whom they may be shown and at what date they can be released (Booker, 1991, p. 373).

Defining accessible records

To create an appropriate access policy the archivist must be familiar with the development, structure and strategy of the company. This will allow the archivist to understand the nature of the records in his or her care and their likely sensitivity and importance. A food manufacturing company or brewery, for example, may hold sensitive recipes (the 130-year-old recipe for Coca-Cola is perhaps one of the most closely guarded secrets of this kind); an engineering firm may have designs, such as those for nuclear power stations, which need to be carefully controlled; and a financial services company may have to keep customer records confidential. A few companies may have no record types that can be safely produced other than those that are already in the public domain, such as annual reports, advertising and the like.

In the past many business archives have observed the same periods of closure as those used by national or other public archives. In the United Kingdom the former 30-year rule used by The National Archives, presently being incrementally reduced to 20 years, has proved popular. Such a policy of availability by date has advantages, but that date may need to vary from one class of records to another. For example, customer and staff records will be more sensitive and regulated than other record types and the archivist will need to consider carefully the implications for the business of producing particular records for users.

This can be frustrating for researchers, as it means a business may sometimes be unable to define clearly which records are closed, and which are open. Often, however, researchers can be helped, in spite of closure periods, by providing access on the basis that only aggregate information is noted down, or by covering parts of or redacting copies of records to avoid confidential information being shown. Where potentially confidential information relates to a company still in business, or to a living person, they can of course be consulted, but an archivist is usually required to take a view on how far an obligation to confidentiality survives after a company is wound up or a person dies. So the extent to which record confidentiality is necessary varies with the nature of the business and can change over time. Often confidentiality may be legally enforceable or a regulatory requirement and archivists need to understand fully the constraints affecting their own business.

Box 9.1 Case study: banking records and confidentiality in the United Kingdom – *Tournier v. National Provincial & Union Bank of England*, 1924

In 1922, a United Kingdom bank disclosed to a customer's employer that an unpaid cheque had been drawn in favour of a bookmaker. As a result the employer did not renew the customer's contract. The action led to a legal case which went to the Court of Appeal. The Court ruled that an implied term of a customer's contract with a bank meant any information relating to a customer acquired by keeping his account should not be divulged unless compelled by law, public duty or the bank's interest, or where a client had given consent. It was a landmark legal case which resulted in banks owing confidentiality to their customers in perpetuity, even after customers died, and making them liable for resulting losses in the event of a breach. This case still affects the access United Kingdom banks can give to the customer records in their archives today.

Source: [1924] 1 K.B. 461

In 2014 a useful guide to managing records, which are not open to the public, *Technical guidance on managing archives with restriction*, was published by the International Council on Archives (International Council on Archives, 2014). This guidance recognises that some records must be closed for a period of time and provides advice to archivists on how to implement restrictions.

Dealing with enquiries

Very few enquirers, internal or external, will actually visit a corporate archive and policy and process must be developed to determine how any long-distance enquiries received will be handled. The number of postal, telephone and email enquiries an archive receives will partly shape policy about what kind of responses can be provided. Most corporate archives prioritise internal enquiries, so the treatment of external enquiries may be impacted by the extent of internal demand.

A service level agreement (SLA) should set out how long enquirers will have to wait for a response. Internal users should be offered a rapid response, perhaps offering a same or next-day service, and external enquiries should be dealt with as soon as possible and ideally within a few days. Setting such objectives will also allow the archive's performance to be measured. All enquiries will need to be answered eventually and there is little point in building up a huge backlog when an immediate response has a far more positive impact on the archive user's perception of the department or the company.

All enquiries and responses should be recorded in case the same enquirer or enquiry returns, as well as to track the performance of the archive team. If this involves storing personal information the archive must be mindful of local privacy legislation.

Internal enquiries

A corporate archive is usually maintained primarily for the benefit of the business. Consequently employees of the company are generally allowed to see archives freely if they have a reason to do so, although care must be exercised with regard to recent records that are closed by the depositing department, particularly in an organisation subject to such legislation as the United Kingdom's Official Secrets Act or which has Chinese walls.[6] In practice, due to pressure of work and geographical location, nearly all internal enquiries will be answered by the archivist rather than by staff visiting in person to undertake research in the archives themselves. This fact makes it easier to control access, but also engenders a need for the archivist to understand that he or she is constantly making access choices on the enquirer's behalf. An archivist will rarely want or be able to provide everything that has a bearing on a particular issue, but chooses what will succinctly provide the best and most appropriate information.

Certainly, all internal enquiries need to be answered swiftly and fully. Some will be matters of fact that simply require to be quickly checked, others will demand much lateral thought and employment of broader knowledge and experience to provide appropriately packaged fit-for-purpose heritage answers that support advertising claims, promotional efforts or other business-led investigations or initiatives. Some very complex or wide-ranging enquiries, involving considerable research, retrievals or copying, may require additional resource to be provided by the enquirer. Indeed, some internal cost allocation can be useful to avoid enthusiastic colleagues requesting archive-related work that is in fact either unnecessary or never used.

The enquiry service the archive can offer should be promoted extensively within the company via the intranet, staff magazines, displays and publications and by building relationships with potential users. Excellent customer service will also encourage information about the value of the archive in answering certain kinds of enquiry to be spread by word of mouth.[7]

External enquiries

Most members of the public who contact an archive with questions about a company's history or archives, due to distance, work, time and other constraints are also generally unable to, or uninterested in, visiting the archive themselves. Most external enquiries arrive by telephone, mail or email. Again it is important to answer such enquiries promptly, accurately and fully. A high standard of customer service will result in the company being perceived as efficient, helpful and having attention to detail. Indeed, it may surprise enquirers that it has such expertise in the minutiae of its own past. In this way the archive can contribute positively to brand reputation. This is one of the reasons why corporate archives rarely charge fees for answering enquiries, although this may often be as much due to the fact that such small monies are simply not practical or cost-effective to collect.

Genuine historical enquiries should be treated promptly and sympathetically, regardless of their source and without judgement regarding either the calibre of the enquirer or the content of the enquiry (Booker, 1991, p. 375). However, there is a need to prioritise and limit the resources spent on each enquiry and to be able to distinguish a legitimate enquiry from one disguised as historical, but with more sinister intent such as investigative journalism and industrial espionage. Procedures need to be put in place to manage such difficult enquiries appropriately.

As time goes on it will become apparent which enquiries are made repeatedly, so that fact sheets or template replies can be formulated to save time and effort going forward and to ensure consistency of response. Some complex enquiries can take a large amount of time to answer and whilst this is acceptable for internal enquiries, the archive will have to decide just how long it is prepared to spend on supporting an external individual's research project. Some archives impose a predetermined time limit on compiling a response, say 30 minutes or an hour. At some point external enquirers may have to be advised that they must come in to carry out any further research themselves or given clear guidance about just how much more can be done for them. It may be useful to offer a list of local research professionals who enquirers can engage to carry out research in the archive on their behalf.

In order to mitigate the risk of providing public access to the archive the archivist needs to develop a sense of which enquiries should be referred on before a response is given, because they are in some way opposed to the company's interest. Enquiries from disgruntled customers or former staff, legal firms or media organisations can be tricky, and the archivist needs to develop a network of colleagues with sufficient knowledge and authority to assume responsibility for pursuing the enquiry or advising the correct course of action in cases where a response or researcher might have the potential to adversely affect the business. This is important, as a single misjudgement with a seriously detrimental outcome may change a company's willingness to allow future public access at all. Conversely, some enquiries may present an opportunity from which the business might unexpectedly benefit, and these enquiries also need to be identified. A company's communications, legal and human resources teams are often better equipped to deal with certain kinds of enquiry.

Access policy and process

A formal access policy, which is freely available, consistently adhered to, and signed off by senior management should be at the heart of a corporate archive's framework for managing access. It should be a clear statement of the available services and how to use them and should reflect the overall purpose of a corporate archive. Such a policy is desirable for researchers and archivists alike as it identifies and mitigates the risk of offering access. These risks are discussed more fully in Chapter 11. Many access policies of individual archive repositories are available online, along with guidance about creating such a policy. There is, for example, a sample access policy in the International Council on Archives' publication, *Principles of access to archives. Technical guidance of managing archives with restrictions* (International Council on Archives, 2014).

Once an access policy has been approved and documented processes and resources need to be put in place to support it. These may include application forms, search room rules and print or online materials that provide potential users with information about the service and archive. Procedures for answering enquiries from remote researchers, internal and external, and for managing reproduction also need to be established.

A key document is the conditions of access form, which is signed by the researcher and ensures that both researcher and archivist have a shared understanding of their respective rights and responsibilities and a record of the researcher's details. This should

Box 9.2 Access policy – content elements

Introduction:

Describe the purpose of the archive and its attitude toward access. For example, the company supports and promotes access to the archive and the information it contains, both internally, as a corporate resource, and externally, as a research collection of interest and value to individuals and organisations worldwide.

State any code of ethics or similar that the archives complies with, for example the code of ethics adopted by the International Council on Archives in 1996, but note that all access must be consistent with conservation; security against misplacement and theft; and compliance with commercial, regulatory and legal requirements.

Access/engagement channels:

- List the ways in which the company provides access to its archive, for example via publications, websites, exhibitions, research visits, answering enquiries and so on.
- State whether access is provided free of charge.
- State whether outreach initiatives are undertaken to promote the collections and attract new users.
- State where information about the archive and guidance for users can be found and how access can be arranged.

Archive responsibilities:

Set out details of the company's commitment to:

- respond to internal and external enquiries about its history and archives, including identification of potential research sources. Define service level standards, for example answering enquiries within a certain number of working days;
- provide facilities for the public to access its archives and publish information on the terms and conditions of such access;
- customer care, ensuring all stakeholders receive courteous, efficient and effective service.

User responsibilities:

Set out each user's responsibility to:

- complete a form requesting access and abide by the terms and conditions it sets out;
- provide, if visiting in person, proof of identity and abide by the reader regulations displayed in the search room;
- handle all archives with due care in a way that promotes their preservation, including statement of where guidance is provided (for example in the search room regulations and by the archivists);

- use information derived from the archives for private study and research only and in conformity with copyright law;
- seek the required permissions if such information is published and use the correct form of citation.

Finding aids:

- State whether archives are catalogued and, if so, whether in compliance with international or national archival professional standards.
- State whether direct public access to the catalogue is allowed or whether, for reasons of confidentiality only information from the catalogue can be provided.
- State when new accessions are catalogued and how backlogs of unlisted material are dealt with and whether access is allowed to unlisted material.

Access restrictions:

- State that all access to the archive is at the company's discretion.
- Note any access restrictions, for example access to original records may not be given if surrogates exist, if they are confidential for commercial or legal reasons, if they are not catalogued or if they are physically unfit for production.
- Provide any standard closure periods, for example for customer or staff records.
- Describe any special exceptions, for example that access to closed records may be granted in some circumstances for the purpose of aggregate statistical analysis if the anonymity and privacy of individuals is maintained.

Copying and reproduction:

- State if photocopies or scans can be supplied, subject to the preservation needs of the material and completion of the appropriate application form.
- State if photographs of archives can be provided and reproduced, subject to completion of the appropriate application forms and whether a fee will be charged.
- State whether personal visitors are allowed to photograph archives subject to the completion of the appropriate application form.

Feedback and complaints:

- Describe how complaint can be made and feedback given and how it will be dealt with.

Review and update:

- State how often the access policy is reviewed and the date of the last review.

be used for visiting researchers and those for whom a significant amount of information from the archive is provided remotely, transcribed, photocopied or scanned. The form should capture or provide the following:

- Researcher's name, address and contact details.
- Details of his or her research project, including date of publication if relevant.
- Terms and conditions of access to the archives.
- Search room regulations if relevant.
- Instructions on how to cite sources in the archive (how to name the archive organisation and describe the document).
- Signature of researcher and date signed.
- Archive's contact details in case of future enquiries.

This document allows the archivist to hold researchers accountable for how they handle records and what they publish that is derived from them, and also to track information about the archive's use. It should be compiled in line with local privacy or data protection legislation. Proof of identity and address should be requested from visiting researchers or those being provided with significant information from the archive.

In a public archive that holds collections of business archives, access should be managed in line with the repository's wider policy, but may need to be tempered by specific requirements imposed by the depositing business regarding records that the depositor might require to be closed due to commercial secrecy or confidentiality.

Promoting and supporting access

Despite efforts by archive bodies and individual archives to promote the importance of the historical records of business and the existence of corporate archive services, business archives tend to be less familiar and discoverable than national and local government archives. In order to give researchers the best opportunity to find and access a corporate archive, it needs to be promoted by providing appropriate print and digital signposts.

Researchers will need information about the kind of records a business archives holds, and how to enquire about them or visit to see them, so it is useful to offer potential users information about the collection and archive service. This can be offered most efficiently online and should include information about how to submit an enquiry; how to make an appointment to view the archive; how to find the archive, perhaps including a map and public transport links; contact details; opening hours; facilities for the disabled; and guidance on the nature of the records in the collection.

In the past several corporate archives in the United Kingdom have offered online archive guides,[8] but, in contrast to public collecting archives, few felt able to make their complete archive catalogue available online due to issues of commercial confidentiality. A simple guide to the history of the company and its key subsidiaries, plus a summary of the principal surviving records open for access, have had to suffice to give researchers an idea of whether the collection may be of use. Instead, researchers have been encouraged to make contact, explaining their subject of research in more detail, so that the archive itself can advise what is held that may be relevant. Such guides are far from universal amongst corporate archives. More common are heritage websites of prepared content – chronologies of companies in various countries, histories of important products or

Box 9.3 Typical conditions of access form

Name:_____

Address:_____

Email address:_____

Full details of project, publication or thesis for which access is requested:

_____

Approximate date of publication/completion: _____

Names and addresses of referees (if appropriate): _____

_____

I request access to the archives of X *[company]* solely for the purpose detailed above, and if access is granted, I agree to be bound by the following terms and conditions and reading room regulations and to cite the archives appropriately. I have retained a copy of this form for my own records.

Terms and conditions of access to the archives of X [company]

Access to the archives or to any particular records shall be at the absolute discretion of the company's archivists, who may refuse access to any document. The archives are open to readers by appointment only.

1   The reader shall supply full details of the project or thesis for which access is required and shall only extract, or otherwise convey to a third party, information which is pertinent to that research. If the nature of the research changes over time then a new conditions of access form should be completed.
2   The reader shall provide proof of identity and one or more references as required.
3   The reader shall submit a draft of any text which he/she proposes to publish which cites or uses information from the archives. Submission of a thesis to a university or other establishment of higher education or presentation of a conference paper is regarded as publication.
4   If publication is approved the reader shall ensure that the required acknowledgement to the company is included and advise the date, place and manner of intended publication.
5   The reader shall abide by the archive's reading room regulations.

Citing sources from the archives

References to items in the archive should be cited in the following form: Reference no, Archives service name. For example, *[sample reference number]*.

Signature of applicant:_____ **Date:**_____

Note: Reading room regulations (see Box 9.6) can be included on the reverse of the conditions for access form.

Acknowledgement: Royal Bank of Scotland Archives.

> **Box 9.4 Key elements for an online archive guide**
>
> - Histories of the company and its key subsidiaries.
> - A description of the kinds of records held.
> - How to arrange a visit to the archive – opening hours, notice required, fees, and so on.
> - How to make enquiries, including guidance on what kind of enquiries can be answered and what information should be provided.
> - How to order and seek reproduction permission for images.
> - Access policy.
> - Archive contact/location details.

services, biographies of key players, stories of landmark buildings and so on – which suggest historical records survive, but do not describe them.

However, in recent years some companies have begun to go further, not only to demonstrate transparency and the significance of their heritage beyond the business itself, but also to make discovery more efficient for both users and archive staff. A number of United Kingdom businesses have recently put full archive catalogues online for the first time, including the Bank of England (Williams, 2012, pp. 30–31), BT, The Postal Museum, Marks & Spencer, Sainsbury's and Unilever.[9] This trend has tended to be led by archives that are set up as charitable trusts or which hold public records and consequently place particular emphasis on research access. Other corporate archives around the world are also following suit, such as the World Bank in 2015.[10] On the other hand, at least one company has had to withdraw an online catalogue having found it led to unwelcome investigative journalism. Corporate archives, which have pioneered online catalogues, report that the online access saves considerable staff time in answering enquiries about what records are held and what they contain and in helping visitors decide what they should look at and whether a visit is worthwhile. After launching its online catalogue the Bank of England archive reported that more than 16 per cent of enquirers quoted the catalogue.

Providing an online catalogue does, however, require careful planning and the following issues should be considered:

- Why is an online catalogue needed? What is the audience and purpose?
- Is sufficient staff resource available? Setting up the catalogue will be a hugely time-consuming and complex process involving several teams (such as archives, IT, legal and digital delivery), each with differing resources and priorities.
- What can be learnt from existing online catalogues? Assess what does and doesn't work online and seek structured feedback from staff and users about what they want.
- The catalogue interface may be compromised due to constraints imposed by the corporate website templates and/or cataloguing software and technology is still evolving at a rapid pace.
- Can the cost be supported? The website will be expensive to set up and will require on-going funding to maintain.

- Assess the risks, such as ensuring none of the catalogue data contravenes privacy or other legislation and that corporate servers are not compromised.
- Test the site thoroughly prior to external publication, perhaps on internal users via the corporate intranet.
- Make the site intuitive to use and search. Most users won't read instructions.
- Promote the site effectively. Signpost the site on your own and other websites and promote it in social media and print wherever appropriate. Also ensure the site is as accessible as possible via web search enquiries.

A few other corporate archives have gone further than offering online guides and catalogues and digitised the records themselves for self-service access too. These initiatives range from digitising a small selection of records for a particular purpose, such as Sainsbury's old staff journals[11] for educational use, Coca-Cola's past advertising for promotional purposes and the Royal Bank of Scotland's digitisation of the bank account of the eighteenth-century landscape gardener Lancelot 'Capability' Brown to mark his bicentenary in 2016,[12] to digitising much bigger and more diverse collections.

The first United Kingdom corporate archive to digitise records on a significant scale was BT in 2013 in collaboration with The National Archive and Coventry University. The site offers over half a million photographs, advertisements and letters as 50 terabytes of freely available content.[13] Likewise, in 2014, the Bank of England launched a site providing digital versions of key records as part of its accountability, public understanding and international debate agenda (see Box 9.5). The following year Barclays Bank also made selected records available online,[14] including many of its old branch bank photographs. Photographs particularly lend themselves to online access. Consideration should be given by all corporate archives to making particularly significant records digitally available online or at least providing online indices to key records so researchers can self-check their relevance.[15]

To promote external use of the collection signposts should be provided on key national websites used by researchers. In the United Kingdom, Discovery,[16] The National Archives' online guide, and the corresponding Scottish website, SCAN,[17] are well used by would-be researchers. In addition, when the archives publishes leaflets or delivers exhibitions, URL or QR code links should, where appropriate, be offered to any website providing more information about the archive.

When external researchers make initial contact most business archivists will want to find out some detail about each user's research interests to establish whether they can assist at all; whether the enquiry is more easily answered by the archivist consulting the archives on the enquirer's behalf, and, if not, which records need to be retrieved. Most business archives will take the view that if it is quicker to answer the enquiry for the researcher by reviewing or transcribing records, this may be less time-consuming for all parties than hosting a visit. As a business archive's main customer is the business itself, it is the responsibility of the archivist to ensure staff time is used appropriately and efficiently in answering external enquiries. Most business archives, as visitors are few, require appointments to be made in advance as the search room facilities are usually small and staffed only as required.

Box 9.5 Case study: the Bank of England Archive and digital access, United Kingdom

The Bank of England Archive introduced an online archive catalogue in 2012 and began to publish selected archival records on its website as part of its broader move toward greater transparency from 2013. Records are generally provided as whole scanned documents up to the archive's 20–year closure period.

Key features:

- Available on the Bank of England's own website.
- Offers scans of whole records, including book covers, as single PDFs.
- Includes indexes where available.
- Confidential information redacted or obscured where necessary.
- Maximum download size of 38MB.

Available records include:

- Court (board) minutes.
- Committees of Treasury, Inspection and Building minutes.
- Governor Montagu Norman's diaries.
- War records and images.
- Annual reports and other key publications.

Risks/issues:

- Download sizes.
- Application of redaction can be time consuming.
- Increased online discoverability means sensitivities should be reassessed even where records are already open.
- Only records known to be Bank of England copyright could be published.

Outcomes:

- Increased transparency and accountability.
- Improved researcher access.
- Greater awareness of the Bank of England's archive collections.
- Ability to promote records via links and images on social media.

Website available at www.bankofengland.co.uk/archive/Pages/digitalcontent/digitalcontent.aspx [Accessed 20 August 2016].

Acknowledgement: Bank of England Archive.

Search room management

For those researchers who visit in person, a public search room facility has to be offered and managed. One of the main objectives must be to ensure the security of records from theft, damage or archival re-arrangement. Often in a business 'search room' is far too grand a term, as the best that can be afforded occasional visiting researchers may be a spare desk in the office area.

If an archivist is lucky enough to have a separate room or area set aside for researcher use, this space should ideally allow the archivists to view the researchers, perhaps by use of a sound-proof glass wall, so the archivist can continue working while office discussions and telephone conversations can continue unheard. The room should have appropriate lighting and environmental control and tables large enough for researchers to look at archive records of all kinds, yet still have space to take notes. Power supplies for laptop computers or notebooks should be provided, as well as foam wedges or book cushions and book weights to allow volumes and plans to be viewed at least risk of damage. Any reference books and catalogues to which researchers might need access should be provided nearby. A microfilm reader is also required if records have been filmed for conservation reasons, as such films should always be shown to users rather than originals.

The following procedures should be observed:

- Require visitors and colleagues to show some form of identification.
- Require visitors to sign a visitor book each day, providing name, address, nature of research.
- Ensure researchers are not permitted into the storage areas and any bags are left in lockers.
- Ensure each document is produced with a slip noting the reference number, location, date, brief description and retrieving archivist. A copy should be kept with the record, a copy in the archive box and a copy filed so that the archivist can ensure the item is returned to the correct storage box and track use.
- Restrict the number of records produced for a researcher.
- Supervise researchers to avoid damage to or theft of records. The use of closed-circuit television cameras could be considered.
- Provide appropriate book rests and weights for use of bound or large volumes.
- Undertake any photocopying for the enquirer and re-file all records.
- Provide written search room regulations (see Box 9.6) setting out the terms and conditions of access and provide it in the search room and as part of the application form.
- Facilitate disabled access by providing an adjustable-height desk as well as wheelchair access.

Many business archives hold records in a format that may require equipment for viewing including film, audio tapes, microfiche and born-digital or digitised records. Guidance needs to be agreed on how and where access can be offered. Film and audio records, for example, may be better converted to electronic formats. In a corporate context with networked PCs and password-protected personal profiles, offering access to digital records to the public may be difficult and require non-standard solutions. Ideally, of course, the increasingly digital nature of many business archive collections should lead

Box 9.6 Typical search room regulations

1 A reader wishing to inspect documents must complete a form applying for access and sign the visitors' register. Signing the form implies an agreement to observe these regulations, and their infringement shall render the reader liable to exclusion.

2 Readers may not eat or drink (including chewing gum, cough sweets or bottled water) in the search room. Mobile phones should be switched off.

3 All bags, including handbags, and outdoor coats must be left in lockers and no non-essential items may be taken into the search room.

4 Readers should work quietly and be considerate to other search room users.

5 Readers should use pencil to make notes. The use of any kind of ink pen is forbidden in the search room. Laptops may be used, provided their use does not disturb others.

6 The greatest care must be taken when handling documents. Book supports should be used where necessary and any defect in, or accident to, a document must be reported at once. Readers should not:
   - lean on documents or rest any other items on them other than weights supplied;
   - write on or mark a document;
   - fold or crease a document;
   - place documents on the floor;
   - handle photographs without using the gloves provided;
   - fan through a document's pages;
   - use an instrument or moistened fingers to turn document pages;
   - change the order of loose documents in a bundle or file or remove tags or paperclips.

7 Only three items will be issued at any one time.

8 No documents must be removed from the search room. Theft of material is an offence and offenders will be prosecuted.

9 Readers are permitted to take photographs of documents in the search room with prior permission, but the use of flash photography or scanners is not allowed. Such photographs must be used for non-commercial research or private study only. They may not be reproduced or published without prior permission.

10 A limited number of photocopies of documents may be provided at the discretion of the duty archivist. Such photocopies are supplied for non-commercial research or private study only. They may not be reproduced or published without prior permission.

11 Readers must comply with relevant copyright and data protection legislation when using information from the archives.

12 Certain classes of documents are closed to readers for a fixed period of years and the company retains the right to deny access to documents.

to greater provision of remote access, thereby reducing the need for researchers to visit search rooms in person. This could be achieved through the publication of digital records on a company website, as explored above in the Bank of England case study. An alternative strategy, deployed by the archivists at the Associated Press Archives for example, is to harness the power of social media platforms by publishing content via YouTube.[18] If the main aim is to meet the needs of internal users of the archive material could be made available via a company intranet. Some off-the-shelf digital archives management systems will include access functionality as part of the overall product.

Where remote access platforms are not in place, it may be necessary to fall back on simpler solutions. A non-networked PC could be set up in a search room, for example, with offline, read-only copies of the records made available to researchers. In all cases, the archivist needs to ensure digital records are not compromised by providing access so all the usual policies need to be applied around sensitivity, copyright, data protection and so on. It is considered good practice to keep archival and access copies of digital records separately. Access copies typically need to be ready for use so may need to be migrated from older to newer forms. For more information on managing access to digital records see Chapter 10 and Adrian Brown's *Practical digital preservation* (2013, ch. 9).

The search room could include a research library of useful publications that users can refer to on a self-service basis, such as duplicate copies of the company's annual reports or staff magazines and relevant trade directories or journals. Any commonly used parts of the finding aid or indices that can be shared could also be made freely available, alongside any published or locally created guides to support the use and understanding of particular record types.[19]

Copying and reproducing archives

Any archive open to the public will certainly receive requests for the reproduction of archives. These will fall into two kinds – images for reproduction in theses, presentations, books, journals, websites and so on, or copies to quicken and support the research process. Increasingly users expect to be able to procure copies rather than spend time making notes, and often want to take their own photographs, rather than request photocopies as in the past. An archive needs to be clear about what copy formats can be offered, if they are charged for, what can be self service, what needs to be undertaken by archivists or by external suppliers, and how ordered copies will be delivered.

Where photocopying services are still offered to visiting researchers, it will be helpful to allow a limited number of photocopies to be made, free of charge, where such copying will not damage the document concerned. Such copies should, however, be made by an archivist to avoid damage during the copying process and corporate archives may want to limit the number of photocopies allowed, in order to avoid staff spending large amounts of time at the copier. Fortunately the arrival of digital and smartphone cameras has allowed researchers to take photographs themselves which, if the flash is turned off, is often less harmful than scanning or photocopying. However, this development also means that researchers often get through archival material more quickly, creating a great deal of work for the supporting archivist and presenting a higher risk of accidental damage to the records from rapid handling. This risk can be mitigated by clear handling guidance and careful supervision. Additionally, an understanding needs to be reached regarding exactly what can be photographed and the reproduction rights attached to photographs taken by researchers.

If images are going to be published, it may be in the interests of the company to ensure that their quality reflects well on the archive, in which case a service for scanning or professional photography should also be provided. An order form for digital photography should be created, requiring a further application form or license to be completed in cases in which reproduction rights are also sought. This should set out the terms and conditions, which may include an acknowledgement of the provenance and copyright ownership of the image. This may be offered as a chargeable service or the company may decide that fees should be waived because the reproduction acknowledgement in itself has significant promotional value.

Copyright

Copyright protection can be regarded internationally as arising from natural justice. The 1948 Universal Declaration of Human Rights says that 'everyone has the right to the protection of the moral and material interests arising in any scientific, literary or artistic production of which he is the author' (Padfield, 2010, p. 1). In the United Kingdom, as in the United States of America and Commonwealth, copyright is an intellectual property right that subsists in a work. This may include literary, dramatic and artistic works, films or sound recordings. Authorship, rather than ownership, generally determines the duration of copyright, which descends on the death of an author to his or her legal heirs. It is commonly thought of in relation to published works, but copyright also subsists in unpublished works. As a result a single file of correspondence can embrace many copyright owners. Archivists need to consider copyright permissions carefully when publishing their own archives, copying documents for others, and agreeing terms of deposit.

When the author of a work is an employee it may be the staff member, rather than the company, that owned the copyright. In the United Kingdom determining the duration of copyright may involve making assumptions about how long a person is likely to live based on the age of the author and the date of the work created.[20] An employer is the first owner of copyright in a literary or artistic work made on or after 1 July 1912, if made by an employee in the course of his or her employment under a contract of service (Padfield, 2010, p. 310).

The whole area is, however, complex. For example, is the firm the copyright owner of post-1912 works created by business partners or non-executive directors if there is no surviving contract of service? Can a pragmatic assumption be made that an employer is the first owner of copyright of a proven employee's work if no agreement is known to exist to the contrary? It may be wise to seek advice from a company's own legal or intellectual property team. Such teams may, however, have little experience of copyright issues in relation to archive collections and may prove quite conservative and risk-averse. Additionally, corporate archivists need to consider if there is reputational risk in reproducing items, or allowing them to be reproduced, even if they are out of copyright if they seem to reveal personal information.

Archivists need to provide clear guidance to researchers describing copyright constraints or procedures and understand the implications for their own use of the archive too.

It may be simplest to advise that all copies are provided for personal research or study only, that a further application is required to license other use, and that the onus is on the user to check copyright status where this is unclear to the archive itself. In the United Kingdom there is a good published, and regularly updated, guide for archivist to this complicated subject area (Padfield, 2015). The National Archives also provides useful advice (The National Archives, 2013).

Data protection

Privacy issues and legislation, known in the United Kingdom as data protection, also affect archives. These constrain the availability of personal information about living individuals, which must be obtained only for specified purposes, not further processed in a manner incompatible with them and kept no longer than necessary for that purpose. United Kingdom law[21] does, however, allow 'research exemptions' permitting personal data to be stored indefinitely for research provided the data is not processed to support measures or restrictions in relation to particular individuals or damage to the data subjects. This provides legal justification for the permanent retention of personal data in archival collections and is essential for retaining records relating to staff, customers, shareholders and so on in the longer term. Most archivists would hesitate to close any files forever, and although data protection legislation applies only to living individuals, some archives have chosen to apply it to the deceased in cases where extremely sensitive information, which could cause distress to living relatives, is held.

Archivists should be aware that both personal data in its own administrative records and personal data in the archive's collections are affected, so there are various implications for how access to archives containing personal data is managed. The publication of personal data in archives comes within the definition of processing within the Act and must comply with the data protection principles.

Data subjects have the right to be informed of the identity of the data controller and the intended purposes of processing. Consequently any form used to collect personal data, such as applications for access or reproduction licenses, whether paper or electronic, should provide the person contributing the data with: the identity and address of the data controller; a brief description of the purposes for which the data will be used; and any further relevant information. Personal data should not be kept for longer than is needed. Data subjects also have the right to access personal data held about them and it should be stored securely so that confidentiality is maintained at all times.

Securing feedback

Every company's reputation depends upon the quality of its customer service. So too does its archive. Offering archive access to internal and external users in the right way can impact perceptions of both the archive and the company as a whole. In order to ensure that an archive meets the actual needs of enquirers and researchers, rather than their presumed needs, it is important to seek feedback from users on a regular basis in order to assess the needs of the archive's stakeholders and decide whether plans need to be put in place to change and improve the way access is offered.

Securing feedback can range from a casual conversation with visiting researchers to a campaign involving the issue of crafted questionnaires that seek information from different

---

Box 9.7 User feedback questionnaire content

Content and layout should depend on whether the questionnaire is aimed at internal and external remote enquirers or personal visitors and on the medium used, but should include some or all of the following elements:

- Name (anonymous if user prefers).
- Date of initial contact.
- How users contacted the archive, for example by email, telephone, post, social media.
- Whether users had contacted the archive on a previous occasion.
- How users found out about the archive, for example internet search, archive website, publication, social media, word of mouth.
- Reason for contacting the archive.
- What type of records were consulted.
- Rating of satisfaction regarding, for example archive website information, ease of contact, speed, clarity and quality of response, reproduction ordering process, helpfulness of staff, overall service provided.
- Suggestions for improvement of the archive's customer service.
- Explanation of how to submit the questionnaire and thanks for completing it.

---

kinds of users about their experience, either in person or remotely. Tick boxes are easiest for users to complete and encourage participation, but it is always useful to provide respondents with at least some space to add freestyle comment and suggestions about changes they might like to see. Online survey tools such as Survey Monkey or in-house Web tools may prove useful. Often there will be good reasons why some feedback requests cannot be fulfilled, but it is important to keep in touch with users' views and wish lists.

Deposited archives and access

Many companies decide to deposit all or part of their archives in a public repository in order ensure that their important historical records are properly preserved and can be accessed by researchers. This allows a business to provide access to its historical records without having the responsibility for supervising researchers. This can be helpful where there is no in-house archive team or expertise. In the United Kingdom and internationally many local and specialist repositories welcome deposits of business archives.

However, both parties need to understand and manage the access and copyright implications of deposit. Archivists on both sides need to be aware, for example, that archive collections, which pass into ownership of, or are held by, a repository, which is subject to the Freedom of Information Act in the United Kingdom, are likely to become subject to the act. The legal position is far from clear cut and must be clarified on a case-by-case basis. Such deposited records may also be subject to Environmental Information Regulations 2004 and Data Protection Act 1998. Useful guidance has been published by The National Archives (Healey, 2007; The National Archives, 2005; 2006).

A clear unambiguous gift or loan agreement should be drawn up with legal advice, which is mindful of all the implications and sets out the terms of the deposit. It should define, among other things, how the collection should be made available for public study – how requests for access will be dealt with; whether they should be referred to the depositor or handled by the repository. In practice, it may be difficult to maintain an ongoing relationship and allowing the repository to control the access process, albeit in line with pre-agreed guidelines, may prove more satisfactory for both parties. However, some repositories do manage fruitful ongoing liaison with corporate depositors.

Similarly it must be agreed for how long records should be closed, if copies can be provided, whether the material or extracts from it can be published or exhibited without reference to the depositor, whether access can be charged, whether surrogate copies must be made for viewing, whether the owner retains data controller responsibilities and the legal authorisations required for copyright purposes. These are all matters that need to be considered and provision made.

Loaned records are usually deposited for a specified period, with an opportunity for review at the end of the period, or on indefinite loan. An agreement should be set in place to allow the company to borrow back records if needed internally for a promotional initiative or legal case.

External repositories unfamiliar with business archives understandably may be concerned by the large volume of, for example, accounting or customer records and reluctant to manage access in a different way to other holdings. However, there are a number of successful deposit models that can be pointed to, for example, the arrangements made by Glasgow University's Scottish Business Archive in the United Kingdom and Harvard Business School's Baker Library in the United States with their corporate depositors.

Conclusion

Business archives are preserved for use by the creating business and by the public in the present and the future. The access service links an archive to its users. The way in which access is provided must, nevertheless, be underpinned by clear policies and procedures that are consistent with business needs, professional ethics, legal requirements, equity and fairness. The access process should be as transparent as possible, yet put firm controls in place that prevent unauthorised access to restricted records. Providing information from the archive, both internally for business use and externally for research use, should also be seen as a huge opportunity to advocate on behalf of the collection and through excellent customer service to raise the reputation of both the company and the archive service.

Acknowledgements

Thanks are due to Lesley Richmond, Paul Lasewicz and Graham Smith for kindly commenting on the chapter as a whole; to Mike Anson for providing information on online catalogues and on the Bank of England Archive's catalogue in particular; to Victoria Stobo for review of the sections on copyright and data protection; and to William

Kilbride, James Mortlock and Tina Staples for commenting on the provision of access to digital records. I am also indebted to Dr John Booker who wrote a seminal chapter on providing access to business archives in *Managing business archives* (1991).

Notes

1 From 2003 United States banks, including J. P. Morgan, Chase & Co, Lehman Brothers and Citizens Financial, were required to investigate and disclose all their historical links with the institution of slavery to satisfy disclosure ordinances issued by certain United States cities.

2 From 1996 Swiss and British bank archives were involved in supporting the identification of the expropriated assets of Jewish victims of the Holocaust by painstakingly searching relevant archives.

3 In the late 1990s Ford Motor Company faced legal action for profiting from the use of forced labour in Germany under the National Socialist regime prior to and during the Second World War. The company's archive team led an objective project to research and publish related information. European corporate archives have long been aware of the need for openness regarding the National Socialist regime legacy.

4 In 2014 the Bank of England released archives relating to the 2007–08 financial crisis period much earlier than normal in the interests of openness and international debate.

5 It may also cover public records held by formerly nationalised businesses and business archives held by public bodies such as local government archives. For example BT, once a government-owned organisation, was privatised in 1984 and despite a general 30-year closure rule, some public records held by BT Archives less than 30 years old are accessible under the Freedom of Information Act 2000.

6 An information barrier within a business to prevent exchanges or communication that could lead to conflicts of interest.

7 For further guidance on advocacy and outreach see Chapter 12.

8 For example, online collections guide to the Rothschild archive available at https://guide-to-the-archive.rothschildarchive.org/welcome-to-the-guide and to the Royal Bank of Scotland Archive available at http://heritagearchives.rbs.com/ [Both accessed 20 August 2016].

9 See The Postal Museum available at www.postalheritage.org.uk/collections/catalogue/ (launched 2006); the Bank of England at www.bankofengland.co.uk/ARCHIVE/Pages/default.aspx (launched 2012); Marks & Spencer at https://archive-catalogue.marksandspencer.ssl.co.uk/home (launched 2012); BT at www.dswebhosting.info/bt/ (launched 2013); Sainsbury's at http://catalogue.sainsburyarchive.org.uk/calmview/ (launched 2014); and Unilever at http://unilever-archives.com (launched 2015) [All accessed 20 August 2016].

10 Washington-based World Bank 'Access to Memory' website available at http://archivesholdings.worldbank.org (launched 2015) [Accessed 20 August 2016].

11 The Sainsbury Archive, a charitable trust with archives on long-term loan to Museum of London, offers JS Journal Online, 600 past issues of the company's in-house journal available at https://jsjournals.websds.net/ [Accessed 20 August 2016].

12 See http://heritagearchives.rbs.com/subjects/list/lancelot-capability-brown-bank-accounts.html [Accessed 20 August 2016].

13 See www.digitalarchives.bt.com/web/arena [Accessed 20 August 2016].

14 Barclays Bank makes thousands of items from the archives freely available online, including branch photographs, advertising material and annual reports, at www.archive.barclays.com/ [Accessed 20 August 2016].

15 For example the Royal Bank of Scotland's archive offers an online index to the United Kingdom's oldest surviving banking records, the customer ledgers of London goldsmith Edward Backwell, 1663–72 at http://heritagearchives.rbs.com/people/list/edward-backwell.html [Accessed 20 August 2016].

16 Available at: http://discovery.nationalarchives.gov.uk/ [Accessed 20 August 2016].

17 Available at: http://catalogue.nrscotland.gov.uk/scancatalogue/welcome.aspx [Accessed 20 August 2016].

18 See www.youtube.com/c/aparchive [Accessed 20 August 2016].

19 See Chapters 4 and 5 on understanding and managing different kinds of business records. Some useful guides to understanding certain records typically found in business archives are available, for example, Boyns, R., Boyns, T. and Edwards, J., 2000. *Historical accounting records: a guide for archivists and researchers*. Northampton: Society of Archivists.
20 Governed in the United Kingdom by the Copyright, Designs and Patents Act 1988, amended by the Duration of Copyright and Rights in Performance Regulations 1995 (Statutory Instrument 1995/3297).
21 Governed in the United Kingdom by the Data Protection Act 1998.

References

Booker, J., 1991. Access policy. In: A. Turton, ed., 1991. *Managing business archives*. Oxford: Butterworth-Heinemann. Ch. 14.

Brown, A., 2013. *Practical digital preservation. A how-to guide for organizations of any size*. London: Facet Publishing.

Healey, S., ed., 2007. *Code of practice for archivists and records managers under Section 51(4) of the Data Protection Act 1998*. [pdf] The National Archives. Available at: www.nationalarchives.gov.uk/documents/information-management/dp-code-of-practice.pdf [Accessed 20 August 2016].

International Council on Archives (ICA), 1996. *ICA Code of Ethics*. [pdf] ICA. Available at: www.ica.org/en/ica-code-ethics [Accessed 20 August 2016].

International Council on Archives (ICA), 2012. *Principles of access to archives*. [pdf] ICA. Available at: www.ica.org/sites/default/files/ICA_Access-principles_EN.pdf [Accessed 20 August 2016].

International Council on Archives (ICA), 2014. *Principles of access to archives. Technical guidance on managing archives with restrictions*. [pdf] ICA. Available at: www.ica.org/sites/default/files/2014-02_standards_tech-guidelines-draft_EN.pdf [Accessed 20 August 2016].

National Council on Archives (NCA), 2008. *Standard for access to archives*. [pdf] NCA. Available at: www.archives.org.uk/publications/other-useful-publications.html [Accessed 20 August 2016].

Padfield, T., 2010. *Copyright for archivists and records managers*, 4th ed. London: Facet Publishing.

Padfield, T., 2015. *Copyright for archivists and records managers*, 5th ed. London: Facet Publishing.

Society of American Archivists (SAA) and American Library Association (ALA), 1994, updated 2009. *ALA/SAA joint statement on access to research materials in archives and special collections libraries*. [online] Available at: www2.archivists.org/statements/ala-saa-joint-statement-of-access-guidelines-for-access-to-original-research-materials-au [Accessed 20 August 2016].

The National Archives, 2005. *Guidance on assessing whether deposited private archive collections are covered by the Freedom of Information Act 2000 (FOI)*. [pdf] The National Archives. Available at: www.nationalarchives.gov.uk/documents/information-management/guidance_private_archives.pdf [Accessed 20 August 2016].

The National Archives, 2006. *Loan (deposit) agreements for privately-owned archives*. [pdf] The National Archives. Available at: www.nationalarchives.gov.uk/documents/archives/loanagreement.pdf [Accessed 20 August 2016].

The National Archives, 2013. *Copyright and related rights*. [pdf] The National Archives. Available at: www.nationalarchives.gov.uk/legal/copyright.htm [Accessed 20 August 2016].

Williams, L., 2012. The new online Bank of England archive catalogue – 'do you have any records on gold? *ARC Magazine*, 277 (Sep.), pp. 30–31.

Further reading

Bettington, J., *et al.*, 2008. *Keeping archives*, 3rd ed. Canberra: Australian Society of Archivists. Ch. 11, pp. 351–378.

Booker, J., 1991. Access policy. In: A. Turton, ed., 1991. *Managing business archives*. Oxford: Butterworth-Heinemann. Ch. 14.

Business Archives Council, 2015. *Access guidance notes*. [pdf] Business Archives Council. Available at: www.businessarchivescouncil.org.uk/materials/bac_access_to_business_archives_guidance_notes.pdf [Accessed 20 August 2016].

Shepherd, E. and Yeo, G., 2003. *Managing records. A handbook of principles and practice*. London: Facet Publishing. Ch. 7, pp. 216–245.

The National Archives, *Online access*. [online] Available at: www.nationalarchives.gov.uk/archives-sector/online-access.htm [Accessed 20 August 2016]. [Case studies of how collections have been made more accessible online].

Williams, C., 2006. *Managing archives. Foundations, principles and practice*. Oxford: Chandos. Ch. 5, pp. 117–145.

Chapter 10

Managing digital business archives

William Kilbride, James Mortlock and Tina Staples

Introduction

With the reassuring rustle of parchment in the reading room, archivists have tended to move at a slow and steady pace for centuries. But traditional principles and practices have undergone a considerable overhaul in recent years thanks to the advent of digital archives. The methodology surrounding digital archives, requires new skills, innovative techniques and fresh mind-sets. The greatest challenge lies in the fact that today's methodology will require constant adaption to keep up with the fast-paced technological environment. Nothing stays still for long in the world of information technology (IT). On the plus side, this surely has to be one of the most exciting times to be a professional archivist. The dynamism of current record keeping and variety of file formats would stun our forebears, while our capacity to make archives accessible to audiences around the world has never been more empowering.

Digital records are, of course, fundamentally records: evidence of a transaction. What sets them apart is that they are not directly or independently intelligible to the reader. They have a technological dependency, being stored, manipulated and accessed through a combination of hardware and software. Indeed, some digital records, such as databases and 3D models, are completely novel digital forms that simply could not exist in physical form. The terms 'digital' and 'electronic' are often used interchangeably when discussing the management of records. For the most part electronic records are digital, though analogue electronic records – especially audio-visual recordings – are common.

Typically, companies have been creating the majority of their business records in digital format for around three to four decades. Although the truly paperless office remains an elusive dream, the tendency to print to paper has been gradually waning. Almost all modern workplaces feature Microsoft Office applications (for example Word, Excel and PowerPoint) in addition to a host of other programs, web browsers, websites and bespoke database systems. The variety of born–digital formats is therefore likely to be vast, even in the most generic of offices. Of course, the more specialist the industry – the greater likelihood of additional, specialist considerations (for example, Computer-aided Design (CAD) file formats in architecture and engineering, video file formats in media institutions).

Digital archiving is a multi-faceted challenge. This chapter will begin with important background information about the field of digital preservation. It will then move from theory to practice, beginning with practical advice on how to get started in digital preservation and an overview of typical challenges and potential solutions. The final section focuses on steps involved in developing a robust, sustainable digital archives management system in a business or business-like environment. The term *born-digital* will be used to distinguish these records from *digitised* records, which are digital copies of physical records such as a scan of a photograph, or a digital conversion of a sound recording on an audio cassette. Digitised records are subject to the same digital preservation challenges as born-digital records: digitisation is not digital preservation.

Naturally, there will be no 'one size fits all' solution. Business archivists operate across a huge variety of industries, and work in organisations, which differ dramatically in size and scope. Experience suggests that it's not the size of the organisation so much as the complexity of the requirements that dictate how challenging digital preservation will be in any given context: large, complex businesses are likely to face complex challenges but small specialist agencies can have equally complicated encounters with digital archiving, especially in heavily regulated sectors. Nonetheless there are likely to be commonalities across the business archive spectrum; and in some cases these may differ considerably from the environment and needs of archivists in alternative sectors, such as national archive bodies and other heritage institutions. This chapter aims to provide advice that should support the development of a comprehensive, sustainable digital archives system. Smaller-scale projects, or projects involving more of a phased approach, will obviously be able to select and modify the advice in accordance with their requirements.

It is also important to state from the outset that this chapter cannot hope to cover fully the detailed technical knowledge involved in this vast and fast-moving topic. An annotated bibliography has therefore been provided to recommend current sources for further information. Furthermore, as any professional archivist knows, effective archival management is not achieved through a tick-box list of technical rules and regulations. Policy, culture, procedure and process all underpin the success of an archival service. Similarly, a comprehensive digital preservation solution cannot be simply procured off the peg. This chapter therefore aims to cover a wide range of considerations involved in a digital archives project, rather than focusing solely on technical matters.

Digital preservation and business

Business improvement has been one of the principle drivers of innovation within information technology (IT), so in a strange way the processes and requirements of digital preservation are both a cause and effect of radically changed business practice. The role of computing in military or scientific endeavours is rightly celebrated, but the business origins of computing are often overlooked. In fact, business improvements, such as automated accounting machines and telephone switchboards, developed originally to support commercial functions, have been central to much of the history of computing. It is these industrial and commercial developments, not the scientific or cryptographic ones that have made digital technologies mainstream.

If business has been instrumental in the development and adoption of digital technologies, it has not so far had a leading role in digital preservation. The prime movers in digital preservation have typically been in the public sector where shared standards to support library, archive and research functions have made particular progress. Foundational texts like *Reference model for an Open Archival Information System (OAIS)* (Consultative Committee for Space Data Systems Secretariat, 2012) have emerged from the need of the scientific community to preserve and share unique research data sets, while large-scale programmes like web archiving have developed from the changing role of memory institutions to preserve cultural memory (Pennock, 2013). Significant digitisation programmes, typically framed to provide surrogate access to cultural or historical objects and texts in museums and archives, have created a need for preservation strategies to guarantee long-term success. While there are some noted examples of digitisation for commercial uses, their processes and workflows have typically been adapted from the public sector. So although the public sector only holds a small proportion of the digital universe, it has been disproportionately represented within the digital preservation community. Early collaborations, like the National Digital Information Infrastructure and Preservation Program (NDIPP) in the United States, were predominantly run by public universities and public agencies: it is only relatively recently that business archives have become more active and more prominent in organisations such as the Digital Preservation Coalition (DPC).

Business innovation has however introduced some of the key components of digital preservation often under different names. Digital resilience, continuity management and cyber-security are fundamental priorities of any successful corporation – and likewise any successful digital preservation system. Business requirements have driven considerable engagement in these areas, resulting in associated technologies such as digital asset management (DAM) systems, electronic document and record management systems (EDRMS) and enterprise content management (ECM) systems. Other elements of the digital record lifecycle such as retrieval and distribution are also particularly well-served by the myriad of technology that businesses invest in today, whether provided directly on the desktop, via servers within the corporate infrastructure, or remotely via cloud services. Off-the-shelf digital preservation repository systems have frequently utilised many of these technological advances in order to improve their own products' resilience, security, user experience and accessibility.

Key standards in digital preservation: an evolving framework

This section provides a high-level overview of the current standards, certifications and attainable improvement models that exist for digital preservation systems. Standards attempt to provide a shared systemic overview of good practice that can be adapted and deployed in diverse contexts. They are therefore a shared currency across much of the computing and information management industry, and properly deployed can help digital preservation processes integrate well with wider organisational infrastructure. Generally speaking, standards, certificates and models will be an important area of consideration whether developing a digital preservation system from scratch or ensuring that an off-the-shelf solution is capable of fulfilling an organisation's requirements. Archivists engaged in such a project should certainly refer to the bibliography provided at the end of the chapter for further information and analysis.

The one standard for all archivists to be familiar with is the *Reference model for an Open Archival Information System (OAIS)* (Consultative Committee for Space Data Systems Secretariat, 2012). Typically cited as the key standard in digital preservation, it offers a systematic framework for understanding and implementing the archival concepts needed for long-term digital information preservation and access, and for describing and comparing architectures and operations of existing and future archives. For a sound introduction to the standard see Brian Lavoie's introductory guide to the reference model (2014).

OAIS is a reference model, not a manual, so implementation is an iterative rather than a linear process. It is constructed out of three more detailed models: a Functional Model, an Information Model and an Environment Model. Arguably the most important of these, the Information Model identifies the constituents of a 'submission information package' (SIP), an 'archival information package' (AIP) and in turn a 'dissemination information package' (DIP), recognising that a variety of packaging and descriptive information are required to support the different functions of receiving, preserving and disseminating data. The Environment Model outlines the different roles associated with the OAIS while the Functional Model, the most frequently quoted section of the OAIS reference model, outlines six broad functions and breaks these down into individual components (see Table 10.1). Although it outlines mandatory responsibilities (see Table 10.2), OAIS does not provide tools to assess compliance.

As OAIS was never intended as a 'how-to guide' for digital preservation, it is perhaps as remarkable for what it leaves to the discretion of the archivist. For example, OAIS is neutral on the question of emulation or migration (see below): both approaches are in scope. It offers no discussion about how material finds its way to an archive or any advice on metadata standards.

Metadata is the term used in IT to refer to information about other information, and it is a familiar concept within archival practice. It is most familiar as 'resource discovery metadata' – information such as finding aids, collection descriptions or catalogues that help archivists and end-users to locate and retrieve information from an archive, though other types of metadata are relevant. Administrative metadata might advise when a file can be opened and by whom; technical metadata might describe what types of files are present and what software is needed to render them; transactional metadata might record who has seen a file and what changes they made to it. In an IT environment, metadata is typically highly structured, following predefined rules for how it is constructed, managed and shared. The rules governing metadata are normally defined in a metadata scheme or schema, which defines the elements of a metadata collection, including which elements might be compulsory or unique. Moreover, the elements of any metadata scheme can be further governed by controlled vocabularies or thesauri. Using these schema and controlled vocabularies makes it possible to share and understand metadata from multiple different sources, thus allowing for 'interoperability': the capacity of procedures, systems or products to work with other systems, procedures or products. This can be further supported by a 'data dictionary', a document that describes the contents, format and structure of a database and the explicit relationship between elements, or a data model, which defines how individual atoms of data connect to each other and how they are processed and stored.

Significantly, OAIS contains detailed guidance on how to document a collection but does not provide an actual metadata schema. It has long been recognised that simple 'resource discovery' metadata will not be sufficient for preservation purposes so OAIS outlines rather exacting requirements for the construction of an AIP, which includes a distinctive concept of representation information necessary to render and understand the bit sequences constituting the content (Lavoie, 2014, p. 14). Representation information is one of the critical factors for long-term access to data and it could even be described

Table 10.1 Open Archival Information System (OAIS) at a glance

Functional Model	Information Model	Environment Model
The Functional Model outlines the six core mechanisms that an OAIS uses to fulfil its requirements. There is a seventh special case.	The Information Model is a high-level description of the three main information packages that an OAIS manages.	The Environment Model describes the three main entities that interact with an OAIS.
Ingest – the processes responsible for accepting information and preparing it for the archival store. **Archival Storage** – manages the archive's long-term storage and maintenance of digital materials.	**Submission Information Package (SIP)** – the information package received by the OAIS from the producer at ingest.	**Producers** – individuals, organisations, or systems that transfer information to the OAIS for long-term preservation.
Data Management – databases of descriptive and administrative data identifying the archived information and supporting finding aids. **Preservation Planning** – the process that maps out preservation strategy and monitors the evolving conditions in which the OAIS operates. **Access** – the processes by which consumers – especially the designated community – locate, request, and receive items in the archival store.	**Archival Information Package (AIP)** – the information package preserved by the OAIS. It consists of the information that is the focus of preservation with sufficient metadata to support preservation and access. AIP is the information which the OAIS is committed to for the long term and the focus of preservation actions.	**Consumers** – individuals, organisations, or systems that consume, or use, the information preserved by the OAIS. A special subset of consumers is the 'designated community', the primary users of the system.
Administration – manages the day-to-day operations of the OAIS, as well as co-ordinating the activities of the other five functional entities. **Common Services** – a special category to represent the computing and networking backbone of any OAIS-type archive.	**Dissemination Information Package (DIP)** – the information package delivered to consumers in response to access requests.	**Management** – responsible for formulating, revising, and enforcing, the OAIS's high-level policy framework.

as the feature that distinguishes OAIS from any other kind of digital asset management system. However, OAIS makes no recommendations for how it should be coded or presented.

Consequently, Preservation Metadata Maintenance Activity (PREMIS) was set up in the early 2000s by the digital preservation community to define a core set of implementable, broadly applicable preservation metadata elements, supported by a data dictionary to provide guidelines and recommendations for populating and managing the

Table 10.2 Mandatory responsibilities of an Open Archival Information System (OAIS)

Negotiate for and accept appropriate information from information producers.
Obtain sufficient control of the information in order to meet long-term preservation objectives.
Determine the scope of the archive's user community.
Ensure that the preserved information is independently understandable to the user community, in the sense that the information can be understood by users without the assistance of the information producer.
Follow documented policies and procedures to ensure the information is preserved against all reasonable contingencies, and that there are no *ad hoc* deletions.
Make the preserved information available to the user community, and enable dissemination of authenticated copies of the preserved information in its original form, or in a form traceable to the original.

elements. The resulting *PREMIS data dictionary for preservation metadata* (PREMIS, 2015) offers a data model consisting of five entities associated with the digital preservation process: intellectual entity, object, event, agent and rights (for more see Gartner and Lavoie, 2013).

The emergence of the PREMIS data dictionary as the *de facto* international standard for preservation metadata means that much of the significant implementation work in the area of digital preservation has coalesced around PREMIS. However, PREMIS does not formally provide a standard mechanism for wrapping metadata with the content objects to which it refers. This can become problematic because with large quantities of content, and periodic updates to metadata, the two can rapidly become decoupled. Therefore the Metadata Encoding and Transmission Standard (METS) is frequently used alongside PREMIS as the practical expression of the OAIS information model and can ensure that metadata and its content objects do not become decoupled (METS, 2010). It is possible for METS to package an entire AIP (archival information package), linking four elements: a file inventory, an administrative description, a content description and a detailed structural map. These four elements can be expressed as XML and may express relationships of considerable complexity.

The triad of OAIS, PREMIS and METS can be seen to encompass many of the challenges of digital preservation, from high-level and abstract through to practical and shareable implementation. However, readers should be advised of four weaknesses implicit in this section so far. First, this is an incomplete description of a large field. Second, the standards that have been described are in flux; their constant evolution means that any description is likely to be superseded relatively quickly. Third, specific business environments and processes have different emphases. In aeronautical engineering, for example, a significantly greater importance will be placed on industry specific standards like LOTAR (LOng Term Archiving and Retrieval),[1] which complements OAIS but addresses specific issues relevant to product lifecycle management within CAD environments. OAIS has also been criticised for the way that the scientific community dominated its development. Its resulting 'imperialistic tendencies' are charged by some with closing down debate, not just about revisions of the standard but more worryingly within the historical record that results, blocking the creation of any 'mechanism for the interpretation of differences' (Bettivia, 2016). Finally, critics of OAIS complain that, while consistent in its own terms, it pays only lip service to the process of content creation and ingest and thus integrates poorly to wider business processes. So, for example, if elements of AIP construction could be transferred from the archive to the points of object creation then the process of ingest and quality assurance could be streamlined.

Certifying digital preservation

Assessing whether or not digital preservation actions have succeeded has been the subject of debate for more than two decades and it remains in flux. There is a proliferation of standards and initiatives, which can be somewhat off-putting to a new reader. The European Commission has attempted to structure certification efforts by proposing an incremental approach from relatively simple peer review to formal external audit. More recently in the United Kingdom the Archive Service Accreditation Scheme has investigated whether a simple maturity model – the 'NDSA levels of preservation' (see below) – might integrate with their existing assessment mechanisms.

A core concept within the standards discussion is the notion of a 'trusted digital repository'. The trusted digital repository should provide reliable, long-term access to managed digital resources to its designated community, now and in the future (RLG/OCLC, 2002). A *Trustworthy repositories audit and certification: criteria and checklist* (CRL/OCLC, 2007, referred to as TRAC) allowed agencies to substantiate claims to being a trusted repository using 86 criteria in three sections: organisational infrastructure; digital object management; and technologies, technical infrastructure and security. TRAC has been largely superseded by the Repository Audit Certification (RAC), also known as *ISO 16363* (International Standards Organization, 2012). While TRAC was mainly directed to self-assessment of digital libraries, *ISO 16363* is designed to form the basis for an external audit process of all types of repositories, from cultural to science to commercial.

Simultaneously, the DIN (Deutsches Institut für Normung) standards committee in Germany adopted a set of 34 criteria that define standardised requirements for the setup and management of digital archives. *DIN 31644. Information and documentation – criteria for trustworthy digital archives* (Deutsches Institut für Normung, 2012) is intended for use by all institutions that aim to preserve information in digital form.

In 2008, the Digital Curation Centre proposed a Digital Repository Audit Methodology Based on Risk Assessment (DRAMBORA) (see McHugh et al., 2008). DRAMBORA was designed to facilitate internal audit of repositories by providing a means for managers to assess their digital preservation capabilities, identify their weaknesses and recognise their strengths. Because it is based on a process of risk assessment, it forced the repository to be explicit about its own assumptions and expectations, so the local and specific context of the repository formed the basis for the assessment, setting it apart from a generic checklist.

Also in 2008 Data Archiving and Networked Services (DANS) released the Data Seal of Approval,[2] a self-assessment process for research archives with guidelines for the creation, storage and (re-)use of digital research data in the social sciences and humanities. The assessment is renewed every year through a modification procedure, and in this way it supports ongoing peer review and practical service improvement. A relatively large number of repositories have been 'awarded' the Data Seal of Approval.

Despite the increase in audit mechanisms, the value of external audits remains unclear. On one hand, participants report the generation of considerable amounts of paperwork that it involves. One commentator noted a major reason of failures in digital preservation have been hard economic realities and that 'diverting resources from actually preserving content into side issues such as certification is counter-productive' (Rosenthal, 2014). More worrying for business archives, there are questions of the practical competency of the standard outside narrowly defined contexts. Anthea Seles has recently observed that 'little attempt has been made to question whether these standards, entirely developed in one context, are actually transferable or applicable to another' (Seles, 2016, p. 4).

Perhaps in rejection of the burdensome expectations of audit, or the relatively opaque development process associated with *ISO 16363*, a number of agents have returned to the question of maturity modelling to assess preservation capability (see for example Becker *et al.*, 2011; Brown, 2013; Dollar and Ashley, 2014). Maturity models provide an accessible means for an organisation to assess its capabilities against a benchmark. Users are invited to score themselves or their institution against a range of criteria, whether relating to organisational activities or procured services. The result is a rapid assessment of strengths and weaknesses. As organisations can assert their own requirements the resulting framework aims to be responsive to the size and complexity of the organisation in question. The assessment can rapidly be adapted to become an action plan, and it can further become a detailed collaborative tool across an organisation, directing investment and delivering improvement. A good, user-friendly example is provided by the United States-based National Digital Stewardship Alliance (NDSA). Their 'levels of digital preservation' (see National Digital Stewardship Alliance, 2013) help to assess a programme against five key capabilities: storage, file fixity and integrity, information security, metadata and file formats. Organisations are invited to assess themselves at levels 1–4 with increasing skill and competency being assumed at the upper levels. Recently a sixth criterion – access – has been proposed.

The NDSA 'levels' have a number of features to recommend them for integration into existing processes in archive services. They focus largely on the technical capabilities, ignoring the policy- or resource-based organisational requirements, which are already expressed in the context of the wider archival service. They have been developed openly by a large and representative coalition, and the owners are open to suggestions for changes. They encourage agencies to adopt requirements that are appropriate – and scalable – to their organisation. Moreover, the whole standard sits on a single sheet of A4 paper so is readily accessible. The NDSA 'levels' have been actively explored to supplement the digital capabilities described in the Archive Service Accreditation Scheme in the United Kingdom. Therefore, self-assessment against the NDSA 'levels' is likely to be a worthwhile activity for many business archives in the short term.

Training and skills

Digital preservation is a continually emerging challenge: because the drivers for change in IT are outside the control of any one archive, digital preservation solutions require constant refreshment to ensure that they are not subject to the same obsolescence which they are designed to offset. Therefore, business archives engaging in digital preservation will need to review their approaches on an ongoing basis ensuring that staff skills are up to date. This is one area where the digital preservation community can report significant success. Not only is there an accessible range of training opportunities, but digital preservation is characterised by a supportive, international and vibrant community which is growing rapidly. Cross-sector and interdisciplinary collaborations are highly valued and they create the conditions for creativity, innovation and exchanges of ideas in the face of shared challenges. Practitioners are encouraged to be outward looking and connect to relevant training.

Given the wide range of skills required very few individuals encompass the full range of skills necessary to deliver a complete digital preservation infrastructure on their own. Even knowing in detail what those skills might be can be hard to identify. To this end the DigCurV project established in 2012 a curriculum framework that matches the different kinds of roles in digital preservation with different types of skills or aptitudes (Moles and Ross, 2013). Three different levels of employee – executive, manager and practitioner – were matched against four different attributes – knowledge, personal qualities, professional conduct and quality assurance, leading to a detailed breakdown of the skills and qualities required at each level. Not surprisingly, the executive level needs only enough knowledge about digital preservation to make confident decisions in the context of an organisation's strategic direction; while a practitioner needs detailed knowledge of content and systems to create and follow digital preservation plans. The DigCurV framework provides a basis for a skills audit within an organisation as well as the foundations for job descriptions, but it is not inherently a training resource. However, there are numerous resources available to suit a range of requirements and budgets.

The Digital Preservation Coalition (DPC), for example, makes considerable resources available to help develop professionals. It offers training workshops of its own and grants to attend training provided by others. It collated and published the *Digital preservation handbook* (2016) with the help of a large international expert advisory committee, offering a comprehensive introduction to the topic. For more detailed commentary, the DPC also produces a series of *Technology watch reports* providing an advanced overview to key challenges in digital preservation. The DPC also supported the establishment of the Digital Preservation Training Programme[3] in 2005, an initiative led by the University of London Computer Centre. This long-running programme, still supported by the DPC, has now provided introductory and advanced training to many hundreds of professionals in the United Kingdom and around Europe.

In the United States, The Digital Preservation Outreach and Education Programme (DPOE), based at the Library of Congress, delivers workshops for digital preservation professionals. Their 'train the trainer' approach is designed to ensure that good practice is cascaded through organisations using a baseline curriculum framework. In this way, DPOE has created a network of around 150 trainers, primarily in the United States, Australia and New Zealand, who have not only participated in DPOE events but are commissioned to extend DPOE resources and training into their own institutions and networks.

Underpinning these and other initiatives is a lively, ongoing cross-sectorial and cross-professional dialogue. Professional bodies such as the Business Archives Council, the Archives and Records Association, Society of American Archivists and the International Council on Archives offer a range of activities and fora that support development opportunities for digital preservation. So the aspiring digital archivist is well advised to explore their own professional network and, because digital preservation is not uniquely an archival problem, to extend their network to include a range of different professional perspectives. The informal and generous exchange of know-how between practitioners is invaluable in building confidence, and expertise and is one of the salient features of the digital preservation community.

From theory to practice: key actions and common challenges

Digital archivists face a proliferation of challenges, the foremost of which is to secure and stabilise content in their custody. This section gives practical advice of how to get started in digital preservation, followed by a rapid reconnaissance of commonly encountered preservation challenges and how they have been addressed.

Getting started

The most useful single resource in digital preservation is practical experience. Delaying or deflecting challenges is not only futile and more expensive in the longer term, but as information grows in size and complexity it means that the challenge becomes progressively more daunting.

The risks that digital archives need to address are complicated and intricate, some of them (such as loss of context) are familiar to archivists, others (such as the suppression of malware) are entirely technical. Some typical risks are described below (see Table 10.3).

Knowing how and where to start can be overwhelming, but the most basic advice can be boiled down to three core tasks:

- Assess the practical capabilities of your organisation, especially the IT section and the archive.
- Understand the goals and mission of your wider organisation and where digital archives fit within that mission.
- Find out a little about the digital objects you need to look after.

In practice, any one of these steps can be elaborated into substantial projects in their own right, so an important objective in the early stages will be to build experience and confidence with achievable goals. Thereafter digital preservation can be propelled programmatically within the organisation to more challenging areas with enhanced skills, tools and relationships.

Table 10.3 Typical digital preservation risks

Storage media failure	Disaster	Lost encryption key
Storage media obsolescence	Broken dependency	Poor version control
Software failure	Failed system integration	Inadvertent deletion
Software obsolescence	Data theft	Malicious deletion
Inaccessible file format	Virus or malware	Poor file naming
Format migration error	Poor documentation	Failure of copying
Loss of storage device	Poor rights management	Link rot
Failure of service provider	Loss of context	Loss of authenticity

An early, rapid assessment of the data collections held by the archive is almost always the best place to start (see Table 10.4). Perhaps the single most useful early action is to create a digital asset register to assess the extent and significance of digital holdings, identifying priorities and planning preservation actions. By identifying size and significance it's possible to alert senior management to the risks that an organisation is running; by identifying vulnerable collections it is possible to prevent immediate loss; by identifying priorities a preservation plan will be tailored to have the greatest impact with the least possible resource. An outline of the collection will also help with more detailed mapping later: a comprehensive and detailed audit could be daunting and likely to change. So, at an early stage the asset register can be quite simple.

Having assessed the collection, it may be necessary to take some early remedial actions if required and feasible in the circumstances. A simple workflow is provided below (see Table 10.5) to demonstrate steps that could be taken if the current environment does not provide basic anti-virus safeguards or disaster back-up to prevent loss. Each step has the potential to become quite elaborate. So it may be worth starting with a simple pilot for a relatively simple component from the collection, or securing a component of the collection that is at immediate risk. Building confidence with small iterative steps is better than losing confidence by trying large or complex tasks.

Further assessment can be supported by a number of simple, free tools designed to help an archivist characterise their collection. The United Kingdom's National Archives' DROID tool performs automated batch identification of file formats. It uses internal file signatures – not simply file names or extensions – to identify many standard digital formats, linking this identification to a centrally maintained registry of technical information about formats and dependencies called PRONOM. These signatures are stored in an XML signature file, generated from information recorded in the PRONOM technical registry. The information generated by the DROID report will provide an understanding of the range of formats that require preservation. Since DROID generates a unique checksum value for each file, it can also help identify duplicates, or where files appear identical but are in fact different.

IT infrastructure in the corporate environment will frequently discourage the use of open source tools, such as DROID. However, it is worth persevering with the request (or seeking out an alternative option) since the deployment of a relatively simple characterisation tool will help in a number of ways. On the practical side, the output provides an immediate item–level catalogue of the whole collection (albeit from a

Table 10.4 Assessing an archive's digital records

Questions supporting rapid assessment of an archive's digital records
What digital records are currently being held?
Where did they come from and how were they received?
Where are they stored and what kinds of media are used?
Why does the archive have these records?
Who is responsible for the data; who are the users and who are the subjects?
How is the data accessed?
What digital records have not been collected yet and what has prevented their transfer?
How is the data likely to change and grow in the near future?
What digital records would the archive like to collect in the future?

Table 10.5 Securing digital records: a simple workflow

Scan for viruses and malware with an up-to-date virus scanner to make sure there are no unwanted surprises in the collection. Perhaps keep the collection in quarantine for a period – on a PC or removable hard disk not connected to your main network – until you have checked for viruses.

Check all expected files are present. If you have a list of files and directories, check the files against it and check that the file sizes look right. Any files with '0 bytes' are a problem and empty directories should be noted to ensure that documents or records have not been lost.

Open a random selection to verify their integrity and/or expected quality levels.

Check also the contents of the random selection, noting any immediate security concerns.

Request immediate replacements for any damaged or missing files, where possible, and ask about any empty directories.

Generate a more detailed listing using tools like DROID that identify file types and give you a 'checksum' value for each file – a 'fingerprint' that will show you if a file has changed.

Start creating copies.

Ensure that (at least) one back-up copy is accessible to you (in compliance with local IT security policy). You will need to regularly revisit your material to ensure its integrity.

Make sure there is (at least) one additional copy on a different media, if necessary on a less accessible, but cheaper storage medium such as tape. Use standard back-up procedures for this.

Keep at least one copy in a different geographical location to the others to mitigate against disaster.

Now update the digital asset register with the information you have generated about the digital assets and the locations of the various backups.

Make sure the digital asset register is also properly backed up. Store it alongside the digital assets.

Source: Digital Preservation Coalition, 2016.

technical perspective). This catalogue will go a long way to the development of the metadata, which you will need in the long term and is invaluable for assessing the technical risks you face and thus the broad thrust of an initial digital preservation plan. Moreover, these tools provide a simple test case about the capacity of the IT service to support archival activities. For example, some corporate networks have complicated security or acceptance-testing requirements. A relatively simple tool like DROID will be a good indicator of the amount of advocacy required before a more complex or comprehensive system can be deployed.

These simple steps provide a business archivist with some initial safeguards to help start assessing and securing digital records in their custody. This offers some valuable breathing space to then go on to look at wider institutional planning and the development of a full digital preservation solution. Policy development, advocacy, business planning, solution building, training, procurement, collaboration and professional development will all be necessary: but this can proceed on the basis that the collection will be relatively secure in the interim. This not only builds confidence but it provides the basis for a robust business case. By demonstrating the underlying business problem, the aspiring digital archivist can illustrate the sorts of efficiency gains and risk mitigation likely to be derived from investment in the digital archive.

Emulation and migration

Broadly speaking there are three approaches to digital preservation: emulation, migration or hardware preservation. These are often presented as alternatives, though in reality they are mutually compatible and in almost every setting some small component of each is likely to be required.

Migration is the most widely adopted approach as it has the smallest initial overhead to implement. In the context of digital preservation, it is understood as the process of transferring digital resources from one generation of hardware or software to the next. It preserves the intellectual content of digital objects and the capacity to access this in spite of changes in hardware or software. Migration is attractive because it is relatively easy to open a file and 'save as' another format. But this may also result in loss of functionality or changes in appearance, meaning that the authenticity and integrity may be compromised and quality assurance in migration becomes vitally important. Moreover, successful migration depends on making accurate predictions of user needs or obsolescence. Most agencies following a migration plan will retain the originals so they can track how the small changes aggregated through time may have compromised the intellectual content of a file. This also enables 'on demand' migrations directly from the original. Migration strategies in a digital archive typically distinguish between archival and dissemination packages. An original file will be retained within the archival information package and dissemination copies derived in advance or on demand depending on the use case.

Emulation is less widely adopted but is becoming more practical with cloud computing. Emulation intervenes at a software or operating system level to imitate obsolete systems on contemporary equipment. It is particularly attractive where the look and feel of a file is important, or where the archival use case requires some functionality to be available. Unlike migration, the original files are not changed and so their integrity is not compromised. However, it requires a considerable amount of technical metadata and information about technical dependencies to create an emulation. Moreover, the emulation itself will need some form of verification, which can be challenging. It has therefore been less widely adopted to date, but the advent of cloud computing – in which it is possible to create and access a wide variety of 'virtual machines' – means that it is now possible to offer 'emulation as a service'. So emulation is likely to become a more practical digital preservation solution in the near future.

A small number of agencies have addressed the digital preservation challenge by attempting to create a back catalogue of obsolete but functioning hardware, allowing them to read old disk drives or reconstruct desktop environments. This is unlikely to be a practical preservation option for most archivists. However, the approach can be useful for the process of digital archaeology or as a test environment for emulation; and in some cases the maintenance of hardware is necessary for business purposes or can be intrinsically justified as a heritage activity in its own right.

Storage, backup and preservation

Digital preservation requires robust storage but it is a common fallacy that digital storage or simple backing up is the same as digital preservation. This error often arises in the IT industry where the preservation of content is confused with the longevity of the storage

Table 10.6 National Digital Stewardship Alliance's breakdown of different approaches to storage

Level 1	Two complete copies stored in a systematic way at different locations, with one of them being offline.	Provides basic capacity to recover from media failure, loss or damage and because materials are stored in a consistent way they become easier to manage.
Level 2	Three complete copies, one geographically remote, with documentation describing how to use the system.	Protection from major disasters, high level of safety and clarity on policy and procedures.
Level 3	Three complete copies, one in a location with different kinds of disaster threat. Active process of obsolescence monitoring for media and storage system.	Mitigates longer-term risks from obsolescence and greater protection from major external threats.
Level 4	At least three copies in different geographic locations with different disaster threats. A comprehensive plan to keep files and metadata on accessible media or a storage system.	Full range of risks addressed. Content highly available and costs predictable and manageable.

Acknowledgement: National Digital Stewardship Alliance. See https://ndsa.org/activities/levels-of-digital-preservation [Accessed 10 October 2016].

device or the data bits stored on it. Robust storage can deliver bit preservation; but digital objects need a great deal of contextual information to be rendered useful. This is sometimes termed as the difference between active preservation where steps are taken to protect the intellectual and informational content and passive preservation where the focus is merely on the bitstream. The question nonetheless arises as to what storage media or backup strategy is the most appropriate for digital preservation. There is no single answer to this question since there are many competing requirements and many different approaches. In short, it is less a question of the technology than how effectively it is deployed.

The NDSA 'levels of digital preservation' (National Digital Stewardship Alliance, 2013) discussed above, addresses the question of storage directly. It proposes, as shown in Table 10.6, that requirements can be grouped into four levels of sophistication and that archivists should consider what is most appropriate to their own setting.

Storage should be tested and updated on an ongoing basis. In many cases a conversation with the IT department will allow you to take advantage of existing business resilience systems that protect IT from disaster. Many organisations have their own data centres and existing disaster management plans pertaining to them. The teams managing these can be contacted and it should be possible to check the plans in place and determine what level of support will be provided for a digital repository's storage. Some organisations will rent space in a commercial data centre, which may also provide applications to use and access the data (for example they may host a Microsoft Word application that is used when accessing Word documents). Such arrangements are often referred to as 'the Cloud'. As these are remote it is normally not possible to approach them directly, so it may become important to interrogate the contractual arrangements you have with the service provider and establish which 'level' these are intended to achieve. In some cases, it will be prudent to amend the contract or to take local copies to ensure preservation functions are delivered.

File formats and preservation

A great deal of attention has focused on file formats in the context of digital preservation on the premise that selection of the 'right' file format reduces dependency on one or other technology. Moreover, standardisation to one or a small set of favoured formats means that preservation efforts can be more targeted and economies of scale achieved. Fortunately, early fears of wholesale file format obsolescence seem to have been overstated. There are relatively few examples of genuinely unrecoverable or un-documented file formats and even the most exotic formats can usually be rendered where there is sufficient time and intent. But at the same time, the sheer numbers of files are expanding prodigiously, and so while obsolescence might not be the challenge it once seemed, the capacity to deal with non-conformant or exotic formats is coming under pressure.

In most cases, an archivist will have little or no control over what file formats are presented to the archive. In some business environments they may be able to control production processes, or specify requirements in EDRMS, but these involve quite complicated conversations with partners for whom preservation is a low priority. Moreover, as data becomes more complicated, a simple decision over which file format to pick seems naive. Archivists today are facing incredibly complex preservation challenges posed by digital objects such as websites, email, social media content and large corporate portals involving data streams with multiple components served together from diverse, distributed locations

This complexity is likely to increase as more traffic abandons the desktop for on-demand cloud computing instead. In the cloud environment, data is created and accessed through services that are leased on a utility basis online. These applications have update and maintenance schedules that are hidden from the user; and they in turn depend on other remote services. Applications are in constant flux, which has a consequence for file formats. These have a tendency to be highly dynamic, add an additional layer of opacity in file format management and can make format verification and detection hard. A tool that has been selected because it is trusted to produce a strictly conformant file may, through variation in some unseen dependency, at any point in time deviate from the standard. So, as systems become more sophisticated managing file format conformance is becoming progressively harder. All of this is not to discount the importance of understanding and managing file formats. Instead it emphasises that we cannot 'adopt a file format' and hope that this will resolve preservation functions by default.

Establishing a digital business archive

The previous section presented simple, 'quick-fix' solutions to stabilise collections and address commonly encountered challenges with digital content. This section examines the steps necessary to deploy an ongoing, sustainable digital preservation solution. Some of the project management and system deployment advice is generic, rather than specific to the business archive setting. It has been included since this is likely to be the

---

Box 10.1 Case study: PDF and PDF/A

A classic example of the problem with file formats is the Portable Document Format (PDF). This widely used format has many features to recommend it for preservation, not least because it is so ubiquitous. Recognising that earlier versions were not robust for longer-term preservation, a specific effort was made to generate an archival version of the standard – the PDF/A. This is effectively a constrained version of the PDF standard with additional rules that minimise external dependencies. So, for example, PDF/A files are required to embed information about the colour of a document or the fonts used so that letters and symbols will render reliably.

These additional rules make the PDF an attractive choice as an archival format, but they are not without challenges. To start with PDF/A is only really an option for material that is already conformant with the PDF standard. Even so, converting PDFs to PDF/A is not trivial because there is no guarantee that the requisite font or colour information is available while other functional components like applications or embedded video are not permitted within a PDF/A file and will be removed during the conversion.

Perhaps more importantly, PDF and PDF/A are not a digital preservation strategy. Storage, retention and disposal matters will still need to be addressed; rights management and metadata are still required; relations between objects need to be maintained (Fanning, forthcoming). Adoption of a single-file format, however well designed, does not exonerate a business from dealing with all the other elements of a digital preservation plan.

---

first time that many business archivists have encountered an IT project of this size. Naturally, the guidance will need to be scaled up or down according to the scope of an individual project.

Building the case

When planning a digital archive solution one of the most important aspects of preparing to launch the project is to ensure that the archivist has a firm understanding of the current IT landscape of their business. Some archivists may be in the fortunate position of having a well-established relationship with their IT colleagues – perhaps as part of an information management department – or maybe due to the fact of working in a smaller organisation where it is relatively easy to get to know everyone. Other archivists may face greater challenges in pinpointing relevant contacts and building relationships from scratch. While an in-depth technical analysis of IT infrastructure is not essential, understanding the organisation's approach to data management is vital. It is important to become familiar with current systems in place in other parts of the business (for example DAMs, EDRMS systems, or video and picture libraries), archive tools already present (such as existing archival cataloguing systems) and knowing what, if anything, from the current IT infrastructure could be adapted to serve digital archiving purposes. Gaining this information is as much about asking the right questions as providing the correct context.

Long before any detailed requirements are written, a digital preservation project should identify and engage with the most relevant IT representatives. IT is probably the most important relationship of all in terms of stakeholder management, since their level of cooperation has the potential to make or break the entire project. It is therefore critical that a common understanding is established between the archivists and IT professionals. If there is not a strong and supportive relationship already in place – now is the time to begin working on that. It may be a good idea to share with them a basic introduction to the role, working practices and value of archives management, before the specific subject of digital archives is even discussed. This could be achieved through an invitation for a special behind-the-scenes visit to the archives service. A walk-through of core activities, such as collecting, cataloguing and access, will illustrate the key requirements behind any digital archiving project. Illustrating these processes face-to-face should enable IT to see the underlying goals of the project from an archival perspective, rather than from an exclusively computing perspective.

At the very least, it may be worth considering some form of glossary to support communication between the two disciplines at the outset (see Table 10.7). Differing interpretations of key words such as 'archive', 'data' and 'record' could prove extremely confusing in the long run. The table below contains terms that may need to be covered in a shared glossary in order to prevent misunderstanding amongst those who work outside of the archive environment. A more complete glossary of digital preservation terms can be found in the *Digital preservation handbook* (Digital Preservation Coalition, 2016).

Aside from explaining the need for a digital archiving platform, the other key focus of early meetings with relevant IT contacts should be for the archivist to gather a deeper understanding of the policies and practices in place for the storage and access of digital records within the organisation as a whole. Investigating their organisation's approach to long-term preservation of digital records may reveal a lack of engagement with the issues. The presence of these systems can also mean that the business is of the erroneous view that it has 'dealt with the problem' of digital records and their governance, even though the current EDRM and DAM systems do not provide long-term retention security. However, even if the business has not effectively planned for the long-term retention of digital records, it may already have some of the tools that could serve as building blocks for a digital preservation system, such as a DAM system. The archivist will need to understand these systems and how they plug into the business's wider IT infrastructure in order to target any proposals for a digital preservation system most effectively. Even if the archivist ultimately decides to dismiss existing options, it is important to demonstrate to stakeholders that all avenues of development from within the company's existing infrastructure have been investigated.

Working closely with IT should aid investigation of opportunities for integration with existing infrastructure, be it a DAM, EDRM or other information management platforms. If these opportunities do not exist then it is important to be aware and respond accordingly when framing plans for what a digital archive system should accomplish, which could be to address the larger gap in the electronic records governance and preservation infrastructure within the business. When making a case for a digital archives system these early conversations will help shape the approach that your pitch for the budget and system requirements will take. IT will be the gatekeepers for beginning any

Table 10.7 Glossary of terms typically used to support the planning of a digital archives project

Terms/abbreviations	Description
Access	The act of obtaining access to a record to view content.
Accession	The process of registering a record or records into the Archives on receipt of a deposit.
Appraisal	The process of selecting which records, deposited with Archives, have sufficient value to be accessioned and catalogued for permanent preservation.
Archive	The overall collection managed by the Archive team, when used with the definite article. It can also be used with the indefinite article to denote individual records within the Archive (for example, an archival record)
Archival description	Comprehensive (non-technical) data in the catalogues, for example the records' provenance, functional use, content, date, extent, format and catalogue reference code.
Archival management processes	The workflow involved in managing the records in perpetuity, namely to capture, store, secure, preserve, appraise, accession, catalogue (or destroy if not required), track and make accessible.
Arrangement	The intellectual and physical organisation of records in accordance with accepted archival principles – particularly provenance and original order – in relation to other records and related collections.
Born-digital records	Records that are created, stored and disseminated digitally.
Catalogue	Descriptive index or 'finding aid' to the company's Archive.
Company external users	Users external to the Archives team, but company employees with access to internal systems; allowed to search, request and view records, subject to access approval by the Archive team members; and existing access restrictions in place on the records themselves.
Data	An information object expressed in machine-readable form composed of structured bit streams.
Deposit	A record or records transferred into the custody of Archives.
Depositing users	Record-owners who are responsible for transferring records into the custody of Archives.
Digital copies	Copies of physical records in digital format. For example, scans of documents/photographs or audio recordings migrated from cassette to .wav files.
Digital storage area	Secure disc space for the storage of digital copies and born-digital records.
Document	An information object in digital form, typically the product of desktop publishing (for example, Microsoft Powerpoint, Excel and Word).
Embargo	Access restriction and closure period placed upon a record during which time it can only be accessed by authorised users.
Non-company external users	Users external to the company (that is the general public), allowed to search, request and view records, subject to access approval by the Archive team members and existing access restrictions in place on of the records themselves, via external interface.
Physical records	Hard copy records, held by the Archives in a variety of formats including, but not limited to, paper, photographs, audio tape, film and artefacts.
Record	Unit of information in any format including physical records, digital copies of physical records and born-digital records.
System	Archival management system which incorporates the catalogues and the digital storage area; and which facilitates the archival management processes.
Technical metadata	Data specific to digital copies and born-digital records such as version of file format and audit trail of record modification.

digital archives project, regardless of whether the solution is found to be in-house or from an external vendor. The questions that the archivist asks at this stage will provide excellent foundations for moving forward to the next stage of planning for a digital archive project.

Understanding risks and benefits

At this stage in the digital journey, it may be tempting to rush headlong into pressing for a procurement decision or hands-on, internal development. But it is worth spending a little more time analysing the findings from the initial research carried out already. Here, risk-management techniques[4] can play a key role in identifying and estimating the dangers involved in simply maintaining the *status quo*, due to lack of resources, skills or impetus to deal with digital archives.

There may be immediate threats such as the security risk of non-authorised access to poorly stored digital records lacking suitable audit trails. It may be possible to pinpoint wider-ranging deficiencies such as the inability to guarantee preservation following organisational upgrades to software or operating systems; or the inability to provide access to records in accordance with the service's publicised access polices. A corporate archivist should not be timid in making senior executives aware of relevant risks posed by poor digital archives management, since these risks can only be appropriately addressed when the risk has been evaluated and potential mitigations considered, in accordance with the organisation's underlying risk appetite and risk management strategy.

At the same time, it is important not to lose sight of the fact that good digital archives management has the potential to offer significant benefits. A successful business case for digital archives investment is most likely to involve this combination of risks and benefits – 'carrot and stick'. For example, the risk of failing to provide access to modern records in accordance with existing access polices, has potential to be addressed with investment in digital infrastructure, which could lead to vastly improved access to a remote and global audience. Opening up access to unique, archive assets in this way can provide brand-enhancing benefits to an organisation. In another example, it might be possible to highlight the operational risk of poorly regulated storage on standard network drives that is making it difficult for the archivists to retrieve information effectively. The introduction of well–managed storage, possibly with direct links to a well-structured archival catalogue, could bring significant efficiency gains by improving search results and reducing the time it takes to retrieve required records. Likewise, the preservation risks of fragile media storage can be mitigated with a server-based storage solution and robust disaster recovery back-ups. This is likely to be more dependable than traditional flood and fire defences for physical collections, which have been all too easily breached in natural disasters. By addressing risks, the organisation sometimes has the potential to vastly improve upon its current position.

The archivist should be prepared to articulate the risks and benefits in business terms in order to resonate with an audience, which may not be familiar with the technicalities of digital archives management. Simply repeating that the current set-up is not 'OAIS compliant' may be understood by fellow archivists, but it is unlikely to resonate with senior executives who hold the purse strings. Naturally, the business case is also likely to be dependent on the success of wider, ongoing advocacy initiatives of the archives service. If there is no overall appreciation of the relevance and benefit of the service within the company, it may make more sense to start with a general profile-raising programme, before then going on to seek for specific investment in digital archives.

Working with stakeholders

The risk and benefit analysis must be driven by a thorough understanding of the strategic aims of the organisation as a whole, and a clear vision of the long-term objectives of the archive service. It should also take into account the views of all relevant stakeholders. The list is likely to include at least some of the following functions or individuals:

- Line managers and budget approvers.
- IT function.
- Records managers and other information management professionals in the business.
- Risk function, particularly regarding information security.
- Legal and compliance function.
- Procurement function, if the project is going to involve vendors.
- Collaborative areas such as marketing, brand and communications.
- Internal users of the archive service.
- External users of the archive service such as advertising agencies and researchers.

Some stakeholders will have a vested interest in backing the project and their voices could lend crucial support to the business case. In many organisations a key step will be to find a project sponsor who understands and supports the project's aims. This individual will need to be willing, and in the right position in the organisation, to be able to champion the initiative and influence eventual decision-makers.

There will be other stakeholders who have the power to block or stall the venture. Their backing will also be vital and it is crucial they are consulted at an early stage to ensure the project does not rely on assumptions, which later turn out to be incorrect. For example, there is little point spending time considering open source options and internal development, if an organisation's IT strategy demands that out-of-the-box, vendor-supported software is deployed. Similarly, a timetable that fails to take into account the need to address potential risk or legal concerns will inevitably prove unrealistic in the long run.

Alongside users, IT is probably the most important relationship of all in terms of stakeholder management, since their level of cooperation has the potential to make or break the entire project. It is therefore critical that a common understanding is established between the archivists and IT professionals. Ideally this should get underway during the very early research stages, as recommended earlier in this chapter.

Information security (IS) has been a growing area of risk management concern within the corporate digital environment. IS departments are typically concerned about the risks caused by factors such as unauthorised access, disclosure and modification of data or systems. The introduction of a system for the storage, processing and management of digital archives is likely to be of considerable interest, even if IS has never previously registered concerns over the management of physical archives. These hazards are inevitably perceived as more menacing in the digital environment compared with the paper environment, and periodic, well-publicised IT breaches in major corporations only serve to compound that. Many of their fears will be shared wholeheartedly by archivists and indeed, it could be argued that archivists have long been practicing a form of information security risk management in their role as guardians of valuable records. This is therefore an important part of the organisation with which to engage. Close collaboration between the archivist and the IS department should strengthen the outcome of the project overall.

Having said that, in many large corporations, the IS risk appetite is often so low that it can lead to a myriad of rigid rules and time-consuming regulations. The legal department is likely to be working in tandem with IS and will add further precautions to ensure the project also follows the letter of the law. Their combined involvement may impact on the project in a number of ways. For example:

- The construction of user profiles to determine access to the system (for example access to the digital archives themselves and other aspects such as administration and test servers).
- The categorisation of digital archives based on content, in order to determine which user roles may access them.
- The acceptance or rejection of particular file formats or systems in accordance with the company's approved 'white lists' or 'black lists'.
- Approval or refusal to utilise cloud storage.
- Determining the geographical location of hosted servers.
- Approval or refusal to transfer records cross-border.
- Selection of the vendor, based on the vendor's own IS standards.
- Approval or refusal to share data with vendors during testing and any migration support.
- The requirement for internal service agreements if the system is going to be providing a service across different entities within a group of companies.

It is difficult to offer specific advice about the types of IS issues that will arise since it depends on the nature of the business and the information held. In preparation for engagement with these areas, it is wise to ensure that the archive service has clear, up-to-date policies and procedures – particularly with regards to the collection and appraisal of records, and their storage, security and accessibility.

Presenting a business case

Having completed the steps above, it should now be possible to develop a high-level business case to take things to the next stage. Early research and peer benchmarking should have opened up ideas on the aims and aspirations of the project. An initial survey should have established current problems and future concerns. Detailed analysis of risks and benefits should have explored the project's scope and priorities. Stakeholder consultation should have refined the scope and the ranking of those priorities. Of course, in the fast-moving corporate environment, there is a good chance the process will not have run nearly as smoothly as this. Best laid plans will need to be flexible and unexpected opportunities should always be seized upon. However, one should not underestimate the time and energy that needs to be spent on these preliminary steps, in order to develop a truly robust business case.

A high-level business case will not contain answers to all the problems. But it should articulate the overall direction of the project; identify logistical and resource considerations;

and set a clear brief for all involved – thereby enabling the key decision-makers to assess its feasibility. The document is likely to include many of the following pieces of information:

- Outline of the proposal.
- Strategic drivers, based on identified risks and benefits.
- Key deliverables and measurable success criteria.
- Any known assumptions, dependencies and risks.
- Budget, agreed or requested, covering both project costs and longer term running costs.
- Timetable.
- Project sponsor.
- Project manager, who may be drawn from outside the archive team, depending on the scope of the project.
- Project team, which will inevitably include IT and the archive team, but may also include other stakeholders such as business analysts and test managers.
- Training requirements, which may be in the field of digital archives management itself, or perhaps the development of project management skills within the archives team.
- Next steps.

A business case template, case studies and supporting guidance can be found in the DPC's Digital Preservation Business Case Toolkit.[5]

Producing detailed requirements

Assuming a robust business case is made and the green light is given – the project will now be able to start defining its requirement in more detail. This tends to be an IT-driven procedure in most business settings and there are likely to be formal document templates, which need to be completed by the archivist in collaboration with IT professionals. A formal detailed requirements document is particularly important if the project is going to be engaging with external vendors in a Request for Information (RFI) and Request for Proposal (RFP) process. But this exercise can still be extremely valuable if the project is going down the route of internal development or open source technology. If the business does not have templates in place it is possible to seek examples online or via project management training courses.

The detailed requirements phase requires the clear articulation of every deliverable that the archivist wishes to achieve through the new digital archives solution. It may be tempting to rush through this stage to get the project moving quickly. However, this is usually a never-to-be-repeated opportunity for the archivists to articulate all that they need from this new system. It forms the basis for all subsequent discussion and agreements. Therefore, it is crucial that the archivists set aside time and resources in order to tease out all the requirements – and to ensure they are communicated and understood in sufficient detail by the entire project team.

A detailed requirements document must provide a comprehensive wish list, which is then broken down into varying degrees of priority (for example High/Medium/Low). This is essential in order to establish that the scope of the project will be technically feasible. Priority settings will need to weigh up the benefits gained, against the technical complexity of the request. Compromise is inevitable and some 'must haves' may need to be relegated to 'nice to haves' if the project is to progress on time and on budget. There are likely to be some deliverables that, on further consideration, are dropped entirely or at least put to one side for the time being. This should not cause too much disappointment since the very process of documenting an expansive wish list for the perfect solution is likely to be time well spent. A truly comprehensive list of requirements should help IT colleagues to 'future-proof' the system by ensuring that the initial design or product will not compromise future development, if more resources become available, or technological advancements introduce new functionality on the market. For example, it may not be immediately feasible to link to an EDRM system, but that can remain an aspiration for the future when there is more budget or time; or there may not be preservation paths identified for certain file formats at the time of implementation, but these migration options may be developed subsequently.

It is good practice to separate 'functional' and 'non-functional' requirements. Functional requirements (FRs) focus on things that the system should do; its behaviours (for example ingest, storage and metadata capture functions; the application of authentication levels to facilitate access; reporting functions). These are most likely to be defined by the archivist. Non-functional requirements (NFRs) focus on the way the system performs, its quality attributes (for example performance response time; capacity for concurrent users; recoverability arrangements). These are likely to be highly dependent on the IT environment of the organisation but the archivist should familiarise themselves with the content and ensure any concerns are addressed. Some examples of functional requirements are given in Table 10.8.

Computer software is logic-driven and relies on known causes and effects to drive transactions, whilst traditional archival methodology is nuanced and involves significant human judgement to carry out key tasks such as appraisal and cataloguing. It can therefore be extremely challenging to have to develop consistent, programmable archival workflows for a digital archives solution. Consequently the involvement of an independent expert, such as a business analyst, may be beneficial to help map out these functional requirements with sufficient clarity and flexibility.

A business analyst could help to analyse and document each precise step in a workflow to ensure the process is valid, comprehensive and as efficient as possible. Their fresh pair of eyes on archival management issues can add considerable rigour to the archivist's way of thinking about a potential digital archives solution. For example, the deletion of a digital record from archival storage may seem a relatively straightforward prospect at first glance. After all, appraisal and de-accessioning are common practice with physical archives. But a business analyst will be pressing for step-by-step answers on questions such as:

- How is the correct file identified and verified?
- Who takes the action to delete the file in the system?
- Is an approver required before the deletion can be completed?
- Can safeguards prevent deletion if the file is subject to legal holds?
- Can the action be applied to more than one record at once, and is there a limit to how many at once?
- What confirmation is received if the deletion is carried out successfully?
- What happens if the deletion is not carried our successfully?

Table 10.8 Outline of how a functional requirements document might be organised

FR/NFR reference number	Requirement	Priority	Vendor response	Outcome
FR 1	Storage: area must be secure and not lose digital records or compromise their integrity, irrespective of medium or system failure.	Critical	Out-of-the-box functionality	Delivered
FR 2	Thumbnails: system should, where possible, provide thumbnail images of digital copies and born-digital records, as users are browsing/searching in the system.	Important	Requires minor customisation	Delivered
FR 3	Records management compatibility: system should have the ability to interface with existing EDRM to enable automated and secure transfer of born-digital records to archives at the end of their agreed retention period.	Desirable	Requires significant customisation	Deferred to a later phase
NFR 1	Support: system must be supported during implementation and for a defined period after implementation schedule.	Critical	Included as standard in contract	Delivered
NFR 2	Concurrent usage: the system should be able to handle increased capacity of up to 20 users.	Desirable	Additional licences need to be acquired	Deferred to a later phase

• Can the deletion trigger an automated update to archival metadata in the corresponding catalogue entry?
• If the file was deleted by mistake can it be retrieved from back up during a temporary 'cool-off' period?

This close analysis should also factor in the differing needs of all potential users of the system, and the potential uses of data and assets from the system, which may extend beyond the system itself (pushing catalogue data through to a separate online catalogue, for example). Unless background knowledge of users and usage (in OAIS terms – a 'designated community') is assessed early, the process will fail before it has begun.

This level of detail will be essential if the solution is going to be a bespoke development, perhaps undertaken by the organisation's own IT department. Likewise, it is very important for any project going down the route of purchasing an off-the-shelf solution, where some level of customisation is being considered. It can even be beneficial when the solution is expected to be out-of-the-box software, since it allows the archivist to identify where it may be necessary to adapt current practice to fit the precise workflows programmed by the vendor. Plenty of projects will not have professional business analyst resources on board. Where this is the case the archivist would do well to familiarise themselves with this questioning mind-set and apply it as they are working through the detailed requirements.

If the archivist already has a potential system in mind, it will be very easy for that to influence how the detailed requirements process plays out. Certain functionality may be included or excluded accordingly. Be very wary of 'solutionising' in this way though, as it may lead to significant oversights. For example, there may be an intention to link an existing archive cataloguing system to a digital archives management system, with an assumption that all searching will continue to be carried out in the catalogue because that has performed sufficiently as a search engine to date. But what if the digital archives management system is able to provide additional or better search functionality across both physical and digital records? To avoid solutionising from the outset, the archivist should frame the requirement around the need for firm sophisticated search functionality across the platform, without specifying exactly how and where that functionality should play out – even if some initial ideas have been mapped out through business analysis. Similarly, and as highlighted earlier in this section, it is important to 'future-proof' the system as much as possible. A rigorous detailed requirements phase will see the archivist focused only on posing the problems (current and future), leaving the IT experts to offer up the potential solutions. There is always the possibility that IT professionals will come up with a totally new and effective approach to a problem, which is unanticipated by an archivist caught up with traditional theories and practice.

Going to tender

Once the requirements have been drawn up, debated and decided, full attention can turn to finding the preferred solution. If the project is going out to external vendors for tender there are likely to be formal processes in places, which must be followed. This may begin with an initial Request for Information (RFI) stage to scope out potential suppliers, before moving on to an in-depth Request for Proposal (RFP) stage with shortlisted contenders. It will be important for the archivist to understand, and comply with, any vendor management guidelines set down by the business (for example clear identification of roles and responsibilities in the process, following official channels of communication). However, generally speaking, this stage of the project is likely to be led by IT, with legal and/or procurement colleagues, who will have far more experience of the questions that need to be considered and the negotiations that need to be undertaken, to secure the best solution with the resources available.

The detailed requirements document will provide vendors with a clear list of expectations, which they need to respond to during an RFP. This will begin a process whereby their vision is combined with the aims and aspirations that the archivist has drawn up so far. The vendors should be keen to establish a thorough understanding of the requirements; the digital records that the solution will need to handle (for example formats, volume, size and structural organisation) and the general working practices of the archive service (for example user roles, access rights and controls and integration with other systems in the organisation). Making time to meet with vendors in person can therefore be time well spent in order to start building the relationship. Good rapport and professional respect will be key to a successful project. It is also worth asking for meetings with vendors' existing clients in order to gather their feedback on both the solution and the vendors themselves.

Responses to each requirement can be scored in order to evaluate vendors' ability to meet the brief and differentiate between contenders. Written responses as opposed to practical demonstrations of the technology – or promises that certain functionality is in the pipeline – should not be taken at face value. There should be detailed discussion to ensure there is common understanding of the problem and to check that the proposed solution really does meet the need of that requirement. Any reliance on future development may need to be covered separately in contractual negotiations.

A large part of the conversation will also need to take place around the IT environment itself (for example server set-ups, storage configuration, user recognition and security). At this point, the archivist is likely to have to take a back seat and depend on IT colleagues to make recommendations and take the right decisions. Once again, this reiterates the need for a strong working relationship and plenty of trust between the archivist and IT professionals to drive this project. There will also be a significant reliance on legal and/or procurement colleagues to nail down the finer details of the contract. This has the potential to be a protracted process, particularly if the solution is going to involve elements of customisation or a combination of different vendors. A generous allowance should be included in the project timetable accordingly. Crucially, towards the end of this process and before a final contract is signed, both parties should document a detailed description of how the project is expected to proceed, including considerations such as:

- How the proposed technical solution meets the requirements.
- Project management methodology including roles and responsibilities.
- Testing and acceptance methodology.
- Change control methodology.
- Timetable.
- Costings.
- Provision for system training.
- Post-implementation support.

This documentation will still be relevant even if the solution is going to be developed internally, rather than supplied by a vendor.

Development and specification

To begin the development phase of a digital archives project it is important for all parties to agree a series of milestones with clear delivery dates. This timetable will enable everyone, including the archivist, to plan their resources accordingly. The development schedule will have quite precise stages with quite distinct activities and inputs. The whole experience might be regarded as a bit like a tennis match with information being passed back and fore. The tight scheduling means that staff need to be available to ensure the project progresses smoothly, understand the questions being asked and respond promptly. This is especially true if sections need approval from senior management. Developers often work in tightly integrated schedules so even a brief delay can set the project back significantly. Throughout this section, the term 'developers' refers to both in-house IT staff and external vendors.

The following sequence of events is typical of many system deployments, but the stages and weightings will inevitably vary from project to project. The technical infrastructure overview may be a very straightforward process, for example, if the system is being developed by internal IT developers who are entirely familiar with the relevant set-up.

Likewise, there will be no building or customising of components, if a totally out-of-the-box solution has been selected from the options available:

- **Review of requirements (5%)** – Harmonisation of the original requirements with what is technically and financially obtainable.
- **Technical infrastructure overview (5%)** – Survey by the developers of the internal IT infrastructure; identifying necessary hardware and how it will be installed.
- **Building of new components (30%)** – The core of the development work. The building of new processes that are key to the functional requirements.
- **Customisation of existing components (20%)** – Development work customising existing out-of-the-box or open-source tools.
- **Internal testing (10%)** – Developer-led testing to provide quality assurance on their work.
- **Installation of test system (5%)** – Many IT departments choose to install a separate test environment on a test server. This ensures that testing and modifications during the development stage are performed on a system that is not exposed to the business' main IT infrastructure. It also allows for changes to be made more quickly due to less stringent security procedures being in place.
- **User testing (15%)** – The test period that allows for examination of the system and ensure that it functions according to the agreed requirements.
- **Production installation (5%)**
- **Pre-launch activities (5%)** – These will include production installation checks, user training, agreement of a support model, etc.

This process can often involve a lot of waiting time as development and testing takes place behind the scenes. Weeks may go by without having any tangible progress to view. During this time it is important to request regular updates with the developers and then disseminate key project developments to stakeholders. These updates should include positives and negatives, reasons for any delays, and perhaps even milestones completed ahead of a deadline! Keeping stakeholders in the loop will allow them to see the complexity of the project and hopefully avoid undue surprise or concern if deadlines slip. The archivist should be prepared to encounter and manage delays during the project. Be pragmatic about project disruptions and fully understand the reasons behind them. Armed with all the facts, an archivist is going to have a better understanding of the cause and potential resolutions, and can therefore apply appropriate judgement on how best to address the problem. Coping with development changes mid-project is also a potential risk that will have to be dealt with. Developers may start work according to the points outlined in the requirements document, only to find later down the line that the design is not technically feasible. Resolving these problems typically involves returning to the original drivers behind a requirement in order to review the implications of potential tweaks to the design. Real stalemates may prompt deferred delivery or even cancellation of that particular requirement altogether. Adaptability and openness should help to deal with problems swiftly, with the final system delivering on expectations, albeit potentially via different routes than originally anticipated. Adaptability in this stage is to be praised, but the archivist should be mindful that this is the point in the project that the dangers of increasing the original scope should be resisted. Developers could return with comments and suggestions for functionality that might be beyond the initial requirements.

It may be tempting to think that expanding the scope of what the system will do will offer some 'quick wins' and save future development costs later on, but with new features come new delays, new compromises and potential new costs. Justifying these delays to stakeholders might be more difficult given that they are outside the project's initial scope.

The end of the development phase should result in the production of a detailed specification document by the developers. This should fully describe the functionality of the planned digital archive system, including planned customisations and configurations. It should also explain any interactions and adaptions required of existing infrastructure. If using an external vendor the specification document has the added importance of being regarded, in most cases, as the contractual description of the system that the project must deliver. Ultimately the testing phase of the project will be based on the functionality of the digital archive system as described in this document, therefore it is important that all parties agree upon its contents.

Testing

Once development work has been completed and a test version of the system is available, the archivist should begin carrying out a thorough regime of tests to ensure the installation meets what was agreed upon in the specification document. This is therefore an opportunity to identify and fix problems that will affect daily usage. If an external vendor is involved then it is also a stage that exists before the support agreement for live use starts and, crucially, will be before final payment for the system is delivered. Therefore, identified errors are likely to be taken more seriously and responded to more quickly. For those opting for a cloud-based vendor solution this should be a shorter process as testing of the virtually hosted applications that a cloud system will offer will be the responsibility of the vendor. In these circumstances testing should focus on any customisation that has been configured for your organisation via the cloud-hosted system.

When planning for the test phase there are some important steps to be taken, which the rest of this section will discuss in greater depth. A detailed test plan should encapsulate the following areas:

- Setting test objectives.
- Choosing how many test stages there will be.
- Scheduling of the testing period and assigning resources for executing test scripts.
- Writing test scripts.
- Agreeing defect management.

Before entering the testing phase it is important to confirm testing expectations (what is going to be achieved). These objectives should be circulated within the testing team, internal IT staff, and, if desired, to external vendors. The list will vary from project to project, but should be tailored to ensure key areas of the requirements document have been met. Each area should be analysed for specific business risks. These risks should then be graded in terms of severity and appropriate weighting assigned in terms of the number and rigour of test cases that are applied to that area. Objectives should not be limited to archivist's requirements, but must extend to other key stakeholders in the project – particularly the IT and IS functions. The following objectives would be typical for many digital archives testing phases:

- **Technical infrastructure must support the solution**. Prior to testing, development may have taken place offline from the infrastructure that will ultimately host the system (for example on an external vendor's server rather than on an internal server behind the company's firewall, or a third party cloud storage set-up). This phase is therefore likely to be the first time the system runs on the correct, technical infrastructure. This must therefore be thoroughly tested to ensure that response times are adequate for the workload and security requirements demanded of it.
- **Expected volumes of data, and numbers of users, can be supported**. This is a technical objective and is essential for ensuring that the scale of the digital archive system can cope with its expected volume and usage. Excellent preservation software is of little use if there is not the capacity to handle the large volume of digital records, and the large file sizes, that will actually be flowing through it. Users should certainly flag slow response times, given that digital archive systems are meant to bring with them efficiency gains.
- **Functionality meets functional and non-functional requirements**. Clearly one of the key objectives in testing is to hold the solution to account against what was agreed during the development and specification phase of the project This is, in essence, holding the developers to account for the core work that has been produced.
- **Access permissions work correctly and meet security criteria**. If the testing process is unable to demonstrate that the system can securely manage data, then it is unlikely to be allowed to launch as a live solution.
- **The data stored meets security criteria**. This applies to the integrity of data stored on the digital archive system (for example, changes to data are recorded and logged in an audit trail).
- **Internal interfaces work correctly**. Many digital archive systems will be based around multiple components (for example, user authentication may be dependent on a company directory system, or there may be a link to a company EDRM or separate archive catalogue). This objective is designed to ensure that the test phase will cover the inter-connecting and synchronisation of relevant systems.
- **External interfaces (both input and output) work correctly**. This objective is designed to ensure that what the users of the system see and are able to access meet security requirements stipulated in the specification document.

Most IT testing strategies will have at least three test stages: systems integration testing (SIT), user acceptance testing (UAT) and operational acceptance testing (OAT). Pursuing these phases will ensure that testing covers key areas of functionality, integration with existing systems and the ability to work in an operational environment.

- **The systems integration test** verifies the overall system design, demonstrating that it operates as specified and that it interacts effectively with existing business systems. It is an 'end-to-end' test of functionality and is best carried out by an independent team, such as the IT department and it will likely involve the archives staff. It should be relatively brief and will not include in-depth test cases.
- **The user acceptance test** addresses the whole project and the business processes that it supports (namely ingest, storage, preservation and access of digital records). It validates the business use, processes and user documentation, which should be in draft form by this stage. It ensures that the system is fit for use by end users. UAT

is usually managed by a sample of the users (including the archivists) as it requires knowledge of both system design, functional requirements and the specification document. This phase is crucial as it represents the completion of functional testing. Test scripts should be carefully designed to test the requirements and all the end-to-end workflow processes that the system offers.

- **The operational acceptance test** is usually the final test phase. This tests underlying processes that support the availability of the system within the business's wider IT infrastructure. It is usually performed by IT and ensures non-functional requirements are met (for example, bandwidth, security, disaster recovery, back up).

Effective testing can be a lengthy process, particularly if the system has been built from scratch, or contains a high degree of customisation. It is therefore important to be realistic when setting the schedule and budgeting for the resources required to complete it efficiently and successfully. When assigning a schedule it is necessary to estimate testing times for activities within the system. The project team should have had access to some form of development system and consequently have a rough idea of how long key functions take to execute within the system. It is important to factor in delays as it would be almost unheard of to test a complex infrastructure, which most digital archive systems will comprise, without finding any errors or divergences from agreed requirements. The schedule is a vital component since it can be referred to when pushing for any defect resolutions once testing us underway. It will also help to keep stakeholders updated with the latest news on the progress of the digital project and will ensure that it is easier to justify delays that are experienced.

Writing test scripts is the process of designing a series of scenarios ('scripts') that examine all the functional and non-functional requirements that were agreed upon during the development and specification stage. The testers (likely to include the archivists) should guide the production of the scripts, but also take the advice of developers to ensure that their workings are realistic and practical. Tests are usually built around 'inputs' or user actions (for example, running an ingest workflow or running a search formula) and 'outputs' or results of an input (for example, an ingest workflow completes/fails, or search result are found/not found). For each input, the following points should be considered for the script the tester must follow: the value of the input, whether it is a valid or invalid input, and the precision and accuracy of the input. The order, method and timing of each test should also be included in the script as there are likely to be some tests that require other tests to have been completed, prior to their own execution. For example, it will not be possible to successfully search for an ingested record, if the script to ingest that record into the system has not already completed first. Against each input, the required or expected output should be specified. The script should consider: the value of the output, the precision and accuracy of the output, how the system should react if the input is invalid, (for example, what error message should be produced). In planning scripts, the testers also need to consider all the test data required for each test. Testing should be representative of the full range of data and resources that the archive will handle, including faulty or problematic sources. In principle, the system should detect these flaws and resolve or report them. Test scripts will likely have multiple steps and should be designed to be easy to follow. Step-by-step scripts not only make test execution easier, they will also be clearer when identifying the point that a test might fail, allowing for quicker defect management response times. Many tests will have prerequisites that have to be met prior to their execution, detailed scripts allow these prerequisites to be clearly marked and reduce the risk of unnecessary failures. In addition, they can later be adapted to provide the basis for a detailed user guide, which will be needed for the system's live launch. Table 10.9 provides an example of a test script used by HSBC Archives during a UAT phase for their digital archives system.

Table 10.9 Extract from part of the test script from the HSBC UAT scripts

Description for details tab	Step name	Step description	Expected results execution risk	Script
Objective – to create a new workflow context that allows archivists to carry out various preservation actions on records stored within SDB (subject to relevant access rights). User is logged into SDB with Admin User rights.	Step 1	Login to Digital Archive System. Open the Preservation tab from main menu		Medium
	Step 2	Click on the Manage tab	The system will then display the Define Workflow Context dialog box	
	Step 3	To create a new workflow context, select a workflow definition from the drop-down list and then press the Add button.		
	Step 4	Complete the define workflow context box as follows – Name – Preservation Workflow Description – Test preservation workflow for UAT Email address – test.user@test.com Ensure that the following two boxes are ticked: – Send email notification on error – Allow concurrent workflow instances All other dialogue boxes should be left unticked. Once this information has been entered, click on the Create button		
	Step 5	Back on the manage tab, click on the tick box beside the newly created workflow to activate it	Workflow should appear on the Start tab of the preservation menu	

Another key area to plan is the policies surrounding defect management and entrance/exit criteria. Entrance criteria are conditions that should be met before commencing execution of a particular test phase. Exit criteria are conditions to be met to signify the completion of a particular test phase.

Entrance criteria are key in preventing premature testing that will most likely result in defects (for example, if parts of the system have not been built, or connections have not been made to related systems). Points for consideration may include:

- Some form of user training should have taken place for the test team.
- Data that was used during any preparatory development should have been removed. This will ensure that there is a 'clean sheet' on which to run test scenarios.
- The developers should provide confirmation of delivery of all the functionality that was agreed upon during development and specification. Testing will confirm that these deliverables actually work, but confirmation of their presence in the system should be sought – it isn't possible to test what isn't there.
- Test scripts should all be documented and agreed, formulated as described in the earlier section above.
- Ensure that the test environment (which may differ from the development environment) is configured correctly and access rights have been provided to all applicable members of the test team.
- Ensure all test data has been defined, generated and made available, as required by the test scripts.
- It may also be helpful to generate a traceability matrix to verify that the functionality specified at the beginning of the development stage has been appropriately tested in the delivered software. This exercise allows the archivist to consider how they are going to record the results of tests.

In an effective test plan it is also crucial to agree how the developers will manage defects. It is highly unlikely that everything within a test system will be working according to the expectations and agreements reached during the development and specification. Therefore it is important to establish how defects will be classified, what is the total failure threshold for each defect classification (for example how many minor defects is it acceptable for the system to have to still be considered to have passed the testing phase?) and what is the minimum expectation for how each defect type is handled and fixed.

A defect classification scheme is typically used to help formulate an agreement with the developers. There will be many different classes of defects, from some that stop the system working completely, to minor issues such as text rendering in the wrong position. The number of serious defects that the archivist should be prepared to accept would normally be zero, but there can be negotiation on how many less urgent defects are required to be fixed by the developers before exit criteria is met. See Table 10.10 for an example of a test defect classification scheme.

The end of testing brings about the acceptance phase. The test plan should clearly illustrate the exit criteria required. Points to consider may include:

- That exit of the test phase will only occur if the numbers of unfixed defects during acceptance testing do not exceed the thresholds specified in the classification scheme.
- All test scenarios should have been executed according to the test plan and any deviations documented and approved by all parties.
- All defects should have received a final disposition. This means that there is no outstanding work due on any defect that has been raised. Either the developer has fixed it or will not fix it during the test period or the tester has agreed to close the defect for some other unspecified reason.
- Sign-off should be obtained from designated stakeholders indicating test completion. It might be necessary to include an agreement to talk to key stakeholders before

Table 10.10: Example of a test defect classification scheme

Classification	Description of error	Acceptance threshold
Critical (A)	A problem that causes total system or significant failure endangering business.	0
Urgent (B)	A facility can be used without major impediment but cannot be used in full operational service without corrections or improvements to specific areas of operation. The problem has a business impact.	5
Normal (C)	A problem that does not prevent the use of a facility in operational service or for which a locally identified cure or circumvention is available.	25
Minor (D)	A problem that is deemed to be within the specification but could be improved as an enhancement. All documentation and text errors (help text, field text and so on).	No limit

ending testing to allow for any concerns outside of the testing team to be raised, before it is no longer possible to raise development queries.
- There is likely to be a set of actions that have to happen immediately after testing. For example, the development team agrees to immediately proceed with installation and loading activities within the live production environment (putting the information in the system that will be used from the beginning – for example any existing digital records, or importing existing catalogue metadata).

The test phase is likely to be the most demanding phase of the project for the archivists as they should be intrinsically linked to all of the testing process. This is the last stage of the project to raise defects and insist on fixes prior to launch, and it is much easier to make modifications to a system that is not live. Planning is absolutely crucial. Create a plan that maps out the objectives, test phases, a clear schedule, test scripts, processes for dealing with defects and key entrance and exit criteria. This will allow for stakeholders to stay well informed and expectations to be clearly understood.

Going live: implementation

Implementing a digital archive system, or 'going live' as it is often referred to, is the stage at which a digital archive project is finally used by its intended audience. It marks the stage that the product is released to users and the system should function to support BAU (business as usual) archival activities, namely providing a means to ingest, store, preserve and provide access to digital records. Ultimately this is the stage of the project that key stakeholders will have been waiting for and the launch is a time to promote the system and highlight all the benefits you originally outlined when making the business case. Launching the system, however, is a stage that cannot be taken lightly and significant planning must occur in order for it to proceed smoothly. This section will cover the important launch activities that should take place both prior to your 'go live date' and in the months following.

Before launch, it is important to establish support level agreements with all parties that will be providing support to the system (for example, external vendors, internal IT operations or a combination of the two). A detailed service level agreement (SLA) is necessary to ensure the smooth maintenance of the system and should provide a clear chain of action to follow when errors within the system occur. This may have already been discussed as part of any contract negotiations if the project went out to tender. Now is the time to document and finalise the arrangements. Key considerations include:

- **Categorisation of defects/issues**. Similar to the defect classification of UAT issues, the support agreement should provide an outline of how defects are categorised. These categories should be organised based on how the defect affects the running of the digital archive system. For example, the most serious category would be reserved for defects classified as an incident that causes significant, or even total system failure, which endangers the business (such as data loss).
- **Response times and availability of support**. Wait times for general support (for example, answers to questions about functionality) and response/resolution times for all defect types need to be agreed. This is particularly important if external vendors are involved. The archivist will need to ask questions such as whether the support team are located in the same time zone as their office hours, and if not, what are the hours of support coverage.
- **Areas of the system covered by support**. Clarity will be needed on exactly what is covered under the support arrangement. Is it simply issues with the software, or is the underlying technical infrastructure of the system supported?
- **Escalation measures**. A senior point of contact will be required for both parties (users and system providers) so that matters can be escalated if necessary. These points of contact should be senior people in both areas, who do not have day-to-day responsibilities for system use or maintenance, but are used to resolving IT concerns between two different parties (for example, an IT relationship manager and a vendor's customer services manager).
- **Support divisions (internal/external)**. If using an external vendor to provide your digital archive system, it is important to understand the demarcation lines between use of external and internal support mechanisms. There are likely to be some issues that should be handled internally due to data security reasons as well as internal knowledge of the infrastructure that supports the digital archive system. Whilst other issues will need to be primarily dealt with by the vendor.
- **Contact procedures**. The method by which support enquiries are raised should be defined. Is there an issue resolution system that will be used to log faults? Should communication in the first instance be via telephone or email?
- **Support term**. Where applicable, it is also important to establish the exact duration, and associated fees, of the support agreement.

Training the users, meeting needs and managing expectations

Whereas tools, technologies and systems can absorb huge quantities of attention, the only meaningful measure of success in the longer term will be the extent to which a digital archive solution is adopted by the intended users. The IT industry is littered with stories of ideal systems carefully designed and scrupulously engineered that failed because there was too little input from users at the start, too little consideration during development, and too little effort to introduce them at the end. Even the most robust system can fall foul of user-resistance, under-deployment or unmanaged expectations. Fundamentally, introducing a new system to a work place is a change and managing change can be tricky.

Much of the process so far – especially stakeholder analysis, requirement gathering, user acceptance testing – is designed to ensure that users are formally represented and informed about the project. A communications plan may be required to keep users informed on progress and key dates, ensuring that their needs are met and their expectations are managed. Towards the end of the project – before or immediately after launch – this will move to a new and potentially intensive phase of training to support adoption. Training of users and administrators is vital.

Archivists on the project team are likely to have experienced some training on the system via the development and testing stages of the project. But there may be other end-users, not part of the project team, who now need to receive training. The archivist will need to decide whether they feel that their team is experienced enough with the digital archive system to provide the training sessions, or whether they will need support from the developers. Looking ahead, the archivist may have to provide training updates to users, and new user training, throughout the life of the system. So if external training is used in the first instance, it is often worth learning from this session to then develop in-house resources for future deployment. Regardless of who provides the training, the following points should feature in an effective training programme for the life of the system to ensure all users are familiar with how the system works, and how key activities are executed.

- **Create a user guide**. Developers should have provided some form of user instruction manual with delivery of the system. This often is not enough, or is not in a format that many users will understand. It is crucial that a digital archive system has an accompanying, user-friendly guide that provides instruction on how to complete different tasks that constitute key functions (namely ingest, preservation and access). This should be the primary source for all users when they need step-by-step instructions. Few archivists possess hands-on experience of digital archives management and this guide will therefore provide a reassuring safety net. Preparing the document may take time, but it is very likely to reduce the level of individual queries post launch. The production of a user guide is also a key element of risk mitigation and future planning. It should be continually improved and updated to reflect future developments; and it offers an important future-proofing tool in the event of key digital archives personnel leaving the business.
- **View training as an ongoing process**. Training for a complex digital archive system, that will likely receive many updates throughout its shelf life, should be regarded as a constant process. In the initial training sessions for new users, the archivist should not be intending to provide instruction on all parts and functions of the system, but rather laying the building blocks of the key aspects of the system. Further training should then be provided in the weeks, months and years ahead to build expert knowledge in the user. Providing too much information in the early training sessions can make the system seem inaccessible and overwhelming.
- **Targeted training sessions**. Training sessions should be precise and to the point. An archivist managing the digital archive system will know their users, not all of

them will require knowledge of every area of the system. Training should be sub-divided into modules focusing on key areas of the system. Users should then be assigned to the most relevant modules based on their role.

- **Refresher training**. Training should be refreshed where necessary. Just because a user has completed initial training and has not subsequently asked for help, doesn't mean that they are necessarily up to speed. If the learning isn't put into frequent practice it can be easily forgotten.
- **Use of multiple media to conduct training**. Whilst it is a good idea to conduct introductory training sessions face-to-face if possible (due to the advantages of being able to monitor users as they complete the training), subsequent training could potentially be delivered remotely via webinars, online presentations, through setting users 'homework' on a development system or by creating videos that show users how to complete various actions. Recorded webinars or training videos, for example, can be distributed and digested at the users' convenience. This means that the trainers do not have to run multiple sessions for different trainees, and trainees can complete the learning at their own pace.

It is important to keep users aware of the projected 'go-live' date and the fact there may be some set-up work for them to complete, such as user registration or software download activities. Between the end of testing and launch there is likely to be a series of checks that need to be performed to ensure that the final installation is functioning as expected, plus key tasks to undertake to ensure all users have appropriate access (for example, password set ups, assigning security groups to different users).

Up and running: launch day and beyond

When all pre-launch activities and checks have been completed the archivist can move forward with their launch date for the digital archive system. This should be a day of celebration with as much internal promotion of the system as possible, after all this day marks the culmination of a huge amount of hard work – from the initial requirements stage, through development and testing, to actual launch within the business. Key stakeholders, such as senior managers and project sponsors should be informed. Key participants in the project should be thanked for their contributions. It may also be appropriate to mark the launch by sharing the project's goals with the wider archival community.

Post-launch the archivist and support teams should prepare themselves for minor issues that the system is likely to throw up when first exposed to mass use. The support agreement should ensure that these are dealt with in a consistent and smooth manner, but it is important to keep a record of the issues and press for speedy resolutions. Throughout the resolution process, the archivist should be pushing for regular updates and feeding these back to their users to ensure that they understand that any issues that they have found with the system have been taken seriously and measures are in place to rectify them.

Moving forward in the months and years ahead, the archivist may consider circulating regular updates to stakeholders regarding the system's progress and development (for example, new collections being opened up to greater access, or statistics demonstrating the growth of digital content that is being securely preserved). These updates can be used to reinforce the live, evolving nature of the system, so that stakeholders appreciate there will be need for further development in due course. Ideally this can be harnessed to ensure there is resource for future investment to keep pace with technological progress within the wider business, and to help tackle requirements that may have been dropped initially because of timetable or budget constraints. Other development priorities may also become apparent when observing how the system is used in its early life and identifying potential efficiency gains. Ideally, the digital archives programme will continue with the proactive development of a strategy for future improvements to the system (for example, enhancement of security, efficiency and access). The constantly evolving world of digital preservation will mean that there are always new strategies and technologies to research across the sector. There will also be opportunities for development within a business's own internal infrastructure, such as new systems coming online with the potential to plug into the digital archive. Once the system has launched much of the hard work and months of development and testing will be over – however the development of the archive's digital repository will have only just begun . . .

Conclusion

Digital archives are a challenge for any archivist. The complexity and sheer volume of digital records that need to be managed is daunting for starters, whilst the profound dependency on IT and IT colleagues can seem precarious in comparison with the solid bricks and mortar of a traditional repository. The business environment can certainly amplify and add to these concerns. Certain industries may present highly unusual and unstable file formats for preservation, and it can be notoriously difficult to justify IT resources in a corporate setting if you are unable to demonstrate tangible and immediate return on investment. Taking on the challenge will require a clear focus and resources over the long term. There is no once-and-for-all quick fix, and a truly sustainable digital archives programme is likely to need dedicated input by staff with a very specialist skill set.

With digital preservation an evolving practice, and the differing needs of individual sectors and institutions, there is certainly no single route to follow. Moreover, because IT changes so quickly, standards and definitions of best practice need to constantly adapt. It is important to start somewhere though. As demonstrated in this chapter, there are plenty of educational tools and training options to consider. There are also a host of small, practical steps to be taken, in order to avoid the dreaded digital black hole. These offer an ideal introduction to some of the key issues and help to pave the way for more ambitious projects looking to implement more rigorous digital archives management as 'business as usual'.

The key advice, as ever, is to understand and remain relevant to the wider aims of the organisation. Build relationships and consult with stakeholders along the way. Be open to – and willing to share – new ideas that may well challenge traditional archival theory and practice. Keep up-to-date with the latest developments in standards and research, and in the marketplace. As the industry grows, the vendor options should increase and costs should come down.

Now is an opportune moment to embrace the challenges and opportunities associated with digital preservation. Business archivists should articulate their requirements, transform their practice and help to lead the way. There is a clear need, an abundance of support, and a lively, welcoming community of practitioners out there with which to collaborate.

Acknowledgements

Thanks are due to Adrian Brown and Vicky Stretch for kindly commenting on the chapter and to Alison Turton for support and patience during its completion.

Notes

1   *Long Term Archiving and Retrieval (LOTAR)* website available at www.lotar-international.org [Accessed 3 September 2016].
2   Data Seal of Approval (DSA) website available at www.datasealofapproval.org/en/ [Accessed 3 September 2016].
3   See www.dptp.org [Accessed 19 August 2016].
4   For further information see Chapter 11.
5   Available at: http://wiki.dpconline.org/index.php?title=Digital_Preservation_Business_Case_Toolkit [Accessed 17 August 2016].

References

Becker, C., Antunes, G., Barateiro, J. and Vieira, R., 2011. A capability model for digital preservation: analysing concerns, constraints, capabilities and maturities. In: J. Borbinha, R. Buddharaju, C. Khoo, S. Sugimoto, S. Foo and A. Jatowt, eds., 2011. *8th international conference on preservation of digital objects: proceedings – iPRES 2011 – Singapore*, 1–4 November. Singapore, National Library of Singapore and Nanyang Technological University, 1–10 [online] Available at: https://phaidra.univie.ac.at/detail_object/o:294293 [Accessed 9 August 2016].

Bettivia, R. S., 2016. *Encoding power: the scripting of archival structures in digital spaces using the Open Archival Information System (OAIS) reference model*. Unpublished PhD Thesis, University of Illinois, Urbana. [pdf] Available at: https://dl.dropboxusercontent.com/u/39731228/Bettivia_Dissertation.pdf [Accessed 16 August 2016].

Brown, A. D., 2013. *Practical digital preservation: a how-to guide for organizations of any size*. London: Facet Publishing.

Center for Research Libraries (CRL)/Online Computer Library Center (OCLC), 2007. *Trustworthy repositories audit and certification: criteria and checklist*, [pdf] Available at: www.crl.edu/PDF/trac.pdf [Accessed 22 August 2016].

Consultative Committee for Space Data Systems Secretariat (CCSDS), 2012. *Reference model for an Open Archival Information System (OAIS): recommended practice*. Washington: Magenta Book. [pdf] Available at: http://public.ccsds.org/publications/archive/650x0m2.pdf [Accessed 8 August 2016].

Deutsches Institut für Normung (DIN), 2012. *DIN 31644. Information und dokumentation – kriterien für vertrauenswürdige digitale langzeitarchive*. Berlin: DIN.

Digital Preservation Coalition (DPC), 2016. *Digital preservation handbook*. Glasgow: DPC. [online] Available at: http://handbook.dpconline.org/ [Accessed 8 August 2016].

Dollar, C. M. and Ashley, L. J., 2014. *Assessing digital preservation capability using a maturity model process improvement approach*. [pdf] Available at: www.securelyrooted.com/s/DPCMM-White-Paper_Revised-April-2014.pdf [Accessed 9 August 2016].

Fanning, B., forthcoming. *Digital document preservation using PDF/A. DPC technology watch report 16–03*. [online] To be made available at: http://dx.doi.org/10.7207/twr16-03.

Gartner, R. and Lavoie, B., 2013. *Preservation metadata. DPC technology watch report 13–3*. 2nd ed. [online] Available at: http://dx.doi.org/10.7207/twr13-03 [Accessed 8 August 2016].

International Standards Organization (ISO), 2012. *ISO 16363:2012. Space data and information transfer systems – Audit and certification of trustworthy digital repositories*. Geneva: ISO.

Lavoie, B., 2014. *The Open Archival Information System (OAIS) reference model: introductory guide. DPC technology watch report 14–02*. 2nd ed. [online] Available at: http://dx.doi.org/10.7207/twr14-02 [Accessed 8 August 2016].

McHugh, A., Ross, S., Innocenti, P., Ruusalepp, R. and Hofman, H., 2008. Bringing self assessment home: repository profiling and key lines of enquiry within DRAMBORA. *International Journal of Digital Curation*, 3(2), pp. 130–142.

METS Editorial Board, 2010. *METS Metadata encoding and transmission standard: primer and reference manual*. Washington, DC: Library of Congress [online] Available at: www.loc.gov/standards/mets/METSPrimer.doc [Accessed 8 August 2016].

Moles, N. and Ross, S., 2013. *Digital curation framework briefing paper (D4.3)*. DigCurV Project. [pdf] Available at: www.digcur-education.org/eng/content/download/10837/166031/file/D4.3%20Briefing%20paper.pdf [Accessed 8 August 2016].

National Digital Stewardship Alliance (NDSA), 2013. *The NDSA levels of digital preservation: an explanation and uses*. [pdf] Available at: www.digitalpreservation.gov/documents/NDSA_Levels_Archiving_2013.pdf [Accessed 8 August 2016].

Pennock, M., 2013. *Web-archiving. DPC technology watch report 13–01*. [online] Available at: http://dx.doi.org/10.7207/twr13-01 [Accessed 8 August 2016].

PREMIS, 2015. *PREMIS data dictionary for preservation metadata*. Version 3.0. Washington, DC: Library of Congress. [pdf] Available at: www.loc.gov/standards/premis/v3/premis-3-0-final.pdf [Accessed 8 August 2016].

Research Libraries Group (RLG)/Online Computer Library Center (OCLC) Working Group on Digital Archive Attributes, 2002. *Trusted digital repositories. Attributes and responsibilities. An RLG–OCLC report*. Mountain View, California: RLG. [pdf] Available at: www.oclc.org/research/activities/past/rlg/trustedrep/repositories.pdf [Accessed 8 August 2016].

Rosenthal, D. S. H., 2014. *TRAC audit: lessons*. DSHR Blog. [online] Available at: http://blog.dshr.org/2014/08/trac-audit-lessons.html [Accessed 8 August 2016].

Seles, A., 2016. *The transferability of trusted digital repository standards to an East African context*. Unpublished PhD thesis, University College London. [pdf] Available at: http://discovery.ucl.ac.uk/1473881/1/Seles_Anthea_thesis.pdf [Accessed 8 August 2016].

Further reading

Digital Preservation is a fast-moving challenge and it is not possible to provide a complete guide in this one chapter. However, there is a vast body of literature available to provide more detailed insight on specific aspects of the topic.

Digital preservation overview

The following publications will assist readers seeking a more comprehensive insight into digital preservation:

Brown, A. D., 2013. *Practical digital preservation: a how-to guide for organizations of any size*. London: Facet Publishing.

Digital Preservation Coalition (DPC), 2016. *Digital preservation handbook*. Glasgow: DPC. [online] Available at: http://handbook.dpconline.org/ [Accessed 8 August 2016]. [Includes an extended glossary of key terms].

Planning and advocating digital preservation

The following publications will assist readers in planning their digital preservation actions and consider how they may be integrated into any given work environment:

Charlesworth, A. J., 2012. *Intellectual property rights and preservation. DPC technology watch report 12–02* [online] Available at: http://dx.doi.org/10.7207/twr12-02 [Accessed 8 August 2016].

John, J. L., 2012. *Digital forensics and preservation. DPC technology watch report 12–03.* [online] Available at: http://dx.doi.org/10.7207/twr12-03 [Accessed 8 August 2016].

Redwine, G., 2015. *Personal digital archiving. DPC technology watch report 15–01.* [online] Available at: http://dx.doi.org/10.7207/twr15-01 [Accessed 8 August 2016].

Todd, M., 2009. *File formats for preservation. DPC technology watch report 09–02.* [online] Available at: www.dpconline.org/component/docman/doc_download/375-file-formats-for-preservation [Accessed 8 August 2016].

Standards

The following provide a ready introduction to key standards in digital preservation:

Gartner, R. and Lavoie, B., 2013. *Preservation metadata. DPC technology watch report 13–3.* 2nd ed. [online] Available at: http://dx.doi.org/10.7207/twr13-03 [Accessed 8 August 2016].

Lavoie, B., 2014. *The Open Archival Information System (OAIS) reference model: introductory guide. DPC technology watch report 14–02.* 2nd edn. [online] Available at: http://dx.doi.org/10.7207/twr14-02 [Accessed 8 August 2016].

Preservation solutions by format

The following reports, all freely available, provide an advanced introduction to particular format-based preservation challenges:

Ball, A., 2013. *Preserving computer-aided design (CAD). DPC technology watch report 13–02* [online] Available at: http://dx.doi.org/10.7207/twr13-02 [Accessed 8 August 2016].

Beagrie, N., 2014. *Preservation trust and continuing access for e-journals. DPC technology watch report 13–04.* [online] Available at: http://dx.doi.org/10.7207/twr13-04 [Accessed 8 August 2016].

Day Thomson, S., 2016. *Preserving social media. DPC technology watch report 16–01* [online] Available at: http://dx.doi.org/10.7207/twr16-01 [Accessed 8 August 2016].

Day Thomson, S., 2016. *Preserving transactional data. DPC technology watch report 16–02* [online] Available at: http://dx.doi.org/10.7207/twr16-02 [Accessed 8 August 2016].

Fanning, B., forthcoming. *Digital document preservation using PDF/A. DPC technology watch report 16–03.* [online] To be made available at: http://dx.doi.org/10.7207/twr16-03.

Kirchhoff, A. and Morrissey, S., 2014. *Preserving ebooks. DPC technology watch report 14–01* [online] Available at: http://dx.doi.org/10.7207/twr14-01 [Accessed 8 August 2016].

McGarva, G., 2009. *Preserving geo-spatial data. DPC technology watch report 09–01.* [online] Available at: www.dpconline.org/component/docman/doc_download/363-preserving-geospatial-data-by-guy-mcgarva-steve-morris-and-gred-greg-janee [Accessed 8 August 2016].

Pennock, M., 2013. *Web-archiving. DPC technology watch report 13–01.* [online] Available at: http://dx.doi.org/10.7207/twr13-01 [Accessed 8 August 2016].

Prom, C. J., 2011. *Preserving email. DPC technology watch report 11–01.* [online] Available at: http://dx.doi.org/10.7207/twr11-01 [Accessed 8 August 2016].

Wright, R., 2012. *Preserving moving pictures and sound. DPC technology watch report 12–01.* [online] Available at: http://dx.doi.org/10.7207/twr12-01 [Accessed 8 August 2016].

Chapter 11

Managing risk

Sara Kinsey

Risk management

Question: what do all these have in common – a torrential rainstorm, an economic downturn, a journalist in search of a scandal? Answer: they all pose potential risks to business archives. Although archivists are experts in managing the past we have not yet evolved the ability to predict the future and avoid all the risks it may bring. However, we can develop skills and procedures to help us cope with anything nasty lurking around the corner. Risk management is a way of looking at the activities, processes and projects we undertake and finding strategies to increase our prospects of success in an uncertain world.

Risk management was for many years seen in the very narrow context of accident and disaster prevention. The modern approach now puts risk management at the very heart of business strategy where it covers a much wider spectrum of activities, and examines both the downsides and upsides of these activities. A quick glance at any company's current annual report will provide a wealth of detail on the types of risks it considers could impact on its business; the risk governance structure employed to identify and manage those risks; and the actions taken to prevent those risks adversely affecting progress. Most large companies have a separate risk management function, and the work within this department is usually divided by category of risk. Typical categories of risk include market risk, reputational risk, information security risk and operational risk.

In addition to the ongoing activities of monitoring and managing risk, companies will also take a strategic view on just how much risk they are prepared to accept – often termed their 'risk appetite' or 'risk tolerance' level. This in turn influences the business objectives and processes. Risk appetite varies depending on the nature of particular businesses, the wider economic environment and the proclivities of the senior management. Companies may be happy with high levels of certain kinds of risks but have no appetite at all for other, different risks. For instance, a financial services organisation may be willing to buy subsidiaries in regions which carry high levels of political risk, but will be rigorous in controlling information security risks – mismanagement of customer information and data carries severe penalties in terms of fines by regulators and potentially severe consequences in terms of loss of trust, reputation and business. This very low appetite for information security risks in turn influences the measures put in place to prevent these risks occurring: strict guidelines and rigorous procedures to govern the creation, use, transfer of and access to customer records; training programmes to ensure that staff adhere to these procedures and thorough internal auditing to check ongoing compliance. Any risk management strategies formulated by a company archive unit must always take into account the broader risk management strategy and appetite of the parent organisation, which will broadly dictate those risks that can be tolerated by the archivists, and those that can not.

Risk management speaks a language that is understood and respected by senior managers, and addresses issues within a framework that is taken seriously by businesses. Archivists may find that existing risk management functions within their parent organisations contain natural allies for certain aspects of their own work, and archivists can use existing risk-reporting communications channels for articulating their own concerns. For instance, the business case for an efficient and effective records management system can be made by addressing the information security risks arising from uncontrolled information and non-existent records management. Similarly, the need for research into a potentially contentious area of a company's past can be flagged up by stressing the reputational risks that may arise if the issue continues to be ignored.

In addition to being aware of the parent company's risk management framework, and using it to escalate concerns, archivists can also use risk management as a means of ensuring success in their own work. The discipline of risk management formalises procedures and decisions that may previously have been taken in a more reactive and *ad hoc* fashion and seeks to embed a more strategic approach to managing and planning work. The procedures of risk management can be as simple or complicated as an archivist wishes to make them, but even a basic approach will allow an archive to plan its activities better; allocate resources to where they are most needed; and request support from other areas of the organisation where it is most appropriate.

Risk management processes

Risk management is a well-established discipline with accepted standards and procedures – although these may vary between country and industry sector. In 2009 the International Standards Organisation (ISO) attempted to codify the many different risk management standards that exist in *ISO 31000:2009* (International Standards Organisation, 2009a) and related works such as *ISO Guide 73:2009* (International Standards Organisation, 2009b), which proposes a common vocabulary.

The starting point for risk management is that not all risks are equal, and that those that present the most danger need to be identified and dealt with. The initial part of the process is therefore identifying and describing all the potential risks associated with a certain activity or project. These risks are then evaluated by estimating how likely it is that they will occur, and how harmful their consequences would be. This evaluation will then result in a ranking or scoring of the risks. How then to treat the risks identified? There will be a range of decisions that can be taken on each risk. At one end of the scale will be the decision that the risk is too high to accept, and that the activity should not be undertaken at all. At the other end of the scale will be the decision that the risk is low enough to accept and that no further action is necessary. In between these two extremes are a variety of actions designed to lessen the probability of the risk occurring, and activities aiming to mitigate the consequences of the risks. Some of these actions can be taken as preventative methods, others are held in reserve as contingency measures, which only need to be mobilised if the risk occurs.

It is important to remember that risk management should not be a one-off activity. Once the initial assessment and evaluation has been carried out, then ongoing monitoring must continue to ensure that any actions are effective, and to monitor any new risks that arise or old risks that are untreated. A simple flowchart of the processes involved in risk management is given in Figure 11.1.

Perhaps one of the hardest parts of the risk assessment process is the evaluation of the potential risks. This evaluation is usually split into two sections: estimating how likely the risk is to occur; and estimating the impact of the risk occurring. These estimations can either be a qualitative judgement – for instance high, medium or low risk; or they can be given quantitive measurement – for instance, given in percentages or ranked on a 1–5 scale. A typical scale for measuring probability and impact of occurrence is given in Table 11.1.

The estimations for both the probability of occurrence and the impact are considered together to give a final risk evaluation. If either a numerical or percentage measurement has been used, then these scores are usually multiplied together to give a total risk number, which makes it simple to see at a glance which risks present the most problems. Some methods of risk evaluations also use a traffic light system of colour-coding (the

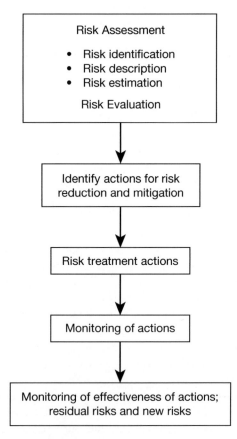

Figure 11.1 The risk management process

Table 11.1 Risk evaluation impact and probability scale

Score	Impact	Probability of occurrence
1	Negligible	Extremely unlikely to occur
2	Minor	Not impossible but unlikely to occur
3	Moderate	Fairly likely to occur
4	Serious	More likely to occur than not
5	Disastrous	Almost certain to occur

red–amber–green, or RAG system) to highlight those risks that have the highest scores and which need action.

Estimating the probability of a risk occurring and the severity of its consequences is not an easy task and will require a certain amount of thought from the archivists. However, working through the following checklist of questions can help with any assessment:

- Has this risk occurred before during a similar activity?
- If it has occurred before, how frequently has it occurred?
- If it has occurred before, what were the consequences?
- What costs might be incurred if this risk occurs?
- Has this risk occurred on a related project?
- Have your peers reported on this risk?
- Is there any guidance in professional literature or internet resources?
- What is the advice from colleagues or fellow professionals?

In the end, your professional judgement, your experience and research and whatever expert advice and guidance you can solicit will all help to decide on these areas.

Risk management and project management

The most obvious place that archivists can productively use risk management techniques is as part of the process of project management. An assessment of the potential risks to a project should be done before it even begins – and should be part of establishing whether the project itself is a viable piece of work and a worthwhile use of the archivists' time and resources. Once a decision is reached whether or not to give a project the green light, then risk management is an essential part of the ongoing project management. The success of any project is threatened by the potential risks, which may impede its progress, prevent it from fully achieving its aims, or even from being completed at all. Ongoing monitoring and treatment of risks is essential to make sure that the project stays on track and achieves its objectives within the required timescale and within the required budget.

For instance, a typical major project for a business archive might be the production of a new history charting the story of the parent organisation in time for a particularly significant birthday. Before the project starts, it will be very helpful to undertake a risk assessment of the potential pitfalls in this project – factors, which will hinder the success of the project, including issues of costs, timetable and quality. A typical risk assessment of such a project is given in Table 11.2.

Table 11.2 Risk assessment of production of new history of 'Historic Company'

Description of risk	Probability of occurrence (1–5)	Scale of impact (1–5)	Final risk assessment score
Content of book contains revelations that could damage reputation of business	2	5	10
Publication date missed due to late delivery of manuscript	2	5	10
Senior management changes whilst book in progress and new management does not support publication	3	3	9
Archivist working on project leaves the company during the project	3	3	9
Book manuscript of poor quality	2	4	8
Book's author is unable to finish the book	1	5	5
Content of book contains criticism of major customer or suppliers and loses business goodwill	1	4	4

If this kind of risk analysis is done at the very beginning of the project then ways of preventing the risks occurring and mitigating their consequences can be built into the project's management from the outset. For instance, in the example given above, the contract drawn up with the author of a company history can contain specific clauses, which will attempt to lessen the likelihood of particular risks arising. To ensure that the manuscript is delivered on time the contract can specify that regular payments to the author will only be forthcoming on the delivery of a specified number of chapters of the book to an arranged timetable. The contract can also specify that the authors must not take on additional publishing projects, or work for major competitors without permission. To protect the company's reputation, the contract can ensure that the final manuscript is delivered in time to allow for a thorough approval process by the company. To ensure the final manuscript is fit for purpose, the initial brief given to the author should detail exactly what the company wants the book to look like including numbers of words, the kinds of financial details it wants included, and the number of illustrations. Being aware of these risks at the outset means that you can build ways and means to manage these risks over the life of the project and ensure its eventual success.

To track such risks, most project management methods – for instance the PRINCE2 methodology – recommend that a risk register, or log, should be kept as part of the essential project management documentation. The risk register looks at each identified risk in turn, and usually contains the following information:

* Risk number – each risk is normally given a unique identifier.
* Description of risk – a clear description of the risk and its impact.
* Date risk identified – at the beginning or during the lifecycle of a project.
* Risk owner – who is responsible for managing the risk.
* Probability score – either a numerical measure or qualitative judgement.

- Impact score – either a numerical measure or qualitative judgement.
- Proximity – the date on which the risk may come into effect.
- Chosen action – how the risk will be prevented or mitigated.
- Action owner – who is responsible for implementing the chosen action.
- Risk status – whether closed or open.

This risk register should be regularly reviewed as part of the ongoing management of a project. This review will track the actions taken, update the register with any new risks that have been identified and initiate new actions where they are needed. In certain cases, a risk may have to be escalated to a more senior member of staff to deal with. Having the appropriate documentation – in the shape of your risk assessment and your risk register – at hand and up to date, will make this process a lot easier.

Risk management in business archives

The remainder of this chapter deals with some specific areas of archive management, which contain a number of potential risks, and suggests how the risk management discipline can be applied to ensure positive outcomes. These areas have been organised into four groupings – information security risks; operational risks; reputational risks; and strategic risks – reflecting the usual categorisation of risks with businesses. Each section seeks to describe some of these risks, and what can be done to mitigate their consequences and to lessen the probability of their occurrence. Some of the risks arise because of conflicting pressures on and clashing objectives of the archives – for instance the aim of making the archives themselves more accessible and more used by the public may also increase physical handling of the archives, and thus raise the risk of harm and damage to the archives. In these cases, the experience and judgement of the archivist is vital in weighing up the different risks and opportunities, and deciding on a course of action that takes all the risks into account, but also takes into account the professional ethics and standards of the archivist, and the aims and risk appetite of the business.

Information security risks

One of the most obvious categories of risk in the work of business archives is risk to the security and integrity of the records themselves, in whatever format they exist.

Disaster planning and prevention

At one end of the scale of risk we find those rare and unexpected but utterly catastrophic and disastrous events. These could be caused by natural disasters such as earthquakes or floods; building or structural failures such as roof leaks or floor subsidence; and disasters caused by human action that could be deliberate or accidental such as fires, computer viruses and acts of terrorism. While these events would score low on the scale of probability of occurrence, they would chalk up a very high on the scale of harmful consequences and impact.

If an archive service already undertakes some kind of risk management, it is likely that these are just the kind of events that are included in such work. Most archives will have, and all should have, a disaster plan relating to the storage of its physical records.

The traditional disaster plan usually covers such areas as the recovery and salvage operations in an archive, which has suffered a disaster, and attempts to mitigate consequences by ensuring that staff are trained and prepared to deal with such a situation; that equipment is available and that all help and support is ready and primed. Guidance on the content of such disaster plans is freely available and a list of helpful sources is given in the references at the end of this chapter. Disaster planning is also discussed in more detail in Chapter 8.

Disaster plans usually focus on the response to, and recovery from, a disaster. A thorough risk assessment should also seek to identify the potential risks to the archives, and attempt to prevent these risks ever occurring so that the disaster plan never need be used. As part of disaster prevention work, a regular audit of risks to the archive storage area should be carried out by examining the building and its surroundings. A typical audit form for such an activity is given in Box 11.1.

Box 11.1 Risk audit of archive storage

Potential risk

- Is the archive repository close to a river for which flood warnings have been issued within the last 12 months?
- Is the archive repository in a neighbourhood in which arson has been a problem within the last 12 months?
- Has the electrical wiring of the archive repository been checked within the last 12 months?
- Have any of the water pipes within the archive storage area leaked within the last 12 months?
- Have any problems occurred with the roof of the building in the last 12 months?

Although the box above deals only with physical records, such an exercise could also be undertaken for any digital storage area that houses electronic records. This audit would cover areas more appropriate to digital storage such as attempts at unauthorised access; corruption or loss of data and critical systems failure. More details of the management of electronic records is given in Chapters 8 and 10, but it is necessary to note here that any risk assessment and audit of storage areas within a business archive should include all records, regardless of format, and the digital repository should be treated as another storage area – albeit one with different risks associated with it.

Protection of vital records

Vital records are those records, in any format, that contain information that is essential to the survival of the organisation. The archives themselves will contain not only records that are essential to the survival of the parent organisation, but they will also contain records that are vital to the survival and ongoing operations of the archive unit itself. It can be helpful to view vital records as those records that you would need to reconstruct a business in the aftermath of a disaster, which would establish its legal presence, rights and extent, and which would govern and direct its operations.

The first phase in the protection of vital records is their identification. Each archive will probably contain a small minority of records, which could also be classed as vital records for the business itself. Records series such as foundation charters; memorandum and articles of association; certificates of incorporation; licences to do business; proceedings of annual general meetings and the signed minutes of the board of directors would be essential in establishing the legal entity and rights of the business and its continuing strategy. Archive collections may also contain records which are essential to the ongoing operations of the business – for instance product specification, formulations or recipes; and which are essential in establishing legal ownership of property, both physical and intellectual. It may be helpful to consult with the legal team, the company secretary's office, the records management function and the business continuity planning function to decide which of the records held by the archives are vital records for the business itself. Once identified these records may need to be recorded on a central list of vital records, and plans drawn up for their ongoing protection.

In addition to these records of importance to the parent organisation, the archives will certainly contain records which are vital records in terms of their importance for the work of the archivist. These records will be both the original records consulted by archivists and users, but also the records created by the archivists in the course of their work. If there were any kind of emergency, then the archivists need to consider what records they would need to access and use in order to carry on their work. These records would normally include such items as the catalogue of the collections held and any kind of location guide to those collections. These kinds of records should have back-up copies as a matter of course, and these back-ups – whether hard copies or digital versions – should be accessible quickly and easily in the event of an emergency.

The original records that the archivists consider are most valuable and important to the continuing use of the archives will vary between repositories. How the archivist judges what is most important will be guided by such factors as the nature of the business, the past use of the records and the monetary value of the records. Typical original records series which might be considered as vital records by the archivists are annual reports (often seen as the backbone of any chronological account of a company's history), staff ledgers and records of successive company chairmen or chief executives. There may also be records that have a high value either measured in terms of the worth to the company – for instance, the first minute book of the company; or measured in monetary terms – for instance, a banknote collection in a bank archive.

Once the vital records have been identified, a plan should be drawn up for their protection and for their recovery in a crisis. This plan should ensure that they are easily retrievable and so may affect where such records are stored within the repository. For instance, the following locations within the archive store could be considered for vital records:

- Adjacent to a door to make it easier and quicker to remove them from a store that is suffering from fire or flood.
- Not directly beneath any water pipes that could potentially leak.
- Not on the top shelves on shelving units in case of roof leaks.
- Not on the bottom shelves in case of rising floodwater.

In some circumstances it might be advantageous to group all the vital records together for ease of recovery, but it might also be more harmful to put them all in the same spot in case a localised disaster destroys them all. Some archives make sure that their vital records are dispersed throughout the store for this very reason. Additionally some archives scatter archives of high monetary worth throughout the store to make it harder for a thief to strike it lucky and make off with one valuable haul.

The list of vital records and their locations will be an important part of the disaster plan, which often prioritises these records in any salvage operation. It can be useful to highlight the locations of these vital records within the archives storage area – for instance with fluorescent stickers – for ease of identifying them for recovery in an emergency.

Repository environment

At the other end of the scale from the sudden and immediate damage caused by disaster events, is the risk of long-term harm to records from their poor storage environment. The optimum conditions for the storage of archives is laid down in different standards around the world, and some details of these are given at the end of this chapter. In the United Kingdom, these conditions are laid down in the British Standards Institution's *PD 5454:2012* (2012), which deals with factors such as relative humidity, temperature, light and air-borne pollutants. These factors can all contribute to the deterioration of archives. For instance, for every 10 degrees Celsius rise in temperature, the rate of chemical degradation reactions that affect traditional paper archives is doubled. Any assessment of risk to the physical condition and integrity of traditional archives must take into account such factors. Traditional methods of controlling risk caused by environmental factors have focused on monitoring and regulating the environment. Such monitoring is vital in assessing the level of risk; in alerting the archivists to changes in the environmental conditions and to allow the archivists to judge whether or not the existing climate control equipment such as de-humidifiers are working as expected. Monitoring and documenting the environmental conditions also provides the archivists with evidence, if it is needed, to support any request for an upgrade of environmental control equipment.

Where resources allow, archive repositories should attempt to have the optimum conditions of *PD 5454:2012* in all of their storage areas. However, where resources do not allow, then the archivist must take a pragmatic, real-life approach and decide on the areas where they are prepared to accept a certain amount of risk, and areas where they are not. Using the risk assessment method it is possible to identify the records most at risk, and those, which if lost or damaged, would have the greatest impact on the archives. This will help to focus work where it is most needed. For instance, high value records, which are most at risk, could be moved to a part of the archive store, which has the best conditions, and the packaging of the items could be improved.

As well as the long-term risks that are posed by the storage environment there are also long-term risks inherent in the format of certain records. Archivists have long been aware of the dangerous nature of certain film formats, but there are other formats which are also prone to decay, although not perhaps in such a dramatic fashion. The tendency of iron-gall inks to corrode; for faxes to fade; for colour photos to deteriorate; for paper clips to rust – all these qualities put the corresponding archives at higher risk. How are we to prevent and mitigate such risks? Systematic identification and assessment goes a long way towards the answer. When you know the scale of a problem, then you can make a plan to deal with it. Papers with iron-gall ink can be photographed, scanned or transcribed; faxes can be scanned or photocopied onto acid-free paper; paper clips can be removed. A survey of repository holdings using a sample of records can give an idea of the scale of the problem. Surveys can be used to compare one part of the collection with another, or to benchmark with other organisations. The results will allow the archivist to make a realistic appraisal of the problem, prioritise areas for action and estimate costs of remediation work. The British Library's Preservation Assessment Survey has been successfully used by many repositories in the United Kingdom as a tool to quantify preservation needs. Further details of this methodology are given at the end of the chapter. For further information on preservation risks and issues refer to Chapter 8.

Operational risks

The archive profession does not fit the usual perception of a risky business but the routine day-to-day work of the archivist may bring with it an array of risks. For example, let us imagine that a business archivist has put some images from the archives onto their company website to illustrate a feature about a famous customer. What risks are there in this activity? There could be the risk of copyright infringement and ensuing legal action if the archive does not actually own the copyright of the images. The images may inspire new visitors to the archives to view the items in question, which then suffers damage from insensitive handling. The grandchildren of the famous customer may complain that they have not been consulted and that they object to their ancestor being used in a public relations exercise by the company, and they may want to withdraw any items that relate to him from the archives. A little thought about everyday archival activities, and some simple planning and risk management can prevent situations such as this arising.

Handling and security risks

Using archives always carries a risk. From the moment a record is removed from its usual store – whether that is in a box on a shelf, or in a folder in a secure digital repository – it is exposed to a higher level of risk of being lost, damaged or altered. However, archivists have a variety of tools at hand to prevent such consequences.

An assessment of the condition of the archive collections can assign levels of risks of damage and alteration depending on the condition and format of each item. This assessment can be a systematic survey of the archive collections, but where this is not possible, then an on-the-spot decision by the archivist will ensure that records are not produced for research that could put them at significant risk of harm. Prevention is the only way to deal with records which carry a very high risk of harm or alteration – which means that for those records, which are extremely fragile or unstable, then no access or handling can be permitted at all to the original. However, it is possible to use a surrogate to allow access to the information contained within the record. For instance, a digital scan of a particularly fragile nineteenth-century photograph could be used instead of the original to prevent further damage to it; or a read-only copy could be made of the contents of a digital file to prevent a user altering the original.

Those records, which pass the initial risk assessment and which can be produced and used by researchers should be protected from harm and loss with simple measures and clear guidelines for use. Business archive units do not tend to have the same volume of visitors as a large and busy public-sector repository, but that is no reason to have any less a professional environment for researchers to consult the archives. Most countries have guidelines relating to the use of archives – and some details of these are given at the end of the chapter – and, where possible, business archivists should implement such guidelines.

Researchers should always be made familiar with any rules in place governing the handling of original material, and should be aware of the vigilant presence of the archivist on duty. The rules should aim to prevent any accidental damage to the original records and also contain measures attempting to deter would-be thieves. The rules should be sensible, defensible and enforceable, and should be applied consistently to all researchers. Suitable search room rules are further discussed in Chapter 9, but the items set out in Box 11.2 are normally included.

Box 11.2 Typical search room rules

- Respect the original records.
- Only pencils to be used.
- No marks to be made on the original records.
- Any papers in a file or bundle to be kept in their original order.
- No bags or coats in the search room.
- No eating or drinking in the search room.
- No more than a certain number of items for use at one time.

Some archives operate much more stringent security measures, which include searching the bags of researchers as they enter and leave; using closed-circuit television cameras; only using glass desks in the search room; and weighing items in and out to ensure that pages have not been removed. Whichever measures are chosen, they should be appropriate and proportionate to the assessed level of risk. It is also good practice to verify identities of researchers; and to keep a record of visits and items consulted. This audit trail could be invaluable in providing leads to track down thieves, and evidence in case it is needed to prosecute.

As well as being consulted by researchers, items from business archives are often used by the business itself – for example in exhibitions, displays, presentations, as props on film shoots and as evidence in court. This can lead to challenging professional dilemmas for the archivist as different priorities and risks collide. For instance – the marketing department may want to use some of the oldest records in a film about the heritage of the company. This may expose them to a higher risk of damage, but not permitting the items to be used in this way puts the archivist at the risk of seeming unhelpful, obstructive and may ultimately lead to loss of management support and threaten the survival of the archive. Conflicting risks need to be weighed up and assessed thoughtfully by a business archivist, who must not abandon the big picture by concentrating on small-scale risks.

The risk of damage, alteration and loss increases when an archival item is loaned, either internally or externally, and leaves the care of the archivist. However, loans are sometimes necessary and the benefits can outweigh the risks, especially if careful management lowers those risks. A clear policy on loans, which sets out the responsibilities of the borrower, the conditions of the loan and any possible penalties for damage or loss, is an essential tool in safeguarding items that are out of the care of the archivist. It is always important to make the recipient of the loan responsible for its care and to impress on that individual that it is vital for the item to be returned in the same condition in which it was lent. Documenting the loan, including photographing it before it leaves the archivist's care and ensuring that the recipient signs a loan form to acknowledge that it has been received in a certain condition will tend to focus the mind of the recipient on the responsibility that they have taken on. Items should also always be protected in archival packaging – which in addition to serving a practical protective purpose will also underline to the loan recipient that this is an item that needs special care. In certain circumstances, the archivist may be able to insist that the item can be loaned on the condition that it is moved and accompanied by a member of the archive team at all times. It is usual practice to have a standard form that must be filled out for all external loans of material that covers such matters such as insurance, transport, storage and display. Box 11.3 shows typical conditions that may be attached to a loan.

Box 11.3 Typical loan conditions

1. Insurance:

Insurance should be arranged at the borrower's expense. Details of insurance policy must be provided prior to any loan. A condition report will be made by the archive team before any items are loaned and checked after their return. Any damage may be the subject of an insurance claim.

2. Transport:

Items are normally transported by a member of the archive team at the borrower's expense. For large or fragile items, such as paintings, specialist shippers should be used. Details of transport arrangements must be provided prior to any loan.

3. Display and storage:

A member of the archive team will normally be present at the installation and removal of items from their exhibition setting. Items on display should not be removed from their exhibition setting except in cases of emergency such as fire or flood. The following details must be provided prior to any loan:

- Address and location of display of item.
- Details of locks and alarms on display cases.
- Details of environmental controls within display cases or area.
- Details of lighting within display cases or area.
- Security staff and arrangements within the building.
- How the building or display area is protected when security staff are absent.
- Smoke detection/fire suppressant/sprinkler systems.
- Location, security and access details of areas where items may be stored prior to or after use.

Access risks

Access to business archives must always be a delicate balancing act upholding the rights and interests of the archive owners, whilst also taking into account those of researchers and users. In most business archives external users do not have any automatic right of access to records, and access is usually granted at the company's discretion. In the United Kingdom, there are a few exceptions to this rule, which include:

- Businesses which were once nationalised industries may hold records that are classed as public records and that the public has a right to see.
- Under the Data Protection Act 1998, living data subjects may have the right to see information kept about them.
- Businesses which have been granted external funding for projects that improve access to their records, may be obliged to grant access to those records as part of the funding conditions.
- Shareholders may have the right to see certain records such as the records of annual general meetings.

In practice, most company archives operate within a broad access framework that has been approved by senior management, but which delegates to the archivists the final decision on how to interpret the framework. In the United Kingdom, many business archivists have been guided by the 30-year closure rule, which previously governed the closure periods of government records. This 30-year rule is often extended to 100 years in the case of records relating to particular individuals. United Kingdom bank archivists also need to take into account the duty of confidentiality that a bank has relating to information about its customers. The Court of Appeal's 1924 judgement in the case of *Tournier v. National Provincial & Union Bank of England* declared that this duty of confidentiality is part of the contractual banker–customer obligation, which is enforceable in law; most bank archives interpret this in practice by not permitting access to customer records that are less than 100 years old. However, in some business archives, the archivists do not apply strict closure periods but make access decisions on a case-by-case basis.

Whichever method is chosen, it is highly desirable – both for researchers and for the archives team – to have a formal access policy, which is freely available, consistently adhered to and signed off by senior management. This will manage the expectations of researchers, and protect the archivist from charges of discriminatory treatment of researchers, attempting to hide documents or subvert access. An access policy will also be necessary if business archives are deposited with an external collecting repository. Some businesses will only deposit records on the condition that all access requests are still vetted by the business, others are happy to sign-up to the general access conditions of the collecting repository. Whichever procedure is used, it is essential that the conditions be agreed in writing as part of the deposit agreement to prevent the risk of unauthorised access at a later date.

A conditions of access form, which is signed by researchers to show that they agree to abide by certain conditions, is also a useful tool in mitigating risks that arise after access has been granted to original records. For instance, most conditions of access forms state that the researcher should submit a draft of any work that they propose to publish that is based on material from that particular archive. This gives the archivists the chance to check that the work does not disclose any confidential details either about the company's business, operations and strategy or about individuals and other businesses. Chapter 9 includes a useful discussion on the contents of conditions of access forms and related policies and procedures.

What potential risks are there in allowing access to and use of company archives? Perhaps the most obvious risk – that a user may discover something damaging to the company – is covered below under reputational risks. But there are other risks. For instance, the archives may contain designs, recipes, research and other intellectual property, which constitute part of the company's competitive advantage – access to this material by external researchers may impair future company performance, and access to these items would clearly be against the interests of the company. In another scenario, researchers may uncover information, opinion and comments on individuals, which may cause hurt or offence to those individuals, or their families, if they were published. The archivist can reduce the risk of accidental access to these kinds of records by ensuring that any catalogues clearly detail the kind of information they contain – knowing exactly what you have in all those boxes is the first line of defence against this kind of risk.

Understanding exactly what a researcher is interested in, and perhaps even why they are interested, is also key to finding relevant records for their research. This understanding should be coupled with a thorough knowledge of the records, which will allow the archivist to anticipate risks, and suggest practical solutions. For example, a user at a bank archive who is researching his family business may want to access branch records that also contain confidential material about other customers. Once the archivist knows exactly what information the user is looking for, and has previewed the records, they can suggest practical measures – such as only allowing the user to see certain pages, or giving them copies of those pages with parts blacked out – that will circumvent this problem. When identifying any risks associated with access to original records it is also useful to view the risks in terms of the outputs of the access, rather than on the process of access. For example, some academic researchers may want to use records that contain confidential customer or staff data but are actually interested in gathering data, which will then be aggregated and analysed *en masse*. Any publications or outputs based on this research will not mention any individual by name and so poses a minimal risk in terms of breaching an individual's confidentiality. In this case, access to records that contain information on individuals, which are less than 100 years old, could be allowed with very little risk.

There are certain records that are more likely than others to have contentious content, and to which it may be necessary to have very restricted access. Staff records – where they include judgements and opinions on the individual concerned, or contain information on the individual's conduct (or misconduct) can be among the most sensitive records. Oral history records may also contain statements and judgements about colleagues or customers that may be unflattering at the very least. To protect those individuals who are named, and may be defamed, in this way, it may be necessary to restrict access to certain items in the archive, or certain parts of those items. Again, accurate catalogue descriptions and an in-depth knowledge of the records is the first line of defence against inadvertently allowing access to these records. Knowledge of the records, good communication with researchers to understand their requirements and a healthy dose of common sense can help to prevent and mitigate many everyday risks of access.

Accountability risks

Business archives usually define their role with a simple mission statement. This mission statement will normally include the aims of identifying, collecting and preserving records of enduring value, and making these records available for research. These very broad aims have the advantage of giving the business archivist freedom to pursue a variety of activities within this general framework. However, they also leave the door open to differing interpretations of the mission of the archive service from record creators and record users who have their own, sometimes opposing, views on exactly what a business archive is for, and how this influences what it should be keeping.

Richard Cox (1995, p. 98) describes the archive's mission as 'the identification, preservation and use of archival records on behalf of the institution it serves and society'. It is this dual role – of serving the parent institution and of serving society – that creates potential accountability risks for the business archivist. The expectation of the business records creators is that the archives service keeps a selection of their records for ongoing legal, regulatory and operational reasons; the expectation of some members of the public may be that the archives service is keeping records to document the actions of the company and its interaction with customers and the wider community. In reality the business archivist treads a tightrope between these viewpoints. Most business archives keep more than the bare essentials needed to satisfy audit and regulatory requirements. They also attempt to document the company's progress, policies, procedures, personalities and culture – to capture what makes this company different from any other. Additionally, there is usually an attempt to predict what records will be useful for future enquiries and researchers, and to transfer these to become part of the archive collection. What risks does the business archivist run with this hybrid approach to accountability and collecting?

In stretching the remit of the archives service to provide records that might be useful to researchers in the future, then the archivist may skew the collections to their own interests and may neglect the core functions of collecting records that are needed for enduring regulatory and operational reasons. If the archives are not keeping the records that the business needs, then this undermines the case for an archives service at all. When successive business archivists have different views on what should be kept, or have had varying resources to devote to this activity, then the result will be patchy archives – rich sources on some business functions in certain time frames, and paltry sources on the same function in a different time period. The resulting inability to provide consistent documentation, and meet the expectations of business users, can again undermine the claims to efficiency and effectiveness of the archive service. As well as these risks of not keeping the right records, or not having enough of them, there is also the risk of a surfeit of records. What if the archives have kept records that may prove a liability to the company in the long term? The legal discovery process may winkle out records from the archives that can be used against the business.

The business archive service can mitigate these risks by having a clear mission statement, which is signed off by senior management. This mission statement will then influence the collecting policy of the archive, which again should be signed off by the relevant departments within the business. The collecting policy can be supported by individual agreements with departments and individuals who detail which records, created by which department or individual, will be transferred to the archives for permanent preservation. These individual agreements can also include any information about the confidentiality of the material transferred, and any Chinese walls that need to be preserved around the information in the records. The top level collecting policy and the individual agreements should be regularly reviewed to make sure that they are still fit for purpose.

Intellectual property risks

Business archives will almost certainly contain items that have Intellectual Property (IP) rights. Each country will have their own detailed IP law and some pointers of where to find more information are given at the end of this chapter. The kind of IP that most concerns archivists is usually copyright, and it is very helpful for archivists to have a basic understanding of copyright law and how it can affect them and their activities.

Copyright law is concerned with literary, musical and artistic works – which includes photographs – and gives the creators of these works the right to control the way in which their work may be used. These rights usually remain in force for a certain number of years from the end of the year in which the creator dies, or a certain number of years from the year of creation if the author is unknown. However, United Kingdom copyright law also states that, from 1912 onwards, an employer owns the copyright of any work made by an employee in the course of his or her employment. So, for instance, a graphic designer who worked for a company producing packaging designs, does not own the copyright to those designs. Business archives do not usually though just contain records produced by employees in the course of their employment, they may also contain records deposited by families of employees, by board directors, or by third party suppliers who were commissioned to produce specific work by the business. In these cases, if the deposit agreement does not specifically assign copyright to the company, then it is retained by the creator. Good examples of the kinds of archival items that this can affect are photographs of sporting teams in action taken by a family member, diaries kept by members of staff, a photograph taken of an event by a professional photographer and advertising films produced in partnership with an external production company.

Table 11.3 Mitigating actions for risk of infringing copyright

Description of risk	Copyright holder is unknown so it is impossible to request permission to use the item. Business may be later prosecuted for infringement of copyright.
Preventative actions	Find another item to use for which the archives does hold copyright instead of the item in question.
Mitigating actions	• Attempt to find copyright holder using existing documentation about item; searches on the internet; contacts in the pensions department if ex-member of staff; adverts in relevant newspapers/journals.
	• Keep detailed records of your efforts to trace copyright holder to demonstrate you have acted in good faith.
	• Use the item in copyright with a statement stating that you have tried to trace the rights holder and invite the legitimate rights holder to contact you.
	• Set aside contingency sum to cover potential payment to copyright holder.

Copyright law allows for the use of material in copyright under certain conditions – for instance it is possible to provide copies for private and research purposes; and for educational purposes. However, if a business archive is planning to use items for which they do not own copyright in other ways – for instance as illustrations in a publication, publishing them on the internet or using them in an exhibition – then they should obtain permission from the copyright holder. This can be tricky in situations where the only clue to the identity of the depositor is a small label tied to an item, which says 'Donated to the archives by Mrs Jones on 2 January 1973'! A risk assessment of this kind of situation will allow you to weigh up the likelihood of being prosecuted by the copyright holder and its possible impact, against the benefit of using the item in question. The archivist can then put in place strategies and actions that will mitigate the possible impact of the risk. Table 11.3 details some of the actions that can be taken to offset any risk arising from using items without the permission of the copyright holder. Issues relating to copyright and access to business archives are discussed further in Chapter 9.

Reputational risks

There is an old saying in public relations that 'image is created but reputation is earned'. Companies work very hard to position themselves and maintain their image in the public's mind, and modern brands are now one of a company's most delicate – but valuable – assets. Reputation, however, is less within the control of the company and reflects how the company acts towards its customers, staff and society as a whole. The reputation of business in general has come under increased scrutiny in recent years in the wake of corporate scandals and economic crises; an anti-corporate story has become an easy one to sell. These factors have led to the management of reputational risk becoming a higher-profile activity within businesses, and the company archivist needs to be aware of any potential risks in this area and manage them accordingly.

Business archives have the potential to play a very positive role in public relations – helping companies to build brands and underpinning relationships between customers and the company. In the financial services industry, archives are used to support claims of longevity, of reliability and stability. In the retail sector, archives can be used to build a story around a brand, to add heritage, colour and depth to products. Classic examples of this include the use of old photographs by Jack Daniel's to emphasise the traditional way in which their Tennessee Whiskey is distilled and produced; and the zeal with which many big companies celebrate significant corporate birthdays and anniversaries.

The flip side of this emphasis on the traditions and heritage of a company is that it may also encourage investigation into areas of which the business is not so proud. How should a business archivist deal with such skeletons in the cupboard if they exist? Can a business archivist defend their employers' view of history – whilst also maintaining professional integrity as an independent steward of the archives? If a business archive does contain material that is potentially damaging to the reputation of the parent company then what should the archivist do? Shred it? Hide it? Expose it?

These kinds of questions are the ones that are most frequently asked of the business archivist by fellow professionals. In reality, the business archivist's working life is not as exciting as these questions assume. Any deliberately criminal or malicious acts will probably not have been documented in the first place, and if they were, it is highly unlikely that the perpetrators would be foolish enough to pass those records to the archives rather than destroying them themselves. However, this is not to say that business archives may not contain records that have the potential to embarrass a business. These records are likely to be evidence of past policies, procedures, and transactions, which could be damaging to the company when seen in the context of present day attitudes, behaviours and ways of doing business. The items themselves may be perfectly standard documents recording normal day-to-day business of the time – but taken out of context and held up to the scrutiny of modern standards they could be used to tarnish the company's reputation.

The potential risks here are twofold. First, there is the risk to the company's reputation, but there is also a secondary risk to the archivists who mishandle these kinds of issues. If the archivist's actions are responsible for exposing the company to reputational risk, then the archivist's own reputation within the company will suffer too. Archivists work hard to create their own brand image within their parent organisation, and to earn their own reputation. Errors of judgement can undermine trust in the archives and management support for them.

To manage these kinds of risks it is useful to follow the standard risk management process. First, identify any potential risks. What issues are there in the company's past that could be contentious? A basic checklist of questions relating to potentially problematical areas that should be considered is provided in Box 11.4.

Each industry will have its own specific questions to add to this general list. For instance, chemical businesses will need to consider their historic procedures for testing products and for disposing of industry waste; banks will need to consider their historic procedures for dealing with dormant accounts generally, and accounts of victims of the Holocaust specifically. Just like any other kind of risk, reputational risk is a constantly changing landscape. New issues may arise or old ones be resurrected. Keeping an eye on the news will help to keep abreast of such developments – for instance the commemoration of the bicentenary of the abolition of the slave trade in the United

---

Box 11.4 Potential reputational risks

- Are there any historic links between the business, its directors or employees and any political party?
- Are there any historic links between the business, its directors, employees, customers or suppliers and certain regimes – for instance, Nazi Germany or apartheid-era South Africa?
- Are there any historic links between the business, its directors, employees, customers or suppliers and the slave trade?
- Have the historic working practices and operations of the business been dangerous or harmful to employees, customers or the communities in which they operate?
- Have the historic working practices and operations of the business been disrespectful or discriminatory towards certain groups of employees or customers?
- Has the company sold products in the past which it knew to be of harm to its customers?

Kingdom in 2007 prompted many businesses to search their archives to identify any possible historic links to the slave trade.

To gain a realistic evaluation of the risk posed by each issue, it is also necessary to know exactly what material is held in the archives relating to each issue, and exactly what information and evidence this material contains. Forewarned is forearmed, and it will not reflect well on the archivist's reputation if a researcher uncovers evidence relating to any of these risks of which they were unaware. Fellow professionals within the business – such as the public affairs, communications, press office and reputational risk teams – may help to evaluate any potential risks, and to guide the archivist on the appetite of the business for these kinds of risks.

Actions to prevent the risks occurring, and to mitigate their effects can take a variety of forms. Good documentation on the processes of the archives – such as collecting policies, lists of accessions, retention schedules and lists of records destroyed – will provide a defence against charges that the archivist has secretly shredded any evidence on a particular issue. Statements on particular issues that have been identified as having potential reputational risk – such as the company's involvement in the slave trade – can be written and pre-approved by the relevant personnel within the business. These statements would seek to put any records in their historical context and can be used in response to any enquiry about this subject. Any request from external researchers to access records that contain potentially damaging material do not have to be refused – any decision on access would need to take into account why the researcher wants to access this material, what form the outputs of their research will take and what the appetite of the company is for such revelations. It is worth remembering that refusing access to business archives leaves the archivist and the company open to accusations of trying to enforce a cover-up, and in some cases it may be more harmful to refuse access than to grant it. The most extreme form of prevention would, of course, be the destruction of the relevant material. It is unlikely that archivists in a modern business environment would be asked to implement such a measure, and if they are then each individual will have to weigh their loyalty to their employer against the professional standards expected of them, their responsibility towards the records in the care, and the dictates of their own conscience.

Where there are very serious issues at stake many businesses have found that getting the facts out in the open as part of a policy of controlled disclosure is often the best method of managing the potential risks to a company's reputation. For example, companies in Germany have had to wrestle with their historic links with, and support for, the Nazi regime. Many companies have decided that a policy of openness is far more beneficial, both to themselves and to society as a whole, in attempting to come to terms with the past and move forward into the future. Allowing access to the relevant records can serve to underline the historical nature of the events, and place a distance between past and present. Some companies have also decided to allow access to external historians who have subsequently published authoritative, yet objective, accounts of the company's history, underlining its transparency and its readiness to accept its past.

Dealing with the media

Reputational risks are harder to manage when they are unexpected, forcing the archivist to react rather than pro-actively plan for a situation. Unexpected risks can arise from many quarters but are most likely to emanate from the media who are looking for a

---

Box 11.5 Case study: Deutsche Bank and its history, Germany

In 1995 Deutsche Bank published a new history of the bank to coincide with its 125th birthday. The bank's management decided to invite a team of external expert historians to write the history with unparalleled access to the bank's archives. This decision was taken in the full knowledge that what the historians might find might not always be easy reading. The independence of the team of historians was underlined by holding an academic conference prior to the publication of the book, where historians were invited to discuss the manuscript that had been produced so far.

The final book was widely applauded in Germany by commentators, including the media, for its openness and approach to a difficult period in the bank's history. The bank's monumental history covered in great detail the bank's involvement with the Nazi regime including such details as the financing of the firms which built Auschwitz.

One of authors wrote in the book's introduction that 'At no time, between the inception of the project and its realization, has the bank sought to censor or influence the content or judgement of the contributors'. The bank's chairman, Hilmar Kopper, echoed this sentiment in his foreword in which he emphasised, 'No instructions were given nor guidelines laid down. Those members of the Deutsche Bank's Management Board who initiated the project were moved only by a single desire – that it should serve the truth'. (Gall, *et al*., 1995, p.xii and pxviii).

---

speedy response, a story with an angle or a telling sound bite. This is especially true in a digital world where the internet and social networking sites mean that a story can be passed on to millions of people around the world whilst you are pouring yourself a cup of coffee, patting yourself on the back and mistakenly thinking that you coped pretty well with that difficult phone call from a journalist!

Dealing with the media can be a potentially risky, but also a potentially rewarding business. The two phrases: 'No news is good news' and 'There's no such thing as bad publicity' show the opposing viewpoints quite nicely. Involvement with journalists and broadcasters can be a positive experience, showcasing the work of the archives, raising their profile and allowing others to see them in a new light or re-assess their value. However, records from the archives can also be used to give credence to a version of events that the business does not support. How can you improve the chances of your brushes with fame falling more into the former camp than the latter?

Co-ordination with a business's media team, press office, marketing department or reputational risk department is usually essential in these situations, and in many companies the press office will act as the gatekeeper for all media enquiries, and may have their own guidelines for any media work including offering training to those who may be required to act as spokespeople from time to time. It is possible to reduce the risks inherent in involvement with the media by following some simple guidelines and preparing in advance. The simple checklist given below can help with preparation for an interview with a journalist by identifying any potential risks:

- What story is the journalist seeking?
- Want angle are they likely to take?
- What is the overall attitude of the media organisation to the subject in general?
- What is your key message?
- What difficult questions might you be asked?

If the interview is going to be taped for broadcast then it is usually possible to discuss with the journalist in advance the areas that will be covered and the kinds of questions you will be asked. Talking these issues through with a member of the press team can be very useful, and may be essential depending on the accepted practice of the company involved. Practising with colleagues can also be very constructive, and can help confidence and fluency in the final interview. Remember to have a good story to tell, and keep it simple. Beware of the last question, which is often casually thrown in at the end but that may be about an issue that the journalist has not pre-warned you about, and so may lure you into saying something that you later regret. Finally, never fall into the trap of making 'off the record' remarks – there is no such thing as 'off the record' with journalists.

Strategic risks

Perhaps the greatest risk that any business archive must face is the risk to its own survival – to the maintenance of an archives unit staffed by professional archivists managing the archive collections of the company. It is difficult to measure the archivist's contribution to the bottom line, and such notions as improving corporate efficiency, maintaining the corporate memory, supporting a company's brands and building employee and customer engagement are difficult to quantify. Archivists need to anticipate business change – and the ripples that spread out from such change – in order to plan for a sustainable future. Business change can be a result of both external and internal drivers – a list identifying risks that may affect the ongoing survival of the archives would include the following:

- Changes in key senior management.
- Mergers and acquisitions.
- Restructuring.
- Relocation.
- Change in business strategy and focus.
- Cost-cutting.
- Recession and economic downturn resulting in any of the above.

What actions can the archivists take to prevent any of these risks having a negative effect on the professional management of the archives?

The company archivist must stay relevant to the current business objectives and aims, and align their work programmes accordingly. As Peter Emmerson (Dearstyne, 2008, p. 91) ruefully observes: 'Many record keeping programs have not been sufficiently responsive to, and aligned with, these strategic objectives. This inevitably makes them vulnerable to changes in fashion'. Business archivists must be proactive in offering their services, and tailoring them to specific audiences. For instance, if a company's new image focuses on emphasising its ability to innovate and produce new cutting-edge products, then the archives should have information, images and stories prepared on how the company has innovated throughout its history. From this resource bank, the archivists can prepare their own range of products – for example, information and fast facts for speeches; slides for management presentations; training modules for internal training; input into company induction programmes; and online exhibitions for intranets to engage staff.

Any strategy for survival should also include building a network of high level support within the company – having friends in high places and agents of influence at all levels can make sure that any case to be made for the archives' survival falls upon friendly ears. Building long-term relationships with key departments – such as company secretary's, legal, research and development, marketing and the press office – and with key individuals – such as the chief executive, the chairman and board members – will give the archivists clear channels of communication to decision-makers, and allow the archivists to prove their worth through their own work. Traditional profile raising activities – such as offering open days, tours of the archives, providing exhibitions and talks – are important in building this network of influence, but just as important is providing an efficient and effective service that adds value to the business, and, which builds the reputation of the archive service. The company secretary's office may be interested in attending an open day, but they will probably be more appreciative of the value of an archives department, which never loses any item transferred to it, can return promptly any item that needs to be consulted, and can give expert and reliable advice on what records need to be kept in perpetuity. Each department within a business will have its own criteria for what constitutes a successful archive service, and the business archivist will need to fulfil these different criteria as best they can – taking some tough decisions along the way about the best ways to achieve this end, and where to focus efforts for maximum effect both for the business and for themselves.

In addition to emphasising the value of their function, the archivists can also demonstrate the value of the archive collections themselves. Most business archive collections are of local importance; some are of national, or even international, importance. For instance the archive collection of a colliery in a South Wales mining valley would be of immense importance for the history of that region – the majority of jobs in the area at one time would either be in the mine, or connected in some way to the mine; and the colliery workings would have had a profound and ongoing impact on the landscape and environment. On a larger scale, many business collections contain records that illuminate social and economic history at a national level. The archive collections of certain businesses in the United Kingdom document the whole history of that particular industry – for example, BT's history is synonymous with the history of the telecommunications industry in Britain. By emphasising the value of the archive collection beyond the creating business – to the communities where the business operates, to the people it has employed, to its customers, to society as a whole – then the business archivist can make a case that by maintaining the archive, and facilitating access to it, the company is demonstrating good corporate responsibility.

It is also possible to gain external validation of the value of the archives through international schemes such as United Nations Educational, Scientific and Cultural Organization's Memory of the World Register (UNESCO, 2016), or a similar national scheme. Such schemes do not come with any funding or guarantee of survival, but the fact that the collections have been acknowledged to have such importance may cause the parent organisation to pause for thought before closing the archives, and may allow the archives to gather a wider constituency of supporters. A number of business archive collections have now been granted this prestigious status, and have used it to gain recognition internally of the worth of the archive collections, and strengthen support for the work of the archivists. Even without such formal external accreditation, business archivists can make the case for the value of their collections. An appraisal of the collection's worth from a respected academic, an exhibition of highlights from the collection in partnership with a respected public institution, an online exhibition including feedback and interactivity with the public – all these activities can underline a collection's value, and provide estimation of its worth from outside the business. However, it is worth pointing out that there is a risk in emphasising the value of the collections to the wider world. It begs the question: if society values the collection so highly, then why doesn't society pay to look after it? Have a handy answer ready to such questions.

Major business events such as mergers and takeovers present serious external risks to the archivist who could be at the sharp end of the cost cutting and synergy programmes that are often part and parcel of the aftermath of such events. A risk assessment of such a situation can enable the archivist to see the advantages and disadvantages of the various options for their future, and to focus on what actions they need to take to achieve their desired outcomes, and what actions they can implement to prevent the least favourable outcome materialising. In such a situation the following strategies can mitigate the risk to the future of the archives service: present a clearly argued business case for your preferred option; marshal the facts and statistics that demonstrate your value; use your network of support to get your case to the right people; try to influence events rather than let decisions be made in your absence without your input.

It can also be useful to have a plan B up your sleeve. Would it be possible to establish a charitable trust to takeover the ownership of the archive collections? Some companies in the United Kingdom, such as Rothschild, Sainsbury's and Cable & Wireless have discovered that this route has allowed them to safeguard the archive collections for the future, whilst also permitting the trust to bid for public money to improve the stewardship of the collections. Can the archive collections be deposited in a public sector archive – such as a university repository? Such an agreement can depend on the fit with the collecting policy of the public sector repository, the money required to fund the deposit and the size of the collection. Successful partnerships along this model in the United Kingdom include the deposit of the Marks & Spencer Archive with Leeds University and the partnership between University of Teesside, Teesside archives and Corus to safeguard the future of the British Steel Archive. Mounting a campaign to save an archive collection can galvanise support, increase the profile of the archives and make its survival a matter of pride for those connected to it. For example, the archives of the Equitable Life Assurance Society in the United Kingdom were saved by the actuarial profession who recognised the importance of the archives to the development of their profession and to actuarial science. In an unprecedented move, members of the profession joined together to donate money to a successful campaign to prevent the archive being split up and sold. The campaign was able to buy the archive and arrange for its deposit in London's Guildhall Library and in the library of the Institute of Actuaries. For further discussion of advocacy in the context of archival survival see Chapter 12.

Conclusion

Risk management helps archivists to decide where best to focus their efforts in a world where there is never enough time or resources to do everything they would like. It offers the opportunity to stand back from everyday concerns to look at the big picture, and then to prioritise, plan and act in a way that will improve the certainty of the outcome. Foreseeing risks is one thing, but knowing how to respond to them effectively is quite another. 'Predicting rain doesn't count', said Warren Buffet, 'building arks does'.

Acknowledgements

Thanks are due to Elizabeth Adkins and Alex Bieri for kindly commenting on the chapter as a whole.

References

British Standards Institution (BSI), 2012. *PD 5454:2012. Guide for the storage and exhibition of archival materials.* London: BSI.

Cox, R., 1995. Archives and archivists in the twenty-first century: what will we become? *Archival Issues*, 20, 2(1995), pp. 97–114.

Emmerson, P., 2008. From cultural luxury to 'The way we do things . . . ?' The influence of leadership in archives and records management. In: B. W. Dearstyne, ed. 2008. *Leading and managing archives and records programs.* Chicago, IL: Neal-Schuman Publishers.

Gall, L., Feldman, G. D., James, H., Holtfrerich, C. and Buschgen, H. E., 1995. *The Deutsche Bank 1870–1995.* London: Weidenfeld & Nicolson.

International Standards Organisation (ISO), 2009a. *ISO 31000:2009. Risk management – principles and guidelines.* Geneva: ISO.

International Standards Organisation (ISO), 2009b. *ISO Guide 73:2009. Risk management – vocabulary.* Geneva: ISO.

United Nations Educational, Scientific and Cultural Organization, 2016. *Memory of the world.* [online] Available at: www.unesco.org/new/en/communication-and-information/flagship-project-activities/memory-of-the-world/register/ [Accessed 3 September 2016].

Further reading

Risk management

Crouhy, M., Galai, D. and Mark, R., 2014. *The essentials of risk management.* 2nd ed. New York: McGraw Hill.

International Standards Organisation (ISO), 2009. *ISO 31000:2009. Risk management – principles and guidelines.* Geneva: ISO.

Purdy, G., 2010. ISO 31000:2009. Setting a new standard for risk management. *Risk analysis*, 30(6), pp. 881-886.

Managing risk as part of project management

Carpenter, J., 2011. *Project management in libraries, archives and museums: working with government and other external partners.* Oxford: Chandos Publishing.

Jutte, B., 2012. *Project risk management handbook.* Bloomington, IN: Xlibris Corporation.

Archive buildings

Kitching, C., 2007. *Archive buildings in the United Kingdom 1993–2005.* Chichester: Phillimore. [Contains both a guide to good practice in the design and construction of archive buildings and a number of case studies.]

Pacifico, M. F. and Wilsted, T. P., 2009. *Archival and special collections facilities: guidelines for archivists, librarians, architects and engineers.* Chicago, IL: Society of American Archivists.

Disaster management

Dadson, E., 2012. *Emergency planning and response for libraries, archives and museums.* London: Facet Publishing.

Harwell Documentation Recovery Service, 2009. *Template disaster plan.* [online] Available at: www.hdrs.co.uk/templateplane.html [Accessed 3 September 2016].

Matthews, G., Smith, Y. and Knowles, G., 2009. *Disaster management in archives, libraries and museums.* Aldershot: Ashgate.

National Archives (United States of America). *Disaster response and recovery.* [online] Available at: www.archives.gov/preservation/disaster-response/ [Accessed 3 September 2016].

The British Library. *Collection care.* [online] Available at: www.bl.uk/blpac/disaster.html [Accessed 3 September 2016].

Repository environment

British Standards Institution (BSI), 2012. *PD 5454:2012. Guide for the storage and exhibition of archival materials.* London: BSI.

National Archives of Australia, 2014. *Standard for the storage of archival records (excluding digital records),* [online] Available at: www.naa.gov.au/records-management/publications/standard-for-storage/index.aspx [Accessed 3 September 2016].

Preservation assessments

Patkus, B., 2003. *Assessing preservation need: a self-survey guide.* Andover, MA: Northeast Document Conservation Center. [pdf] Available at: www.nedcc.org/assets/media/documents/apnssg.pdf [Accessed 3 September 2016]. [A comprehensive guide to assessing all aspects of the preservation of archives.]

The British Library. *Collection care.* [online] Available at: www.bl.uk/blpac/disaster.html [Accessed 3 September 2016]. [Information and case studies relating to the standard methodology used by many archives in the United Kingdom as developed by the British Library Preservation Advisory Centre.]

Access guidelines

International Council on Archives (ICA), 2012. *ICA code of ethics.* [pdf] ICA. Available at: www.ica.org/en/ica-code-ethics [Accessed 3 September 2016], principles 6 and 7.

International Council on Archives (ICA), 2014. *Principles of access to archives. Technical guidance on managing archives with restrictions.* [pdf] ICA. Available at: www.ica.org/sites/default/files/2014-02_standards_tech-guidelines-draft_EN.pdf [Accessed 3 September 2016].

Public Services Quality Group (PSQG), 2008. *A standard for access to archives.* [pdf] National Council on Archives. Available at: www.archives.org.uk/ara-in-action/publications/journal-of-the-ara-sp-1111397493.html [Accessed 3 September 2016].

Society of American Archivists (SAA) and American Library Association (ALA), 1994, updated 2009. *ALA/SAA joint statement on access to research materials in archives and special collections libraries.* [online] Available at: www2.archivists.org/statements/ala-saa-joint-statement-of-access-guidelines-for-access-to-original-research-materials-au [Accessed 3 September 2016].

Intellectual property

Padfield, T., 2015. *Copyright for archivists and records managers.* 5th ed. London: Facet Publishing. [Includes details of copyright law in selected other countries including Australia, Canada and the United States of America.]

Strategic risks

Dearstyne, B. W., 2008. *Leading and managing archives and records programs.* Chicago, IL: Neal-Schuman Publishers. [Includes a particularly interesting contribution from Peter Emmerson reflecting on the risks of succession planning.]

Reputational risks

Business Archives Council, 2016. *Managing business archives.* [online] Available at: www.managingbusinessarchives.co.uk/ [Accessed 3 September 2016]. [Includes case studies about different ways of exploiting business archives.]

Faraday, J., 2007. Doing the business: the promotion of business archives in the private sector. *Business Archive: Principles and Practice*, 93, pp. 1–13.

Giffen, L. and Shields, K., 2010. Going back to our roots: the partnership between the Marks and Spencer Company Archives and the University of Leeds. *Business Archives: Principles and Practice*, 100, pp. 27–40.

Goodwin, M., 1999. Preserving and promoting history in a fast-changing environment: an example from Cable and Wireless. *Business Archives: Principles and Practice*, 77, pp. 47–56.

Heggie, J. K., 2009. The British Steel Archive project: forging new kinds of partnerships to preserve significant business archives. *Business Archive: Principles and Practice*, 98, pp. 16–32.

Parkinson, V., Steel, A. and Strickland, J., 2008. Business archives and the MLA designation scheme. *Business Archives: Principles and Practice*, 95, pp. 21–31.

Sienkiewicz, M., 2008. Asset or liability: the value of an archive to a company's reputation. *Business Archives: Principles and Practice*, 95, pp. 32–43.

Part 4

Using business archives

Chapter 12

Advocacy, outreach and the corporate archivist

Paul C. Lasewicz

Introduction

> Don't focus on the costs. Examine the activities that drive costs. Look at all the reports and 'services' the overhead departments provide to their 'clients' (typically inside the company). Examine how useful these end products really are. Look for ways to reduce, eliminate or streamline the end products, or the activities that generate them.
>
> John Neuman, management consultant, 1975

Managerial principles such as these have been the bane of a corporate archivist's existence for more than 40 years. But the indomitable archivist embraces these perspectives, because they bring stark clarity to what the primary goal for any corporate archive needs to be. They reduce that goal to the most simple, most base objective – survival. Why is survival the single most critical objective for an archive? Because the core organisational contributions of any archive – preserving information of long-term value, leveraging that information for business utility, documenting that corporation for societal use – none of that occurs if the archive doesn't survive (Steele, 2014).

However, as Neuman makes abundantly clear, in a corporate environment archival survival is not a given. Cut-throat corporate realities mean that unlike its counterparts in government or academia, corporate archives need to continually justify their existence. The business case for a corporate archive is usually based on its ability to make significant but intangible contributions to company activities, as archives often struggle to place a tangible monetary value on their organisational contributions. Since the 1970s, however, corporate management strategies that have focused on increasing profits by reducing the size of non-revenue generating functions have placed tremendous pressure on corporate archives, which traditionally are not a core mission of their larger parent organisations (Neuman, 1975). In fact, rarely are they considered core even to the organisational units to which they report. This peripheral nature of a corporate archive creates significant exposures for the function in that it ranks as a lesser priority for its direct management, placing it at risk in times of corporate upheavals – budget and headcount cutbacks, reorganisations and management transitions.

Survival can be serendipitous – the archive might have the good fortune to be located in an organisational structure that doesn't attract a lot of cost-cutting attention, such as the legal function. Or it might have a champion with the organisational heft to protect the function in times of corporate transition. But an archive aspires to permanency, and these are temporary protections – departments get reorganised, and champions move on.

Rather than leave archival survival to chance, the enduring corporate archivist takes a more proactive approach to ensuring survival by crafting a comprehensive advocacy and outreach (A&O) programme. What is an A&O programme? Simply put, it is a strategic and ongoing initiative to justify the continued existence of a corporate archive. When The Postal Museum, an independent charity operating with an uncertain budget to provide heritage services to Britain's Royal Mail organisation, felt its very existence was threatened by the spectre of the privatisation of Royal Mail, it aggressively created what was essentially a survival plan. The Postal Museum took its message – 'don't forget the heritage' – to influential politicians, civil servants and journalists, and succeeded in getting its concerns addressed by Parliament. It was then able to leverage that governmental sanction and increased visibility to acquire new facilities and a greatly expanded role in governmental archive circles (Steele, 2014).

As The Postal Museum example demonstrates, A&O is not merely a short-term, one-off exercise in acquiring additional funding or protecting current headcounts. Instead, a well-designed and well-executed A&O plan gives a corporate archive the best chance for long-term survival because it raises awareness among an institution's resource allocators of the value an archive can hold, and it creates a user base that generates that value. Moreover, because it is an ongoing endeavour, it is flexible enough to adapt to meet changing corporate needs and realities.

A&O Overview

In corporations, it is not just what you do, but why you do it, for whom you do it and how often you do it for them that defines success. An archive can do great work supporting corporate activities, but if resource allocators aren't aware of it, then the value of the archive is a moot point – when budget-cutting time comes, there will be nobody sitting at those tables that can speak for the function. In this atmosphere, the best path to long-term functional success is to be connected to the institutional centres of influence. One archivist has suggested that A&O is as vital to the success of a private institutional archive as the more traditional activities of acquisition, processing and reference (Haws, 2011, p. 186). Another notes that most corporate archives spend more time providing business services such as research than more traditional archival activities such as processing (Markley, 2008, p. 22). This perspective is perhaps best summed by a long-time corporate archivist for a major global brand, who stated that corporate archives must be 'aggressive self-promoters, seeking every opportunity to sell the use of the archival record for business enhancement' (Mooney, 1997, p. 62).

Archival literature does not often distinguish between the two concepts of advocacy and outreach. Usually the terms are used interchangeably, because both concepts overlap in that each aims to strengthen an archival function within an institution. Both require constant attention and both have cumulative impacts that grow over time.[1] However, while they are highly complementary, they are in fact separate rather than interchangeable concepts. Where they differ is in their target audiences and in their messaging.

Advocacy strategically seeks to educate key influencers, both internal and external, about the institutional value of an archives programme in order to create powerful allies who will act on its behalf (Hackman, 2011, p. 3). Advocacy is an entirely proactive process aimed at developing and nurturing an archives support base, one that is in place before it needs to be accessed in times of crisis. Defining advocacy is often contentious, because it is a broad, inclusive concept. So describing it may be more useful than trying to define it. One archivist succinctly but accurately describes it this way: 'Advocacy is you playing offense' (Society of American Archivists Issues and Advocacy Roundtable, 2015).

Likewise, outreach is also a form of archival promotion that is aimed at creating an archives support base. But rather than targeting key influencers such as advocacy, outreach focuses primarily on building grassroots support by strategically growing the use of the archives. The basic goal of an outreach programme is to enlarge the archive's reach and impact by growing its usage by raising awareness among key but underserved constituencies – both internal and external – of the relevance and value of archival content and services. In some companies the archive actively courts external constituencies, particularly in Europe. In North America, corporate archives are traditionally focused on growing internal usage.

When used together, advocacy and outreach can create an organic, balanced, enterprise-wide support community. For example, the Transport for London Archives included in its plan such advocacy goals as establishing vocal support for the archive and raising the internal and external profile of the service. Similarly, Transport for London Archives' outreach goals included increasing the ease of access to its services and collections as a way to increase the number of internal and external users (Thornhill, 2013). Combining both advocacy and outreach into a coherent programme can help justify a corporate archive's existence as well as mitigate the negative impacts on it caused by broader turmoil in the parent organisation.

But what defines a successful A&O programme? Frankly, that is an unknown. While much has been written in professional literature about both advocacy and outreach, this body of content tends to focus on the specifics of A&O activities – we did this, they did that. There is little empirical evidence that captures the impact of A&O, that is to say there is no best practices data that demonstrates in a compelling way if an archive specifically does this, it will most certainly accomplish that. In short, there are no A&O silver bullets evident in the literature.[2] Therefore, for a corporate archive, A&O success is less about applying a universal template and more about finding what works best within an individual organisation. Ownership structure, organisational structure, geographical locations, cultural heritage, corporate values and business principles, and last but not least people themselves are among the many factors that will have significant impact on what will and will not create archival success.

Given this lack of a universal solution, it may be more useful to frame an A&O discussion as a metaphorical tool belt, filled with tactical A&O tools that the intrepid archivist can select to use in the circumstances that are best suited for their institution. Each of these tools must be considered as part of a larger, strategic A&O programme – they are not, in and of themselves, the complete solution to an archive's promotional needs. Whatever A&O tools an indefatigable archivist chooses to use, they need to be programmatically deployed, built into a coherent A&O framework of daily-weekly-monthly-annual archival activities in order to facilitate a departmental culture of proactive promotion. For it is only through the consistent and regular application of A&O that an archive can position itself for long-term survival (Freivogel, 1978; Finch, 1995).

Advocacy

There are four primary steps to developing an advocacy plan. They are:

1   determining the value equation for the archives in the institution;
2   identifying the primary stakeholders in the archives;
3   developing goals that meet stakeholder needs and advance an archives agenda;
4   developing and executing a series of action steps to meet those goals.

The first step in developing this programme is identifying the strategic value of the function. Unlike government or university archive services, where the function's mission is organisationally mandated, clearly defined and relatively unchanged from institution to institution, corporate archives exhibit much less institutional support and much more variety.

For example, the strategic value for an archive in a firm that is closely aligned with the family of the founders will likely be oriented around preserving and promoting the personal legacies of those iconic personages along with subjects that support the purpose and mission of the business. Therefore the firm's A&O will be oriented towards results that consider the family interests as well as developing an enterprise-wide network; the two do not preclude each other. Contrast that scenario with an archive that is aligned with a records management function that focuses on corporate governance. The A&O for that function would likely be slanted toward raising awareness amongst senior management and the records community at large of the role and value of the archive in managing long-term information assets. Or to a scenario of an archive aligned with a knowledge management function, where A&O goals would include building an executive business case for the collection and reuse of knowledge as well as developing an enterprise-wide network of users to maximise the return on the investment in knowledge development and dissemination.

As a rule of thumb, the closer an archive's value proposition is to the company's revenue streams, the better. Where those revenue streams lie depends on the type of company. In a marketing organisation it is the sales force that gets the annual meetings in exotic locales. In a multi-line insurance company, it is the divisions that cater to large corporate accounts that get the big expense accounts. In a technology company, it is the high-margin product lines that receive VIP treatment. Regardless of the scenario, every corporate archive should aspire to be an integral component of the day-to-day operation of the money-making parts of the parent organisation – to be perceived as a provider of an 'essential service' (Treanor, 1994, p. 6). The more essential services the function can provide, the stronger is its justification for existence.

There are numerous examples of corporate archives that are integrated into revenue-generating processes. At Solvay, a chemical company, the archive helps the company capitalise on its older intellectual property, and brings historical context to current innovation projects assessments. It also improves the efficiency of environmental rehabilitation efforts by providing records that document the evolution of company sites over time (Coupain, 2016). At the brewer Guinness, the archive helps the company tap into its 250-year history to provide creative inspiration for current product development and marketing initiatives.[3]

It is this palette of strategic options that makes each corporate archive unique, and makes determining a value equation for any given institution so challenging. It is important to note that these value equations can and will change over time, as organisations are reshaped by the forces of market economies – business units are sold, companies are merged, corporate strategies shift. For example, the Aetna Life & Casualty Corporate Archives had a thriving and revenue-relevant business providing the international division with old policy documentation that was repurposed for use in new markets in less developed countries around the world. That is, it did until the company sold off the international division. So it is important that the archivist be adept at reading the winds of organisational change and flexible enough to adapt the archives to catch and ride those changing winds.

Regardless of which way the wind is blowing, determining a viable value equation is absolutely critical for a corporate archive, for this deep understanding of the value that a corporate archive brings to the institution is foundational to any advocacy programme. It will serve as the business justification for the function's continued existence. And it will indicate who its primary stakeholders are.

Being cognisant of those stakeholders, and identifying what their needs and drivers are, is crucial to an advocacy programme, because the long-term success of an archive depends on how well its agenda matches up with the larger objectives of the parent organisation. For example, the New York Philharmonic is a non-profit organisation that will never be blessed with a large annual operating budget. Therefore the financial function at the Philharmonic is always a key stakeholder for the organisation. Recognising this reality, the archive crafted an advocacy plan that had as one of the core components what it calls 'defensive advocacy' – keeping its annual budget small so that in times of financial stress it doesn't become a target for cutbacks. When larger archive projects are approved, they are budgeted as one-time expenses that fall outside the scope of annual operating costs (Haws, 2011, p. 189). In this manner, the function keeps a low cost profile, which makes one of its stakeholders – the folks controlling the purse strings – happy.

Once these stakeholder drivers are understood, they will guide the process of defining advocacy objectives. Absolutely critical in the setting of these goals is the recognition that the archives do not operate in a vacuum. As its very existence is tied to its ability to contribute to the larger organisation, so too its goals must not just be for its benefit. The goals with the greatest potential for success and impact are the ones that benefit other functions as well. For example, when the chief executive of retailer Marks & Spencer was invited to review the firm's archives in 2009, he wasn't looking to move the function from a hard-to-find upstairs space over a small, out-of-the-way north London M&S store to a badly-needed, much larger facility. But he did once he discovered that the archives collection could inspire new product designs, provide brand protection, and contribute to the firm's reputation building activities. The M&S story is a wonderful example of how advocacy – in this case, raising executive awareness of an archive's value – can link the archive's agenda (acquiring a more suitable physical space) to the objectives of other constituencies, for the benefit of both (Houston and Carter, 2012). At another company, this concept of mutual benefit is called 'synergistic success' (Wagner, n.d.).

With these advocacy objectives established, a set of A&O action steps for each objective should be set. In the Marks & Spencer example, the archives invited nearly every board member and senior department head to the archive for a tailored tour that demonstrated how an investment in the archives could turn the function into a unique asset capable of adding value to their specific responsibilities. Similarly, the Marks & Spencer Archives also approached the company's 125th anniversary – which was arriving fast – as an enterprise-wide outreach opportunity, a rare chance to demonstrate the utility and impactfulness of heritage content on an enterprise-wide basis. Collectively, these steps generated unanimous board support for and approval of the new facility project (Osborn, 2011).

As the Marks & Spencer example demonstrates, A&O steps should be ambitious but achievable within the context of daily archives workloads. They should address the pain points of the organisation and they should not be one-time endeavours but a consistent concerted effort, for the real impact of A&O is built up over time and multiple activities. The collective effect of these is cumulative, which means that in order to generate maximum impact these activities need to be persistent, a ubiquitous aspect of the culture of the archives function. Otherwise hard-earned momentum can be lost, which will be difficult to recreate.

Nor should an archive wait until a crisis to reach out to its supporters – even if they were inclined to help, it will likely be too late for them to do anything. By the time an archive realises it is at risk, it is probably already too late to reverse course. The real value of an A&O programme is in its pre-emptive ability to reduce risk by removing an archive from the cutback conversation by developing a clear-cut recognition of the value the function adds to ongoing business processes.

Since the impact of A&O is cumulative, these action steps will require a commitment on the part of not just the archivist but also the entire archival staff. It could involve such individual commitments as dedicating time each week to networking within the organisation, or proactively cultivating and nurturing internal advocates. James O. McKinsey, the founder of one of the world's leading management consultant firms, strongly believed that the lunch hour was one of the most productive parts of an individual's day – it was his practice to schedule a lunch meeting every day solely for the purpose of expanding or strengthening his personal network. Also, as Larry J. Hackman, the American archival advocacy pioneer, notes, 'effective advocacy is a team sport' (Hackman, 2011, p. 9). Empowering archives staff to advocate for the function not only expands the reach of the function, it has the added benefit of ensuring that they remain focused on the appropriate value equations and functional behaviours in their day-to-day work.

Advocacy targets

Functional management

Advocacy starts close to home. It is critical that the business unit the archives reports into values the archival function, understands archival imperatives and needs, and is able to advocate effectively for the archives within the upper levels of the organisational hierarchy, where funding, headcount and other decisions are made. Functional management will also be an important source of organisational information for the archivist. It will be a source of key contextual knowledge that could potentially impact the archive's agenda – staying in close contact with local leadership will help the intrepid archivist to stay ahead of organisational change.

Every organisation has those employees who are renowned for knowing how to get things done within the bureaucracy, and functional leadership can often provide valuable guidance in directing the archivist towards these bureaucratic wizards. Often these wizards are mid-level managers who are blessed with an acute sense of organisational politics or an equally outstanding knack at building successful business cases for getting additional resources. A savvy archivist will seek these people out and solicit their assistance in reviewing an archive's plans and pitches.

Senior management

While it is critical to have the support of functional management, it is a reality of corporate life that functional management rarely has the power of departmental life and death. The decision to reduce headcount and even eliminate functions is often made several levels above the archives manager and handed down as a final decision, without discussion or recourse. So it is critical for archivists to identify and cultivate advocates from the ranks of senior management.

It is equally important to recognise that not all senior leaders have the same level of influence in the organisation. For example, in most corporations, organisational power follows revenues – the opinions of those leaders whose functions generate revenues will carry more weight than those who oversee corporate support functions. Even within corporate centres, currying favour from those executives who do not control the purse strings in the archives reporting structure (or anywhere else for that matter) does not carry as much weight as cultivating a relationship with those who do.

Special attention may be needed to address the potential threat posed by new hires in senior positions in the organisation. Corporations often seek to attract leadership talent from outside the organisation. Home-grown talent would have the advantage – as seen from the archivist's perspective – of having risen through the ranks and having good knowledge of the company's values, history and even the archives function. However, a new senior manager from the outside will have his or her attention on the immediate business tasks at hand, and few will prioritise what they may see as the softer cultural aspects of the new job. Or, even worse, they may feel that existing culture is part of the business problem that they need to change, and they may engage in an effort to revamp that culture by eradicating established traditions and values – the sweet spot of any archive. Advocacy in these circumstances should focus on identifying how the archive can support the new directions and raising management's awareness of the archive's ability to help.

While a sophisticated advocacy programme will seek to cultivate the support of the more powerful figures in the organisation, observing proper organisational protocols in arranging to contact these executives is critical. Many hierarchical organisations frown upon personal initiative that does not follow appropriate channels – sidestepping these protocols could damage the reputation of the archivist and the function. So the successful advocacy plan is often a patient one, one that builds its advocacy base in a culturally appropriate fashion – because cutting corners by jumping directly to the source can leave a poor initial impression with a power broker.

In addition, it is a mistake – perhaps even a fatal one – to assume that every business leader automatically values the archive and the work it does. In fact, the opposite will more likely be true – they will assume that the function is just another part of a bloated corporate centre that stands as a drain on corporate earnings (Lasewicz, 2015). So before approaching these individuals, the archivist must do their homework to identify specific ways in which the archives can help this particular organisational leader better meet their business needs. This involves researching the business operations of these figures, and identifying places where the archives can help improve a business activity or perhaps even alleviate a business pain point. For example, for companies with international operations, managing exposures caused by inconsistent global records management can be extremely problematic. Knowing that there is a records professional in-house that already has an enterprise-wide records perspective can prove to be a win–win situation for the company and the intrepid archivist (Lasewicz, 1994).

It is also a mistake to phrase the archives business case in archival terminology. The savvy corporate archivist will couch their presentation in the language of business, including supporting the specific assertions with tangible metrics whenever possible. These value statements could range from a detailed analysis of reference requests to social media metrics to testimonials from client account teams that used archival content to close deals or improve client relationships. It is important to remember that not all metrics carry equal weight with executives – statistics that delineate cost avoidance savings are useful, but not as compelling as numbers that support revenue generation. Speaking the language of business will make the concepts easier for executives to relate to, and will increase the business credibility of the archivist (Lasewicz, 2015). True, not every senior manager will be initially convinced of the benefit of an archive, but that shouldn't stop a proactive archivist from continuing to try to think of ways to develop that relationship over time.

For those executives who are receptive to the benefits of the archives, the objective is not for the archivist to become a known quantity to them. The ultimate objective is to earn business credibility by helping those executives with their needs. The archivist does this by demonstrating the archive function's deep knowledge of the contents of its collection and of their relevance to business operations, and by incorporating archival assets and competencies into solutions for their pain points. This is not a one-off relationship – it is critical that the archivist continues to stay in regular contact with these individuals. Only in this way will an archivist achieve the status of a trusted advisor, somebody an executive can turn to when they have a problem. Developing these kinds of relationships is daunting work – not every corporation has a CEO as enlightened as Unilever's Paul Polman, who early in his tenure immersed himself in the company's history, and clearly saw the connection between the firm's past, present and future (Unilever, 2015). So these kinds of relationships need to be continually tended to if they are to provide the kind of support the function needs in times of crisis. But when done well, they can make all the difference.

Advisory boards

Advisory boards can be a powerful tool for an archivist. Composed of either decision-makers or of people with ties to decision-makers, an advisory board can serve as an influential carrier of the archival message, using the personal networks of others to expand the reach of the archives. It can also provide valuable insight into current corporate priorities and initiatives, and it can help an archive best position itself for future organisational directions. Additionally, by association with these influential people, an archive can enhance its own credibility (Hedlin, 2011, p. 311).

The composition and function of this body will necessarily reflect the unique circumstances of an institution, but some universal aspects of organisations make it possible to offer some guidance on how to craft an effective board. There are obvious corporate functions that should be represented on an advisory board – legal, communications and human resources among them. These functions are natural customers for a corporate archive, and so can serve as a conduit for current information on ongoing functional initiatives and priorities.

But while corporate function representatives are valuable and indeed essential advisory board members, they are not likely to be true power brokers because – like the archives itself – they are removed from the revenue generation process. With this in mind, the strategic archivist will identify and solicit members from where the true organisational power lies. While it may be presumptuous to solicit the participation of the absolute powers that be, it should be possible to identify influential individuals from these power centres who can still adequately represent the interests of their business units when it comes to discussing the contributions an archive can make to their organisation.

It may be counterintuitive, but it is not essential that every member of the advisory board be a supporter of the archives. In fact, there may be a danger in having advisors who are unabashed supporters of the function, for the objectivity of these choir members may be held in question by the broader organisation. While having staunch critics on the advisory board may create undesired difficulties for the archivist, it could benefit the function in the long run by forcing the archivist to build stronger business cases. If these arguments prove solid enough to pass the muster of these non-choir members, then they will have a better chance of succeeding in the larger organisation.

External stakeholders

Internal stakeholders are the most important advocates for the use, success and survival of the archive, but an entrepreneurial corporate archivist also needs to consider external agents of influence who might be useful advocates for the archive. These may prove particularly important at times of crisis, when the future of the archive and the survival of the records within it are under threat.

Recruiting external supporters may involve embedding a corporate archive within the national archive network so that professional bodies will rally round to champion the importance of the collection and its survival if a need arises. Corporate archivists playing an active and public role in national and regional professional bodies raises the profile of their archives and can win unexpected allies. In the United Kingdom several corporate archives have also sought and won accreditation of their archives under the national archive service standards scheme or achieved recognition of their collections on the national Memory of the World register sponsored by the United Nations Educational, Scientific and Cultural Organization (UNESCO). Such schema provide both a quality mark to recruit internal advocates and also encourage corporate archives to be seen as a natural and important part of the national archival landscape.

Some corporate archives may also be able to engage external vested interests, such as university professors or government officials, as influential supporters who will be prepared to argue that the archive is regionally or nationally important and that the company has a social responsibility to look after the archives and to make them available. This approach was used to great effect by the Marks & Spencer Corporate Archives in their drive for a new facility, where the Archives engaged a business historian to academically assess the external value of the collection. His report, which stated that the collection 'had the potential to become one of the finest business archives in the United

Kingdom', proved to be a useful tool in the campaign to upgrade the archive's facilities, as it assured the board that the archive's holdings had external value and that there would be academic demand for the content (Osborn, 2011, p. 17).

Providing research facilities and excellent customer service to the general public can also create a compelling argument for investing in an archive. Indeed, in today's customer-driven brand environment, securing great feedback from external customers can be another way of persuading the company that the archive service creates brand value by providing a much appreciated, if unusual, information service.

Outreach

If advocacy is largely aspirational, outreach is operational – it is where a corporate archive fulfils the promises it has made. Outreach is focused on generating organisational value by developing approaches to meet stakeholder needs. An outreach programme has three key characteristics:

1   identifying audiences and processes that fit the stakeholder value equations;
2   negotiating a role and objectives for the archive;
3   creating a programme of action steps to achieve those objectives.

Advocacy efforts will have identified significant stakeholder drivers to target with outreach. For example, a company with an underutilised brand heritage indicates that the marketing, design and external relations functions should be outreach targets for the archivist. A firm that struggles with retaining employees in emerging markets indicates human resources and employee communications in those regions are potential customers for the archives. Organisations that face challenges with managing intellectual property points to legal, records management and business units as prime outreach targets.

While advocacy efforts will have identified significant stakeholder and outreach targets, obtaining buy in from the stakeholder organisations does not necessarily follow. Change is hard, and people are busy. With already full plates, they are rarely interested in tweaking processes or adding new responsibilities – especially for something with unproven value, like archival content. Employees who are supporters of corporate history in principle may still be reluctant to incorporate archives into their work processes because they aren't convinced it has any value beyond nostalgia. Even with stakeholder support, the archive often faces an uphill battle in negotiating a role for inserting itself into company processes.

Beyond earning critical functional credibility through the daily impact of providing excellent customer service, the quality and effectiveness of a planned outreach programme will be a close result of how well it is designed and executed. The design starts with the purpose and goals of the programme itself – they should be meaningful and of sufficient consequence. It is important, however, not to confuse an overarching objective – for instance, the acquisition of adequate physical space – with outreach goals. Outreach goals are action steps that collectively contribute to overarching objectives. But they themselves should target specific, measureable issues and opportunities, because a specific goal will define a specific audience, which in turn will define specific audience needs assessments that will in turn define the most relevant and most effective content, messaging and communication channels to address those needs.

One example of a specific goal could be building relationships with parts of the corporation that are under documented in the archives in order to increase accessions from those units. Another could be to grow archive usage from revenue generating parts of the organisation by raising awareness of how heritage can deepen client conversations through the celebration of past relationships between the two firms. Another example could be to help human resources processes such as recruiting and employee retention by using the firm's heritage to differentiate it from its competitors or to increase employee loyalty by growing pride in the company.

In each of the goals listed above, a corporate archive has the potential to create value add by partnering with specific business functions to address organisational pain points. The experience of the Delta Air Transport Heritage Museum is a great example of this. When Delta and Northwest Airlines merged in 2008, the museum was enlisted to create a heritage programme that was used by corporate leadership to help facilitate the consolidation of the two corporate cultures. Even though budgets were tight in a tight economic environment, such was the significance placed on creating this merged heritage that the museum was able to solicit funds from a variety of business units for this effort. In return for their good work, the museum was able advance its own agenda by collecting materials to create a Northwest Airlines corporate archives. It also found its visibility at an all-time high, with usage at record levels (Force, 2011).

The expectations of the archives emerging from such collaborative partnerships place a premium on the proactive provision of content, so the enterprising corporate archivist will want to improve the function's capacity to support this objective by creating tools that will promote rapid, comprehensive archival access. Ideally, that means creating highly granular control over the collection, but that is often a luxury that perhaps only start-up archives can aspire to. More realistically, established archives will want to invest resources in preparing content compilations to speed access, both for research and daily use in communications. Specifically, the archives should develop: timelines for offices, business lines and country organisations; lists of key personnel, cultural activities and achievements associated with product lines and organisational entities; thematic narratives around key company traits such as innovation, diversity, and leadership; and chronologies such as 'On this day in history'.

Sometimes this may be purely a matter of routine departmental activities. For example, in the case of Transport for London, where the archive was seeking to improve access to the collection in order to grow internal and external use, its expressed outreach action steps neatly fit into traditional archival workflows of processing, arrangement and description. This focus on leveraging archives content, knowledge and capabilities by aligning the function with stakeholder interests can generate the kind of archival impact that enhance the function's business credibility, which will go a long way towards justifying its existence and even increasing its budget.

After the goals have been set and specific activities established to meet those goals, an effective outreach plan will have a timetable and a plan for measuring impact and assessing success. While outreach itself is never ending, it needs to be periodically re-evaluated for continuing relevance and efficiency. Any number of variables can affect the efficacy of an outreach plan – organisational and departmental priorities shift, target audiences change, messaging gets stale or falls off point, communications channels get superseded by newer content vehicles, even external events can impact the relevancy of content.

So a realistic outreach plan should anticipate its own inevitable obsolescence, and factor that timetable into the ongoing planning process.

The recognition of an outreach lifecycle naturally lends itself to a periodic evaluation of an outreach plan's effectiveness. As part of the outreach goal-setting process, the archivist should establish clearly measureable objectives against which the success of the plan can be assessed. The goals don't have to be complicated – they can be quite straightforward, such as increasing year-to-year reference requests by X per cent, growing website visits by X per cent in one year, or getting X number of followers on Twitter. But they should be measureable, because having a defined target will drive execution as well as assist in post-activity analysis.

Outreach targets

Requestors

The single, most critical aspect of a successful outreach programme is excellent customer service. It doesn't matter how thoughtfully crafted and carefully executed an archive's A&O activities are – they can all come undone if the function doesn't back up its promises with great service.

Most corporate employees are unlikely to ever see the inside of their company's archive. For them, their primary and possibly only contact with the archives will be through reference requests. Every email responded to, every phone call answered, every information asset delivered becomes a customer touch point that can either enhance or harm an archive's reputation. Through these information transactions, the archive builds organisational trust and credibility in the function. In a very tangible sense, an archive's reference work shapes its brand (Conway, 2003, p. 6).

In addition, institutional archivists need to be aware that they are not the only information resource in an organisation. Comparisons to other internal content providers such as libraries and online resources can affect how a corporate archive is perceived – for better or for worse – by both users and funding sources. Initially, the archive at the Royal Bank of Canada steadfastly adhered to traditional archival reference practices that had served the scholarly world well. But when the function began to suffer a negative reputational impact when its turnaround times were contrasted against other, quicker information repositories, the archive knew it had to make changes if it wanted to survive in the faster, more demanding pace of the corporate world (Rabchuk, 1994).

So the archive must set a high bar for its promised service levels . . . and then exceed it. To clear that bar, the function must take ownership of the requestor's problem and partner with them to solve it. Astute archivists will never say no. Even if they don't have the specifically requested information, they will strive to find something that can still help the requester in some manner. This could be related content in the archives that the requester didn't think to ask for. Or it could be that the information exists outside of the archives – in the company, or possibly outside the company. In those cases, the diligent archivist doesn't leave it to the requesters to find the information for themselves, as they may not have the organisational knowledge to find this content efficiently. Instead, the strategic archivist will increase the value add of the archives (and grow its base of organisational knowledge) by performing the research to find that information for the requester. The requestor will appreciate the help, and the reputation of the archive will grow correspondingly.

The archive will also benefit by this investment of staff resources in performing this research. Over time, the cumulative, enterprise-wide organisational knowledge the archive acquires though this work will become a *de facto* service offering in and of its own – as very few corporate functions will have this kind of enterprise-wide internal contact network. Ultimately, the archive can find itself becoming a 'go to' institutional resource for these kinds of requests. One North American archive became so adept at obtaining this information that the corporate call centre began referring non-archive-related calls directly to the archivist when they were at a loss to find the right contact.

This breadth of organisational knowledge – and the personal contacts that come with it – can also be leveraged to archival advantage. The information flow in these transactions does not need to be in one direction. The proactive archivist can turn the tables on requesters by starting a dialogue with them about archival matters. Did they know the archive has information related to their function? Do they know they have a function anniversary coming up in the near future? Do they have concerns about managing information with long-term value in their functions?

By looking at each information request as an outreach opportunity – a chance to grow the archive's reputation, to add a friend to the archive's support community, to gain organisational knowledge, and to advance the archive's agenda – the archivist will be well on their way to developing a successful outreach programme.

Process owners

This is where the archival value equation begins to transcend mere nostalgia – when an archive begins to contribute to ongoing business processes. Ideally, these processes are tied to revenue streams, and the business case for incorporating an archival component to these processes is clear-cut. This business case should strive to build a compelling argument for ongoing archival involvement – while one-off projects are still meaningful, lasting value comes from the integration of an archival component into existing processes. For example, at Gap Inc., a speciality retailer, the archive built a compelling case for owning the digital asset management system that was used to manage the product lifecycle, from the initial design phase to the permanent preservation of resultant intellectual property. Not only was the archive integrated into the revenue stream process, it actually owned a key part of that process.

Not all archives can aspire to owning the technology that hosts a product development process. But often-archival content can become a key part of the process. Since the 1990s, major manufacturers from automobiles to fashion to food products to insurance policies have been incorporating retro styling touches into their product lines, using their archives for design inspiration. For example, when BMW acquired the rights to the Mini, the company launched a completely new car from a technical perspective, but gave the vehicle a retro-cool look by taking design cues from the classic Mini bulldog design. Likewise, Volkswagen revived first the Beetle and more recently its campervan, tapping into nostalgic memories of past driving experiences. And Fiat similarly sought to leverage its heritage by bringing back to life its famed 500 model, which had been moribund for more than 35 years.

Other examples of companies looking to drive sales by leveraging consumer nostalgia for bygone eras can be found in looking at trends in retro-packaging. When Diageo launched a limited edition premium blend whisky, they successfully leveraged the Walker family's unrivalled history to illustrate and support the 'luxury' status of the new brand. When John Lewis, the United Kingdom's largest omni-retailer, marked its 150th anniversary in 2014, it used its heritage to create retro-products to mark the occasion. Kellogg's, the cereal company, as part of the 50th anniversary celebration of Froot Loops in 2013, designed a well-received series of retro boxes for its Froot Loops and Cocoa Krispies, Rice Krispies and Frosted Flakes brands. In 2014, Miller Brewing Company reintroduced its original 1970s-era beer can design, to much fanfare, with consumers going so far as to say that even though there was no change in recipe, the beer tasted better in the new packaging (Business Archives Council, 2012; John Lewis, 2014; Tselentis, 2014).

Similarly, there are examples of times when archival content can drive new products. Boots the Chemist sought to create a new global beauty brand, with an authentic 1920s look and feel. Research in the company archive identified original 1920s product formulations and merchandising that were subsequently adapted to create a new product line. This innovative use of Boots design and packaging archive delivered a global brand to market, quickly and cost-effectively (Business Archives Council, 2012). Likewise, the previously mentioned International Division of Aetna Life & Casualty is another example of a company integrating older intellectual property into its product design process. In the 1990s, Aetna's International operations relied on the archive to supply it with decades-old product content – policy language, forms, marketing material, and so on – that could be reused to inspire and speed the creation and introduction of new products into less developed markets. In these cases, use of the archival collections inspired and reduced the time to market cycle for new products.

While being close to revenue streams is the best defence against corporate cutbacks, significant value can be created by integrating the archive into non-revenue generating processes. Helping the marketing team better leverage its brand heritage contributes significant value to a corporate reputation. Helping the legal function better manage corporate intellectual property and compliance exposures by assuming responsibility for preserving and providing long-term access to documentation with ongoing relevance addresses a major pain point for many companies. Helping human resources win the war for talent by improving the effectiveness of employee recruitment retention through the provision of content that increases employee pride in the company ties the archives to a mission critical objective. Helping support media relations and internal communications teams by providing historical proof points adds credibility and authenticity to key messaging.

These examples illustrate ongoing corporate processes that can use an archival component, which makes the owners of these processes ripe targets for archival advocacy. These targets are specific individuals or small teams, and so the best way to work with them is through face-to-face meetings. At these meetings the archivist must be prepared to demonstrate deep knowledge of the process and the process owner's pain points. The archivist must also have a compelling case for integrating the archives into the process in order to address those problem areas.

Employees, history community

Most corporations have an amorphous group of history aficionados – long-time employees, employees with history degrees or people who just love history. The rise of social media technology over the last two decades has not only given a shape and a voice to a crowd, it has made it a credible practice among corporations to cultivate and leverage that voice to business advantage. The archivist can take advantage of that by organising an internal 'history community' that can help the archives shape and meet its agenda.

Using internal communications vehicles such as print and intranet communications, virtual team rooms and forums, social media technologies such as internal blogs and micro blogs, and even email distribution lists, the archives solicit individuals to join a virtual community of firm history fans . . . *archivinistas*, if you will. This community could serve as a sounding board for the attentive archivist, providing feedback and advice on the archive's projects and initiatives. The community can be used to help advance the archive's agenda by serving as informed advocates within their own work sphere, raising awareness of the archive and promoting its use. They can look out for the archive's interests by alerting the archivist to records or business activities that require archival participation.

They can even be marshalled to help with archive projects or difficult reference requests, as was the case with the HSBC war card project. When the HSBC Archives was faced with the prospect of transcribing more than 4,000 index cards that documented the service of the employees of a predecessor bank who fought during the First World War in time for the 100th anniversary of the start of the conflict, they were able to recruit 275 employee volunteers to perform the transcriptions. While this content was donated to the Imperial War Museum as part of a larger initiative to document the First World War, the donation and the information found was promoted on the HSBC News web page, and served as an archive win (Schindler, 2014; Porter, 2014; Porter, 2015).

Employees, general

The bulk of reference requests for most corporate archives come from the general employee population, so if number of requests is a key measurement for evaluating an archive's corporate contributions, then it behoves the archivist to broadly target employees with content designed to first, raise awareness of the archives, and second, demonstrate how the function is relevant to day-to-day business operations.

The first of these two goals is perhaps the easiest. Many employees have a soft spot for their institution's history, and so are likely to be interested in seeing firm history on display in almost any form – exhibits, presentations, company publications, internal social media and intranet sites. Internal communications teams regularly look for new and interesting content to spice up their more routine content mix of business and employee information, so they too are often open to company heritage material. The combination of the existing readership and internal communications imperatives means that in many companies, getting access to internal communications vehicles – both online and in print – is often quite easy.

Another way to promote the archives internally is by serving in non-archival roles such as joining corporate task forces, participating in one-off corporate projects, or helping with event planning. By participating in divisional events such as the roll out of a new product line or the kick off of a new organisational entity, helping out with site events such as 'Take your child to work day' or site anniversaries, or assisting with enterprise-wide events such as task forces or diversity days, archivists can put a face on the archives. In so doing they can raise the archival awareness of groups that may not have had occasion to think of the function before. In addition, archivists can enhance archival credibility by demonstrating the capabilities of the function's staff.

A former corporate archivist for American International Group insurance company participated on a corporate task force that focused on knowledge sharing within the firm. Not only did she participate in a highly visible senior management-driven project, she was exposed to the leadership of and issues associated with all the major information flows in the company. At the same time, she was able to bring an archivist's perspective to the work, and greatly enhance the visibility and credibility of the archive function among potential clients and supporters (Maclin, 2000). The archivist at another North American insurer regularly helped with annual philanthropic fund drives and divisional kick-off meetings. He also served on the firm's first intranet committee and its Y2K (year 2000 problem) committee.

Another excellent example of this non-archival outreach activity is the Durst Organisation Archives, where the staff skills sets include photographic expertise. One of the ways they've generated value for the organisation is by serving as an internal photography resource, taking employee portraits and documenting major construction projects. Not only does this activity address a corporate need, it benefits the archive as well, for the function owns the image creation process, an important component of the Durst documentary record. In addition, the archive also has acquired new photographic equipment at no cost to itself, earned credibility for the function, and broadened its network of internal contacts (Bojorquez, 2015).

Similarly, the curator at the Roche Historical Collection and Archive supported a corporate change management initiative by participating on an interior design team to shape facility interiors that reinforced key cultural messaging (Bieri, 2016). Other corporate archivists have taken on company records management responsibilities, helped design content frameworks for corporate intranets, served on industry study teams and helped reengineer corporate information flows. These opportunities not only serve to grow a polymath archivist's personal skill sets, but they also enlarge their reputation outside normal archival circles as an employee with competencies that extend beyond the archival box.

Harder than raising awareness of the archive's existence is convincing the employee population that an archive is relevant to their work. The challenge for the corporate archivist is to avoid perpetuating the unfortunate perception that while company history can be interesting and perhaps even fun, it is not relevant to current business activities.

The best way to combat this is by clearly tying archival content to strategic imperatives. While posting nostalgic images on 'Throwback Thursdays' can generate many views and comments, these are metrics that don't necessarily influence resource allocators. However, if an internal publication doing a special edition on a topic of current business significance includes an article on the historical background to the current situation that supports the company's key messaging, that is a different matter. This is the kind of heritage usage that does raise awareness of archives' business value.

Convincing employees of the business utility of an archive will be a never-ending struggle, requiring a thoughtful form of outreach – strategic and patient. The forbearing archivist needs to be strategic in what and how archival capabilities are promoted, informed about specific business needs and clear about what value the archive adds. Patience will be at a premium, as cultural change is hard for even chief executive officers – the archives needs to set its expectations appropriately. Sadly, it is likely that the average employee will not be convinced of the relevance of an archive to their work until they actually use the archive during the course of their business.

External stakeholders

While North American business archives rarely encourage external research in their collections, their European counterparts are more transparent in this regard. European corporations consider providing access to their histories as part of their social responsibility. As a result of this, European corporate archives are more open to making their collections available to external audiences than their North American counterparts, whose concerns about litigation and damaging publicity far outweigh their sense of responsibility for enriching national historical narratives. While European corporate archives have these same risks, their social responsibility drivers make them more amenable to finding ways to increase their transparency.

European regions or countries also can be home to clusters of corporations within a certain industry, which often leads to the development of professional programmes in universities and specialist interest from academia, in museums and in the educational systems. One such example is Denmark, which despite its relative size in terms of population and national economy, plays a significant role as an international ship-owning and -operating country. Along with the historical development of a range of companies in the shipping industry, universities, business schools and even upper secondary schools have adopted shipping as a major subject in their curriculum. Such institutions are very open to interactions with knowledgeable resources in the shipping companies, including those with special knowledge about shipping history.

In this manner, Europe has a plethora of centres for business history. As of 2013, such centres – usually associated with universities – could be found in Copenhagen, Glasgow, Milan, Oslo, Reading, Rotterdam, Uppsala, Ultrecht and York (The Alliance of Centres for Business History in Europe, n.d.). A non-academic example of these institutions can be found in the Centre for Business History in Stockholm. Originally founded by the municipality to preserve and present local business records, the organisation now has a national agenda, with over 300 member companies and 7,000 individual corporate archives (Husebye, 2015).

With this external obligation in mind, European corporate archivists target external audiences with historical content that supports larger corporate objectives as well as meeting the needs of their own archives. For example, the Scottish Southern Energy Archives was featured in a corporate video in 2015 that had the dual purpose of introducing the archives to the general public and publicising the development of a new corporate visitor centre at the same location, the site of an historic dam and power station (Scottish Southern Energy, 2015).

Friends groups

There are external communities that have shared or even vested interests in the success of a corporate archive. For example, due to the technological significance of its historical collection, IBM has numerous groups that follow developments with its archives, ranging from local and industry museums to scientific associations. These organisations are ready to – and have in fact – reached out to IBM management whenever they have concerns about the fate of the archives.

Often companies produce items that have collectible value, which in turn fosters affinity groups such as collectors' associations. The Coca-Cola Company Archives has very close ties with its global collectors community, with staff attending collector conventions. Similarly, motorcycle manufacturers Ducati and Harley-Davidson actively support rider clubs and events for their customers and fans.

Reaching out to and cultivating relationships with these organisations can not only help expand the reach and influence of the archive, it can also help increase key metrics – website visits, site visits and processing totals. It will also tie the archive into customer support objectives, a key focus for many corporations.

Volunteers

Volunteers have always been a mixed blessing for archives, as the impact of their knowledge and passion in working with archival collections is often lessened by other factors – irregular schedules, the need to and challenges in building consensus among the staff and the volunteer team, and the obstacles in maintaining standards. There can be even more difficulties working with volunteers in a corporate environment – even if the volunteers are current employees, there can be issues associated with what content they are allowed to see. Additionally if the volunteers are not employees – such as company retirees or industry experts – there are often irresolvable physical, content and network security issues that present themselves.

But social media technologies potentially offer a way for corporate archives to solicit volunteer contributions in ways that don't conflict with corporate priorities. Company alumni are often a wonderful resource for a corporate archive. One study demonstrated the ability of an archives-based social media project to generate enthusiasm and goodwill among the alumni of a North American university as well as helping the archives with a difficult description project. Numerous corporations are trying to activate their alumni base – both retirees and former employees – as unofficial industry advocates. To the extent that a corporate archive can tap alumni as a potential resource, it could also serve the larger corporate objective of improving alumni relations (Baggett, Gibbs and Shumar, 2014). Not only are they founts of historical knowledge, they can be a valuable source of volunteers – motivated by their passion for the company and its products, and already familiar with the firm's culture and archives content. They also can be useful advocates for the archives as well – thoughtful archivists can leverage this broader trend to advance their own cause by adding another knowledgeable and credible voice to their support base.

The Archives of American Art at the Smithsonian Institution over a period of a few years developed a relationship with volunteer Wikipedia experts to improve user access to the museum's online collection content by reviewing and creating links on relevant content pages in the world's most popular online encyclopaedia. The skilled Wikipedians utilised their knowledge of tools and techniques to dramatically increase traffic to the museum's online content – Wikipedia forms the single largest referrer to the museum's websites. The museum returned the favour by providing rights-free images to WikiMedia Commons (Snyder, 2014).

Tools

The corporate archivist has many tools in their organisational tool belt through which to advance and implement their A&O programme. Existing organisational information channels – both analogue and increasingly digital in nature – can be utilised to great effect by thoughtful, creative, proactive archivists. All of these tools have strengths and weaknesses – for example, in-person presentations are great for humanising key messages, but don't scale very well if reaching a large audience is an objective. Social media can scale upwards very easily, but sometimes key messaging can get lost in a sea of cyber content. So the strategic archivist should invest some thought in identifying the tools best suited for achieving the desired results.

Any assessment of the tools should start with a clear objective in mind. As previously discussed, outreach activities are the tactical implementation of larger advocacy objectives. Therefore, each objective should have specific target audiences in mind. In addition, beyond targeting specific audiences, each outreach activity should have specific goals in mind. These goals should target specific areas for improvement, and they should have clearly defined definitions of success. They should have set timeframes so that the degree of success can be more readily assessed. And they should be realistically framed, stating what can reasonably be expected to be achieved with available resources and be defined so as to have measurable results.

With these definitions in mind, the archivist can begin to identify the tools most likely to achieve the desired results. If one is seeking to influence the centres of organisational power, face-to-face meetings are likely to be more effective than a Twitter campaign. If one is seeking to solicit volunteers, lectures or electronic newsletters will be more effective than historical displays. If one were looking to raise public awareness of the archives, press releases or a Facebook page would be more useful than an elevator speech. It is important to note that while many of the 'tools' listed are discussed in their external application, most have internal corporate counterparts that can be similarly utilised to reach key internal stakeholders.

Implicit in the concept of tools is the notion that no 'one tool fits all' – it may very well be that the archivist will need to use multiple tools in order to maximise the breadth and degree of their A&O impact. For example, the role that the Delta Air Transport Heritage Museum played in facilitating the successful 2008–2010 consolidation of the Delta and Northwest Airlines merger demonstrates the impact of both incorporating archive content and the effectiveness of a co-ordinated multi-pronged approach to outreach. Faced with a double enterprise-wide strategic objective, the museum utilised classic analogue approaches like physical exhibits, posters, articles in company publications and even a vintage employee uniform week to bring key messaging to the employees of both companies. The museum also utilised social media vehicles such as regular blog posts and internal and external websites to increase the reach and impact of this heritage content (Force, 2009).

Similarly, the United States Library of Congress' Personal Digital Archive initiative shows how effectively social media can be combined with more traditional outreach activities such as presentations, brochures and partnerships. This initiative merged the reach of the online media such as a website, a blog, Twitter, Facebook and webinars with in-person public events to raise awareness among underserved constituencies of the challenges to preserving digital family history. The Library of Congress also partnered with other organisations such as the American Library Association, and leveraged existing promotional vehicles such as National Preservation Week to raise awareness of the issue and available solutions. The takeaway for institutional archives is how a thoughtfully crafted and co-ordinated multi-tool outreach effort can greatly expand the reach of an archive (Lefurgy, 2014).

Once these desired results for an A&O activity have been defined, it becomes easier to identify the tools to be employed for this specific effort (see Table 12.1). While many of the tools have both internal and external versions, the internal iterations require less procedural scrutiny and therefore are less laborious. Content disseminated internally is entirely focused on an internal audience, and that affords archivists a little more freedom to operate – they need only keep their internal brand in mind when making decisions about content selection, confidentiality and rights, and presentation formats. Good judgement is still important – the archive does itself no favours by disregarding internal corporate communications and cultural standards. But generally internal communications require little in the way of formal approvals.

External content, however, requires more care because it is by definition a part of the parent organisation's larger brand. Here the adroit archivist needs to ensure that archival

Table 12.1 A&O tools

A&O Target	Meetings	Presentations	Print materials	Displays	Digital communicators	Internal social media	External social media	Intranet	Internet	Blogs	Wikis	Mobile apps	Online apps
Advisory board	*	*	*	*	*								
Management	*	*	*		*								
Business process owners	*		*			*	*	*					
Employees, history community		*	*	*	*	*	*	*	*	*	*	*	*
Employees, general		*	*	*		*	*		*	*	*		
External, stakeholders	*	*	*		*		*		*	*		*	*
External, general				*			*		*	*		*	*

A typical corporate archives A&O programme will feature many of these 'tools'. Differences in target audiences and the various strengths and weaknesses of typical A&O approaches require archivists to be thoughtful about which tools they employ to advance their agendas.

content posted externally does not conflict with the parent organisation's broader image and messaging. One of the unexpectedly troublesome aspects of posting historical content online externally is that it can't be recalled – it remains widely accessible for a very long time. This poses fairly unique challenges to archivists. For example, many companies operate in politically unstable countries. If one of those country organisations were marking an anniversary, a commonplace scenario would have an archive posting on various external channels a laudatory chronology of firm milestones in that country. However, what is seen as a positive marketing initiative today could quickly become a public relations negative if a future change in government in that country results in a decline in the country's international reputation. Then the company may not want to call attention to its long-standing relationship with that country.

Regardless of what the company wants, that scenario may present an unavoidable exposure for an archive. Nevertheless, it is always best practice to partner with external relations teams to ensure all content is approved. In other situations, however, it may be impractical to get formal approval for each piece of archival content posted to a company's internet history pages. In those cases, it is important that the archives have earned the trust of the external relations teams by demonstrating its awareness of and ability to operate within corporate standards. For example, the IBM corporate history website has several thousand pages of archival content, few of which were formally reviewed and approved. But the archives managed that exposure by having most of those pages written by a former member of the company's public relations function, a writer well-schooled in IBM's external messaging practices.

Ultimately, the single greatest determinant of the assessment process for outreach is available resources. Costs always factor into determining what an archivist can and can't do, and it is no different when it comes to A&O. Not every institution will fund the development of a regional attraction such as the Porsche Museum in Stuttgart, or a sophisticated online heritage portal such as the history section on the Coca-Cola Journey website. But there are many low cost channels that can be leveraged for A&O by less well-funded archives, ranging from internal collaboration tools such as blogs and wikis, to external applications such as Twitter and Facebook. What the archivist needs to determine is which tools will generate the most impact from the allotted resources, that is the greatest return on investment.

Low cost, high scale

Figure 12.1 illustrates a comparative way of assessing the potential impact of the tools, by placing them in the context of the number of people reached versus the relative cost of production. The upper left quadrant is a sweet spot for corporate archives in that it contains tools that produce the greatest impact for the least amount of money and effort. Not surprisingly, the tools placed there are internal and external social media technologies.

In recent years the use of social media by the general public has exploded. For example, user statistics in the United Kingdom for 2013 indicate that 83 per cent of adults were online. More than two thirds of them had social media profiles. Similarly, 43 per cent of businesses had a social media profile, a figure that rose to 80 per cent for firms with more than 1,000 employees (King, 2014).

Partnering with corporate social media teams has proven to be a highly impactful use of archival content and resources, one that raises both the visibility and credibility

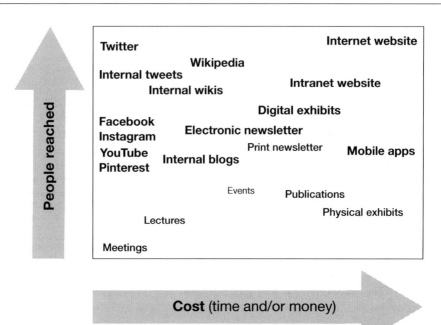

Figure 12.1 A relative impact matrix of various A&O tools. This graphic is illustrative only, and is not to scale nor is it based on scientific data.

of the archive function. The use of heritage in social media appears to tap into a collective goodwill for brands that is proving surprisingly powerful from the perspective of corporate communications personnel. Heritage is a tool that communication professionals are increasingly interested in using on social media platforms because it allows them to tell a brand's unique story to a global audience in a way that is authentic and credible. Over the past few years, companies have learned that heritage content drives more social media interaction than current business content. For example, American Express posted heritage imagery on several social media venues under #AmexArchives and saw user engagement levels jump significantly, noting how 'offering up grainy, decades-old pictures has created superb social engagement without any ad spend' (Heine, 2013).

There is a natural affinity between archival content and social media. Social media teams are content desperate and digital vehicles are ideal channels for repurposing readily available archives content such as interesting images or video clips and already prepared timelines and leadership quotes. For many archives, much of this content is already available and requires little reworking – chronologies, timelines, milestone lists all lend themselves to be readily repurposed in this fashion. For example, existing chronological content such as 'On this day in history' factoids are ideal for reuse on Twitter. Iconic corporate images with captions that may have been written decades ago find new audiences on image-sharing applications like Flickr and Instagram, while dedicated company channels on YouTube and Vimeo are perfect venues for posting clips on historic video.

With this in mind, it is clear that social media technologies are best used to raise awareness among a general audience of archival content and capabilities, and to tap into the goodwill that brand heritage engenders in the general population. It is less suited for reaching more narrowly defined constituencies, with the exception of demographically differentiated groups – social media experts have noted that specific social media technologies appeal to specific demographics. For example, recent studies have shown that 79 per cent of LinkedIn users are 35 years or older, and Instagram's most followed brand is MTV. Similarly, specific technologies are more in line with certain objectives. To wit, if growing a community is one of an archive's goals, then social sites like Facebook (with over a billion users) and Twitter (with its largest penetration in the United States) are good tools for raising awareness of the archives. If reaching out to women is a goal, then Pinterest with 68 per cent of its users being female would be a recommended tool. Other applications excel at sharing AV materials – YouTube for video and Instagram for images and graphics. Table 12.2 provides a social media assessment table summarising the attributes of the most useful social media channels for corporate archives.

In addition, as an online technological tool, social media excels at data collection, which makes it relatively easy to capture data that measures progress and impact. For example, one of the reasons the University of Tennessee selected Historypin and Pinterest for mounting their special collections online was because of the strong metrics platforms each application had for measuring their effectiveness as outreach vehicles (Baggett, Gibbs and Shumar, 2014).

Numerous examples exist of corporate archives using social media to advance the interests of their programmes. In the summer of 2011, the Royal Bank of Scotland Archives began tweeting real time excerpts from the 265-year-old diary of a bank employee in conjunction with the loan of a portrait of that employee to the Scottish National Portrait Gallery. The diary entries documented one person's view of a significant period in Scottish history, the Jacobite occupation of Edinburgh, and presented the archive's collections in a new and attractive light. This initiative, and others like it, have created new relationships for the archive, and earned the function internal credibility as a 'forward-looking, bold and creative team' (Yeoman and Reed, 2012, pp. 21–22; Reese, 2010, p. 3).

Forward-looking teams can take advantage of social media's metrical core capabilities – the collection and analysis of user metadata is a strong feature of the technology. A particularly creative example of archival social media analysis is the American Heritage Center's (AHC) 'Name the Tribble' contest, where it sought to meet its goal of engaging users by soliciting online suggestions to name its 1960s artefact from a classic episode of *Star Trek*. The contest inadvertently tapped into a rich vein of pop culture fandom, and attracted national interest and participation. While AHC is not a corporate archive, its forays into social media outreach are revealing. The Tribble contest was by far its most successful online outreach activity, and AHC used the experience as a learning opportunity 'to look more closely at our online audience, evaluate our outreach strategies in the realm of social media, and gain a more concrete sense of what might be effective in future outreach efforts' (Dreyer, 2014, p. 138).

Several archives have used social media video-sharing platforms to great effect. HSBC posted on the firm's YouTube channel a series of high quality company history videos to mark its 150th anniversary in 2015. Although videos like these are clearly event-driven creations, social media applications can give them long lives. For example, the IBM

Table 12.2 Social media channels assessment

Channel	What is it?	Tips	Examples of use
Twitter	An online service for sharing news and content with other users. It allows for instant communication with followers through brief (140 character) tweets. It is an excellent way to build a community around an archive's activities and raise profile externally. Be aware that the brevity of tweets often mean they lack context and may lead to the 'dumbing down' of archive content by neglecting its potential depth and storytelling capability. Twitter had 313 million active monthly users in 2016.	Share images – tweets with images have higher engagement. Embed Twitter feeds in websites or blogs. Make the most of hashtags and join conversations. Popular hashtags, such as #onthisday or #throwbackthursday (or #tbt) can be used by businesses as a hook to showcase heritage items.	Marks & Spencer Archives – @MandSHeritage; BT Archives – @BTArchives; Coca-Cola Archives – @coke_archives. Project accounts include: John of the Bank (Royal Bank of Scotland); Edwardian postcards; and WWI Foreign Officer.
Flickr	An image sharing platform. Flickr allows for more curation than Twitter, as content can be given detailed context in descriptions and organised into albums or sets. Be aware of copyright issues and the limited control over future image use when planning to upload images. Flickr had 112 million users in 2015.	Use Flickr as a shop window to attract an audience to a repository's collections. Create communities for collections and track engagement with images. Ask for crowd-sourced help with the identification of unlabelled photographs. Embed slideshows on other online platforms.	The Postal Museum; Library of Congress; National Library of Scotland; The National Archives (United Kingdom).
Blogs	A regularly updated website or web page, written in an informal or conversational style. Blogs are a way to regularly share detailed news and information about an archive service and its collections. A blog post is typically made up of 2–3 paragraphs with supporting images and links. Be aware that blogs demand more thought and time, a consistent voice and regular content, but are a great way to share detailed information.	Promote new blog posts via other social media accounts. Consider creating an archive slot on the main corporate blog. This will require less time and resources than maintaining a dedicated archive blog. Project blogs work well for anniversaries or cataloguing projects as they have defined content end times.	Laura Ashley; Liberty; Coca-Cola; Levi Strauss & Co; The Postal Museum; GEC Traction Archive Project.

Platform	Description	Examples
Facebook	A social networking platform that allows images, links and more detailed posts to be shared in a similar way to a blog, but within the framework of the Facebook community. In 2016 Facebook had 1.7 billion users. An enterprise version for workplace collaboration, Workplace by Facebook, launched in 2016.	Share news and updates about an archive service and its collections. Facebook is very easy for people to comment or 'like' what archive repositories are submitting or doing. Provide heritage/archive content for the corporate Facebook account.	The Postal Museum; Unilever Archives; Coca-Cola Archives; Society of American Archivists Business Archives Section; The Henry Ford.
YouTube	A video sharing service that allows users to watch videos posted by other users and upload videos of their own. Vimeo and Vine are other examples of similar platforms. YouTube had over 1 billion active monthly users in 2016.	Give new life to digitised content in the archive. Archive material is a source of unique content for corporate brands. Showcase the archive to employees and/or external users with specially made 'introduction to' or 'behind-the-scenes' films. Embed films on other online platforms.	BT Archives; Unilever Archives (30 years of the archive); IBM; HSBC (150th anniversary); Coca-Cola Archives; Coors beer; Marks & Spencer Archive; Scottish Southern Energy.
Instagram	An image sharing site, one of the fastest growing platforms that excels at brand engagement. However, there is some doubt over meaningful engagement as individuals view images and move on without knowing where they are from or entering into further inquiry. Instagram had 500 million active monthly users in 2016.	Support corporate accounts and provide images for #throwbackthursday-type posts. Make the most of hashtags and join conversations. Embed image feed in websites or blogs.	Coca-Cola Archives – @coke_archives; Archives Foundation – @archivesfdn; White House History – @whitehousehstry; New York Public Library – @nypl. Corporate accounts include Guinness, Clarks and Harper Collins.
Pinterest	A service where users can upload, organise and manage media through collections known as pinboards. Pinterest encourages a high level of engagement and its content has the longest half-life of any social media platform (3.5 months compared to 90 minutes on Facebook). Pinterest had 100 million active monthly users in 2016.	It can act as a shop window for collections by creating boards based on collection themes and links to catalogues or websites. Showcase how collections have been used by others by pinning examples of research, exhibitions or publications. Create meaningful descriptions and they are likely to be kept when repinned by others. Support your corporate account with a heritage board.	The Postal Museum; Ballast Trust; AGA Rangemaster; Maersk; John Lewis (150th anniversary); Loewe; P&O (175th anniversary); The Henry Ford.

Source: Table provided by Kiara King by private communication.

Centennial Film '100 x 100' that was posted on the IBM YouTube channel in 2011, received nearly 1.2 million views over the following five years.

Despite successes such as these, corporate archives should think long and hard about whether social is right for them. While social is an A&O tool that can deliver archival content and messaging to an audience of a size that was unthinkable just 20 years ago, it is also a content monster with a voracious appetite, placing similarly unprecedented demands on an archive's time and resources.

Social media's focus on user engagement requires close, dedicated and skilled attention – the technology and user expectations demand that posts by users need to be monitored and if needed responded to at internet speed. So the resource demands of the care and feeding of social places on an archive's staff can be a significant addition to and potentially disruptive of daily archival routines. For example, the world of social media demands that different social platforms require different content – repeating the same content across multiple platforms is considered lazy by tech savvy audiences. With this in mind, providing content that is timely, platform appropriate and on message can be a challenge over time. Similarly, maintaining a consistent voice and high editorial standards can be difficult as well. It is important to note too that much of the benefit from the use of heritage on social can be unwound by a failure to sustain the interactive aspect of the effort, both in terms of provision of fresh compelling content as well as failing to maintain a two-way dialogue with the newfound audience.

To avoid being sucked into the maw, the successful corporate archivist must thoughtfully recast departmental processes to incorporate the demands of the new workload. The archive should look for ways to leverage existing departmental and corporate routines to produce content for social. To wit, the processing and description of new accessions should include a review for content suitable for use on social. The archive should also look to leverage existing corporate social resources rather than recreate the wheel. For example, the archive should gain access to the corporate communications content calendars so that they will know what topics they should target for research over the course of the year. In addition, they should look at the framework of their social activities – does it make more sense to provide content to corporate social accounts, rather than create dedicated archives accounts? Can the archives use existing corporate social editorial processes to address issues of voice and grammar?

Lastly, the notorious inability of corporations to control where the interactive dialogue goes once content is posted requires careful consideration of the heritage topics chosen to highlight (Borison, 2014). An example of an often-troublesome social media vehicle for corporations is Wikipedia. An internet search of almost any topic imaginable usually returns a Wikipedia entry in the first few results, so it is likely that most companies have some version of their history mounted on Wikipedia. At first glance, this sounds like it should be an ideal place for corporate archivists to post about their companies.

Alas, it is not. Wikipedia's clearly stated policies strongly discourage content creation that smacks of advertising, marketing or self-promotion. They also discourage contributions that can be viewed as conflicts of interest. This is not to say that Wikipedia is off limits to corporations, but the digipreneurial archivist needs to collaborate with rather than dictate to Wikipedia page owners. To this end, corporate archivists seeking to leverage Wikipedia's expansive reach to convey accurate and relevant historical information to the general public need strictly to adhere to Wikipedia's participatory model. Any prospective corporate contributor must become deeply conversant with

Wikipedia core editorial policies, behaviours and guidelines, for those edits should follow appropriate Wikipedia cultural precepts and processes. There is a lot to learn in this regard, but it is knowledge that is critical to safely negotiating Wikipedian culture.

At all times, archivists must keep realistic expectations. Looking for anything more than improving the accuracy of a company's pages is asking for trouble and potential media backlash. Wikipedian antennae are acutely sensitive to spin – even the slightest promotional wording can create a mini-firestorm (Hafner, 2007; Snyder, 2014; Wikipedia (a), 2015; Wikipedia (b), 2015). Corporate archivists must recognise and accept that adding even purely factual content may be a lengthy process. They should expect that the consensual nature of Wikipedia might produce end results that are less than hoped for.

High cost, high scale

They say money can't buy love, but it certainly can buy A&O results. There are a number of costly tools that – if resources are available – can be effectively utilised as components of an A&O programme. Two of them are large physical exhibits and corporate history websites.

Corporate history content is built into corporate destination sites such as the Autostadt and Volkswagen Factory, the World of Coca-Cola, Guinness Storehouse and Cadbury World; corporate museums such as Porsche, Mercedes Benz, Harley Davidson, Campari, Shiseido and Wedgwood; or smaller, largely internal yet still significant exhibits such as history exhibits at headquarters and other key corporate sites.[4] For a review of the use of corporate museums in Italy see Box 12.1.

Attendance figures for the destination sites with significant corporate history themes like the World of Coca-Cola and Hershey Park are in the millions. Similar data for corporate museums or history exhibits is unavailable, but is likely to vary widely. An example of a large exhibit would be HSBC's partnership with the Hong Kong Maritime Museum to produce 'Made in Hong Kong: our city, our stories', which ran in 2015 and attracted over 100,000 visitors. The exhibition, part of HSBC's 150th anniversary programme, successfully met two objectives – to emphasise the shared history of HSBC and Hong Kong, and to give something back to the community of Hong Kong to thank them for their support over the last 150 years.

While even small physical exhibits require an investment of archival time and resources, a couple of display cabinets in a key location, which feature archival content tied to current corporate strategic priorities, can be a great way to showcase the value of the function by demonstrating how an archive can provide background and depth to contemporary issues. Refreshed regularly, such exhibits can be an impactful and ongoing reminder to passers-by of the relevance of history.

The scale, scope and financial cost of these types of projects are usually well outside the sphere of archival responsibility, so for those archivists involved in these kinds of projects, excellent collaboration skills are a must. It is likely that the expert archivist will be a part of a larger team, with the ability to influence but not determine direction. So if they are to ably represent their function in these kinds of efforts, they must be able to recognise the various drivers that other vested interests have in the project, and to work within those parameters to make sure the archival agenda is met.

For example, one typical archival agenda item in externally-facing corporate history projects is to make sure the content is accurate. This can be easier said than done when

Box 12.1 Case study: reaching stakeholders through corporate museums in Italy

One vehicle for disseminating and leveraging corporate history is the corporate museum. These range from small, in-company facilities to external charitable trusts and massive destination tourism sites. Regardless of size, they can play an important role in representing a company and advancing its A&O agenda with its key stakeholders, internal and external alike.

Perhaps no other place in the world celebrates corporate museums as intensely as Italy, where corporate history is a widely accepted mechanism for merging the interests of companies with those of their stakeholders. According to one recent study, more than half of the corporate museums in the world are located in Italy.

The basis for this national appreciation is rooted in two characteristics of Italian business: the strong regional identity that Italian companies often develop (and the resultant 'made in Italy' pride the larger region derives from that association), and the worldwide renown that many Italian products have achieved. This appreciation, combined with the strong social awareness that is characteristic of Italian corporations, has resulted in the creation of a relatively large number of corporate museums. The corporate museums of two legendary Italian companies – Ferrari and Ducati – illustrate the business benefits of making corporate history available externally.

The Ferrari Museum was founded in 1990, and aspires to be the authentic custodian of Ferrari history – the development of legendary cars, the evolution of an iconic brand, and the role of the entrepreneurial founder, Enzo Ferrari, as a paramount example of Italian innovation. Attracting some 250,000 visitors per year, it has become a destination site for the region. These visitors are exposed to Ferrari's key messaging – not just the company's legendary history, but also the company's role in developing Italy's automotive sector and advancing the nation's technological capabilities.

Like the Ferrari Museum, the Ducati Museum, established in 1998, serves as a shrine to 'Ducatisti', as fans of the brand are known. Ducati motorcycles are another iconic Italian product, long renowned for the aesthetics of its design. The museum was conceived of as a cultural component of a corporate effort to revive the brand through the preservation and display of its history, both to inspire current designers and to grow internal and external awareness of the uniqueness of the Ducati brand.

In the case of both Ferrari and Ducati, both museums closely tie corporate history into larger corporate objectives. Not only do they perform public relations and marketing roles, they also support social responsibility efforts. They serve as educational centres, teaching visitors from near and far about Italian technological innovation and design leadership. They enhance the attractiveness of the region to national and international visitors, a tourism bump which benefits local economies. They raise awareness of not only the corporate brands in national and international cultural networks, but also of Italian brands in general. In so doing, they help the parent companies satisfy the needs and demands of a variety of internal and external stakeholders.

For further information see Bonti, 2014.

faced with marketing personnel and creative agencies that are prone to rewording and reinterpreting archival facts and sources to conform to viewer attention spans, to maximise the impact of the content, and to better align history with key points of emphasis. So one role the archivists should position themselves to play in these projects is as one of the editors of the final copy to ensure that the final product is accurately presented.

But before they can play that role, they need to have the personal credibility as the recognised subject matter expert on all things corporate history. It is important to note that an archivist's corporate credibility is not entirely tied to their professional knowledge and skill. It is well known that corporate employees rarely know or care about how an archive works. What they do know is how the archive has partnered with them to help them do their jobs better. So an archivist's ability to influence how corporate history is used is ultimately tied to their skill at tying corporate history to current business agendas. The more effective they are at finding historical proof points that support current business activities, the greater their personal credibility will be.

Similarly, it doesn't do the archive any good for the archivist to develop a reputation as being difficult to work with. This means that the archivist needs to know which battles to fight and which ones to walk away from. Some fights over historical accuracy require an archivist to dig their heels in and go all out to win. Others may be things that aren't quite ideal from the archival perspective, but nonetheless are things they can live with – especially if waging the good fight means harming the archive's reputation as a helpful partner. Still others are fights that the archivist cannot win. The shrewd archivist needs to be able to distinguish between these situations if they want to develop and maintain a reputation as *the* 'go to' source for corporate history.

Having a seat at the project table also gives the archivist a chance to advance the archival agenda in ways that go beyond enhancing the function's reputation. A savvy archivist will look to leverage project funding to benefit the archive collection. For example, project funding may be made available to digitise important parts of the collection, or to process key parts of the backlog. As part of the IBM Centennial, the corporate archive received funding to build a centennial digital asset management system (DAM) to provide digital archival content to centennial projects around the world. It also received funding to digitise and create metadata for some 10,000 images and nearly 1,000 audiovisual titles to populate the DAM. This was an event-driven investment in archive content that will pay dividends long after the anniversary passed.

Of course, a great reputation and high credibility can also be a curse for the overworked archivist, as it means they will become a trusted resource that will be asked to take on more work than they have the bandwidth for. So a big part of having a seat at a large project table is setting expectations about what the archive can and can't do. For example, while the role of content editor on heritage projects is a high priority and worth the added work, the role of researchers and fact checkers is perhaps one that could be foisted upon contractors. So the prudent archivist will work hard to raise awareness with management of the staffing limitations of the archives, and position the function so that it is not unduly burdened with extra work during the development period and fabrication phases of the project.

Another 'high cost high scale' outreach vehicle is a website. It is an older technology than social media, and is one that is decidedly more difficult and expensive to use. But it remains a highly effective information dissemination vehicle, forming a necessary part of every corporation's reputational and marketing effort. A 2009 study indicated that among the Fortune 100 companies of 2008, only 17 did not have company history pages on their corporate websites (Force, 2009). Such ubiquity indicates that most companies see at least some value in making their history an accessible part of their brand. It also indicates that most companies are willing to allocate some resources to the development of history-oriented sites, which can be relatively costly to build and maintain within a corporate IT environment. Even if a corporate archive may not always be considered the 'owner' of a company history site, it nonetheless should position itself to ensure the accuracy of the information posted there, and to use these pages to promote its content and its own agenda.

The externally-facing archivist should strive to prioritise positioning themselves in this role, because an external history website is a terrific A&O vehicle. Web technology offers the potential opportunity to disseminate archival information to tens, even hundreds of thousands of visitors each month. The United Kingdom's National Co-operative Archives uses its website to increase access to its collections by publishing a series of interactive resource guides – from factories in the First World War to global commerce – designed to raise awareness of specific areas of their collections among a wider audience (Stewart, 2015). Similarly, the Baring Archive worked to create an interactive website that educates schoolchildren on the basics of finance and Baring's history by drawing on Baring Archive content that documents some of Baring's most notable deals, such as the financing of the Louisiana Purchase and the flotation of Arthur Guinness Son & Co. (Harrow, 2012). These website visits can be easily tracked and documented, providing insightful metrics that can bolster business cases and shape future content selection. A careful crafting of the content that is promoted on the site – such as credible timelines and topical narratives, archive guides and finding aids, and authentic images and FAQs – can strategically augment the reference process by creating a self-serve access to most requested content, thus freeing up internal resources for other tasks. This content can also be curated to support key corporate messaging, thus enhancing the function's strategic value. It can also be optimised for search engines, to ensure that a company's history pages are among the top returns for any search for that information. By creating a site that meets user needs and supports key corporate messaging, an archive is performing the best kind of outreach – it is tangibly demonstrating its relevance.

For all their benefits, websites are not without their flaws. If social media–like interactivity is an archives goal or a corporate web policy, then that requires a more complicated technology back-end than static html pages – which raises the cost. This additional complexity also makes the pages harder and more costly to maintain and migrate going forward, as back-end software and front-end look and feel standards grow obsolete and change. So the juggling archivist will need to balance design aesthetics – building in current technologies bells and whistles in tune with corporate design guidelines – against future prospects of obtaining the necessary funding to preserve and migrate those feature functionalities and capabilities to future web standards. Ironically, just as it is with analogue records – the stone tablet, rag paper journals, photographic negatives, microfilm, *et alia* – older, less sophisticated software such as flat html pages is easier to preserve.

For example, the Prudential plc corporate history site[5] has typical historical content – timelines and so forth – but also taps into current user expectations by presenting historical content in interactive formats such as games. These pages are less about conveying deep access to Prudential historical content, and more about providing a positive user experience through an entertaining and attractive overview of the firm's history (Porter, 2016). While the content is presented in a format that will better resonate with younger audiences, it is not a given that future web technologies will be backwards compatible with today's features – so without adequate funding for full migrations, it is possible that some current content and site functionality will eventually be abandoned.

On the other hand, the IBM archive website was designed to meet the needs of individuals seeking ready access to very specific IBM historical content. So the IBM site is composed of more than 1,600 primarily flat html pages that cover a wide range of content but are optimised for granular page-level access. It is a cumulative site, filled with pages that had been added since 2000 yet still featuring the same look and feel throughout (with the exception of the centenary pages, which have their own unique design). While the user experience of the IBM site is decidedly dated, it nonetheless successfully meets the needs of its audience, as annual metrics consistently indicate the majority of users on average open fewer than two pages per visit, but spend nearly a minute on the site per visit. This suggests site users are looking for specific content, and they are successfully finding it. As the Prudential and IBM web pages demonstrate, there are numerous approaches to the web presentation of corporate historical content. The prudent archivist will need to decide where the balance point is between designing to cater to current and future audiences and designing to maximise the value of the archive's investment in web technologies.

Another consideration is that websites that encourage user engagement require, like social media, constant monitoring and rapid responses. For example, when the Royal Bank of Scotland created a large website, 'RBS Remembers 1914–1918', exploring the wartime experience of its banks and bankers as part of national commemoration of the centenary of the First World War, users of the site were offered the opportunity to post comments or condolences for the fallen on every page and the bank's archivists were empowered to respond to them directly on the site. This active interface with the public is an exposure for corporations and a challenge for archivists, who often are not trained communications professionals. But increasingly, as corporations attempt to enhance their external reputation by allowing non-communications professions to participate in public venues as subject matter experts, companies are establishing social media guidelines to help define the parameters of appropriate employee public interactions. These policies to help prevent public missteps by employees can also guide archivists who are attempting to create social media engagement.

As with physical exhibits, archivists will likely receive additional budget funding to develop a website. A practical archivist will use this funding in ways that advance the archive's agenda. For example, a dynamic 'On this date in history' page could be developed that might drive the digitisation of a valuable but as yet unindexed company publication to support the web feature. In addition, the creative use of web technology can convey significant historical content in less costly ways. To wit, an archives blog on the website could bring timely, more in-depth looks at aspects of the company's history or archives function without the added expense of developing more permanent physical or digital topical exhibits.

One last consideration for the judicious archivist is to decide not only how to spend their web page budget allocation, but where. The value of external web pages as part of the corporate brand experience and meeting external requester needs is undeniable, but from an A&O perspective, having internal intranet pages may be more useful. While company employees can still use an internet corporate history site to find the content they need for their purposes, on an intranet site the aggressive archivist can market the archive to employees in a more blatant manner than would be appropriate externally. They can post content designed to raise the profile of the archive among employees – raising awareness of what the archive is, what it does, and how it can support employees in their work.

The question for the extroverted archivist is one of priorities – is it better to focus entirely on developing and maintaining an external site, or split precious IT funding to cover the costs of both an external and an internal site? The answer to that question will be found in the specifics of the individual circumstances. Does the archive cover web costs entirely out of its own budget, or are other funding sources involved? What is a greater priority for the function – enhancing the brand and reaching external audiences, or using internal web technologies to encourage internal usage? Does the corporate culture support or discourage the use of departmental funding to support internal marketing initiatives? These variables and others must be weighed and factored into the decision to create an intranet website.

The ultimate 'high cost high scale' outreach vehicle is an enterprise-wide anniversary promotion. A major anniversary represents a rare business opportunity to define, validate and communicate a company's key messaging, and promote that message with key constituencies – clients, industry analysts, shareholders, media, local communities, employees – in order to drive revenue/share, grow brand awareness, and raise and shape public perception of the firm. Therefore, the proactive archivist will be quick to raise management's early awareness of the strategic value of an upcoming anniversary. There are a number of ways that a corporation can leverage its anniversary to business advantage:

- *Heritage is a competitive advantage*: Few competitors can boast of a comparable track record of business success, industry leadership, and social impact. Heritage is an industry differentiator.
- *An anniversary can drive marketing and brand awareness*: A major corporate anniversary is an ideal platform from which to strengthen existing customer and partner relationships, draw media attention, and generate interest across of broad base of constituents and the public at large.
- *An anniversary will create an extremely receptive audience for corporate messaging*: Media and public interest in the company will be at its highest point ever, which presents a unique opportunity to shape corporate image and promulgate key messages.
- *An anniversary can improve community relations*: The achievement of a significant corporate milestone presents the opportunity to reaffirm company commitments to the communities it does business in.
- *A coherent, unified heritage platform can facilitate the integration of new acquisitions and the transition to a global company*: Communication and celebration of a common past will strengthen bonds across country, organisational and employee cultural divides.
- *Heritage messaging can strengthen employee relations, increase employee retention, and facilitate recruiting*: Growing pride in the company will improve climate and increase employee motivation.
- *Anniversary preparations will improve the retention of global intellectual capital*: Anniversary-driven research activities will improve records processes and help preserve the information a corporation needs for future reuse.

For a case study of one corporate archive's contribution to large-scale anniversary promotion see Box 12.2 for the story of the IBM centennial.

High cost, low scale

While it may be impractical to invest in expensive activities that reach relatively few individuals, there are times when it makes sense to do so. If an A&O approach targets a select demographic that is important to an organisation – clients or potential recruits, for an example – then it may be considered worthwhile for a corporation to make that financial outlay.

Traditionally, these kinds of efforts revolve around physical items like publications, videos, heritage branded items, and small, site-specific physical exhibits. The company history book, often created around a significant anniversary when the business rationale for a tangible corporate tome makes sense and the significant required funding is available, remains surprisingly frequent in this digital age – perhaps because print is still a medium that that current generation of corporate leaders remain comfortable with. While the writing of a book or producing a video or designing an exhibit is often – but not always – assigned to either an internal communications professional or an external consultant, this practice does not necessarily lessen the impact such a project would have on an archive's resources. Often the archive conducts much if not all of the necessary content research, and is likely to be involved in the editing and fact checking processes as well. So as was discussed earlier in regards to destination sites, corporate museums and large exhibits, the challenge will be to make sure the archive appropriately manages what responsibilities it takes on, and what roles it passes on to other funding sources.

The use of internal physical exhibits for outreach purposes can catch the eye of the employee population, but it is important that they be done well so as to represent the archive function as a capable and professional corporate asset. Exhibits that look as if they were created on a shoestring budget will not project the image of expertise and impact that the capable archivist aspires to. Similarly, the exhibit topics should not be esoteric or entirely nostalgic, for those will not project the image of current business relevance that the strategic archivist desires. Ideally, the theme and content of such exhibits will tie into and support broader corporate initiatives, such as innovation, impact or diversity. It is also important to recognise that to do physical exhibits well will place stiff demands on an archive's resources. The Transport for London Corporate Archives did a series of annual internal exhibits for employees, and one of them – 'The story of the bus' – required 1,000 hours of staff time in research, design and installation (Thornhill, 2015). But if an archive wants to reach its employees through a physical presence, it needs to be aware that a poorly executed display will create a negative impression of the function's business relevance and capabilities.

In the past, corporate archives have used posters, pamphlets and brochures to promote awareness of the function and its capabilities. While the printed item has a nice tactile quality, it is relatively more expensive than other communication vehicles, and can create a negative impression among employees who are cost-conscious and/or stalwart supporters of corporate green initiatives. It'll probably come as a surprise to many that corporate archives have been using online vehicles to promote their function almost as long as it has been possible to be online. IBM had a dedicated company history internal electronic forum dating at least to 1984, although that was an online history community that served

---

Box 12.2 Case study: celebrating the centenary of IBM, 2011, United States of America

The IBM centennial is an excellent example of a corporation using a major anniversary to strategically address business needs. In 2005 the IBM's Corporate Archives raised senior management's awareness of a looming centennial, and the ambiguities associated with the company's official start date. Arguments could be made for dates ranging from the 1880s to the 1920s. To help management resolve the matter, the archivist authored a corporate position paper that outlined the business case for the company's potential start dates. The paper's recommended start date – the 1911 date of incorporation of the business entity that evolved into the modern IBM – was selected as IBM's official start date.

The following year the IBM Corporate Archives was moved from the Corporate Secretary's organisation into Communications specifically for centennial purposes, and the archivist prepared a paper which benchmarked best practices for corporate anniversaries, including potential strategic and tactical objectives. In 2008, IBM's Marketing and Communications function began market research and strategic planning for the event.

From the very beginning, senior management saw the centennial as a stra-tegic business opportunity, one which held the potential to improve IBM's current position in the marketplace and to support the company's future aspirations. They saw the centennial as an opportunity to address weaknesses in IBM's brand and market position with key global constituents. Specifically, these included information technology decision makers, investors, employees and the general public. Management decided that core centennial messaging was to focus on three key brand attributes that IBM trailed its competitors in: innovation, leadership and social impact.

Tactical planning for the centennial started in 2009 and continued into 2011. Major deliverables were identified – a global forum on the challenges of the twenty-first century that was hosted in New York City and featured heads of state and other world leaders, high visibility executive speeches, a global day of employee voluntarism, several films, a book, a website, exhibits and innumerable local events. The archivist was selected as a member of the centennial core team, and the archives provided curated heritage content and imagery that supported the key messaging and strategic objectives of the majority of the deliverables. This heritage content was closely aligned with the three strategic centennial themes – innovative technologies, inventing the modern corporation, and making the world work better.

The centennial initiative launched in January, 2011, and continued until October of that year. By any account, the business results were spectacular. They provide a compelling and – perhaps more importantly – a measurable demonstration of the business value the strategic application of heritage can generate for a company. The results fell into four categories: employee relations, media relations, selling environment, and the bottom line.

Employee relations

One of the more strategic aspects of the centennial initiative was increasing the appreciation IBM employees had for the company. With about half of the company's more than 400,000 employees being with IBM for less than five years, few had a sense of how historically important the company has been. Employee loyalty, particularly in growth markets where IBM was a less familiar brand, was not as strong as the company would like. So the centennial was seen as a vehicle that could revitalise employee morale and strengthened employee ties to the company.

On both accounts the centennial was a success. 'Pride' and 'proud' were two of the most used words in employee feedback on the centennial and it also markedly improved employee attitudes about the company, especially in growth market areas. An end-of-year global employee survey quantified these improvements. Of the more than 30,000 employees who responded, 90 per cent felt they had a better appreciation of IBM's impact on the world, and 70 per cent felt more confident of IBM's future. More than 65 per cent of respondents felt they had a better understanding of what it meant to be an IBMer, and 60 per cent were more willing to recommend IBM as a place to work.

Media relations

The statistics for the media relations side of the business were equally impressive with more than 5,700 traditional media articles in 100 major publications from around the world. More than 77 per cent of these were feature stories, which exceeded the target number by 50 per cent. More than 70 per cent of this coverage was positive, which also exceeded the pre-centennial goal. Additionally the articles successfully hammered home the three message objectives: 71 per cent portrayed IBM as a technological innovator, 41 per cent portrayed the company as a transformational leader and 37 per cent portrayed IBM as having a positive social impact. These were impressive results, exceeding expectations in terms of both reach and message penetration. Significantly, all three of these public relations focal points were heavily grounded in heritage content.

The centennial book also exceeded expectations, selling 625,000 copies by the end of the year. It continued to demonstrate its influence by continuing to sell well into 2012 as well. It was printed in eight languages, and reached Top 10 lists in Canada, Germany, Japan and the United States. On the social media side, the centennial films on YouTube received 1.2 million views. The centennial website received 2.3 million views, and visitors spent 80,000 hours on the site in 2011. IBM trended Top 20 on Twitter on its 16 June anniversary date, with more than 43,000 tweets.

Selling environment

The impact the centennial had on the IBM brand and selling environment is perhaps the most important part of the centennial puzzle. The Interbrand survey – an accepted global measurement of corporate brand value – had their annual valuation of the IBM brand increasing by eight points, an impressive jump for what was already the world's second most valuable brand.

But perhaps a better assessment of extent of the contribution corporate history made to IBM in 2011 is found in a third quarter global survey of 5,600 information technology decision makers at companies with more than 100 employees. The third quarter timing of this survey is important. While the centennial was a year-long programme, its messaging and content was heavily weighted toward heritage in the first half of the year. The numbers captured in this survey, coming as they did so soon after IBM's target selling audience experienced their deepest exposure to IBM's heritage content, stand as a clear, tangible assessment of the impact that IBM history had on the brand and sales environment.

The survey revealed that with regard to IBM's key brand differentiators, those respondents who were aware of the centennial rated IBM 15 percentage points higher than those who were familiar only with IBM's primary marketing campaign, Smarter Planet. Those who were aware of the centennial were 60 per cent more likely to say that their consideration of IBM as a vendor had improved, as opposed to those who were unaware. And – most significantly – those who were aware of the centennial rated themselves 40 per cent more open to doing business with IBM than those who were aware solely of Smarter Planet.

These numbers demonstrate that IBM's centennial dramatically enhanced the impact the company's primary marketing campaign had on its most important target audience.

Bottom line

Ultimately, though, the most powerful proof point of the success of a corporate initiative is its impact on the bottom line. During IBM's centennial year, the company's revenues and net income reached record levels in 2011 of $106.9 and $15.9 billion. Both were up seven per cent in a difficult economy.

Can the Archives claim credit for this? Not entirely. There's no clear measurement of the value the Archives added to these record numbers. But clearly the use of IBM heritage was foundational to a very successful effort to improve the company's standing with key constituencies and to produce tangible fiscal returns. IBM's senior executives wielded the company's past as a strategic asset, a significant marketplace differentiator that their competitors couldn't counter. They also understood the role that IBM's Archives played in managing and making this asset accessible. That understanding will go a long way towards justifying investment in the Archives for years to come.

as a discussion vehicle for topics in company history rather than an archives-sponsored programme. But as early as 1994, the archive of another computer company, Digital Equipment Corporation (DEC), was using the firm's electronic communications vehicles as part of a formal outreach programme. The DEC archives incorporated its inventory into the company's online library catalogue so that searches of any topic would turn up both current content from the libraries and historical content from the archives. In addition, the archive used the company's computer communications network to raise awareness of the archives and its capabilities (St Clair, 1994). About the same time as DEC's electronic outreach programme, the Aetna Life & Casualty Corporate Archives started distributing a set of serial company history email instalments to a distribution list. Meant to raise awareness of the interesting and relevant content in the archives, the instalments proved to be highly popular and often had a second life, getting forwarded to people not on the original list. Some of these secondary recipients in turn would request to be added to the list.

Today, the HSBC Archive creates an electronic archive review every six months. It circulates this report to a distribution list of key stakeholders, a list that is updated constantly as the Archive comes into contact with new influencers. The NBC Universal Archives is an example of an organisation that communicates digitally instead, using a weekly electronic newsletter that includes video productions, which personalise the function and raise internal awareness of the nature and relevance of the archive's holdings (Chin, 2015).

Another example of a large resource investment is an event, where the outlay could involve both money and labour. While events tend to attract a much lower number of participants than say a corporate history website, the experience is much more personalised. For example, a number of institutions from Portland, Oregon, banded together to create an archives version of an immensely popular local event – the Portland pub crawl. Rooted in a desire to broaden community awareness of local archives in an era of shrinking resources, the Oregon Archives crawl featured 36 institutions working from four host institutions to create an event designed to acquaint 'a broader, atypical audience with the resources of the large and small archival institutions' (Banning, Hansen and Prahl, 2014).

Increasingly, these events are becoming digitally conducted. For the digital generations and their increasing mobile technologies, the world of mobile applications is an admittedly expensive but increasingly accepted way to reach a younger demographic. In 2011, an iPhone app, 'Navigating Nightingale', was launched by the Florence Nightingale School of Nursing and Midwifery at King's College London. The application cleverly provides users with a guided walking tour along the banks of the River Thames, using current sites to teach about the life and impact the noted health pioneer had in sanitation, nursing and hospital reform more than a century ago (King's College, 2011). Similarly, in 2013, Unilever Archives launched an app called 'Port Sunlight: walking with William Lever', a guided tour of the factory site and industrial village built by Lever to mark Port Sunlight's 125th anniversary. It was based on maps, photographs, film and documents from the company's archive, and sought to use technology to both enrich the visitor experience and expand the reach of the Port Sunlight site beyond those that tour the site (Unilever, 2013).

Low cost, low scale

Scale is not the only measurement of impact of A&O activities. The effectiveness of reaching out to smaller groups or even individuals to raise awareness of and support for the archives agenda cannot be overemphasised. The power of face-to-face meetings, the convenience and relevance of business lunches, the compelling nature of a well-executed elevator speech – all can do much to advance the archival cause.

The challenge is to be completely prepared. Know your audience. Target those stakeholders that have archives-relevant activities but may not be aware or what an archive does or how it can add value. Have a clearly expressed value equation, one that highlights your knowledge of their needs and can be presented simply but compellingly. For example, one of the things the Modern Political Archives at the University of Mississippi did to promote the opening to the public of a new collection was to participate in a continuing legal education programme, which raised awareness among Mississippi's legal community of the archives and the relevance it had to their ongoing work (McWhite, 2014, pp. 46–60). The Durst Corporation's Archive hosts a quarterly internal 'Lunch and learn' presentation series, which provides employees with overviews of the archive function, updates on archive activities, and topical talks on company history (Bojorquez, 2015). Both of these initiatives feature attendance figures of less than 75 people per session, so the scale is much smaller than A&O activities on social media. But the impact is likely to be longer lasting, as the impression of watching professionals representing their function well will personalise the experience for attendees in ways that reading tweets or reviewing a historical display will not.

While a targeted outreach approach can be very effective, this is not to say that there is no value in outreach to broader, more general audiences. The Unilever Archives took the occasion of its 30th anniversary to host an internal spotlight event at Unilever headquarters, where staff fielded queries from and demonstrated processes to their fellow employees, including how to use the new online archive catalogue. As part of this 30th anniversary outreach effort, the archive also created 12 videos – done entirely by the staff with just an iPad – with a variety of key archives contacts on the theme of the 'What the archives means to me', which were posted on an internal video sharing site. This anniversary-based outreach initiative was deemed a success in that it developed new staff skills, strengthened and broadened the function's internal network, and grew departmental pride by giving the archive team the opportunity to reflect on 30 years of accomplishments (Tunstall, 2015).

Similarly, provision of in-person access that leverages an archive's physical facility itself can be an impactful outreach tool. A programme that brings key A&O targets into the actual archive space, with tailored presentations and displays showcasing how the archive can support the specific work of that particular department, can play a huge role in raising awareness of the strategic value of the archive. More broadly, conducting 'behind the scenes' tours of an archive operation for more general audiences like new hires can give people a tangible sense of what content is in a collection, what is required to make it accessible, and how it can help them do their jobs better. At the new John Lewis Partnership Heritage Centre in Cookham, the archive offers its space for departmental off-site meetings – as part of the meeting experience, they give a presentation on the history of the bank, conduct a tour of the repository, and even put on exhibitions – all of which raise awareness of the function and its current business relevance.

For those archives with interesting artefactual collections, setting up the storage space to facilitate living storage tours can help bring an archive to life for visitors. The IBM Archives, with a collection of artefacts dating to the 1600s and no formal corporate museum to display them in, laid out its storage floor plan in a chronological manner to allow visitors to walk the aisles and experience how technology had evolved over the centuries. While something less than a formal museum experience, the scale and scope of the collection still provided visitors – from senior management to new employees to external constituencies – with a 'wow' experience that they would long remember.

Conclusion

In the rough and tumble world of corporate centres, a well-executed archival A&O programme can have a prophylactic effect on the function's fortunes. It can protect an archive from the proverbial budget axe by compellingly demonstrating that the function is too valuable to chop. But to be successful, A&O needs to be an ingrained part of an archive's departmental culture. It needs to be a routine part of daily departmental practice, rather than something that is focused on periodically. In this respect, outreach is a marathon, not a sprint. Success is often composed of a series of small wins, pilot A&O projects that can serve as templates to be replicated throughout the organisation. Through the accumulated impact of many such small A&O steps, an archive can create the lasting business credibility that will enable it to ride out cost-cutting cycles. An archive's long-term viability, and even its survival, depends on it.

Acknowledgements

I owe an immense debt to several colleagues whose collective input has dramatically improved this chapter. First and foremost, I would like to thank Alison Turton – her efforts on my behalf went above and beyond editorial obligations, and the depth of my gratitude for her knowledge, diligence and patience is immeasurable. As she has many times in the past, Katie Dishman once again lent her editorial savvy and all-seeing eyes to the hopeless task of mitigating my authorial sloppiness. Sara Kinsey and Henning Morgen provided thoughtful insights and wonderful suggestions. Last but not least, Kiara King graciously allowed me to include her brilliant guide to social media, which greatly enhances the operational utility of this chapter.

Notes

1   The notion that creating a wider user base for archival materials is a professional responsibility is a relatively recent one in North American archives, corporate and non-corporate alike, dating in the United States only to the 1970s. 'Until recently, outreach has been the poor stepchild of reference and access. When I first entered the profession, it was seen as a frill, or an add-on; something that was done only when the other or "real" work of acquiring and processing collections was under control. Archivists prepared exhibits, gave talks, and compiled printed guides to their collections, but marketing was considered crass and somehow mercenary. There was definitely an "if you build it, they will come" attitude toward developing an audience or selling the value of our services' (Duff, et al., 2010, p. 582; Bain, et al., 2011 pp. 4, 19, 33–40). A 1985 study indicated that few archives collected even the most rudimentary information about use. A later study indicated that there is a growing body of research in North American

archival journals that focuses on advocacy, as a small but growing number of articulate archivists began persuasively arguing for a pragmatic reorientation of archival perspective from the collection to the use of the collection and, by extension, the current and future users of the collection (Banks, *et al.*, 2011, p. 8). For an early discussion of outreach, see Applegate, *et al.*, 1997.

2   This topic is too big for the scope of this chapter, so consider this a two-pronged call for additional academic research. The key to survival in a cost-centric environment is increasingly value, not volume. So I would like to see future studies that focus on valuation metrics as a way of justifying archives. For example, see Duff, *et al.*, 2010, and Yakel, E., Duff, W., Tibbo, H., Kriesberg, A. and Cushing, A., 2012. The economic impact of archives: surveys of users of government archives in Canada and the United States, *The American Archivist*, 75, Fall/Winter, pp. 297–325. In addition, A&O is not just a challenge for corporate archives, it is a challenge for many institutional service functions with enterprise-wide mandates. With this in mind, I believe much benefit could be derived from a systematic survey of A&O writings from non-archives professions, such as special libraries. For example, when reviewing the institutional outreach challenges facing medical librarians, archivists find themselves on very familiar ground. See Fama, J., Berryman, D., Harger, N., Julian, P., Peterson, N., Spinner, M. and Varney, J., 2005. Inside outreach: a challenge for health sciences librarians, *Journal of the Medical Library Association*, 93(3), pp. 327–337. This avenue of research would greatly expand the knowledge base available to archivists on the topic of A&O, and enable them to a) identify best practices, and b) expand their tactical tool belt of specific actions.

3   Colgan, E., 2016. *Case study: the brewer's project*. Unpublished paper delivered at International Council on Archives Section on Business Archives Conference, Atlanta, United States of America, 4–5 April 2016.

4   For a useful overview of corporate museums, see Seligson, J., 2010. One part education, one part sales: this is the corporate museum, *Museum*, November/December. [pdf] Available at: www.wiu.edu/cas/history/pdf/Corporate-Museums.pdf [Accessed 11 September 2016].

5   Available at: www.prudential.co.uk/who-we-are/our-history [Accessed 11 September 2016].

References

Applegate, H. L., Brown, R. H. and Freivogel, E. F., 1997. Wider use of historical records, *The American Archivist*, 40(3), pp. 331–335.

Baggett, M., Gibbs, R. and Shumar, A., 2014. 'Pin'pointing success: assessing the value of Pinterest and Historypin for special collections outreach. In: K. Theimer, 2014. *Outreach: innovative practices for archives and special collections*. Lanham, MD: Rowman & Littlefield. Ch. 5.

Bain, G. W., Fleckner, J. A., Marquis, K. and Pugh, M. J., 2011. Reference, access and outreach: an evolved landscape, 1936–2011, *The American Archivist*, 74, pp. 1–40.

Banks, B. S., Conway, P., Zimmelman Lenoil, N. and Suarez, M. F. S. J., 2011. The view from here: perspectives on educating about archives, *The American Archivist*, 74, 306, 1–32, p. 8.

Banning, D., Hansen M. and Prahl, A., 2014. The Oregon Archives crawl: engaging new users and advocates. In: K. Theimer, 2014. *Outreach: innovative practices for archives and special collections*. Lanham, MD: Rowman & Littlefield. Ch. 1.

Bieri, A., 2016. *Using archivists' core competencies in building a company culture*. International Council on Archives Section on Business Archives Conference, Atlanta, United States of America, 4–5 April 2016. [online] Available at: www2.archivists.org/groups/business-archives-section/ica-presentations [Accessed 11 September 2016].

Bojorquez, C., 2015. Lunch and learns. *Society of American Archivists Business Archives Section website, advocacy success stories*. [online] Available at: www2.archivists.org/groups/business-archives-section/bas-advocacy-success-stories [Accessed 11 September 2016].

Bonti, M., 2014. The corporate museums and their social function: some evidence from Italy, *European Scientific Journal*, Nov., special edition 1.

Borison, R., 2014. The top 10 social media fails of 2014, *Inc.* [online] Available at: www.inc.com/rebecca-borison/top-10-social-media-fails-2014.html [Accessed 11 September 2016].

Business Archives Council, 2012. *Managing business archives.* [online] Available at: www.managing businessarchives.co.uk/materials/2785_managing_business_archives_lr.pdf/ [Accessed 11 September 2016].

Chin, E., 2015. Internal newsletters, videos and site posters, *Society of American Archivists Business Archives Section, advocacy success stories.* [online] Available at: www2.archivists.org/groups/business-archives-section/bas-advocacy-success-stories [Accessed 11 September 2016].

Conway, P., 2003. Talking to the angel: beginning your public relations program. In: E. F. Finch, 2003. *Advocating archives: an introduction to public relations for archivists.* Lanham, MD: Scarecrow Press.

Coupain, N., 2016. *Archives for a sustainable chemistry.* International Council on Archives Section on Business Archives Conference, Atlanta, United States of America, 4–5 April 2016. [online] Available at: www2.archivists.org/groups/business-archives-section/ica-presentations [Accessed 11 September 2016].

Dreyer, R., 2014. Happy accidents and unintended consequences: how we named our Tribble. In: K. Theimer, 2014. *Outreach: innovative practices for archives and special collections.* Lanham, MD: Rowman & Littlefield. Ch. 9.

Duff, W. M, Yakel, E., Tibbo, H. R., Cherry, J. M., McKay, A., Krause, M. G. and Sheffield, R., 2010. The development, testing, and evaluation of the archival metrics toolkits, *The American Archivist,* 73, pp. 569–599.

Finch, E. F., 1995. Archival advocacy: reflections on myths and realities, *Archival Issues,* 20(2), pp. 115–127.

Force, M., 2009. Company history: corporate archives' public outreach on Fortune 100 company websites, *Journal of the Society of Georgia Archivists,* 27(1). [online] Available at: http://digital commons.kennesaw.edu/provenance/vol27/iss1/5 [Accessed 11 September 2016].

Force, M., 2011. Flying together: use of company heritage in Delta/Northwest, *Society of American Archivists Business Archives Section Newsletter,* 28(1), p. 5.

Freivogel, E. F., 1978. Education programs: outreach as an administrative function, *The American Archivist,* 41(2), April, pp. 147–153.

Hackman, L. J., ed., 2011. *Many happy returns: advocacy and the development of archives.* Chicago, IL: Society of American Archivists.

Hafner, K., 2007. Seeing corporate fingerprints in Wikipedia edits, *New York Times,* 19 August. [online] Available at: www.nytimes.com/2007/08/19/technology/19wikipedia.html?page wanted=all&_r=0 [Accessed 11 September 2016].

Harrow, C., 2012. New website uses archives to open the world of finance to young people, *ARC Magazine,* 277, p. 18.

Haws, B., 2011. Advocating within the institution: twenty-five years for the New York Philharmonic Archives. In: L. J. Hackman, ed., *Many happy returns: advocacy and the development of archives.* Chicago, IL: Society of American Archivists.

Hedlin, E., 2011. What the case studies tell us. In: L. Hackman, ed., *Many happy returns: advocacy and the development of archives.* Chicago, IL: Society of American Archivists.

Heine, C., 2013. AmEx's social data shows that nostalgia is just swell 19th-century pics push engagement through the roof, *Adweek,* October 11. [online] Available at: www.adweek.com/news/technology/amexs-social-data-shows-nostalgia-just-swell-153053 [Accessed 11 September 2016].

Houston, A. and Carter, K., 2012. The M&S company archive on the move, *ARC Magazine,* 277, pp. 10–12.

Husebye, A., 2015. 'This is the Centre for Business History in Stockholm'. ICA SBA presentation, 15 June. [online] Available at: http://naringslivshistoria.se/en/cfn-news/this-is-the-centre-for-business-history-in-stockholm-2/ [Accessed 11 September 2016].

John Lewis, 2014. *150 years never standing still.* [online] Available at: www.johnlewis.com/john-lewis-150-years/c6001170154?rdr=1 [Accessed 11 September 2016].

King, K., 2014. Access to business archives: the opportunities and pitfalls of social media. In: Business Archives Council, *Access guidance notes. 'Let the right one in? Challenging perceptions of access to business archives'.* [online] Available at: www.businessarchivescouncil.org.uk/materials/bac_access_to_business_archives_guidance_notes.pdf [Accessed 11 September 2016].

King's College London, 2011. *School launches 'Navigating Nightingale' iPhone app,* press release, 3 April. [online] Available at: www.kcl.ac.uk/nursing/newsevents/news/2011/Schoollaunches NavigatingNightingaleiPhoneapp.aspx [Accessed 11 September 2016].

Lasewicz, P. C., 1994. Strangers in a strange land: archival opportunities in a multinational corporation, *Archival Issues,* 19(2), pp. 131–141.

Lasewicz, P. C., 2015. Forget the past? Or history matters? Selected academic perspectives on the strategic value of organizational pasts, *The American Archivist,* 78(1), pp. 59–83.

Lefurgy, W., 2014. Taking preservation to the people: educating the public about personal digital archiving. In: K. Theimer, 2014. *Outreach: innovative practices for archives and special collections.* Lanham, MD: Rowman & Littlefield. Ch. 12.

Maclin, S., 2000. Knowledge sharing at American International Group, Inc.: a case study in participation and perspective by the archivist, *Society of American Archivist Business Archives Section Newsletter,* 6, p. 6.

McWhite, L., 2014. Working within the law: public programming and continuing education. In: K. Theimer, 2014. *Outreach: innovative practices for archives and special collections.* Lanham, MD: Rowman & Littlefield. Ch. 3.

Markley, G., 2008. The Coca-Cola Company Archives: thriving where Dilbert, not Schellenberg, matters, *Journal of the Society of Georgia Archivists,* 26(1), p. 22.

Mooney, P., 1997. Archival mythology and corporate reality. In: J. M. O'Toole, ed., 1997. *The records of American business.* Chicago, IL: Society of American Archivists. Ch. 3.

National Council on Disability, 2004. Outreach and people with disabilities from diverse cultures: a review of the literature, *Washington, National Council on Disability.* [pdf] Available at: www.ncd.gov/publications/2003/nov302003 [Accessed 11 September 2016].

Neuman, J., 1975. Make overhead cuts that last, *The Harvard Business Review,* May.

Osborn, K., 2011. Advocacy and the Marks & Spencer company archive, *ARC Magazine,* 259, p. 16.

Porter, J., 2016. Reaching new audiences: gamification and the Prudential archive, *ARC Magazine,* 321, pp. 10–12.

Porter, R., 2014. *Untold stories from the front line.* [online] Available at: www.hsbc.com/news-and-insight/2014/untold-stories-from-the-frontline [Accessed 11 September 2016].

Porter, R., 2015. Crowdsourcing at the HSBC Archives, *ARC Magazine,* 306, pp. 24–25.

Rabchuk, G., 1994. Reaching out for survival: The Royal Bank experience, *Society of American Archivists Business Archives Newsletter,* 11(2), p. 1.

Reese, M., 2010. How one archivist broke the surface at Nationwide Insurance, *Society of American Archivists Business Archives Section Newsletter,* 27(1), p. 3.

St Clair, C. G., 1994. Electronic outreach in the archives: bringing them in at Digital Equipment Corporation, *Society of American Archivists Business Archives Newsletter,* 11(2), p. 4.

Schindler, A., 2014. Staying connected: engaging alumni and students to digitize the Carl 'Pappy' Fehr Choral Music Collection. In: K. Theimer, 2014. *Outreach: innovative practices for archives and special collections.* Lanham, MD: Rowman & Littlefield. Ch. 4.

Scottish Southern Energy, 2015. Introducing the SSE Archive at Pitlochry, *Vimeo* [online] Available at: https://vimeo.com/135448373 [Accessed 11 September 2016].

Snyder, S., 2014. 'Wikipedia is made of people!': revelations from collaborating with the world's most popular encyclopedia. In: K. Theimer, 2014. *Outreach: innovative practices for archives and special collections.* Lanham, MD: Rowman & Littlefield. Ch. 7.

Society of American Archivists Issues and Advocacy Roundtable, 2015. *Blog 23: agreeing on advocacy.* [online] Available at: www2.archivists.org/groups/issues-and-advocacy-roundtable/blog-entry-23-agreeing-on-advocacy [Accessed 11 September 2016].

Steele, A., 2014. Keep me posted: advocacy and the British Postal Museum & Archive, *ARC Magazine*, 300, pp. 17–19.

Stewart, S., 2015. Archive learning resources from the National Co-operative Archives, *ARC Magazine*, 306, p. 33.

The Alliance of Centres for Business History in Europe, n.d. [online] Available at: www.ebha.org/?seite=business%20schools [Accessed 11 September 2016].

Thornhill, T., 2013. Advocacy for business archives, *ARC Magazine*, 292, pp. 23–24.

Thornhill, T., 2015. 'The story of the bus': 1000 hours in the making, *ARC Magazine*, 306, pp. 7–9.

Treanor, J., 1994. Essential services as outreach: confessions of a Catholic diocesan archivist. *Society of American Archivists Business Archives Newsletter*, 11(2).

Tselentis, J., 2014. *Retro design, retrovores + throwback packaging*, 8 December. [online] Available at: www.printmag.com/featured/retro-design-retrovores-throwback-packaging-design/ [Accessed 11 September 2016].

Tunstall, C., 2015. Thirty years of Unilever Archives and Records Management, *ARC Magazine*, 306, pp. 14–15.

Unilever, 2013. *Unilever launches app in celebration of 125 years at Port Sunlight*, press release, 20 September. [online] Available at: www.unilever.co.uk/news/press-releases/2013/unilever-launches-app-in-celebration-of-125-years-at-port-sunlight.html/ [Accessed 11 September 2016].

Unilever, 2015. Celebrating 30 years of archives, *YouTube*. [online] Available at: www.youtube.com/watch?v=18afeDrrhnw [Accessed 11 September 2016].

Wagner, S., n.d. Building relationships to preserve the legacy around the globe, *Society of American Archivists Business Section Newsletter*. [online] Available at: www2.archivists.org/groups/business-archives-section/building-relationships-to-preserve-the-legacy-around-the-globe [Accessed 11 September 2016].

Wikipedia, 2015a. *Conflict-of-interest editing on Wikipedia.* [online] Available at: https://en.wikipedia.org/wiki/Conflict-of-interest_editing_on_Wikipedia#Jimmy_Wales [Accessed 11 September 2016].

Wikipedia, 2015b. *WikiScanner.* [online] Available at: https://en.wikipedia.org/wiki/WikiScanner [Accessed 11 September 2016].

Yeoman, L. and Reed, R., 2012. A little bird told me, *ARC Magazine*, 277, p. 21.

Chapter 13

The business history discipline

Leslie Hannah

The subject matter of business history is the business past. It follows that business history is as old as civilisation and much older than the first accumulations of business archives. Humans always earned a living (first by foraging and hunting, later by farming and trading) and tales told in families and social groups have long been an efficient way of passing on the lore of how to do so. The Bible, the Norse sagas and the Confucian analects were not *centrally* focused on the more advanced agricultural, crafts and trading businesses of their day, but they contain stories and analytical reflections on making a living by providing goods and services to others. Accounting records on stone date back thousands of years, and archaeologists and classical scholars have proved far more adept at reconstructing the business past of pre-modern eras than scholars in those fields once considered either possible or desirable. The oldest accounts of the activities of businesses that still survive today have been preserved by courtesy of the precocious literacy and above-average longevity of religious organisations and businesses that served them in both Europe and Asia.[1] In the light of these and millennia of previous business storytelling, it is unwise to attempt to identify the 'first' business history.

By the same token, discussions of the proper boundaries of the subject quickly become tedious. Since the *only* data we have on business is *past* data, *any* empirical discussion of business must in a fundamental sense be *either* historical *or* baseless.[2] It may be true that data for the last 30 years is more prone to be discussed by economists, sociologists, management specialists or financial journalists, while historians typically venture on recent events with some modesty and circumspection, but that boundary is a matter of habit, increasingly transgressed (as the case study in Box 13.5 on HSBC's recent history shows).

The development of the subject

The early origins of the subject as an academic discipline are indistinguishable from those of economic history, with important milestones delineating some central themes of the subject such as Arnold Toynbee's lectures on the Industrial Revolution at Oxford (Toynbee, 1884).[3] Recognisably differentiated corporate histories (which remain an important constituent of the broader field of business and economic history) came earlier and originally derived from individual capitalists or firms becoming self-conscious about – and usually viscerally proud of – their own origins. Of course, for most of human history businesses were collectively or personally owned and small scale. Although corporate businesses, of sorts, were known in ancient and medieval times, joint-stock companies of the recognisably modern type date from fourteenth century France (Le Bris *et al.*, 2014; see also Scott, 1910–11 on later English cases). The earliest of these large, incorporated businesses soon attracted their publishers of archival records and chroniclers,[4] and, with general incorporation in the nineteenth century, corporate biographies multiplied.[5]

Business biographies of individuals rather than companies remained the main literary manifestation of business history well into the nineteenth century. Typical of the genre was the biography of the railway constructor, Thomas Brassey, by the civil servant, essayist and popular historian, Sir Arthur Helps (1872). Providing a wider interpretation, commentators such as Samuel Smiles (1869) distilled homiletic versions of such business tales, explicitly framing them to elevate the ambitions of their contemporaries.

The foundations of business history as a self-consciously differentiated *academic* subject are traceable to the early decades of the twentieth century in economics and history departments and proto-business schools, when academics in other fields began writing works that constitute business history of sorts. The economist, Sydney Chapman, the first Dean of the Faculty of Commerce at the University of Manchester in 1904, wrote on the development of the cotton industry and included modern history and commercial geography among the subjects to be studied for his new commerce degree (Keeble, 1992, p. 104). The Frankfurt-based *Gesellschaft für wirtschaftliche Ausbilding* – a private organisation of professors of engineering, economics, business economics and public administration and businessmen with an interest in business management – sponsored a conference in Cologne in 1913 on the organisation of business archives. Alfred Marshall's *Industry and trade*, published in 1919, resembles modern business history more than modern industrial economics, though he would perhaps have been somewhat surprised to be labelled a business historian rather than a political economist. In Europe, America and Asia, the first university chair in the subject of business history,[6] the first organisation devoted to the preservation of business archives,[7] the first publication of journals specialising in business history,[8] the first creation of specialist business history research units[9] and the first formation of specialist associations of practitioners[10] can be dated to the decades between the 1920s and the 1960s. There are, however, still enormous international differences in the degree to which the subject is formally recognised in universities. Very few German or British professors of business history actually have that title, while there are over 300 with that title in Japan. Yet business history is alive and well in all three countries!

In European universities, business history increasingly attracted the attention of leading economic historians after the Second World War. Sometimes, as with the histories commissioned by the Wallenberg family in Sweden, the origin was a desire to counter the influence of left-wing critics, though they were careful to choose critical professional historians whose work could be respected (Olsson, 2013). Professor Charles Wilson of Cambridge similarly wrote a commissioned corporate history for Unilever (1954), tracing it to the chairman's desire to counteract what he considered the desperately ill-informed nature of Cambridge economists' understanding of business.[11] Later, one of the most prolific British corporate history writers was William Reader, one of Wilson's pupils at Jesus College, Cambridge, who completed histories of, *inter alia*, the stockbrokers, Foster & Braithwaite, the international chemical groups Huntsman and Imperial Chemical Industries, and other manufacturers such as Bowater and Metal Box. Some of his assistants and their colleagues later became providers of business history writing services in their own right (Slinn, 1984; 1988; 2013); and Professor Theo Barker and Stephanie Zarach founded one among many commercial providers, Debrett's Business History Research (Zarach, 1987). In the United States similar services developed: George Smith and colleagues founded the Winthrop Group and Professor Louis Galambos the Business History Group.[12] In Japan Professor Tsunehiko Yui's Business History Institute developed a similar intermediary role between academics and companies requiring historical services. Journalists worldwide also entered the market as competitors.[13] This has generated a wealth of publications in corporate history, though the quality of such histories varies considerably. Their quantities also vary roughly in line with the size of a country and the length of its experience of capitalist corporations: thus Japan early this century could count about 13,000 volumes of corporate history while China had only 1,200 volumes.[14]

What sense have we made of the business past after all this activity? For individual organisations, placing themselves historically is an end in itself, or a source of inspiration for the future. Some businesses (notably banks) found it worthwhile to identify their venerable age as a sign of stability (not always with accuracy). Others (Hovis, Bisto) found that an image of old-fashioned wholesomeness could be derived from nostalgic glimpses of a recent lost world of country values. Some commemorative company histories are quite informative but it must be admitted that many are publicity 'puffs' and have little value for the professional historian or serious business analyst.[15] Companies also differ in their attitudes to access, a problem that from the first concerned historians given privileged access: their sources were uncheckable unless companies developed proper general access policies. Commissioned histories of companies whose archives are organised to provide official access to all researchers – given the importance of the possibility of verification for scientific history – will, usually, be taken most seriously by professional historians and business analysts. While some corporate lawyers may argue against that (indeed in favour of widespread archival destruction), the fact that more sunlight can safely and productively be allowed to shine on the past, than is usually possible (for commercial secrecy reasons) for current corporate records, gives historians a huge comparative advantage over other analysts of business.

Theorising in the subject

Perhaps the most ambitious attempt to distil broader wisdom from the study of business history was the foundation by Joseph Schumpeter and Arthur Cole of Harvard's Research Center in Entrepreneurial History in 1948, in an era when development economists and historians alike shared a belief that this was one way the forces of capitalist development could be understood. A roll call of those who passed through in its brief 10-year life is a list of some of the most productive scholars in the disciplines of economic and business history over the next 40 years: Thomas Cochran, Bernard Bailyn, Alfred Chandler, Henry Rosovsky, Barry Supple, Lance Davis and Douglass North (the latter a Nobel Memorial Laureate in Economics, for his work on institutional economics).

Of these the most revered among modern business historians was Alfred D. Chandler Jr., who did more than anyone to liberate business history from inconsequential antiquarianism. Charles Wilson was sufficiently doubtful about his own dabbling in the field to suggest that 'it is not necessary to say that business history is the highest form of history', but Chandler had no time for such priggish apologetics. He went on to claim a place not only as one of the great and original twentieth-century historians, but as a

Box 13.1 Case study: using archives to research a company's history, Renault, France, 1960s

In 1972 Patrick Fridenson published a history of the automobile manufacturer Renault, from its origins in 1898 to the outbreak of the Second World War. Based on a previous PhD, it was the first study of a second industrial revolution company in France, the first business history to venture frankly into recent history and, despite its visible emphasis on the coming of large-scale enterprise, and a multinational, it was one of the first histories of a French family business.

The subject was suggested because Fridenson's supervisor knew that there were records of Renault, with a typescript catalogue, in the Company Archives Department of the Archives Nationales. Fridenson quickly realised that understanding the history of the archives themselves was of the essence. Here were the huge archives of a family enterprise which in 1939 had become the largest French firm by its turnover. They were classified by senior managers' departments of 1940, yet the company had never had an organisation chart and they were by no means complete. Parts had been destroyed by British bombing of the factories in 1943, erasing many traces of the early years. Parts were retained by the company, either because they were still current (legal records, patents, model studies, factory plans) or sensitive (First World War profits taxation) or had not interested the Archives Nationales curators (lists of early customers), but they were in worse shape. The archives of the founder himself were missing. There was also a political dimension in this archival landscape: the family had been stripped of power and deprived of property by a postwar nationalisation (1945), most paper traces of the family firm were in the Archives Nationales, the company itself was now state-owned and the realm of enterprising engineers and technocrats, who cursed the name of the founder, kept it only for marketing reasons.

The press and other printed sources were vital, but Fridenson also needed external archives to have other views of the company, of its financing, of its suppliers, of its markets, of its competitors and of alternative means of transportation. He was denied access to the two most obvious external sources: the private Protestant bank Mirabaud, which had been Renault's financial partner, which was traumatised first by its conflicts with the founder then by the nationalisation, and the trade association of car manufacturers, long stricken by oppositions between its private and public members. He consequently had to depend on the giant archives of a bank with a department of stock certification (Crédit Lyonnais) and on the archives of the army and of various ministries with which the firm had to deal. Latterly Fridenson also embarked on some oral history and benefitted from information collected by lower-level managers who created an association for the history of the company, collecting sources and recollections.

Since then the archival context of the company has changed dramatically. In the late 1970s the managers' historical association persuaded Louis Renault's widow to deposit about half of his archives with them on open access. In the 1990s the trade association opened its archives, and so too did the Banque Mirabaud, while the

Renault family gathered the remaining archives held by family members and later made them available online. A business historian writing today would have more than twice the sources Fridenson enjoyed. In the late 1980s the Archives Nationales handed back the Renault files to the company, but it became more and more unable to care for the needs of historians or to develop an archive policy. Other automobile manufacturers moved more positively: in 1982 the Berliet family created an archive and library in Lyons (a private foundation) and in 2010 the Peugeot family opened in Hérimoncourt an up-to-date facility for the archives of Peugeot, Citroën (part) and Panhard.

Fridenson, P., 1972, 1998, *Histoire des usines Renault, vol. 1. Naissance de la grande entreprise 1898–1939*. Paris: Editions du Seuil.

Source: Information provided by Patrick Fridenson by private communication.

name respected in disciplines as varied as economics, sociology and management. He began his career by writing business history in its oldest and most traditional form, with a business biography of his own great-grandfather, Henry Varnum Poor, the founder of the modern rating agency, Standard & Poor (Chandler, 1956). He is, however, better known for his 1962 book *Strategy and structure*, which broke new ground in analytical business history. He again did this by mining the most traditional methodology: immersing himself in the archives of four major United States corporations – General Motors, Du Pont, Sears Roebuck and Standard Oil – in order to understand how they managed their remarkable twentieth-century expansion as diversified large-scale companies.[16] He showed that their strategy of geographical and/or product diversification was facilitated by their (separate) invention in the 1920s of a multidivisional management structure, in which the head office focused on strategy and monitoring, while the divisions focused on the operational details of production and marketing for specific geographical areas or business lines. There was already a large management literature, at the time he wrote, discussing decentralisation of management, but Chandler's distinctive view based on archival research was bolstered by his (non-archival) analysis in Chapter 7 of more than 70 other United States corporations in the 1930s to 1950s, showing that there was a pattern explaining why some did and others did not adopt the multidivisional structure.

Chandler's research was deservedly influential among a wide range of social scientists, management theorists and historians. The multidivisional structure was found by many independent researchers to be related to successful diversification and management of large-scale organisation in a wide variety of cultures (and where that was not already the case, leading business schools and management consultants peddled it as a solution to the managerial problems of large-scale companies, so it became even more widespread). Business history thus begat business policy and policy analysis in turn validated historical conclusions. Chandler's growing reputation led to his appointment to the Straus business history professorship at the Harvard Business School, at that time the only endowed chair in the field. There he published in 1977 another remarkable work, *The visible hand* (1977), which ambitiously interpreted much of nineteenth- and twentieth-century American

Box 13.2 Case study: using archives to research a company's history, Barclays Bank, United Kingdom, 1990s

In the 1990s the author of this chapter (with Margaret Ackrill, both then at the London School of Economics) was commissioned to write the history of Barclays Bank, a major enterprise, which at one time had been, variously, the largest bank in Africa, in the United Kingdom and in the world, and the largest interstate bank in the United States.

The bank was generous in providing funding, open access and guarantees of the authors' freedom to publish (except on most recent matters). Thus the authors had the advantage of a free run of the bank's archives from the 1720s to the 1990s, not to speak of records of the hundreds of other banks Barclays had absorbed (though those of some one-time subsidiaries, now divested, were in the possession of the acquiring banks). The guidance of present managers and archivists as well as the existing banking history literature were all vital in deciding what to prioritise: no research team could possibly have covered the archive comprehensively and many other specialist historians were simultaneously researching the subject firm.

The archives of competitors like the Midland (now HSBC) were also invaluable and some early records of apprenticeships were traced in London's Guildhall Library and other fragments even as far afield as Swarthmore College Archives (the founders had helped finance William Penn's development of his transatlantic Quaker colony in the seventeenth century). Eclectic use of complementary archives has become immeasurably easier in the last ten years due to internet archive indexes and guides, so more carefully triangulated judgements, less beholden to the perspective of one archive, are now more possible. One unusual result of the external research was that it clarified that the bank was not as *young* as it used to claim (more typically, banks claim to be *older* than can plausibly be established!).

Historians had already published much on the bank's first two centuries, so the authors decided to focus on the twentieth century, which was less well covered. This was an age when the bank was bureaucratised, so extensive typewritten, printed and photographic archives were available. Sources used ranged from consultancy reports, accounting records, merger proposals, committee minutes, head office circulars, to records of regional boards and individual branches (though the bank's archivists were just beginning to scratch the surface of digital record-keeping). The state was increasingly involved in regulating banking, so The National Archives and those of the Bank of England also proved invaluable. Central archives such as Barclays' board minutes were used exhaustively, but others could only be selectively sampled. Some issues like the nature of industrial lending, changing bad debt ratios, and reaction to government controls were (with varying degrees of success) prioritised, as they had not been well treated in the existing literature. Existing archives were supplemented by interviews with surviving staff members, though only notes rather than recordings were preserved.

One feature distinguishing the resulting book from other bank histories was its comprehensive statistical appendix, providing a distinctive framework for the analysis of business developments in the main body of the book. Key measures were changing profitability and sources of value added, as banking was transformed by changed regulatory constraints and by modern technology. Barclays installed the world's first 'hole in the wall' cash dispenser – a forerunner of the modern ATM – in 1965, not to speak of issuing the United Kingdom's first major bank credit card.

Ackrill, M, and Hannah, L., 2001. *Barclays: the business of banking 1690–1996*. Cambridge: Cambridge University Press.

business history as the story of the replacement of Adam Smith's invisible hand of the market by the visible hand of corporate management.

The diversification of the subject

The twin forces of corporate demands for sponsored histories and Chandler's prestige in leading the discipline led to a remarkable efflorescence of work in business and company history in the last three decades of the twentieth century; and also to growing dissent from what threatened to become the Chandlerian orthodoxy. Both labour and political historians felt that Chandler underplayed corporate labour relations and the role of regulation in business development, though many other historians willingly filled these gaps. When Chandler attempted comparative European business history, notably an extension of his interpretation to Germany and the United Kingdom in 1990 in *Scale and scope* (Chandler, 1990), he stumbled badly.[17] The reasons were largely ideological: he came to the subject with a Progressive/Whig conviction that he had identified the 'magic' managerial ingredient that differentiated successful from unsuccessful business cultures, and Germany was identified as a land where professional managers took over from personal owners, while in Britain fewer large-scale enterprises were formed. He also devised a half-plausible explanation of British exceptionalism: business families liked control and refused to cede their prerogatives to professional management hierarchies.

Europeans were quick to point out the weaknesses of this framework: family firms were ubiquitous and not always inefficient. If anything, they were *less* tenacious in Britain than Germany, while quantitative studies showed no British shortfall in the number – or sustainability – of her large twentieth-century enterprises. Apart from his ideological prejudice, however, Chandler's failure was archival: while he dipped into a few British archives such as Cadbury or British Steel, the serious engagement in case studies that had informed his earlier work was simply missing, leading to multiple errors and egregious misinterpretations of much of the secondary European business history literature. With increasing European dissent, more American scholars looked again at some Chandlerian generalisations and found anomalies there too. Thus does scientific history progress.

One leading United States business historian, Louis Galambos, contrasted European open-mindedness and eclecticism with Harvard's stultification first under N. S. B. Gras, and then under Chandler: 'the Harvard Business School was and still is a powerfully consensus-oriented institution. It encouraged elaboration, not dissent, in much the same way that most modern bureaucracies do' (Galambos, 2003, p. 18). Yet the fact remains that Europe produced no business historian of the stature of Chandler, whether judged by the breadth, innovativeness or influence of their work.

In Eastern Europe, although totalitarian regimes liked their historians to warm to the theme of the exploitation of the working class, some scholars there bravely wrote some proper history within that constraining framework,[18] while others migrated and kept the flame of the business history of their countries alive in the west (Teichova, 1997). Marxist business historians were more part of the intellectual mainstream and produced some distinguished work in the West, too, notably in Italy and France. Partly in reaction to Chandler's misinterpretation, some historians produced more robust defences of small firms and family firms, culminating in two books aimed at a wider market: *Dynasties* by David Landes (2006), which looked at contrasting family fortunes in banking, automobiles and resource industries, and *Family capitalism* (2006), by Harold James, which followed the trajectory of German, French and Italian business families through the nineteenth and twentieth centuries.

More generally, a thousand flowers have bloomed in the field. There have been specialised histories of every business function, from personnel management, through strategic planning to operations research, marketing, public relations, government relations, accounting, investor relations, office politics and finance. Interpreters of business have called in aid every conceivable human and social science – not just old stalwarts like economics – but anthropology, Freudian psychoanalysis, semiology, political science or organisational behaviour to enrich their theoretical credentials. Neighbouring specialisms – gender history, cultural history, technological history, social history, industrial archaeology, management research – have been ransacked for ideas and case studies to enrich business history writing. Illegal cartels, asbestos abuse and insider dealing have been tracked in history as well as by modern regulators. Each country's business historians have pursued their own ghosts, whether the less reputable aspects of imperialism investigated by the British, French and Americans (though there is also a partial rehabilitation of some aspects of dependency in promoting growth, from both sides of the imperial divide), or of Nazi business exploitation and anti-Semitism, recently more honestly reappraised by the Germans and Swiss. Traditional topics – like entrepreneurship, education for business, the family firm and multinationals – all have their modern interpreters. Those with postmodern tastes will find critical business history refreshing, even if older hands see it as not notably different from old-fashioned anti-capitalist or Marxist business history. Every profession, from the oldest, prostitution, to the newest, management consultancy, has its business historians. While manufacturing, banks and railways once seemed to dominate business history, the businesses studied increasingly span a wider range, including department stores, commodity exchanges, electric utilities, merchant firms, patent agents, telecoms operators, gangsters, drug dealers, venture capitalists and advertising agencies. There are now multiple dictionaries of business biographies and dictionaries of corporate histories (Ingham, 1983; Jeremy, 1984–86; Slaven and Checkland, 1986; Torres, 2000; Daumas, 2010). There were earlier attempts to generalise about entrepreneurial and managerial careers (Newcomer, 1955; Erickson, 1959), but the new dictionaries have facilitated more attempts at generalisation from

Box 13.3 Case study: using archives to research a company's history, Toyota Motor Corporation, Japan, 1990s

In Japan companies rarely disclose their own archives to the public and Toyota is no exception. The company established the Toyota Commemorative Museum of Kuragaike in 1974, the Toyota Automobile Museum in 1989 and, with its closely related companies, the (Toyota) Commemorative Museum of Industry and Technology in 1994. These museums often held special exhibitions focusing on real automobiles and other artefacts. Toyota thus expends more energy than most Japanese companies on corporate museums, but has only small libraries, focusing on published magazines and books about automobiles and related topics. Historians wishing to investigate archive materials – such as board minutes – would find it extremely difficult to access such materials.

In the early 1990s Kazuo Wada, and the editor of Nagoya University Press, approached Toyota Motor Corporation with a view to publishing documents written by Kiichiro Toyoda, founder of the Toyota Motor Corporation. At that time the museums held no archives, but during the following seven years Toyota set up a department to bring together old documents and photos. As a result Wada managed to compile and edit *Corpus of Kiichiro Toyoda's documents* to commemorate the opening in 1999 of Kiichiro's old house, which was removed and rebuilt at the Toyota Commemorative Museum of Kuragaike.

In the last stage of publishing *Corpus*, Wada was commissioned to write Kiichiro Toyoda's biography, jointly with Professor Tsunehiko Yui. The company arranged interviews with many old employees as well as with Shoichiro Toyoda, the first son of Kiichiro Toyoda and then honorary chairman. In writing Kiichiro's biography, Toyota gave Wada the opportunity to read his diary and some reports circulated in the nascent years at Toyota. He also visited the Platt Brothers archives (now part of the Platt-Saco-Lowell archive at the Lancashire Record Office), to understand some early steps in Lancashire's improving engineering technology, and thoroughly read local newspapers of the period as well as Toyota's in-house newspaper and magazine. Kiichiro Toyoda's biography was published in 2002.

Even after the publication of the biography, it was difficult to access and review the company's original documents including board minutes or other reports freely, though the company helped with collecting in-house newspapers and magazines. As Toyota had a profound effect on its local community, local and national magazines and newspapers yielded much information about Toyota and its related companies. Through such time-consuming research, Wada managed to write the prize-winning *The fable of manufacturing: from Ford to Toyota*, published in 2009.

Wada, K., 1998. *Corpus of Kiichiro Toyoda's documents*. Nagoya: Nagoya University Press. Wada, K. and Yui, T., 2002. *Courage and change: the life of Kiichiro Toyoda*. Tokyo: Toyota Motor Corporation. Wada, K., 2009. *The fable of manufacturing: from Ford to Toyota*. Nagoya: Nagoya University Press.

Source: Information provided by Kazuo Wada by private communication.

such collective biography both in the United States of America and in Europe (Kaelble, 1985; Berghoff, 1991; Joly, 1996; Nicholas, 1999).

Businesses have been studied not just as single entities but as networks, members of trade associations and a rich variety of otherwise defined business groups (by main bank, by regional cluster, by supplier relations, by interlocking shareholdings). And of course hundreds of corporate histories – sponsored and independent, and of big, medium or small firms – continue as a publishing mainstay of the discipline and constantly expanding quarry for case studies, whether for the more stylised (sometimes quasi-fictional) offerings of business school case studies to the more cerebral offerings of business historians. Print is not the only medium used: some firms maintain their own sound and film archives and the National Life Stories Collection at the British Library preserves the oral recollections of businessmen, with projects on retailing, banking, technology, electricity and many others already completed or under way.[19]

It would be a challenge to document all this output and it is some years since the last comprehensive bibliographies of the subject were attempted (Derdek, 1988–present; Goodall, Gourvish and Tolliday, 1996; Japan Business History Institute, 1996; Beltran, Daviet and Ruffat, 1995), but an excellent selective and critical guide to the literature is the multi-authored and authoritative *Oxford handbook of business history*, first published in 2007, and since 2009 available in paperback (Jones and Zeitlin, 2007). Textbooks have also been produced, some dealing with the business histories of particular countries (Jeremy, 1998; Kirby and Rose, 1994; Bliss, 1987), others developing a more ambitious international approach (Boyce and Ville, 2002; Jones, 1996). The review pages of the leading journals in the field – *Business History, Business Archives, Business History Review, Technology and Culture* and *Enterprise and Society* – also bear witness to the extensive productions and eclectic interests of the profession.

It is invidious to select from the rich panoply of work in the field, but in your present guide's personal taste, one of the most intriguing users of business archives has been JoAnne Yates, who has explored not only their content but their physical structure (not all of which is preserved by modern archival practice). She shows that the rise of the Chandlerian corporation was facilitated by new technologies such as the vertical filing cabinet: 'Procedures, rules and financial and operational information were documented at all levels, making organisational rather than individual memory the repository of knowledge. Impersonal managerial systems – embodied in forms, circular letters, and manuals – replaced the idiosyncratic, word-of-mouth management of the foremen and owners of earlier periods' (Yates, 1989, p. 271). An insight into the less conventional uses of business archives is provided by Alan McKinlay (2013, pp. 137–154), who skilfully uses an unusual cache of cartoons in the Lloyd's Bank archive produced by staff (together with records of court cases) to understand how managerial hierarchies were initially viewed (readers of today's 'Dilbert' cartoon strips, lampooning modern management practices, will get the general idea).

Some of the most refreshing recent work has been in internationally comparative business history. The groundwork for this was laid by the Fuji international conferences sponsored by the Japanese Business History Society and the Taniguchi Foundation,[20] but it has also been greatly enriched within Europe by the European Association of Business Historians conferences, encouraging many young researchers to venture into comparative fields. It has become traditional for Young Turks of the discipline to bemoan the fact that Chandler's successors have failed to produce a modern synthesis of these varied

Box 13.4 Case study: using archives to research company history, British Oxygen Corporation/ Linde Group, United Kingdom/Germany, 2000s

British Oxygen Corporation (BOC) was acquired by the German-based Linde Group. BOC, founded as Brins Oxygen Company in 1886 and renamed British Oxygen, was a long-established, globally active market leader in the industrial gases industry, specialising in production of purified air gases and other gases as well as in related plant and equipment.

In the complex process of merger and acquisition, the future of the corporate archives of the acquired company – to the extent they exist – is often not high on the agenda. This case, though, was different. The Linde Group decided to commission an archive-based history of BOC and approached Ray Stokes to carry it out. He suggested instead that the history of BOC should form part of a business history of the international industrial gases industry, examining its evolution and dynamics from its start in 1886 through 2006 based on archival material from its major component firms, including BOC and Linde, but also AGA (Sweden), Air Liquide (France) and American-based Air Products and Praxair (formerly part of Union Carbide). Linde duly commissioned the research and writing to be carried out by Stokes and Ralf Banken. As part of the agreement, the German firm gave extensive access to its own records and those of two other key members of the Group, AGA and BOC. Linde also agreed to facilitate contacts with other firms to gain archival access.

In the case of BOC, though, two issues arose immediately. First, the BOC acquisition was quickly followed by a relocation of the Surrey-based former headquarters of the British firm to Guildford where there would be no room for the small collection of archival material in Surrey. A new home had to be found fast; when it proved impossible to find space for the collection in the United Kingdom at short notice, the documents were shipped to the Linde company archive in Munich. Second, the researchers knew from a survey of BOC's records from the mid-1980s – then located in Hammersmith – that the documents sent to Munich did not include crucial items, including board minutes (Richmond and Stockford, 1986, pp. 387–393). They were eventually located in a storage facility and shipped to Glasgow for consultation. Digital photographs were then taken of many of the documents, which included all board minutes from 1886 to 1990 and a collection of key documents and interviews associated with preparation of a publication (which was never written) to celebrate the firm's centenary in 1986. This collection of digital documents is held by the authors and by the Linde archive in Munich. These and materials collected from other company archives formed the basis for the history of the industry from its origins to 2006, which appeared in 2016.

Stokes, R. and Banken, R., 2016. *Building on air: the international industrial gases industry, 1886–2006.* Cambridge/New York: Cambridge University Press.

Source: Information provided by Ray Stokes by private communication.

strands, but this criticism is arguably wide of the mark. The key point about the Chandlerian experiment was that it over-reached itself and became a prison rather than an inspiration for its followers. His later work was flawed precisely because it tried to establish an over-arching application of a theory which, in fact, could not be so widely applied. If we have a large number of smaller insights – and a not-very-clear idea of how they fit together to explain business success and failure – that may reflect the inherent nature of the subject rather than our incompetence in developing explanatory frameworks.

Indeed, there is a good reason why no empirical regularity discerned in business, whether by historians or others, and however modestly framed, is likely to be immutable. It is the genius of capitalism that it proves wrong what clever people of many different stripes think right. There are many research directors who have been told by a distinguished science professor in their field that they are unlikely to produce the breakthrough they are looking for, but occasionally ignoring such hegemonic experts pays off. J. R. Winfield and J. T. Dickson, at the Calico Printers Association, by doing so, in 1941 invented polyester fibre, which, after the war became the world's most widely-used man-made fibre (Jewkes, Sawers and Stillerman, 1960, pp. 388–391; Owen, 2010). During the internet bubble, I saw ludicrous business plans from my students getting generous venture capital support, and felt suitably smug when the boom collapsed, but I would have been less smug if one of them had been the founder of Amazon or Google.

Academics try to make sense of such matters, so a high-powered team at MIT, in their famous book, *The machine that made the world*, in 1990 explained what Japanese lean production had done to transform the competitive world of motor manufacturing and how America could catch up. In the following years, firms following their recipe improved their performance and had temporary success, but by 2009 not only were General Motors (once the most archetypally successful firm in the world) and Chrysler in the bankruptcy courts, but Toyota itself reported large losses. Appropriately the professor explaining the complexity that led to this outcome chose, as his title, *The world that changed the machine* (Freyssenet, 2006). What works in the world in one state might not work so well when it changes.

'Magic' ingredients for business success rapidly become ineffective in a diverse and competitive economic environment. Stuff happens, the world changes, and we delude ourselves if we think we can anticipate everything, or even fully explain things retrospectively. Capitalism is therefore not an organisational mode in which only academic genius thrives (though it often does and successful companies recruit the best graduates for good reason), but it is also a system, which brings out the extraordinary in ordinary people. Since most of us are ordinary, that diversity is its strength. But not all business historians are sufficiently aware of the contingent elements in the stories they tell. There is a temptation – famously attacked by Herbert Butterfield (1950) in the political sphere – to write 'Whig' history. The American business historian Daniel Raff (2013), has shown most clearly how contingent narratives give us a better feel for the nature of decisions taken at critical moments when decisive choices were made, than the typical business history based on hindsight which makes success seem inevitable.[21]

For many business archivists and business historians the use of archival material in the writing of history appears unproblematic. One is interested in a topic and one looks for the evidence in the business archive. The goal of many corporate historians (and of many economic and social historians using business archives) is simply to develop a

Box 13.5 Case study: using archives to research a company's history, HSBC, United Kingdom and Hong Kong, 2010s

In March 2015 HSBC marked its 150th anniversary with a programme of events which included publishing a new history of the bank, *The lion wakes*, by Richard Roberts and David Kynaston. The book covered the modern period of HSBC's story – from 1980 until 2011 – and was well received both within and outside the bank. A review in the *FT* praised it as 'expert and thoroughly readable' and *Financial World* magazine called it 'required reading.' Inside HSBC the book was used not just for corporate gifting, but also as a crucial tool in staff engagement and induction. How was this successful outcome achieved?

Choice of authors: HSBC invited a range of specialists in financial, business and banking history to tender for the job of producing their new history. The final choice was for two authors who brought complementary skill sets and approaches to the book. The use of external specialists guaranteed an objective and expert account.

Book brief: The contract with the authors contained a detailed brief for the book which stipulated among other details its tone ('accessible and authoritative'), length and content.

Governance and support: The book was supported at the highest levels of HSBC – commissioned by the bank's chairman, who became the chair of the History Committee which oversaw the project. This high-level support ensured co-operation from employees throughout the bank.

Project management: The project began in 2006 allowing plenty of time for research, writing and editing. The day-to-day running was co-ordinated by the archives department and the project was supervised by the History Committee which met twice a year to consider progress, give feedback on chapters written to date and advice on research areas and relevant individuals to interview. Regular payments to the authors were linked to satisfactory progress reports and writing of specific chapters within a given timescale.

Research support: The authors were given comprehensive support from the archives department. The archivists also pro-actively sought out modern sources within the bank and arranged for their transfer to the archives. A full interview programme was arranged – around 200 individuals interviewed – and the archives department provided interview organisation and transcription services. The authors were allowed unfettered access to the archives and to confidential modern board papers.

Publishers: The bank chose to publish the book with a small independent publisher which provided a commercially-aware service ensuring that the book was not just produced to timetable, but was also designed to be an attractive and readable book and the cover retail price was kept as low as possible.

Roberts, R. and Kynaston, D., 2015. *The lion wakes*. London: Profile Books.

Source: Information provided by Sara Kinsey by private communication.

historical narrative, telling some story 'wie es eigentlich gewesen' – as things really were – as the nineteenth-century realist historian Ranke famously put it. Generations of historians brought up since then on *What is history?* (my copy is E. H. Carr's 1965 Penguin, but the later edition with an introduction by Cambridge's Professor Richard Evans is now widely used) (Carr and Evans, 2002) have dutifully learnt that life is not so simple. Our (conscious or unconscious) priors, often derived from the present, drive our selection of evidence and all archives contain untruths and distortions as well as what we judge to be historical 'facts'. Yet historians often forget some of their theoretical training when they get down to the practicalities of writing. Stefan Schwarzkopf of Copenhagen Business School was not far wrong when he suggested that business historians are among the most irredeemably 'realist empiricists' still practising the historical trades (2012, pp. 1–9). Without necessarily navigating too far down the road of extreme 'postmodern' relativism, any sensible business archivist or historian will still recognise the sense of points that Derrida made in 1995 about the potentially misleading nature of archives, individually or as a collectivity (1995, pp. 9–63). Archives tend to privilege the treatment of large managerial hierarchies that survive (which originally had the resources to generate them and still retain the capacity to preserve them) at the expense of bankrupt firms (for whose liquidators archival preservation is rarely a priority or profitable) or of networks and markets (which inherently generate less bureaucratic remains than formal organisations).[22]

Some of the practical issues arising in writing a company history are admirably covered in John Orbell's *Guide to tracing the history of a business* (2009).[23] His lessons, though based on British case studies, apply more generally and the book has sold widely abroad, where local needs are less well catered for (judging by its appearance in many international university library catalogues). Finally the boxed case studies (on pages 431, 433, 436, 438 and 440) provide vignettes of some histories of individual companies in the UK (Barclays Bank), France (Renault), Japan (Toyota), United Kingdom/Germany (British Oxygen/ Linde) and an autonomous region of China (HSBC), showing an eclectic range of approaches to the commissioning and writing of corporate histories.

What can we say of the future of business history writing? Will archivists be serving different demands from historians in the future than in the past? Of course, the only reasonable conclusion from experience so far is that we cannot possibly tell. The hallmarks of the best past works in business history – grounded theory, good empirics, liberal archival access, big questions, international comparisons – will no doubt continue to be important. Business historians will continue to challenge the stylised facts of over-ambitious social scientists with richer empirical case studies, insisting on understanding the complexity of change. Let variety thrive.

Acknowledgements

The author is grateful to the contributors of the case study panels on the histories of Renault (Patrick Fridenson, Professor Emeritus, Ecole des Hautes Etudes en Sciences Sociales, Paris), Toyota (Kazuo Wada, Professor Emeritus of Economics, University of Tokyo), British Oxygen/Linde (Professor Ray Stokes, Chair of Business History, University of Glasgow) and HSBC (Sara Kinsey, archivist, HSBC) for permission to reproduce their work.

Notes

1　The Japanese constructor of Buddhist temples, Kongo Gumi, was founded in 578 and lost its independence in 2007, when the 40th generation, heavily indebted following financial miscalculations, sold out to a rival, Takamatsu (Hutcheson, J. O., 2007. The end of a 1,400-year-old business, *Business Week*, 16 Apr.). This left Hoshi Ryokan in Komatsu, Japan, as claimant to the title of the oldest independently surviving family business. The oldest family business in Europe is probably the Fonderia Pontificia Marinelli (an Italian bellfounder dating from around 1000) and in Britain, John Brooke, the Huddersfield wool manufacturer founded in 1541. One can trace older 'businesses', run by surviving monarchies or monasteries.

2　One might exempt from this generalisation recent developments in experimental economics (for example Kahneman, D., 2011. *Thinking fast and slow*. London: Penguin); it would be stretching a point to call data so constructed 'historical'.

3　For other milestones, see Harte, N., ed., 1971. *The study of economic history: collected inaugural lectures, 1893–1970*. London: Cass.

4　For example, Shurtleff, N. B., ed., 1853–54. *Records of the Governor and Company of the Massachusetts Bay in New England*. Boston, MA: White.

5　Company employees with an interest in history were often the authors of such volumes. There are, for example, multiple nineteenth-century histories of railways. Typical examples include Williams, F. S., 1877. *The Midland Railway: its rise and progress*. London: Strahan & Co and Wilson, W. B., 1899. *History of the Pennsylvania Railroad Company*. Philadelphia: Coates.

6　N. S. B. Gras at Harvard in 1927.

7　The United Kingdom Business Archives Council was founded in 1934. Amatori, F. and Jones, G., eds, 2003. *Business history around the world*. Cambridge: Cambridge University Press usefully summarises the histories of the discipline within different countries.

8　The *Bulletin of the Business Historical Society* was first published in 1926 and later transmuted into the *Business History Review*. In Britain, the University of Liverpool began publishing *Business History* in 1958.

9　The Research Center in Entrepreneurial History at Harvard was founded in 1948.

10　The Japan Business History Association was founded in 1964, the United States-based Business History Conference in 1971.

11　He cannot have been thinking of Keynes, whose knowledge of business was impressive, but rather was irked by Maurice Dobb and other Cambridge Marxists. Wilson published three volumes on Unilever with Cassell, taking the story to 1965. The commissioned Unilever story was later extended by Geoffrey Jones (see Jones, G., 2005. *Renewing Unilever: transformation and tradition*. Oxford: Oxford University Press).

12　See www.winthropgroup.com and www.businesshistorygroup.com [Both accessed 20 August 2016].

13　For example the history of GEC was written by Robert Jones and Oliver Marriott (Jones, R. and Marriott, O., 1970. *Anatomy of a merger*. London: Cape).

14　Lee, P. T., 2013. The history of Bank of China: a critic on the documentation and research, *Asian Research Trends* (New Series), 2013, 8, pp. 85–114, which also discusses quality problems. See also Murahashi, K., 2002. *A study of company history* (in Japanese). Tokyo: Diamond Press, p. 1; Kanemaru, Y., 2008. *The cultural lands and technology transfers for Chinese business corporations* (in Chinese). Kyoto: Ritsumeikan University, pp. 6–24.

15　They have their place, for certain business purposes. A good compromise is to commission a scholarly history, which can be taken seriously as analysis, while also producing a shorter 'picture-book' version for staff, shareholders, customers and retirees (as has been done, for example, by Unilever, HSBC, Barclays and Toyota).

16　Hannah, L., 2008. Business archives and the life cycle of the business historian. *Business Archives: Sources and History*, 97, p. 14.

17　For a recent critical re-evaluation, see Hannah, L., 2009. Strategic games, scale and efficiency, or Chandler goes to Hollywood. In: Coopey, R. and Lyth, P., eds, 2009. *Business in Britain in the twentieth century*. Oxford: Oxford University Press, pp. 15–47.

18　For example Nussbaum, H., 1966. *Unternehmer gegen Monopole*. Berlin: Akademie-Verlag.

19　See www.bl.uk/projects/national-life-stories [Accessed 20 August 2016].

20 The many volumes of its proceedings were published initially by the University of Tokyo Press and latterly by Oxford University Press.
21 See also Lamoreaux, N., Raff, D. M. G. and Temin, P., 2004. Against Whig history. *Enterprise and Society*, 5, 3, pp. 376–387; Hannah, L., 1999. Marshall's 'trees' and the global 'forest': were 'giant redwoods' different?. In: Lamoreaux, N., Raff, D. M. G. and Temin, P., eds, 1999. *Learning by doing in markets, firms and nation*. NBER and University of Chicago Press; and Fridenson, P. and Scranton, P., 2013. *Re–imagining business history*. Baltimore: Johns Hopkins University Press.
22 Decker, S., 2013. The silence of the archives: business history, post-colonialism and archival ethnography. *Management and Organizational History*, 8, 2, May, pp. 155–173) discusses some of the problems of archival selection biases. Fridenson, P., 2004. Business failure and the agenda of business history. *Enterprise and Society*, 5, 4, Dec, pp. 562–582) discusses the importance of studying failing firms as well as success.
23 See also Fase, M. M. G., Feldman, G. D. and Pohl, M., 1995. *How to write the history of a bank*. Aldershot: Scolar Press.

References

Beltran, A., Daviet, J. and Ruffat, M., 1995. L'histoire des enterprises en France: essai bibliographique. *Les Cahiers de l'IHTP*, 30.

Berghoff, H., 1991. *Englische Unternehmer, 1870–1914: eine Kollektivbiographie führender Wirtschaftsbürger in Birmingham, Bristol und Manchester*. Göttingen: Vandenhoeck & Ruprecht.

Bliss, M., 1987. *Five centuries of Canadian business*. Toronto: McClelland & Stewart.

Boyce, G. and Ville, S., 2002. *The development of modern business*. Houndmills: Palgrave.

Butterfield, H., 1950. *The Whig interpretation of history*. London: Bell & Sons.

Carr, E. H. and Evans, R., 2002. *What is history?* Houndmills: Palgrave Macmillan.

Chandler, A. D., Jr., 1956. *Henry Varnum Poor: business editor, analyst and reformer*. Cambridge, MA: Harvard University Press.

Chandler, A. D., Jr., 1962. *Strategy and structure: chapters in the history of the American industrial enterprise*. Cambridge, MA: MIT Press.

Chandler, A. D., Jr., 1977. *The visible hand. The managerial revolution in American business*. Cambridge, MA: Harvard University Press.

Chandler, A. D., Jr., 1990. *Scale and scope: the dynamics of industrial capitalism*. Cambridge, MA: Harvard University Press.

Daumas, J. C. *et al.*, eds, 2010. *Dictionaire biographique des patrons français*. Paris: Flammarion.

Derdek, T., ed., 1988–present. *International directory of company histories*. Andover: Gale Cengage Learning. Multiple volumes published annually. Information about online availability at: http://solutions.cengage.com/Gale/Catalog/Fact-Sheets/CompanyHist.pdf [Accessed 20 August 2016].

Derrida, J., 1995. Archive fever: a Freudian impression. *Diacritics*, 25: 2.

Erickson, C., 1959. *British industrialists steel and hosiery, 1850–1950*. Cambridge: Cambridge University Press.

Freyssenet, M., 2006. *The world that changed the machine. An essay about the car history*. Paris: GERPISA.

Galambos, L., 2003. Identities and the boundaries of business history: an essay on consensus and creativity. In: F. Amatori and G. Jones, eds. 2003. *Business history around the world*. Cambridge: Cambridge University Press.

Goodall, F., Gourvish, T. and Tolliday, S., eds, 1996. *International bibliography of business history*. London: Routledge.

Helps, A., 1872. *Life and labours of Mr Brassey, 1805–1870*. London: Bell & Daldy.

Ingham, J. N., ed., 1983. *Biographical dictionary of American business leaders*. Westport, CT: Greenwood Press.

James, H., 2006. *Family capitalism: Wendels, Haniels, Falcks and the continental European model.* Cambridge, MA: Harvard University Press.

Japan Business History Institute, 1996. *Kaishashi sōgō mokuroku* (General Index of Company Histories), 2nd ed. Tokyo: Japan Business History Institute.

Jeremy, D. J., ed., 1984–86. *Dictionary of business biography, 1860–1980.* London: Butterworth.

Jeremy, D. J., 1998. *A business history of Britain, 1900–1990s.* Oxford: Oxford University Press.

Jewkes, J., Sawers, D. and Stillerman, R., 1960. *The sources of invention.* London: Macmillan.

Joly, H., 1996. *Patrons d'Allemagne. Sociologie d'une élite industrielle, 1933–1989.* Paris: Presses de Sciences Po.

Jones, G., 1996. *The evolution of international business: an introduction.* London: Routledge.

Jones, G. and Zeitlin, J., eds, 2007, 2009. *Oxford handbook of business history.* Oxford: Oxford University Press.

Kaelble, H., 1985. *Social mobility in the 19th and 20th centuries: Europe and America in comparative perspective.* Leamington Spa: Berg.

Keeble, S. P., 1992. *The ability to manage: a study of British management 1890–1930.* Manchester: Manchester University Press.

Kirby, M. W. and Rose, M. B., eds, 1994. *Business enterprise in modern Britain from the eighteenth to the twentieth century.* London: Routledge.

Landes, D., 2006. *Dynasties.* New York: Penguin.

Le Bris, D., Goetzmann, W. N. and Pouget, S., 2014. Testing asset pricing theory over 600 years of stock returns: profits and dividends of the Bazacle Company from 1372 to 1914, *NBER Working Papers*, no.20199, June.

McKinlay, A., 2013. Following Foucault into the archives: clerks, careers and cartoons. *Management and Organizational History*, 8: 2.

Marshall, A., 1919. *Industry and trade*, 2 vols. London: Macmillan.

Newcomer, M., 1955. *The big business executive. The factors that made him, 1900–1950.* New York: Columbia University Press.

Nicholas, T., 1999. Clogs to clogs in three generations? Explaining entrepreneurial performance in Britain since 1850. *Journal of Economic History*, 59: 3.

Olsson, U., 2013. En värdefull berättelse Wallenbergarnas historieprojekt (A valuable story. The Wallenberg history project). *Göteborg Papers in Economic History*, 16.

Orbell, J., 2009. *Guide to tracing the history of a business.* Chichester: Phillimore & Co.

Owen, G., 2010. *The rise and fall of great companies: Courtaulds and the re-shaping of the man-made fibres industry.* Oxford: Oxford University Press.

Raff, D. M. G., 2013. How to do things with time. *Enterprise and society*, 14: 3.

Richmond, L. and Stockford, B., 1986. *Company archives: the survey of the records of 1,000 of the first registered companies in England and Wales.* Aldershot: Gower.

Schwarzkopf, S. 2012. Why business historians need a constructive theory of the archive. *Business Archives: Sources and History*, 105, Nov., pp. 1–9.

Scott, W. R., 1910–11. *The constitution and finance of English, Scottish and Irish joint stock companies to 1720*, 3 vols. Cambridge: Cambridge University Press.

Slaven, A. and Checkland, S., eds, 1986. *Dictionary of Scottish business biography. 1860–1960.* Aberdeen: Aberdeen University Press.

Slinn, J., 1984. *A history of May & Baker 1834–1984.* Cambridge: Hobson's.

Slinn, J., 1988. *Linklaters & Paines: the first 150 years.* London: FT Law & Tax.

Slinn, J. and Spira, L. F., 2013. *The Cadbury Committee: a history.* Oxford: Oxford University Press.

Smiles, S., 1869. *Self-help with illustrations of character, conduct and perseverance.* London: John Murray.

Teichova, A., 1997. *Central Europe in the twentieth century: an economic history perspective.* Aldershot: Ashgate.

Torres, E., ed., 2000. *Los 100 empresarios Españoles del siglo XX*. Madrid: Lid Editorial Empresarial.

Toynbee, A., 1884. *Lectures on the industrial revolution in England*. London: Rivingtons.

Wilson, C., 1954. *The history of Unilever*, 2 vols. London: Cassell.

Yates, J., 1989. *Control through communication: the rise of system in American management*. Baltimore, MD: Johns Hopkins University Press.

Zarach, S., ed., 1987. *Debrett's bibliography of business history*. London: Macmillan.

Index

References in italics refer to figures and tables.

For Product Safety Concerns and Information please contact our EU
representative GPSR@taylorandfrancis.com Taylor & Francis Verlag GmbH,
Kaufingerstraße 24, 80331 München, Germany

Printed and bound by CPI Group (UK) Ltd, Croydon, CR0 4YY
10/05/2025
01866284-0001